Western Ways to the Center

Major Religions of the World

	Christianity
	Islam
	Buddhism
	Hinduism
	Animism (includes Shamanism)
	Judaism

Substantial minority religions are indicated with the following symbols:

A Animism   B Buddhism

C Christianity   H Hinduism

J Judaism   I Islam

O Chinese religious blend (Buddhist, Confucianist, Taoist, and other elements)

0   5,000
Kilometers
0   3,000
Miles

Pacific
Ocean

Atlantic
Ocean

Pacific

Ocean

1. Japan mixes Buddhism and Shinto.

2. China mixes Buddhism, Confucianism, Taoism, Islam, and Marxism.

3. Eastern Europe mixes Marxism and Orthodox Christianity.

4. USSR mixes Marxism, Orthodox Christianity, and Islam.

Approximate Populations of the Major World Religions 1988 (in millions)

Religion	Africa	East Asia	Europe	Latin America	North America	Oceania	South Asia	USSR	World
Christianity	283	82	413	403	233	22	133	105	1,674
Islam	254	24	9	.7	2.7	.1	560	33	883.5
Hinduism	1.5	.01	.5	.7	.9	.3	660	.001	664
Buddhism	.01	155	.3	.5	.2	.02	157	.3	313
Judaism	.3	.002	1.5	1	8.2	.09	4.2	3.1	18.3
Confucianism	— *	6.2	.001	—	.02	—	.002	—	6.2
Taoism	.01	165	.05	.05	.1	.001	8	—	173
Baha'ism	1.2	.05	.07	.6	.3	.006	2.4	—	4.5

Source: *1989 Britannica Book of the Year.* Figures are conservative.
*— = negligible

OF RELATED INTEREST

BETWEEN TIME AND ETERNITY: THE ESSENTIALS OF JUDAISM, *Jacob Neusner*
JUDAISM: DEVELOPMENT AND LIFE, third edition, *Leo Trepp*
CHRISTIANITY: AN INTRODUCTION, second edition, *Denise Carmody and John Carmody*

THE RELIGIOUS LIFE OF MAN SERIES   *Frederick Streng*, Editor

UNDERSTANDING RELIGIOUS LIFE, third edition, *Frederick Streng*

THE HOUSE OF ISLAM, third edition, *Kenneth Cragg*

THE WAY OF TORAH, fourth edition, *Jacob Neusner*

THE HINDU RELIGIOUS TRADITION, *Thomas J. Hopkins*

THE CHRISTIAN RELIGIOUS TRADITION, *Stephen Reynolds*

CHINESE RELIGION, fourth edition, *Laurence G. Thompson*

JAPANESE RELIGION, third edition, *H. Byron Earhart*

THE BUDDHIST RELIGION, third edition, *Richard H. Robinson and Willard L. Johnson*

NATIVE AMERICAN RELIGION, *Sam D. Gill*

ISLAM FROM WITHIN, *Kenneth Cragg and R. Marston Speight*

LIFE OF TORAH, *Jacob Neusner*

CHINESE WAY IN RELIGION, *Laurence G. Thompson*

RELIGION IN THE JAPANESE EXPERIENCE, *H. Byron Earhart*

THE BUDDHIST EXPERIENCE, *Stephen Beyer*

NATIVE AMERICAN TRADITIONS, *Sam D. Gill*

WESTERN WAYS TO THE CENTER

An Introduction to Western Religions

Second Edition

Denise Lardner Carmody
UNIVERSITY OF TULSA

John Tully Carmody
UNIVERSITY OF TULSA

Wadsworth Publishing Company
Belmont, California
A Division of Wadsworth, Inc.

Religion Editor: Sheryl Fullerton
Editorial Assistant: Andrea Varni
Print Buyer: Martha Branch
Designer: Detta Penna
Compositor: Weimer Typesetting Company
Cover: Cynthia Bogue

Cover art: Adapted from *Violet Snowflake* by Jeanette Stobie © 1991

Printed in the United States of America

1 2 3 4 5 6 7 8 9 10——95 94 93 92 91

LIBRARY OF CONGRESS
Library of Congress Cataloging-in-Publication Data

Carmody, Denise Lardner, 1935–
    Ways to the center : an introduction to world religions / Denise Lardner Carmody, John Tully Carmody. — 3rd ed.
      p. cm.
    Includes bibliographical references.
    Includes index.
    ISBN 0-534-13980-9
    1. Religions.   I. Carmody, John, 1939–   . II. Title.
BL80.2.C343 1990
$291^1.09182^11$—dc20   90-34460
                                               CIP

IN MEMORY OF

Catherine R. Carmody

Stephen J. Carmody

Denis Lardner

Martha Comen Lardner

CONTENTS

PREFACE

In preparing this second edition of *Western Ways to the Center*, we have concentrated on updating the scholarly base, clarifying the logic and language, and correcting factual mistakes and problematic interpretations. To make recent scholarly trends available to undergraduate students and teachers, we have again focused on sources likely to be widely available, in this case articles in the *Encyclopedia of Religion* edited by Mircea Eliade (New York: Macmillan, 1987).

Many of our interventions aim at clarifying the expository prose have been small, but, in the words of an interesting article by Jonathan Z. Smith some years ago, *"Adde Parvum Parvo Magnus Acervus Erit"* ("Add a Little to a Little and there will be a Great Heap") (*History of Religions*, 1971, 11:67).

Major additions to this edition include three new chapters: on the ancient religious mind, the religions of recent nonliterate or oral peoples, and general alternatives to religion (secularist and humanistic systems). We have also added considerations of the source-critical bases for studies in the major Western religions, of methodological issues, of the philosophical foundations of comparative religious studies, of spirituality, of sociological factors in the rise of the Western traditions, of secularizing trends in each major tradition, of the problematic character of the term *center*, and of the problematic character of the term *Western*, especially concerning Islam.

Concerning pedagogical supports, we have greatly expanded the glossary and placed the glossary items at the end of each chapter. We have also updated the annotated bibliography and the demographic data, added some schematic charts, and on occasion added historical details to clarify what had been too concise an exposition. Finally, we have expanded the questions and oriented them toward discussion (they can now serve as topics for either homework or in-class discussions).

Overall, however, the basic design of the book remains a twofold exposition of the major Western religious traditions in terms of historical and structural (philosophical) analyses, incorporating the changes developed for the third edition of *Ways to the Center*, the parent text that treats the full span of traditions, East and West. As well, this text retains a fairly demanding linguistic and conceptual level. We hope that this will be unobjectionable at the beginning of the 1990s, when numerous studies have lamented the decline of literacy among college students and urged a reinfusion of rigor and challenge.

There comes a point at which diluting the vocabulary, imagery, and conceptual equipment one uses to display complex phenomena such as the world religions is simply pandering to the baser educational instincts. Certainly one has to sympathize with students who have been ill-prepared for adult study in the humanities. On the other hand, one does them little good by dumbing things down to their beginning level of underachievement. If a college degree is going to be worth the parchment on which it is issued, students have to have been stretched beyond the proficiency they had when entering as freshmen and have to have worked hard. In a nutshell, they have to have spent some time with an unabridged dictionary and extended the range of what they initially could name and so think about. Wittgenstein's famous epigram is remorseless: The limits of our language are the limits of our world. Having tried to clarify and sharpen the language of our text, we make no apologies for the challenges that remain. All the religions insist that there is no lazy person's way to enlightenment.

Finally, we are happy to acknowledge our gratitude to the readers of this second edition, who have offered much useful criticism and suggestion:

J. Dell Johnson
Department of Religious Studies
Stonehill College
Tuscaloosa, Alabama

Michael Rende
Gonzaga University
Department of Religious Studies
E. 52 Boone Avenue
Spokane, Washington

John Crossley
University of Southern California
School of Religion
Los Angeles, California

Western Ways to the Center

INTRODUCTION: ON THE STUDY OF WORLD RELIGIONS

A contemporary sign for friendship between man and woman

The religious life of humanity is a vast spectacle hard to keep in perspective. Therefore, we should make our goals and methods clear from the outset. Our primary goal is to make clear how the Western religious traditions have oriented billions of human lives. Our primary method is to place the study of religion in the context of the humanities and approach the traditions with a consistent format. Let us explain these notions in more detail.

THE NATURE OF RELIGION

Picture yourself in New Delhi. You are outside *Rajghat,* the memorial to Mahatma Gandhi, the politician and holy man who led India to freedom from British colonial rule. Before you, squatting on the broken sidewalk, are three small boys with wooden flutes. They are piping tunes toward round wicker baskets. When they lift the baskets' covers, three silver cobras slowly weave their way out. You watch for several minutes, fearful but entranced. Then the boys shove the cobras back into their baskets and approach you for their fee.

Date	Text
ca. 1500 B.C.E.	Vedas
ca. 1360	*Hymns of Akhenaton*
1000–500	*Redactions of* Pentateuch
800–400	Upanishads
750–550	*Hebrew Prophets*
550	*Oldest Parts of Zoroastrian* Avesta
500	*Oldest Parts of* Analects
400–250	Job; Ecclesiastes; Bhagavad Gita
ca. 350	*Plato's* Laws; Tao Te Ching
ca. 330	*Aristotle's* Metaphysics
ca. 160	*Buddhist* Prajna-Paramita
ca. 80	Lotus Sutra, *Key Buddhist Text*
ca. 50	*Buddhist* Dhammapada
ca. 50–90 C.E.	New Testament *Writings*
413–426	*Augustine's* City of God
425	*Buddhist* Visuddhimagga
ca. 500	*Babylonian* Talmud
ca. 650	*Canonization of the* Qur'an
712–720	*Shinto* Chronicles
ca. 1100	*Al-Ghazali's* Revivification of the Sciences
1175	*Chu Hsi's Neo-Confucian Synthesis*
1190	*Maimonides'* Guide for the Perplexed
1270	*Aquinas's* Summa Theologica
1536	*Calvin's* Institutes
1581	*Compilation of* Adi Granth, *Sikh Scripture*

A few rupees seem fair enough—you don't want to upset those cobras.

Does this picture shine a light on the exotic East? Is it a minor *revelation* of Indian culture? Yes, but only if you know a little background. In India, as in many other countries with ancient cultures, serpents have been potent symbols (think of the story in the third chapter of Genesis). Perhaps because they appear menacing or phallic (penislike), they have stood for something very basic, something very close to the life force. For centuries, groups of Indians have specialized in snake handling, and the skills have been passed along from father to son. Their profession has combined show business and a bit of crude religion. It has been both entertainment and an occasion to shiver about the implications of death and life.

Now picture yourself in medieval England. In 627 C.E. ("common era" = A.D.) the monk Paulinus came to King Edwin in northern England and urged him to convert his people to Christianity. After some debate, one of Edwin's counselors stood up and said: "Your majesty, on a winter night like this, it sometimes happens that a little bird flies in that far window, to enjoy the warmth and light of our fire. After a short while it passes out again, returning to the dark and the cold. As I see it, our human life is much the same. We have but a brief time between two great darknesses. If this

Figure 1 *Corpus Christi, Spanish, second half of the thirteenth century. Wood with polychrome, 72 in. high. The crucifixion was a central focus of medieval Christian piety. The Nelson–Atkins Museum of Art, Kansas City, Missouri. (Nelson Fund)*

monk can show us warmth and light, we should follow him."[1]

For most of medieval Europe, the warmth and light that made life seem good radiated from Jesus Christ. At the core of Europe's complex and in many ways crude culture at that time was a *faith* that a personal father *God* so loved the world he had given his son to heal and enlighten it. When they shared that faith, European monks, kings, and kings' counselors largely agreed on their conception of life. Monks, for instance, were willing to give up family life in order to bear witness to God's love. Kings tried to show that their rule derived from what God had done through

Jesus, and counselors tried to show commoners how the rule of kings mediated God's will. Often, of course, monks and kings and counselors did things that we find hard to square with Jesus, pursuing wealth and power by means of guile. But their culture forced them all to confront Christian warmth and light, as Indian culture forced Indians to confront sex, death, and life.

Our two pictures are not quite compatible. The modern Indian scene stressed rather primitive sexual or vital energies, while the medieval English scene stressed lofty love and vision. Westerners have tended to view Indian and European life in that way, as the writings of early Christian missionaries to India suggest. However, the past century of scholarship in religious studies has shown the deficiencies of such an attitude, so we must add a few comments on the two scenes.

First, drawing a picture of medieval Europe that is raw and *primitive* would not be hard. In Ingmar Bergman's movies about the medieval period, such as *The Seventh Seal* and *The Virgin Spring,* death and sex and life are jammed together like serpents in a basket. Because of the Black Death, the plague that killed about three-quarters of the late medieval European population, monks and commoners marched in processions beating themselves, scourging their flesh with whips to do penance for their sins and keep death away. The harshness of medieval life also led to brutal wars and brutal rapes. The knight and the squire of *The Seventh Seal,* who watch the procession of penitents, have kept company with death since they went to war as Crusaders. The rape and murder of the young girl in *The Virgin Spring* sums up medieval primitiveness. Sex and death pour out in her blood, and only after her father has slain the rapists do we see hope for new life trickle forth in a fresh spring. Medieval Europe, Bergman suggests, was as raw as India has ever been.

Second, were we to go inside the memorial to Gandhi and look at the scene at his commemorative stone, the sublimity of Indian culture and its visions of warmth and light might rise up and parallel those of Christian Europe. *Rajghat* blends green grass, elegant black marble, and fresh flower petals of orange and pink. They symbolize the beautiful spirit of the Mahatma, the little man of great soul. Gandhi was a politician who moved people by *satyagraha*—the force of truth. Without military arms, much money, or even much respect from British leaders, he forced the whole world to take notice. When he vowed to take no food until India's just claims were met, the world held its breath. When he led groups of nonviolent *satyagrahis* into the midst of club-swinging soldiers, he upset the conscience of the world. By the simple rightness, the sheer justice, of his cause, Gandhi showed how his Hindu conception of God could be very powerful. His God was "Truth," and it finally shamed the British into withdrawal.

Snakes and scourges, love and truth—they have shot through India, Europe, and most other parts of the world. In contemporary America, they or their off-spring live with us yet. For instance, our nuclear missiles are for many citizens and analysts eerie phallic symbols. Like cobras we are trying to get back in their baskets, the missiles give us shivers. Many people see the missiles' thrust, their destructive power, and the claims that they give us security or economic life as brutalizing and raping our culture. From Hiroshima to Three Mile Island, nuclear power muddles our wellsprings and hope.

So too with the ways that we whip ourselves for guilt, the ways that we still crave love, the ways that we search after light. Our guilt keeps psychiatrists in business. Our searches for light fill churches and schools. Clearly we are sisters and brothers to religious Indians and medieval Europeans. Clearly their snakes and saviors relate to our own.

Religion is the issue of ultimate meaning that this discussion of cobras and monks spotlights. It is the part of culture—Eastern, Western, or contemporary American—that we study when we ask about a people's deepest convictions. For instance, Hinduism is the animating spirit, the soul, the way of looking at the world, that has tied snake handling and *satyagraha* together for most Indians. Christianity is the way of looking at the world that joined scourging to Jesus for most medieval Europeans. Religion, then, is what you get when you investigate striking human phenomena to find the ultimate vision or set of convictions that gives them their sense. It is the cast of mind and the gravity of heart by which a people endures or enjoys its time between the two great darknesses of prebirth and death.

Because of the recent increase in the use of the term *spirituality* to designate such a cast of mind or gravity of heart, among nonreligious as well as religious people, it may be well to relate our venture here to "spirituality." Briefly, we verge into the domain of spirituality whenever we deal with the personal, existential dimensions of people's lives. Such activities as prayer, work done in a spirit of serving God, giving alms to the poor, visiting the sick, and visiting the imprisoned traditionally have focused people's personal sense of commitment to their religious tradition and the deity it mediated. So have such activities as preparing the bodies of the deceased for burial, teaching children the rudiments of faith, making pilgrimages to holy sites, fasting, and holding processions and celebrations in honor of saints or religious holidays. In Western religious history, all these have been ways that ordinary believers have expressed their commitment to their Jewish, or Christian, or Muslim faith.

Thus, on the occasion of dealing with such religious activities, perhaps especially the different types of prayer and *worship,* we venture into the ultimately personal character of *religion.* Without denying the significance of the sociological aspects of each tradition, the fact remains that some of the deepest significances of religion come out of solitude, when the individual realizes his or her unique relationship to the God who might answer burning questions about human meaning: how to wrestle with evil, how to hope for fulfillment, how to cope with suffering and death. In our discussions of the center of each Western tradition, we keep this personal dimension prominent.

Mention of the sociological aspects of religion anticipates the discussion of scholarly methods of studying religion that occurs later in this introduction. Suffice it to say now that the personal and social aspects of religion are never separable. In its very *nature* religion embraces both the unique individual and the common group. People's religious lives are shaped by their economic class, their gender, their race, their ethnic heritage, their age, and the many other factors by which they may be characterized. Just as the historical period in which they live is significant, so is the geographic locale. Religion is so closely tied to people's bedrock *humanity*—their fundamental sense of who they are and where they stand in the universe—that it is bound to be shaped, and to shape in return, all the significant worries, experiences, convictions, sufferings, and so forth that people can share. As well, all religions are passed down by the groups, formal or informal, that shape them. If many religious traditions develop formal mechanisms for controlling doctrine, liturgy, ethical precepts, social action, and the like, they also sponsor neighborhood clubs, sewing guilds, recreational associations, and similar groups that express their religious convictions informally. To get a complete sense of what religion means in any tradition, one has to remain sensitive to both such formal and informal group influences. Indeed, ideally a religion will finally make plain how it expects individuals to contribute to the ongoing transmission of the religion's beliefs and practices, as well as how it believes that membership in its given religious community provides the context or atmosphere in which individuals can flourish best.

Finally, we should note that modern experiences of religion are colored so regularly by secular influences that nowadays religion itself has to be analyzed as dialectically engaged with secularism, if not as a factor in the processes of secularization. In the past, one could suggest that religion pointed to otherworldly realities and secularism named an antireligious process pressuring people to pay more attention to this-worldly matters than to God or heaven. Scholars knew that such a dichotomy was simplistic, especially concerning the Western religions, because they knew that the Mosaic covenant, and the Incarnation of the Logos in Jesus Christ, and the Qur'anic revelation given through Muhammad all carried immense implications for this-worldly living. At their origins, Judaism, Christianity, and Islam all thought holistically. None made the distinctions between church and state, the religious and the secular, that arose in modern times. Each thought that its God touched every reality. Curiously, therefore, each of the major Western *traditions* wanted to take root in the structures shaping daily life—marriage, education, business, politics—and so could be said to have encouraged a practical, applied, this-worldly side of faith. All could be said to have thought of themselves as increasing the significance of space and time, of what human beings did or did not do concerning their neighbors, of money, and sex, and power.

While the modern proposals to confine human significance to the realm of space and time horrified the Western traditions, especially when they explicitly rejected the significance of God and the afterlife, those proposals became challenges with which the synagogues, churches, and mosques had to deal. Under the pressure to show how they improved the lot of human beings, the synagogues, churches, and mosques (in different ways, related to the pace at which modern secularism became a factor for them) all became more secular—in the sense of more concerned to sharpen the this-worldly implications of the faith they preached. Each tradition brought forward fuller appreciations of the physical world, the human body, the arts, the sciences, work, politics, and the other this-worldly human occupations. Each had to think harder about how to correlate the otherworldly dimensions of its confession of faith with the secular dimensions. Thus, nowadays, the secularizing features of the traditions' past histories, as well as of their present movements, bear watching. Nowadays, the this-worldly, secular character of much religious thought and activity seems obviously part of the very nature of religion.

STUDYING RELIGION

Certain attitudes should be cultivated in all study, but the study of religion demands more self-awareness and personal engagement with its materials than most other disciplines do. For instance, although reducing physical science to "objective" observing and testing is simplistic, since all knowledge is ultimately personal,[2] physical science does not make great demands on a student's inner experiences of suffering or love. The humanities (those disciplines that study our efforts at self-expression and self-understanding) involve more of such inner experiences, because suffering and love shape so much of history and literature, yet even the humanities seldom deal with direct claims about ultimate meaning. Only in philosophy and religion does one directly encounter systems about God, evil, and humanity's origin and end. Philosophy deals with such concepts principally in their rational forms, while religious studies meet them more concretely in the myths, *rituals, mysticisms,* behavior patterns, and institutions through which most human beings have been both drawn to ultimate meaning and terrified of it.

More than in any other discipline, the student in a religious studies course is confronted with imperative claims. The religions are not normally warehouses where you pay your money and take your choice. Rather, they are impassioned heralds of ways of life. More than most people initially like, the religions speak of death, ignorance, and human viciousness. However, they also speak of peace and joy, forgiveness and harmony. Whatever they discuss, though, they are *mystagogic,* which etymologically means "mystery working." The religions work *mystery.* Their preoccupations, when they are healthy, are nature's wonder, life's strange play of physical death and spiritual resurrection, and the possibility of order in the midst of chaos. The religions say that the kingdom of God is in your midst, because you are a being who can pray, "Abba, Father." They say that the *Tao* ("the Way") that can be named is not the real *Tao.* Above all, they say that the person who lives divorced from the mysteries of rosy-fingered dawn and wintery death is less than fully human. So Sioux Indians revered the East, because dawn symbolizes the light of conscience. So Jewish scripture speaks of love as strong as death. So, finally, Islam speaks for all religions when it says that

Allah—Muslim divinity—is as near as the pulse at our throats. Clearly, then, we cannot study the religions well if we are afraid of mystery or are in flight from death and life.

We also cannot study the religions well if we insist on forcing them into the categories of our own faith. We must first take them on their own terms, giving their experiences and problems a sympathetic hearing. After we have listened to the wisdom of a scripture such as the Hindu *Bhagavad Gita,* we may and should compare it with the wisdom of our Western faiths. Even then, though, unless we can say with the Christians' Saint Peter, "I see now how true it is that God has no favorites, but that in every nation the person who is God-fearing and does what is right is acceptable" (Acts 10:34), we risk acting with prejudice and condescension.

A second reason for remembering life's mystery, then, is that it helps us clear away prejudice. Talk of the New Testament superseding the Old or of revealed religion besting paganism—without strong qualifications—is self-serving and naive. Used as a word of God, Jewish scriptures open onto a divinity ever new, ever fresh, and ever free. Taken in its experiential vividness, a Zen Buddhist's enlightenment *(satori)* tears the veil of ignorance and comes as revelation and grace.[3] As Thomas Aquinas insisted, we do not know what God is. As John Calvin knew, the mind without mystery is a factory of idols. The most authoritative Western theologians have fought against prejudice.

Third, it is worth pointing out that the religious studies course offered here is not theology, at least not the theology of a church. Church theology tends to be a search for an understanding of one's own faith that is directed by the particular creed or commitment of an individual or group. Spontaneously the search spreads to a probing of all life's dimensions in terms of such a commitment. So there develops a theology of art, a theology of history, and even a theology of the world religions.[4] In these theologies, however, the main goal is to square data with one's own faith or religious group. Moreover, a church theology's ultimate goal is to promote its own faith. It studies art, history, or the world religions to beautify, advance, or defend its own vision of things, whether the "church" be Muslim, Buddhist, Jewish, or Christian. The understanding that theology seeks in such study is not necessarily distorted, but it is in the service of preaching, ministering, and counseling. When it is not in such service, church theology becomes divorced from the life of its community.[5]

In a university, however, neither students nor teachers are expected to confess their faith (or non-faith). We, the authors, have argued elsewhere[6] that it is proper and healthy to make clear one's position on the *implications,* for thought and action alike, to which a course's studies lead. In other words, there is nothing wrong and much right with teachers and students becoming personal—dealing with concrete, practical implications. There is much wrong, however, in university courses that place their own values on other people's art, history, or religion and thereby distort them. One must listen with an open mind before judging and deciding.

So we urge you to get inside the religions' experiences and values and compare them with your own. In fact, we very much hope that your study will enrich your appreciation of nature, will increase your wonder about life's meaning, and will increase your resources for resisting evil. But we do not set these hopes in the framework of any one faith. We are not, in other words, doing church theology. You may be Christian, Jewish, Buddhist, agnostic, atheistic, or anything else. To us such labels do not matter. What matters is that you be human: a man or woman trying to hear the Delphic oracle's "Know thyself," a person humble with the Confucian virtue of sympathy or "fellow feeling" *(jen).*

Fourth, what benefits will this effort to study humanistically bring you? At least two spring to mind. First, you will have the chance to grapple with some of the most influential, wisest personalities of the past. Second, you will better understand the world of the present, in which all peoples on the globe are much closer than they have ever been before.

To illustrate the first benefit, let us call on the Chinese sage Confucius. In his time (551–479 B.C.E.) some people were advancing the proposition that it is better to pay court to the stove (to practicalities) than to heaven (to ideals) (see *Analects* 3:3). Confucius battled their proposition back. If you do not pay court to heaven, he said, you will have no recourse when practicalities fail to bring you good life. In other words, the mystery of life is more than food and drink, more than shelter and pleasure. Important as those things are, they do not make the truly good life. Only moving in the Way *(Tao)* of heaven makes us human beings what we ought to be, what we most deeply want to be. If we settle for the stove, we halve our human potential.

To illustrate the second benefit of the humanistic study of religion, we must comment briefly on current history. Today it is a commonplace observation that the world is becoming one. That does not mean that all peoples are agreeing on a common government, economy, or philosophy. It does mean that communications, transportation, economics, and other forces are tying all nations together. Thus, commentators speak of a "global village" or a "planetary culture." They remind us of the novelty of the twentieth century, the only time when it could have happened that when Gandhi fasted, the world held its breath; that when Mao died, his funeral reached every capital. Furthermore, in our nuclear age all curtains can be raised. In our age of escalating population and hunger, all the silos of Kansas cast shadows on East Africa. In our age of ecological pollution, the wastes of one country foul the air, water, and land of others.

The implications of this current state of affairs are too numerous to detail. We may be on the verge of a new phase of evolution; the human sciences may just be approaching their maturity. The outer complexity of human affairs may just be developing a self-consciousness among human beings so that we will be able to cope with these affairs. Or we may devastate the entire planet through nuclear war or ecological disaster. In either case, religion acquires an added significance, because we cannot learn much about the evolution or self-consciousness of the global village unless we listen to its members' deepest perceptions and convictions. We cannot understand human motivation unless we study what people have considered the highest good. Religion shows a people's deepest perceptions and convictions. Hinduism, Buddhism, Christianity, and Islam form the souls of a majority of the world's population today. To live together in the future, we human beings will have to understand the world religions very well.

SCHOLARLY METHODS

In pursuing such understanding, it is well to take note of the different methods that scholars of religion have developed. W. Richard Comstock, the author of a useful introduction to religion, once offered a list of five basic methods.[7]

First, there is the *psychological* perspective. Since the time of Freud (1856–1939), who was quite interested in religion's parallels with neurosis, Western scholars have been sensitive to the inner drives that set people to work, parenting, religion, and the many other aspects of human culture. For example, sexual satisfaction, acceptance by our peers, and a sense of control all play a part in our development of human culture. C. G. Jung (1875–1961) broke with Freud over the interpretation of sexual and religious drives. For Jung the second half of life tends to be a pursuit of meaning (giving one's time and experience coherence). Often the symbols people use in pursuing meaning are religious, so even today psychoanalysts probing patients' dreams can come upon archetypal symbols reminiscent of ancient religious mythologies.

If we generalize the sensitivity that recent psychological studies sharpen, the main point seems to be that we must stay alert to the complexity of human motivation. For example, in studying a holy man from the Hindu tradition, such as Mahatma Gandhi, we should realize that his asceticism had a basis in his adolescent sexual traumas and that his political ambitions were forged by his experiences of racial discrimination in young adulthood. At these formative times in his life cycle, Gandhi was tested to an unusual degree. He found himself unready for the erotic aspects of marriage, and his experience as a "colored" person in South Africa told him he had to champion India's oppressed.[8]

On the one hand, if we so focus on psychological issues such as these that we neglect the history, sociology, economics, politics, and other aspects of Gandhi's life and times, we become reductionists, trying to squeeze all of reality onto the psychoanalyst's couch. On the other hand, if we neglect such inner demons and angels, we divorce ourselves from a powerful tool of understanding (perhaps because we do not want to face the similar demons and angels warring in our own souls). As usual, a balanced use is the ideal.

Just as scientific psychology is a fairly recent development, not available to scholars of religion a century ago, so is *sociology*. And just as the pioneer psychologists were quite interested in religion, so were pioneer sociologists such as Max Weber (1864–1920) and Emile Durkheim (1858–1917). In both cases, their interest was religion's role in making a group cohesive. The religious ideas of a tribe, or even a large culture, are always in part a projection of the tribe's or the culture's sense of its own identity. For example,

Hindus have been people stratified by traditional wisdom into four main social classes. Chinese have been people living at the center of the world in accordance with the *Tao* they thought moved both nature and the wise ancients. Americans have been high-minded refugees come to make a place of justice and freedom in a new world. Thus neither Hindu caste nor Chinese misogyny nor American racism could be the patent inhumanity an outside observer might think it. Sacralizing the way they talked about themselves, all three peoples claimed heaven had approved their customs.

Recently, cultural anthropologists such as Clifford Geertz and Victor Turner have tuned the interests of the classical sociologists more finely. Living in the midst of the societies they wanted to interpret, they have sought the deep structures and threshold moments through which a people reveals how it constructs its world view. Geertz's study of the Balinese cockfight,[9] for example, is a marvel of sophisticated participant observation. Sensitive to the drama of what he calls "deep play," Geertz makes the cockfight a microcosm of the Balinese thought-world.

A third methodological orientation popular in recent religious studies is the *historical*. One of the drawbacks of the psychological and sociological approaches is that they can seem to bracket time past (and time future), as though their analyses were moved by an Archimedean lever standing outside the flowing stories of either their subjects or themselves. But such ahistoricism obviously is fallacious. The self always enacts a story, a unique version of the common life cycle, and a society is always being pushed by its past and lured by its future. Since the modern discovery of evolution, and the rise of modern retrieval techniques such as archeology, the study of religion has become more historical, and so more faithful to the traditions' ongoing changes. Even the most conservative tradition alters in at least small ways, generation by generation. Though they perform the same rituals and tell the same myths, a people of any era understands itself somewhat differently than its forebears did or its children will.

The good historian's goal is telling the story of these changes. Representing the past as it most likely was, good historians bring their readers from point alpha to point omega. Thus a Buddhist historian might muse: In the beginning, at the earliest point we can reconstruct, Buddhists understood Gautama in such and such a way. A thousand years later, when controversies inside the community had caused much debate, there were the three following major interpretations. Today, in Japanese Buddhism, the third of these interpretations prevails, due to such and such factors.

One thinks, then, of a continuum or a map. In the image of the continuum, the historian grants all centuries a certain equality, showing how Buddhism changed century by century. In the image of a map, the historian plots the journey from the Buddha's India to modern Japan, showing the geographic and cultural routes the Teaching (dharma) traveled. The result should be a sense of perspective and interrelationship. Alpha led on to beta, because of factor alpha prime, just as today omega seems to be leading on to omega-plus-one, because of factor omega prime.

Comstock's fourth methodological perspective is *phenomenological.* Referring to the work of scholars such as Geradus van der Leeuw (1890–1950), who have concentrated on the different *forms* that many religious traditions seem to share, one can emphasize the concern many phenomenologists have to find *typical* patterns that show up repeatedly across the full range of religious data. So, for example, sacred people appear in most traditions. East and West, monks or ascetics or yogis have won great veneration. One can distinguish among these three categories of holy people, but they share an orientation away from worldly affairs, toward contemplation and self-discipline. The typical Hindu holy man fits the pattern of withdrawal, as does the typical Buddhist monk. In China and Japan, both Buddhism and Taoism prized withdrawal from worldly affairs, seclusion in order to grow better attuned to the dharma or the *Tao.*

Phenomenological studies tend to stress the sameness of certain structural features, providing a basis for discussing how Hindu yogis differ from Buddhist monks in cultural details, or how Eastern ascetics differ from Western ascetics. By grouping functionaries together in general terms, we are stimulated to ask how they differ in particulars. The results of such generalizations can seldom be ironclad, since there are usually exceptions to general trends, but phenomenological inquiries can be very stimulating.

Comstock's fifth methodological perspective is *hermeneutical.* If anything, this perspective has increased in importance since the time he made his survey. *Hermeneutics* is the study of interpretation. It concerns processes such as that by which a teacher from Maryland tries to explain to a student from Oklahoma what it was like to live in medieval Europe or India. In one sense, hermeneutics applies to all parts of this communication. Even the gap between Maryland and Oklahoma can be significant, but the gap between twentieth-century America and medieval Europe or India is enormous. Thus, hermeneutics tends to be most concerned with how we can tease from texts or artifacts reliable interpretations of past or foreign cultures. The cultural anthropologists we mentioned have come to the forefront of the hermeneutical debates, but historians, psychologists, sociologists, and philosophers of language have also been prominent. These debates tend to get very technical, generating schools such as structuralism and subdisciplines such as semiotics and deconstructionism. Thus, the scholarly end of the hermeneutical "turn" is not yet in sight and its overall significance is still emerging.

For undergraduates, though, the gist of the hermeneutical perspective is clear enough: Try to be quite sensitive to the sources and ranges of the meanings you are studying. Above all, realize that in studying a text, or any other cultural artifact, you are involved in a two-way conversation. A text is not a brute object whose meanings are obvious to any beholder. Physically, a text is simply some marks on a piece of paper or some impressions in clay. To convey meaning, these marks have to "speak" from the mind of the person who set them down to the minds of people like you who are trying to pick them up. Thus, the languages and assumptions of both minds come into play, your own as much as the author's. You can assume that you and the author share a great deal, since you are both human, but you must be careful about how you use this assumption. The death of a child in ancient China was both very like the death of a child in contemporary America, and very different. Boiled down, hermeneutics is walking the tightrope between the sameness we have as members of one species and the differences we have as individuals, people of different cultures, and people of different historical eras.

One might suggest how these five different methods complement one another by trying to apply them to a single religious phenomenon. Suppose, for example, that one were studying the place of Torah, Divine Instruction, in Judaism. Psychological methods could help one probe what Torah has meant to the millions of men and women formed in traditional Judaism— how it consoled them in hard times, why they clung to it with might and main, why trying to enter into the thought-world of an ancient text proved fascinating, how Torah barred the door against meaninglessness. Sociologically, one might probe the status accorded those who became expert in Torah, moving on to study why bright little boys traditionally were encouraged to become masters of the text and why little girls were not encouraged. One might also analyze how the community divided when modernity called much of traditional Judaism's docility to Torah (regarding diet, keeping the Sabbath, resisting assimilation into the gentile culture, and the like) into question.

Historical studies could teach us about the original conception of the Torah in biblical times, how this conception changed when Jews were cast out of Jerusalem in the first century C.E., what Torah had come to mean by the time the Babylonian Talmud had been collected and edited (about 500 C.E.). We might study the connection between Torah and the Jewish philosophy of a great medieval thinker such as Moses Maimonides, between Torah and the devotional fervor of the Baal Shem-Tov (who founded Hasidism in eighteenth-century eastern Europe), and between Torah and Zionism, the twentieth-century movement to return to Israel. In each case, we would be rounding out the notion of "Torah" by tying it to specific coordinates on the map of space and time.

Phenomenological studies of Torah could lead us to compare it with other instances of Divine Instruction, such as the Hindu Vedas, the Buddhist Tripitaka, the writings of the Confucian Canon, the Christian scriptures and creeds, and such Muslim analogues as the Qur'an and the *Shariah* (Law). Or, within Judaism itself, we might study how Divine Instruction was both the same and different for the prophets and wisdom writers of biblical times, for the early rabbis and the later Hasidim, for Reformed Jews and Jews who in reaction to Reform became "Orthodox." Phenomenology could help us see both what emerges as common to all these instances and what proves variable, maybe even contradictory, among the different instances.

Last, hermeneutical studies would engage us directly in the task of interpreting the Torah, of trying to bridge the centuries between the Five Books of Moses, or the early rabbinic codes known as the Mishnah, and the twentieth century. We would have to try to get inside the "system" of the Torah, to see how it comprises an integral, consistent world view. We

would also have to criticize the assumptions behind that world view, so that we came to appreciate how the choices the biblical authors and rabbis made were free and full of consequences—things they might have taken in a different direction.[10]

Three further issues pertaining to the scholarly methods now favored for studying religious phenomena beg consideration. The first is the matter of the source-critical basis for studies of ancient texts, personalities, movements, and the like. The second is the matter of such descriptions as "Western" and "Eastern" used in this text and many other places. The third is the matter of the philosophical foundations for studies that compare different religious traditions, even to the modest extent that we do in this text.

Concerning the question of the source-critical basis for studies of ancient texts, personalities, movements, and the like, the frank answer is that although scholars have made significant advances in editing primary written sources, much remains less exact than what present-day ideals of reliability require. Judaism, Christianity, and Islam all stem from periods when oral tradition was more significant than written tradition. What one finds in the Bible and the Qur'an, for example, is more mythic, poetic, indebted to memories handed down for generations, and less "scientific" than what present-day critical history requires. The same judgment holds for nonscriptural materials from these three traditions, as well as for sources bearing on the origins of Greek, Iranian, Mesopotamian, Egyptian, Native American, Eskimo, and African traditions. The modern development of critical study postulated a detached point of view, according to which one could sift competing claims and assemble an account of a given action, belief, or career that could stand up to outside, skeptical scrutiny. Much of the spirit behind modern critical scholarship likened it to legal proceedings in court. Evidence and cross-examination were highly prized. The text or traditional memory was subjected to scrutiny from the viewpoint of those trying to prove its innocence (reliability) and from the viewpoint of those trying to prove its guilt (unreliability). Indeed, the presumption developed by source-critical studies has tended to be in favor of unreliability rather than reliability, lest the credulity so powerful in religion infect humanistic scholarship.

The result of this modern mentality has been both to sharpen judgments about the historical reliability that a given piece of evidence carries and to make it plain that some of the most crucial sources of evidence are simply never going to yield testimony able to stand up to the demands of critical history. In other words, there is no way that the Bible or the Qur'an can be turned into a witness acceptable in a contemporary courtroom, because neither the Bible nor the Qur'an ever wanted to be a detached observer, a disinterested party. In addition to all the lapses in memory and corruptions in copying that specialists can sniff out in the scriptural texts, there remains the more fundamental problem that the materials always assumed and required faith. By definition, the religious studies scholar cannot give such faith, so the religious studies scholar, trying to establish the humanistic credibility or sense of key texts, is always going to come up short. The problem is not that the Bible or the Qur'an or the other, analogous sources on which the historical representation of Western religious experience depends have been mendacious, deliberately trying to conceal or mislead. The problem is that the sense of reality, of what actually happened and what that happening meant, operative in the most important sources bearing on Western religion has been shaped by convictions of faith that God was doing such and such. Therefore, careful scholarship in religious studies always has to put many qualifications on the conclusions it draws about actual, historical happenings when its primary sources have been documents or other artifacts forged in faith.

Second, concerning the use of "Western" religions, one has to confess that it is at best a useful convenience, at worst a significant distortion. Christianity now has a presence in all 254 of the countries represented in the *1989 Britannica Book of the Year*'s statistical chart on the populations of the world's religions.[11] Does the fact that the majority of the Christian population still resides in the West, along with the fact that Christianity has had more impact on the historical development of the West than the East, continue to justify describing Christianity as a "Western" religion? Perhaps so, but only with the qualification that the 82 million Christians in East Asia and the 132 million Christians in South Asia are not insignificant populations. Even more significant are the 282 million Christians resident in Africa. These populations are changing the traditionally Western or European visage of Christianity, as befits a global culture in which West and East increasingly interpenetrate and so dilute many of their differences.

One could argue that Christianity, and even more Judaism and Islam, are better described as "Near Eastern" religions, in view of their places of origin, than they are as "Western" religions. All of them arose in what we now call the Near, or Middle, East. Christians and Jews continue to have sizable fractions of their populations there, even though they have spread to many other geographic areas. About 84 percent of present-day Jews are Ashkenazim (people of German/European cultural background), so "Western" continues to be defensible in the Jewish case.

It is harder to defend the use of "Western" in the case of Islam, because the vast majority of Muslims live in Africa (253 million) and South Asia (560 million). The Indian subcontinent and Indonesia house hundreds of millions of Muslims. On the other hand, there are two good reasons for considering Islam along with Judaism and Christianity and so casting the mantle of the term "Western" over it. One reason is the family relationship among the three traditions, all of which consider Abraham their father. Christianity confessedly derives from Judaism, while the Qur'an clearly is concerned to position Islam in relation to Judaism and Christianity. Muslims speak of Jews and Christians as "people of the book," and Islam thinks that the prophecy given to Muhammad perfected the prophecies that structure Judaism and Christianity. Inasmuch as Judaism and Christianity fall into the category "Western," Islam may be placed there too, as a topographical convenience.

The second reason is more pragmatic. In dividing the world's major religious traditions, it makes some sense to consider their place of origin as the first demarcator. It follows, then, that Buddhism, Hinduism, Confucianism, Taoism, and other Asian religions end up in the "Eastern" half of a simple division, while Judaism, Christianity, and Islam are left for the other part of the division, which inevitably gets labeled "Western." For our purposes, the main lesson to draw is that the term "Western" is quite loose and debatable, and that we are using it more for reasons of convenience than for strong theoretical reasons.

Third, concerning the philosophical foundations for the comparative study of the world's religions, suffice it to say that we follow a philosophical anthropology (an understanding of human nature) indebted to thinkers such as Eric Voegelin and Bernard Lonergan, according to which religion expresses drives of human consciousness found in all people. Because all people press forward to know the structures of their world and find something worthy of their wholehearted love, all people exhibit some similarities in their religious traditions (which tend to be the parts of their culture where ultimate concerns most clearly focus). From the side of the human agent, then, one can postulate a likeness sufficient to permit the side-by-side comparison of Confucians and Jews, Muslims and Hindus. Granted the assumption (itself based on empirical observation) that all human beings desire to know and love ultimately, the religious traditions may be studied, and compared, in terms of the myths, rituals, artifacts, social structures, and the like that their desires have generated. Alternatively, they may be studied in terms of the fourfold delineation of reality that analyses of human consciousness such as Lonergan's and Voegelin's have disclosed: nature, society, the self, and divinity.

So, the basic assumption behind our comparative efforts is the transcendental (ever ongoing) character of the human spirit, while the basic diagram of the objective correlative of the human spirit (the world with which it is always involved) considers reality to have four irreducible dimensions: divinity (ultimate reality), human society, the physical world, and the human self. These are the main philosophical pillars undergirding our comparative work, and they position us as "critical realists." That is, we believe that one can gain some purchase on reality (what is so objectively) if one strives to be attentive, intelligent, judicious, and responsible. By disciplining one's senses, imagination, judgment, and will, one can gain reasonable confidence that what one finds making sense of one's data in fact obtains in reality.

THE CENTER

Difference and sameness apply to all our interactions with other human beings, so the study of Native American religions is not radically different from the study of the child-raising practices of the people next door. Still, one can lean more heavily on difference or sameness, make the people one is studying stranger or more familiar, depending on one's point of view. Generally speaking, sociological, historical, and phenomenological approaches tend to stress differences. Concerned with other people's customs, stories, and distinguishing features, they tend to detail things peculiar to Japanese, or Nigerians, or Italians. Psychological and hermeneutical studies perhaps lay greater stress on sameness. Because motivation plays an im-

portant role in psychological studies, and because the meaning of a people's customs or the assumptions behind their rituals loom large in hermeneutical studies, the common humanity that observer and observed share is emphasized. This is not to say that sociologists, historians, and phenomenologists neglect motivation and meaning. It is not to say that psychologists or hermeneuticists neglect external behavior or detail. It is simply to suggest that studying other people involves an outside and an inside, a blend of alien details and perhaps more familiar motivations, and that different methods may stress either the alien or the familiar.

Suppose, for instance, that you were an anthropologist, living in the midst of an Indian tribe in the Amazon jungle. If you witnessed a ritual boxing match, in which each man clouted the other as hard as he could, winding up to deliver a mighty blow to the opponent's chest, you might at first think this a strange way to while away an evening. Then, when you learned that the purpose of this ritual was to test the power of each man's spirits, the vitality of the *hekura* lodging in his chest, you probably would find it making a little more sense. Nonetheless, it likely would remain a quite foreign, if not bizarre, custom until you got a handle on the concern of this (rather typically shamanic) tribe to build up vitality, the power to resist disease and other enemies, by drawing on the forces of its surroundings, the spirits of the plants and animals that shared its habitat. At that point, you might sense a parallel to the psychosomatic concerns of modern Western medicine, the efforts of your own people to feel sturdy and confident.

In any study of the religion of other people, we do well to move back and forth between their differences from us and their likenesses to us. If we respect the ways that they conceive of the world, give their own reports a fair hearing, we can move on to try to assimilate their reports to our own experiences and convictions. Then a process of dialogue can develop that may grow richer and richer, showing the people we are studying to be both stranger and more familiar than probably we found them at our first meeting.

In an ideal study, however, one finally verges upon the center of the other people's experiences. Florinda Donner, an anthropologist who went to the Amazon, observed the strange boxing matches, and learned about the *hekura,* was fortunate enough one day to grasp the beauty of her subjects' world and so come to understand their tendency to live almost completely in the present: "An overwhelming sense of awe brought me to my feet as the sky in the east glowed red and purple along the horizon. The clouds, obedient to the wind, opened to let the rising disk through. Pink mist rolled over the treetops, touching up shadows with deep blue, spreading green and yellow all over the sky until it changed into a transparent blue. . . . Like the Iticoteri [the tribe she was studying] I had learned to live in the present. Time was outside of me. It was something to be used only at the moment. Once used, it sank back into itself and became a perceptible part of my inner being."[12]

One's inner being verges on one's center. One's center is what produces the sense of a self, a coherent identity, a whole entity. Certainly it is difficult to translate the metaphor "center" into anything anatomical. Certainly both the heart and the brain have their rights. Yet, from ancient times, people have always used the term "heart" as something holistic, something able to sum up the entire personality. And from ancient times people have spoken also of the "soul," the spiritual presence that gives form to the entire entity.

Our greatest interest in this book is suggesting something of the centers, the hearts and souls, of the different Western religious traditions. In doing that, we hope to suggest also the center of religion, which we suspect is close to, if not coincident with, the center of being human. So after we have discussed historical and structural details, and sometimes during our discussions of historical and structural details, we try to indicate, evoke, the center of the religious tradition in question. Implicitly, we are also trying to indicate, evoke, what it is in that tradition that most reveals the human striving of its people, their greatest efforts to verge upon the best of what their experience has shown them. Finally, when we have made such an indication, we feel justified in inviting the reader to consider what the center of the tradition in question has to offer to outsiders. For example, what can, should, the overtones of Muslims' efforts to serve Allah carry to the ears of Jews, Christians, and Western secularists, who would have to be tone-deaf to miss all of their beauty and longing? What can, should, the overtones of the Christian center—the profound sense that the flesh of Christ reveals the unsurpassable love of God— carry to the ears of Muslims, Jews, and Western secularists, who are also searching for ways to anoint their space and time, their bodies and spirits, with a sense of beauty and revelation? These are the sorts of questions we hope our interest in the center will raise.

THE STRUCTURE OF THIS BOOK

In this book we try to build our descriptions of other people's outside features and inside convictions into a climactic presentation of the sort of peak experience, vivid and peaceful, that gives their world a center. Thus, we try to present the Western religions as various "ways to the center."

Where the data allow, we begin our chapters with a sketch of the history of the tradition in question. Behind this historical section lies the conviction that one gains valuable insights into a people's sense of reality by learning the story of where they have come from, how they were formed into a people, what crucial experiences forged their deeper senses of who they are and what they believe. Such historical sections afford us the opportunity to mention many of the people's external characteristics. Sketching where they have come from and where they now seem to think they are going, we can try to move them from "once upon a time" to today.

Following on the historical section will be a "structural analysis" of the tradition's view of reality. Assuming that each religion has a certain consistency, a drive to make sense out of reality as a whole, we shall indicate some of the major pillars of the adherents' world view. The schema that we have found most adequate for this work has four headings: nature, society, self, and ultimate reality. Both the external data of the world religions and an internal analysis of human experience East and West seem to justify using this schema as a loose working format.

For example, all peoples must contend with nature. The physical world affords all of us our food. The skies and the seas and the plains provide all of us our environment, spiritual as well as physical. Indeed, it is characteristic of most ancient peoples to strive for a close harmony with physical nature. As though they instinctively knew many of the lessons that scientific studies in ecology have been teaching our contemporary world, ancient peoples typically sought kinship with the plants and animals of their area, knowledge of their area's weather and terrain. Nor is it hard to find connections with our own situation as twentieth-century individuals. If we find that we tend to perform differently on a high pressure day (when the skies are open and the sun is bright) than on a low pressure day (when the skies are low and gray), we have half the stimulus we need to become interested in the ecological sensitivity of other people, in how they pictured their weather and environment.

More easily than with ourselves, we find that most ancient peoples sacralized at least portions of nature: treated them with reverence or even worship. This tended to be a rallying point for the people, whether the people was at the stage of hunting and gathering or had unified itself under an impressive king. Through their rituals and ceremonies, most people have tried to move with nature's annual flow and ebb. Spring awakening and Fall harvest, Summer heat and Winter cold, have all cried out for recognition. In giving nature such recognition, people have helped define who they were: people of the forest, or people of the mountain. Depending on the way that it has pictured reality as a whole, a people usually has appointed headmen or shamans or priests to deal with these important matters. We shall see more of this in our first chapters, but it brings us to a point worth underscoring from the beginning: In most religions, the people's attitudes toward nature and their own social organization have fit together, have been complementary pieces of a single puzzle.

The same with a people's attitudes toward self and *ultimate reality.* When religious people the world over have asked "Who am I?" their answers have reached out to include situating themselves in the physical cosmos, placing themselves in the history and social structure of their tribe, and making at least fumbling attempts to connect themselves with the ultimate power or reality they have considered the origin, destiny, or most important feature of the whole, the universe, of what human beings can see and conceive. Nature, society, self, and ultimate reality are not artificial or isolated categories, fashioned simply for the convenience of teachers and textbook writers, who must try to give the mass of data about the world religions some shape. We are convinced they are interconnected dimensions of each human life that become more significant and fascinating as our exposure to human history expands and we continue our descent into the depths of our own consciousness.

So, for example, you can find in any bookstore writers telling you that: you are what you eat, your American nation is in peril, your self will flower only through physical love, and "God," a benevolent ultimate power, numbers every hair of your head. Behind each of these assertions is both knowledge and questioning. For centuries people have studied diet, national history, sex, and the mystery of the universe.

Today these topics continue to imply vital questions, matters that any of us would be better for having probed. Moreover, we can use them to build bridges to other people, other eras, other faiths. That is how we plan to use them in our structural analyses: as useful ways of presenting some of the most important aspects of ancient, nonliterate, Egyptian, Iranian, Greek, Mesopotamian, Jewish, Christian, Muslim, and secular experience.

At the end of our structural analysis we conclude each chapter with a short summary essay on the heart of the tradition's convictions, the center of the tradition's world. Admittedly, such essays are always just our own interpretations, but we have felt we owed students the best parting word we could write. If you use our structural analyses and summary essays comparatively, noting how a given tradition both is like the others and differs from them, you should close this textbook with a fairly adequate sense of Western humanity's worldwide religious beliefs.

One does not get to the center of a religious tradition by methods (controlled ways of approach) strictly so called. One works more by intuition or a sense of where the different weights of a tradition come to rest. Among the approaches that hone such intuition, however, one can mention philosophy and mystagogy. Philosophy, in the Platonic sense of the love of wisdom, involves contemplating and trying to come into harmony with the highest good a tradition reveres. Mystagogy, as we have previously described, is sensitive to the mystery (fullness and perplexing character) of existence—to ultimate reality or God. By trying to reflect back upon the coherence of a tradition with philosophical and mystagogical attunement, one often finds one's own judgments about the tradition's center emerge rather clearly.

Discussion Questions

1. What is the difference between a humanistic and a theological approach to world religions?

2. Why does the interconnected character of today's international scene spotlight the significance of religion?

3. What are the main methods scholars recently have used to study religion?

4. How does "religion" relate to peoples' approaches to the mystery of human existence?

5. Why does an adequate view of a religious tradition require attending to its "center"?

6. Briefly sketch the history, world view, and center of your own religious tradition.

7. How would you counsel your friends to increase their openness to people of other religious traditions?

Glossary

faith: belief; commitment or assent beyond factual surety or proof. All religion, if not indeed all of life, requires faith, for we are always having to go beyond what is empirically certain. The religions spotlight the demand for faith, because they deal with a mystery one cannot measure, asking that we trust prior travelers on the way to gaining a healing relationship with such a mystery. The intellectual side of religions, their theologies and philosophies, do good work by offering faith a serviceable language and conceptual scheme, but faith itself always remains rounder, closer to the ineffable core of the personality and the mystery it encounters, than what any theology or philosophy can render.

God: the supreme being, holy and creative, that Western religions have considered fully personal and unique. Precisely what "God" names is a question that has long exercised both theologians and philosophers, both of whom have seen that the word intends something beyond the empirical or everyday order. In religious perspective, the word points toward the sense of transcendence and holiness many people feel, suggesting that these common stirrings of human beings are best explained by there being an objective correlative—a Being who corresponds to them as their potential fulfiller. God then becomes imagined and conceived as full of truth, beauty, justice, love, mercy, and the other qualities that human beings frequently long to meet in pure, unlimited, deathless form.

hermeneutics: the study of interpretation—how to extract the legitimate meanings of a text or artifact. The hermeneutical "turn" of recent religious studies has greatly enriched our awareness of the complexity and sophistication of the exchanges among writer, text, and readers. On the other hand, sometimes hermeneutical works get so complicated that they seem to call impossible what manifestly has happened in many times and places: effective communication of meaning from a writer or speaker to an audience. In the case of religious communication, the mysteriousness of many of the references only heightens the need for hermeneutical scholars to test their own range of experiences, feelings about religious symbols, and assumptions about the ultimate construction of both reality as a whole and religious consciousness in particular, asking that those who would preside over how meaning is established come clean about their own theoretical and personal prejudgments.

humanism: an appreciation of human virtues and needs that leads to focus on human concerns, sometimes to the neglect of divinity or ultimate reality. Humanism may go hand in hand with religion, or it may appear to be religion's enemy. The social programs of the religions, and their appreciation for the wonders of human nature, tend to make them humanistic. However, when humanism becomes delimiting—a way of saying that human beings are the measure or the limit—religion usually must protest. Religion lives from transcendence: going beyond any present attainment, reaching out to the infinite. Humanism can define itself so as to be compatible with such transcendence, but frequently it does not. Secular humanism expressly does not, taking its name from the this-worldly horizon that at best brackets divine transcendence.

mystery: something that has not been explained or cannot be explained. The religious philosophers tend to agree that the divine mystery is a fullness, a surplus, that no amount of human scholarship—indeed, no amount of divine revelation to humanity—will ever remove. So, for example, there is the Christian notion that the beatific vision of God in heaven can be endless (eternal), because the fullness of the divine intelligibility is endless—literally without limit. Theologians also speak of mysteries when in fact they might better speak of surdities: things that appear intrinsically irrational. Evil may be such a surdity or mystery. Why should people do what is to the hurt not only of others of their kind but also of themselves, since it closes them to the divine life for which they have most basically been made? Perhaps the most difficult mysteries are the natural disorders (earthquakes, cancers) that cannot be held to the account of free human beings and seem to bring God into the dock. On the testimony of Job, one can only confess one's nescience and let the problem remain with God, neither denying the ways that God seems guilty nor presuming to be certain that God can't still be bringing goodness out of what human perception can only call evil.

mysticism: experience of or direct communion with ultimate reality. Mystics come in different garbs and may be found across the religious traditions, monotheistic and polytheistic alike. Problems of definition abound, but most commentators stress an ineffable experience that brings the person into direct contact with ultimate reality or God. How important union with ultimate reality is, or how lasting the indubitable character of the experience must be, can be debated. What mystics commonly share is the conviction that the world open to the senses is only a fraction of total reality, as well as the conviction that direct communion with ultimate reality, through gracious divine love or human enlightenment, is the most precious experience any human being can have.

nature: physical reality in its totality; whatness or character. Nature in the sense of the physical world or cosmos virtually coincides with divinity in many religious traditions. Not everything in nature is divine, because divinity has depths or boundaries that escape the cosmos—transcend the natural matrix. On the other hand, nature tends to be perceived as having come from a divinity stronger and less perishable than itself. Nature therefore remains mysterious, something whose foundations, rhythms, purposes, and willfulness human beings cannot fathom. Nature in the sense of essence or whatness stems from rather refined philosophical analysis. When people distinguish between the fact that something is and the character of that thing (the way that it exists—as human or rabbit, tree or rock), they have begun to press beyond commonsensical naming and started to wonder about how things give up their whatness, how mind correlates with names and essences, and so forth. Philosophy, poetry, and natural science differentiate from a primordial wonder about this process, taking humanity in several different enriching directions and then asking to be correlated again.

primitive: original or underived; undeveloped. This word clearly can have at least two quite different connotations. As pointing to religious ways that are original, not derived from long-standing cultural traditions, primitive can suggest vitality, creativity, raw power, closeness to a nature or a divinity that has not been tamed by convention. Thus the primitive theology of the Yahwist gives the Pentateuch much of its religious power. However, as undeveloped, unsophisticated, unrefined, primitive religion is liable to con-

fusion and shallowness. Its myths may be incredible fantasies rather than lovely poetry. Its rituals may be crude exhibitions or orgies, rather than artful expressions of how the world was born, how the deities move, what human beings need to hear, say, and do to be reconciled. Scholars generally have dropped the designation "primitive religion," because the nonliterate or small-scale cultural complexes with which it dealt proved too admirable to justify risking the condescending or negative possibilities in the term.

religion: communion with, service of, or concern for ultimate reality. The etymological origins of the term stress binding or tying, to the gods or holy forces. Religion traditionally has been little distinct from the mores of a people, naming most of what has animated its art, legal conventions, ethical expectations, role models, and senses of destiny. Religion inevitably traffics in mystery, contending with the Beginning and Beyond that the human mind cannot comprehend, but religious people come in various personality types, some inclining more to social service (as their expression of devotion to ultimate holiness) and others inclining more to solitary contemplation.

revelation: disclosure (of sacred truth). The core image is of tearing or removing a veil that previously has shrouded the truth. People can make self-disclosures that merit being called revelations, but for religions the primary revelations always come from the ultimate powers. The paradox hanging over the theology of revelation is that even when divinity unveils itself, as in the Incarnation of the Logos or the gifts of the Qur'an, it remains so mysterious that one has to continue to say that what human beings do not know about it outweighs what they do know. Philosophical theologians have gained some insights into the process of revelation by appropriating the views of thinkers such as Martin Heidegger, whose essential notion of truth (*a-letheia*) was the unveiling of bits of reality that comes when a word enters the mind as a fresh naming.

ritual: prescribed, formalized religious action or ceremony. With myth, ritual constitutes the typical and basic way traditional humanity spoke to itself about the world, who it was as a people, individual destiny, and the divine forces responsible for its world and fate. Rituals tend to dramatize existence, and their appeal is holistic: to the senses, memory, feelings of social solidarity, symbolic or artistic faculties that engage people's feelings and make their experiences vivid. Few people are thoroughly convinced of truths that have not been communicated ritualistically, and instinctively most peoples have employed music, dance, special costumes, and the like to make ritualistic occasions the more impressive. Rituals carry the danger of becoming overly aesthetic, ends in themselves, antagonistic to doctrinal clarity, and rubricized (legislated in all their details), but many commentators think that the repristination of myth and ritual is essential if present humanity is to reacquire the feelings necessary to have a beautiful and fully meaningful existence.

tradition: teaching and practice that have been handed down. Religions generally look to the past for their standards, models, and wisdom. Indeed, many religions are nostalgic for a golden age when relations with the gods supposedly were better than they have been recently. Tradition can imply a precious connection to this better past and the way a people stays in touch with the paradigms given by the gods at the creation of the world. In religions that look back to a historical revelation, tradition tends to make that revelation its starting point and golden age. Thus Moses, Jesus, and Muhammad all launched strong traditions. Philosophically, tradition depends on and expresses the historicity of religion and the rest of human culture. Faith and morals, as well as art and scientific lore, are always evolving. As well, every people has to contrive ways to pass its culture on to the next generation. So tradition intersects with a people's ways of educating its young. The religious problems raised by traditioning boil down to finding a balance between neglecting the past, and so being condemned to repeat its mistakes, and being immobilized in the past, afraid or unwilling to make the adaptations necessary if what was believed in the past is to continue to be vital in the future.

ultimate reality: the endpoint the mind reaches when it seeks the source of the being, intelligibility, and goodness it experiences. This term may also indicate divinity in an impersonal mode. Religious traditions that shy away from calling themselves theistic sometimes are comfortable speaking of ultimate reality. Generally the term does not depend on revelation and may represent a philosophical or mystical extrapolation from the sense that finite realities do not furnish their own reason to be. The so-called proofs for the existence of God frequently amount to explorations of ultimate reality. The cosmological proof argues from contingency to a necessary being. The teleological proof argues from efficient action to goals and purposefulness. The ontological argument argues from the inclusion of existence in the concept of a supreme or perfect being to the actual reality of such a First, Source, or Divinity. When religions confess an ultimate reality, they virtually confess the presence of that reality to all proximate beings and situations, whether ontologically or in the sense that one cannot fully estimate the significance of any proximate reality without taking the ultimate reality into account.

worship: adoration and veneration, usually offered directly to God or truly ultimate reality. Worship can provide for prayers of petition and sacrifices aiming to dispose the deity to grant favors, but most liturgists place the heart of worship in praise and thanksgiving. Religious traditions concerned about idolatry and polytheism usually insist that only the One God merits worship. Thus biblical Judaism, Protestant Christianity, and Islam have all had iconoclastic impulses designed to protect the purity of their worship. More sacramental religions have thought worship ought to engage the senses, employ material elements, and invite nonhuman creation to participate. Iconographic traditions usually have distinguished between the veneration accorded their saints and the worship rightly offered only to God. So, for example, Catholic and Orthodox Christian theologians have separated the *latria* suitable for God from the *dulia* one might offer the saints or the holy images.

CHAPTER 1

THE ANCIENT RELIGIOUS MIND

Egyptian sign for divine wisdom

We begin our study of the Western religions by trying to understand the mentality of prehistoric human beings. *Prehistoric* implies having no literature or writing, because we moderns require writing for a critical, trustworthy account of what happened—a history. The ancient religious mind is the mentality that we hypothesize characterized humanity when it was without written records. It is the oldest human mentality, because the first human beings did not write. It is also the newest human mentality because it is the "beginner's mind" with which human beings meet the world most freshly.[1]

To feel sympathy for the earliest religionists, we must be convinced that they were as human as we are. In a way, the description that follows will argue this case, but it will also assume it. Right now, then, we need a quick and brilliant proof—a case that will banish all doubt. Consider the cripple of Shanidar.

From excavations at a Paleolithic cave ("Shanidar cave") in northern Iraq, archeologists have described the skeleton of a man whose arm had been severed in his youth. He must have been useless for hunting or self-defense. He could not have dragged fuel, extended a territory, stalked or stunned a foe. Life in his time was hand-to-mouth, and there was little extra food to go around. Surely, then, he was a liability. Like animals, his fellow cave dwellers should have let him die

Key Dates Continued

1.5 million years ago	Homo Erectus; *More Sophisticated Tools*
500,000 years ago	*Use of Fire*
100,000 years ago	Homo Sapiens; *Ritual Burial*
75,000 years ago	*Mousterian Cave Dwellers; Clothing to Survive Northern Winters*
40,000 years ago	Homo Sapiens Sapiens, *"Modern Man," Full Hunting Culture*
35,000 years ago	*Clothing Adequate for Life in Siberia*
30,000 years ago	*Prehistoric Painting and Sculpture*
30,000–25,000 years ago	*Migrations across Bering Strait to New World*
20,000 years ago	*Colonization of Europe, Japan*
15,000 years ago	*Extensive Cereal Collecting*
10,500 years ago	*Humans throughout South America*
9,500–6,500 years ago	*Cereal Cultivation, Domestication of Animals*
8000 B.C.E.	*Full Withdrawal of Glaciers*
8350–7350 B.C.E.	*Jericho, First Walled Town (10 acres)*
6250–5400	*Catal Huyuk (Turkey), Large City (32 acres)*
ca. 6000	*Rice Cultivation in Thailand; Pottery and Woolen Textiles in Catal Huyuk*
ca. 5000	*Irrigation of Mesopotamian Alluvial Plains*
ca. 4000	*Bronze Casting in Middle East*
ca. 3500	*Megaliths in Brittany, Iberian Peninsula, British Isles; Invention of Wheel*
ca. 3100	*Pictographic Writing in Sumer*
ca. 3000	*Spread of Copper Working*

where the accident occurred. They did not. There must have been something about the cripple, something more than the ability to hunt and gather. Maybe he sang, bringing cheer to the dark night. Maybe he loved children—was patient, kind, quick to tell stories. Maybe he was a great wit, or a great lover, or a great reader of signs. Or maybe he was just a good man in pain—a man whose smile broke your heart. Whatever, his family kept him on, made sure he got food and clothing. He did not die by famine or by beast. He died in a cave-in, at home in his family circle.

The Ancient Religious Mind: Twenty-five Key Dates

4.6 billion years ago	*Formation of the Earth*
3.6 billion years ago	*Rise of Life*
4 million years ago	Australopithecus, *Advanced Hominid in Africa*
2 million years ago	Homo Habilis; *Stone Tools*

Such a valuing of humanity for itself, with little concern for pragmatic benefits, indicates that prehistoric people were more than our peers. Sometimes they were our betters.[2]

In this chapter we deal with four places where one can observe important stages of humanity's first period of religious evolution: earliest religion, hunting and progress toward agriculture, the period after agriculture, and the period when many people built great stone constructions (called megaliths) on the order of Stonehenge in England.

EARLIEST RELIGION

What we are calling earliest religion begins with the oldest remains of human culture. Since humanoid beings have been walking the earth for perhaps 3,500,000 years, and since true humans *(Homo sapiens)* surely existed 100,000 years ago,[3] this is an enormous time span. On the basis of archeological evidence, scholars are persuaded that religion is virtually as old as humanity itself.[4] The earliest forms of religion are quite vague, but since the time of what we might call "developed" human beings (beings capable of abstraction and calculation), which began at least with the Aurignacian era 32,000 years ago,[5] there probably has been a reflective religion that we ourselves could recognize.

Indeed, as we shall show, we moderns continue to manifest many facets and interests of ancient religion, and psychoanalytic theory suggests that strata of early evolutionary experiences live on in our unconscious.[6] Because we have become aware of this, and because anthropological studies have shown that contemporary nonliterate tribes probably have as much native intelligence as we, contemporary attitudes toward ancient religion are very different from attitudes during the formative years of academic religious studies, when the so-called classical approaches emerged.[7] Then a scholar such as K. T. Preuss, who flourished at the turn of the century, could locate the beginnings of religion in what he called "primitive stupidity" *(Urdummheit).* Bedeviled by the evolutionary perspective that had burst on the scene with Darwin's *On the Origin of Species* (1859), many of the classicists considered nonliterate peoples to be savages, more bestial than rational.

SOME CORRELATIONS AMONG PHENOMENA OF PREHISTORIC RELIGION	
Earliest existence	Burial rites Interest in soul
Hunting	Kinship with animals Life taking life Study of game Importance of men Eventual domestication of animals
Gathering	Kinship with plants Appreciation of nature's cycles Importance of women
Agriculture	Control of crops Basis for settled life Emphasis on mother earth Source of wealth and leisure Stimulus to new technology
Megaliths	Permanence of stone Honoring of dead Bones of mother earth Ritual centers

But rational they were, and such remains as cave paintings and rock incisions lead us to conclude that they were thoroughly absorbed in making religious sense of their condition. It is perilous to generalize about a regular or typical prehistoric religious mentality (in North America alone, before the coming of whites, there were up to 2,000 separate cultures, many of them based on mutually unintelligible languages),[8] but Native Americans, Africans, Australians, and oth-

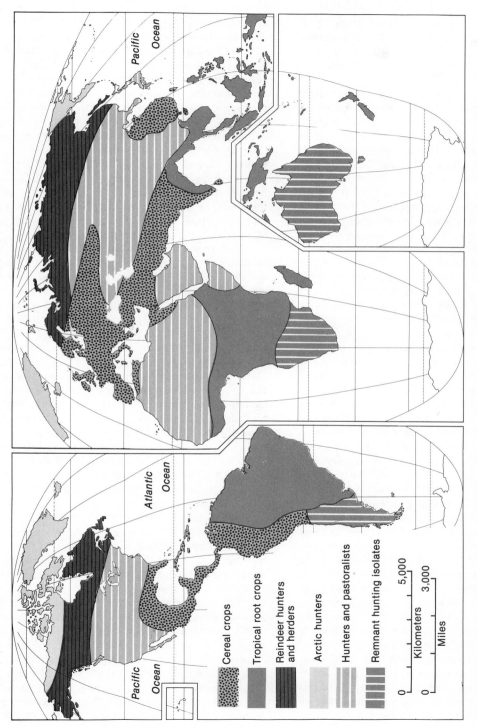

Figure 2 *Original economies of the world. Adapted from The Times Atlas of World History, edited by Geoffrey Barraclough, 1979.* © Hammond, Inc., Maplewood, New Jersey. Reprinted by permission of The London Times, New York, New York.

Cereal crops

Tropical root crops

Reindeer hunters and herders

Arctic hunters

Hunters and pastoralists

Remnant hunting isolates

Pacific Ocean

Atlantic Ocean

Pacific Ocean

Kilometers

Miles

0   3,000   5,000

ers do seem to have shared some basic beliefs. From these beliefs we can tender a few hypotheses about the earliest human cultures, which similarly had no writing, usually depended on hunting and gathering, and sought intimacy with nature.[9]

What do scholars of prehistoric religion say about the earliest human mentality? That its most absorbing issues were probably birth, subsistence, and death.[10] The first human concern probably was survival, which meant food and children. The first religious interest, consequently, probably was how to get the mysterious surrounding powers to provide food and children. Developing this thesis, the British scholar John Bowker has proposed that early religion clarifies the general biological or evolutionary situation, in which a species must sufficiently crack its "compound of limitations" to gain another generation's worth of life.[11] By "compound of limitations" Bowker means the set of factors that threaten a species' existence. This includes needing food, being liable to disease, being vulnerable to natural disaster, and the like. For human beings it also includes spiritual vulnerabilities: madness, loss of hope, and noncooperation.

At first Bowker's theory, which owes much to computer science, seems very sophisticated, but it soon works out to be rather basic: The first human beings strove mightily to survive. They hunted and gathered for food; they did what they could to avert sickness and cure disease; they begot children and tried to protect them. Part of their recourse in these efforts, though, went beyond what we might call practical means. Part of it was religious in the sense of reaching out to the unseen. There is evidence, for instance, that more than 500,000 years ago, in the Dragon Bone Hill caves of China near Beijing, people buried bodies in the hope of an afterlife.

Some of the earliest peoples, then, tried to break death's stranglehold by imagining that something in them survived death. That something might be the part that traveled in dreams, that could fantasize and construct realities other than the physical. It might be like the smoke that wood releases when it is destroyed by fire, or like the part of plants that makes them flower again after winter. Whatever, these prehistoric peoples used their imagination and at least rudimentary reflection to project meanings that could overcome their biological weakness and mortality.

At this stage of human existence, the hard distinctions between nature and human beings that we have been taught did not exist. Rather, the art of pre-

historic caves suggests that animals and plants were intimate fellow creatures, close links to humans in the chain of life. What happened to plants in the spring might well illumine what would happen to human dead in the next turn of their cycle. So as the earliest people mourned their dead, treasured their frail offspring, or marveled at sexuality, they probably drew on a sense of the life chain, the continuum of plants, animals, and themselves. We know that they anointed their dead with substances like red ochre, which resembles life-giving blood. As well, they probably saw hunting and gathering as sacred affairs, dealings with nature's awesome powers of life and death. Nature, then, was the great interest and educator of the earliest people. Much more than we moderns, they felt part of the seasonal cycles, dominated by sun and cold.

This concern with nature seems to have made certain objects related to fecundity, hunting magic, and the cult of the dead potent symbols. Whether ancient peoples thought in terms of a single, overarching power (a *"god"*) that would organize these symbols is still debated. More likely, their most general conception was of a universal bounty—a source of life that kept replenishing the animals and plants. Two apparent locations of this life-power were the sky and the earth. The sky, vaulted over everything, was in a position to observe and perhaps control everything, and it contained the sun and the rain; thus, it regularly attracted the mind's search for an ultimate principle. From the experience of human birthing, people seem to have given the earth a maternal modality very early—to have thought of it as a *Great Mother.*

Much of the *cult* of early humanity, much of its worship, probably focused on generative powers and the Great Mother. Relics from a swath of land extending from Siberia to the Near East attest to the prehistoric use of figurines of pregnant women and to the likely conception of God as a woman.[12] In the same way, numerous relics attest to a concern with hunting magic and animal fertility. In the cave called Trois Frères, near St. Girons in Ariège, France, explorers found the head of a lion engraved on a stalactite. The presence of numerous arrows suggests that the lion head functioned as a target in a ritual of hunting magic. The famous "sorcerer" painting discovered elsewhere in the same cave depicts a figure who may have presided over such hunting magic. His legs are human, his eyes are those of an owl, and he has reindeer antlers, the paws of a bear, the tail of a horse, and prominent genitals. Some scholars suggest that he is a "master of the animals,"[13] who led a dance or ritual in which his people expressed their needs and hopes for the hunt.

So prehistoric peoples probably understood their world largely in terms of quite concrete, emotion-laden interactions with the life-powers. From nonliterate peoples living today, we can hypothesize that the earliest peoples probably developed stories about the origin of the world and of themselves based on their observations of human and animal birth. Moreover, because they could create by making things, and so sensed their special powers of consciousness, prehistoric peoples may frequently have claimed to have a special soul—a source of psychic or spiritual life. Such a soul may have been thought to linger after death, giving ancestors a semiphysical presence, making them more than just their children's memories. Because of this conception of a soul, they may have thought of death as a passageway, a threshold to a new level of existence. As one passed thresholds at birth and puberty, so one might pass a last threshold at death. In death one might even curve to a new phase in a circle that led the soul back to earthly life—one's life force might animate another breathing creature, even another human body.

In this way, the fascination and dread experienced by early human beings in their encounters with death could have generated a rudimentary philosophy. As a result, they may have tried to explain both the interconnectedness of living things, which often take life from one another, and the apparent end signified by an individual's death. Because they felt so dependent on the sky and the earth, early human beings probably petitioned their aid, asking the sky and earth to carry the dying across to a new life. Thus, the interplay of life and death probably formed the center of prehistoric religion.

HUNTING AND PROGRESS TOWARD AGRICULTURE

For the more prosaic, and more certain, aspects of the history of religion before the rise of civilization, a useful guide is the first volume of Mircea Eliade's history of religious ideas.[14] In it, Eliade, a very influential

historian of religion, summarizes the major religious advances from prehistory to the time of the city-state. At the beginning, more than two million years ago, our ancestors may have pondered life's mysteriousness in terms of the implications of hunting. Living off animal flesh, they both established a bond with the animal world and made a significant change in their own evolution: "Hunting determined the division of labor in accordance with sex, thus reinforcing 'hominization'; for among the carnivora, and in the entire animal world, no such difference exists."[15] Thus, well before 500,000 B.C.E. (the date of the first documented use of fire), human beings had moved into a world of new meanings by specializing in hunting.

The earliest remains believed to have been used for religious purposes are bones, and those from the Mousterian period (70,000–50,000 B.C.E.) suggest the practice of burial with hopes for an afterlife. The problem in interpreting ancient artifacts (many of them much older than the Mousterian), though, is that they are "opaque"; their meanings are uncertain. Without written texts or at least semididactic ("teaching") art, we can only imagine how the earliest people used such artifacts—what they thought when they laid the dead in the ground, why they sang and danced, and so on. The situation is somewhat better in the Paleolithic period (30,000–9000 B.C.E.), since many cave paintings reflect the theme of animal life. They make it clear that Paleolithic peoples were bonded to animals out of need, reverence, and fear.

Some of the motifs in the cave paintings correspond to what we know from shamanist hunting peoples of modern times. For instance, many paintings combine animal and human forms (the *shaman* often identifies with a bird or wolf), and certain "x-ray" paintings manifest an interest in skeletal structures (many shamans meditate on skulls and bones, which they consider the crucial animal elements). Other motifs emerge in remains from the Mesolithic period, after the last glacial period (about 9000 B.C.E.). For example, there is a new concern with women and human fertility, as evidenced by many statues of females who either are pregnant or have exaggerated sexual features. Along with excavations of a village in Siberia, in which men and women lived in different quarters, this motif suggests an increased interest in human procreation and sexual complementarity. Such complementarity no doubt had more than human significance. Probably it meshed with the hunters' views of animal life, calculations of astronomical cycles, dances, mythic-ritualistic accounts of creation, and so on.

If the apparent similarities between certain early remains and the arts of hunting peoples living today are valid, we can infer that Mesolithic tribes had a complex world of signs and symbols—a cosmos (ordered whole) with many sacred layers. We know that shamanist ecstasy goes back to prehistoric times. We can guess that wonder about human language lent great imaginative power to such ecstasy, as it did to ritual and myth. From at least Mesolithic times, then, human beings probably have tried to coordinate sex, sacrifice, death, animals, the moon, the stars—all the striking, impressive phenomena of their lives.

Moreover, the end of the Ice Age seems to have marked a division among prehistoric peoples. From Mesolithic times there is mention of a golden era, a paradise when human relations with **heaven** and the animals were more harmonious. Probably this idea represents the culmination of hunting peoples' myths and reflection—an early form of mythic speculation on the ways things ought to be. In any case, when the glaciers melted, the flood brought the world's strangeness into sharper focus. Also, questions arose of moral responsibility and guilt: What caused the flood? How did we lose paradise? Ancestors, believed to linger on as ghosts or spiritual presences, also stimulated such questions: What is our relationship to our predecessors who knew better times? To increase their chances of living in a good age, ancient hunters probably developed a code of behavior and a cluster of taboos that they attributed to their ancestors: "Live this way and you will prosper."

Just as hunting trained people to pay close attention to the characteristics of the game—where they fed, when they migrated south or north—so gathering trained people to pay close attention to the characteristics of plants. Gatherers, the majority of whom probably were women, had to know where to find the roots, nuts, berries, fruits, and other plant products that furnished the staple portion of the earliest peoples' diet (meat from hunting was unreliable). Moreover, gatherers experimented to learn the different properties of the plants in their area—which ones yielded savory spices, which ones had healing or hallucinogenic properties, which ones could be boiled or dried to produce dyes, decorative hangings, or good fuel for the fire.

All of this attention to the cycles and characteristics of plants paved the way to agriculture: the control of plant production. With agriculture human beings made a great leap in their mastery of their environment. Like the domestication of animals, agriculture meant people no longer were at the whim of natural cycles they did not understand. They could stabilize their food supply, lay in better stores for winter, and free some members of their group for artistic work, for developing religious lore, or for planning how to dominate neighboring peoples. The very successes of hunters and gatherers therefore moved these earliest people toward a significantly different way of life (and so toward significantly different religious interests and concepts).

AFTER AGRICULTURE

The great practical advances of the Mesolithic period were the settled communities made possible by the domestication of plants and animals. In the Near East, especially in Palestine, these advances created a period of strong cultural activity, as people strove to understand and express the far-reaching changes in their life-styles. The remains of the Natufian culture at Wadi en-Natuf, for instance, show a people who built a village of circular huts, harvested wild cereals with stone sickles, and ground seeds with mortar and pestle. (There is evidence that cereals were a dietary staple in the valley of the upper Nile as early as 13,000 B.C.E.) By 6500 B.C.E. different Near Eastern communities had domesticated sheep, goats, and pigs. The Mesolithic period also produced numerous important inventions, among them the bow, cords, nets, hooks, and boats.

In Eliade's view, such inventions have more than just practical or economic effects. When people work with different materials imaginatively and creatively, they develop a sophisticated sense of the many possibilities in matter—the many analogies between tools and artifacts, between human work and natural processes. Then they easily create rich symbolisms or mystiques. Thus ancient peoples often gave mining, harvesting, or weaving a densely symbolic value. A fairly direct line runs from their prehistoric world to that of the medieval alchemist and even that of the modern engineer, in that all have been absorbed with the changes one could work on matter and through matter on social life.

Before the Mesolithic turn to agriculture and a more settled life, nomadic cultures depended on hunting, blood sacrifices, and a close identification with animals. In later times, these Paleolithic themes continued to play in the background. Through military groups, myths of the days of nomadic life, hunting for sport, and occasional orgies (with frenzied tearing of animals and eating of raw flesh), agricultural peoples kept contact with their past. Nonetheless, along with village life came "vegeculture" (the cultivation of roots, tubers, and rhizomes) and then agriculture (the cultivation of cereals and grasses). The religious impact of these cultivations was revolutionary.

For instance, to be steady producers of food, human beings had to calculate the seasons much more accurately. This led to astronomical calculations, astrology, and the worship of planets and stars. Furthermore, agriculture led to a more intimate knowledge of the natural cycle of death and rebirth. In the myth of Hainuwele, from New Guinea, we can see the ancient struggle to comprehend this new set of mysteries.[16] By her murder and dismemberment, the semidivine Hainuwele allowed tuberous plants to spring forth. In other words, vegeculture was thought to have depended on a primordial murder. More deliberately than hunters, who found available animals, cultivators buried life to secure their food. Summarizing the psychic impact of this new situation, Eliade says, "All responsible activities (puberty ceremonies, animal or human sacrifices, cannibalism, funerary ceremonies, etc.) properly speaking constitute a recalling, a 'remembrance,' of the primordial murder. It is significant that the cultivator associates with a murder the essentially peaceful labor that insures his existence, whereas in societies of hunters the responsibility for slaughter is attributed to *another,* to a 'stranger.' "[17] Thus, as people reflected on their new relations with nature, they had to confront their own responsibilities in the cycle of nature's fertility.

Succeeding the mystical solidarity between hunters and animals, then, is a mystical solidarity between cultivators and plants. Whereas in earliest times blood and bone were the essential, most sacred elements of life, in agricultural times the generative elements— masculine sperm and feminine blood—became the most sacred. Above all, women dominated agricultural life, and "mother earth" was the prime focus. Through the millennia before the biology of reproduction became clear, the earth was believed to give birth independently, without need of any male. Because women developed agriculture and controlled it, and because women issued all human life, Mesolithic culture connected women to mother earth. Thus, from this period

came the best known great goddesses. Sexuality became a sacred drive and process, because all nature— the whole cosmos—moved through a religious cycle of conception, gestation, birth, nurturance, growth, decline, and then death (which could be a new conception).

Houses, villages, shrines, and burial vaults all reflected the womb architecturally. The earth itself seemed uterine: From it we come, to it we return. Accordingly, very old myths of human creation speak of first ancestors crawling forth from mines or caves, and funerary rituals consign the dead offspring back to the Great Mother. Finally, during this initial period of agriculture, there was an increased stress on polarities—earth and sky, dirt and rain, yin and yang (the Chinese dual elements).

This focus on the earth in the Mesolithic era continued into *Neolithic* times, when village life developed into city life, agriculture became more extensive and secure, and arts and crafts such as pottery, weaving, and tool manufacturing were established. Also, in the Neolithic period, cults of fertility and death assumed even greater prominence. From sanctuaries excavated in Anatolia (modern Turkey), we know that around 7000 B.C.E. worship involved skulls and various gifts, such as jewels, weapons, and textiles. The principal divinity was a goddess, who was manifested in three forms: a young woman, a mother, and a crone (old woman). Figurines represent her giving birth, breasts adorn her cave sites, and drawings portray her among animals, especially bulls and leopards. In many caves the double ax, symbol of the storm god, underscores the fertility theme (stormy rain fecundates mother earth).

Representations of bees and butterflies relate this fertility theme to the burial skulls and gifts, since both bees and butterflies pass through distinct stages in their life cycles. Worshipers likely tried to fit death into such a scheme—to see it as another transformation of the life force, another stage. Subordinate to the goddess was a male god, a boy or youth, who seems to be her child and lover and who has some correlations with the bull.

With the discovery of bronze about 3500 B.C.E. in the Middle East, new weapons and tools came into use. Also, more specialized work developed, such as mining, smelting, and casting metal. In turn, this work created more efficient farming implements, which led to the production of surplus food. Surplus food allowed a new class of religious specialists (who were agriculturally unproductive) to arise, while the metals "industry" stimulated the exploration and colonization of new territories for raw materials.

From 1900 to 1400 B.C.E., following the Hittite invention of tempering, iron came into widespread use, and the production of bronze and iron further stimulated the human imagination and increased the symbolic content of mother earth. Whereas the earliest iron was a gift from the sky (coming in the form of meteorites), mined iron came from the womb of the earth. Indeed, miners developed regimes of fasting, meditation, and purification, since they had to go into sacred depths and extract a new form of life. Their mythology spoke of elves, fairies, genies, and spirits who inhabited the underground, assisting or witnessing the slow gestation of mother earth's strangest children, the ores. Metallurgists, like blacksmiths and potters, had to be "masters of fire," which associated them with the shamans, who were masters of inner, magical heat. Also, metallurgists took on some of the paradoxical nature of metal itself. Coming from mother earth and being a boon to humanity, metal was sacred. However, being invulnerable and easily made into an instrument of death, metal was too close to evil for humans to handle comfortably. Thus, the smith entered the mythology of the gods, fashioning weapons for their heavenly battles and tools for their heavenly enterprises. In India, Tvastr made Indra's weapons for the fight against Vrtra; in Greece, Hephaestus forged the thunderbolt that enabled Zeus to triumph over Typhon.

MEGALITHS

The Bronze and Iron ages begot the first great Near Eastern civilizations, which we discuss in Chapter 3. Here, however, we survey one last prehistoric phenomenon, the megaliths. *Megalith* means "great stone," and it brings to mind the prehistoric European cultures that left remains such as the famous cromlech (circle of huge stones) at Stonehenge in England. Actually, prehistorians speak of a megalithic cultural complex, centered at Los Millares in southeastern Spain and covering Portugal, half of France, western England, and parts of Ireland, Denmark, and Sweden. In some cases, prehistoric peoples in these areas arranged either cromlechs or *dolmens* ("immense capstone[s] supported by several upright stones arranged to form a sort of enclosure or chamber")[18] from slabs weighing as much as 300 tons.

What was the point of all this labor? Apparently the megalith was the major symbol for a cult of the dead. For Neolithic peasants of the fifth and fourth millennia B.C.E., stone was the symbol of permanence—of resistance to change, decay, or death. Unlike peoples in central Europe and the Near East, who strictly separated themselves from the dead, the megalithic tribes of western Europe sought close communion with the deceased, probably because they regarded death as a state of security and strength. To these people, ancestors could be powerful helpers and great allies. With the discovery of agriculture, human life perhaps seemed even more frail than it had before. Like that of the plant, it was ephemeral, bound to a cycle of birth, life, and death. By associating with "ancestral" stones—the bones of mother earth—humans might overcome their frailty and impermanence.

The megaliths represent burial vaults or ritual areas where this faith was practiced. At Stonehenge, for instance, the cromlech was in the middle of a field of funeral mounds. (Stonehenge was also a sophisticated instrument that could be used for making astronomical calculations.) At Carnac in Brittany, there was an avenue large enough for thousands to parade. Both sites likely were ceremonial centers or unenclosed temples—areas of sacred space for communing with ancestral stones.

Practically the whole island of Neolithic Malta was a megalithic sanctuary system. There a great goddess presided as the guardian divinity over a cult of the dead. One necropolis, now called the Hypogeum, has yielded bones of more than 7,000 people. Previously, scholars thought that this cultural complex, like the European ones, derived from a cultural basin around the Aegean Sea. However, radiocarbon datings show that the megaliths are older than the remains from the prehistoric Aegean, so western Europeans apparently developed their megalithic death cult independently.

Moreover, megaliths later cropped up in a vast geographic area extending from Algeria to Korea and North America. Thus, huge stones probably prompted in many different peoples similar ideas about death, ancestors, permanence, and escape from time and decay. If most prehistoric peoples were moved to ponder their mortality more deeply because of agriculture, perhaps they tended to use stone to assist them in this contemplation. Indeed, studies of megalithic societies that continued into the twentieth century C.E. confirm this hypothesis. In Indonesia and Melanesia, stone monuments defended the soul during its journey to the beyond, ensured an eternal existence after death, linked the living and the dead, and fertilized the crops and animals through their sacred durability. Certain customs of European peasants in megalithic areas further confirm this hypothesis. As late as the early twentieth century, peasant women in parts of France slid along stones or rubbed themselves against stones to stimulate conception. For them as for women who lived in their locales 5,000 years earlier, stone was powerful and fertilizing.

SUMMARY: THE CENTER OF THE ANCIENT RELIGIOUS MIND

We said earlier that the cyclical conflict between life and death probably formed the center of prehistoric religion. With a life expectancy less than half our own, the earliest human beings knew death as an intimate partner. So they probably struggled to make friends with the forces that seemed to oppose death: the sun, the rain, the personages they pictured as controlling the animals. They probably prayed to these forces, offered these forces things good to eat or beautiful to behold, and tried to purify themselves of evil or abusive thoughts that might alienate the powers of life. When they themselves had to kill, to secure food or ward off enemies, they probably did so with some uneasiness, feeling a need afterward to purify themselves. Indeed, the killing power of warriors probably seemed to conflict with the nurturing power of mothers, so prehistoric people perhaps kept these two powers apart, insisting that both mothers and active warriors seclude themselves from the community at large.

One can interpret the various religious rites that the remains in prehistoric caves suggest as ways to try to make contact with the powers of life that controlled the world of prehistoric peoples. In their stories and dances, the earliest peoples probably identified themselves with different natural forces and animals that impressed or appealed to them. The link between human beings and other living things would have been strong—human beings, for instance, feeling that they held as many things in common with animals as they held apart. Thus to dance in the gait of a bear, to prowl in the step of a tiger, could be to associate oneself with the bear's strength, to take on some of the tiger's deadly grace. Similarly, to draw these animals, or other life-associated forces, could be to project oneself into the world of their vitality, as could chanting, dancing, or making drug-induced voyages of the spirit.

Björn Kurtén, a scholar of prehistory, has written a fine novel about life 35,000 years ago, when the European glaciers thawed. Using his scientific knowledge to give his literary imagination a solid footing, Kurtén has brought to life a very full mental, social, and ecological existence that the earliest members of our species may well have led. In his portrait, one glimpses the identification with animal power that the artistic remains of the European caves seem to suggest. A man named Tiger has watched two tigers slowly and masterfully isolate a mammoth calf from its mother and then kill it for food. Thinking about his own name, and the need he feels to avenge his father against an enemy who had killed him, Tiger decides to put his artistic talent to good use.

Then one morning the tigers were gone. Their tracks showed that they were heading north. Tiger was tempted to follow them, but he kept his head. He knew that he had things to do, and now he thought he knew how to do them. He would appear gentle and innocent, but behind that mask he would be as swift and deadly as the tigress. There was one thing he had to do before he went on. Not far away, he found what he was looking for: a great granite hogback with a smooth, ice-polished surface, where the wind had swept away much of the snow and the sun had melted the rest. Tiger built a great fire and, armed with charcoal and mammoth fat, went to work.

He sketched out a great picture of the scene he had witnessed. The immense black mammoths took shape under his hand. Then came the tigers. He worked in ecstasy to reproduce in sensitive lines the flow of power, the clownish insolence, the mastery of the male tiger; to catch the ur-

Figure 3 *Prehistoric "Standing Stones" on the Isle of Lewis, Scotland, at Callanish. Photo by J. T. Carmody.*

gency and precision of the female, her single, high-rising attack, the one unerring stroke of violence in the whole combat. . . . Then he drew a different image, which came from another secret place in his mind. There were only two figures here: one, a majestic *shelk* [the name and symbol of his murderous enemy]; the other, a black tiger moving in to attack. The shelk, for all its glory, was touched by the premonition of death, while every line in the tiger was alive with implacable anger.

After days of toil, all was finished. Exhausted, yet with a consciousness of purpose and resolution that was new to him, Tiger contemplated his work. "That is the way it will be done," he said. The pictures sealed his compact with the great Guardian.[19]

This is an imaginative reconstruction, of course, taking considerable literary license. Nonetheless, it has the great advantage of making Tiger, one of the earliest members of our line *(Homo sapiens sapiens)*, seem as intelligent and sensitive as we are. The differences between Tiger and ourselves, which quite likely represent the actual historical differences between ourselves and people of Tiger's prehistoric era, pivot on his greater immersion in the forces of nature. Not having literacy to mediate between him and nature, he more closely identifies himself with the interactions of the other members of his natural environment than we do. For him the changing of the seasons, the migrations of the herds, the flights of the birds were both economically and aesthetically more absorbing. Consequently, they were more significant religiously. Thus the mysterious sources of life seemed to be directing the interactions of human beings and tigers to some inscrutable purpose. Feeling intensely alive, Tiger referred his whole natural ecology to a guardian power. Feeling alive, or lonely, or bewildered, many of us living tens of thousands years later reach into the darkness with spiritual efforts not so very different. Quite like Tiger, we continue to dance around life and death.

Discussion Questions

1. What do the grave sites of very ancient peoples suggest about the earliest religious interests?

2. How does literacy serve as a shield between human beings and nature?

3. Why have the sky and the earth always been religiously significant?

4. How did religion shift with the rise of agriculture?

5. What did early peoples probably make of the killing power of the hunter and warrior?

6. How did women and mother earth function in symbolisms of the cycles of life, death, and rebirth?

7. What were the main functions of the megaliths?

8. What was Tiger doing in making his great drawing?

Glossary

archetype: a first form that serves as a model for later members of the same class. In most religious mythologies primal figures and events, such as Adam and Eve and the Fall, serve as archetypes through which later members of the tradition interpret their own experiences. Archetypes therefore have something paradigmatic about them, offering themselves as basic patterns that will always prove illuminating about human weakness, possibility, mortality, and the like.

cult: this word can mean worship, usually in the sense of the formal thanksgiving, praise, and petition that a religious group offers its deity on a regular basis. The word also can mean an idiosyncratic group that in effect offers its founder or leader so intense an obedience that the life of the group verges on idolatry and seems a worship of the will of its leader. Cult in the first sense has been at the foundations of culture, implying the leisure (both physical and psychological) in which to create and appreciate works worthy of God.

god: written with a small *g,* the word implies a partial possessor of ultimate holiness, power, and the like,

and so something considerably less than the fullness of divinity intended by the monotheistic religions. Whether polytheism—profession of many divinities—is best considered a defective religious option opposed to monotheism or an alternate outlook intent on stressing the many manifestations of what might be the single source or font of holiness and creative power is a difficult question. Much depends on one's definitions of terms, especially on what one wants "monotheism" to denote and how one is going to express the presence of divinity in all creatures, each of whom may well only exist because of the direct grant of being God makes to it.

Great Mother: the female divinity found in many ancient cultural areas who seems to stand for ultimate reality in the mode of a fertile, nourishing, and perhaps kindly personification. Archeological excavations in central Europe and Asia have yielded many artifacts suggesting veneration of a Great Mother in Mesolithic and Neolithic times, if not before. Scholars usually associate such veneration with the great interest prehistoric peoples had to have in fertility of all sorts—human, animal, and vegetative. As the manifest sources of human life, human females would have suggested a Great Mother as the source of all the life in the cosmological whole—or at least as the One people did well to imagine interested in their problems of life and death and so properly honored with sacrifices, prayers, and faith.

heaven: the realm of the gods or the force that oversees human affairs. It seems an almost universal human tendency to associate the sky and its forces (light, from the sun and moon; rain, from the clouds) with the ultimate powers shaping creation, observing human activity (and so able to pass judgment upon it), and calling the human spirit to ascend toward greater vision and purity. Heaven, therefore, stands in tension with earth, sometimes as a pure zone judging a corrupt zone, but other times as symbolic of a reality needing union with earthly (maternal) powers of fertility if it is to co-create a fully vital and truly human (or truly saving) religion.

megalith: a prehistoric monument constructed of huge stones. Scholars debate the origin and intent of most aspects of the megalithic remains scattered over a large range in western Europe (but found as far east as Indonesia). The major conjectures include their use as ceremonial sites, places for burying the dead, and astronomical laboratories for making solar and stellar calculations. Clearly, they depended on sizable outlays of labor, and possibly they had social ties to promoting the significance of a chieftain class, somewhat the way the Egyptian pyramids dovetailed with the status of the pharaohs. Stone may have appealed as seeming the most immortal of substances, or as representing the bones of mother earth. Either way, it could symbolize a transhuman sort of "life" that represented something sufficiently other or transcendent to focus numinous powers.

Neolithic: relating to the latest period of the Stone Age, beginning in southwestern Asia around 8000 B.C.E. in many locales. The Neolithic period was when agriculture came firmly into human control, along with animal husbandry and village life. Writing tended to occur at the end of the Neolithic or the beginning of the Bronze Age. Nonetheless, social and ritual patterns derived from older hunter days continued to be influential, as did various mother goddesses.

prehistoric: before written history. In one sense, there are no prehistoric beings, in that all true human beings have had memory and language and so have defined themselves through stories of their origin and destiny. In another sense, writing clearly leads to a different sort of history, based on archival records and the possibility of much later reconstructing a synoptic view of events from many different sources. But we should not exaggerate the difference between these two sorts of histories and so sorts of existence, because even well-documented events always remain elusive— never can be reconstructed in their full impact nor set in a larger narrative framework that is free of assumptions and prejudices.

shaman: a specialist in ancient techniques of ecstasy. The shaman normally is a functionary for a nonliterate community, serving as its healer, intermediary with the gods, guide of the souls of the dead to their rest, and custodian of traditional tribal lore. The typical shaman comes to this role through either heredity or having manifested idiosyncratic traits (epilepsy, sexual ambiguity, poetic sensitivity, dramatic dreams). Psychologically, shamans depend on an ability to function in two worlds, the ordinary reality of daily life and the extraordinary reality they encounter through their ecstatic journeys. As well, they serve their tribe as a defense of meaning, by incarnating a contact with the powers thought to hold the tribe's destiny.

shelk: Björn Kurtén's term for a magnificent prehistoric deer. Kurtén's novel develops the scientific views that paleontologists have of the entire life of prehistoric Europeans, from the plants and animals of their environment to their hunting, gathering, art, and religion. His shelk is both an actor on the physical scene and a totem—an animal that symbolizes powers a given human tribe or individual reveres.

CHAPTER 2

RELIGIONS OF RECENT NONLITERATE PEOPLES

Australian aboriginal hunting symbol

COMMON THEMES

Let us begin by describing some of the basic characteristics of the religious lives of recent nonliterate peoples, focusing on three topics: the sacred, myth and ritual, and the shaman.

The Sacred

As we saw, life and death dominated prehistoric religion, as they dominate much religion today, but the broadest notion in the prehistoric mind perhaps was what we call the sacred or the holy. The Oxford English Dictionary defines *sacred* as "set apart for or dedicated to some religious purpose." For recent nonliterate people it has meant the realm of the truly real, the realm of the gods or venerable powers.

This idea of the sacred probably was vital among the first human beings. We believe this because recent nonliterate peoples have sensed that one can live in passionate connection with what is most real and valuable or in dissociation from it. They have sensed that they ought to be in harmony with the power that courses through sky and earth and sea and that often they were not. Furthermore, they, and no doubt the

Religions of Nonliterate Peoples: Twenty-five Key Dates

100,000 years ago	Homo Sapiens *in Africa*
70,000– 50,000 years ago	Homo Sapiens *in Australia*
30,000– 25,000 years ago	*Mongoloid Peoples Cross Bering Strait*
8500 B.C.E.	*Mongoloid Peoples throughout South America*
5000	*Agriculture and Domesticated Cattle in Nile Delta*
4000	*Intense Hunting, Gathering, Fishing in Boreal Regions*
3000	*Farming in Central Africa*
2000	*Metalworking in Peru*
1500	*Maize Farming in Central America*
1100	*Lapita Civilization in Polynesia*
1000	*Colonization of Arctic*
900	*Foundation of Nubian Kingdom of Kush*
500	*Iron Making in Sub-Sahara; First Hieroglyphic Writing in Mexico*
300	*Rise of Hopewell Chiefdoms in Illinois and Ohio*
300 C.E.	*Rise of Mayan Civilization*
700	*Islamic Domination of North Africa; Rise of Empire of Ghana*
800	*Polynesians Reach Easter Island and New Zealand*
900–1500	*Emergence of African States*
1000	*Reindeer Hunting in Boreal Regions*
1200–1300	*Eskimos Appear in Greenland*
1325–1470	*Aztec and Inca Civilizations*
1526–1870	*Ten Million Slaves Shipped from Africa*
1645	*Tasman Circumnavigates Australia*
1741	*Russian Traders Cross Siberia to Alaska*
1880–1913	*Western Powers Partition Africa*

first human beings, have seen the destruction that disharmony can bring—natural disasters, disease, slaughter, and death. So the realm of ultimacy, the realm of power and the truly real, has been both concrete and mysterious. Either way, it has been the massive given with which ancient peoples have had to contend. They may not have abstracted the powers of the sacred into a "realm" or personified it as an expression of a primordial will, but they have completely turned their spirits toward its puzzles and sway.[1]

The experience of the sacred, in Rudolf Otto's celebrated description, involves the sense of a mystery that is both fearsome and fascinating.[2] It has been most vivid in nature's manifestations of power, but it might also occur in initiation rites, ceremonial ecstasy, or other intense experiences. With modifications, we can glimpse the experience of the sacred in accounts of enlightenment and peak experiences from religious and psychological literature. The visions of Isaiah (6:1–13), Ezekiel (1:1–29), and Revelation (1:1–29) show some of the biblical expressions of the sacred. In all these cases, we can see human imagination dazzled by the pure power that makes everything that is. Perhaps this power, Van der Leeuw has argued, is religion's central object.[3]

As many scholars have shown, the sacred can touch any aspect of creation or life. Van der Leeuw

LEADING NONLITERATE RELIGIOUS FUNCTIONARIES

American Indians*	Shamanic Visionaries	Healing, guiding tribe
Eskimos	Shamanic Visionaries	Guides for dead, healing Intercessors with deities Keepers of tribal lore
Australians	Medicine Men	Healing Guidance in ceremonies Guidance into the dreamtime Keeping tribal lore
Africans	Diviners	Foretell future Determine cause of troubles Keep tribal lore
	Witch Doctors	Healing
	Priests	Sacrifice
	Kings	Sacrifice Keep fertility of people
	Prophets	Express divine voice Guide social change

*Most North American Indians sought shamanlike visions and intimacy with animal spirits. South American Indians tended to accept them but not seek them.

KEY ASPECTS OF NONLITERATE RELIGION

Sacred	Order of Being	Main social goal: Harmony with what was considered most real, most holy
Myth	Order of Thought	Group defining its identity by telling stories about how the gods made the world and human beings
Ritual	Order of Action	Ceremonies to enact the myths, bring people into contact with the original order of creation, dramatize progress in the life cycle, unite the tribe
Shamans	Order of Salvation	People with access to the sacred who could heal and mediate restoration to right order

himself deals with stones, trees, water, fire, sky, mother, father, demon, angel, king, life, death, preacher, *priest,* community, family, church, nation, soul, and more. The sacred may even focus on human hair and fingernails.[4] Clearly, ancient humanity felt the power of creation, the awesome force of life and being, everywhere. During a storm, the power could be manifested as thunder and lightning. More tranquilly, it could play on the waters.[5] Regularly it would rush in at birth and death. Hunting, planting, weaving, metalworking—all occupations felt the touch of sacred power. Thus, ancient peoples lived with a fact that the early Greek scientist Thales only glimpsed in a vision: "The world is full of gods." For them nothing that one saw or did was without its heavenly archetype.[6]

This omnipresence of sacred power is perhaps our best thread through the labyrinth of the nonliterate religions. To dramatize such omnipresence, let us draw on some examples of sacredness that Mircea Eliade has assembled in his thematic sourcebook *From Primitives to Zen.*[7] The Dayak of Borneo, for instance, thought of themselves as a sacred people. Their land was sacred, too, because it had been given to them by the divinity, which made it from the remains of the sun and the moon. For the Delaware Indians of North America, the four directions of the compass were sacred and merited prayers of thanksgiving. They thanked the east for the morning, when the light is bright and everyone feels good. They thanked the west for the end of day, when the sun goes down and everyone can again feel good. To the north they owed thanks for the wind, whose cold coming reminds us that we have lived to see the leaves fall again. To the south they owed thanks for the warm winds that make the grass turn green.

Thus, the land and its directions were regularly thought of as manifestations of creation's holy power. So, too, were the phases of life. The Ngaju Dayak of South Borneo saw marriage as a sacred stage in life's unfolding. Therefore, the two marital partners were made to die symbolically so that they could be reborn by sticking the stem of the Tree of Life, represented by a spear, in a human head taken in a raid or from a slave. Thus, the couple was made vividly aware that their new state dealt with awesome powers. (Recently the head has been replaced by a coconut.)

For the Naskapi Indians of Labrador, hunting was especially sacred, since it was their most important occupation. The Naskapi believed that the animals they hunted had emotions and purposes like their own, and that in the beginning animals could talk like humans. So the Naskapi would sing and drum to them as to friends. Similarly, they would take great care not to mutilate certain bones of the elk or beaver believed to enclose an inner soul, a spirit like the hunter's own. Indeed, they thought that at death the animals gathered in their animal realm, just as human spirits gathered in the human realm. Both realms were conceived as stages in a cycle of reincarnation (rebirth in a new form), and so both sets of spirits were bound together. If the hunters did not know the behavioral principles governing their sacred connections with the animals, all sorts of misfortune could ensue. The hunt would be fruitless, the people would be without food, sickness or even death might descend.

As hunting peoples have considered their pursuit of game sacred, so agricultural peoples have considered farming sacred. The Native Americans who raised corn (maize) reverenced it as the gift of the Corn Maiden and harvested it ceremonially.[8] Other Native Americans insisted on treating the earth especially gently in the spring, for then it was like a woman pregnant with new life. To plow it, even to walk or run on it without care, would have been to mistreat a full womb.

In a word, just about every aspect of human experience has at some time been held sacred. Thought and sex, trees and waters, stones and ancestors—all have been considered manifestations of power or holiness. We can say, therefore, that the sacred is the ultimate or deepest significance that any thing, place, or person can manifest if seen at the right angle. For instance, the beggar can seem to wear a coat of holiness. On the other end of the social scale, chieftains and kings have regularly been reverenced as sacred. In fact, the king has been not only a ruler by divine right but also frequently a sacrificial figure, killed for the sake of his people.[9]

More understandably, perhaps, the shamans, yogis, and medicine men who have been prominent in nonliterate societies' dealings with the sacred have taken on the aura of holiness. Because they have been *mediums* for encountering the venerable powers, they themselves have been venerated and feared. Normally nonliterate peoples have felt that the sacred itself was a good or at least an indifferent force. If one was not in harmony with it, however, it could be destructive. Therefore, one had to approach sacred functionaries with some caution.

A story by the contemporary Native American storyteller Durango Mendoza captures this feeling of caution.[10] Two children make fun of an old man. He has a reputation for witchcraft—the ability to turn special powers against his enemies. When one of the children later becomes sick, the story suggests an almost palpable presence of evil: The old man is taking revenge. As studies of Navaho witchcraft have shown, this evil (power turned malevolent) is often a strong component of the American Indian world view.[11] In dealing with the holy, human beings risk being consumed in burning flames. If humans are not protected, the holy can destroy them.

Many ancient aversions and *taboos* (irrational or magical forbiddings of contact with items thought to be dangerous) can be explained by the belief that the sacred demands purity. Contact with the dead, for instance, is often a source of *pollution*. Because many ancient peoples considered contact with a menstruating woman to be polluting, ancient woman was a powerful figure.[12] In neither case is the pollution something moral—it is not a matter of bad will, bad choice, or sin. Rather, it is a matter of being out of phase with the sacred and so endangered.

It is difficult for us in modern technological societies to appreciate this ancient sense of the sacred. However, our own interests in the occult, astrology, demonology, and parapsychology indicate that we still sense part of its world. Indeed, the ancient world portrayed so effectively by Carlos Castaneda forces us to realize how much our own reality is the product of social consensus and the inner dialogue that we constantly carry on.[13] If we lived in the midst of people who were awestruck by the sun, we, too, would likely reverence its rays.

Today, what science tells us about simple vegetative forces is capable of humbling us. For instance, Annie Dillard reports that a single plant of winter rye grass can send forth 378 miles of roots with 14 billion root hairs. One cubic inch of its soil can contain 6,000 miles of root hairs.[14] The power coursing through the natural world is staggering, and when we are staggered, we are open to the sacred.

Myth and Ritual

Nonliterate peoples have usually described the sacred through myth and ritual. A myth is a story, an explanation of what has happened. History began in the tendency of peoples to tell myths explaining how they came to be where and what they were. Of course, our present-day critical history distances itself from myth

by rigorously controlling sources and arguments. Nonetheless, critical history could not have developed without the capacity of human beings to remember what had happened to them and what it meant.

Ritual refers to the conduct of ceremonies. In the nonliterate context, it consists of the dances and dramatic presentations by which tribes have displayed their mythic histories and realities. Together, myth and ritual constitute the characteristic means by which nonliterate peoples have explained the world, interacted with the sacred, solidified their community, and baffled many scientific observers. If one takes ancient cultures seriously, without presuming that they are inferior or subhuman, one has to search for the meaning of their myths and rituals.[15] Let us see what that might entail.

Until the French anthropologist Marcel Griaule was tutored by a blind tribal elder, he could only deal superficially with the culture of the Dogon, an ancient tribe living near the Upper Volta region of northwestern Africa.[16] But when Ogotemmeli, the elder, led him through thirty-three days of indoctrination, Griaule came to realize that this "primitive" people had an amazingly complex traditional lore through which they explained all the important facets of their life. Essentially, their explanations were stories of how each thing or practice had come to be.

Weaving and smithery, for instance, were considered activities of heavenly origin. The weaver's ginning iron and the smith's hammer both reflected the celestial granary, which symbolized the whole world system. Because the granary contained seeds, and the heavenly smith had brought these seeds to human beings on his hammer, and because the ginning iron both resembled the smith's hammer and dealt with seeds (cotton), the smiths (men) and the weavers (women) could both be confident that their work had come from heaven and was supremely significant. In the same way, the weaver's carding stick was like the rod by which the archetypal smith had sprinkled water on his fire, while the skin on which a woman spun was like the sun, because the first leather had belonged to the bellows of the smithy, and the smithy had contained the solar fire.

Clearly, the mythic mentality of the Dogon gave them a reality that is very different from what modern imagination gives us. The logic governing the Dogon world, like most mythic worlds, was a logic of correspondences. Blacksmithing and weaving corresponded because their tools were similarly shaped and their materials were used in similar ways. Furthermore, they both fit into more comprehensive patterns used by the heavenly forces who had formed the world by design. As a result, things were more "alive" than they are in a scientific culture. A scientific culture tends to fix relationships to universal patterns rooted in the sensible world. Unless items correlate according to these patterns, they are not considered real but merely imaginary or fabulous. Like the centaur, the phoenix, or the unicorn, they can be represented but are not truly real.

Ogotemmeli did not follow such patterns. His ancestors had explained the world to him in terms of what the Nummo, the heavenly forces, had done in creating and ordering it, and this explanation had served him well. It had given smithery, weaving, harvesting, and his people's other occupations dignity and coherence. What could be more dignified than a work designed by the gods? What could be more coherent than a culture in which all occupations related, in which all occupations were strands in a single tapestry? Ogotemmeli's world was not simply a cartoon that was colorfully imagined. His mythic mentality knew as well as the scientific mentality that human relations and farming are objective and demand common sense. But often his mentality brought a different, indeed a more creative, mythic sensitivity to such common sense.

For example, the Dogon viewed speech as a means of organization, and as such thought it essentially good. Nonetheless, from the start of the world, speech had loosed disorder. This was because the jackal, God's deluded and deceitful son, desiring speech, had laid hands on the skirt (where speech was hidden) of his mother the earth and so had begun an incestuous relationship that set the world careening. As a result, there were many bad words whose utterance had quite physical effects. To Ogotemmeli they actually smelled, and their smell traveled from the nose to the throat and liver, and then to the sexual organs, where it affected potency and procreation. Was this not a vivid way of symbolizing our human psychosomatic constitution? Might it not make us rethink the effect that bad words of lust or hate have on children, both in the womb and outside?

Creation Myths. The myths of other nonliterate peoples prompt similar thoughts. For example, though American Indian creation myths are no scientific competition to current astronomy, they offer considerable insight into our condition as creatures. The Winnebago, for instance, pictured creation as a process of pure divine thought. When the Father, the Earthmaker, came to consciousness, he cried because he did not know what to do. Noticing that his tears, which had fallen from heaven, had become the waters, he realized that by wishing he could make other things become. So he wished light and earth, which became. Then he made a likeness of himself from earth, and when it did not answer him he made for it a mind and soul and breathed into it so that it could reply. Thus, in one myth, the Winnebago taught that the world was made by design and that humans were made in God's image to converse with him.

Creation is the subject of the most basic myth, which ritual frequently uses to integrate a people with the sacred. Scholars have lavished much attention on this type of myth and have found explanations of creation involving thought, sacrifice, masturbation, a cosmic egg, diving into the primeval waters, and many other motifs. Indeed, the Boshongo, a Bantu tribe of central Africa, said that the creator Bumba produced the world because he had a stomachache. In pain, he vomited up the sun, the moon, living creatures, and finally humans. Thus, again and again, in tales both funny and sobering, nonliterate people have oriented themselves in the world and suggested why things are as they are.

Rites of Passage. As a final mythoritualistic motif common to many peoples, we mention what scholars call "rites of passage." *Rites of passage* are ceremonies of the life cycle, religious dramas for birth, puberty, marriage, and death. For nonliterate peoples, each of these times has been the threshold to a new stage of development, a new stage of intimacy with the sacred. As the gods did at the beginning, so human beings have given birth, passed over to adulthood, married, and buried their dead. Most impressive have been the rites for puberty. Rites for young men regularly have stressed enduring suffering. Those for young women have stressed preparing for feminine tasks, as the particular society conceived of them. For both sexes, puberty has been a time to learn about sexuality, the tribal gods, and the discipline that adulthood demands.

In Black Elk's account of the seven rites of the Oglala Sioux,[17] the pattern for the female puberty rite was set by a vision of a buffalo calf being cleansed by its mother. Out of this grew the traditional ways that young women were cleansed (as the Sioux thought necessary for their fertility power) so that they could bear children and raise them in a sacred manner, and so that their fertility power would not conflict with the killing power of Sioux males (who were hunters and warriors).

For the BaMbuti, the forest pygmies of the northeastern Congo, female puberty rites have been less solemn. These rites, called the *elima,* have consisted of dancing and singing in praise of life.[18] Since the BaMbuti have had a quite positive view of the life that their forest gave them, the *elima* has been but one of a number of occasions on which they sang with their *molimo* (a long tubal instrument that produced hauntingly beautiful sounds and was thought to represent the forest animals' collective voice). What has emerged in the *elima* is the equality of men and women among the BaMbuti. This was reflected in the economic cooperation among the pygmies, but during the *elima* it emerged as something more basic—an instance of androgyny, of the ancient conviction that both sexes are needed for a complete, fully human life that will mirror divinity.[19]

The Shaman

The central figure of nonliterate religion, found in many areas, is the shaman, who offers the most striking example of what happens when one meets the sacred with a mythoritualistic consciousness. According to Mircea Eliade,[20] the shaman is a specialist in archaic techniques of ecstasy. Specifically, tribes of Siberia and Central Asia (which some scholars consider the most purely shamanistic) often select their shamans for psychological features and capacities that render them apt for ecstasy—for going outside themselves. The typical candidate is sensitive, introverted, inclined to solitude, and perhaps sickly (perhaps epileptic or given to fainting). By adolescence he (males predominate in Siberian shamanism) is thought to be different—peculiar, brooding, religious. If he has an emotional crisis or something strange happens to him (such as getting very sick or being struck by lightning), elders will consider him appropriate for initiation into shamanism. That will entail learning tribal lore and ecstatic techniques and then passing an initiatory ordeal.

In Siberia the initiatory ordeal amounts to a ritualized experience of suffering, death, and resurrection. The candidate's body is dismembered; he dies and is transported to the realm of the gods. There his organs are replaced or renewed, sometimes with special stones or other tokens of his visit added. Depending on the beliefs of his tribe, he may fly to heaven as a bird, climb a sacred pole or tree (the *axis mundi* connecting earth to heaven), or travel up the rainbow. Which organ is replaced seems to depend on what his tribe thinks is the organ that ultimately quickens human beings. Bone and blood are popular choices. The constant feature of the ordeal is bodily sundering and death. As noted, the death usually takes place in the realm of the gods, after a flight or ascent, and a benefactor god or ally typically reconstitutes the candidate's body (replaces the removed organ) and returns him to life.

This experience takes place while the candidate is in ecstasy, outside his normal consciousness. If the initiation is public, the community gets a running narration of how it is going, with descriptions of the ascent, the celestial realm, the dismembering, and sample voices of the gods. A modern Westerner would probably call the proceedings imaginary, but nonliterate peoples tend to equate the real with the vividly experienced, so they consider it quite real.[21] Furthermore, studies show shamans to be the healthiest members of their tribes psychologically, not the most schizoid, hysterical, or neurotic. Performing his duties makes the shaman feel good and heals him of his ills, so whenever he is out of sorts, the shaman will sing or drum and go out of himself to the gods.

When the candidate has passed his initiatory ordeal, he is usually accepted by his community and can start functioning as a shaman. His principal functions are healing, guiding the dead to the afterworld, and acting as a medium between the living and the dead. These functions show much of what a shaman's tribe believes, which is essentially that the universe and the human being are both dualistic. The universe is dualistic because it includes the human realm, where the shaman's body remains, and the spiritual realm, to which his spirit travels. The human being is dualistic because he or she has both a bodily and a spiritual part. The spirit's "travel" is the shaman's colorful experience of ecstasy.

Ordinarily, a shaman goes into ecstasy to gain knowledge or power. He must find out from the gods what is ailing a patient or what the right medicine is. (For nonliterate peoples, illness is as much a spiritual matter as a physical one.) Similarly, to find where the game has gone, the shaman must be able to go to the gods who keep the game. For example, to the coastal Eskimos, this meant the shaman's swimming to the depths of the sea, where the goddess Sedna, who ruled the seals and the fish, had fenced them in. To guide the souls of the departed, the shaman must also be

Figure 4 Eskimo mask, Alaska, nineteenth century. Wood, feathers, paint; 15 in. high. This seal mask, with bubbles extending upward, depicts what a shaman saw in a vision. The Nelson–Atkins Museum of Art, Kansas City, Missouri (Nelson Fund).

able to travel to the land of rest. If a tribal member suffers soul loss (which causes sickness), the shaman must be able to trace the soul and retrieve it.

Wherever he goes, the shaman reports on his progress. His functioning therefore re-creates the community in two senses: (1) He helps his people reassert their view of the world, and (2) he gives them an entertaining account of his plunge to the bottom of the sea, his fight to get past Sedna's vicious watchdog, and so forth. When he returns from a mission, he often requires the community to renew itself. Sedna may be withholding the fish because someone has broken a taboo—a hunter may have mistreated a seal, two brothers may have had a violent fight, or spouses may have aborted a fetus. Such a violation of the tribe's ethic must be atoned, for it has ruptured their harmony with nature. Thus, the skillful shaman creates a forum in which his people can confess their guilts and express their regrets and fears. He tries to reconcile

enemies and convince the whole tribe to reaffirm its ethical ideals.

How do shamans gain their tribe's confidence to do this? Some develop paranormal powers, including clairvoyance and clairaudience (seeing and hearing beyond the normal range). Others possess an impressive knowledge of herbs, drugs, tribal traditions, or special vocabulary. Probably the shamans' greatest success, though, comes from their mastery of techniques of suggestion, which are especially effective with peoples of vivid imagination.

Eliade's description of shamanism stresses ecstasy and the shaman's ability to go into a trance and travel to the realm of the sacred powers. Other scholars interpret shamanism more loosely, stressing its social dynamics. Overall, though, it is clear that the shaman has been a very important figure in many nonliterate tribes.

In contrast to the Siberian shaman, some functionaries in nonliterate societies give guidance by taking in a spirit. In other words, rather than going out to the gods, the gods come into them. That is the case for much of the spiritualism or shamanism in China and Japan. Typically shamans there sing songs and go into a trance as a way of being taken over, being temporarily inhabited or possessed. Significantly, such shamanism has been practiced more by women than by men. In China, the female shaman's song to her guiding spirit often has had a romantic tone, as though a beloved were pining for her lover.[22] In Japan, the *kami,* or spirits, who come can be erotically intimate. In both places, the possessed shaman performs divination, discerning what the spirits want or what the future will require. Additionally, the Japanese shamans used to band together and walk a regular beat through the local villages, offering personal advice and medical healing. In performing this work they developed teaching techniques that contributed to Japanese theater and dance.[23]

I. M. Lewis's anthropological study of spirit possession and shamanism[24] reveals important sociological aspects. Lewis finds that many of the spirit-possessed live on the margins of society. This contrasts with Eliade's theory, in which the shaman is a key social figure. Part of the contrast may lie in the fact that Lewis deals more with modern societies, whose power structures are more differentiated and complex. Another part may lie in Lewis's concentration on the "enthusiasm" of "little people" (marginals) in highly developed religious traditions (including Islam and Christianity).

Etymologically, *enthusiasm* means "being filled with the god." In Lewis's study it tends to mean emotional exaltation, as we can observe in rural American religion, where the devout may swoon, sing ecstatically, or dance. Interestingly, societies that grant women little status tend to have a substantial number of female enthusiasts. Most likely, such women use their religious experience to gain a little respect and influence. So, too, with the powerless people prominent among other groups of ecstatics. Their religion may be genuine, but the attention they receive can be very welcome.

If shamanism is to be considered in general terms, the phenomena of visions and tutelary spirits must be included. Among Native Americans the vision quest is a regular feature of an adolescent's passage to maturity. This quest is especially clear for men (it is less clear for women), and some of its most famous examples occur in *Black Elk Speaks*.[25] There we read that even before adolescence and without a quest, Black Elk was taken into the air on a cloud, saw groups of prancing horses, was told by "grandfathers" about his people's sad future, and finally was taught the sacredness of his nation's hoop—the circle representing all the Sioux.

This vision stayed with Black Elk throughout his life, dominating his interpretation of all that he observed and experienced. After he had grown old and witnessed many sadnesses, he climbed Harney Peak (for the Oglala Sioux the center of the world), prayed to the grandfatherly spirits, and confronted for the last time the broken hoop, the withering of the tribal tree. As if in answer to the tearful conclusion of his life, a raincloud appeared in the clear sky—a dramatic expression of the Great Spirit. Perhaps a majority of Native Americans were shamans like Black Elk (though not necessarily in such dramatic fashion), for many of them lived by a personal vision and spirit.

Not all shamanist figures have been exalted personalities or seers. Some have been charlatans who performed for applause or money, and some "black" shamans, who solicited the powers of evil to inflict harm. In fact, shamans have run the full gamut: from holy persons, expert in venerable lore, stooped from bearing the tribe's burdens, to quacks and half-mad mutterers. (Films show Nepalese shamans performing the crudest of cures, with filthy fetishes—objects believed to have protective power—and the blood of cocks. No doubt they offer some psychological comfort to their people, but they must be hygienic disasters. Similarly, films of Yanomamo shamans, who practice

among the fierce people living at the border of Venezuela and northern Brazil, indicate that their visions come from ingesting hallucinogenic snuff. The snuff induces visions of *hekura,* tiny humanoid figures who may be used for healing friends or making enemies sick. The Yanomamo shaman's vocation demands some dedication—periods of celibacy, for instance—but most Yanomamo shamans practice in order to ingest snuff and fight.[26])

Shamanism is so widespread that it cannot be explained by cultural diffusion from a single original center. Eliade's study treats central and northern Asia, North and South America, Southeast Asia and Oceania, central Europe, Tibet, China, and East Asia. Edmans's volume *Studies in Shamanism* studies Eskimos, North Americans, Nepalese, people of Kalash-Kaffir, Israelites (on the basis of biblical evidence), Hungarians, and Swedes.[27] Other studies have dealt with Greek and Malay cases. If the definition of shamanism is extended to include divination by trance, we could cite many African instances, including some influenced by devotional Islam (Sufism).

What does this worldwide phenomenon suggest? That shamanist ecstasy accomplishes something that most peoples have desired. To go out of oneself to deal with supernatural powers is a way of extending one's world. Many peoples have found it a way to encounter the sacred, a way to experiences both tremendous and fascinating. Surely that is why so many different tribes have employed shamanism.

We have seen something of the prehistoric religious mind. In the rest of this chapter, we examine four nonliterate peoples from different parts of the world: American Indians, Eskimos, Africans, and Australians. Each area has many cultural subgroups, so what we can say about each group as a whole is limited. Nonetheless, this chapter should give us a better understanding of how several aspects of the prehistoric religious mind have endured to the present.

AMERICAN INDIANS

Because of their contact with white culture, which has altered their reality markedly, few American Indians now live as their great-grandparents did. However, on the western reservations enough of the old traditions and native mentality remains to distinguish Indian children from those of other ethnic groups. At least, that is what child psychiatrist Robert Coles concluded after extensive contacts with Pueblo and Hopi children of New Mexico.[28] They showed an instinctive reverence for the land, a living relationship with their departed ancestors, and a revelatory dream life that he had not found in black, white, or Chicano children. All these characteristics indicate ancient beliefs, but the most significant is the orientation to the land. As Coles himself puts it:

> There is a seemingly impersonal quality to the words and gestures a Pueblo or Hopi parent uses when pointing at some element in the surrounding landscape. There is a pantheistic side to Indian life—an emphasis by parents upon the sacral quality of *both* the living and the inanimate world. And, too, there is a subdued but persistent eroticism that is expressed in the contemplative wonder and awe that Indian children learn to feel when they stare at the sky, the horizon, the land both near and far. A thunderstorm, a windstorm, or simply a bright, clear day—and the Pueblo or Hopi child is happy, is ready (if it were possible) to reach out and touch with great satisfaction the sun, the dark clouds, the air rushing by so noisily.[29]

Consider what the life of a Pueblo Indian even fifty years ago might have been like. For years, he or she would have been living "on the roof of the world," at a high elevation, absorbed by the sun, the sky, and the mountains. In youth, there would have been leisurely, wonderful ceremonies that drew the young person into the meanings and mysteries of the sun, the sky, and the mountains. In adulthood, much of life was arranged so one could contemplate these elements— think on them from the heart. Increasingly the elements came to dominate one's life. The sun, was it not a great god? Were not all human beings children of its light and warmth? The mountains—did they not give us water and make us the streams necessary for life?

All that such an Indian cared for came together in such ceremonies and contemplation. Dancing and gazing, the Indians did their part of the holy work. Ultimately, the Pueblos believed the world itself would cease to function if they did not practice their religion: The sun would not travel the sky, the mountains would not stand tall. In the utterly clear air, this belief was absolutely certain. Without thanks from human beings and exchanges with human beings, the forces

of the world would not abide human beings, would not function. Indians and sun, then, kept a holy compact. All that gave Indians life came from the sun, the sky, and the mountains. Yet Indians had great dignity, for Indians kept nature going, kept furnishing it a reason to be.[30]

For our purposes, these attitudes link recent American Indians with their most ancient forebears, who probably began to come from Siberia across a land bridge at the Bering Strait as much as 30,000 years ago. Upon contact with Europeans in the fifteenth century, native North Americans comprised several distinct geographic groups.[31] In the East were woodland tribes, who both hunted and planted. Southeastern tribes cultivated the land extensively, midwestern Plains tribes were primarily buffalo hunters, and southwestern tribes lived in pueblos or were nomads. Along the Pacific northwest coast, fishers predominated. In each case, the tribal economy determined the life-style. Depending on the buffalo meant a life quite different from that which depended on salmon or corn. Nonetheless, scholars think that some basic attitudes were held by all North Americans.[32]

At the core of these attitudes lay belief in a primary holy force. For the Sioux it was *wakan;* for the Algonquin, *orenda.* Other tribes gave it other names. But shamans throughout the continent agreed that a holy force held all things together. North American Indian life largely revolved around this force. It made nature alluring and intimidating, a source of benevolent influences that on occasion turned severe. Perhaps the key goal of most American Indians was to keep harmony with such holy natural power, to move with its cosmic pulse. Harmony was the way to fertility of both tribe and field, to success in both hunting and war, to a full life. By contrast, disharmony led to disaster: ruined crops, sickly children, defeat in war. As a deliberate exercise in disharmony, witchcraft caused a perceptible shudder. It strove against the natural rhythm, willfully tempting power to run amok. Death was too good for a witch.

As noted, these ideas probably had originated many millennia in the past. In fact, many of the myths, rituals, and beliefs of the native North Americans resemble those of Siberian tribes, and the two groups share numerous physical characteristics. The North Americans' original myths, rituals, and beliefs likely developed in a culture centered on hunting, warfare, and shamanistic activities, which North Americans pursued until recent times.[33] Even today Navaho ritual attempts cures by singing, and Zuñi ritual

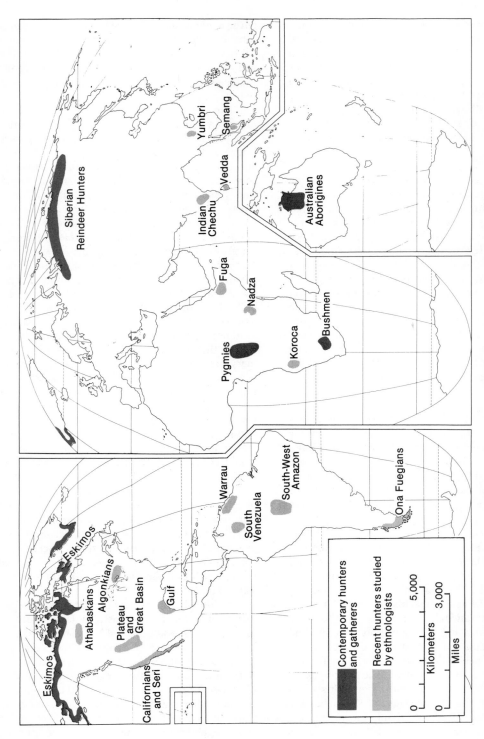

Figure 5 *Modern hunters. Adapted from The Times Atlas of World History, edited by Geoffrey Barraclough, 1979. © Hammond, Inc, Maplewood, New Jersey. Reprinted by permission of The London Times, New York, New York.*

Figure 6 *Indian boy by George Catlin (1796–1872). Oil on canvas, 49⅛ in. × 39½ in. Seminole prince Nikkanochee is shown as a young warrior. The Nelson–Atkins Museum of Art, Kansas City, Missouri (Nelson Fund).*

shows traces of hunting ceremonies (though the Zuñi have been settled agriculturalists for some time).

Divinity

For the most part, native North Americans have not worshiped a supreme "God." For them, the categories "nature" and "divinity" have been largely indistinguishable. Some of the agricultural tribes thought of a supreme power associated with the sky or the sun, but most peoples have worshiped several powers. For instance, scholars studying Indian myths find a vari-

ety of creator spirits. Earth Diver (an animal or bird who brings the earth up out of the water) is a common one, but the Zuñi tell of numerous workers who disappeared once the world was organized. According to the creation myth of the Maidu of California, a turtle collaborated with a heavenly spirit called "Earth Initiate" to pull the land up out of the waters. The turtle wanted a place to rest from his ceaseless swimming, so he volunteered to dive down for some earth. Earth Initiate held a rope tied to the turtle's left arm. The turtle went down, stayed six years, and returned covered with green slime. Under his fingernails was some sand, which Earth Initiate rolled into a ball that swelled up and became the earth.[34] In the slightly different version of the Yauelmani Yokuts of California, a duck and an eagle replace the turtle and Earth Initiate.

Less revered than creative deities are the culture heroes celebrated in myths, whose function was to socialize the tribe. Often they are twins to whom the people trace their arts and crafts. Another superhuman figure in many tribal mythologies is the spirit who owns the animals. Unless the people reverence this spirit, they will not have good hunting or fishing. A third power in North American mythology is the antihero called *Trickster.* He is both a cunning person and a dupe, a principle of both order and disorder, the founder of convention and yet its chief defier. Typically, he has enlarged intestines, an insatiable appetite, and an extended, uncontrolled penis that goes off on adventures of its own. Trickster will not control his bowels or bladder, and he makes practical jokes and humbles the haughty. In short, he is human impulsiveness, the psychoanalytic id, set free to be an entertainer.[35]

By contrasting *wakan* with lesser figures such as Trickster or culture heroes, we can focus on the more comprehensive North American notions of divinity. These include the Dakota Wakan Tanka, the Lenape Mani, and the Pawnee Tirawa. Wakan Tanka is the oneness of all holy *(wakan)* beings. Mani, on the other hand, is the chief among many gods who function as his agents. Most Lenape prayers address these agents, but the greatest ceremonies address Mani himself. Tirawa seems more like Wakan Tanka than like Mani. Though "Father Above" is one of its titles, Tirawa is usually impersonal. Perhaps we can best conceive of it as the power in all creation that sustains all things.

These native divinities, of course, were not principally ideas. If we imply that they were philosophical conclusions or abstract inferences, we misrepresent them. Rather, they have been the stuff of storytelling, song, and dance. North Americans have lived with them, spoken to them from the heart, and sought access to their sacredness through traditional ceremonies. Perhaps such ceremonies are the best introduction to American Indians' sense of both society and self.

Ceremonies

Some ceremonies, which we might call negative, have emphasized the dangers of falling out of harmony with sacred power. For instance, warriors and homicides have had to be purified, lest they infect the tribe; relatives of dead persons have had to be protected against ghosts. Even scalping ceremonies were negative, insofar as they were efforts to tame and tap the male spirit power, which resided in the head. Death, then, was a time of crisis demanding ritual protection to restore the harmony it had upset.

Much other Native American ritual, however, was positive, aiming at intimacy with a benevolent supernatural power. A good example of this is the vision quest. Many North American Indians strenuously sought a vision of a guiding spirit. (South Americans accepted visions that came but tended not to pursue them.) The vision quest became a rite of passage, a threshold to maturity. Without a vision as a guiding experience, one could not walk with direction or live with full purpose. If a young man's vision quest failed, he might become a tribal marginal, forced to dress in women's clothing and barred from male roles.

Along the Great Lakes and Mississippi Valley, the vision quest was largely used to train boys. In the Plains, men used it throughout life, whenever they felt the need. On the Pacific coast, it often took the form of spirit possession.[36] When the vision quest was used as training, children as young as seven years learned to fast. Boys heard that they would amount to nothing if they did not see a spirit and obtain its guidance. Girls could quest until puberty, when a different kind of power came, the power of motherhood.

As Charles Eastman, a Santee Sioux, tells it, a young man would begin the vision quest with a steam bath, putting off all worldly thoughts. Then he would ascend the most commanding summit, strip to his moccasins and breechcloth, and stand erect and motionless for several days.[37] To prove his sincerity, he might cut off his little finger or offer strips of flesh from his arm. When his vision came, it usually included a promise for his tribe, a glimpse of a tutelary

animal (often a wolf or eagle), and a token (perhaps a feather or hair) that became his most prized possession. Finally, the youth would also receive his song—the particular chant that he alone could sing on important occasions. If he had other visions in the future, he could accumulate a "medicine bundle" of tokens. Often shamans who were great healers relied on such tokens to work cures.

An important variation on this vision theme was the Hopi representation of spirits through ceremonial masks. In that tribe, children up to eight or nine believed the *kachinas,* or masked dancers, were real spirits in their midst. The crisis of the Hopi passage to adulthood occurred when the dancers dropped their masks, for then the young person had to accept that the reality of the *kachinas* was not physical but completely spiritual. In a painting by Louis Aiken,[38] the *kachina* has horns, a marionette face, a block nose, speakerlike ears, and a collar of fur. Emory Sekaquaptewa has described how Hopi adults assumed the characters of the masks they wore by projecting themselves into the spirit world and becoming what they were representing.[39]

Other tribes achieved such projection through the use of narcotics. Peyote is the best known, but at the time of Columbus, American Indians used perhaps a hundred different substances.[40] Far fewer were available in the Old World, which may explain why the vision quest was much less common there.

Largely through their visions, Native American shamans functioned as healers, prophets, and diviners. As healers, they tended to suck from victims' bodies objects thought to be the tools of witches or ghosts. Shamans from the Navaho and other tribes of the Southwest stressed healing by ritual singing, while holy people of planting tribes specialized in spells for crop fertility. The Pueblos of New Mexico were agriculturalists who shifted from shamanist, rather individualistic, ceremonies to more formalized, priestly rituals. However, even their lengthy chants for healing and fertility retained ecstatic elements from a preagricultural, nomadic, and shamanist past.

Constantly, then, American Indian peoples interacted with spirits, divinities, and animals, since their principal goal was to be in balance with them. Tribal rituals served this end, for they kept human beings on the right path. No North Americans seem to have thought in terms of original sin or a fall, but all tribes recognized a need for discipline and renewal. A religious ceremony such as the punishing Sun Dance of the Sioux combined such social and personal functions, renewing the tribe's good standing with sacred nature and giving warriors stoic courage.

The Self and Destiny

Among hunting tribes, the concept of the self or soul was not well defined. Human beings were thought to have several souls, one or more of which might live on after death. In fact, the Sioux were exceptional in not fearing the dead. Other tribes would have a child "adopt" a deceased relative to tame the relative's loosed soul. Reincarnation was a common belief, and the Hopi buried dead infants in the hope that their souls would return in future children. The Pueblos had a singularly clear and happy conception of the afterlife. For them the dead would either join the *kachinas* or become rain clouds. More typical was the Hopis' muted hope—they buried women in their wedding dresses, anticipating the women's passage to the next world.

Despite the importance of these notions, most Native Americans were less concerned with salvation in a future heaven than with a good life in the present. Happiness or success was to enjoy the beautiful land, to have many children, and to know the spirits intimately. Our modern notions of getting ahead would have meant little to a traditional Native American. Far more important than possessions was the power to see.

Recent Movements

In the nineteenth century, a pantribal movement called the Ghost Dance responded to Indians' depression and being subjugated by whites and temporarily lifted their spirits. The Ghost Dance was a cult based on trance and a spiritual message promising that if the Indians renewed their old ways and danced the new dance, they would defeat the whites and witness the return of the buffalo. In 1886 a Paiute named Wowoka rallied hundreds of Paiutes, Kiowas, and Cheyenne in Nevada. By 1890 the Sioux, who had lost nine million acres of their best land, turned to the Ghost Dance as a last resort. Across the country, Indians sang of the message brought by a spotted eagle: The dead are returning; the nation is coming; the Father will return the elk, the deer, and the buffalo. But the whites killed Sitting Bull, and the movement ended in the tragedy of Wounded Knee.[41]

Today one of the most interesting Native American religious movements is the Peyote religion. It was introduced in the late nineteenth century by Apaches, who traded for peyote across the Mexican border. Slowly a body of rituals developed, many of them from the Plains Indians, until there was a complete ceremonial of confession, singing, drumming, and praying. The movement incorporated some Christian elements, reached many tribes of the Plains and the Southeast, and filled some of the void left by the Ghost Dance. Today, incorporated as the Native American Church, the Peyote religion offers Indians the legal right to take peyote as their ritual sacrament.

In these and other ways, some of the tribes are preserving their traditions. Pueblos, Navahos, and Hopis have returned to some of their rituals, while in the Plains the Sun Dance ceremony of dedication and endurance is being revived. On the reservations, though, the main heritage seems to be the intimacy with nature that Coles witnessed and the concern for living at the center of nature that has so impressed some Christian observers.[42] With the Native American understanding of suffering,[43] this heritage makes for a powerful, underappreciated religious resource. However, American scholars still have a hard time appreciating the holistic, more than rational character of American Indian religion.[44] Perhaps for that reason, foreign scholars have worked more vigorously to show the importance of American Indian religion.[45] But a desire for greater intimacy with earth powers has brought feminist writers such as Margaret Atwood close to an American Indian psychology,[46] and ecological concerns may bring more of us to it in the future.[47]

ESKIMOS

Far north of the American Indians, but having some contact with them and sharing a common Siberian past, have lived the Eskimos, our next ancient religious group. The Eskimo groups differ significantly among themselves, especially the coastal and inland groups. However, most of the 50,000 or so who called themselves "Inuit" understand one another. From Greenland, across Canada and Alaska, and to the Bering Strait, their life has traditionally revolved around fishing and hunting. Naturally, their culture has been most shaped by their environment. Because sheer survival is a formidable feat, Eskimo children learn to disregard egocentric or self-indulgent impulses. From their earliest years, they are part of a group dominated, regulated, and challenged by the wind, the river, the tundra, and, above all, the snow and ice.

What sort of a personality does a child brought up in such a world have? Were you to ask Eskimo children about the world, you might be discomfited by the answer. They might quietly summarize the ruin that whites have brought Eskimo culture (especially Alaskan Eskimo culture), and they might describe a confrontation with death that the elements seldom force on those living in warmer climates.

If the children draw you pictures, the pictures will probably strike you as abstract: no people, a few uncontrolled lines, and a few bleak colors. Such a picture may well represent a storm that no one survived or the last moments of a village, or the child's own final day. Frequently, it will show only a little blue fighting an immensity of white. The white is winning—the snow, the ice, the cold.

In a strange way, this clear acknowledgment of icy death may liberate Eskimo children. They see the harshness of life so clearly that the behavior demanded by their parents makes sense. Furthermore, the opportunities to express kindness and friendliness are all the more precious. Wary, yet full of grace, Eskimo children can grow up to carve wonderful seals or spirits in ivory or stone. Or they can grow up to try to drown their pain in alcohol.[48]

The Supernatural

The full history of the Eskimos' habitation in the far north is beyond recovery. Their location, physical characteristics, and culture argue for a north Asian origin. Like that of traditional, shamanist Siberian tribes, traditional Eskimo life was dominated by the supernatural. Spirits and powers were as real as ice and snow. Eskimo notions of creation, however, were rather vague. For example, north Alaskans held that when Great Raven was sitting in darkness, he came to consciousness and was moved to create trees and humans.[49]

Eskimos of northern Canada had a myth of Sedna, goddess of the sea and source of the sea animals. Originally, Sedna was a handsome girl who proudly spurned prospective suitors. One spring a fulmar flew in from across the ice and wooed her; his song de-

Figure 7 *Alaskan house post: Haida; Sukkwan Island, about 1850. Wood, paint; 11 ft., 11½ in. high. The post is designed to placate friendly spirits and to ward off the unfriendly. The Nelson–Atkins Museum of Art, Kansas City, Missouri (Nelson Fund).*

scribed the soft bearskins she would rest on and the good food she would never lack were she to become his wife. However, the fulmar never fulfilled his promise, and the new bride found herself in the most wretched conditions, bitterly lamenting her rejection of previous human suitors. To avenge her, Sedna's father killed the fulmar; but he and Sedna then became objects of the other fulmars' wrath. While Sedna and her father were fleeing from their attack, a heavy storm arose, and the father decided to surrender Sedna to the birds by throwing her overboard. She clung to the side of the boat, but he cut off her fingers. The first joints became whales, the second joints became seals, and the stumps became ground animals. The storm subsided and Sedna returned to the boat with a fierce hatred for her father. While he was sleeping, she had her dogs gnaw off his feet and hands. He cursed her, the dogs, and himself, whereupon the earth opened and swallowed them all. Ever since, they have lived in the nether world, where Sedna is mistress of sea life.[50]

In a Greenland version of this myth, Arnaquagsaq, the old woman living in the ocean depths, sits in her dwelling in front of a lamp and sends out the animals that Eskimos hunt. Sometimes, however, parasites settle on her head, and in her anger she keeps back the game. Then the *angakoq* (shaman) must brave the way to her and remove the parasites. To do this, he must cross a turning wheel of ice, negotiate a kettle of boiling water, skirt terrible guardian animals, and finally navigate a bridge as narrow as a knife's edge.[51] He narrates this journey to the community, who follow the tale breathlessly in their mind's eye.

On the traditional Eskimo earth lived the goblin people—dwarfs, giants, trolls, shadows, and the like—who could either help travelers or carry them off to torture. Below the earth was an underworld—a warm, comfortable place where the dead could enjoy what they liked in life. The sky was usually considered a good place, too, although western Greenlanders pictured it as being cold and deserted. When the northern lights appeared in the sky, the dead were believed to be playing football with a walrus head.[52]

Eskimos traditionally regarded rocks, animals, food, and even sleep as alive. Their whole world was alive, though only humans and animals had true souls. The basic image for those souls was either a shadow or a breath. The souls were miniatures of what they animated; thus, they were pictured as tiny humans, tiny caribou, and so on. A child was named for a dead person in the belief that he or she inherited that person's soul and qualities. For that reason, the Caribou Eskimo called a child who had inherited an ancestor's name "grandmother" or "grandfather." Many Eskimos also believed in animal reincarnation. For instance, the fish soul was thought to dwell in the intestines, so they threw fish intestines back into the water to replenish the schools.

The most general Eskimo religious conception, however, was "Sila." Najagneq, a shaman whom the explorer Knud Rasmussen met in Nome, described Sila as "a great spirit, supporting the world and the weather and all life on earth, a spirit so mighty that his utterance to mankind is not through common words, but by storm and snow and rain and the fury of the sea; all the forces of nature that men fear."[53] On the other hand, Sila could also express himself gently, by sunlight or calm of the sea. Frequently, he spoke to small children. Since many of his messages warned of danger, children were directed to alert the shaman. When all was well, Sila dwelt in endless nothingness, apart from everything. He was a mystery, whether he was close or far away. Thus, Najagneq concluded, "No one has ever seen Sila; his place of being is a mystery."[54]

The Eskimo Shaman

Normally, the shaman mediated between Sedna or Sila and the tribe. Another of Rasmussen's informants, Igjugarjuk, said this about shamanist power: "All true wisdom is only to be learned far from the dwellings of men, out in the great solitudes; and is only to be attained through suffering. Privation and suffering are the only things that can open the mind of man to those things which are hidden from others."[55] The hidden powers themselves chose the people who were to deal with them, often through revelations in dreams.

Igjugarjuk, for instance, became a shaman because of strange visions he had at night, which marked him as a potential *angakoq*. He was therefore given an instructor. In the dead of winter, his instructor placed him in a tiny snow hut and left him without food or drink. His only provision was an exhortation to think of the Great Spirit. Five days later the instructor returned and gave him some lukewarm water. Again he exhorted him to think of the Great Spirit and left. Fifteen days later, the instructor gave Igjugarjuk another drink of water and a small piece of meat. After ten more days—a total of thirty days of nearly complete solitude and fasting—Igjugarjuk saw a helping spirit in the form of a woman. For five months after this he was kept on a strict diet and forbidden sexual intercourse, to consolidate his new power. Throughout his later career, he fasted whenever he wanted to see his spirit and gain her help.

Other Eskimo shamans have reported initiations involving being shot through the heart or drowned. One who was drowned described being tied to a pole and carried out onto a frozen lake. His instructor cut a hole in the ice and thrust him into it, so that he stood on the bottom with his head under water. He claimed to have been left in this position for five days, and when he was hauled up, his clothes were not wet. He had overcome death and become a great wizard.[56]

In these accounts, we can see that the Eskimo shaman's way to power is through an initiatory ordeal that often has had a death-resurrection motif. Eliade's materials on Eskimo shamans detail other initiatory techniques.[57] For instance, a neophyte might have to rub stones over and over until helping spirits came, or an older shaman might extract the neophyte's soul from his eyes, brain, or intestines, so that the spirits could determine what was best in him. Through this process, the neophyte learned how to draw out the soul himself, so as to travel on mystical journeys. Still another initiatory motif focuses on sudden illumination. In the shaman's brain flashed a sort of searchlight or luminous fire that enabled him to see in the dark, perceive coming events, or read others' secret thoughts. Finally, Iglulik Eskimos spoke of the shaman's ability to see himself as a skeleton, all of whose parts he could name in a special language. The skeleton represented elemental human stuff, that which could best resist sun, wind, weather, and even death. By going in spirit to his skeleton, the shaman stripped himself of perishable flesh and blood and readied himself to deal with the holy.

World View

In traditional Eskimo religion, then, divinity, nature, and self were all related. Although Sila was a force moving through the universe, it could be personified as a woman who was especially concerned that humans treat the animals kindly. The mythic Eskimo mentality sensed Sila or divinity in a wide variety of places, and it did not nail down the status of spirits, ghosts, or Sedna. More important was the typical ancient conviction that nature was alive, willful, holy, and dangerous. Because the shaman came into con-

tact with this dimension of life most directly, the shaman best exemplifies the Eskimo self. "Animistic," "impressionable," and even "hallucinatory" are tags that commentators have used, but these terms are probably more confusing than explanatory. Quite simply, these very practical people, who often expressed themselves in exceptionally skillful hunting, sewing, and art, were, like American Indians, extraordinarily aware of the elements' impact on their psyches.[58]

Traditional Eskimo society focused on survival: gaining shelter against the cold and obtaining the seal, fish, or deer that furnished food and clothing. The basic social unit was the married couple, and the male hunted and the female sewed. Both the hunting and the sewing took place in the midst of complex taboos. As interpreted by the shaman, these taboos formed a system for dealing with the spirits. Shamanist ecstasy, then, served social as well as individual ends. The shaman fasted, danced, or ingested tobacco to gain for the tribe access to the control center of the natural world.

This culture may go back beyond the Bronze Age.[59] Since that time, Eskimos have been hunters, and the elaborate taboo system that they developed seems to have been designed to conciliate the game who had to suffer so that the Eskimos could live. As one Iglulik shaman put it, "Life's greatest danger lies in the fact that man's food consists entirely of souls."[60] Therefore, great precautions were taken to placate the spirits of the game and avoid their anger. For instance, Eskimos poured water on the snout of the ringed seal when they killed it, because it lived in salt water and was thirsty. The harpoon had to stand by the blubber lamp the first night after the kill so that the soul still in the harpoon head might stay warm. If one killed a bearded seal or bear, no one could work for three days; also, such a prize deserved presents—for example, sole skin for the bear, because bears walk so much. The Bering Sea Eskimos spent a month preparing for their festival of the bearded seal, during which they returned to the sea the bladders of all seals caught in the preceding year.[61] In honor of the whale, they held masked dances and gave gifts.

The Eskimos of central Canada had taboos to separate land animals from sea animals. For instance, eating walrus and caribou meat on the same day was forbidden. Before seal hunting on ice could begin, the hunters had to smoke their weapons over fires of seaweed to remove the smell of the land. Similarly, all sewing of caribou skins had to cease on a particular day.

Such a taboo system depends on a network of relations among the different forms of life. Because of those relations, many Eskimos carried amulets or *fetishes*—bits of bone, feathers, or the like. An amulet represented a power bond between the wearer and the animal of origin. One might give a baby some owl claws so that the baby would have strong fists. A man would wear a piece of caribou ear to gain sharp hearing. Even soot was given to impart strength, since it is strong enough to extinguish fire.

Many analyses of Eskimo culture linger somewhat pruriently over marriage.[62] According to Freuchen, Eskimo marriage traditionally began by the man's "capturing" the woman (carrying her off more or less against her will). It was not sexually exclusive, for a man might offer his wife to a visiting friend, regularly arrange to share her with other men, take another man's wife on a hunt with him if his own were pregnant, and so on. Some groups practiced polygamy, and the general attitude was that sexual desire is just another appetite like hunger.

In part, these marital arrangements usually reflected a shortage of women. Fathers prized male children, and many female infants were killed by strangling or exposure because raising them and providing a dowry loomed as too great a burden. In daily life, however, women were indispensable. They cooked the food and made all the clothing, often chewing for hours on an animal skin to soften it for sewing. Women went on dogsled trips, and some could handle the dogs better than men. Eskimo men feared menstrual blood, so women were forbidden contact with game. For the same reason, men isolated women who were in labor. In fact, both birth and death were awesome events involving dangerous forces. A new mother was restricted in what she could eat, whom she could see, what clothing she could wear, and more. Only certain persons could touch the dead, and, if possible, a person died outdoors. If death occurred indoors, everything in the house had to be destroyed.[63]

The "spirit songs" recorded by Rasmussen offer our final glimpse into the Eskimo mind.[64] They breathe both loneliness and sensitivity. Fighting their vast, barren land, Eskimos remind us about how many trials ancient peoples endured. Their lives were short, their labors heavy. Eskimo children often died in birth, and Eskimo hunters were frequently lost at sea or frozen in storms. Nonetheless, the Eskimo human spirit devised implements for building igloos at breakneck speed and for hunting, fishing, and traveling by sled. It also produced a somber yet poetic thought-world.

Although that world was poorer mythologically than those of the American Indian or African, it was equally impressive in imagining life's elemental forces. Sitting on their ice floes and working animal skins, Eskimo men and women did what had to be done to survive. Their wisdom about Sila was no cheap grace. Sila was in both storm and quiet. It moved the bear as well as the child. Knowing Sila, one could call life good. Knowing Sila, one could be glad to be an Inuit.

AFRICANS

As American Indians and Eskimos have been shaped by their environments, so traditional Africans have been shaped by their land. They have been forest people, such as the BaMbuti, or mountain people, such as the Ik. In fact, the habitat of Africans has even determined their sense perception, how they see and hear the world. Anthropologists have found Africans from the forest who could not see things in perspective at far distances. For instance, one anthropologist took a BaMbuti friend from the forests of Zaire on a trip to the Ruwenzori Mountains of Uganda. At home in his forest, the Pygmy was a skillful hunter, able to pick his way through the dense growth with ease. He knew dozens of plants at a glance, and very little escaped his gaze. The trip was a great adventure for the Pygmy, who was shrewd, alert, and interested in every detail.

In the mountains, however, for the first time no trees blocked the Pygmy's view. The anthropologist only realized how significant this was when they stood looking down over miles of grassland. Several miles away, yet clearly in view, was a herd of grazing buffalo. "What are those insects?" the Pygmy asked. The anthropologist thought he was joking until he realized that the Pygmy had never had to make much allowance for distance when he judged something's size. The same thing happened later when they were viewing a distant lake; the Pygmy refused to believe that a large boat was in the middle, insisting that it was just a floating piece of wood.[65]

The Africa most germane to our study in this chapter is south of the Sahara.[66] In the north, Islam is now the major influence, while in the south, ancient religion mingles with Christianity. A 1990 census estimated that 294 million Africans were Christians, 263

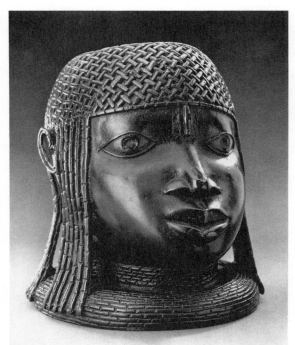

Figure 8 *Memorial head of an* oba *(king), Africa, sixteenth century. Heads such as this were placed on the king's altar to propitiate his ancestors' spirits while he was away. The Nelson–Atkins Museum of Art, Kansas City, Missouri. (Acquired through the generosity of Donald J. and Adele C. Hall, Mr. & Mrs. Herman Robert Sutherland, an anonymous donor, The Nelson Gallery Foundation, and the William Rockhill Trust [by exchange].)*

million were Muslims, and 66 million adhered to traditional ancient ways.[67] However, those figures are deceptive. Ancient notions persist so strongly that African Islam and Christianity differ markedly from their counterparts elsewhere.[68]

Because traditional Africans were not literate, no written materials are available for a history of the cultural development. Still, some analysts of African mythology find indications of very ancient thought patterns, as well as of extensive cross-cultural influences. For instance, one analyst sees in Dogon thought evidence of a time of hunting and gathering, a time of early land cultivation, a time of grain cultivation, and a time of contact with Hellenistic culture.[69] Another analyst, in a famous study of Near

Eastern kingship, draws extensive parallels between Egyptian notions more than 4,000 years old and twentieth-century African views.[70] A third, like scholars of ancient peoples generally, underscores the conservatism and tenacity of oral traditions. Some African tribes have kept a ritual language that is different from contemporary speech and that goes back countless generations, just as liturgical Latin or Old Slavonic does.[71]

World View

In analyzing traditional African religion, one first notes that most tribes have had a supreme being. In East Africa, its most common name has been Mulungu, which connotes an impersonal spirit that is far away.[72] Mulungu is creative, omnipotent, and omnipresent. It may be heard in thunder and seen in lightning. Originally Mulungu was intimate with the world, but in later days it withdrew. When personified, Mulungu is envisioned as having a wife and family. He molds human bodies and gives all life its breath.

Under Mulungu are subordinate powers.[73] Africans have reverenced both these powers and their own departed ancestors. The most important of the subordinate natural powers are the spirits of the storm, but earth spirits, water spirits, and spirits associated with crafts (such as blacksmithing and weaving) exert considerable influence, as do gods associated with divination.

Traditional West Africans have families of gods and build temples. They tend to pray every day, using simple, personal words, and frequently they pray at one of the many shrines that dot the countryside. Usually their prayers are quite practical—petitions for health, security, good farming, or safe travel. They commonly sacrifice something to a god, usually offering a liquid or cereal. The first-fruits offering at harvest time is especially important. Special occasions may prompt an animal sacrifice, and in ancient days humans apparently were sacrificed, largely to provide companions for deceased kings.[74] (Kings were crucial mediators of cosmic harmony, and so somewhat divine.)

The ox sacrifice of the Nuer shows African religious ceremony in high style. It only takes place on such important occasions as weddings or feud settlements. Once the ox has been brought in, the ceremony unfolds in four phases: presentation, consecration, invocation, and immolation (killing). The animal is tethered to a stake; officiants rub ashes on it to con-

Figure 9 *Sacred Ashanti stool, Ghana, about 1860. Wood and silver, 15 in. high ×
23½ in. wide. According to tradition, the power and well-being of the Ashanti state
were vested in a king's stool thrown down from the heavens. The Nelson–Atkins
Museum of Art, Kansas City, Missouri (Nelson Fund).*

secrate it; a priest raises his spear and invokes the
spirit; he then spears the animal, and all members of
the community eat from it.[75] (Africans in general
show great regard for cattle, and the main idea in cattle sacrifice seems to be to revere and tap the powers
of procreation that bulls and cows represent.)

Traditionally Africans also emphasize rites of passage, investing birth, adolescence, marriage, and
death with religious significance and giving the self a
sense of development. Usually these rites are performed at home under the guidance of a family elder.
At a birth, the family will make offerings to the ancestors. They will also divine to which deity the child
should be dedicated. Adolescent ceremonies stress endurance. They are ordeals designed to toughen children into adults and to impart adult sacred lore.

Frequently they take the form of circumcision or
clitoridectomy.

Many tribes are polygynous, and so African
women often are co-wives. As the operation of a wom-
en's society such as the Sande of Sierra Leone shows,
one of the purposes of clitoridectomy is to develop
deep sisterly ties, lest husbands play women off against
one another. Thus, the painful excision of the initiate's
clitoris is performed amid strong group support; other
women console the initiate with food, songs, and
dances, promising her that her present suffering will
ensure her future fertility and be a sign to her husband
of her moral and religious maturity. It is also likely
that clitoridectomy is thought to remove any maleness
(since the clitoris is perceived as a penislike organ),
allowing the woman to fit into her female social status

more easily.[76] Understandably, feminist scholars have suspected a patriarchal desire to control women's sexuality. Anthropologists also furnish interesting accounts of African circumcision.[77]

Almost all Africans consider marriage a sacred duty and children a great blessing. For that reason, the menarche (first menstruation) can be a time of tribal rejoicing and for such celebrations as the Pygmies' *elima* feast for young women. Indeed, female fertility is linked directly to tribal prosperity. With no social security system, African parents see many children as their hedge against old age. Thus, polygyny and large families are frequent. Westerners trying to lower the birthrate sometimes find themselves upsetting an old economic system.[78]

Funeral rites are intended to separate the dead from the living without offense. One must perform them most carefully, for they can influence the dead person's peace in the spirit world. Funerals keep the living in view, too, stirring up consoling memories and reminding the bereaved that all life is fleeting. Africans have tended to place great stock in dreams, often because there they could meet their departed ancestors.

Representative Myths

African religions are especially rich mythologically, so studying the tribes' tales has become a preferred way of understanding the African social outlook. In a Yoruba creation myth, the supreme God sends to a marsh an artisan who is carrying a bag that lay between the great God's thighs. From this bag the artisan shakes out soil and then a cock and pigeon, which scratch the soil until the marsh is covered. Thus, the land is holy, given from above. The Dogon say that God created the sun and moon like pots with copper rings. To make the stars he flung pellets of clay into space, and he also made the earth of clay. The Fon think that a great snake gathered the earth together after God made it and that the earth still rests on this snake's coils. For the Kikuyu of Kenya, God is the divider of the universe. He made Mount Kenya, the "Mountain of Brightness," as evidence of his wonders and as a divine resting place. The Luyia say that God first made the moon brighter and bigger than the sun. The sun became jealous, and the two fought. The moon was thrown into the dirt, resulting in its muddy face.[79]

Through many images, then, traditional Africans made their world sacred. It was a living whole, not modern science's objective collection of matter. Perhaps relatedly, African art tends to avoid representing the supreme God. Indeed, there are numerous myths of his withdrawal to the distant heaven. The Mende of Sierra Leone say that God moved away because humans were always bothering him. Ghanians and Nigerians say that humans became too familiar with God. Originally God's heaven was just above their heads, but children came to wipe their hands on it, women hit it when pounding grain, and finally a woman with a long pole hit heaven in the eye. God then moved away. The Burundi of central Africa say that God went off because a crippled baby was born, and some humans wanted to kill God, whom they held responsible. In African mythology, God often leaves by climbing a spider's thread. If there were a great emergency, humans might be able to find the thread and obtain God's help again.

Though these stories stress God's distance and so reflect an African sense of a fall from heavenly grace, African prayers show that divinity is still thought to be present and operative, in ordinary times through intermediary gods and in times of crisis through the high God. Thus, a prayer to Imana, creator God of the Ruanda-Urundi, begs, "Give me offspring, give me as you give to others! Imana, what shall I do, where shall I go? I am in distress, where is there room for me? O Merciful, O Imana of mercy, help this once."[80]

A hymn to Mwari, God of the Mashona of southern Zimbabwe, recites his attributes and accomplishments (he piled the rocks into mountains and sewed the heavens like cloth), then asks a hearing and mercy. A South African Bushman asks his God Gauwa for help in hunting, complains that Gauwa is cheating him, but concludes on a note of hope: "Gauwa will bring something for us to kill next day, after he himself hunts and has eaten meat, when he is full and feeling well."[81]

The African God, then, is both far and near, both inscrutable and able to be petitioned. In general, he is considered kind and good, a father or friend. He creates and sustains all things, but no one has ever seen him. In a number of myths, he creates humans out of the ground. The Zulu of South Africa and the Thonga of Mozambique both have a tradition that the first man and woman came out of an exploded reed bed. A Pygmy story says that the chameleon heard a strange, whispering noise in a tree. When it cut the tree open, out came a flood of water, which spread over the earth, and the first humans, who were light skinned. The Ashanti of Ghana revere Mondays and Tuesdays, because the leopard, who is sacred to some clans, emerged on those days. Also, the first human leader consoled his followers, who were frightened on coming out from under the earth. Because that leader was killed on Wednesday, Wednesday is a feared day.[82]

Overall, Africans seem to experience nature as being bountiful and good, unlike the Eskimos. Perhaps as a result, Africans show little tendency toward asceticism. God's heavenly world is but a larger and happier version of their present good life. Many tribes hope that after death there will be a rebirth from the world of ghosts into another part of the sunlit earth.

Because nature is bountiful, natural processes, including sex, are accepted without great question. The Ashanti of Ghana say that sexual knowledge came when the python sent man and woman to lie together. Consequently, many Ashanti thank the python for their children. If they find a dead python, they sprinkle it with white clay and give it a ritual burial. Africans tend to fear abnormal births, however, and disfigured people become outcasts. Twins are regarded differently by different tribes. Some tribes expose them to die, but others welcome and honor them. Like Eskimos, Africans think that souls are numerous, that the world is alive, and that a new child may inherit a soul from an ancestor.

Several of the most poignant African myths deal with life's troubles. A Zambian story tells of an old woman who wanted to follow her dead relatives because she had been left all alone. First she cut down tall trees and piled them on top of one another, trying to reach the sky. When this failed, she went looking for the road to heaven, which appears to touch the earth at the horizon. She could not find it, but in her travels she met many tribes. They assured her that suffering is normal. A myth of the Chaga of Kenya tells of a man determined to shoot God because his sons had died. When he found God, however, there were his sons, more glorious than they had been on earth.

From these and other sources, it follows that many Africans have attributed death to a mistake. The Kono of Sierra Leone, for instance, explain death as the failure of a messenger dog. God gave the dog new skins for human beings, but the dog put them down in order to join a feast and a snake stole them. Since then the snake has been immortal, changing skins, while human beings have died—and tried to destroy snakes.

Divination

The African religious functionary who merits most attention is probably the diviner. One scholar has sug-

gested that there are several levels of African *divination,* and that the diviner at the deeper levels is equivalent to a profound shaman.[83] The two polar categories this scholar uses are "possession" and "wisdom." In possession, the diviner is filled by a spirit that reads omens, interprets movements of sacred animals, and so on. In wisdom, the spirits, gods, and the diviner's own personality are subordinate to the cosmic order. Thus, wisdom is a protoscience or protocosmology—an effort to set the facts of nature and experience into some overarching scheme. Often through wisdom the diviner arrives at the notion of a Supreme Being who intelligently controls all cosmic flux. In other words, the diviner of wisdom is an intellectual, not an ecstatic or spirit-possessed functionary. His or her religious talent is to conceive a comprehensive view of how all events fit into a sacred scheme.

However, possession and wisdom are not clearly differentiated. Intermediate forms lie between them. The Mwari cultists of the Matopo Hills of Zimbabwe, for instance, believe that God speaks through mediums whom he possesses deep in certain caves, and that these messages give a comprehensive view of his operations in the world.

Also, there are numerous African intuitive diviners, famed for their ability to find lost articles, identify thieves, recognize witches, and so on. Whether they are inspired by a spirit or instinctively sense particular events is unclear. Perhaps neither explanation is adequate. These diviners show high intelligence, can pick up oblique clues from their clients' stories, and give evidence of extrasensory perception.

Evan Zuesse suggests that the typical Dogon sage is a wisdom diviner, insofar as the mythoscientific scheme that he reveals functions, with its archetypes and creation accounts, as the Dogon's most profound way of situating themselves in the world. The myths of the scheme's first level, which are made known to noninitiates, have themes such as the loss of paradise and the withdrawal of God, which are common to hunters and gatherers. A second level deals with the marriage of heaven and earth, which is a theme typical of early cultivators. The third-level myths of the cosmic egg have been found among grain cultivators, while the highest esoteric knowledge, concerning the "Word," suggests the Logos (Word) of Hellenistic culture. Therefore, through the centuries Dogon sages probably assimilated the deepest insights of each new culture with which they came into contact, weaving them into their own philosophy.[84]

Another evidence that African world views reflect centuries of cultural exchange is the common divinatory systems that stretch from Zaire to South Africa. In one system, for example, a basket containing 205 pieces of bone or wood represents all reality. To answer a question, the diviner shakes the basket and analyzes the pattern into which the pieces fall. The possible combinations are enormous, so students travel long distances to study with famous teachers. In effect, the basket and its pieces are a microcosm of the African world's social institutions and forces. The diviner can feed into this system the problem at hand and then read out an answer. As with the shaman's report from the gods, the diviner's answer often becomes a means to healing or reconciliation.

Like the African witch doctor, who is a sort of physician, the diviner supports the forces of good, just as *witches* (to be distinguished from witch doctors) and *sorcerers* are agents of evil. Most tribes think that witches work at night, are usually women, and inherit or buy from demons a power to inflict harm.[85] The sorcerer taps the power that witch doctors use, but turns it to harm. He or she may make potions, cast spells, or put pins in an image of the victim. Needless to say, sorcerers and witches are greatly feared and hated.[86]

African religion, therefore, is a good example of the "undifferentiated" consciousness we meet throughout nonliterate cultures. On the whole, it presents a compact sense of reality in which material, imaginative, and spiritual components more run together than they are clearly distinguished. The positive effect of such compactness or lack of differentiation is that the African reality has been rich and weighty. Africans have lived close to the earth, at ease with their bodies, in the midst of spiritual forces that could touch their bodies by touching their minds. The African psychology has been holistic and full of feeling, little sundered by wars between body and spirit.

The negative potential in all compact consciousness, African included, has been a vulnerability to irrationality—such fear of witches and spirits that people could die, such immersion in dreams and sensation that neither technology nor theology could make clear, consistent progress. Thus we have seen the African tendency to solve the problem of making God both transcendent of the world and immanent to the world by postulating a high God aloof from the world and lesser gods immersed in daily activity. Most

other nonliterate religious cultures have worked out similar solutions, never quite appreciating how the otherness of full divinity, its lack of the limitations we find in all nondivine realities, makes it the realest, closest of beings. On the other hand, most other nonliterate cultures have shared with African cultures a solid love of the world in which they have found themselves and so an enviable realism and mental health.

AUSTRALIANS

Australians lived far from the influence of the madding European crowd until the end of the eighteenth century. Of the settlement that followed Cook's exploratory voyage of 1770 it has recently been said: "The spread of settlement proved a disaster to the delicate ecology of aboriginal civilisation, which perished from all but the centre and far north almost before it was noticed, let alone understood."[87] Consequently, the reconstruction of how native Australian religious culture must have first appeared takes considerable imagination.[88]

The prime impression that the natives made on observers was of living in a different sort of time. Australian natives were not just sensitive to the seasons—they seemed to have a different set of aspirations. Their apparent listlessness seemed to grow more intense with age. A young man or woman who was manifestly alert and able to solve practical problems steadily became more dreamlike.

The first European observers did not know that this psychological makeup had a firm rationale. Were the native informants clearly to have spoken, they might have said something like the following: "In our religious ceremonies, we are initiated ever more deeply into the dream time of the eternal ancestors. That is the world's own time, by which creation moves. Around us, at the places in the landscape that we memorialize, the ancestors exert the pull of this dream time. Slowly, they return us all to our origins, to where we were before this life. How strange that you whites rush and bustle. You must not know the dream time, must not want to return. Too bad. Life is for returning. We are as the ancestors have dreamed us."

Historically, the Australian aborigines probably migrated from Southeast Asia (southern India and Sri Lanka) about 50,000 years ago. They spread throughout the continent and were isolated from outside influences until the arrival of Europeans in the eighteenth century. From the time of Cook's voyage interest grew, and in 1778 the British settled a penal colony in the area that is now Sydney. At the time of European contact, the aborigines probably numbered about 350,000. Some aspects of their culture suggest that they had had contact with peoples of Melanesia and New Guinea. Presently they number about 120,000, and about 45,000 are of pure stock. In the semidesert northern region, they maintain much of their original culture, which is based on hunting and gathering and which was fairly uniform across the numerous tribes.

World View

The secrecy and foreignness of much Australian lore have made it hard for Western investigators to penetrate its history or philosophic structure. Nevertheless, E. A. Worms has suggested a list of the original religion's essential features, which include the belief in a personal sky being, belief in helpful spirit beings, belief in holy, powerful objects left by the sky being, ritual drama to renew divine creativity, initiation rites for both sexes, sacrifice and prayer, and a medicine man leader.[89]

T. G. H. Strehlow has complemented this list by sketching the beliefs that were held over the entire continent.[90] According to Strehlow, most tribes believed in eternal supernatural beings, whom they linked with totemic animals, plants, or natural phenomena. In fact, the concept of totem came into religious studies largely as a result of research in Australia.[91] As Webster defines it, a *totem* is "an animal, plant, or other object serving as the emblem of a family or clan." The eternal supernatural beings were therefore ancestors and clan founders.

In the beginning, many tribes say, these supernatural beings slept under the earth's crust. Time began when they were "born out of their eternity" and burst to the surface. According to the Unambal of northwestern Australia, in the beginning Ungud lived in the earth as a snake, while in the sky was Wallanganda, the Milky Way. During the night they created everything through a creative dream. Ungud transformed himself into the beings that he dreamed; Wallanganda threw out a spiritual force, shaped it into

images, and projected them onto the rocks of the present landscape.[92] Next, spirits arose, shaped as either animals or humans and based on Wallanganda's images. In turn, they shaped the rest of the earth— mountains, sand hills, plains, and so on. The ancestors were also responsible for the aborigines' sacred songs and rituals, which were preserved with great care.

The ancestors were restrained only by a vague superior force that could punish any crimes, although they were also subject to age, sickness, and decay. Eventually they sank back into their first state of sleep, having produced the sun, moon, stars, death, labor, and pain. In the Northern Territory, scholars have found cults and art honoring the ancestors' fertility. In other regions, natives venerate rocks, trees, and *tjurunga* (distinctive slabs of wood) as sites where ancestors left supernatural powers.

Thus, Australians parceled divinity out among several supernatural figures. Central Australians believed that human beings came into existence as semi-embryonic masses that were joined together by the hundreds. The totemic ancestors then sliced these masses into individual infants. The traces of these masses left in the landscape became a principle of human life, for pregnant women would receive them and pass them on to the unborn. In other words, a soul could enter the fetus from a certain point in the landscape. It would be an immortal gift from one of the ancestors, the ancestor's own reincarnation. The newborn was thus a being of high dignity. Also, the newborn had strong links to a particular rock or tree, since from it had come the ancestor's spirit.

If humans were linked with eternal ancestors, why did they die? According to the Wotjubaluk of southeastern Australia, originally the moon raised the dead. Then an old man said, "Let them remain dead." So now only the moon itself returns to life. An Aranda myth says that the dead used to emerge from the grave for a second round of life, but a magpie who witnessed this became angry, grasped a heavy spear, thrust it into the neck of a dead man, and shoved the man back into the grave, saying, "Remain rooted down for all time."[93]

Now mortal, humans pass through a temporal circuit. Life begins when one's parent perceives the coming of the ancestor's spirit to the womb. This most often occurs in a dream but may be prompted by morning sickness or even birth pangs. During initiation into maturity, one partially reenters the dreamtime—the time when he or she originated out of eternity. Adult life means returning deeper and deeper into this time through religious ceremonies. At death one crosses the final threshold and again becomes a sacred spirit in the sky.[94]

Ritual

Puberty rites were a crucial occasion. Scholars first thought that they existed only for men, but more recent scholarship suggests that menstruation and childbirth were ritualized as religious experiences.[95] Puberty rites took place in considerable secrecy on sacred ground. Often this sacred ground represented the world as it was in the beginning, for in the puberty ceremonies the participants relived the time of creation. The puberty rites of the Kamilaroi, for instance, reenacted the time when their god Baiame was on earth and founded their ceremonies; in this way the tribe reactualized his presence and regenerated the world.

Accordingly, the Kamilaroi prepared the sacred ceremonial ground in terms of a cosmic symbolism. The dominant features were two circular enclosures. The large enclosure, about twenty-three meters in diameter, had a pole about three meters high with emu feathers on top. In the smaller circle were two young trees with their roots in the air. The Kamilaroi drew figures on the ground or modeled them in clay. The largest was a five-meter representation of Baiame. Then they pantomimed the sacred history of Baiame's creative acts. For the adolescent initiates, this was their first exposure to the tribal lore about how things were in the beginning. For the adults who directed the ceremony, it was a renewal of faith.

One tribe, the Kurnai, separated adolescent boys from their mothers matter of factly, but most tribes even today begin the ceremonies with much weeping and lamentation. Initiates may vary in age from six to fourteen, and they undergo various bodily operations. Most ceremonies follow a regular pattern of segregation of the initiates, instruction, bodily operations, revelation of some sacred objects and ceremonies, washing, and returning to ordinary life.[96] The dominant symbolism of the entire ceremony is death and resurrection. The novice dies to the child's world of irresponsible ignorance and is reborn as a mature, spiritual being. Supposedly the mothers take the death motif literally. Thinking hostile supernatural beings have killed their sons, they mourn as at a funeral. When the boys return, the women treat them as new beings, quite different from what they were as children.

During the ceremony, the boys are covered with branches or rugs. They may not use words, only sounds and signs. In the ritual operations deadly supernatural beings act upon them. When the bullroarer (a slat of wood tied to the end of a thong that roars when whirled) is sounded, the supernatural beings may knock out a tooth, pull out hair, or scar the body. Circumcision is the key act, however, because it is a direct slash at a life source.

Six months to three years after circumcision, many tribes perform a second operation called subincision. Students of Australian religion debate its significance. Subincision involves slitting the underside of the penis and permanently opening the urethra. Some tribes give it overtones of bisexuality, likening the wound to a vulva. In that case, it may represent males' efforts to arrogate powers of mothering. Supporting this is the sociological fact that the boys pass from female to male control at this time. Other evidence indicates that subincision is a way to gather blood, which is needed for other ceremonials. From this perspective the act approximates menstruation. Eliade explains this ritual as follows: "Just as the women get rid of 'bad blood' through menstruation, the initiate can expel his mother's blood by laceration of the subincision wound."[97] The deeper goal of all these initiation ceremonies, however, is to instruct the young men in the sacred lore necessary for an adult male life.

Girls' initiations are tailored more for the individual, since they are triggered by the onset of menstruation. In seclusion older women teach the girl songs and myths relating to female dignity and duties. After this instruction, they lead the young woman to a lagoon for a ritual bath and then display her to the community as an adult. In some tribes, a girl's initiation includes defloration with a sort of dildo, followed by ritual intercourse with a group of men. No doubt this act has more than a sadistic or carnal motive, but its exact religious significance is unclear. Certainly nonliterate peoples sometimes treat sexuality as an impersonal dimension of tribal life, so perhaps this aspect of the ceremony is a way of tying the potential mother to the gods' and tribe's forces.

The female puberty rite is only the first rite in an Australian woman's life. Marriage, childbearing, menopause, and old age occasion further instruction in the nature of the sacred. As the revelations become more profound, the ceremonies become more secret.

Figure 10 *Ritual mask, Sepik River, New Guinea, twentieth century. Basketry, clay, bamboo, feathers, paint; 42 in. high. This mask was used in men's ceremonies, hanging high on the gable of the man's house to represent a helpful spirit. The Nelson–Atkins Museum of Art, Kansas City, Missouri (Nelson Fund).*

Westerners have found a pattern in the women's rituals similar to that in the men's—the reenactment of mythical events from the time of creation.

In early times, women apparently played important parts in the men's rituals. Myths speak of female ancestors who were more powerful than male ancestors and of men stealing songs, powers, and artifacts that had belonged to the women. The bullroarer is one of the artifacts that the men supposedly stole. Women may have originally functioned in the male circumcision rites, for among some tribes today the initiate gives his foreskin to his sister, "who then dries it, anoints it with ochre, and suspends it from her neck."[98] No myth speaks of women stealing important religious items or doctrines from men. Most likely,

then, in earlier times religious collaboration between the sexes was greater than it has been recently. In modern times, women have not been privy to male lore. For that reason, men say that women do not progressively reenter the sacred dream time—that female ceremonies are not a steady return to spiritual existence in the sky.

The Medicine Man

The principal figure in traditional Australian ritual life has been the medicine man, who derives his healing powers from visionary contacts with supernatural beings. Usually he possesses magical items that symbolize these powers: quartz crystals, pearl shells, stones, bones, or the like. Mircea Eliade has described the ecstatic, highly imaginary making of a medicine man among the Wiradjuri of southeastern Australia.[99] First his father places two large quartz crystals against the boy's breast. They disappear into his body, making him clever and "able to bring things up." These crystals felt warm, but other ones that the boy drinks look like ice and taste sweet. From this time on, the boy can see ghosts.

During the boy's puberty rites, after a tooth has been knocked out, he learns to go down into the ground and bring up quartz crystals. The initiators take him to a grave, where a dead man rubs him to make him clever. The dead man also gives him a personal totem, a tiger snake. By following the snake, the boy and his father find the living places of various gods. At the initiation's climax, they climb a thread to Baiame's place in the sky. Baiame looks like an old man with a long beard, and from his shoulders extend two great quartz crystals.

Evidently, the medicine man is a sort of shaman whose healing powers derive from his ability to "travel to heaven." They are represented by his quartz crystals, which are part of divinity itself, and his animal spirit, the tiger snake, helps him in his tasks. An Unmatjera medicine man from central Australia reported that an old doctor threw crystals at him during his initiation and then cut out his insides. He was dead until the old man put more crystals in his body, covered it with leaves, and sang over him. The singing caused him to swell up. Then the old man gave him new internal organs and brought him back to life. From that time the medicine man was able to produce quartz crystals within himself at will, and they gave him the power to heal.

Thus, the Australian ancient religion over which the medicine men ruled bound people to the land and to one another through imaginative myths and rituals that brought them into contact with ancestral totemic spirits or divinities. Its basic goal was to keep harmony with these powers. By integrating themselves with them through ritual, participants supported nature as well as personal and tribal life. Death broke one's ties with the supernatural beings, so funeral rites had two functions—consoling the bereaved and helping the deceased to find his or her new station. The Aranda believed that finding one's new station entailed the immortal soul's going back to the place where it first passed into the fetus. The dead person's second, mortal soul turned into a ghost and was capable of malicious acts. Consequently, the mourning ceremonies tried to mute any anger that the deceased might have borne against relatives and friends. After a stated time, the ghost was incapable of mischief, because it departed for other haunts or faded away.

THE PERSISTENCE OF ANCIENT THEMES

When we observe our contemporaries interested in the occult, astrology, and witchcraft, we should get an inkling that the world of our prehistoric and nonliterate ancestors is not so far away as we tend to think. When we find ourselves longing for a pace that would be more humane, a medicine that would treat the mind and the body as fully integral to our holistic self, a technology that would try to go with nature rather than thinking it had to assault nature, we may realize that in any dialogue between such ancestors and our contemporaries the ancients would have things to teach as well as things to learn. But perhaps the clearest indication of how ancient themes continue in current Western culture emerges when we consider the three topics with which we began this chapter: the sacred, myth and ritual, and the shaman.

The sacred peeks through whenever people turn toward the mysteries of being and goodness. For example, when people respond to a philosopher such as Martin Heidegger, whose ruminations about being continue to command respect, they find their minds quieted and pointed toward something both basic and potentially holy: the mystery that anything at all should exist, that creatures should continue to step out of the void of nonbeing.[100] When people follow the wry yet troubling narratives of a novelist such as Walker Percy, they find themselves confronting very old questions about good and evil, about God and the demonic, about what true holiness, and so true humanity, entail.[101]

Clearly, therefore, many of our writers still work under the allure of the old questions that set the agenda of our early ancestors' discussions around the campfire.

The question of being plays less philosophically but no less actually in Florida sunsets, in otters sporting off Point Lobos, in a lover's eyes. Indeed, there is no place we can fly, the Psalmist says, where the divine source of being does not hover. The very structure of our minds, some religious analysts say, implies the question of God.[102] Certainly the structure of our hearts, their constant search for what is truly worth loving, what is stable in goodness, keeps open the question of the sacred, of that which might be wholly good, untouched by the evil that compromises our worldly experiences. So our own senses, minds, and hearts continue to present us with mysteries quite like those that dominated ancient human cultures.

As a consequence, we also retain a sense of the *profane,* the nonsacred. It comes from losing oneself in cooking, clerking, welding, or tennis—from gaining bread or freeing sweat. Our surfeit of busy-ness and pragmatism is a major form of profanity. Perhaps because of it, we have few awesome shrines, our woods are not full of helper spirits. We still intuitively distinguish the sacred from the profane, however, for we still sense that some things are truly real and others are but passing.

We also still make myths and ritualize the life cycle,[103] though few commentators find our myths effective or our rituals profound. For decades, we Americans lived a civil myth now called "manifest destiny." It began with the Pilgrims' errand in the wilderness, moved west to establish a New Israel, and finally led us to think we were guardians of the free world, able to destroy villages in order to save them. The shattering of this myth was close to a national trauma, suggesting how powerful ancient peoples' self-definition through stories must have been. Whether we shall fashion a new myth or a ritual cycle to make our children brave remains to be seen. We could do better than the current New Year's Day, Memorial Day, Fourth of July, and Thanksgiving or the current American way of wedding and dying. We might learn from feminist religionists' revolt from tradition and return to the goddess.[104] We could tell stories from E. F. Schumacher's *Small Is Beautiful*.[105]

Last, what about shamanism today? Are there still ecstatic people able to communicate with the sacred? The poet T. S. Eliot was rather doubtful. In *The Cocktail Party*, he made the psychiatrist our priest. One could do worse, though, than a Robert Coles or an Erik Erikson. They know a great deal about the spirit's quests. Similarly, Michael Polanyi and Eric Voegelin suggest the religious import of creative scholarship; Doris Lessing, Lawrence Durrell, Walker Percy, Patrick White, Isaac Singer, Saul Bellow, and many others show the art and mystery of modern love. Shamanism is not dead. Its essence lives in such tribal comforters.

To be sure, these people offer no panacea, no unguent for every bruise. With Aeschylus, they know that wisdom comes through suffering. But they keep heaven open, so they are deeply encouraging. Beating their drums, spinning their tales, they climb the cosmic pillar. Had we eyes to see, we might follow them to an ancient beauty, a wonder viable yet.

SUMMARY: THE CENTER OF NONLITERATE RELIGIONS

In an interesting book, whose title alone reveals a great deal about the progress of scholarship in dealing with nonliterate peoples, Sam Gill has tried to summarize the salient findings of recent researches. Gill's book is entitled *Beyond the Primitive,* and near its conclusion he reflects:

> The most general concern of this book has been to demonstrate: (1) the immense variety of religions which may be found among nonliterate cultures and (2) the complexity and sophistication of the religious beliefs and expressions. We have shown that these religious systems are comparable in many ways to those of literate peoples and to the great religious traditions which have a worldwide influence. And we have found that the religions of nonliterate peoples are not different in kind, nor in any single distinguishing feature, from the rest of the religions of humankind. How-

ever, this is not to say that there are not distinctions to be made nor that all religions are the same. Indeed, we have seen that there is a whole set of religious categories in which certain tendencies may often be associated with nonliterate peoples. Furthermore, we have shown that at least one way to address and understand these tendencies is to focus on the fact of nonliteracy, the lack of a written counterpart to the spoken language. Yet we fully acknowledge that this tie is perhaps only one of many ways these tendencies may be meaningfully associated and understood.

> Nonliteracy is linked with limits on the potential size of a culture, its forms of economy and political system, its modes of thought, and its forms of expression. Nonliteracy also shapes conceptions of time and space, fundamental to the process of religious conception and expression. We can see this fact clearly when we consider the various forms which are so ingeniously used to express complex ideas—art, artifacts, architecture, colors, odors, verbal arts, and symbolic movements. We can see how belief is both shaped by and expressed through the most commonplace aspects of sustenance activities. Nonliteracy shapes relationships and orientations within time. It encourages the face-to-face, person-to-person transmission of culture in forms especially appropriate to the needs of such processes—stories, songs, prayers, and other aspects of oral tradition.[106]

In other words, the center of nonliterate peoples' religions is much the same as the center of prehistoric and literate peoples' religions (life and death, the sacred, enlightenment, or God), but nonliterate peoples tend to color this center distinctively, because of their very nonliteracy. Not having the means to fix their histories, traditions, myths, rituals, and beliefs in unchanging form, they tend to have quite flexible histories, traditions, myths, rituals, and beliefs. They may have marvelous memories, capable of retaining orally matters that go back hundreds of years; but the sharp accent of their cultural life, and so of the faiths that inform them, is on the present, the immediate, the interpersonal.

Where literate peoples always run the risk of becoming bookish, abstract, cut loose from the living immediacy of the sacred, nonliterate peoples run the risk of quite opposite dangers. For them the problem is gaining sufficient critical distance or control over their ceremonies and beliefs to *differentiate* the various aspects of the complex reality in which their dreams, hunts, memories, and economic needs all whirl together. The shaman may well touch psychic depths that technical, literate modern cultures have neglected. The way of the shaman may well have a lot to teach modern Western medicine.[107] But the nonliterate shaman has only a slippery hold on the distinction between imagination and reason, knows only a little bit, and that intuitively, about the distinctions that might separate the sacred, the psychic, the aesthetic, and the therapeutic.

Beyond the nonliterate lies the objectifying mentality that can make these distinctions, for both weal and woe. For weal, the distinctions lead to modern science, modern political theory, modern economic arrangements. For woe, they lead to alienation, bureaucracy, systemic injustices, institutionalized neuroses. The center of nonliterate religions is a vividly sacral world, an impressively mysterious nature, that might teach aberrant modernity a great many lessons in what is necessary to regain a healthy, peaceful human nature. It would be sheer romance to make the nonliterate life of the American Indian or central African the measure of human achievement, but that sort of life often had satisfactions, healths, that literate peoples came to lose. How many modern Westerners, for example, have a vividly sacral world? What percentage of Europeans and North Americans find nature alluring, welcoming, hospitable, daunting, pacifying, as most nonliterate peoples have?

For most nonliterate peoples, nature has not been cut off from the divine or ultimate reality. It has not been raw material to be exploited, developed, subdued as human beings saw fit. It has rather been a milieu, an environment to be reverenced and enjoyed, respected and celebrated. The spirits of the trees and the animals have made nature round rather than flat, alive rather than inert, impressive rather than factitious. The beauty of the forests, the jungles, the rivers, and the skies has made nature most centrally a benevolent mystery. The world's core force or greatest divinity has been awesome, worthy of great thanksgiving and applause. Because they could not write their emotions down and be done with them, nonliterate peoples have told stories and composed dances to express their thanksgiving, petition, and applause. Because they could not separate out the part pertaining to the brain from the parts pertaining to the body, they have had to make a religious return that was whole. As we struggle to gain a postmodern wholeness, we would do well

to keep nonliterate peoples' wholeness toward the front of our minds.

Discussion Questions

1. Describe your reaction to Figure 6, "Indian boy," by George Catlin.
2. What was the significance of the Eskimo concept of Sila?
3. Why would traditional Africans consider marriage a *sacred* duty?
4. Explain the significance of the Australian medicine man's crystals.
5. Explain the sentence "The power coursing through the natural world is staggering, and when we are staggered, we are open to the sacred."
6. What are the assets and liabilities in Ogotemmeli's myth about speech?
7. What is the function of the shaman's ecstasy?
8. How does profanity, the lack of sacredness, influence contemporary Western culture?
9. Why does nonliteracy encourage a stress on the here and now?
10. What does a romantic view of nonliterate cultures tend to forget?
11. How does sacredness relate to wholeness?
12. Compose a religious myth about the Fourth of July.
13. Create a religious ritual for Thanksgiving.

Glossary

angakoq: an Inuit term used to denote the major religious figure, a shamanic healer, keeper of tribal lore, intermediary with the deities, guide of the souls of the dead, and general protector of the tribe's psychological peace against the forces of nature, the spiritual world, and the gods and goddesses that might threaten chaos.

divination: the art of discerning future events, the cause of sickness, the will of a god, and the like, practiced by the majority of archaic peoples. Diviners—specialists in this art—have used innumerable methods in their work: studying the entrails of special animals, determining the flight of birds, reading the cracks in tortoise shells, shaking out yarrow stalks or chits in a basket, and much more. Regularly the "system" developed has been a miniature of the social structure, if not the whole world view, of the tribe involved and has served the diviner as a framework for intuiting many psychological and social aspects of personal, familial, and tribal tensions.

fetish: an object believed to have protective powers. Fetishes, like geomancy, flourish in an animistic world, where one needs protection from powers that may be either malign in themselves or sent on malign errands by one's enemies. By giving the frightened personality something specific upon which to fix its hopes for defense, the fetish provides a measure of psychological comfort. Although the technologies of the sophisticated religious traditions certainly can bring forward other rationales, the beads of pious Muslims, mezuzah of pious Jews, and icons of pious Christians all draw much of their impact from the same need and psychodynamics that earlier peoples fixed on fetishes and amulets.

kachina: a masked dancer prominent in Hopi Indian ceremonies such as that for coming of age. The dancer usually stands for an ancestral spirit, and part of the revelation made to those in the process of becoming adults (full human beings) was that the *kachinas* were "actually" human beings. On the other hand, when wearing their masks the dancers themselves felt they had entered upon a different identity, so the revelation about their humanity was not just a debunking. Rather, it probably served to free the borders between "spirits" and "human beings," opening to the newly minted young adult the possibility, the wonder, that traffic crossed both ways. As in other societies that used masks in their rituals, the Hopi aimed at an ecstasy that would both expand their sense of "reality" and renew the wonder of the entire created world.

medium: a go-between, usually in the sense of the person who goes into trance to transmit messages from the dead or from intelligent spirits. Mediums flourish in shamanic milieus, for their practice depends on accrediting their ability to work in a nonordinary mode of consciousness. Most mediums appear to be passive instruments taken over by the deceased or the spirits in question. They may employ ouija boards, divination baskets, tarot cards, and similar methods, in which case they become mediums between the present and the future (or the fate that exists outside of time). One might say that premodern con-

sciousness regularly was more fluid than what we usually see in the West nowadays, and so that "travel" or "possession" was less remarkable.

myth: a storied form of explanation, usually traditional, that may discard the limits of ordinary experience and portray divine or ultimate realities acting beyond the constraints of space and time. Scholars distinguish myths into different kinds. Usually a people's most important myth concerns the cosmogony—how the world was born. This sets the pattern for all the things in creation, tends to be renewed at the turning of each new year (often through rites of dissolution [orgy] and reformation), and may be invoked at any other new start, such as erecting a house, passing from childhood to adulthood, marrying, or passing from the living to the dead. Etiological myths explain the origin of particular aspects of the natural or cultural world; teleological or eschatological myths deal with the goal of history and the end of time. Myths of judgment describe what will happen after death to reward the good and punish the wicked. Myths often are sung, danced, and ritualized. Overall, they make people's basic notions vivid, memorable, capable of empowering human beings to live with direction and conviction.

pollution: being sullied or rendered unfit for participation in sacral activities, because of some action (for example, murder) or some state (for example, menstruation) thought incompatible with proximity to the divine or ultimate reality. Pollution frequently is not a moral matter but rather a matter of what a people "feels," psychosomatically, is not compatible with divine power. The concept is of energies or vitalities whose collusion would bring disaster. However, one also can be polluted through sin, which also frequently is pictured as being out of kilter, disharmonious, with both one's better self and the legal or sacral order ordained by the divinity (either through positive precept or through the natural laws it has encoded in the human tribe or conscience).

priest: a religious functionary usually primarily concerned with performing sacrifices, rituals, and at least semiofficial interpretations of doctrine and morals. Priests tended to arise alongside writing and to become the custodians of the religious lore that multiplied after writing, but one can find ritualists in oral societies who fit most of the rest of the priest's profile. Priests may be innovators, prophets, or mystics, but as priests they tend to have debts to tradition and the current religious establishment that make them conservators rather than innovators. Frequently, priests become specialists in law and other verbal occupations—preaching, teaching—and sometimes this leads them to overstress the mental, conceptual, or semantic sides of religion. As concerned with sacrifice, priests mediate between heaven and earth, trying to placate the deity and sympathetically represent human needs before the heavenly throne.

profane: the opposite of sacred; that which exists outside the shrine or realm of the holy; ordinary reality when taken without reference to its ultimate source or goal. Scholars debate the usefulness and applicability of the twin terms *sacred* and *profane,* usually agreeing that many traditions themselves have equivalent notions but disagreeing about how precise or ultimate the notions are. For on the one hand virtually all peoples have separated off certain times and places as special—holy, given over to divinity, deserving of respect or even awe—whereas on the other hand they have thought that the divine could invade any realm and so have put brackets around mental or physical efforts to make airtight distinctions between the holy and the ordinary or even the depraved. Modern Western consciousness has increased humanity's general sense of profanity by removing many portions of reality from the divine influence. Thus the processes of nature, and many of the processes of the human mind and social consensus, now tend to be viewed as implying nothing sacred—nothing showing the direct imprint of the transcendent, other, holy reality traditionally called God. How much here is perception and how much ontology remains unclear. What presently is very clear is the difference, if not antagonism, between secular outlooks in terms of which virtually everything is profane and religious outlooks that suspect that everything positive is a gift of God and that with a properly contemplative or mystical spirit normal people could appreciate them as such.

rite of passage: a ceremony in which one moves from one state to another, for example, from puberty to adulthood, or from life to death. The great stages regularly ritualized as passages through the life cycle have been birth, puberty, marriage, and death. Many peoples have conceived of human time as an ongoing initiation, and the rituals of traditional peoples have carried the motif of further disclosures of tribal wisdom. The rites themselves tend to create a free zone, different from ordinary existence, in which people may bond in fresh and deeper ways and their ordinary identities are laid aside. One finds analogies to rites of passage, therefore, in such other ritual occasions as the Islamic Hajj and the Western Mardi Gras.

ritual: ceremonial action designed to express a people's beliefs, fears, and hopes. Rituals allow people to participate in their myths and dramatize their beliefs, so that they make a full, psychosomatic impact.

sacred: holy, more real and significant than ordinary reality, purer and deserving purer handling. The sacred stands in contrast to the profane, which is experienced as nonultimate, secular, business-as-usual, perhaps even sullied. Sacredness often elicits piety, as people experience the goodness of what is most ultimate and perhaps has been merciful to them. Awe, fear, and intoxication also may result from dealings with the sacred, as the exalted spirit either appreciates the blinding holiness and power of the sacred or loses its footing in the world. Cultures differ as to how they conceive of the sacred, but virtually all premodern cultures agreed that sacredness was the crux of meaning. In modern times secularity has risen to challenge and purify sacredness, but also to tempt humanity to try to do without sacredness—a move most religious people think disastrous.

sorcery: the use of power gained from evil spirits. Sorcery is like black magic or negative witchcraft in seeking to use its powers for harm. It usually depends on a world view in which impersonal powers can be brought to one's side or spiritual forces may be divided into those serving evil spirits and those serving good. Thus in some situations sorcery has meant diabolism—the attempt to gain and serve satanic powers.

taboo: a Polynesian word used to designate something one should avoid because of its sacral or dangerous character. Scholars tend to associate taboos with nonliterate or tribal religious traditions, but one easily finds analogies in literate and civilizational traditions. Thus, while it is clearly a taboo when Eskimos avoid contact with the seals in certain periods, or when any tribal group segregates menstruating women, it is arguably something quite the same when Jews establish kosher laws and Muslims, Buddhists, and some Christians proscribe alcohol. The common denominator in most taboos, when they are viewed psychologically, is that one is to avoid particular items not because it can be shown they are simply evil or opposed to sacredness but because cultural factors have linked these items with the human spirit's general needs to defend itself against violations of nature's strange (never fully knowable) laws, or to keep its tribe distinctive, or to preserve a sense of cleanliness that it tends to equate with godliness.

totem: an animal, plant, or other object that serves as a clan emblem. The totem suggests the symbiosis between human and animal life. A clan usually thinks of its totem as a helper, as well as a symbol of its special qualities. Thus an eagle could be a messenger from heaven, as well as a symbol of freedom and speed. A bear could be a source of wisdom about the ways of the forest, as well as an emblem of strength. It would be natural to speak to the clan totem, venerate it in regular rites, and let it summarize the whole animal economy on which one's people depended for food and clothing.

Trickster: a figure found in many nonliterate societies who usually plays a part in founding the tribe's culture and shows a deceitful, clownlike, yet powerful character. Trickster has struck some psychoanalytically inclined observers as a projection of the id—the faculty or source of irrational human impulses. Often the myths about Trickster deal with inordinate appetites—for food, sex, rascality. Trickster tends to perform gross, scatalogical pranks, and overall may often have been a safety valve—a way for a people to project their animal appetites, mock law and order, and tame with humor the destructive potential in their instinctual makeup. The pranks played by Susanoo, the wind, on the Shinto sun queen Amaterasu are a good example of tricksterish behavior.

witch: one who performs sorcery or magic with evil intent; or simply a wise woman rooted in the pre-Christian traditions of European religion. Witches could be advocates of naturalistic methods of healing, childbearing, and worship. They could be people stigmatized as social deviants. Some were men (warlocks), but most have been women. When engaged in sorcery, witches tried to tap powers of animals or malign spirits. In societies that both accredited witchcraft and feared it as a source of black magic, people proven to be witches could be marked for death.

CHAPTER 3

RELIGIONS OF ANCIENT NEAR EASTERN CIVILIZATIONS

Zoroastrian fire symbol representing purity

We begin our study of traditions that began in the Near East with four great ancient cultures: Mesopotamia, Egypt, Iran, and Greece.

MESOPOTAMIA*

Ancient Near Eastern culture began in Sumer, which lay in the southern part of what is now Iraq, where the Tigris and Euphrates rivers come together and flow into the Persian Gulf. (The term *Mesopotamia* means "between the rivers.") The Sumerians arrived there as colonizers in prehistoric times and were not related either racially or linguistically to their neighbors to the north, the Akkadians. Sumer was a flat, marshy region, and the first settlements consisted of huts built on mud. Flood was a constant, potentially devastating threat. Silt made the land fertile, however, and the

*We are indebted in this section to Professor Eugene Webb of the University of Washington, who furnished us his materials on Mesopotamian religion. Any defects, however, are entirely our responsibility.

Religions of Ancient Near Eastern Civilizations: Twenty-five Key Dates	
ca. 6500 B.C.E.	*First Farming in Greece and Aegean Countries*
ca. 5000	*Agricultural Settlements in Egypt*
ca. 3100	*Unification of Egypt; Memphite Theology; Rise of Writing in Sumer*
2700–2200	*Old Kingdom in Egypt*
2590	*Great Pyramids at Giza*
2050–1800	*Middle Kingdom in Egypt*
2000	*Beginning of Minoan Civilization in Crete*
1570–1165	*New Kingdom in Egypt*
ca. 1500	*Iranian-Speaking Peoples Rise*
1370	*Akhenaton's ''Monotheistic'' Reform*
1200	*Collapse of Mycenaean Civilization in Greece*
776	*First Olympic Games*
750	*Homer's* Iliad *and the Poetry of Hesiod*
ca. 588	*Zoroaster Begins Prophetic Work*
550	*Cyrus II Founds Persian Empire; Zoroastrianism the Official Religion*
525	*Persian Conquest of Egypt*
525–406	*Aeschylus, Sophocles, Euripides*
521	*Persia Extends from Nile to Indus*
469–332	*Socrates, Plato, Aristotle*
332–329	*Alexander in Egypt, Persia, India*
323–30	*Ptolemaic Dynasty in Egypt*
312	*Start of Seleucid Era in Persia*
247	*Arsaces I Founds Parthian Empire*
224 C.E.	*Foundation of Sasanian Dynasty*
637	*Muslims Invade Persia*

Sumerians were able over the millennia to transform the swamp into a garden. They were highly creative people, and by the time they developed cuneiform (wedge-shaped) writing—approximately two centuries before the Egyptians developed hieroglyphics—they had already built great terraced, multistoried temple towers (ziggurats) with bricks, and they were using sailboats, wheeled vehicles, animal-drawn plows, and potter's wheels. The country included a dozen small cities, each belonging in principle to its god and centered upon his temple. These cities included Eridu (traditionally considered the earliest, dating from about 4000 B.C.E.), Ur, Nippur, and Uruk or Erech. Sumerian kings served as representatives of the gods, enforcing their justice and promoting wealth to be used in their service. Cuneiform writing developed primarily as an instrument for recording contracts and accounts in the affairs of the temples, which controlled up to one-third of the land and owned great wealth.

It was also in Sumer, toward the middle of the twenty-fourth century B.C.E., that the idea of imperial rule was born, when a king named Lugalzaggesi (Zaggesi the Great) conquered a large part of the valley. An inscription that Lugalzaggesi placed on a monument in Nippur tells how Enlil, the supreme god and king of all countries, gave dominion to Lugalzaggesi, who

Figure 11   Egypt, Iran, and Greece.

MAJOR CHALLENGES TO THE COSMOLOGICAL MYTH		
Egypt	Akhenaton Amon hymns	"Monotheism" Negative theology
Iran	Zoroaster	Interior, spiritual experience as source of divine attributes
Greece	Philosophy	Correlation of mind and reality; rationality as crux of reality

then prayed that his rule might be peaceful and prosperous forever.

Sumerian political power never extended northward into Akkad, but Sumer had enormous cultural influence there. Over the centuries the Akkadians learned writing from the Sumerians and adopted much of their mythology and technology. Despite Lugalzaggesi's prayer for perpetual dominion, he was later defeated in battle and taken captive by an Akkadian, Sargon I, who founded an empire of his own—and also claimed the authority of Enlil. Sargon's rule was short-lived, however, and the Sumerians regained their independence for a while. But by the time of Hammurabi in the eighteenth century B.C.E., the Sumerians were completely absorbed into the civilization that is now known as the Babylonian, after its principal city, Babylon (*Babilani* or "the gateway of the gods"), which grew to prominence after the demise of Ur.

Although we have some Sumerian fragments, most of the writings now available come from the Babylonian period, so we see Sumerian myths through Babylonian eyes and with Babylonian adaptations. One reason that the evidence is so fragmentary, in addition to its enormous antiquity, is the fact that the cuneiform tablets were not used primarily for the recording of myths, but for business accounts. In many cases the tablets with myths seem to have been the exercise books of schoolboys learning to write by copying out stories. Still, we have enough evidence to provide a fairly clear picture of the religious conceptions not only of the Babylonians, but also of the Sumerians.

Sumerian Creation Myths

The great legacy of Mesopotamia is its mythology. To begin with the beginning, let us consider one of the earliest Sumerian creation myths, the story of Enki and Ninhursag in the land of Dilmun.[1] Dilmun, the poem tells us, was pure, clean, and bright, free from death and disease, until the mother goddess, Ninhursag, was impregnated by Enki, variously interpreted as the god of earth or of water. These events took place in primordial time, the time of the ordering of the cosmos. In the myth, Ninhursag and Enki produce a daughter, with whom Enki also mates and who then gives birth to another daughter, with whom Enki also mates. This last birth brings Uttu, Enki's great granddaughter. Ninhursag warns the girl that Enki lurks in the marsh and lusts for her, and that she should not yield herself to him until he offers her the appropriate gifts for a bride. He does so, however, and she gives herself to him joyfully.

At this point it seems (the text is broken) that Ninhursag intervenes, takes Enki's semen, and uses it to bring forth eight plants. Enki, noticing the eight new plants, decides he must "know" them and decide their fate, and therefore he eats them. Ninhursag becomes furious at this usurpation. She curses him and says she will no longer look on him with the eye of life. Enki then languishes and the land becomes dry and dusty. Alarmed, the other gods, with Enlil as their spokesman, intercede through the help of a clever fox to get Ninhursag to restore Enki. She does so by placing her vulva next to the ailing parts of Enki's body and bringing forth eight goddesses, each of whom heals the part with which she is associated. The eight goddesses evidently replace the eight plants that Enki had misappropriated. The poem ends with the naming of the goddesses and the assignment of their destinies. It is not clear who speaks at that point, Enki or Ninhursag, but since the ending is one of reconciliation and restoration of life, it seems that the naming takes place with Ninhursag's approval. The last line of the surviving text praises Father Enki.

It is not easy to interpret a text that comes to us from a time so distant, in fragments, and possibly with many layers of revision along the way, but the main outline is not too difficult to discern. Clearly the myth depicts the beginning of the ordered world (or "cosmos") as we know it— a world in which nature brings forth living creatures. Before natural life with its cycles of birth, fertility, and death begins, there is no death or disease, but with life comes the problem of evil in its various forms. The form of evil that this story emphasizes is the evil of disorder. Exactly why Enki's claim to preeminence (that is what his eating of the plants seems to imply) is a source of disorder is not altogether clear. Many ancient myths take the preeminence of the father god for granted, but this one does not. Possibly, therefore, there was an earlier version with a matriarchal emphasis, that is, with the idea that the female principle is preeminent in generation. At any rate, what we see is a struggle between the male and female sources of life to define their relative dignity.

When Enki, the male principle, claims eminence that Ninhursag finds excessive, she demonstrates her own importance by withdrawing her life-giving power. The other gods subsequently realize her importance, as does Enki himself, who must ask her to heal each part of his body that is afflicted. At the end an appropriate balance seems to emerge. The masculine principle's usurpation of knowledge and power is represented as a sort of fall that must be purged through suffering and the reestablishment of proper order.

Thus we see a fairly typical mythic pattern in which disorder in creation is repaired by dissolution, and right order is established through a new act of creation (the healing of Enki and the birth of the goddesses who replace the plants). Since this sequence of creation, death, and rebirth is also the pattern of the annual cycle of vegetation, the myth seems to do double duty as both a story of creation and commentary on the cycles of nature.

Case Study: Enuma Elish.   Another widespread motif is that of a battle between creative and destructive forces. In the Dilmun myth this motif takes the form of a personal conflict between mother and father deities. In the famous *Enuma Elish* myth, it becomes a regular military campaign. Both myths explain the seasonal renewal of nature and also the continuing need for the creative forces in the cosmos actively to counter threats of disorder and returning chaos. (*Cosmos* and *chaos* are Greek terms that have come to be used generally to refer on the one hand to the ordered totality of things, including all the levels of being and even the gods, and on the other hand to a state of unformed, unordered being. The term *chaos* originally meant an abyss and comes from the verb "to yawn." *Cosmos* originally referred to the village as compared with its surrounding wilderness. Eventually it came to refer to whatever was harmonious, civilized, beautiful, and constituted an ordered whole.)

The *Enuma Elish* (the title means "When on high" and is from the first words of the Akkadian text) has come down to us mainly in its Babylonian form, but some fragments of a Sumerian original have also survived. In the Sumerian version everything begins with the union of sky and earth, represented by the first "thing," a cosmic mountain whose base is earth (female) and whose summit is the sky (male). The Babylonian version begins with the precosmic chaos: "When on high the heaven had not been named. Firm ground below had not been called by name. . . . No reed hut had been matted, no marsh land had appeared. . . ."[2] Neither gods nor humans had yet been created. There was only the primordial pair, Apsu (male, associated with fresh water) and Tiamat (female, the sea), "their waters commingling as a single body." Time and the world begin when they give birth to the first gods (perhaps representing the accumulation of silt where the river water meets the sea). These beget other gods and goddesses who mate in turn to produce the gods of earth (Ea) and sky (Anu) and so on. (Interestingly enough, earth and sky are here both represented by male gods, evidently because the Babylonians wanted to give honor to the earth god, Ea, progenitor of their own special god, Marduk. They seem to have been more emphatically patriarchal than the Sumerians.)

As the story proceeds, the younger gods annoy their original ancestors through their poor manners and overbearing character. Apsu complains that he can gain no rest by day or by night because of their incessant noise and he proposes to annihilate them. Tiamat, though she too is angry with them, urges restraint, but he ignores her. When the younger gods hear of his plans, they become virtually paralyzed with fear, except for Ea, who casts a spell of sleep on Apsu and then slays him. Afterward Ea builds his home on

Apsu's body and begets Marduk. (The image suggests earth, perhaps mud from the river, building up above the level of the water so that habitations may be built and the Babylonians eventually generated.)

The poem proceeds with lavish praise of Marduk (the sun), who is said to be the tallest and strongest of the gods. Marduk himself creates the four winds and produces streams, both of which annoy Tiamat. She decides to put an end to all of this nuisance and to avenge Apsu. She takes a new consort, Kingu, and raises an army with which to make war on the younger gods. When they hear of this they are at a loss until they think of asking Marduk to lead them. Ea bids Marduk come to the assembly of the gods. Marduk promises to be their champion but asks in return that he become supreme among them and receive all their authority to "determine the fates." They willingly proclaim him king and confer on him throne, scepter, and royal vestments.

When Tiamat sees Marduk ride into battle against her, she goes wild, taking leave of her senses and shaking to her lowest parts—an image not only of a stormy sea, but of chaos itself. Slaying her, Marduk splits her in two like a shellfish and thrusts one-half upward to make the sky and the other downward to make the sea, setting guards to ensure that her waters will not escape and threaten the world again. He makes the dome of heaven correspond to earth as its heavenly counterpart. Then he executes Kingu and creates human beings from his blood so that the gods will have servants to maintain the earth when they have withdrawn to the heavens. As their final work of creation the gods build Babylon and at its center, as a temple to Marduk, the great ziggurat of Esagila, described as reaching as high as Apsu, as high as the primordial waters were deep.

Notice in this myth that the gods need human beings that they may rest from labor. The gods are not unlimited in power, but constitute only a part of the larger system of things that is the cosmos as a whole. They themselves must struggle to establish creation and keep it in proper order. Also, they do not create the world from nothing but make it from a preexisting reality. The world as we know it comes from the body of the subdued Tiamat, and human beings come from the blood of Kingu. One might say that the gods do not "create" the world in the same sense that the God of the Judeo-Christian-Islamic tradition creates. Rather they are the world, and we are of the same substance as they. Theogony (the birth of the gods) and comogony (the birth of the ordered whole) are here one and the same.

Order

The plot of the *Enuma Elish* describes both the creation of the cosmos as a whole and the evolution of the political order of Mesopotamia, as seen from the perspective of Babylonians in the second millennium. The authors are looking back to the origins of an order in which they have preeminence over their neighbors but are themselves under the authority of the gods and divine justice. The movement from a democratic assembly of gods to a centralized monarchic system under the rule of Marduk, god of Babylon, parallels the historical movement from independent city-states in Sumer and Akkad to the Babylonian Empire. That the Babylonian emperors interpreted their own authority as subordinate to and representative of an overarching divine order can be seen, for example, in the preamble to the Law Code of Hammurabi (approximately 1750 B.C.E.), which opens with a description of how Anu and Enlil, lords of heaven and earth, committed lordship ("the Enlil functions over all mankind") to Marduk and then called Hammurabi personally to enforce their justice in the land.

The underlying idea in this picture of historical development seems to have been that earthly kingship was conferred from a superhuman source and was an imitation of and participation in the ordering power of a divine original, the order established by the gods of the empire at the beginning of the world. This meant that royal rule was intended to be sacred rule in the service of true justice. It also meant that human life and its order were connected with the cosmic order and the life of the gods. If human farmers did not cultivate their crops, if reverent worshipers did not offer sacrifices, if justice among human beings was allowed to deteriorate, then the life of the gods would also suffer injury.

This interpretation of the relationship among human beings, the world, and the gods is a good example of cosmological symbolism: symbolism in which human life and society are interpreted by analogy with the cosmic order. That was the predominant pattern of symbolism in ancient Mesopotamia, and we will see it again in Egypt. It is not the only possible pattern of symbolic interpretation, but all over the world it seems to have been the first to develop.

Anthropomorphic symbolism, such as that which flourished in classical Greece, likens society and the cosmos to a human existence. Specifically, it depicts reality in terms of the inner order of a wise and virtuous person. Anthropomorphic symbolism usually develops after cosmologically symbolized societies have broken down and disappointed their members so deeply that the members feel the need for an entirely new way of discovering meaning and purpose. This sort of disappointment never seems to have afflicted the ancient Mesopotamians, at least not enough to have caused a radically new development in their culture. Most of the myths the Mesopotamians have left us suggest that they found the evil of the universe intelligible in terms of the basic model we have seen: a precarious balance of interdependent forces.

Case Study: Gilgamesh Nonetheless, the Mesopotamians did finally wrestle with the problem of a suffering that is genuinely personal and calls the cosmological principle into question. The epic of Gilgamesh is their famous meditation on personal suffering. It concerns a famous early king of Uruk in Sumer and probably dates from the late third millennium B.C.E. The most complete surviving text is in Assyrian, but there are fragments of earlier versions in Sumerian and Akkadian.[3]

Gilgamesh, the poem tells us, was of mingled parentage, divine and human, but he was a mortal all the same, and his mortality is the poem's main theme. At the opening Gilgamesh is a vigorous and effective ruler, in fact too vigorous: His constant demands for labor and military service lead the people of Uruk to appeal to the gods for relief. The goddess Aruru responds by creating another energetic creature, Enkidu, to attract the interest of Gilgamesh. Enkidu is humanity in its most primitive state. He is naked, covered with hair, enormously strong, and lives among animals in the wilderness. Befriending the animals, Enkidu protects them from hunters, who, unable to fight him themselves, appeal to Gilgamesh. Gilgamesh sends a sacred prostitute, Shamhat, to civilize Enkidu. Shamhat goes to the wilderness to wait for Enkidu by a water hole. When he comes, she attracts his interest by uncovering her body. They enjoy a week of heroic lovemaking, at the end of which Enkidu tries to return to the company of his animals but finds them shying away from him. Shamhat tells him that he no longer belongs among animals but has become wise and godlike. She offers to take him to see the great walls of Uruk and mighty Gilgamesh. Enkidu

decides to go with her and to challenge Gilgamesh. He arrives in Uruk at the moment of Gilgamesh's wedding procession and bars Gilgamesh's path to the bride. The two powerful figures hurl themselves at each other and fight like young bulls, shaking the walls of the bride's house. Gilgamesh turns out to be the stronger of the two, but his generous praise of Enkidu makes them fast friends. Looking for adventure together (Gilgamesh seems to have forgotten all about his bride), they set out to kill a monster named Huwawa. When they return victorious the goddess Ishtar falls in love with Gilgamesh and proposes to him. He turns her down. Furious, Ishtar appeals to her father, Anu, to unleash the bull of heaven. Anu warns her that this monster will be so destructive that there will be a famine for seven years, but she persuades him to unloose it anyway. However, Enkidu gets behind it and twists its tail while Gilgamesh plunges his sword into its neck. Enraged by Ishtar's curses, Enkidu tears off the bull's shank and throws it at the goddess.

This means trouble. The gods hold an assembly and sentence Enkidu to death. Enkidu is horrified and launches into a long lament in which he curses everything that has led to this end: his departure from the animals, his lovemaking with Shamhat, his migration to the city, and even his friendship with Gilgamesh. The sun god Shamash, however, intervenes and persuades him to withdraw his curses and bless his friend before dying. In a dream Enkidu has a vision of Irkalla, the land of the dead. It is a house of dust and darkness, devoid of real life, in which one is no more than a shadow. Far from representing a form of immortality, it is death depicted in the most graphic terms.

After his friend's death Gilgamesh falls into an extreme despondency, not simply due to the loss of his companion, but because death, which had always been a remote abstraction to him, has now become a vivid reality. He realizes that however long and glorious his life may be, death awaits. This thought becomes an obsession, undermining any joy in his own or his city's glory and any consolation from the balance of forces in the cosmos. The thought of his death haunts Gilgamesh day and night. Finally he decides to search for an escape from mortality. He has heard of an ancestor named Utnapishtim who once won eternal life as a gift from the gods and now dwells at the end of the earth. The sun god, Shamash, reproaches him for his lack of moderation, but Gilgamesh is not interested in reasonableness; his heart is set on only one thing: not to die. Eventually he arrives at the shore of the great sea that encircles the earth, where he finds a tavern run by a woman named Siduri. She offers the conventional wisdom, urging him to accept his mortality, enjoy food, drink, and merriment, wear beautiful clothing, bathe in fresh water, rejoice in his children, and give satisfaction to his wife. This, she says, is the task of human beings. Gilgamesh refuses to listen and persuades her to tell him how to find Utnapishtim. She directs him to the boatman, Urshanabi, who takes him to Utnapishtim's island.

The result, however, is bitterly disappointing. Utnapishtim tells Gilgamesh that he did not win immortality through deeds of valor. It happened at a time when the gods had decided to destroy humankind in a great flood. Ea, more foresighted than the other gods, realized that without human beings to maintain the earth the gods would languish for lack of sacrifices. Ea told Utnapishtim to build an ark and save his family and pairs of all animals. (The story is similar in many details to the biblical story of Noah, which, as far as written records indicate, it predates by perhaps a millennium.) After the flood the gods realized the fault of their hastiness and were so grateful to Utnapishtim that they conferred eternal life on him. Unfortunately that was something that could happen only once.

Utnapishtim suggests, evidently mockingly, that if Gilgamesh wishes to conquer death he might begin by trying to conquer sleep. No sooner does Gilgamesh take up the challenge than sleep overcomes him. Utnapishtim would happily let Gilgamesh sleep himself to death, but his wife takes pity on Gilgamesh and persuades Utnapishtim to wake him and let him go home. She also persuades him to tell Gilgamesh about a plant that will perpetually renew his youth. This thorny plant grows in the Apsu, the sweet waters deep under the earth. (In the Mesopotamian cosmology the earth is a great floating island.) Gilgamesh dives for it by tying stones to his feet and sinking to the bottom. When he gets the plant he is overjoyed, thinking his basic goal achieved. On the way home, however, feeling the heat of the day, he decides to take a swim in a cool pond. He leaves the plant with his clothes and while he is swimming a serpent comes out of its hole and eats the plant. Immediately the snake sloughs off its old skin and is renewed, shiny and young.

With that, Gilgamesh completely despairs. Following his despair, however, come resignation and composure. Essentially Gilgamesh accepts the wisdom of Shamash and Siduri that he had rejected earlier. At the end of the poem he takes the boatman around the great walls of Uruk, praising the grandeur of his royal domain.

Is the poem a lesson in moderation and the acceptance of human limitations, or is it a radical protest against those limitations? There is no easy answer. How far did the challenge to Mesopotamian cosmological assumptions proceed? Did anyone seriously doubt them to the point of considering another perspective? The ending of the poem seems designed to reassert the old beliefs. In the perspective of the conclusion, Gilgamesh's obsession becomes a temporary disorder that must be overcome if one is to live in proper harmony with the cosmos and the gods.[4]

EGYPT

Today Egypt is a powerful center of Arab and Muslim culture. Taxi drivers careen through Cairo with a Qur'an on the dashboard to protect them; common people lay rugs in the train station and kneel at the call to prayer. Yet the treasures of Tutankhamen, the Giza pyramids, and above all the Nile tie modern Cairo to the pre-Islamic Egypt of more than 5,000 years ago. Merely follow the Nile by train to Alexandria and you will see in its delta peasants drawing water with buffalo much as they did in the Old Kingdom.

The Nile itself is a principal player in Egyptian history. Its moods, both varying and constant, reflect the Egyptian soul. Historically, the Egyptian soul appears ageless. For the best part of 2,500 years Egyptian life remained the same. At the Great Pyramids near the Sphinx, the desert seems to have mimicked the Nile's behavior. The endless sand, like the river water, changes with the wind. Actually, though, little changes. Sky, sun, sand, and water—they all endure. Like stable props, they are set on every stage.

On the Egyptian stage, pharaohs and peasants enacted a mortality play. As the pyramids show, death kept adamant hold on this people's soul.

Beyond life under the sun, life in the flesh, lay deathlessness. The tomb then was an archway through which everybody passed. Sanity was preparing to pass well.

Standing before the Sphinx, an Egyptian might have offered a prayer such as this: "O god of the puzzle, well do you symbolize our situation. Strong as a lion, winged like thought, you beguile us like a woman. In this flesh, we mainly know contradiction. Body and thought, we go diverse ways. Clearly, though, all ways end in the underworld. Help us stand judgment there before Osiris. Help us enter Re's course through the sky. May our time in the sun go smoothly. May our afterlife be content. Help us solve our riddle."

History

Scholars debate the history of Egyptian religion, but the major events are clear. Unification of Upper (southern) and Lower (northern) Egypt occurred about 3100 B.C.E., and with it began the central Egyptian religious dogma—*divine kingship.*[5] In the prehistoric years before unification, Neolithic culture gradually developed small-town life, characterized by domestic animals, significant crafts (especially pottery), and probably the burial of the dead with hopes of an afterlife. From the beginnings of Egyptian history, local gods had great influence, and throughout the long dynasties they comprised a pantheon (assembly of divinities). It is well established that ancient Egypt was amazingly stable culturally. Divine kingship, concern with an afterlife, and a rather unorganized complex of gods exemplify that stability, for they characterized the entire 2,000 years of the native dynasties.

Egyptian splendor began vigorously in the period 3100–2200 B.C.E., which historians divide into the Early Dynasties (3100–2700 B.C.E.) and the Old Kingdom (2700–2200 B.C.E.). A famous product of Old Kingdom religion is the Memphite theology, developed to justify the new, unified kingdom centered at Memphis. Central to the justification is that the god of Memphis, Ptah, is the foremost creator god. Ptah originated Atum, the supreme god of the older cosmogony, and the other gods by an idea in his heart and a command on his tongue. Scholars are fascinated by this notion, because it suggests that 2,000 years before the Hebrews or Greeks came up with the notion of a first spiritual cause, an Egyptian had more than suspected it.[6]

From about 2200 to 2050 B.C.E., there was an intermediate period of disorder. The social order rooted in the permanence of nature and the gods gave way to chaos. We catch overtones of that upheaval in the famous "Dispute over Suicide," a remarkable text from the end of the third millennium. A man says to his soul, "To whom can I speak today? My fellows are evil, my friends do not love, . . . the land is left to those who do wrong." So, he considers suicide: "Death faces me today like the recovery of a sick man, like going

out into the open after a confinement, . . . like the longing of a man to see his home again, after many years in captivity."[7] Clearly the prehistoric Egyptian hope of a happy afterlife with the gods functioned for this desolate writer as a way to justice—a way to symbolize the friendship and social order that life must have if it is not to seem absurd.

The Middle Kingdom (2050–1800 B.C.E.) was centered at Thebes. It nurtured several trends that brought important changes, although they worked below the surface constancy of Egyptian life. The most important of these trends was a democratization of certain religious rights, as the distance between the pharaoh and the common people narrowed. Also, there was an effort to elevate the more important gods and an increasing inclination to worship gods who were in the form of animals,[8] two phenomena that we shall observe when we analyze the complex Egyptian sense of divinity. The most important religious rights that democratization brought the middle classes were privileges in the afterlife and a chance to participate in ceremonies that had been confined to the king and a few priests.

A second intermediate period (1800–1570 B.C.E.) dissolved the Middle Kingdom and included a century or so of rule by the Hyksos (Shepherd Kings), who were probably Syrians. The New Kingdom (1570–1165 B.C.E.) began with the famous XVIII dynasty, which made Egypt a true empire that stretched to the Euphrates. For our limited review of the high points in later Egyptian religious history, the New Kingdom's speculation on monotheism and a purer divinity is important. In the XIX dynasty under Akhenaton (1369–1353 B.C.E.), there was a move to make Aton, previously just the sun disk, the sole deity. Apparently Akhenaton himself bullied through this change (Egypt quickly reverted to polytheism after his death) because of his own spiritual perceptions (which many of his contemporaries considered fanatical and heretical).

Eric Voegelin calls Akhenaton "a new voice in history, the voice of a man intimately sympathetic with nature, sensitive to the splendor of light and its life-spending force, praising the god and his creature."[9] In a joyful climax, one of Akhenaton's hymns cries out: "The Aton is the creator-god: O sole god, like whom there is no other! Thou didst create the world according to thy desire, while thou wert alone."[10] Moreover, Aton was not the god of Egypt alone. Akhenaton saw that a true creator god must have established all peoples, whatever their country, speech, culture, or skin.

Figure 12 *Great Sphinx near Giza pyramids, outside Cairo, Egypt. Photo by J. T. Carmody.*

This was truly a remarkable leap toward universalism, especially coming from the leader of a resolutely ethnocentric people, and it was the centerpiece in the so-called Armarna Revolution that gave the New Kingdom a great charge of cultural energy.

Another high point of New Kingdom theology consisted of the Amon hymns, which probably date from the reign of Ramses II (1290–1224 B.C.E.). They illustrate a return to Amon and the demise of Aton, as well as a deep sense that the first creator god must be mysterious. Amon is "far from heaven, he is absent from the underworld, so that no gods know his true form. His image is not displayed in writings. No one bears witness to him. . . . He is too mysterious that his majesty might be disclosed, he is too great that men should ask about him, too powerful that he might be known."[11] Along with the hymns of Akhenaton, these praises of Amon represent the greatest advance in Egyptian theology.

For the most part, the Egyptians were not intellectually rigorous. They easily tolerated many gods and relied almost unquestioningly on ethical maxims and proverbs. In the Amon hymns, however, we see traces of a negative theology—a rising of the mind to the true nature of divinity by denying that creatures can represent it adequately. Because negative theology is a paramount way of breaking the cosmological myth, the Amon hymns show how close Egypt came to the revolutions that Israel and Greece accomplished.

In the centuries after the New Kingdom, the capital moved to Tanis, Bubastis, and Saïs—a good indication of the political turmoil of that era. Persians ruled Egypt from 525 to 405 B.C.E., and the last native dynasties (405–332 B.C.E.) ended with the conquest of Alexander. In the period from Alexander to about 30 B.C.E., the Hellenistic Ptolemies ruled, and the city of Alexandria was the luminary of the eastern Mediterranean. Christian influence rose in the Roman and Byzantine periods (30 B.C.E.–641 C.E.), bequeathing Egypt the Coptic church. Since 641, Egyptian culture has been largely Muslim, but its native orientations have never completely died.

Structural Analysis

Ultimate Reality. With regard to divinity, the proliferation of Egyptian gods and symbols is overwhelming. The basic hieroglyph for God is a pole with a flag—the emblem flying in front of major temples, which designated purity and the creative life force. Since the Egyptians sensed purity and creativity in many places, they split divinity into many gods. The gods most important in the old cosmogony were four male-female pairs. The males bore the head of a frog, and the females the head of a snake—symbols, apparently, of self-renewal (the frog begins as a tadpole, while the snake sheds its skin). The belief (before the Memphite theology established Ptah as the creator) was that an invisible wind moved over primal waters and used these four pairs of gods to make life.

Throughout Egyptian history, the most important gods were associated with the sun and death-resurrection. Their names and images varied from cultural center to cultural center, but the most common name for the sun god was Re, symbolized by either the sun's disk or the falcon. Another name was Khepri, represented by a scarab pushing the sun disk; a third name was Atum, whom people at Heliopolis worshiped and represented as the setting sun. In the mythology of Heliopolis, Atum generated himself on the primordial hill of creation (the Great Pyramids of the Old Kingdom represented this hill). He conquered chaos, took charge of the world, and established *maat,* the eternal cosmic order. The *Book of the Dead* (17:3–5), from the New Kingdom, says that Re became king of the gods in the earliest times by defeating all his opponents. Maat is his daughter but also his mother, because in his course through the sky, the sun god follows her cosmic order.

That course determined Egyptian reality. The west was the land of the dead, and the east was where the daily miracle of the sun's return from the dead occurred.[12] On the walls of royal tombs near Luxor, twelve sections divide the night realm, or underworld, through which the sun god's boat travels. Although the sun god is dead during this time, he still possesses the power of resurrection. Middle night is the realm of Sokaris, who appears in human form with the head of

a falcon. His area is a desert through which Re's boat has to be dragged before the sun can reemerge into the light.

It was Osiris, however, around whom developed the funerary cult that made the underworld almost an Egyptian obsession. Nowhere is the myth of his descent to the underworld detailed, but it probably had the following plot. Osiris and Seth were brothers, and Isis was Osiris' sister and wife. Osiris ruled the world as a good regent, but Seth hated him and killed him by guile. He got Osiris into a coffin and sent it down the Nile. Isis recovered Osiris' corpse and uttered a soulful dirge (which inspired litanies used in Osiris' worship). This dirge had a magic power that revived Osiris. Once again Seth moved against Osiris, this time hacking Osiris' body into fourteen pieces and then scattering them. Isis recovered them all and buried each piece properly wherever she found it (this explained the many Osirian sanctuaries). Furthermore, Isis conceived a son Horus by the dead Osiris and brought Horus up in the marshes to hide him from Seth.

When Horus reached manhood, Isis arranged for a trial at which Seth was condemned for murdering Osiris and Horus was recognized as Osiris' heir. Osiris himself remained in the underworld, accepting the roles of lord of the nether realm and judge of the dead. Osiris seems to represent the growing power of vegetation, which roots in the earth, and he relates to all buildings that are set on the earth, to the moon, and to the dead. Isis represents the throne, the sacred seat of the king. As such, she "makes" the king and is his mother. For instance, on a relief in a temple at Abydos, the pharaoh sits on Isis' lap. Thus, Horus and the pharaoh are correlated. As Horus owed his throne to his mother Isis, so did the pharaoh.

Horus had many appearances, but most frequently he wore the head of a falcon. He was the model son but shows traces of an older sky god. In the Osiris myth, Horus fought Seth and lost an eye, while depriving Seth of his testicles. They reconciled, however, to suggest that life and death are paired. Thoth, originally a moon god, was the agent of their reconciliation. Usually Thoth was represented as a baboon or an ibis. He was also a god of the dead and is thought to have found Horus' lost eye and have returned it to him. This eye became a token of life returned from the dead.

The prime attribute of Egyptian divinity, then, was life. It shone in the sun, who daily accomplished the miracle of being resurrected from darkness, bestowing life-giving light and warmth. Life flowed in the Nile, whose annual flooding was necessary for crops to grow. Even the underworld became a realm of life. Osiris ruled there, judgment took place there, and vegetation rooted there.

Nature.   From this association of divinity with life, it follows that nature itself had a potent sacredness. Henri Frankfort, in fact, has analyzed Egyptian divinity in terms of the sun's power of creation, the power of procreation in cattle, and the power of resurrection in the earth.[13] We have seen a little of the sun and the Osirian earth. Apis, the bull god, was a focus of procreative power, as was Min, a mummy with a huge projecting phallus.

By the "cosmological myth," we mean the tendency to run these various sacred forces together so that nature and divinity are coextensive. Apart from the brief ventures behind the hymns to Aton and Amon, Egypt little doubted the cosmological myth. It could support so many gods because, like oral ancient peoples, Egyptians sensed sacredness everywhere. Unlike Jews, Christians, and Muslims, however, they did not fashion a popular, effective negative theology that said, "True divinity is actually in no one place—it is beyond all place, all time, all this-worldly containment." As a result, nature's cycles and changes all represented aspects of the basic Egyptian divinity, which was the world itself. This cosmos of rocks and trees, water and land, living things and dying things—this was the ultimate reality.

The Egyptian people participated in the sacred cosmos through their king, who to them was quite literally divine. The king represented Horus, Re, or Osiris. In the analytic terms of Western scholars, he mediated between nature's divine order and his people. Society and politics were part of one natural circuit; the *maat* (goddess of order) that gave the world its law or reason ran from heaven through the pharaoh to the people. Thus, the *pharaoh* was under *maat* and yet, for the common people, was the source of *maat*. Psychologically, this order was a major reason for the stability of the Egyptian culture. With divinity in their midst, what need the people fear?

Through many agricultural ceremonies and many regal rituals, these beliefs took dramatic form.[14] At first the common people had limited access to most kingly ceremonies, but in the later centuries their participation increased. The greatest threat to social stability, understandably, was the king's death. Consequently, the most influential mythic cycle was that of Osiris and Isis, which explained where the king (identified with Osiris) had gone at death. Relatedly, the most important ceremonies were the old king's burial and the new king's accession. For a hint of how effective this mythic-ritualistic faith was, consider the pyramids. The common people supplied the immense, brutal labor needed to build the pyramids, because they assured the king's happy afterlife and the state's continuance.

Society.   Ancient Egypt had a powerful caste of priests, and at times, despite the dogma of the king's divinity, this caste clashed with the crown. The conflict between Akhenaton and the priests of the old god Amon was a vivid instance of such friction, but conflict was almost always on the verge of breaking out. When Akhenaton moved the capital from Thebes to Amarna, he bruised theological, class, and local sensitivities all at once. The local priesthood, fighting for its own gods and people, consistently defended those sensitivities. As a result, the priesthood was a powerful sociological force.

Women were quite subordinate in Egyptian society, but were not without influence and religious importance. The goddesses Hathor, Nut, Neith, Maat, and Isis represented the feminine aspects of divinity, while the queen had vital roles in the political theology.[15] Hathor, Nut, and Neith were forms of the mother goddess—both sacred representations of fertility and figures of comfort. Maat ruled cosmic justice, while Isis was sister and wife of the god as king. On rare occasions a queen could rule (Hatshepsut, 1486–1468 B.C.E., is the most famous instance), and as the source of the divine king, the queen mother was much more than just another harem wife.

Egyptian proverbs encouraged husbands to treat their wives well so that their property would prosper, but they also pictured women as "frivolous, flirtatious, and unreliable, incapable of keeping a secret, untruthful and spiteful as well as naturally unfaithful. To the storytellers and moralists [women were] the epitome of all sin and an endless source of mischief."[16] Women of the New Kingdom served in the temples and as popular entertainers, but in both cases they risked reputations as prostitutes. In both formal and popular religion, Isis was a focal point for women's own religion, especially in Hellenistic times. Related to Osiris, she was the ideal wife (and a potent exemplar of grief); related to Horus, she was the ideal mother. Through Isis, then, women in ordinary roles participated in divinity.

Perhaps because of this divinity, legal documents from about 500 B.C.E. suggest that Egyptian women had the right to own property, buy or sell goods, and testify in court. They were taxpayers and could sue; they could inherit from parents or husbands.[17] On the other hand, husbands could dismiss wives at their pleasure (but not vice versa), and concubinage, adultery, and prostitution were widespread. Because many Egyptian women worked the fields or had other important economic roles, their lot was better than that of women in other ancient civilizations (Mesopotamia, for instance). Still, women were not equal to men, in part because of a prevailing male suspicion of woman: "She is a deep water whose twisting men know not."[18]

Self. The Egyptian religious conception of the self relates intimately to the Egyptian concern with death, burial, and the afterlife. That concern, John Wilson insists,[19] was a result not of gloom but of optimism. The ancient Egyptians loved life, despite its dependence on such uncertain phenomena as the Nile's proper rising, and they looked forward to another, better chapter after death. The remains of many burial sites, well preserved because of the desert sand and dry climate, show that the departed took with them favorite utensils and even favorite servants. The *ba* was that aspect of a person that continued after death, which contrasted with the *ka,* or vital force, the impersonal power animating the living. A third concept, the *akh,* was the shining, glorious aspect of the dead in heaven. With these three notions, the Egyptians had a sense of what moves the living and what continues on after death.

As indicated in our outline of his myth, Osiris judged the dead in the underworld. The pyramid texts of the Old Kingdom, coffin texts of the Middle Kingdom, and *Book of the Dead* from the New Kingdom show a constant concern with judgment, hence a certain awareness of personal responsibility. The *Book of the Dead* contains a famous "negative confession" that illustrates both the posthumous trial Egyptians imagined and some of their principal ethical concerns. The deceased claims before Osiris: "I have not committed evil against men. . . . I have not mistreated cattle. . . . I have not blasphemed a god. . . . I have not done violence to a poor man. . . . I have not made anyone weep. . . . I have not killed. . . . I have not defamed a slave to his superior. . . . I have not had sexual relations with a boy." In all, thirty-six declarations of innocence are made.[20] Then, to complete his show of religious virtuosity, he gives each of the forty-two divine jurors, by name, a specific assurance. For example, "O Embracer-of-Fire, who comes forth from Babylon, I have not stolen. O Eater-of-Entrails, who comes forth from the thirty [judges in the world of the living], I have not practiced usury. O Eater-of-Blood, who comes forth from the execution block, I have not slain the cattle of the god."[21]

In ancient Egypt, then, the gods were everywhere. Economics, politics, the arts, nature—all aspects of life were religious. In symbolically mythic ways, nobles and peasants alike looked to the king, tried to discern *maat,* and hoped for mercy before Osiris. The sun, the river, and the land all witnessed the interplay of death and resurrection and offered comfort. Each dawn, each annual flood, each spring sprouting was a pledge of hope. Therefore, one could live optimistically and even with good humor; on most days, ancient Egyptian life probably was good.

IRAN

Recently Iran has been a nation in the throes of choosing its identity and direction, as well as a nation wracked by a prolonged war with neighboring Iraq. On first view, the principal choices Iran has faced in determining its identity have been Western secularism (almost unavoidable because of Iran's massive petroleum industry) and a volatile form of traditional Islam. These forces alone are more than enough to bewilder analysts, but the snowcapped mountains rimming Tehran suggest there is much more—the long history of culture that crossed the Iranian plain. When one sees Iranian women draped in black, showing only a panel of dark eyes, something flickers that is more ancient than Islam.

That something is the spirit of Zoroaster, priest and prophet from 2,500 years ago. In the mind's eye, it burns toward Truth. Picture Zoroaster as being fiery, choleric, fierce of face. He is angry that some Iranians do not accept his Wise Lord. In their dimness, they stick to the old vital forces. Zoroaster, though, knows better—he knows the battle between Evil and Good.

Ask about Zoroaster on the streets of Tehran today, however, and you will likely be rebuked. "We are Muslims!" the typical residents will say. True enough, fewer than 30,000 Zoroastrians remain in Iran (perhaps 100,000 remain in India). Nonetheless, Zoroaster was the greatest religious influence in the epochal Persian Empire, the strongest molder of the Iranian spirit. As well, he was the first son of Asia adopted by the West.[22]

Zoroaster first intrigued the Greeks, whose explorers encountered his culture 400 years before Christ. Much later he impressed Western historians, philosophers, and artists as a cultural hero—a founder of civilization and conscience.

History

The historical context for estimating the significance of Zoroaster stretches from the tenth century C.E., when the Arab military conquest of the seventh century began to affect Iranian culture, back beyond 1500 B.C.E., when speakers of Indo-Iranian filtered through the Caucasus Mountains to the Iranian plateau. Before that date, "cave man," as Ghirshman calls him, lived around that plateau in holes dug into wooded mountainsides.[23] Indeed, archeological remains suggest that human beings have inhabited Iran since the beginning of a dry period, 12,000 to 17,000 years ago.

According to Ghirshman, in the primitive agricultural societies that developed on alluvial deposits, such as on the Iranian plateau, women had an economic, political, and religious superiority. Indo-European conquerors who settled in Iran probably adopted their matriarchal social structure from these first inhabitants of what is present-day Iran.

Those first inhabitants were great potters, and archeologists have found among their relics designs and figurines of a naked goddess, whose mate was likely a god who was her son. This belief would be the most direct explanation for the early Iranian customs of marriage between blood relations, descent through the female line, and, in certain tribes (for example, the Guti of Kurdistan), female army commanders. Later archeological remains, dating back to 2000 B.C.E., suggest a people both artistic and hopeful, for impressive pendants, earrings, bracelets, and the like found in gravesites imply a strong belief in an afterlife.

In the second millennium B.C.E., Indo-Europeans, pressured by population shifts in the neighboring geographic areas, left their homelands in the plains of southern Russia and migrated southeast across Iran. Some of them eventually ended up as far south as India.[24] In the west they established the Hittite Empire, sacked Babylon, and confronted the Egyptians. From the east, Indo-European tribes called the Mittani conquered northern Mesopotamia and allied themselves with Egypt in about 1450 B.C.E. Linguistic, religious, and social parallels suggest that pre-Zoroastrian Iranian culture, as well as the culture of the peoples who conquered the Indus Valley in India and produced the Vedic culture, derived from the Mittani, Hittite, and other Indo-European "Aryans" (from an Indo-European word meaning "noble"). In particular, the Iranian and Indian Aryans had similar gods and similar social structures. (French scholar Georges Dumezil has argued that the Aryan gods correlated with a three-part social structure—priests, warriors, and agriculturalists—in which each social class had both a legal and a symbolic aspect.[25])

The native Iranian religion that Zoroaster challenged was probably controlled by Median priests (the Medes were a later Aryan tribe) from western Iran called **Magi.** Apparently that religion was an animistic **polytheism** (devotion to many divine spirits) similar to that of early Aryan India. After Zoroaster's death, the Magi fused their ideas onto his new notions, making Zoroastrianism an amalgam of conflicting gods and practices.

Zoroaster is estimated to have lived from 628 to 551 B.C.E., but the only direct source for his message is a fragment of the sacred Zoroastrian liturgical text, the *Avesta.* That portion, called the *Gathas,* along with later Greek and Persian traditions, suggests that Zoroaster's enemies (Magi and men's societies of the old religion) forced him to flee from his native western Iran westward into ancient Chorasmia (the area today of Khurasan, western Afghanistan, and the Turkmen Republic of the Soviet Union). There, when about forty years old, he found a patron in King Vishtapa and his message began to have social effect.

R. C. Zaehner has suggested the following summary of Zoroaster's main doctrines:[26] (1) There is a supreme God, the Wise Lord (**Ahura Mazdah**), who has thought all things into existence by his Holy Spirit. The Wise Lord is holy, righteous, and generous, and he expresses himself through the Holy Spirit, Good Mind, and Truth—three entities inseparable from his essence. Wholeness, Immortality, and Right-Mindedness are his attributes. (2) The world is divided between Truth and the Lie. Ahura Mazdah made Truth, but Zoroaster does not say who made the Lie. (3) Creatures of the Wise Lord (spiritual beings and humans) are free to choose between Truth and the Lie. Angra Mainyu (the Destructive Spirit), twin brother of the Holy Spirit, chooses to do evil. "This he does of his own free will as do the *daevas,* the ancient gods whom, on account of the violence associated with their wor-

Figure 13 *Beaker with winged lions and bulls,*
Persian, about 1000 B.C.E. *Gold; 6¾ in. high. The*
Nelson–Atkins Museum of Art, Kansas City,
Missouri (Nelson Fund).

radical discovery of reason and that suggests some parallels with such near-contemporaries as the Buddha and the Mahavira, Zoroaster generates his images of divinity and human destiny from the operations of his own spirit. He turns away almost completely from nature toward the inner light of human conscience. In so doing he steps at least halfway out of the cosmological myth.

Two verses from perhaps the most autobiographical of Zoroaster's hymns suggest the religious experience at the core of his preaching:

> As the holy one I recognized thee, O
> Wise Lord,
> When I saw thee at the beginning, at
> the birth of existence,
> Appoint a recompense for deed and
> word:
> Evil reward to the evil, good to the
> good,
> Through thy wisdom, at the last
> turning-point of creation [43:5].[27]

> As the holy one I recognized thee, O
> Wise Lord,
> When he came to me as Good Mind.
> To his question: "To whom wilt thou
> address thy worship?"
> I made reply: "To thy fire! While I
> offer up my veneration to it,
> I will think of the Right to the utmost
> of my power"[43:9].[28]

In Iran in the early sixth century B.C.E., only an exceptional personality could have cut through the welter of Aryan gods, spells, and semimagical practices and discerned a clear religious call to identify divinity with justice. Similarly, only an exceptional personality could have lingered over abstractions such as Good Mind and the Right and made these terms God's best names.

It is true, as most scholars remind us, that Zoroaster's revelations had a social background and significance;[29] for instance, he championed the farmer over the nomad. Nonetheless, the deeper explanation of Zoroaster's religious power is the interior, spiritual experiences indicated by the *Gathas*. Like Jesus and Muhammad, Zoroaster met a holy, compelling divinity or ultimate reality. His mission was simply to spread the truth of this divinity far and wide. The origins of Zoroastrian history, then, are the visions and the reli-

ship, Zarathustra [Zoroaster] considered to be evil powers." (4) Because human beings are free, they are responsible for their ultimate fates. By good deeds they win the eternal reward of possessing Wholeness and Immortality; by evil deeds they merit pain in hell. (5) The great outward symbol of Truth is fire, and the center of the Zoroastrian cult is the fire altar.

When we set these doctrines in the context of Zoroaster's times, they are striking for their interiority. Before this prophet, little in Indo-European, Mesopotamian, or Egyptian religion focused on the mental concepts of truth and lie, the spiritually intuitive concepts of immortality and right-mindedness. In a way that prefigures the Greek philosophers' more gious insights of a founding genius. Through all its later changes, Zoroastrianism and the world religions that it influenced retained something of the dazzling vision of Zoroaster's Wise Lord.

After Zoroaster. The great leaders of the Achaemenid Empire who followed Zoroaster were the Persians Cyrus II (599–530 B.C.E.), Cambyses II (530–522 B.C.E.), and Darius I (522–486 B.C.E.). They conquered eastern Iran, the prophet's initial sphere of influence, and we can read in inscriptions that they left something of Zoroastrianism's function as the religious rationale for a new, energetic empire.

Following Alexander's victory over Darius III in 331 B.C.E., the Achaemenid dynastic line begun with Cyrus II gave way to the Greek Seleucids. Under the Seleucids, for almost a century, Hellenistic cultural ideals blended with Persian. Zoroastrian influence probably declined, being overshadowed by a Greek-Iranian *syncretism* (combination of two forms of belief). While the practice of pure Zoroastrianism seems to have remained in Fars (the southern province called Persis), the old Iranian goddess Anahita, fused with the Mesopotamian goddess Nanai, complicated the religious picture in other provinces.

Also complicating the picture was the Greek hero Heracles, who joined with local gods. Heracles was the patron of the gymnasium, the place of physical exercise, an important feature of Hellenistic culture. Also, he was one of several "savior" gods (gods who made life whole) whose influence grew apace with the disintegration of the previously secure city-state religions. The *Avesta* was probably still evolving at this time, incorporating hymns to the god Mithra, who had existed before Zoroaster and later became an important savior god for the Romans. In the *Avesta,* Mithra's main functions are to preserve cattle, sanctify contracts, and render judgment on human actions.[30]

The Era of Many Religions. The Greek Seleucids yielded to the Parthians, who entered Iran from the area southwest of the Caspian Sea. The Parthians dominated Iran, bit by bit, from the first conquest by Arsaces in about 238 B.C.E. until about 226 C.E. While sources are scanty, Zoroastrianism apparently made some gains against syncretism under the Parthians, achieving a privileged status. Richard Frye relates this to the influence of the Magi: "We may suspect that Magi, in various parts of Iran, upheld the worship of Ahura Mazdah and/or other old Aryan gods in varying forms and degrees of piety."[31] Nonetheless, in Parthian times the cultures of the different geographic areas varied considerably. Coins, art, and other remains indicate different local preferences for a variety of gods. Ahura Mazdah and Mithra certainly were influential, but the cult of the goddess Anahita was probably the most important.[32] The northern Magis' custom of exposing the bodies of the dead on mountains (burial would pollute the earth) spread as far south as Susa, capital of the old Elamite kingdom. We also know that the Parthians were tolerant of religious minorities, so much so that Jews regarded them as great protectors.

The history of Zoroastrianism under the Parthians remains rather vague. Under the Sasanians (ca. 226–637 C.E.), it is more definite, as is the story of Persian culture generally. The early Sasanian king Papak probably was the director of the shrine to Anahita in Istakhr in Persis (south-central Iran), and his successor Shapur had quite liberal religious policies. That soon changed, however, largely because of the influence of Kartir, a zealous Zoroastrian priest. By the last third of the third century, he had made Zoroastrianism the established Persian "church." Kartir favored proselytizing, establishing fire temples for worship and instruction, purging Zoroastrian heretics, and attacking all non-Zoroastrian religions. Consequently, he persecuted Jews, Buddhists, Hindus, Christians, and Manichaeans, destroying their centers and proscribing their faiths. From his time marriage between blood relations became a common Zoroastrian practice, and the Zoroastrian clergy were a political power.

The Manicheans—followers of the native Iranian prophet Mani—were the chief heretics. Under Shapur I, Mani had been free to travel and preach, but soon after Shapur's death the Zoroastrians martyred him. Nonetheless, his ideas gained considerable acceptance, both in Iran and throughout the Roman Empire. They stressed a *dualism* of good and evil, equating good with the spirit and evil with matter. Consequently, Manicheans denigrated the body, sex, marriage, women, and food—anything perceived as carnal. As we shall see, Manicheanism had significant effect on Christians, influencing St. Augustine and spawning several medieval heresies. At the end of the fifth century C.E., Persian Manicheans led a socioeconomic movement called Mazdakism (after its leader Mazdak), which preached a sort of communism that included the division of wealth and the sharing of wives and concubines. Many poor people embraced this movement, but Prince Chosroes Anosharvan massacred the Mazdakite leaders about 528 C.E.[33]

In the last decades of Sasanian rule, the Zoroastrian church sanctioned a rigid caste system based, somewhat like that of India, on an ideal division of society into priests, warriors, scribes, and commoners. Ritual tended toward a sterile formalism, and a number of speculative or gnostic (relating to secret knowledge) tendencies emerged. At the beginning of the Sasanian period, Zurvanism had become the dominant Zoroastrian theology, in good part because of an increasing interest in the problem of evil. Zurvan was Infinite Time. Slowly, he displaced Ahura Mazdah (now called Ohrmazd) as the first principle. Ohrmazd then became identical with Holy Spirit, and Zurvan became his father, as well as the father of Holy Spirit's twin, Destructive Spirit. Thus, Zurvanism begot a dualism: Holy Spirit and Destructive Spirit. However, unlike Mani's dualism, Zurvanism did not make matter evil. For Zurvanite Zoroastrians, nature remained God's good creation.

Muslim Era.   After the Muslims conquered Persia in the seventh century, the Zoroastrian communities that survived continued to have significant influence. Zoroastrian priests were instrumental in creating a renaissance of religious literature in Pahlavi, the native Persian in its "middle" period. They kept alive the notion that the prior Sasanian Empire had been a fortunate time for the "good religion" that had preceded the Muslims, and also for such Zoroastrian doctrines as the coming of the future savior and the approach of an apocalyptic era when Judgment would occur. Zoroastrians also fought against the Arabs, Romans, and Turks in their midst, assuring the faithful that God would soon give them revenge against these interlopers.

However, the actual political revolts that the Zoroastrians attempted tended to be completely crushed. That was dramatically true of an uprising attempted in the city of Shiraz in 979, the result of which was a series of harsh repressions instituted by the Muslim rulers. As a consequence, around the end of the tenth century, Zoroastrians began to leave Iran and head toward India, where their small but successful community became known as Parsis. They left a reduced community in Iran, centered in the regions of Yazd and Kerman. Both these Iranian Zoroastrians and the Parsis have perpetuated the religion begun by Zoroaster, although what one finds practiced nowadays naturally has been deeply transformed by a further millennium of historical changes.

Until the sixteenth century, the Zoroastrian communities in Iran and India had little contact with one another. In the sixteenth century they began to exchange *rivayat,* texts providing answers to questions that had arisen about liturgical and doctrinal matters. The Iranian communities usually felt isolated in the midst of a hostile Muslim environment, but the Indian Parsis flourished and exerted considerable influence on their neighbors, all the more so when British rule gave them special privileges. Bombay has been the center of the Indian community.

In India, the Zoroastrians have had considerable contact with other religions: Hinduism, Islam, Christianity. They have also encountered modern spiritualism: astrology, theosophy (occult systems about divinity based on supposedly direct intuitions). The result of such contact has been pressure to rethink traditional views about monotheism (Ahura Mazdah) and dualism (Truth and Lie). Indian Zoroastrians (Parsis) have also struggled with internal questions of reforming liturgical rites and doctrine, to make them more attractive to modern members. Such matters as the cult of the dead, questions related to the liturgical calendar for religious celebrations, and interpretations of the scriptures (the *Avesta,* rediscovered in the eighteenth century and thereafter studied with modern philological tools) have all been occasions for debate and division.[34]

When British rule ended in India in 1947, a small group of Parsis (perhaps 5000) were isolated in Pakistan. There was also a small community in Sri Lanka. A census in 1976 estimated that there were about 130,000 Zoroastrians worldwide, about 80,000 of them in India, 25,000 in Iran, and most of the others in North America. They held an international symposium in Tehran in 1960 and subsequent, similar meetings in Bombay in 1964, 1978, and 1985. A 1986 estimate of the religious complexion of Iran's 46 million people listed less than 2 percent as non-Muslim, while in India Parsis were less than 0.4 percent of the estimated 777 million. In India Parsis have kept the fire sacrifice, exposed their dead in "towers of silence" where vultures might strip their flesh, and become one of India's best educated and most prosperous groups.

Structural Analysis

Ultimate Reality.   Before Zoroaster, Iranian ultimate reality included a number of *ahuras*—good celestial spirits. The most prominent were lucidity (the brightness that glances off the waters or that leaps from fire); the sacred liquor *haoma,* used in the old Aryan cult; and plain water, symbol of purity and motherliness.

Zoroaster pushed to the fore one wise Ahura, whose special qualities, such as Wholeness and Good Mind, were expressions of divine being. In later Zoroastrianism, these qualities became angelic beings who served Ohrmazd and influenced humans.

Opposing the good angels were powerful, antidivine forces led by the evil one, Ahriman. According to speculation after Zoroaster, Ohrmazd realized that to destroy Ahriman he would have to lure him out of eternal time (Zurvan) into finite time. Zoroastrian theology thus became highly eschatological (interested in the last events of humanity) and developed imaginative doctrines of judgment, heaven, and hell. Ultimately Ohrmazd and goodness would triumph, and hell would cease after the wicked had been purged of their sins.[35]

If Ohrmazd and Zurvan represent the most refined aspects of Zoroastrian divinity, Mithra and Anahita express aspects no less influential. Both relate divinity to nature—Mithra to the sky and sun, Anahita to water. On the folk level, Anahita was very powerful, in effect giving Iran a great goddess. For instance, in one *Avestan* text (*Yasht* 5:17), Ahura Mazdah asks Anahita to make Zoroaster think, speak, and act according to good religion. Clearly, then, there was considerable confusion in developed Zoroastrian theology. Pressed by pre-Zoroastrian traditions and by outside cultural influences, Zoroastrianism tried to accommodate a variety of divinities within its monotheistic stress on Wise Lord. As a result, the goddess of plenty, the god of wind, the star Sirius, the Fravashis (the preexistent souls of good men and women), and more were objects of veneration.

Nature. Though Zoroaster's theology turned away from nature and toward mental processes, the physical elements continued to shape Iranian religion. Mental processes and physical elements conspired in practical living, since the basic ethical imperative was to maintain goodness and life by fighting against evil and death. As a result, Zoroastrianism has frowned on fasting, asceticism, and celibacy. Rather, humans have been counseled to foster the powers of generation in nature and humanity alike. One basis for this view was Zoroaster's own stress on the holiness of agriculture, which to him was a cooperation with Ahura Mazdah. The farmer who sows corn, he said, "feeds the religion" of the Wise Lord.

Society. Ancient Iranian society established a pronounced caste system, but most of its cultic practices cut across class distinctions. Some common people were quite interested in magic, but the orthodox leaders feared the occult, treating sorcerers and witches as criminals. Folk beliefs and totemic practices (for example, rubbing oneself with the wing of a falcon to ward off an evil spell) flourished, in part because of contact with Mesopotamia. Both divination and astrology were common, and other nations considered Persian Magis to be specialists in dream interpretation. Finally, occasionally there was trial by fire or molten lead (if the person survived, he or she was deemed innocent).

Zoroaster himself seems to have disapproved of blood sacrifices, going out of his way to try to protect cattle. Blood sacrifices survived in later Zoroastrianism, though, the most important being the bull sacrifice. Also important to later Zoroastrians was the preparation and offering of *haoma,* the sacred liquor, which until recently served as a sort of sacrament for the dying. The most important sacrifice and cultic focus, however, has been the fire sacrifice. The flame has to be "pure" (obtained by burning "pure" materials such as sandalwood), and it has to pass to another flame before its fuel becomes embers. The fire sacrifice has overtones of an ancient wonder at the source of light and heat, but its major emphasis has always been to symbolize the blazing purity and potential sensing of the Wise Lord.

Self. Through their several sacrifices, Zoroastrians have kept a sense of righteousness before Ahura Mazdah. For individuals, rites of passage at maturity, marriage, and death are important, as are various purifications. At maturity, both men and women have received a sacred thread and shirt. The thread is a compound symbol: Cosmically it stands for the Milky Way, the thread of the stars through the heavens; mythologically, it recalls Ahura Mazdah's gift of *haoma;* personally, it symbolizes taking up adult responsibilities. The shirt is white, to symbolize purity and the garment that the soul dons after death.

Death and bloodshed are prime occasions for purification, because they are prime pollutants. As noted, Zoroastrians have exposed the dead so as not to defile other persons, the earth, fire, or water. In some periods of Zoroastrianism, blood from a cut or from an extracted tooth, or even menstrual flow could render one ritually unclean. Emily Culpepper, who has surveyed Zoroastrian menstrual taboos, suggests a strong ancient element in this concern with purity.[36] (Complicated rites in which bodily impurities were passed through bull's urine, sand, and water also evidence this concern.[37]) In general, women have played only a small part in the Zoroastrian world. Their part in redemption has been to furnish males to fight against Ahriman. Most of the tradition has held that in the beginning women defected to the Destructive Spirit. Theologically, then, Zoroastrianism has viewed the female nature as unholy.

Zoroastrianism is important beyond its own confines. Because its eschatology attracted Jews, Christians, and Muslims, it has influenced perhaps half the world's believers. That is its historical prestige. In terms of philosophical prestige, where the issue is wisdom—the clarification of reality—Zoroaster is a prime religious figure because he made a strong contribution to the discovery of order, the proper perspective on reality that comes when we determine the relations among nature, society, self, and divinity.[38]

GREECE

Mesopotamia calls to mind a rich mythology. Egypt amazes the world historian by the stability of its civilization. Iran-Persia impresses the historian of religion by Zoroastrianism's contribution to the clarification of order and its influence on Judaism, Christianity, and Islam. Greece, the final land of ancient Near Eastern civilization that we study, dazzles both world historians and historians of religion with its cultural diversity and splendor. Like classical Egyptian and classical Iranian religious culture, classical Greek religious culture has passed from the scene. Its influence in modern Greece lies under the surface of Eastern Orthodox Christianity, much as classical Egyptian religion lies under present-day Egyptian Islam and classical Zoroastrianism lies under present-day Iranian Islam. It is dead, but not without its influence.

Moreover, the influence of classical Greek religion is active in a sense different from that of its Egyptian or Iranian counterparts. Through the philosophy, science, literature, politics, and art that it nurtured, classical Greece became tutor to the West. For example, it furnished Christianity and Islam with many of their intellectual categories. Insofar as those categories have been developed in modern science and technol-

ogy, classical Greece has been absolutely instrumental in shaping the present global society.

History

In his world history, Arnold Toynbee locates the beginnings of Greek culture about the middle of the third millennium B.C.E., when Sumerian and Egyptian influences apparently stimulated civilization in Crete.[39] Sir Arthur Evans, the foremost archeologist of ancient Crete, called the Bronze Age culture that had developed by 2000 B.C.E "Minoan," after Minos, the legendary king of Crete. By about 1700 B.C.E. the Minoans had a linear script, and in the period 1580–1450 B.C.E. a splendid civilization flourished. The first true Greeks, called Minyans, were Aryan-speaking Indo-Europeans. They established relations with Minoan Crete, and between 1450 and 1400 B.C.E. (at which time they were known as Mycenaeans) the Greeks had settled at the Cretan capital city of Knossos. The Mycenaean period (1400–1150 B.C.E.) constituted Crete's last glory; a people known as the Dorians invaded from northern Greece and cast a "dark age" over the Aegean from 1100 to 650 B.C.E.

During that period, literacy largely passed from the Greek scene. Consequently, much of our knowledge of Minoan religious culture comes from archeological excavations. These reveal that caves were great cultural centers from Neolithic times, serving as dwellings, cemeteries, and churches all in one. (Insofar as they gave rise to the mythic labyrinth, Cretan caves influenced the religious psyche permanently.[40]) As the archeological excavations show quite clearly, the foremost deity of Cretan cave religion was a goddess, whose primary features were fertility and mastery of animals. This corresponds with remains found on Cretan mountains, where Minoans also celebrated fertility.

However, the goddess cult probably did more than simply venerate natural life. The many burial remains, symbols of butterflies and bees (change-of-state beings), and other artifacts suggest a complex religious interest in life, death, and rebirth. Probably participants underwent initiation into these mysteries, much as tribal Africans or Australians have long done. The remains or artistic representations of bull horns, double axes, trees, animals, cosmic pillars, and blood sacrifices testify to a particularly rich Neolithic agricultural goddess religion like that described on page 29.

Figure 14 *Mycenaean tomb figurine, 1400–1200 B.C.E. Painted terra cotta; 4½ in. high. The figurine may stand for protective spirits or for the departing soul of the deceased. The Nelson–Atkins Museum of Art, Kansas City, Missouri (Nelson Fund).*

In light of later Greek initiations—for example, those into the Eleusinian and Orphic mysteries—it is likely that the Minoan goddess cult aimed at ensuring a happy afterlife.[41] If so, it probably had conceptions of immortality that continued through the dark age and served as a counterpoint to the later Zeus and the Olympian gods. In the Olympian scheme, the afterlife was only a shadowy, dismal existence. The mystery religions that offered a more hopeful view may well have derived from the Cretan earth goddess.

At any rate, as the script that archeologists have discovered and called Linear B shows, people spoke Greek on Crete from 1400 B.C.E. By that time, Minoan and Mycenaean cultural forces were interacting. One important effect was that later Greek religious culture appropriated Minoan Crete as its golden age. For instance, according to Olympian legend, Zeus was born on Crete, and Apollo, Heracles, and Demeter (and even the non-Olympian Dionysus) performed prodigies or had high adventures in Crete. Crete thus be-

came the *omphalos,* the navel or birth center, of the classical Hellenic world. At the end of his life and literary career, when he composed his masterpiece the *Laws,* Plato placed his characters on Crete, walking from Knossos into the hills to the temple cave of Zeus.

Case Study: Olympian Religion. The Cretan or Minoan strand of Greek religious history wove itself deep into the Hellenic fiber. The Mycenaean strand, however, was throughout more predominant. Linear B shows that the Minyan people who came to Crete were Indo-Europeans—the people that shaped both Iran and India. One of the outstanding characteristics of Indo-European religion was its interest in sky phenomena—storms, wind, lightning, the sun, and stars. Zeus, the prime Greek Olympian god, is a close relative of both Vedic and Iranian sky gods. (In proto-Indo-European religion, Mother Earth was polar to Father Sky but less powerful.) Furthermore, the Indo-Europeans were much concerned with the human word—in sacrifices, chanting, spells, and sagas. Their traditions were largely oral, and they opposed writing when they first encountered it among Near Eastern peoples. It is worth underscoring that they had a powerful, double sense of the sacred—the sacred was both charged with divine presence and forbidden to human touch. Throughout its later development, Greek religion never lost this sense of awe-filled untouchability. Last, as we noted in connection with Iran, Indo-Europeans divided their society and gods into three groups. As a result, Vedic India, Aryan Iran, and pre-classical Greece all thought in terms of priests, warriors, and commoners (though in Greece the priestly class was underdeveloped), as did Celts and Romans.

If both Crete and mainland Greece maintained earlier traditions during the dark age,[42] we can assume that the emergence of Homeric, Olympian religion was quite slow. By the time of the great poet Homer, however, the Indo-European religion had a distinctively Greek flavor. For instance, Zeus had acquired a mythological lineage. According to a later work, Hesiod's *Theogony,* he was born in the third generation of gods, after the original period of Earth and Heaven and the second period of the Titans. When Zeus overthrew his father Kronos, the present world resulted. (Eliade sees in the rather violent mythology of the *Theogony* a Greek account of creation. Heaven and Earth separate: nature's forces assume their present order.[43])

Zeus came to preeminence slowly. Most likely, his many liaisons with local goddesses represent a religious and political takeover, as a unified Greek culture emerged out of local traditions. These local traditions did not disappear, but instead entered the large complex of Greek religious notions, enriching both Greek mythology and religious practices. For instance, the local Cretan dances of armed youths during their initiation ceremonies became part of the colorful story of the infant Zeus' birth in Crete. The noise of the youth's clashing shields drowned out the infant's cries, and so saved him from Kronos, who wanted to devour him. Furthermore, the Cretan Zeus merged with the child and lover of the Cretan goddess, linking him to the island's Neolithic past.

In classical Greece, Zeus was first among the gods dwelling on Mount Olympus, as Homer portrayed him. He was the father of humans, the ruler of their destinies, and, despite his own moral waywardness, the ultimate upholder of justice. In addition to Zeus, the roster of the foremost Olympian gods included Hera, Zeus' wife; Poseidon, god of the sea; Hephaestus, the divine blacksmith; Apollo, god of law and order; Hermes, the divine messenger; Artemis, mistress of wild beasts; Athena, patroness of feminine and practical arts; and Aphrodite, goddess of love.

Of these gods and goddesses, Apollo deserves special mention, because he came to symbolize many virtues that seemed typically Greek, such as serenity, harmony, balance, and order.[44] Through his oracle at Delphi, Apollo gave counsel on matters of liturgical propriety and ritual purification. For example, Apollo had charge of purifying homicides, who had to cleanse themselves of their "pollution." One would take serious matters needing counsel to Apollo's pythia (priestess) at Delphi. In trance, she would exclaim the wisdom with which Apollo filled her. The origins of the pythia's exclamation may lie in shamanism, but by classical times Apollonian wisdom had distanced itself from the emotional and irrational, becoming primarily intellectual *theoria*—relatively serene religious contemplation. As epitomized in the Delphic oracle's command "Know thyself," Apollonian religion deified thought and spirit. For that reason, it encouraged science, art, philosophy, and music.

Somewhat the antithesis of Apollo was Dionysus, an eccentric among the gods of the Olympian period. A son of Zeus by a mortal woman, Dionysus apparently always remained an outsider. His cult was not native to central Greece, while psychologically its concern with the irrational and emotional made many fear it. In his well-known study, *The Greeks and the Irrational,* E. R. Dodds associates Dionysus with "the blessings of madness."[45] Unlike the ecstasy of the Apollonian pythia, that of the followers of Dionysus (for example, of the women called maenads)[46] was wild, frenzied, and orgiastic. Such ecstasy represented the enthusiasm (being filled with divine force) that could come from dancing and wine drinking.

For Eliade, Dionysus conjures up "the totality of life, as is shown by his relations with water and germination, blood or sperm, and by the excess of vitality manifested in his animal epiphanies (bull, lion, goat)."[47] Finally, Dionysus was a god of vegetation who would disappear to the underworld and then spring back to life. The most influential literary source on the Dionysian cult, Euripides' play the *Bacchae,* portrays the god's followers as wildly joyous. If the play is accurate, their mountain revels culminated in tearing apart live animals and eating the flesh raw (so as to commune with the god of animal life).

Strangely enough, the Greeks recognized something essential in the non-Olympian Dionysus. Call it the need for madness, reverence for the life force, or the value of temporarily escaping one's moral bonds—they blessed it and called it good. As a result, Apollo vacated Delphi during the three winter months and allowed Dionysus to reign.

Earthly Religion.   The sky-oriented, rational aspect of Olympian religion never was the whole story. From the Minoans and the psyche came an earthly religion to balance the sky. Certainly the Dionysian cult was a major manifestation. So, too, were the many mother goddesses. Hera, Artemis, and Aphrodite, for example, all relate to fertility and mother earth. In Hesiod's *Theogony,* Gaea (earth) actually precedes and produces heaven. In popular religion, Demeter and Persephone were very influential. In fact, Demeter's search for Persephone in the underworld was a major theme of the Eleusinian mysteries, which are described below.

The result of this earth-oriented counterweight to the somewhat overbearing Olympian gods who resided in heaven was a view that humans should aim to become, in Plato's phrase, "as much like God as possible." Through contact with the forces of life and fertility (in the Eleusinians' case) and with the forces of intellectual light (in the philosophers' case), the limits of mortality were challenged. "No," many Greeks said, "we are made for more than a few days in the sun. If we truly know ourselves, we can find undying life."

The Eleusinian mysteries were practiced in Athens from about 600 B.C.E. on, though they clearly originated much earlier. They evolved from the myth of Demeter's search for Persephone in the underworld,[48] which included a subplot about Demeter's unsuccessful (because of human folly) attempt to make Demophoon, the infant prince of Eleusis, an immortal. Thus, the mysteries consisted of rites and revelations that gave initiates precious knowledge in this life and bliss in the world to come.

We do not know the particulars of the mysteries, which were strictly secret, but the *mystery religions* probably grafted Neolithic agricultural ideas onto the Olympian theme that the gods are immortal. If so, the mysteries moved beyond the myths of the Polynesian Hainuwele type, in which agriculture entailed ritual murder and gods that died. The result was a new, powerful synthesis of sexuality and death (as reflected in Persephone being carried to the underworld by Pluto) and of agriculture and a happy existence beyond the grave (as in Demeter representing mother earth). This religious synthesis made Eleusis an important cultic center for almost 2,000 years. Adherents to the Eleusinian mysteries lived in all parts of the Greek world and came from all social classes. Anyone who spoke Greek and had "clean hands" (including women, children, and slaves) could take part. Poets of the stature of Pindar and Sophocles praised the mysteries, and they were a powerful force in Greek life.

The background of the somewhat similar Orphic rites was a mythology like that of Demeter and Persephone.[49] Orpheus was a prominent Thracian hero, the son of Calliope by Apollo. His great gift was for music—when he played the lyre wild beasts grew calm, trees danced, and rivers stood still. Orpheus married the nymph Eurydice, who died from snakebite while fleeing Aristaeus, another son of Apollo. Orpheus could have regained Eurydice from the underworld if he had been able to resist looking at her. But he could not, so he had to wander inconsolably until followers of Dionysus tore him apart (because of his devotion to Apollo). From this background Guthrie concludes: "The story throws light upon the Orphic religion because that is exactly what, in its main features, it stood for, a blend of the Thracian belief in immortality with Apolline ideas of *katharsis* [purification]. From the one it took *ekstasis,* enthusiasm, and a deep spiritual

hope; from the other a formalizing influence, an almost legal atmosphere of rules and regulations."[50]

For eternal blessedness, Orphics preached, one had to follow a strict moral code, abstain from the flesh of living creatures, and cultivate the Dionysian part of human nature. When fully pure, the soul would be reincarnated no more. No more would it drink of the spring of Lethe (forgetfulness), but, light as air, it would live in union with the divine mind. The Orphics appealed to persons of refinement, and Orphism certainly influenced Plato, the natural philosopher Empedocles, and the Roman epic poet Virgil.

Both the Eleusinian mysteries and the Orphic rites sought immortality, the one by a profound ritualization of the life force, the other by purifying the divine soul. Together, they were a strong counterforce to the pessimism fostered by the heaven-oriented Olympianism, which taught that once one passed from the sun everything became a shadowy darkness. Another counterforce to the sky were the *chthonioi,* the spirits who lived in the dark recesses of the earth.[51] Though they were hardly mentioned in Homer, in popular religion they tended to spell out the twofold function of mother earth: fertility and rule of the dead. For the most part, the *chthonioi* were local spirits, concerned with a particular town's crops or deceased. Sometimes their cult blended with the cult of a local hero. Other times sacrifices to the *chthonioi* had overtones of devotion to Gaea, Demeter, Pluto, or Trophonious—divinities of fertility or Hades. Whether the *chthonioi* were gods or shady figures imagined to populate the afterlife is not clear. Regardless, they elicited considerable fear, and the common people tried not to offend them.

Case Study: Philosophy. The common people did not build Athenian culture or make the breakthrough called philosophy (the "love of wisdom"). Rather, an aristocratic elite, working for several centuries, slowly distinguished the realms of myth and reason and in so doing wrote a pivotal chapter in the history of human consciousness. Before philosophy, the concept of reason was vague. We have seen the prehistoric suspicion that something can travel in dreams, rise in shamanist flight, and survive the grave. In Egypt, the Amon hymns exhibited a strong sense of transcendence—of the human mind passing beyond materiality to divine mystery itself. In Iran, Zoroaster's interior dualism (the battle between Truth and the Lie) revealed a striking grasp of the abstract spirit.

Nonetheless, only the culture of the Greek city-state identified reason and controlled it. Only the line of pre-Socratic thinkers—most prominently, Pythagoras, Xenophanes, Parmenides, and Heraclitus—so disciplined their dissatisfaction with Olympian culture that they saw the human mind (*nous*) itself as being divine and real. India approached this belief but never came away with Greece's counterbalancing faith in the reality of the material world.

The story of the pre-Socratics, which weaves into that of the dramatists and Sophists (teachers of shallow philosophy), is a fascinating chapter in religion.[52] Partly from interior experimentation and partly from an empirical study of nature, the early philosophers moved beyond what most previous peoples had meant by the word *god*. As we have seen, peoples believing in the cosmological myth considered the world to be a living whole. With the rise of civilized religion, Mesopotamians, Egyptians, Iranians, and others focused on the political aspect of the cosmos. In other words, divinity to them was in good part a symbolic representation of their own society. Even Ahura Mazdah had a strong political function. For Darius I, Ahura Mazdah sanctioned the building of an empire of Truth.

Out of its dark age, Greek creativity produced a pantheon—a roster of gods—that was neither natural nor political. The Olympians were anthropomorphic, evidencing human aspects. To be sure, Zeus was a sky god and Athena fought for Athens. But although nature and politics played important roles, they did not make the Olympians distinctive. What made the Olympians distinctive was the rich, anthropomorphic mythology surrounding them. In these divine characters or personalities, human passions were blown up to divine stature. Contemplating such divinity, ruminating on the Olympian mythology, the Greek philosophical geniuses clarified where and how *mythos* shatters on *logos*—where story must yield to analytic reason.

Of course, this realization was prompted by historical events. It did not spawn at a seaside resort. Looking around them, the Greek geniuses of the fifth and fourth centuries B.C.E. saw a succession of empires. The decline of Babylon, Egypt, and Persia evoked the question, "What is the meaning of history's process?" As a result, historians such as Herodotus and Thucydides wanted a break with myth, an explanation of the flux in political affairs.[53] As a result, Socrates, Plato, and Aristotle labored heroically to produce such a break.

When the Athenians sentenced his teacher Socrates to death for impiety, they shocked Plato to the depths of his soul. If Athens could reject the one wise person who might save it, what chance did truth have?[54] Eventually Plato correlated the Athenian city-state experience with the flux of empires that had bothered the historian and came to wonder about the very possibility for human beings finding or making order—stable meaning. The *Republic* and *Laws,* which constitute about 40 percent of Plato's writings, testify to how long and deeply problems of political order absorbed him. His great problem, in fact, was the disorder of most humanity—citizens, empire builders, the great and small alike. Grappling with this problem, Plato saw that all order—personal, sociopolitical, and historical—depends on a truth only luminous because given by an incorruptible divinity. Since Plato's great problem remains our own, we do well to attend to his insight.

From instinct, observation, and reflection, Plato decided that history must mean more than wars and power struggles. Restricted to that level, history is literally absurd—a cause for despair—and yields no truth that might give the soul peace and joy (except negatively, as an analysis of cultural destruction).

Rather, Plato thought that we must become aware of a reality not distorted by our lusts, that divine mystery must shine forth an ordering light. Where warmongers and powerbrokers close themselves, philosophers must be receptive and willing to change. Where politicians restrict reality to money and influence, philosophers must go to the center of things—to the soul's passion for justice and love. Like a new Prometheus bringing fire to humanity's soul, the Platonic lover of wisdom wanted to make justice and love humanity's great passion. The presence or absence of that passion made for either health or disease. Plato minced no words. One either admitted divine mystery or one faced disaster.

The fire and order of the Platonic soul clarified human reality. From Plato's time, some people have realized that the meaning of their existence is to move through experience toward the intellectual light of God. Thus, since Plato the process of human questioning—human searching for flashes of insight and then sustained visions—has been a primary task for those seriously religious. The Western development of science, philosophy, and the humanities was possible because of the Greek consecration of this task of seeking wisdom.

Plato himself used myth and symbols to suggest the psychology, politics, and natural philosophy of the newly clarified human consciousness. His uses of

Figure 15 *The Parthenon, remains of a prime symbol of Athens' golden age. Photo by J. T. Carmody.*

them were deliberate, calculated attempts to keep in touch with the whole field of human awareness, to keep from getting lost in abstraction. Aristotle, more prosaic, commonsensical, and scientific than Plato, analyzed the new clarification of consciousness in drier, more technical terms.[55] As he saw it, a person first experiences ignorance about the meaning of human existence. This ignorance, however, is peculiar: It is knowing that one does not know—being aware that one is in the dark. Instinctively we seek release from the tension that this realization produces. Aware of our confusion, upset that we do not know how our lives make sense, we are moved to clarify things. If distractions, whether personal or social, do not interfere, we may pursue enlightenment, and our search may become inner directed. We may grope forward by an intuition or foreknowledge of what we seek, just as we work a math problem by a knowing ignorance that enables us to recognize when our answer is correct.

Likewise, in the profound problem of human understanding that Aristotle was working on, there is a sense of the answer or goal from the beginning. Looking for the reality that will order both ourselves and our world, questioning and following the thoughts of our mind, we slowly advance toward the divine light, the divine mind, the divine being. Indeed, divinity itself, Aristotle finally realized, had been attracting him from the beginning. From the first, his glimmerings of light, of intellectual understanding, had been sharings in God. Developing this Platonic and Aristotelian insight, the Christian theologians Augustine and Aquinas wrote a new treatise on the image of God, stating that our human intellectual light is a share in the activities of the Father, the Son, and the Holy Spirit.[56]

The Hellenistic Religions. Following the cultural flowering of Greek religion in science, the arts, and philosophy, the Hellenistic religions dominated. This postclassical period resulted from Alexander the Great's conquests (*Hellenism* is the term for his vision of an ecumenical, transnational culture). The Hellenistic era extended from Alexander (who died in 323 B.C.E.) well into the Roman and Christian periods. According to historians who love classical Greek culture, it was not a time of glory. Gilbert Murray, for instance, speaks of a "failure of nerve," while E. R. Dodds speaks of a "fear of freedom."[57] From our standpoint, perhaps the most significant feature of Hellenistic religion was its syncretism. In an imperial area populated by numerous ethnic groups, many different gods, beliefs, and rituals swam together. We can conclude our historical survey of the main movements of Greek religion by describing the most important aspects of this syncretism.

Alexander himself was something of a visionary, for what lured him to empire building was the idea of a realm in which conquered peoples "were to be treated not as uncivilized and barbarous members of subject races but as equals with whom one must live in concord."[58] Before Alexander, the Greeks had some knowledge of foreign religions through travel and trade, but, in general, Oriental deities had made little impact on their own piety. (One exception might be Cybele, a mother goddess imported from Phrygia [central Turkey], who was identified with Rhea, the mother of Zeus.) However, from the time of the Diadochi, the rulers who succeeded Alexander, Oriental cults began to spread. By the beginning of the second century B.C.E., they were predominant. The most popular gods were Cybele, Isis, and Serapis. In the later Roman period, Mithra also flourished.

As noted, Cybele was a mother goddess (and mistress of the animals). Usually she was accompanied by her young lover, Attis. (We may hypothesize that to the Greeks Cybele and Attis echoed the Minoan cave goddess and her consort.) She was severe and vengeful, and accompanied by lions. When Attis was unfaithful, she drove him insane. Eventually Cybele became a maternal deity like Demeter, Hera, and Aphrodite—a patroness of life, protectress of particular cities, and defender of women.

In Cybele's ceremonies devotees reenacted Attis' insanity and consequent self-castration. They would take the pine tree (Attis' symbol), bury it, mourn for the dead god, and then observe his resurrection. Resurrected, Attis would rejoin Cybele, which was cause for great feasting. The cult seems to have promoted fertility, and its rituals have overtones of the vegetative cycle and sexuality. Celebrants went to emotional extremes, dancing, scourging themselves, and even on occasion imitating Attis' castration. We could say that the worship of Cybele attracted Dionysian energies.

In ancient Egypt, as we saw, Isis was the wife of Osiris and the mother of Horus. In the Hellenistic period she achieved a wider influence, often in the company of Serapis. Serapis was an artificial creation, the result of the Greeks' aversion to the Egyptian tendency to worship gods in animal form. Fusing Osiris with his symbol (Apis, the bull), the Greeks made a new god: Serapis. He was bearded and seated on a throne, like Zeus, Hades, and Asclepius, some of whose functions he shared (such as rule of the sky, rule of the underworld, and healing). Joined with Isis, Serapis was primarily a fertility god, bedecked with branches and fruit.

Isis rather overshadowed Serapis, for she became a full-fledged, several-sided deity. As the consort of Osiris-Serapis, she was the heavenly queen of the elements, the ruler of stars and planets. Because of such power, she could enter the underworld to help her devotees or to stimulate the crops. Indeed, as a vegetative goddess she blended with Demeter and also the moon goddess Selene. Perhaps her most important role, though, was to represent feminine virtues. In distress, she had sought the slain Osiris and brought him back to life. Sensitive and compassionate, she would do the same for her followers. As the mother of Horus (she was often represented suckling him), she would help women in childbirth and with child raising. Unlike Cybele, the Hellenistic Isis was soft and tender. Yet, as recent scholarship has shown,[59] her devotees assumed a code of high ethics and her cult was strikingly free of orgiastic tendencies.

Like those for Cybele and Attis, the ceremonies for Isis and Osiris-Serapis amounted to a cycle of mourning and rejoicing. Mourning, followers reenacted Isis' search for Osiris and her discovery of his dismembered parts. Rejoicing, they celebrated Osiris' resurrection and the return of Isis' joy. The initiate Apuleius' famous account gives some of the details of the rituals, which included bathings, ten days of abstinence from sex, "approaching the gates of death," and entering the presence of the gods.[60] Clearly, the ceremonies were elaborate and effective, much as the Eleusinian mysteries must have been. Through the cycle of Osiris' death and resurrection, followers would gain confidence that their own lives were in good hands. Through the dramatic symbolization of the afterlife, they could anticipate security and bliss.

Mithra, whom we know from Iran, never took strong hold among the Hellenistic Greeks, but he did become important among the Romans influenced by Hellenism, especially the Roman soldiers. Indeed, his transformation illustrates almost perfectly the religious amalgam that cross-cultural contact produced at this time. In Mithra's Romanization, Jupiter (Zeus) took on attributes of Ahura Mazdah and became a great champion of Truth. Mithra, in turn, became Jupiter—Ahura Mazdah's faithful helper in the battle against the Lie. In this later mythology, Mithra was born of a rock (symbol of the celestial vault), and from birth carried a bow, arrows, and dagger (much like a Persian noble). He shot the arrows into the heavens from time to time to produce a heavenly spring of pure rain water. Very important was his sacrifice of the bull, from whose blood sprouted the corn (symbol of vegetation).

Thus, Mithra was both a celestial deity (later associated particularly with the sun) and a fertility god. His followers would trace his circuit through the sky, reenact the mythology of his birth, and celebrate a bull sacrifice in his name. After the sacrifice they would feast together, believing that the bull's meat and blood contained the substance of eternity. As the Mithraic doctrine developed, it generated a complicated astrology, by which the progress of initiates' souls through the heavens was shown. At its peak, Mithraism ran underground "churches" and schools. Today excavations under Christian churches, including St. Clement's in Rome, reveal statuary, classrooms, and altars used by Mithraists.

In summary, the Hellenistic period was a time of profuse religious activity. Onto Greek and then Roman religious culture, a cosmopolitan era grafted elements from the Egyptians, Persians, Phrygians, and others. We have not even mentioned the Syrian cults of the mother goddess Adonis and of various baals (Canaanite and Phoenician local deities), which constituted another strand of Hellenistic fertility religion.[61] Beyond doubt, a certain cultural confusion underlay all this excitement. Thrown into close contact with foreigners, all people in the new empire had to face new divinities and beliefs. Partly as a result, many people felt great need for signs of salvation or assurances of a happy afterlife. The upshot was a frenzy of mysteries through which devotees could feel stirring emotions or see marvelous sights. With a rush of sorrow, sexual excitement, or hope for rebirth, an initiate would feel passionately alive. In a time of disarray and ceaseless warfare, when the city-state or clan no longer offered security or guidance, such a sense of vitality was more than welcome.

Structural Analysis

Nature and Ultimate Reality. Nature and divinity run together in pre-Christian Greek religion. Throughout its history, the Greek religious mind associated all major natural phenomena with particular gods. As noted, the sky, sea, and earth were powerful deities. The major stress was on fertility (which was the focus of most local festivals), perhaps due to the poor quality of the rocky Greek soil. The Homeric hymns, for instance, sing praise to mother earth, who feeds all creatures and blesses humans with good crops. Relatedly, they make the man with good crops a symbol of prosperity. The earth, mother of the gods and wife of the starry heavens, has blessed him—his children can play merrily.[62] As a result of its prehistoric roots, then, Greece saw much divinity in natural growth.

Society. In *social* terms, Greek religious culture reflects the ethical ideas that bound first the early clanspeople and then the citizens of the city-state. The ethics of the early historical period evolved from the extended family. There was no money, and banditry was rife, so a man's great virtue was to provide food, shelter, and defense—whether by just means or otherwise. Consequently, most men (it was a patriarchal culture) petitioned the gods for material prosperity and success in arms. They called one of their number good (*agathos*) and praised him for excellence (*arete*) if he was a survivor. The more elevated notions of justice later developed by philosophers clashed with the less moral early tradition. Since early Greek religion did not associate godliness with justice, the philosophers called for its overthrow.

Another primitive concept that died hard was "pollution." This was the dangerous state of being unclean, or at odds with the natural powers because of some dread deed. Homicide was especially polluting, but incest, contact with a dead person, or even a bad dream or childbirth could also be polluting, each in varying degrees. Washing in a spring would cleanse away a bad dream; purification by fire and the offering of pig's blood cleansed a homicide. The concept of pollution seems to have been a way for the Greeks to deal with dreadful, amoral happenings that might bring destructive contact with the sacred, even though they were unintentional. Since polluted persons could contaminate others, they were often banished.

Greek cults used magical formulas, prayers, sacrifices, dances, and dramatic scenes—a wealth of creative expressions. Magical formulas probably were most prominent in agricultural festivals, where peasants mixed models of snakes and phalluses with decomposing, organic materials, such as pine branches and remains of pigs, to excite powers of fertility. Greek prayers would recall a god's favors and the sacrifices that the praying person had offered previously. This implied a sort of barter: We will honor you and offer a sacrifice if you give us success in crops (or war, or family life, or whatever). Occasionally texts indicate pure admiration for divine power or beauty, but the ordinary attitude was quite practical. Since the gods were not necessarily rational or holy, they had to be cajoled. Indeed, a Greek tended to pray and sacrifice rather parochially, addressing the family Apollo or Athena, who might remember fat sacrifices offered in the past. Each family or city-state had its own traditions, customs, myths, and gods, which served both to bind the members together and to keep the different tribes from uniting.

Sacrifice was a primary way to keep local religion in good health. By giving the local god good things, one could expect prosperity in return. (Significantly, this implied that the gods blessed those who were wealthy and had good things to sacrifice and that those who sacrificed and met bad luck had secret sins or wicked ancestors. Either way, human success and goodness were rather arbitrary.) In a sacrifice, usually parts of an animal were offered and the rest was consumed. According to a Homeric account, for instance, a pig was cut up, pieces of each limb were wrapped in fat and thrown on the fire, and barley grains were sprinkled on the fire. The meal that followed was a mode of communion with the deities.

Greek cults produced many priests, but their status and functions were limited. In principle, any person could pray and sacrifice to any god, so priests had no monopoly. They tended to be limited to particular temples and were seldom organized into bands or hierarchies. A large clan might have its own officiating priest, and the priest of a prosperous temple might make a good living from sacrifice fees. Otherwise, priesthood was not a road to status or wealth. Priests seldom gave instruction or performed divinations, though some priests in the mystery rites did both.

Many Greek religious authors were rather harsh on women. Hesiod, for instance, reported the myth of Pandora and the box of evils, which made woman the source of human woes. In other places he called woman "that beautiful evil," the "snare from which there is no escaping," and "that terrible plague."[63] Socrates, when asked about the advisability of marriage, balanced the boon of heirs against the woes of a wife: "One quarrel after another, her dower cast in your face, the haughty disdain of her family, the garrulous tongue of your mother-in-law, the lurking paramour."[64] In Plato's *Republic,* women were to be equal to men socially and sexually, having rights to education and rule. Nonetheless, Plato tended to consider women less independent than men, in good part because of their physique: "The womb is an animal that longs to generate children." Aristotle, however, was the most unequivocal misogynist. To him women were simply inferior, both intellectually and morally. In his matter-and-form theory, women supplied only the matter for human reproduction, men supplying everything effective and active.

Women did have legal rights in Athenian society, but their lives were largely circumscribed by male control. Their basic function was to bear children. The playwright Euripides summarized the impact of this socialization, putting into the mouths of the women of his *Andromache* such self-evaluations as: "There's a touch of jealousy in the female psyche"; "For nature tempers the souls of women so they may find a pleasure in voicing their afflictions as they come"; "A woman even when married to a cad, ought to be deferential, not a squabbler"; and "And just because we women are prone to evil, what's to be gained from perverting men to match?"

On the other hand, we have seen that Greek divinity frequently was powerfully feminine. In the Minoan-Mycenaean period, a great goddess was the prime deity. In the Olympian period, Demeter, Hera, Athena, Artemis, and Aphrodite all exerted great influence. In the Hellenistic religions, Cybele and Isis more than equaled Mithra. Psychologically, then, Greek culture never doubted the divinity of the feminine. More than Israelite, Christian, or Muslim culture, Greek divinity was androgynous. Furthermore, certain religious groups offered women escape from social oppression, for example, the Eleusinian and Dionysian sects. There, in a sort of utopian free zone, women could experience equality and dignity. Although these cults never compensated for women's lack of dignity or status in ordinary life, their egalitarianism was an implicit admission that ordinary life was quite imperfect.

Self.   The personal side of Greek religion is perhaps most manifest in myths dealing with human creation. In the most famous collection of myths, Hesiod's *Works and Days,* ancient Greeks read that they were the last and lowest in a series of human generations. During the first ages, races of gold, silver, and bronze had flourished, but they came to various bad ends. A flood intervened, followed by the age of the heroes. Finally the present iron people arose. In other words, Hesiod's myth put into Greek form the widespread belief in a golden age or a previous paradise, with the accompanying message that the present age was a low point, a period of decline.

Partly from this religious heritage, the prevailing mood of many Greek writers was pessimistic. As Sermonides, a writer of the seventh century B.C.E., put it, "There is no wit in man. Creatures of a day, we live like cattle, knowing nothing of how the god will bring each one to his end."[65] Others echoed Sermonides: Human beings have only a short time under the sun; their powers fade quickly, their fortunes are uncertain. By comparison, Delphic wisdom was more positive: Gain self-knowledge and moderation. Self-knowledge, above all, was accepting one's mortality. By moderation, one could avoid hubris (overweening pride) and tragedy. There were overtones of jealousy in this advice from Apollo, however, as though the god feared humans yearning for immortality or resented their craving a life of passion.

Indeed, passion was ever a danger, for the Greeks were competitive and lusty. In the end, they would not give up their dreams of immortality. So becoming godlike became a central theme of philosophy and mystery religion. The philosopher Empedocles, for instance, thought that his wisdom made him a god among mortals. Plato taught that the soul is divine and deathless. The common person would more likely find divinity in one of the mystery rites, through a union with Demeter or a knowledge from Isis, either of which could bring victory over death.

The personal implications of Greek religion were greatest in the philosophers' clarification of reason, universal humanity, and the participation of divinity in human thought. As we have noted, the poets, dramatists, and early philosophers slowly clarified the nature of human reason, separating it from myth. By focusing on mind (*nous*) and its relations with being (*ousia*), the pre-Socratics prepared the way for Plato and Aristotle, who realized how mind and being coincide. Moreover, this work did not take the Greek intellectuals away from either religion or politics. Rather,

it introduced them to an order that set all the fundamentals—nature, society, self, and divinity—in harmony. In other words, it took them to the heart of what it means to be human.

Finally, the philosophers' order meant a new perspective on death. In early times, death was shadowy. For Homer, the dead had only a vague existence around their graves or in the underworld. There was no judgment or punishment for injustice toward one's fellows. Only those who had directly affronted the gods had to suffer. The mystery cults said one could conquer death by union with an immortal divinity, and their great popularity indicates the hold that death had on Greece starting in the sixth century B.C.E. The philosophers spoke of judgment and punishment because they were acutely aware that justice rules few human situations. In quite deliberate myths, Plato symbolized the inherent need we have for a final accounting. Without it, he suggested, reason would lose balance.

In the eyes of many scholars, the Greeks were among the most religious of ancient peoples. From heaven to under the earth, from crude emotion to the most refined spirituality, their great culture put a religious shine on everything. Today, if we find the world "sacred" (deeply meaningful) through science or art, if we find the human being "sacred" (deeply valuable) through medicine or philosophy, if we find the political order alive with counsels to flee disorder and pursue justice—if we ever think in these ways, it is largely because of the Greeks. They made the "transcendental" qualities—unity, truth, goodness, and beauty— part of all subsequent Western religion.

SUMMARY: THE ANCIENT NEAR EASTERN CENTER

We have surveyed the rise of ancient Near Eastern civilized religion. We should now reflect at least briefly on the central patterns that our survey reveals.

First, civilization—culture and social organization at a scale larger than that of the tribal village— developed on the foundations of agriculture. The increase in population, the sedentary life, and the economic and cultural specialization that farming allowed made cities and their cultural advances possible. Not surprisingly, then, many agricultural or earth-related motifs continued on in the religions of the first great civilizations. For all their moments of spiritual achievement, Egypt, Iran, and Greece all remained immersed in peasant views.

Second, the discovery of writing was essential in the advances of civilized religion. Through writing— even the hieroglyphic writing of the Egyptians—came the records that the early civilizations themselves used and that we, their latter-day students, have used to retrieve what they thought and felt. Within the early peoples' own religious horizon, the sense of history that came with writing was a significant development. Of course, oral peoples have memory and tradition, but writing makes historical consciousness more formal.

Writing also raises the possibility of a new attitude toward the realities of the traditional world. For writing makes the realities of the traditional world *mediated,* as they previously were not. Spoken language has a holistic quality, conveying its message immediately, in a rather imperative or at least solicitous way. Written language is more detached and indirect. To the benefit of science, and perhaps the detriment of religion, it tends toward scholarship. For example, once the biblical legends were written down, scholars could dissect them at leisure. In the development of the early civilizations, we catch sizable traditions at their very revealing transition from oral to written religion.

Third, this chapter has mainly dealt with religious traditions that lasted for long stretches of time. Of course, Mesopotamia, Egypt, Iran, and Greece all changed significantly during the times that we studied. Nonetheless, Egypt had a quite coherent religious culture that lasted longer than Christianity has so far, and Iran and Greece both provide impressive instances of religious cultures that endured and evolved through many centuries. Because of their long duration, we can reconstruct and analyze the world views these cultures generated. Concerning nature, they all preserved close ties with a living cosmos. In rites, myths, and popular religion, for instance, they all kept strong agricultural influences. On the other hand, each separated itself from the cosmological myth somewhat. Akhenaton's reform was Egypt's most dramatic separation, but the Amon hymns and man's dispute with his soul about suicide provide additional evidence.

Zoroaster made Iran break with the cosmological myth more sharply than Egypt did, but later Zoroastrianism retreated on this point. Only Greece took the full step toward the realization of spirit. The philosophers discovered the mind; for Plato and Aristotle, what is and what can be thought coincided.

Still, none of the early civilizations broke the cosmological myth entirely. None conceived of a personal creator God wholly independent of the cosmos. All their divinities were world forces, and all their ultimate world views tended to follow nature's rhythms.

Socially, Egypt appears as the most hierarchical and rigid civilization; its culture is remarkably static. Iran appears as a welter of ethnic influences and a welter of religious trends. It was in great turmoil, but few personalities, other than military kings, stand out. Personalities stand out most dramatically in Greece, despite its large patches of social conservatism. Especially in the Athenian golden age, tradition seemed just flexible enough. Thus, Greece fostered geniuses. In art and philosophy, we study them still. If viewed as the culmination of the developments of ancient Near Eastern civilizational religions, they suggest that the center for which these developments were groping was the consubstantiality of mind and holy being, the mutual penetration. In the Greek discovery of reason, human beings glimpsed the possibility that divinity is eminently rational, that the sacred is a holy word. That glimpse changed the history of Western religion and now is rewriting the history of the entire world.

Discussion Questions

1. Why was the sun so prominent in Egyptian religion?

2. How does the myth of Osiris illumine the religious significance of the pyramids?

3. In what sense did Zoroaster differentiate Iranian religious consciousness?

4. What emerges when you compare Ahura Mazdah and the Egyptian Amon-Re?

5 How did the Greek love of wisdom definitively clarify the nature of human reason?

6. Do Dionysus and Apollo together compose a complete symbolization of divinity? Why?

7. Is it fair to summarize the Hellenistic religions as a return to a prephilosophical emphasis on fertility, or did their "salvation" entail considerably more?

8. What is the main lesson in the myth of Gilgamesh?

9. What were the main features of popular, local Greek religion?

10. What significance have the Zoroastrians given to fire?

11. What does Greek religion suggest about the religious significance of death?

12. What were the main feminine motifs in the ancient Near Eastern religions?

Glossary

Ahura Mazdah: the Wise Lord who has been the main Zoroastrian divinity. Ahura Mazdah represents Zoroaster's version of the extrapolation from the demands of a refined conscience to the existence of a good, intelligent first principle one finds in other reflective religious seers.

cosmos: the universe conceived as an orderly system. Opposed to the cosmos is the chaos of a nature that seems unordered and a human realm that defies rational analysis. Religious systems that have posited an intelligent power at the foundations of reality usually have imagined the universe as a cosmos. On the other hand, the irrationalities in creation and its nonhuman scale have kept the specter of chaos alive and influential. The more sophisticated theologies—for example, the Hindu—have sometimes incorporated both aspects into their divinity, and even the theologies (for example, those of the monotheistic Western religions) that have pictured the divinity as wise and loving have had pockets in which the raw power of the deity came close to being an irrationality (or a suprarationality) so strong that human beings could never comprehend it and had always to fear it.

divine kingship: the concept, common to many ancient societies, that the monarch so mediates between the people and ultimate reality that he should be considered a god. Usually the society involved has a rather fluid notion of divinity, applying it to any forceful or crucial entity that mediates relations with the ultimate powers. In the typical scheme, the assumption of the cosmological myth makes the leading ruler the connection between heaven and earth, where the power that keeps the one consubstantial realm in order passes from above to below. Thus the vitality of the king is extremely important, and the moment when the king dies and mediating functions pass to a new ruler is the most dramatic time in the people's existence.

dualism: bifurcating reality, usually so that it separates into forces of good competing with forces of evil. The experiential basis of most dualisms is the complexity of the moral realm, in which goodness and evil seem irreducible (one cannot be collapsed into the other and neither is able to defeat the other decisively). Manicheanism and Zoroastrianism are two dualistic religions that exemplify this tendency. The Christian St. Augustine thought he solved the problem of evil, and so in good conscience could quit Manicheanism, by seeing that evil, rather than being something positive or existent in its own right, is always a privation of the being, order, and goodness that health or virtue demands. Thus sickness is the disordered functioning of cells or bodily mechanisms, whereas sin is the lack of reason and love that rationality and faith demand. Every theism has to contend with the data sparking dualism, either by distancing evil from God or by postulating what in effect is evil at the very foundations of the world (in divinity itself). Hinduism sometimes seems to take this latter position.

Hellenism: the cultural ideals, usually credited to Alexander the Great for their genesis, that dominated eastern Europe and the Near East from the late fourth century B.C.E. through perhaps the first five centuries of the Common Era. Alexander sought an ecumenical empire in which perception of a common humanity would allow different ethnic groups to be citizens of a common political realm. The religious implications included a tolerance of many different gods and cultural traditions, which in turn frequently sponsored a syncretism in which gods from different traditions overlapped or ran together.

maat: an Egyptian term (and goddess) referring to cosmic order. *Maat* was something like the Law or *Logos* guiding creation. Personified, it had the obligation of constraining or persuading creatures to follow the laws natural to them. The pharaoh mediated *maat* to the common people, and the laws of the state sanctioned by the pharaoh spelled out what *maat* was to mean in many concrete circumstances. The pharaoh had responsibilities to *maat,* but he served as well as a metaphysical link between the order of heaven that *maat* expressed and the order of earth that needed ordering. *Maat* had many competitors in the Egyptian pantheon, probably standing psychologically for the rights of reason in competition with will, desire, fertility, and the other urges of both the conscious and the unconscious mind.

Magi: ancient Persian and Zoroastrian priests. If one finds the roots of the Magi in ancient Indo-Iranian culture, they may originally have been a hereditary class like the Brahmins. Their name has overtones of (spiritual) riches, and in later periods they presided over the Persian rituals, including the Zoroastrian rites. By the time of Christ, the Magi had a reputation throughout the Hellenistic world as astrologers and interpreters of dreams.

mystery religions: traditions of the Hellenistic period that focused on ways to gain immortality and used secret sacramental rites. The mystery religions stemmed from various sources—Greek, Egyptian, and Mesopotamian. They influenced Judaism and Christianity inasmuch as they were competitors in a battle for the allegiance of people interested in wisdom and salvation. Many of the recurrent themes dealt with fertility—the dying and rising of nature that might hold promise that human beings would enter a new cycle after death. Others enacted myths of the immortality of the human soul, recalling its divine origin and speculating about its happy afterlife.

pharaoh: the king or presiding figure of ancient Egypt who mediated heavenly power and *maat* to the people. Pharaohship took place within the Egyptian version of the cosmological myth, the pharaoh being less important as an individual than as a mediator between heaven and earth. The pyramids witness to the Egyptian desire to secure pharaohship against death, while the care taken for the transition from old pharaoh to new suggests how the office of the pharaoh served Egypt as a fence against chaos.

polytheism: having many gods, or allowing all the many places or ways in which ultimate reality expresses itself to be venerated. Sometimes polytheists unify the many expressions of the divine by speaking of a single divine substance or of a great divine overlord. Usually, however, they are not metaphysicians and do not trouble themselves greatly about the relationship between the many deities and the one divine power that makes them all kin. Egyptian and Mesopotamian religions are good examples of polytheism in a developed, in its own way quite sophisticated, mode that generally felt little pressure toward henotheism or monotheism.

syncretism: the tendency to run several gods, ceremonies, beliefs, or other aspects of two or more religious traditions together. The result usually has been an undigested mixture or rather infertile hybrid. Syncretism was influential during the Hellenistic period and so presented both Judaism and Christianity many serious questions. One should distinguish syncretism from the acculturation that a religious tradition undergoes when it is transplanted from one geographic locale to another, though in fact such acculturation does sometimes lead to syncretism. For example, the translation of Buddhism from India to China and Japan was not itself syncretistic, but when Japanese Buddhists and Shintoists agreed that *bodhisattvas* and kami could be two faces of the same reality, they were accomplishing something syncretistic.

CHAPTER 4

JUDAISM

Jewish menorah

Judaism is the oldest of the three major prophetic religions. The founding and development of Christianity and Islam could not have occurred without the pre-existence of Judaism. (Zoroastrianism can claim some prophetic equality with Judaism, but its prophecies never became dominant in Near Eastern and Western beliefs. Zoroastrianism's major influence in the West was its eschatology—its ideas of death, judgment, resurrection, punishment, the warfare between good and evil, and so on.) Abraham, Moses, David, Elijah, Isaiah—they are the personalities that dominated the Western prophetic beginnings.

HISTORY

The Biblical Period

In dealing with the roots of Judaism in the biblical period, we encounter serious questions about the sources that any historical treatment must use. The Bible is not a simple, straightforward book, and thus the evidence it provides for the evolution of Israelite faith is not simple or straightforward. The current scholarly consensus is that the Jewish scriptures (Old Testament) come from many sources and represent many different points of view. Circles of priests, prophets, and people interested in wisdom (sapiential circles), for example, probably preserved memories of battles, of traditional laws, of the reigns of different kings, of prayers to be sung on special occasions, and much more. Each such circle had its own traditions, its own political goals, its own understanding of what Israelite history had been in the past and signified in the present. For perhaps a thousand years (from the time of the monarchy of David to the time when the rabbis reached a final rough consensus about what writings should be deemed regulative and so "scriptural"), Israelites (early Jews) worked over records and leavings. Northerners had traditions that differed from southerners. Poets put things one way and chroniclers put things another way. Indeed, in just the first five books of the Bible, traditionally attributed to Moses, scholars have discerned at least four major strands of tradition. Weaving their way through Genesis, Exodus, Leviticus, Numbers, and Deuteronomy, these strands sometimes offer us different perspectives on the same topic. For example, the account of creation that opens the Bible (Genesis 1) stresses the orderly arrangement

Figure 16 *The Near East.*

KEY JEWISH DOCTRINES	
Revelation	Divine will expressed in Torah
	Divine nature shown in history
Covenant	Special bond created between God and Israel
	Chosen people called to a special holiness
Redemption	Divine action to save the people
	Key experiences: Exodus, return from Exile, establishment of the state of Israel
Prophecy	Divine inspiration to announce God's will
	Call to right worship and social justice
Monotheism	Only the God of the ancestors is a true divinity
	Need for vigilance against idolatry
Ethics	Need to follow Jewish Law (Torah)
	Call above all to justice and mercy

of the physical world, while the account that we find in chapters 2 and 3 is more interested in how the first human beings arose and what happened to them.

Materials such as these different strands of the Pentateuch were edited, usually several times, into the order of the biblical "books" that we find today. Each book of the Bible therefore is a composite work, and sometimes one finds conflicts, both within a given book and between one book and another. So, for example, Exodus gives us one view of Moses and Deuteronomy gives us another. Moreover, although the first five books of the Bible have been accorded the most dignity and authority, the second section of the Bible, traditionally called "the Prophets," also has been revered, and this second section contains reinterpretations of the events (especially the establishment of the covenant between Israel and God) suited to later crises, such as the removal of many leaders of the Israelite community to Babylon in the sixth century B.C.E. Still a third section of the Bible, traditionally called "the Writings," collects later and disparate materials, and while as a group it has had less status than either the first five books (Pentateuch, Torah) or the Prophets, its works have still been considered authoritative interpretations of the meaning of Israelite existence. Together, these three sections of the Bible comprised the *TANAK*, an anagram comprised from the first letters for each in Hebrew.

Any sketch of the history of biblical Israel, therefore, both depends on questionable sources and tends to distort what the Bible itself was all about. The Bible itself is about "paradigmatic" history: key events and personages that could serve as three-dimensional lessons about the significance of Israel's experiences sojourning with its Lord though time. As we turn now to such a sketch of the biblical period, it is important to remember that the biblical writers on which we or the authorities we are using depend were themselves usually more interested in the significance a given event had for contemporary existence (the cultural challenges existing at the time of the writer or editor) than in what happened, in a literal sense, originally. In other words, we are always involved in interpreting interpretations—dealing with the meanings, symbolic and historical alike, that people using the Bible paradigmatically found most absorbing.

To begin our historical survey, we take up an "integrationist" point of view, assuming a continuity between biblical Israel and later Judaism. As one prominent Jewish scholar has put it: "From the point of view of the Jew, Judaism and the Religion of Israel are the same, and what is called the religion of [biblical] Israel is but one chapter of a long and variegated historical continuum."[1] We accept this point of view, avoiding the tendency to make a great disjunction between biblical Judaism and Judaism in the Common Era. While the Roman destruction of the Temple in Jerusalem in 70 C.E. changed Jewish religion, the rabbis continued to look to the Torah of Moses for their inspiration.

In the beginning, the Jews were most likely a loose collection of seminomadic tribes that wandered in what is today Israel, Jordan, Lebanon, and Syria. They may have cultivated some crops, but their self-designation was "wandering Aramaeans" (Deut. 26:5). Thus, when scouts returned from Canaan (present-day western Israel) with grapes, pomegranates, and figs (products of settled cultivators), they caused quite a stir.[2]

Members of an early Jewish extended family tended to worship their particular "god of the father," defining themselves largely in terms of their patriarch and his god. The cult therefore centered on clan remembrance of this god, who wandered with the tribe in its nomadic life. The common name for such a clan divinity was *el*. Before their settlement in Canaan, the people seem to have worshiped a variety of *els:* the god of the mountain, the god of seeing, the god of eternity, and so on. Usually they worshiped at altars constructed of unhewn stones, which they considered to be the god's house. In addition to the *els* were household deities and minor divinities and demons of the desert. In later orthodox Jewish interpretation, Abraham drew on whatever sense there was of a unity among these *els* or of a supreme *el* over the others to dedicate himself to a God who was beyond nature. That God, the creator of the world, Abraham called Yahweh (YHWH).[3] (The influence of Exodus 3:14 on the Genesis story of Abraham is clear.)

For later orthodoxy, Abraham became the "Father" of the Jews and his God YHWH ("I am who I am") became their God. In that sense, Judaism began with Abraham. Abraham probably lived around 1800 B.C.E. His descendants Isaac and Jacob, whose stories are recounted in the biblical book of Genesis, kept the Abrahamic faith in the unique name of YHWH, "the Lord." From about 1650 to 1280, the people of Abra-

ham, then known as Hebrews, were in Egypt, subjects of the Egyptian kingdom.[4] According to the Book of Genesis (39–50), the Hebrews' presence in Egypt was due to the success there of Jacob's son Joseph. Their leader at the end of their stay in Egypt was Moses. In later Jewish theology, Moses functioned as the founder of the Jewish people, because God revealed through Moses his will to make a covenant and fashion himself a people. In the incident at the burning bush (Exod. 3), Jewish faith said, Moses experienced God's self-revelation. God then commissioned Moses to lead the people out of Egypt, giving as his authoritative name only "I am who I am" (or "I am whatever I want to be").

Moses then led the Jewish people out of Egypt, an event that dominated the biblical authors' interpretation of everything that preceded and followed it. In the most significant episode in that *exodus,* Egyptian pursuers drowned in the sea. Free of them, the Israelites (the descendants of Jacob, Abraham's grandson) wandered in the desert until they entered the homeland that God had promised them. The deliverance from Egypt through the unexpected event at the Reed Sea (not the present-day Red Sea) marked all subsequent Jewish faith. Looking back to this event, later generations clung to the belief that their God ruled history and would continue to liberate them from oppression.

In the desert, Moses and the people tested the meaning of their exodus experience. They came to believe, through what the Bible pictures as God's miraculous speaking to them, that they were bound to God by a *covenant.* In this compact, based on the relation between a Near Eastern overlord and vassal, God pledged care and the people pledged fidelity. The commandments accompanying this covenant gave the binding relationship (which some later commentators saw as prefigured in Adam, Noah, and Abraham) an ethics. They became the basis of the Law (Torah) and the revelation that bound the people together.

This *Torah* has been the mainstay of Jewish life for over 3,000 years. In the beginning, it encompassed the oral revelation of God, believed to have been given to Moses as a sort of charter or constitution for the life of the covenanted or chosen people. When Jewish religious writings about the formative period (of the earliest ancestors and Moses) arose, they were attributed to Moses. Thus the first five books of the present Bible, now known as the Torah or the Pentateuch, were long considered to have come from Moses' hand (modern biblical scholarship disputes this). When subsequent writings eventually included in the Hebrew Bible (the two groups of writings known as the Prophets and the Writings) gained status as authentic revelation from God, they too partook of the dignity of Torah. Thus the Tanak (Torah-Prophets-Writings) or Hebrew Bible has all been considered Torah.

In the same way, later Judaism came to consider the rabbinic writings (such collections as the Mishnah, the Gemara, and the Talmud [the Mishnah plus the Gemara]) sufficiently authoritative to have the status of God's revelation or direction, so such rabbinic writings also came under Torah. Torah, then, is the expression of the divine will, given through human intermediaries, on which pious Jews have depended for their basic sense of what God is like, what God has done in their history, and how God wants them to live (in keeping with their call to be the special people of a holy deity). From laws about how to keep the Sabbath to traditions about how to sway while praying, Torah has encompassed all the traditions cherished as the basis of the people's identity and way to live worthy of their Lord.[5]

When the Israelites finally settled in Canaan (in the latter half of the thirteenth century B.C.E. under Moses' successor Joshua),[6] they changed from a nomadic to an agricultural people. They were still a group of confederated tribes, but in settlement their bonds tended to loosen, as each group kept to its own area and developed its own ways. Only in times of common danger would the groups weld together, but war was so constant a feature of the period from the Exodus to the sixth-century Exile in Babylon that the people had to cooperate. Settlement also meant religious changes, as local sanctuaries replaced the wandering ark of the covenant as the house of God. A somewhat professional priesthood apparently developed around these sanctuaries, and as the Israelites conquered Canaanite temples, they probably took over the scribal schools attached to the temples. These schools were probably the first sources of written Hebrew religious literature. In addition, the Canaanite religion itself was a great influence on the Israelites. Before long it produced a conflict between Israelites who favored the older God YHWH—the God of Abraham, Moses, and the covenant—and those who favored the agricultural gods (baals) of the Canaanites.

Kings and Prophets. From about 1200 to 1000 B.C.E., the Israelites had a government by "judges"—charismatic leaders, usually men but occasionally women, who took command in times of common danger. However, they eventually adopted monarchical rule, orga-

nizing a sturdy little kingdom under David at a new capital: Jerusalem. This kingdom unified the tribes of both north and south, and under Solomon, David's son, it had a brief but golden age of culture and empire. Some of the most striking narratives of the Hebrew Bible (Old Testament) derive from this period, including the brilliant memoir we find in 2 Samuel, chapters 13–20.[7]

In these narratives, David is portrayed as the ideal king and yet a man undeniably human—lustful for Bathsheba (willing to murder to get her), tragically at odds with his son Absalom. Much later, David's achievements in war and his fashioning a kingdom for peace made him the focus of messianic hopes—hopes for a king anointed by God who would usher in a new age of prosperity and peace. David, then, was the Jewish prototype for sacred kingship. Similarly, David's son Solomon became the prototype for wisdom. Just as many pious Jews attributed the Psalms to David, so they attributed much of the Bible's wisdom literature to Solomon.

Following Solomon's death, the northern and southern portions of the kingdom split apart. The north (Israel) lasted from 922 to 722 B.C.E., when it fell to Assyria. The south (Judah) lasted until 586, when it fell to Babylon. (Both Assyria and Babylon lay to the northeast.) These were centuries of great political strife and military conflict. They spawned a series of important religious *"prophets,"* who dominate the next phase of biblical history. Greatest of the early prophets was Elijah, who preached in the north against the corrupt kings Ahab and Ahaziah and the queen Jezebel. The legendary stories about Elijah portray him as a champion of YHWH and true prophecy against the false prophets of the Canaanite baals. What is clear from these stories is the influence at the time of charismatic personalities who felt that God inspired them to stand up for the old religious ways—even if doing so infuriated the royal establishment.

Around 750 B.C.E., Amos, an originally southern prophet working in the north and the first of the writing prophets, issued a clarion call for justice. Changing the notion that YHWH was simply Israel's protector, Amos made divine blessings dependent upon repentance from sin. His God was clearly in charge of nature, but the key access to divinity was social justice. In other words, YHWH was a God of people and history, especially concerned that human beings deal with one another fairly.

Hosea, another northern prophet, also spoke up for mercy and justice (and for nonidolatrous cult), but he expressed God's attitude as that of a spouse willing to suffer infidelity, unable to cast off his beloved (the people covenanted to him). In the south, the successors to these northern prophets were Isaiah, Jeremiah, and "Second Isaiah" (the source of Isaiah, chapters 40–55). They made the same demands, but with greater stress on punishment by foreign powers. Reading the signs of the times, they thought that God would subject his people to captivity because they had not relied on him in pure faith. However, both Jeremiah and Second Isaiah held out hope for a new beginning, assuring Judah that a remnant of the people would keep faith.

During the reign of the southern king Josiah (640—609 B.C.E.), there was a religious reform that many scripture scholars see as the source of the "Deuteronomic" recasting of the early Jewish tradition. It shaped not only the Book of Deuteronomy but other historical writings as well. Among the influential ideas were that YHWH had elected Israel to be his people; that observing the covenant laws was necessary for religious prosperity; that Jews ought to repudiate contacts with foreigners and foreign gods; that the cult should be consolidated in Jerusalem; and that Israel ought to rely only on YHWH, since he controlled history and oversaw nature.

Case Study: Jeremiah.   It will be useful to consider the personality, career, and message of Jeremiah, for Jeremiah is a striking example of both the prophetic vocation and biblical spirituality. Born in the middle of the seventh century B.C.E. (in 645, according to some scholars), and coming from a priestly family, Jeremiah preached during the reigns of kings Josiah, Jehoiakim, and Zedekiah, until he was deported around 582 to Egypt, where he died. We know more about Jeremiah's personal life than that of the other prophets, and Jeremiah's personal life shows a man completely dominated by God's call. He did not marry, because he wanted to symbolize that most children would not survive the troubles coming because of Israel's infidelities (Jer. 16:1–4). He would not take part in mourning ceremonies or festivals, because soon there would be none left to mourn and nothing good to celebrate (16:5–8).

As one might expect, these dire forecasts made Jeremiah very unpopular. Enemies conspired against his life (11:18–23), he was confined in the stocks (19:14–20:6), and for announcing the coming destruction of the Jerusalem Temple he was tried for blas-

phemy. King Jehoiakim considered Jeremiah his deadly enemy and had him flogged. Jeremiah reciprocated Jehoiakim's enmity, flogging him verbally. Indeed, his indictment of King Jehoiakim reveals so much about Jeremiah's character that the verses are worth reproducing:

> Woe to him who builds his house by
> unrighteousness, and his upper rooms
> by injustice;
> who makes his neighbor serve him for
> nothing, and does not give him his
> wages;
> Who says, "I will build myself a great
> house with spacious upper rooms,"
> and cuts out windows for it, paneling
> it with cedar, and painting it with
> vermillion.
> Do you think you are a king because
> you compete in cedar?
> Did not your father eat and drink
> and do justice and righteousness?
> Then it was well with him.
> He judged the cause of the poor and
> needy; then it was well.
> "Is this not to know me?" says the Lord.
> "But you have eyes and heart only for
> your dishonest gain,
> for shedding innocent blood, and for
> practicing oppression and violence."
> Therefore thus says the Lord
> concerning Jehoi'akim the son of
> Josi'ah, king of Judah:
> "They shall not lament for him,
> saying,
> 'Ah my brother!' or 'Ah sister!'
> They shall not lament for him, saying
> 'Ah lord!' or 'Ah his majesty!'
> With the burial of an ass he shall be
> buried,
> dragged and cast forth beyond the
> gates of Jerusalem." (22:13–19 RSV)

Whence came this lashing tongue, this need to accuse the mighty to their faces? Jeremiah felt his painful vocation had been laid upon him by God, who had chosen him to be a prophet from the moment of his conception (1:5–10). His mission would extend beyond Israel, bringing the Lord's message to all the nations.

Jeremiah apparently came to this understanding of his vocation while still a teenager, and the responsibility it imposed overwhelmed him. But the Lord would hear none of Jeremiah's protests, assuring him that if he spoke divine words he would receive divine support: "Behold I have put my words in your mouth" (1:9). "Be not afraid of them, for I am with you to deliver you" (1:8). So a prophet was formed, a man dominated by "the word of the Lord," the message his God impelled him to deliver.

Along with Jeremiah's calling came two visions (1:11–19). The first vision was of an almond tree. Punning on the similarity of the Hebrew words for *almond tree* and *to watch,* God told Jeremiah that his vision of the almond tree was accurate: The Lord would watch over his word to perform it. The second vision was of a boiling pot, facing away from the north. Just as boiling water spilled out of the pot and swept away twigs and pebbles, so foes would sweep out of the north and inflict evil on Jeremiah's countrymen. Jeremiah himself would face strong opposition for delivering these oracles, but his enemies would not prevail. The Lord would be with him, to deliver him.

From the outset, therefore, Jeremiah was a troubled man. He felt a charge to bring before his people the unpleasant news that hard times were coming, as the just desserts of their irreligion. From the outset Jeremiah was also a poetic man, brimming with powerful imagery. In a few lines he could sketch the whole career of a dishonest king, withering him by contrast with his righteous father. In a few phrases he could etch the king's coming demise, depicting the funeral that none would mourn. The word of the Lord pouring from the mouth of this troubled man riveted his people's imagination and lashed their soul. Jeremiah's passion for justice, his almost obsessive sense that the people had abandoned the very basis of their existence by falling away from the true God, gave him the courage to flay kings and leaders publicly. Thus he asked the people, in the name of God, "What wrong did your fathers find in me, that they went far from me, and went after worthlessness, and became worthless?" (2:5).

As Jeremiah read the political situation, God would punish this worthless people, using Babylon as his instrument. King Zedekiah consulted with Jeremiah about the political situation, but the king's advisers were bitterly opposed to the prophet, feeling that his predictions of woe were destroying the people's will to resist the Babylonians. Babylon did lay siege to Jerusalem, and when in 588 or 587 Jeremiah used a brief break in the siege to leave Jerusalem, his enemies arrested him for desertion. Zedekiah soon released him from the dungeon but had him kept in confinement. Undeterred, Jeremiah continued to proclaim that the Babylonians would defeat the Jews, and for this stubbornness his enemies threw him into a cistern, with the intention that he should starve there. When Jerusalem finally fell in 586, the victorious Babylonians treated Jeremiah well, offering him the choice of living either in Babylon or Judah. Jeremiah .chose Judah, and he urged his countrymen left in Judah to try to live in peace.

Peace was not to be, however, for some discontented Jewish fugitives from the army killed Gedaliah, the governor appointed by the Babylonian ruler Nebuchadnezzar. Most of the Jewish community feared Babylonian vengeance for this murder, but when the community appealed to Jeremiah for a divine oracle on whether they should flee to Egypt or stay where they were, Jeremiah told them to stay in their own country. The people would not accept this oracle, however, so they took Jeremiah and his scribe Baruch with them to Egypt. In Egypt Jeremiah continued his unpopular ways, predicting that the Babylonians would defeat the Egyptians and castigating Jews who fell to worshiping a heavenly queen. The Jews in Egypt rejected this rebuke, and, according to later legend, stoned Jeremiah to death.

Overall, most of Jeremiah's warnings, visions, symbolic actions, and oracles were gloomy. Thinking that his people had enmeshed themselves in secular politics to the neglect of their religion, the prophet saw Judah becoming crushed by the much larger foreign powers surrounding it, and thought this fate a fitting punishment for Judah's defections. Still, not all Jeremiah's prophecies were gloomy. Like the other great prophets, his message balanced judgment with consolation. If God was judging the people harshly, because of their wanton irreligion, God was also assuring the people that the future would bring better times. Jeremiah's most consoling assurances occur in chapters 30–32, which are a high point of biblical poetry and theology.

Chapter 30 begins with the formulaic introductory phrase, "The word that came to Jeremiah from the Lord." This word was positive. The days were coming when God would restore his people's fortunes. He would bring them back to their land, lost when the northern kingdom fell in 722 to Assyria and threatened by Babylon. No matter how great the present pains grew, God would save the people from them. He would break the yoke of their foreign rulers, leading them back to serve him, the Lord their God, and a king like David.

With great poetic skill, the prophet plays variations on this theme. Behind the people's present sufferings is the hand of the Lord, punishing them for their transgressions. But that same hand will punish Israel's enemies: "Therefore all who devour you shall be devoured, and all your foes, every one of them, shall go into captivity, those who despoil you shall become a spoil, and all who prey on you I will make a prey" (30:16).

Similar poetry sings of what the restored people will enjoy: good fortune for the tents of Jacob, compassion on all Jacob's offspring's dwellings, songs of thanksgiving throughout the city and the palace, many voices making merry. "And you shall be my people, and I will be your God" (30:22). Hearkening back to the exodus from Egypt, the prophet has God say that the people who survived the sword and found grace in the wilderness would come to know God most intimately. Why? Because "I have loved you with an everlasting love; therefore I have continued my faithfulness to you" (31:3).

So in the future weeping would be for joy rather than sorrow, walking would be along lovely brooks of water and straight paths of virtue. God would gather his scattered people, like a shepherd gathering his flocks. Maidens would join in the dance, young and old alike would make merry. And the voice of Rachel, lamenting the exile of the northern kingdom, would cease. In the future, voices would not be for mourning, eyes would not be for tears. After the present time of painful chastening, the people would realize that God had never forgotten them, never stopped feeling merciful toward them.

In the good future, no longer would it be said, "The fathers have eaten sour grapes, and the children's teeth are set on edge." Rather, each person would be responsible for his own good or evil. Indeed, there would be an entirely new covenant, better than the covenant the people had entered upon after God led them out of Egypt. The people broke that covenant, though God was their husband. "But this is the covenant which I will make with the house of Israel after those days, says the Lord: I will put my law within them, and I will write it upon their hearts; and I will be their God, and they shall be my people. And no longer shall each man teach his neighbor and teach his brother, saying, 'Know the Lord,' for they shall all know me, from the least of them to the greatest, says the Lord; for I will forgive their iniquity, and I will remember their sin no more" (31:33–34). In all the literature of the world religions, few passages express the divine love more beautifully.

Both the prophets and the Deuteronomic historian-theologians testified to the dangers to survival that Jews of their time felt. Political subjugation by the much larger neighboring powers was ever a possibility, but it was less ominous than cultural assimilation. To preserve their identity Jews would have to keep clear of their neighbors' fertility religion. Only an adherence to a quite different god—YHWH, the God of Moses and Abraham—could keep the people true to themselves.

Thus, the stress on nonidolatrous cult and detailed religious law that we find after the period of captivity to Babylon was most likely a reaction to the threat of adopting non-Hebrew influences. For instance, both adopting kingship and holding agricultural celebrations could be false steps, because they could take the Israelites away from YHWH. When the Israelites were dispersed into Babylon, Jews of the southern kingdom tested the prophets' theology. A few realized what they had lost by playing power politics and relying on new gods. When the Persians gained control of the region from the Babylonians, Cyrus allowed Jews to return to Jerusalem. The relatively small number who did return lived a reformed life under Nehemiah and Ezra, choosing to rebuild the Temple the Babylonians had wrecked and to reestablish themselves on the basis of a strict adherence to the covenant law. Marriage to foreigners was interdicted, and priests strictly controlled the new Temple.

Covenantal Theology. From their *Exile* to Babylon, Jews thought they had learned a capital lesson. They now viewed their history as one of wavering fidelity to the covenant, and this view suggested to them that infidelity to Torah led to national disaster. God had chosen them by covenanting with them in a special way, and unless they responded with signal fidelity, they would reap not blessing but judgment. Consequently, the returnees stressed their isolation and uniqueness. Still, historical experience also suggested, at least to some prophets and religious thinkers, that God himself was universal, Lord of all peoples. His dominion included the foreign nations, for they had obviously served as his instruments for chastening Israel. He had punished through the Assyrians and Babylonians and freed through the Persians.

As a result, conquest, exile, and return made Jews focus more and more on Jerusalem and its cult (centered in the Temple) as the source of their identity. At the same time, they clarified their ideas about God's worldwide outreach, finally realizing that God had to be the Creator of all things. Views of the covenant changed somewhat, but the predominant view was that God would punish Israel for infidelity and reward it for standing firm. However, God was not bound to be merciful. Mercy, rather, was an outflow of his unpredictable, unmeasurable goodness. Somehow, despite all human weaknesses, God would give a new future. Often the Jews envisioned this future as messianic—coming through a holy ruler anointed by God.

The stress on covenant by the Deuteronomic and postexilic leaders exalted Moses as the religious figure par excellence. However much David stood for kingly success, indeed for the very establishment of Jerusalem, Moses stood for the Torah—revelation, teaching, law. The Torah was a much more solid foundation than either kingship or Jerusalem. By the words of God's mouth, the heavens were made. By the words God spoke through Moses' mouth, the Jews were made a people. If the people kept to those words, they would choose life. If they forgot them or put them aside, they would choose death. Thus, Moses had said: "I call heaven and earth to witness against you this day, that I have set before you life and death, blessing and curse; therefore, choose life, that you and your descendants may live, loving the Lord your God, obeying his voice, and clinging to him" (Deut. 30:19–20). In the sober climate that followed the return from exile, the wise way for Jews seemed to be to keep to themselves and their own special laws.

Wisdom and Apocalypse. Two other movements marked the later Jewish biblical period. The first is found in the wisdom literature of the Hebrew Bible. As many commentators point out,[8] Ecclesiastes and Proverbs bear the marks of the prudential, reflective thought, expressed in maxims, that was available from Egypt. Somewhat incongruously, it grafted itself onto Jewish speculation about God's action, which suggests that postexilic Judaism found its times rather trying. At least, the wisdom literature is dour and sober compared with the historical and prophetic sections of the Bible. It retains a faith that God still has his hand on the tiller but it finds the seas gray and choppy. Suffer-

ing had tempered the fire in the Jewish soul for poetry and prophecy.

The Book of Job, however, is an exception. Job probes the problem of suffering, which surely is a wisdom concern, but it reaches poetic depths. Job reveals that the innocent do suffer mysteriously—that we cannot understand our fate, because all human life unfolds by the plan of a God whose mind we cannot know. This God set the boundaries of the seas, made the different species of all living things. He is not someone we can take to court, not someone who has to account to us. Rather, we can only cling to him in darkness and in trust. Because Job does not profess the older theology, in which punishment was in response to sin, instead proposing a mystery beyond legalistic logic, it brings the postexilic centuries some religious distinction.

By the end of the third century B.C.E., however, the constraints on Jewish national life brought about another reaction to the problems of suffering and providence. Job refers to Satan, an "adversary," and, perhaps due to Iranian influences, in the last years before the Common Era, a dualistic concern with good and evil came to the fore. God and his supporting angels fought against Satan and his minions. The world, in fact, was conceived of as a cosmic battlefield, with God and the forces of light against the forces of darkness. For the first time, Jewish religion started to focus on an afterlife. Pressed by the problem that the good do not necessarily meet with reward nor the evil with punishment, Jewish religion raised the notion that a divine judgment would mete out proper justice. Correspondingly, it started to imagine heavenly places for the good who pass judgment and infernal places for the wicked who fail.

The Book of Daniel expresses these concerns through what scholars call "apocalyptic" imagination.[9] This imagination purports to be a revelation *(apocalypsis)* from God about how the future will unfold. Psychologically, it is an effort to comfort people who are under stress with promises that they will find vindication. Theologically, it puts a sharp edge on the question of whether God controls history. The historical context of Daniel was the pressure of Antiochus Epiphanes, the pagan ruler, to profane Jewish worship. The revolt of the Jews led by the Maccabees stemmed from this pressure.

Daniel joins apocalyptic concern with the older prophetic concern with a messiah, casting the future vindication of the Jews in terms of a heavenly being (the "Son of man") who will come on the clouds. His coming is the dramatic climax in the eschatological scenario that Jews developed in postexilic times. Thus, the Son of man came to figure in many apocalyptic writings (most of them not included in the Bible), and among apocalyptic believers he was the preferred version of the messianic king. (Christians seized on this figure as a principal explanation of Jesus.)

Hellenism.   From the end of the fourth century B.C.E., the political fate of the Jews lay in the hands first of the Greeks and then of the Romans. Thus, Greek and Roman influences mixed with Israel's wisdom and apocalyptic concerns. The ideals that some Jews accepted from Alexander the Great are commonly labeled "Hellenistic." They included the notion that all people have a basis for community *(koinonia)* in human reason and so can share an inhabited world *(ecumene).*[10] Contact with Hellenism divided the Jewish community. Some priests and intellectuals took to the notion of a common humanity, as well as to Greek science, philosophy, and drama, but the majority of the people, sensing a threat to their identity, reacted adversely. By the time that Antiochus Epiphanes tried to enforce pagan Hellenism and destroy traditional Judaism, most Jews supported the (successful) revolt that the Maccabees led in 168 B.C.E.[11] Herod the Great, appointed king of the Jews by the Roman Senate in 40 B.C.E., helped to promote Hellenistic influences in Judea after the Roman conquest.

Overall, Hellenism influenced the Jewish conception of law, and it sparked the first strictly philosophical efforts to make the Torah appear reasonable to any clear-thinking person. Philo, a contemporary of Jesus, was a great expositor of this sort of philosophy. In the final decades of the biblical period, however, political and religious differences divided the Jewish communities. Some people, called the Zealots, urged political action, in the spirit of the Maccabean rebellion. These Zealots opposed those (such as the Essenes of the Qumran community around the Dead Sea) who urged a withdrawal from political life and a purification for the coming of the Messiah. The *Pharisees* and *Sadducees,* lay and priestly groups, adopted centrist positions, urging both a political accommodation and a reliance on the Torah.

Rabbinic Judaism

The forces who urged revolt against the Romans suffered a crushing defeat in 70 C.E., when Titus destroyed the Temple in Jerusalem and cast most of the Jews out into the *Diaspora* (in this context, *Diaspora* refers to the settlement of Jews outside Palestine). Despite the heroic resistance of many Zealots at Masada, a fortress of King Herod near the Dead Sea Valley, foreign (pagan) rule stamped down all the harder. The Pharisees and their successors picked up the pieces. The Pharisaic movement owed much of its concern for the punctilious observance of Torah to the lay scribes (lawyers) who arose in the postexilic Hellenistic period, but the Pharisees did not organize themselves as a distinct party until the second century B.C.E. Maccabean revolt.[12] The Pharisees stood for a close observance of the covenant law, applying it in all aspects of daily life, trying to adapt it as new times required. This belief had come to dominate the scribes who preceded the Pharisees, and it dominated the *rabbis* (teachers) who came after them. The Pharisees sponsored vigorous debate about the application of Torah, which became a feature of subsequent rabbinic Judaism.

In the Diaspora these rabbis became the center of communal life. The Temple had fallen and with it the cultic priesthood. So the alternative to cultic sacrifice—an alternative that had begun in the Babylonian exile, when Jerusalem and the Temple were far away—filled the religious void. This alternative was the *synagogue*—the gathering place where the community could pray and hear expositions of the Torah. The synagogue became the central institution of Judaism in exile, and the study necessary to expose the Torah well made Judaism an intellectual powerhouse.

What we call rabbinic Judaism focuses on the synagogue, exposition of the Torah, and study that increases the importance of the teacher (the rabbi). Increasingly, the teachers wanted to base their expositions on the teachings of their eminent predecessors, so they gathered a great collection of commentaries. Eventually, this collection became the *Talmud* ("the Learning"), a vast collection of the oral law that was composed of the *Mishnah* (itself a collection of interpretations of biblical legal materials) and the *Gemara* (commentaries on the Mishnah).[13] As noted, all of these rabbinic materials became part of Torah.

The Mishnah arose at the end of the first century B.C.E. from the new practice of settling legal disputes by a systematized appeal to recognized authorities. This practice prompted a conflict between the Sadducees and the Pharisees. The Mishnah represented a Pharisaic effort to outflank the Sadducees, who denied the binding character of the oral law and relied on the literal biblical text alone. After the Temple fell in 70

C.E. and times became tumultuous, a written record of all the great teachers' legal opinions became highly desirable. The recording took place in Jabneh, a town on the coast west of Jerusalem. Many teachers moved to Jabneh, among them the great Rabbi Akiba (50–135), who later set up his own influential academy at Bene-Berak to the north. They began the real systematization of the Mishnah (the word implies repetition). The Mishnah continued and even intensified the scrutiny of every scriptural jot and tittle, but it went hand in hand with more pastoral activities.

Under the Roman emperor Hadrian, the Jews felt so oppressed, especially by his decision to build a temple to Jupiter on the site of the great Jewish Temple in Jerusalem, that they mounted the short-lived revolt led by Bar Kokhba. The Romans crushed it in 135 C.E., and thenceforth Jews could enter Jerusalem only on the anniversary of the destruction of the Temple, when they might weep at the Western Wall (Figure 17).

In Babylon (present-day Iraq), to which many of the teachers fled, the talmudic work went on. When Hadrian died in 138, Palestinian Jews' fortunes rose, and a new intellectual center soon was established in Galilee in northern Israel. There, under Rabbi Judah, the Mishnah was elaborated to the point where, when written down (around 200 C.E.), it could be both a practical code and a digest of the oral law. It consisted of six parts, whose subject matter reveals a great deal about the rabbis' conception of religious life.[14] The first Order (part) deals with the biblical precepts concerning the rights of the poor, the rights of priests, the fruits of the harvest, and other agricultural matters. The second Order deals with the Sabbath, festivals, fasts, and the calendar. The third Order (entitled "Women") contains laws of marriage and divorce and other laws governing the relations between the sexes. The fourth Order, entitled "Damages," addresses civil and criminal law. The fifth Order deals with cultic matters and the slaughtering of animals, and the final Order concerns ritual cleanliness.

Law and Lore. Perhaps the best-known portion of the Mishnah is the *Pirke Avot* ("Sayings of the Fathers"), the last tractate of the fourth Order.[15] It contains opinions of some of the oldest and most influential rabbis, but it is especially venerated for the spirit, the animating love, with which it infuses both the study of the Torah and the ethical life that the Torah should inspire. Often commentators on Judaism state that the Talmud represents a psychology of defense. It is a "fence" for Torah—a protective device to keep people from violating the Law on which their identity and survival depend.

But the religious spirit of the Fathers forces us to reconsider this interpretation. The Fathers built an ethics and religion that are, if not aggressive, at least positive and constructive. On first reading, the *Pirke Avot* suggests not defensiveness but the thought of sober, disciplined, studious minds—minds not unlike that of Ecclesiastes and the other wisdom writers. However, further study shows that the Fathers' sobriety encourages a study that reaches the heart and brings joy. This is explicit in Johanan ben Zacchai (2:13), but surely it is implicit in Hillel (1:12), Simeon the Just (1:2), and many others.

The rabbis called the legal portion of the Torah *halakah*. Through reason, analogies, and deep thought, halakah made the most minute applications of the Torah. For instance, it concerned itself with the dietary laws intended to keep the Jews' eating practices clean or fitting (*kosher*). It also went deeply into the laws for the observance of the *Sabbath*. For centuries such laws, in their biblical forms (for example, Leviticus and Numbers), had kept the Jews separate from their neighbors. As the scribes, Pharisees, and then the Diaspora rabbis concentrated their legal expertise, however, halakah became very complex. Certainly in the Roman Empire, non-Jews strongly associated the Jews with their laws. Thus, halakah partly contributed to anti-Semitism, insofar as it stressed the sense of "otherness" that often is used to justify bigotry.

Balancing the strictly legal teaching and lore, however, was the looser, more folkloric *aggadah*. This was a treasury of exegetical and homiletic (explanatory and preaching) stories that applied biblical passages to a congregation's present circumstances.[16] Where halakah reasoned closely, aggadah was apt to employ mythic devices, including paradigmatic figures and symbols. Aggadah drew much of its authority from the fact that Jewish theology had always held (at least in the ultimately dominant Pharisaic opinion) that an oral Torah accompanied the written Law of Moses and the other books of the Hebrew Bible. Aggadah often presented unscientific but pious reflection about traditional passages, especially those of scripture, that pictured God in his holy freedom—God at work creating this world in which we live.

Thus, the aggadic tradition tells of Rabbi Hanina bar Pappa's teaching on how God guides conception: "The name of the angel appointed over conception is Night. He takes the seed and lays it before the Holy One, blessed be he, and says to him: Master of the

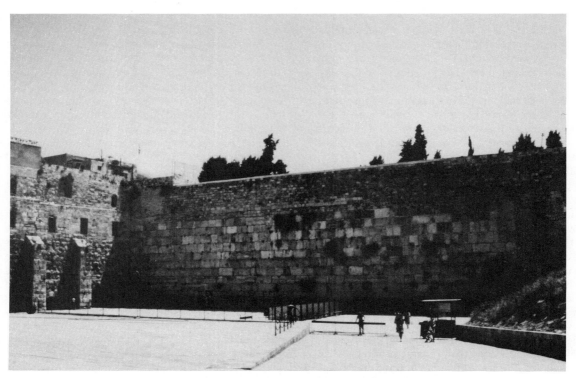

Figure 17 *Jerusalem: the Western Wall, with the Dome of the Rock in the background. Photo by J. T. Carmody.*

universe, what is this seed to be—mighty or weak, wise or foolish, rich or poor? But he does not say 'wicked' or 'righteous.' So according to Rabbi Hanina. For Rabbi Hanina said: 'All is in the hands of heaven, except the fear of heaven.' " In other words, the aggadah tried to explain how a phenomenon (such as conception) was under God's control. It also urged certain attitudes (such as fear of heaven) to make faith consonant with such control. This method probably began with Ezra in the postexilic period, and it dominated what Jewish historians call the Soferic period, when the scribes came to dominate the reassembled community's spiritual life. Aggadah continued to develop side by side with halakah for at least a millennium, ministering to the needs that common folk had for a teaching that was vivid and exemplary.

In Babylon, under the rule of the Exilarch (as the head of the Diaspora community was known in the Common Era), scholars collected the fruits of discussions of Rabbi Judah's Mishnah conducted at various academies. In addition, they immersed themselves in the ideas and *responsa* (masters' answers to questions about the Law's application) that flowed back and forth between Babylon and Palestine. Both halakah and aggadah contributed to this broad collection of legal materials, and the final redaction of the Babylonian Talmud, probably accomplished early in the fifth century, amounted to an encyclopedia of scholarly opinion not only on the law but also on much of the other learning of the day, including biology, medicine, and astronomy, that formed the background for many of the discussions.

Talmudic Religion. In terms of theology proper, the Talmud (whether the Palestinian or the more influential Babylonian version) clung to scriptural faith.[17] Its central pillar was the *Shema* (Deut. 6:4): "Hear, O Israel: The Lord our God is One Lord." A second pillar was the biblical notion of election. The Talmudic view of the Shema was practical rather than speculative.

That is, the rabbis did not spend much energy probing the unity of God, the confluence of the divine attributes, or the like. The oneness of God meant to them God's sole dominion over life. He was the Lord of all peoples, the world's only source and guide.[18] The most practical of God's attributes were his justice and his mercy, but how they correlated was not obvious. Clear enough, though, were the implications for ethics and piety: A person ought to reckon with God's justice by acting righteously and avoiding condemnation. A person also ought to rely on God's mercy, remembering that he is slow to anger and quick to forgive.

Through such righteous living, a person could look forward to God's kingdom, which would come through the *Messiah*. The Messiah would rejuvenate or transform this earthly realm, which was so often a source of suffering. Of the Messiah, Isadore Epstein says, "At the highest the Messiah is but a moral leader who will be instrumental in fully rehabilitating Israel in its ancient homeland, and through a restored Israel bring about the moral and spiritual regeneration of the whole of humanity, making all mankind fit citizens of the Kingdom."[19] This description rejects the Christian tendency to equate the Messiah with a divine son and also provides a foundation for the Zionistic fervor to return to the land. The concept of God's kingdom eventually included a supernatural dimension (heaven), but Judaism rather distinctively has emphasized that personal fulfillment comes through daily life.

The thrust of the Talmud, therefore, is not so much theological as ethical. The rabbis were more interested in what one did than in how one spoke or thought. So they balanced considerable theological leeway with detailed expectations of behavior. One could hold any opinion about the subtleties of God's nature, but how one observed the Sabbath was clearly specified.[20] A major effect of this ethical concern was the refinement of the already quite sensitive morality of the Hebrew Bible. For instance, the rabbis wanted to safeguard the body against even the threat of mortal injury, so they called wicked the mere raising of a hand against another person.

Similarly, since the right to life entailed the right to a livelihood, the rabbis concerned themselves with economic justice, proscribing once accepted business practices such as cornering a market, misrepresenting a product, and trading on a customer's ignorance. In the same spirit, they pondered a person's rights to honor and reputation. To slander another obviously was forbidden, but they reprehended even putting an-

other to shame, likening the blush of the shamed to the red of bloodshed.

Despite the caricature that they were concerned only with legal niceties, their writings show that the rabbis were very sensitive to social interaction. Lying, hatred, infringement on others' liberty—all these were targets of their teachings. The rabbis held that the goods of the earth, which prompt so much human contentiousness, were to be for all people. Thus, after a harvest, the owner should leave his field open for the public to glean; the wealthy are obligated to help the poor; and no bread should ever go to waste. Moreover, the rabbis did not limit their lofty social ideals to the Jewish community. Glossing the injunction of Leviticus (19:34) to love the stranger "who sojourns with you . . . as yourself," the talmudists made little political or social distinction between Jew and non-Jew. Human rights applied to all.

The spirit of talmudic ethics, thus, is both precise and broad. The Talmud goes into extreme detail, but it applies to all humanity. According to the Talmud, the great vices are envy, greed, and pride, for they destroy the social fabric. Anger is also destructive, so the rabbis lay great stress on self-control. On the other hand, self-control should not become gloomy asceticism. Generally speaking, the Talmud views the goods of the earth as being for our enjoyment. We should fear neither the body nor the world.

In fact, God, who gives us both the body and the world, obliges us to keep them healthy and fruitful. To spurn bodily or material goods without great reason, then, would be to show ingratitude to God—to withdraw from the order God has chosen to create. Wealth and marriage, for instance, should be viewed as great blessings that one should accept with simple thankfulness. For the truest wealth, finally, is to be content with one's lot. In faith, the pious Jew tried to raise his sights beyond everyday worries to the Master of the universe, from whom so many good things flowed. The ultimate purpose of religious life was to sanctify this Master's name—to live in such love of God that his praise was always on one's lips.

Hallowing Time.   Through religious observances the talmudists designed the social program for inculcating their ethical ideals. In practice, every day was to be hallowed from its beginning. At rising the faithful Jew would thank God for the night's rest, affirm God's unity, and dedicate the coming hours to God's praise. He was supposed to pray at least three times each day: upon rising, in midafternoon, and in the evening (women were exempt, because of their family responsibilities). Ritual washings, as well as the kosher diet, reminded the faithful of the cleanliness that dedication to God required. Prayer garments such as the fringed prayer shawl; the phylacteries, or *tefellin* (scriptural texts worn on the head and the arm); and the head covering reinforced this cleanliness. The mezuzah (container of scriptural texts urging wholehearted love of God) over the door was a reminder to the entire home to adopt this attitude. Home was to be a place of law-abiding love. When possible, Jews would say their daily prayers together in the synagogue.

The synagogue, of course, was also the site of congregational worship on the Sabbath and on the great feasts that punctuated the year. Primary among such feasts have been Passover, a spring festival that celebrates the Exodus of the Israelites from Egypt; Shavuot, a wheat harvest festival occurring seven weeks after Passover; Booths (Sukkoth), a fall harvest festival whose special feature is the erection of branch or straw booths that commemorate God's care of the Israelites while they were in the wilderness; the New Year; and the Day of Atonement (Yom Kippur).

The last is the most somber and solemn of the celebrations: the day on which one fasts and asks forgiveness of sins. It is a time when estranged members of the community should make efforts to reconcile their differences, and when all people should rededicate themselves to the holiness that God's covenant demands. There are other holidays through the year, most of them joyous—like Hanukkah, a feast celebrating liberation by the Maccabees—and collectively they serve the several purposes of a theistic cult: recalling God's great favors (anamnesis), binding the community in common faith, and expiating offenses and restoring hopes.

In the home, celebration of the Sabbath did for the week what the annual feasts did for the year. It gave time a cycle with a peak that had special meaning. From midweek all looked forward to the Sabbath joy, preparing the house and the food for the day that came like God's bride. When the mother lit the candles and the Sabbath drew near, even the poorest Jew could feel that life was good. Special hospitality was the Sabbath rule; rest and spiritual regeneration were the Sabbath order. Regretful as all were to see the Sabbath end, a glow lingered that strengthened them so they could return to the workaday world.[21]

The principal rites of passage through the life cycle were circumcision, through which males entered the covenant community on their eighth day; bar mitzvah, to celebrate the coming of age; marriage; and burial. Through communal celebration, these rites reinforced the faith that life is good, the Torah is life's crown, marriage is a human being's natural estate, and death is not the final word.

The Medieval Period

From the seventh century on, this talmudic religious program structured the lives of Jews who were mainly under Muslim rule.[22] As a subjugated people, the Jews tended to look inward for their fulfillment. Muhammad himself took rather kindly to Judaism, because he thought that his own revelation agreed with biblical thought: "Hence his uncompromising monotheistic doctrine, his insistence on formal prayers, fasting and almsgiving, his adoption of the Day of Atonement, his introduction of dietary laws (such as the prohibition of swine's flesh), and his [initial] requirement that his followers turn toward Jerusalem in prayer."[23] However, things grew more complicated when the Jews refused to convert to Islam, and under both Muhammad and his successors the Jews had to endure not a little trouble. Nonetheless, Muslims frequently found Jews useful as translators or businessmen, and Muslim countries were generally tolerant. As long as non-Muslim religious groups posed no threat to security or orthodoxy, they could have a decent, if second-rate, civil status.[24]

During the first centuries of Muslim power, the Jewish community's prestigious center of learning was at the heart of its Diaspora in Baghdad (in Babylonia). According to talmudic tradition, the leaders of the Baghdad schools gave *responsa* to points of law and held sway over community religion. They also fixed the pattern of communal worship, which hitherto had been a source of confusion and controversy. During the ninth and tenth centuries, the scholars of the Babylonian schools also standardized the pronunciation for the Hebrew Bible. These scholars (Masoretes) supplied the vowel points, accents, and other signs necessary to make readable a text that had consisted only of consonants. (Pronunciation, consequently, had been a matter of oral tradition.) The same work went on in Palestine, and eventually the version of a Palestinian author named Ben Asher won acceptance as the canonical Masoretic text.

At the end of the first millennium of the Common Era, talmudic scholars emigrated to Europe, North Africa, and Egypt, taking with them the scholarship of the talmudic school to which they felt the closest ties. The Babylonian traditions were more popular, but in countries such as Italy, which had close ties with Palestine, Palestinian influence was great. In Europe, of course, the Jews were largely under Christian rule, although southern Spain and southern France were under Muslim rule.

The two great Jewish traditions, the *Sephardic* (Iberian) and the *Ashkenazic* (East European), can be characterized by their subjugation under either Muslim or Christian rule, respectively. The two traditions shared more than they held separately because of the talmudists, and their different styles in intellectual matters and in piety largely derived from the different cultures in which they evolved. In the tenth and eleventh centuries, the Sephardim in Spain developed a golden culture, with philosophy, exegesis, poetry, and scientific learning at their peak. Toledo and Cordoba were great centers of learning, but so were Avila and Lisbon.

The major internal problem during this period was the rigorist Karaite heresy, which began under the leadership of Anan ben David in the eighth century. This movement rejected the Talmud and based its beliefs on a literal reading of the scriptures. For instance, Karaite Sabbath law forbade washing, leaving the house, carrying anything from one room to another, wearing anything except a shirt, making a bed, or any other activity construed as work. Karaites interpreted the injunction of Exodus 35:3, to kindle no fires on the Sabbath, to mean that one had to spend Friday night and Saturday in darkness and cold. They were so scrupulous about incest laws that finding an acceptable marriage partner was difficult.

Because *Karaism* appealed to individual conscience and had some master propagandists, it mustered considerable support. Anan withdrew from Babylonia to Jerusalem, where he set up a community, and he pushed for a complete break with talmudic Jews (called Rabbanites). In the ninth and tenth centuries Karaism spread to Persia, Egypt, Spain, and parts of Asia and seemed to be on the verge of replacing Judaism. When we add to its appeal the confusion that the Muslim recovery of Greek learning was producing in scholarly circles, we can understand the complexity of the Jewish religious situation and why it came close to crisis. With literalist Karaites on their right and rationalistic Hellenists on their left, the talmudists felt besieged.

The talmudists responded to the Karaites with an intensive campaign of biblical study, which included exegesis, Hebrew grammar, philology, and the other learning necessary to defend their own interpretations of the sacred text. Against the rationalists they took up the tools of philosophy, logic, and physical science in an effort to show the compatibility of reason and faith. The great champion in this talmudic or Rabbanite counterattack was Saadya ben Joseph (892–942), who lived in Upper Egypt. He combined Hebrew and Arabic learning, biblical scholarship, and philosophical erudition. In addition, he wrote halakic *responsa,* codified rules of talmudic logic, resolved problems with the calendar, and composed an order for public worship.[25] The counterattack that he spearheaded was successful, and when the Jews fled from Babylonia at the breakup of the Muslim Empire into the eastern and western caliphates, they took with them at least the beginnings of a renewed talmudic tradition. The golden age in Spain was in no small measure possible because of this renewal.

Philosophy.   The early medieval period thus saw a ferment in talmudic learning. As well, a Jewish philosophical theology arose.[26] While Philo, in the first century of the Common Era, worked at what could be called philosophical theology, trying to reconcile Hellenistic thought with biblical thought, the medieval thinkers, especially Maimonides, brought philosophy into the Jewish mainstream.

Philo, whose strong point had been what he called *allegoresis* (a reading of scripture on several levels, so as to remove the problems that the philosophical mind might have with anthropomorphism), never exerted a decisive influence on his contemporaries. Maimonides did. He was the response that made Judaism competitive in the new arena opened by the Muslim retrieval of Aristotelian logic and science. As such, his work was apologetic, making Judaism a strong contender in the debates that were being conducted by the Western religions on the supposedly common ground of rational analysis. However, Maimonides' work was also constructive, setting talmudic and traditional learning in the context of a philosophical system. Finally, the philosophical services of thinkers such as Maimonides were very useful in internal fights with literalists such as the Karaites, who (despite their fundamentalism about points of biblical law) mocked both biblical anthropomorphism and much of aggadah (because it was poetic and symbolic).

The great questions of this period of philosophical debate were the criteria of biblical *exegesis,* the relation of faith to reason, the nature of the human personality and its relation to God, God's existence and attributes, the creation of the world, and providence and theodicy (God's justice). In debating these questions, the philosophers based their work on the Greek view that contemplation *(theoria)* is the most noble human work. Thus, the Jewish philosophers made rationality the source of human imaging of God. From that they derived an obligation (they would have called it a religious obligation) to develop one's reason—to explore God and his world.

Whereas for the talmudist, study of the Torah was the highest activity, many of the medieval philosophers considered the contemplation of God's eternal forms (through which he had created the world) the highest human activity. Maimonides became the prince of Jewish philosophers largely because he was also learned in the talmudic tradition and so could reconcile the old with the new. For him philosophical contemplation did not take one away from the Torah, because the proper object of philosophical contemplation was the one Law we find in both scripture and nature.

A key teaching in Maimonides' system was divine incorporeality. God had to be one, which he could not be if he occupied a body, since matter is a principle of multiplicity. To rationalize the anthropomorphic biblical descriptions of God, where he has bodily emotions if not form, Maimonides allegorized as Philo had done. The dynamic to his system, however, was the conviction that philosophical reason can provide the key to scripture. As his own *Guide for the Perplexed* puts it, "This book will then be a key admitting to places the gates of which would otherwise be closed. When the gates are opened and men enter, their souls will enjoy repose, their eyes will be gratified, and even their bodies, after all toil and labor, will be refreshed."[27]

Maimonides has probably been most influential through the thirteen articles in which he summarized Jewish faith, and which even today are listed in the standard prayer book: (1) the existence of God, (2) God's unity, (3) God's incorporeality, (4) God's eternity, (5) the obligation to worship God alone, (6) prophecy, (7) the superiority of the prophecy of Moses, (8) the Torah as God's revelation to Moses, (9) the Torah's immutability, (10) God's omniscience, (11) reward and punishment, (12) the coming of the Messiah, and (13) the resurrection of the dead.[28] In this summary a philosopher gave the key headings under which reason and biblical revelation could be reconciled.

However, Jewish philosophy before Maimonides expressed a somewhat contrary position. The lyrical writer Judah Halevi (ca. 1086–1145), for instance, insisted that the God of Aristotle is not the God of Abraham and the biblical Fathers. (Halevi's position is reminiscent of the later Christian philosopher Blaise Pascal, and it draws on the same sort of religious experience that made Pascal visualize God as a consuming fire—no Aristotelian "prime mover" but a vortex of personal love.) Halevi did not despise reason, but he insisted that it is less than full religious experience, faith, or love. Moreover, he was concerned that Judaism remember where it had found God in the past. Concrete historical acts had furnished the Jews their election and destiny as God's covenanted people, not eternal forms or timeless philosophical truths ever available for human contemplation.

Mysticism. The devotional current in influential medieval philosophers shows that the appropriation of Greek rationality did not extinguish Jewish mystical life, any more than it extinguished talmudic preoccupation with law. Law, in the sense of guidance for a daily practice of faith and ethics, certainly predominated over philosophy in the popular religious mind, but both philosophy and mysticism colored legal interpretation. Gershom Scholem has treated the major trends in Jewish mysticism admirably,[29] tracing them back to biblical origins. The major influence, discernible even in Maimonides' doctrine of God, was Ezekiel's vision (Ezek. 1) of the divine chariot *(merkabah)*. Philosophers and mystics alike agreed that under this symbolism lay the most profound mysteries of the divine nature. The talmudists tended to stay away from the subject, lest they fall into impious speculation, but the mystics, even though they cautioned about dangers, repeatedly went back to it.

In medieval Germany a movement arose among people called the Hasidim, who upheld a relatively new spiritual ideal. Biblical religion had spoken of the poor of God *(anawim)*, and from biblical times a *hasid* was one poor in spirit who piously devoted himself to God. The medieval expression of this piety, in which intellectualism was subordinate to devotion, contested rabbinic learning. What characterized the truly pious person, this movement argued, was serenity of mind, altruism, and renunciation of worldly things. The renunciation, implying asceticism, especially ran counter to traditional Judaism, for it seemed to entail turning away from the world. Indeed, Hasidic speech relates to the experience that has always drawn mystics and caused them to neglect the world—the experience of glimpsing the divine being itself, of tasting the biblical "goodness of the Lord." Then the divine love exalts the soul and seems far more precious than anything the world can offer.

Hasidism in its medieval, Germanic form is not the direct ancestor of the modern East European Jewish pietism that goes by this name. Intervening between Hasidism's two phases was a most influential Jewish mysticism, that of the *cabala*. *Cabala* means "tradition," and the cabalists sought to legitimize their movement by tracing it back to secret teachings of the patriarchs and Moses.

Such secret or esoteric overtones stamp cabalism as a sort of Jewish gnosticism (secret knowledge); indeed, several cabalistic doctrines smack of the Gnostic concerns with the divine *pleroma* (fullness), the emanations of different divine aspects, and secret doctrines explaining how divinity intends to redeem the wicked fallen world.[30] Thus, R. J. Zwi Werblowsky characterizes cabalism as a "theosophical" (concerning wisdom about God) movement especially concerned with the *pleroma*.[31] This fullness, which the prophets glimpsed in their ecstatic visions, ordinary human beings can only conceive symbolically. Hence, cabalists engaged in their own brand of allegorical exegesis of scripture, trying to decode secret symbols about divinity that the Hebrew Bible couched in deceptively simple language.

For cabalistic thought, the divine and the human spheres are interdependent. The fallen state of the world (most acutely manifested in the suffering of the Jews, God's chosen people) signals a disruption within the divine essence itself. Human sinfulness, it follows, reflects this divine wounding. On the other hand, human holiness contributes to God's repair, and so every human act takes on cosmic significance. In fact, human life can become a sort of mystery play or theurgy (divine work), in which the significant aspect of people's actions is their wounding or repairing of the divine life.

When the Spaniards expelled the Jews from the Iberian Peninsula at the end of the fifteenth century, the cabalists had the perfect crisis on which to focus their somewhat fevered imaginations. Isaac Luria, who taught in Jerusalem in the sixteenth century, and Sabbatai Zevi, the "false messiah" of the seventeenth century, interpreted the expulsion as an effect of a cosmic disaster that actually occurred before Adam's fall. They had great popular impact.

The paramount book of the cabalistic movement, and the most representative of its symbolism, was the *Zohar*—the "Book of Splendor." From 1500 to 1800, the *Zohar* exerted an influence equal to that of the Bible and the Talmud. Analysis of the work suggests that it was written in Spain at the end of the thirteenth century, most likely by Moses de León.[32] The *Zohar* is similar to aggadic materials in that it interprets scriptural texts symbolically and in pietistic fashion rather than in the legal manner of halakah. What distinguishes the *Zohar* from traditional aggadah is its suffusion with the Gnostic ideas mentioned above. For instance, its commentary on the first verse of the Hebrew Bible (Gen. 1:1) goes immediately to what the divine nature was really like "in the beginning." Within the most hidden recess of the infinite *eyn sof,* the divine essence, a dark flame went forth, issuing in the *sefiroth*. The *sefiroth* were what the philosophers called the realm of divine attributes, but the mystics saw them as the emanations of God's own being. Such a view makes the world alive with divinity. It gives history and human experience eternal implications, because the emanations move through our time, our flesh, our blood.

The *Zohar* turns over each word of Genesis, searching for hidden clues to the divine plan. It concerns itself with the numerical value of the words' letters (for example, a = 1) and correlates clues in Genesis with clues from other visionary parts of the Hebrew Bible, such as Ezekiel, chapter 1, and Isaiah, chapter 6. To align its interpretation with respectable past commentary, it cites traditional rabbis, but the *Zohar*'s immediate concern is not the rabbis' interest in ethics but an imaginative contemplation of divinity and the divine plan.

In other words, the *Zohar* draws people by the splendor of its vision, its graphic display of divinity. With its beauty, the *Zohar* can move the spirit to ecstatic joy. No doubt the cabalists devoutly hoped that such an imaginative and contemplative experience would build up faith and inspire good works. However, they differed from the talmudists (some of whom had secret sympathy for cabalism) in their predilection for visionary appreciation of the Law's source rather than a sober perusal of the Law's applications.

The Modern Period

If the mark of modernity is a turn from rather mythical religious authority to human authority and self-reliance, modernity did not begin for Judaism until the end of the eighteenth century—although some intellectuals realized early on the challenge that the Enlightenment raised to traditional Jewish Law. In fact, thorough exposure to a secularized, technological culture did not come to most of the rural population of the Eastern European *shtetls* (villages), where much of the Jewish population lived, until close to World War II. Until that time enlightenment and reform made little impact, for talmudic and Hasidic orthodoxy kept the tradition basically unchanged.[33]

Cecil Roth[34] and Leon Poliakov[35] have described the constant repression and persecution that Jews endured in medieval and early modern times. What Roth calls "the crowning tragedy" was the Jews' expulsion from the Iberian Peninsula in 1492, since that devastated what had been Jewry's greatest cultural achievement. In its aftermath, the Eastern European ghetto became home to most Jews, and the false messiah Sabbatai Zevi, who finally apostatized to Islam, shows the intensity that Jewish messianic yearning reached by the mid-seventeenth century. Part of the success of Israel Baal Shem-Tov (1700–1760), the father of modern Hasidism, resulted from the effects of Sabbatai Zevi. In his wake lay a void into which apostasy, nihilism, and antinomianism (lawlessness) threatened to rush.

The Baal Shem-Tov (Besht) and his followers taught a religious inwardness, a joyous communion with God.[36] They sought to restore the traditional faith, which they saw as endangered by false messianism, arid intellectualism, and talmudic legalism. Hasidism did not attack the Law and traditional practice itself. Rather, it shifted Jewish religious focus from the "scientific" rabbinic leader to the gifted Hasid or holy person, who manifested divine wisdom and joy. The movement quickly caught fire in Eastern Europe, and thousands rushed to the Hasidic "courts" where charismatic masters presided. In their vivid portrait of *shtetl* life, Zborowski and Herzog[37] have shown the attraction that the Hasidim exerted in the typical village. Many of the villagers (usually men) yearned to go off to the courts for spiritual refreshment, and many would leave their families for substantial periods of time.

Case Study: Hasidic Tales. The Hasidic masters made a deep impression on the Jewish imagination, and some of the tales about them are wonderfully entertaining, as well as deeply instructive. For example, there is the story of the burning of the Torah, which deals with "the terrific struggle between the Baal Shem-Tov and the Enemy, who by foul trickery sought to have the Torah taken away from the Jews."[38]

Satan was tormented by the good he saw the Baal Shem-Tov doing on earth, so he schemed to overcome the Master. Calling all his servants of darkness together, he disclosed to them a wicked plan. He would station devils on all the roads that led to heaven. Whenever a prayer rose upward, toward heaven's gates, the devils would be able to throttle it, and so keep it from getting through. Thus no prayers would come before God's throne. After some days without prayers getting through, Satan would be able to go to God and say, "Look, your people have deserted you. They no longer send you prayers. Even your favorite puppet, Rabbi Israel Baal Shem-Tov, has ceased to pray. Take back his wisdom, then. Take away his people's Torah."

The soldiers of the Evil One listened attentively, and then slunk out to execute the foul scheme. Leaving no bypath unguarded, they lurked silently in wait for any prayer. When a prayer came, they leaped upon it, pummeling and kicking it. They could not kill the prayers, but they flung them sideways into chaos. Thus all of space became filled with wounded prayers, whimpering and moaning, lost from their way. On Sabbaths the flux of prayers was so great that many got through to heaven's gate, but there a great army of devils saw to it that the prayers were rebuffed. Three weeks passed in this fashion, and Satan thought it time to confront God.

Going before the divine throne, Satan said: "Take away the Torah from the Jews." But God said, "Give them until the Day of Atonement." Satan struck a hard bargain: "Give the command today, but hold back on its execution until the Day of Atonement." So God gave the terrible edict, and the Jews were to lose the Torah. On earth, the archbishop issued a proclamation. In ten days, the bishops were to have all the Hebrew books of learning confiscated. Men were to be sent into the synagogues to seize the Torah, and into all the Jews' homes. Then they were to heap all the Hebrew books into a great pile and set fire to them. The bishop of Kamenitz-Podolsky in Russia was the most zealous in obeying, sending his servants into all the Jews' homes. On the Day of Atonement, a great fire would destroy all the books of God's Law.

When the Baal Shem-Tov saw these things happening, he knew Satan was mounting a terrible attack.

Yet he did not know how Satan was accomplishing this great evil, nor how to counteract it. Each day the horror mounted, as Jews were stripped of the Torah. In home after home cries of anguish rent the night. Fasting and sleepless, the Baal Shem-Tov struggled on behalf of his people, sending mighty prayers toward heaven day and night. They rose on colossal wings at incredible speed, but the Enemy himself caught them outside heaven's gate and cast them aside. So the heart of Baal Shem-Tov emptied, becoming a great cave of grief.

At last the Day of Atonement dawned. Rabbi Israel went into the synagogue to hold the service, and the people saw the fever of his struggle on his face. Hope rose in their hearts. "He will save us today," they said. When the time came to sing the *Kol Nidre* ("All Vows"), Rabbi Israel's voice poured out the pain of his heart, freezing all who listened.

It was the custom for Rabbi Yacob to read each verse of the lamentations aloud and then for Rabbi Israel to repeat it. But when Rabbi Yacob read out the verse, "Open the Portals of Heaven!" Rabbi Israel did not utter a word. The people first were confused, and then waited in growing fear. Once again Rabbi Yacob repeated, "Open the Portals of Heaven!" but still Rabbi Israel did not utter a word.

Then, like a trumpet blast into the monumental silence, Rabbi Israel threw himself upon the ground, beat his head, and roared like a dying lion. For two hours he remained doubled over, his body shaking with the force of his struggle. Those watching in the synagogue dared not approach him. They could only worry and wait.

At last, the Baal Shem-Tov raised himself from the ground, his face shining with wonders. "The Portals of Heaven are open," he said, and then he ended the service.

Years afterward, it became known how Rabbi Israel had passed those terrible two hours. He had gone to the Palace of the Eternal, traveling by the road that goes directly to the throne. There he had found hundreds and hundreds of prayers huddled before the gate. Some were wounded, some lay gasping as though they had just ended a terrible struggle, some were emaciated and old, and some were blind from having wandered so long in darkness. "Why are you waiting here?" the Baal Shem-Tov asked them. "Why don't you go in and approach the throne?"

The prayers told Rabbi Israel that only his approach had scattered the dark angels. Before he came, no prayer could pass through the gate. "I will take you in," the Baal Shem-Tov told them.

But just as he started to pass the gate, the Baal Shem-Tov saw the army of evil spirits rush forth to close it. Then Satan himself came forward and hung a great lock, as big as a city, upon the heavenly gate. The Baal Shem-Tov walked all around the lock, looking for a crack through which to enter. It was made of solid iron, however, so there seemed no way he could pass through. Still, Rabbi Israel did not despair.

Now, for each of us living on earth, there is an exact duplicate living in heaven. So, Rabbi Israel called across the gate to his heavenly counterpart. "What shall I do," he asked, "to bring the prayers before the Name?" Rabbi Israel of heaven told him, "Let us go to the Palace of the Messiah."

They went to the palace, where the Messiah sat waiting for the day when he might go down to earth. As soon as they entered, the Messiah told them, "Be joyous! I will help you," and he gave the Baal Shem-Tov a token. The Baal Shem-Tov took the token back to the heavenly gate. When he brandished the token, the heavenly portals swung open, as wide as the earth is large. So all the prayers entered, going straight to the Throne of the Name. Heaven fell to ecstatic rejoicing, and all the angels sang hymns of praise. But the dark angels fled back to their hellish dungeons, routed and fearful again.

On earth, the bishop of Kamenitz-Podolsky was lighting a great fire. Beside him was a mountain of Hebrew books, which his minions had readied for the flames. He took a tractate of the Talmud and hurled it into the fire. He hurled another and another, until the flames leaped high as the clouds. But then his hand began shaking, and he fell down in an epileptic fit. The crowd was seized with terror, and ran out of the central square. The fire soon died down, and most of the books were saved. When the news of this happening spread to other towns, they abandoned their plans to burn the Torahs. Fearing they too would be struck by seizures, the other bishops gave back all the stolen books. That was how the Baal Shem-Tov saved the Torah for the Jews, on the Day of Atonement.

When we reflect on this little story, it reveals volumes about premodern Jewish belief. The Baal Shem-Tov is the central hero, but there are many other actors in the drama. The evil genius threatening Jewish life is Satan, the angel of power and light who had turned bad. Hating God and everything good, Satan is constantly plotting against God's people. If the Jews had not had saints like Rabbi Israel, there was no telling how their misfortunes might have grown. Bad as life was in the midst of unsympathetic Christians, it would have been much worse without the sainted rabbis.

As the story shows, the central treasure of premodern Jewish life was the Torah. Enclosed in the holy pages of the treasured books lay the only wisdom worth pursuing. Without the Torah, the Jews would not have been God's people. Without the Bible and the Talmud, there would have been no faith, no joy, no hope. For the common people, the volumes of Torah were both pledges and holy presences. To destroy a book of Torah therefore was to slash at the central artery, to snuff out the breath of life.

The theater for the drama of Satan against the Torah was not limited to earthly cities. For the popular Jewish mind, heaven was a central factor in the play. Before the throne of God, all parts of Jewish life passed review. God's ways were terribly inscrutable, but no pious Jew doubted the efficacy of prayer. If the people would pour out their hearts to the Master of the Universe, he would find them a way to survive. The Torah spoke of many past acts of salvation and of the coming of the Messiah, the one who would bring lasting peace. Prayer and strict observance therefore became the people's armor. Often helpless in earthly terms, the Jews looked to their learned rabbis as to spiritual generals. By the holy power they generated, the rabbis might storm heaven's gates and keep Satan's dark forces at bay.

Of course, it is hard to say how literally the average person took imagery like that of our story. Whether heaven had a big gate, whether there were roads to heaven, whether prayers could be kicked and wounded—all that is hard to tell. Most likely, all that was quite secondary. Lost in a good, gripping story, most Jews probably indulged their imaginations. To picture prayers like little people, or like swift birds winging up to God, made the act of praying more dramatic. Most people knew they could never picture God accurately. They knew heaven was beyond any tongue's ability to describe. So they let their imaginations paint whatever settings most helped them in their prayers and inner struggles. There had to be close connections between this world and heaven, for otherwise God would not be involved in what his people were doing. But it was the essence of the theology of the covenant that God was always deeply involved in what his people were doing, were suffering, and were hoping. So the life of the Jewish home and the services of the Jewish synagogue encouraged many vivid pictures of heaven. Indeed, the worse earthly life became, the more heaven gleamed in contrast.

Village Life. Hasidism ran the danger of irrationalism and an intolerance of anything modern, but for discerning contemporary Jews such as Martin Buber[39] and Abraham Heschel,[40] it became a valuable resource. Although large portions of the educated, who were desirous of a Jewish enlightenment and emancipation from Christian discrimination, strongly opposed Hasidic piety, it remained vigorous in the villages well into the twentieth century. There it tended to commingle with talmudic faith, blending legal observance with emotional fervor. Indeed, Jewish village life hinged on the Sabbath (in the time-organizing way described above) and on three blessings: the Torah, marriage, and good deeds.

The Torah meant God's revelation and Law. In practice, it meant the exaltation of learning. *Shtetl* parents hoped that they would have learned sons, well versed in the Law, who would bring glory to the family. Thus, the ideal son was thin and pale, a martyr to his books. From age five or so he marched off to a long day of study, beginning his education by memorizing a Hebrew that he did not understand and then progressing to subtle talmudic commentaries. The Torah shaped the economic and family lives of *shtetl* Jews, because men tried to free themselves for study, placing the financial burdens on women. The poor scholar, revered in the *shul* (synagogue school) but master of a threadbare family, exemplified the choices and values that the Torah inspired.

Many men did work in trades (the state usually prevented Jews from owning land and farming), but even they would try to gain dignity by devoting their spare time to learning. Glory for women came from caring for the home, the children, and often a little shop. So much were those responsibilities part of religion for women that no commandments prescribed for them exact times for prayer, fasting, synagogue attendance, charitable works, or the like. Women's three principal *mitzvoth* (duties) out of the traditional 613 were to remove a portion of the Sabbath bread, to light the Sabbath candles, and to visit the ritual bath *(mikvah)* after menstruation.

In the *shtetl,* marriage was the natural human situation and children were its crown. Father and mother were obligated to create a home steeped in Torah and good deeds (fulfillment of the *mitzvoth* and acts of charity). In semiserious popular humor, nothing was worse than an old maid, while an unmarried man was pitied as being incomplete. Of course, kosher rules and keen legal observance marked the devout home, which was but a cell of the organic community. That community supported needy individual members with material goods, sympathy in times of trouble, and unanimity in religious ideals. One had to share one's wealth, whether wealth of money or wealth of mind, and the seats of honor in the synagogue went to the learned and the community's financial benefactors.

Tribulations. The community exacted quite a toll through the pressure it exerted to conform to its ideals and through the gossip and judgment that ever circulated. Nevertheless, most Jews gladly accepted being bound by the common laws and custom, and few Jews could avoid being bound by the equally overt and common suffering. The urban populations in the Russian and Polish ghettos shared an almost paranoid life, with pogroms (persecutions) a constant specter, while the rural populations of the rest of Eastern Europe never knew when some new discrimination or purge would break out. In both situations, Jews' mainstay was their solidarity in faith. Consequently, we can understand how threatening movements to change the faith, such as the reform or enlightenment (described below), must have been. The old ways had been the foundation of Jewish sanity. New conditions, as in Germany and the United States, seemed much less solid than long familiar suffering and endurance.

The bulk of the Jewish population in the late 1700s was in Eastern Europe: the pale of the Russian Empire, Austria, and Prussia. Their life was rather precarious, and attacks by Russians and Ukrainians produced a stream of emigrants to the New World. Yet European Jews contributed to the formation of the notion of the modern, secular state, probably because they hoped that it would offer them greater religious freedom. Thus, the Jewish philosopher Spinoza (1632–1672) suggested such a political arrangement, and Moses Mendelssohn (1729–1786), a German man of letters, plumped for a secular state before the French Revolution. Generally, Jews' civil status seemed to prosper in countries or under regimes that were open to the new, liberal ideas of equality. However, when nationalism prevailed, Jews tended to experience more anti-Semitism, since non-Jews then considered them all the more outsiders.

Jacob A. Agus has noted three principal Jewish reactions to modern nationalism.[41] First, many Jews identified themselves with the people among whom they lived. For instance, German Jews became great supporters of German culture, which was enjoying a golden age in music and philosophy. Second, some of the Jewish intelligentsia embraced the new universalist philosophies that downplayed race or ethnicity and stressed the common humanity all people share through their reason. Third, some Jews incorporated nationalistic feelings into their own group consciousness by thinking of the cohesiveness of the "nation" of Israel. Agus sees these reactions working, respectively, in the time of Emancipation in France (see below), the socialist movements in Europe and Russia [which led to the formation of the Jewish *Bund* (party), influential in Poland during the two world wars, and also to the Reform movements in Germany and the Anglo-American world], and the Zionist movement, which he conceives of as a Jewish nationalistic renaissance.

Dissolution of Traditional Judaism. Jacob Neusner attributes the breakup of traditional Judaism in the modern period to two factors, the enlightenment and Hasidism.[42] The enlightenment, whose main feature according to Kant was the realization that humanity should be guided by its own reason and not by institutional authorities, in effect attacked the legal and philosophical underpinnings of traditional Judaism. By extending political rights to Jews ("Emancipation"), the gentile thinkers of the enlightenment in principle took away the basis of the Jewish community—it was no longer a ghetto or a world set apart from the national mainstream, because all citizens were to be equal.

By its philosophical turn to individual reason, the enlightenment attacked the talmudic assumption that traditional law and its interpretation by the Fathers were the best guides for life. Thus, intellectual Jews who accepted the ideals of the enlightenment tended to abandon talmudic scholarship (or at least deny that it was the most important learning) and devote themselves to secular learning. This movement spawned the distinguished line of modern Jewish scientists, social thinkers, and humanists, but it meant that the Jewish community lost some of its best talent to secular concerns. It also often meant intellectual warfare between the advocates of the new learning and the defenders of the old.

The relation of Hasidism to traditional, talmudic Judaism is more complex. On the one hand, as we have seen, Hasidism accepted traditional assumptions about the Law, the specialness of the people, the coming of the Messiah, and the reality of God's reign over the world. On the other hand, Hasidism set the charismatic holy man rather than the learned rabbi at the center of the community.[43] This new figure, the *tzaddik* (righteous one), Hasidim revered for his intimacy with God, his ability to pray evocatively, and his gifts as a storyteller. (As a storyteller he was an updated version of the ancient aggadist.) But the simple faithful held the *tzaddik* to be a wonder worker.

Thus, as illustrated, the Hasidim abounded with stories of God's coming to the aid of his oppressed people through the special interventions of the *tzaddik*.[44] The story with which the contemporary Jewish writer Elie Wiesel (who explicitly situates himself in the Hasidic tradition) prefaces his novel *The Gates of the Forest* epitomizes the impact of Hasidic faith in the masters' powers:

> When the great Rabbi Israel Baal Shem-Tov saw misfortune threatening the Jews it was his custom to go into a certain part of the forest to meditate. There he would light a fire, say a special prayer, and the miracle would be accomplished and the misfortune averted. Later, when his disciple, the celebrated Magid of Mezritch, had occasion, for the same reason, to intercede with heaven, he would go to the same place in the forest and say: "Master of the Universe, listen! I do not know how to light the fire, but I am still able to say the prayer" and again the miracle would be accomplished. . . . Then it fell to Rabbi Israel of Rizhyn to overcome misfortune. Sitting in his armchair, his head in his hands, he spoke to God: "I am unable to light the fire and I do not know the prayer; I cannot even find the place in the forest. All I can do is to tell the story, and this must be sufficient." And it was sufficient. God made man because he loves stories.[45]

Reform.   Thus, the traditional legal authority at the heart of rabbinic Judaism crumbled because of both the new secular learning and the greater attractiveness of the charismatic *tzaddik*. From within, Judaism succumbed to a desire for more intellectually and spiritually satisfying evidence of God's helpfulness. In response to this crisis of the tradition came a "Reform" of orthodox conceptions. On a popular level (though we are still speaking of the relatively educated), Reform meant an effort to accept modern culture and still remain a Jew. In other words, it meant searching for new definitions of Jewishness that would not necessitate alienation from the intellectual and political life of gentile fellow nationalists.

Among the "virtuosi," as Neusner calls the important personalities of the Reform movement, the effort was not just accommodation but rethinking the tradition to bring it up to date with integrity. A good part of the virtuosi's effort emphasized the Jewish philosophical and ethical beliefs that seemed eminently rational (and so applicable to all people). In effect, emphasis shifted from what was distinctive in Judaism, what gave Jews their unique status as God's chosen ones, to what Judaism could offer to all humanity.

The stress of Reform was ethical. Reform Jews saw their tradition as offering all peoples a moral sensitivity, a concern for the rights of conscience and social justice, that derived from the prophets and the great rabbis but could serve the dawning future age of equality, political freedom, and mutual respect. In part, this ethical stress was the result of wishful thinking. Reform Jews tended to be talented people who were either formally or informally excluded from national and university life. As a result, their visions of a new day led them to stress what in their own religious past might abet equal opportunity.

A response to Reform within Judaism was self-conscious *Orthodoxy*. It tended to recruit those who shared many of the Reformers' perceptions but who disagreed with their reinterpretation of the tradition. Instead, Orthodoxy insisted that the Torah be the judge of modernity and not vice versa. Positively, however, the Orthodox conceded the possibility that living with gentiles might be a good, God-intended arrangement. No doubt, the breakup of Christian control over culture that marked the Western shift from medieval to modern times played a strong role in this reevaluation. That is, the Orthodox saw the wisdom in the Reform argument that, despite its evident dangers to faith, living among modern gentiles might free Jews of the prejudice endemic in medieval Christian faith by letting Christians see that Jews could be amiable fellow citizens (in its most virulent form, that prejudice branded all Jews as "Christ killers").

In their contests with the Reformers, the Orthodox could draw on factors that tradition had driven deep into the Jewish psyche. First, there was the conservatism that was almost intrinsic to a faith built on teaching "Fathers" and the father-figure of the family. Such conservatism made it difficult for the younger generation to convince the older. Second, the Ortho-

Figure 18 *Infamous gate at Dachau concentration camp, outside Munich, Germany, reading "Work frees." Photo by J. T. Carmody.*

dox could claim, much more plausibly than the Reform, that they represented the wisdom and experience of the past by which the people had survived. Third, the Orthodox could seem more genuinely religious than the Reform; although the virtuosi wanted to develop faith, the majority of the Reformers were secularly minded, drawn by goods outside the traditional culture. Last, the combination of these factors gave Orthodoxy the advantage of appearing safer and surer than Reform.[46]

Conservative Judaism represented an effort to find a centrist position between Reform and Orthodoxy. Its founder was Rabbi Zecharias Frankel (1801–1875), chief rabbi of Dresden and later head of the Breslau Theological Seminary in Germany. Frankel's position was that Judaism should change slowly, remaining true to its traditional character and only allowing slight modifications of traditional practice. In the United States, Solomon Schechter of the Jewish

Theological Seminary of America was the central promoter of Conservative Judaism.

Presently Conservative Judaism is the largest of the three main groups of American Jews. Its intellectual center is the Jewish Theological Seminary in New York, its rabbinical assembly numbers more than one thousand members, and its league of synagogues (the United Synagogue) numbers more than one thousand congregations. Building on Reform initiatives, the Conservative worship service has introduced family pews, developed a modernized liturgy in the vernacular, and allowed women a fuller role in the congregation's ritual life.

Reconstructionism, a U.S. Jewish movement founded by Mordecai Kaplan (1881–1983), has taught that past Jewish concern with otherworldly salvation is no longer credible, and that consequently Jews should translate their traditional concern for salvation into this-worldly terms: human betterment in health, political rights, education, and the like. Other reconstructionists have kept the same this-worldly emphasis but focused more on Jewish culture than "salvation."

Zionism.   The movement most responsible for the establishment of the modern state of Israel is *Zionism.* Most of the medieval piety movements anticipated Zionism insofar as their messianism regularly involved the notion of returning to the ancestral land (and to the holiest of cities, Jerusalem). Thus, the Karaites of eighth-century Iraq (Babylonia) emigrated to Israel, and some of the cabalists took up residence in Galilee. In the eighteenth and nineteenth centuries, Hasidim in Poland sent many people to the holy land, with the result that there were circles of devout Jews in Jerusalem, Tiberius, and Safed.[47] The upsurge of nationalism in modern Europe tended to make Jews consider their own national roots, while new movements of social thought, including those led by Marx and Tolstoy, caused many Jews to dream about a new society based on the *kibbutz* (collective).

The greatest impetus to Zionism, however, was the persecutions that convinced European Jews they were in peril on the Continent: pogroms in Russia from 1880 to 1905, Ukrainian massacres from 1917 to 1922, persecutions in Poland between 1922 and 1939, and, above all, the Nazi persecution that began in 1933 and climaxed in the Holocaust of perhaps six million Jews in Nazi death camps. By 1948 about 650,000 Jews lived within the British Mandate of Palestine, and at the birth of modern Israel many hundreds of thousands more emigrated from Europe and from Arab lands (where, after the 1948 war, conditions were difficult). The main ideologist for the modern Zionist movement was a Viennese named Theodor Herzl. His witness of anti-Semitism during the Dreyfus affair in France at the end of the nineteenth century had convinced him and many other Jews that only by having their own nation could Jews be free of constant persecution.

Today Judaism is most vital in Israel and the United States, and in both places the battles over what it means to be a Jew in the modern world continue unabated. Israel has become the spiritual center of Judaism, and what faith can mean after Auschwitz and the Holocaust has become the prime topic of theological discussion.[48] Because of its vigorous intellectual tradition, Judaism disproportionately contributes to the debates about the value of modernity, and its voice is now influencing many Christian thinkers.[49]

STRUCTURAL ANALYSIS

Nature

Generally speaking, nature has not been so important in Judaism as peoplehood. For example, Maimonides did not refer to it in his thirteen articles of faith, and scholars dealing with the biblical period,[50] a historical perspective,[51] or even Jewish values[52] do not focus on nature. That does not mean, of course, that Jews had no consciousness of their land or that the physical world played no part in their religion. Indeed, the promise of a land of their own kept the people going during their wanderings in the desert under Moses and encouraged all Jews during the centuries of the Diaspora.

In the biblical period nature was quite important, because the earliest "Jews" were shepherds or farmers. The earliest theology appears to have been a veneration of different *els* (gods) related to natural powers, and the constant lament of the prophets and other biblical theologians that the gods of the neighboring peoples (the Canaanites especially) were seducing the people away from true religion is testimony that the cosmological myth held considerable attraction.

Still, contesting the cosmological myth (in which divinity is immanent to the world and natural processes are divinity's most intimate operations) were the "great acts" of YHWH in his people's time. Eric Voegelin has argued that "history" itself (our human conception of time) is substantially the product of Israelite theology.[53] For Voegelin, history gets periodicity from the revelations of a God outside the world, and it is those revelations that decisively shaped the Jewish people. So YHWH, the most transcendent of Gods, was also the most interactive. He was the God of the Fathers, Abraham, Isaac, and Jacob. He was the one who had led the ancestors out of Egypt, struck the covenant on Sinai, and ushered the people into the promised land.

From the beginning, the Jewish conception of God, coupled with the Jewish ethnic memory and sense of identification through religious history, combined to deemphasize nature as a religious focus. As the Psalms show, YHWH was the lord of nature as well as of time. He was the creator of the physical world, the benefactor of good harvests, a God who could appear with clouds and lightning. What made him special in Jewish eyes, though, was his redemptive activity and covenanting—actions in which he stepped out of natural phenomena and acted on a personal basis.

For instance, the liturgical feasts, though they began as nature festivals, ran through the agricultural year, and were expressions of gratitude for harvests, reached their peak at Passover and Yom Kippur—celebrations of historical events and of a moral requirement based on the covenant. Furthermore, the sacrificial aspect of early Jewish worship was replaced by the sermonizing and Bible reading of the synagogue. In fact, as the Torah grew in influence, the human qualities of law, reason, study, and ethics came to the fore. Celebrations still involved food, drink, and dance, but they were probably due more to a social sense, from a desire to affirm a common identity, than from a close connection with mother earth or father sky. (Interestingly, though, in their elaboration of the Torah, the rabbis were remarkably sensitive to animals' welfare. They glossed the biblical injunction not to muzzle the grinding ox, and they demanded that ritual slaughtering be as painless as possible.)

Urban Values. Many of the countries in which Jews lived, as a distinct and often inhibited minority, forbade them ownership of land, while their tradition of study tended to lead them into intellectual occupations and business. The tensions between *shtetl* Jews and *goyim* (gentiles) in Eastern Europe, for instance, were due as much to different occupations as to different theologies. The gentile peasants worked the land and valued rather brutish strength. The *shtetl* Jews did not farm very much, tending, rather, to engage in small businesses and study.

As a result, the qualities valued by the Jews were not the goyish qualities of strength and violence. Jews were not to fight, engage in hard labor, drink, or carouse. They were to be disciplined, cultured, and family and community oriented. Because few Jews lived on farms, they had to concentrate on living in densely populated areas. The gentile peasants needed customers for their goods, middlemen for their trades, craftsmen, and doctors, and Jews tended to fill these

roles. Thus, they clearly stood at some remove from nature.

Zionism. With Zionism and the return to the holy land, Judaism has brought back to center stage a theme that was prominent in premodern times—the predilection for Israel and Jerusalem as the most religious places, favoring the prosperity of Jewish faith. In the centuries of Diaspora, the typical Jew felt something of what the first biblical exiles lamented—the inability to sing and rejoice in a foreign land. No doubt that feeling did not afflict the descendants of the actual exiles as intensely, for few of them returned from Babylon when they had the opportunity, but it mixed a certain nature orientation with Jews' desire to have a place of their own. Consequently, Israel became not just a venerable place but also a beautiful, fruitful, arable, desirable land. Thus, the biblical theme of a promised land joined with messianic hopes to link the new age that the Messiah would usher in and the people's return to a place flowing with milk and honey. Zionism drew on these traditional themes, joining them to socialistic (if not utopian) theories of working the land and living together in close cooperation.

Though few American Jews farm or do their religious thinking along cosmological lines, quite a few Israelis live on kibbutzim and work the land (and quite a few American Jewish youths join them for a summer or a year). The land, if not nature, is most important to kibbutzniks. Because of Israel's ancient history and Jews' present need to have their own place in the sun, the Israelis now are more agrarian than their recent predecessors were. How that affects their religious consciousness is hard to determine. Many do not consider themselves religious, and they often view their life on the land, even though it brings them close to nature, in sociological rather than naturalistic terms. Frequently, then, they resemble other idealistic groups who form communes and farm in order to augment their freedom (and often to "purify" their lives). On the other hand, those who do form kibbutzim out of religious motivations are often fundamentalists trying to regain their biblical heritage. Still, that heritage is not so much harvesting God's earth as living where God made the Jews his special people.

Thus, Judaism has tended to view nature rather prosaically. To be sure, some Jews have farmed, and some non-farming Jews have found religious significance in seasons, sunsets, flowers, and stocks of grain. However, the Hebrew Bible, the Talmud, and other products of the mind have been more central to the tradition.

Society

Few religions are as community minded as Judaism. Even when we consider that modern individualism is a historical novelty, the fact remains that the Jews were the chosen *people*—chosen as a group or line rather than as individuals. From tribal beginnings, through kingdom, Diaspora, and ethnic diversification, Jewish religion has always been a group affair. Of course, the Torah is inseparable from this phenomenon, for it is a special law designed expressly for the chosen, covenanted people. It sprang from a group sense that life must flow to "our" God, who led us out of captivity to be his own people. The Torah also specified the theological direction of Jews by giving election and covenant the forms by which they shaped social life.

Thus, the synagogue has been a popular gathering place, uniting the action of the people. The Christian *ecclesia* ("church") has a similar etymological meaning ("gathering," "being called out"), but the building it names has been almost as much a place for private prayer as for public. Perhaps the relative smallness of the Jewish population has helped it to gain a more worldwide sense of community than Christians have had. Perhaps, as well, the relative mildness of its sectarian divisions has helped to keep Judaism a family affair. In any event, Muslims, despite their democratic worship and pilgrimage, have been less united than Jews have been, and Christians, despite their lofty theology of the Church, have been more individual oriented and divided. Finally, nothing in Hinduism or Buddhism prompts a different judgment: Judaism is unified and social to a remarkable degree.

Women's Status.   Jews, then, have focused more on culture than on nature.[54] Anthropologists sometimes use these two concepts as opposing points on a spectrum to determine a people's attitudes toward itself and cosmological processes. For instance, anthropologists have used this spectrum to study sex roles.[55] Women have generally been associated with nature, because of menstruation, childbirth, nursing, and—to male eyes—more instinctive, less cerebral behavior. Men have been associated with culture: craft, art, literature, and politics. It does not take a great deal of research to dispute this construct, but many societies have used it, more or less consciously, to characterize sex roles. Therefore, the construct is useful in analyzing how societies view the play of physical nature in human societies.

This sexual stereotype is somewhat applicable among Jews. As we noted, during many periods of Jewish history women worked or ran the home while the men studied. The biblical portrait of women,[56] and the portrait of women in the Talmud[57] and in the *responsa*,[58] reflect a traditional view that placed women away from law and the mind and toward nature and the body. Separating the patriarchal structure of Middle Eastern society, the Jewish religious conception of God (usually as a husband or father, seldom as a wife or mother), and the Jewish perception of nature is almost impossible. The facts, however, are that women and nature went together and that they were subordinate to men and culture.

For instance, women did not read the Torah in the synagogue (usually they could not read Hebrew), did not have many legal obligations (only three *mitzvoth* pertain only to them), could not be priests or rabbis, were tabooed during menstruation, and were both indulged and criticized for their "flightiness." Under biblical law, Jewish women were partially considered as property—akin to animals and goods. For instance, the laws concerning adultery and rape were principally intended to protect the rights of the male—the injured husband or father. The principal value of women throughout Jewish history was motherhood— a quite "natural" function. They seldom could have careers and usually had difficulty obtaining the education that would have enabled them to be their husbands' best friends. They were the source of the family line and of emotional support, not leaders. In good measure because he enjoyed being the cultural center, the male Jew traditionally prayed thanks to God for not having created him a woman.[59]

Case Study: Jewish Rituals.   Traditionally, Jewish social life has involved many rituals. To begin with, there was circumcision, the ritual through which males entered the covenant community. Herman Wouk, the celebrated novelist, has tried to explain circumcision and other Jewish rituals to sympathetic gentiles.[60] He begins by noting the scorn that often has been directed at circumcision and similar Jewish customs. Thus the French Enlightenment writer Voltaire mocked a God who could care whether people cut off their sons' foreskins. On the other hand, Spinoza, the rationalistic Jewish philosopher, thought that circumcision alone was sufficient to keep the Jews a separate people. However, whether mocked or made a subject of philosophy, circumcision can be a key to Jewish faith.

In the perspective of Jewish faith, circumcision is not a matter of hygiene. It is a sign of the pledge made between Abraham and God, a sign in the very organ of life. For the rest of his life, the man signed this way stands out from the rest of unsigned humanity. Naked, the Jewish man is clearly a Jew. In Wouk's interpretation, the swing of modern medicine to circumcision was but a ratification of the sound policy Jews have always expected God's law to entail. With or without such a ratification, however, Jews would continue to circumcise their males on the eighth day after birth, the time when Abraham circumcised Isaac.

The circumcision ritual is called a *bris,* the Hebrew word for covenant. When most children were born at home, the bris meant a family feast, with crowds of relatives and friends, learned speeches, and general merrymaking. Each step of the ceremony was something to be stored in the memory for later meditation. Contemporary ceremonies retain what they can of this tradition, gathering relatives and friends to celebrate the new birth. The bris intensifies the ordinary joy parents feel at the gift of a child, by emphasizing that the covenant community is being extended another generation.

So the father of the child pronounces a joyous blessing: "Blessed are you, Lord our God, Master of the Universe, who have made us holy with your commands, and have commanded us to bring this boy into the covenant of Abraham our father." Ideally the father would do the circumcision himself, as Abraham did, but the accepted practice has become to employ a *mohel* or ritual circumciser to perform it. The mohel may or may not be a medical doctor, but he has been well trained in medical safeguards and antisepsis. In Wouk's view the mohel is preferable to an ordinary doctor, both because the mohel likely has fuller technical training and because he understands the full meaning of the ritual. Thus, he can stand in for the father more adequately.

Following circumcision, the next rite of passage for the Jewish child is the *bar mitzvah* or ceremonial accession to adulthood. Recently, American Jewish feelings about this ceremony have become quite sensitive, and Wouk reports having received many bitter, even violent complaints about his somewhat humorous depiction of a bar mitzvah in his novel *Marjorie Morningstar.* Where he thought he had portrayed the bar mitzvah accurately and affectionately, many of his fellow Jews thought he had been satirical, even disrespectful. His reply is that when people lose their sense of humor, becoming unable to see the foibles of their tribe, it is time they take themselves to the mirror.

Sticking to his humorous guns, Wouk likens the American bar mitzvah to a Christmas feast orchestrated by Charles Dickens. The lengthy preparations, the incredible eating, the enormous wassailing, and the swirl of family emotions seem parallel in both cases. In both cases, a great deal of purely human gusto dances on top of a religious rationale. In the case of American Jews, the bar mitzvah seems to have become an occasion to celebrate a relative freedom from discrimination. While Wouk applauds this freedom, he wonders whether American Jews aren't in danger of losing the religious significance of the bar mitzvah, much as American Christians are in danger of losing the religious significance of Christmas, through all their buying and partying.

The religious tradition behind the bar mitzvah assumes that a child does not develop the capacity to grasp the concepts of Judaism, nor to fulfill Judaism's disciplines, until the age of thirteen. Before that time, the father is responsible for the child. The bar mitzvah marks the child's transition to personal responsibility. Donning the phylacteries that an adult wears when he prays, the boy bar mitzvahed can now receive an *aliya,* a call to speak the blessing over a part of the weekly reading of the Torah.

The most honorific aliya is the last one, the call concerning the weekly piece from the prophets. In European Jewish communities the custom arose of giving this special aliya (called the *maftir*) to a boy on his bar mitzvah Sabbath, and this custom has been retained in the United States. Often, however, the solid preparation in Hebrew that the European tradition assumed has been lacking. Thus, in Wouk's view, the American bar mitzvah frequently became a time of crisis, the young person feeling that his blitz of preparations was a sham. In a number of communities, this has led to a renewal of Hebrew studies, so that the ceremony can express a genuine mastery of Judaism's foundations.

With the rise of a Jewish feminist consciousness have come rituals for bringing girls into the covenant and adulthood. Thus Judith Plaskow, a prominent Jewish feminist and theologian, has written a bris ceremonial for a girl. It begins with the song Hannah sang on the occasion of the birth of her son Samuel (I Sam. 2:2–8), including the words: "The bows of the mighty are broken, but the feeble gird on strength. Those who were full have hired themselves out for bread, but those who were hungry have ceased to hunger. The barren has borne seven, but she who has many children is forlorn. God creates and destroys; She brings down to Sheol and raises up."[61] With similar adaptations of other scriptural passages, Plaskow weaves together a celebration of a baby girl's entrance into the community's life parallel to that for a baby boy.

Concerning a girl's coming of age, Wouk indicates some of the reasons for the absence of a special ceremony in the past, and why present times have led to coming-of-age ceremonies for girls. Traditionally, women were exempted from most Jewish rituals, that they might be free for family tasks. When the bar mitzvah was a rather minor ceremony, for which boys began intensive studies at the age of five, "a girl would have been out of her head to agitate for the burdens of scholarship." But when the preparation for the bar mitzvah dwindled, and the event came to occasion a great party, there were good reasons for girls to want an equal celebration. Thus, there has arisen the *bas* (or *bat*) *mitzvah* ceremony for girls, an improvised way to ritualize girls' graduation from religious-school training and to recognize their new status as adults. (Wouk seems insensitive to the traditional correlation between learning and religious status in Judaism, as well as to the deeper hopes of feminists for full sexual equality.)

In most religions' ritualization of the life cycle, the third recurring ceremony has been marriage. Judaism has been no exception, giving marriage a great deal of ritual attention. *The Jewish Catalogue,* a high-spirited collection of lore and advice that tries to make Judaism attractive to contemporary Americans, begins its section on marriage with a story from the talmudic traditions.[62] Once a Roman matron asked Rabbi Jose bar Halafta how long it took God to create the world. The rabbi replied it took six days. The woman then asked, "What has God been doing from then until now?" The rabbi answered, "The Holy One, blessed be He, is occupied in making marriages." The matron scoffed at this, saying that marriage should only take a short time. Indeed, she went home and in one night married off a thousand of her male slaves to a thousand of her female slaves. The next day the slaves came before her, broken, wounded, and bruised. Each slave said, "I do not want the one you gave me." So the woman went back to the rabbi and apologized. "I see now that your Torah is beautiful—praiseworthy and true." The rabbi replied, "Yes. God considers making a suitable match as difficult as dividing the Red Sea."

Difficult or not, Jews, like all other peoples, have persisted in marrying, generation after generation, for better or worse, for richer or poorer. Traditionally, their marriages have taken place under a canopy *(huppah)* supported by four poles, the original purpose of which was to provide the ceremony a sacred space. The day itself usually entailed a fast, and other similarities to the Day of Atonement, in the belief that on their wedding day God forgives a couple all their past sins, so that they may begin their life together afresh. Another custom was for the bride and groom to wear white as a symbol of purity.

Jewish betrothal occurred by writing a legal document binding on both parties. The rabbi asked the groom if he was prepared to fulfill his obligations as stated in the contract *(ketubbah),* and the groom answered affirmatively by taking hold of a handkerchief or some other object given him by the rabbi. After the groom signed the contract, the men present surrounded the groom and danced with him over to the bride, who sat regally on a throne. The groom lifted the veil from the bride's face, while the rabbi recited the phrase, "O sister! May you become the mother of thousands of myriads" (Gen. 24:60). The bride and groom then processed to the huppah, the bride circled the groom seven times (entering all seven spheres of her beloved's soul), there were psalms, hymns, a blessing of wine, and then the essential act occurred.

The essential act was the groom putting a ring on the index finger of the bride's right hand and saying, "Behold you are consecrated to me with this ring according to the Law of Moses and Israel." After this the marriage contract was read, seven blessings were recited, and the groom smashed a glass by stamping on it, to conclude the ceremony. Traditionally, the bride and groom then retired to consummate the marriage. Nowadays they retire to break their fast. When they emerge, their families and friends greet them with music, dancing, and celebration.

Funeral rites, the last stage on life's way, have involved Jews in a final confession of faith. Ideally the dying person said, "Understand, O Israel, the Lord our God is One. I acknowledge before Thee, my God, God of my fathers, that my recovery and death are in your hand. May it be your will to heal me completely, but if I should die, may my death be an atonement for all sins that I have committed." After death there was a ritual washing of the body, a funeral dominated by the recitation of psalms, a ritualized burial, a meal for the mourners, and then the *shivah,* a seven-day period of mourning, during which friends were expected to visit

Figure 19 Judith with the Head of Holofernes,
*by Simon Vouet (1590–1649). The Nelson–Atkins
Museum of Art, Kansas City, Missouri (Nelson
Fund).*

and a *minyan* (quorum of ten) was to gather each day. The mourning period concluded with visiting the synagogue the first Sabbath after the shivah.

A Jew has usually prayed in the plural, for the sake of the many. When a student or scholar devoted himself to Torah, it was usually in common. In the *shtetl*, one clearly lived very much with people—at times oppressively so. As we noted, wealth was for the common good and study had teaching as its goal. Unlike Christian society, Jewish society had no monastic alternative (neither solitary nor communitarian) to marriage and family life.[63] (The Essene community at Qumran, if it was an exception to this rule, was short-lived.) Generally, then, Jewish existence has been distinctly social or communal.

Relatedly, the rabbinic mind uncompromisingly intended that all the people live socially. The scholar pondered a law incumbent on all; the working person normally was in business rather than in the solitude of the fields or the forests; in the home, which was largely the woman's province, feelings were gotten "out," almost compulsively expressed. In fact, silence

was considered antisocial and even cruel behavior. The two things that a child could do to punish its mother were not to eat and not to speak. Finally, community conversation buzzed with a detailed analysis of each member's learning, wealth, and family lineage. Small wonder, then, that being called forth to read the Torah before the community was an honor, placing one among the *sheyneh yidn,* the "beautiful Jews."

As we have seen, this communitarian consciousness is rooted in patriarchal times. Jews first identified themselves by their tribal origins, which they tied together under the concept of "the twelve tribes." They attributed their sense of commonness to fatherly figures: Abraham, Moses, and David. Abraham was the source of the seed. To him had been the promise of a progeny as numerous as the stars in the heavens or the grains of sand along the sea. Moses was the founding father, in the sense of being the lawgiver. David was the sacred king, the mediator between heaven and earth, the top of the human pyramid. From his line would spring the Messiah. In a special way, the capital city of Jerusalem was the city of David.

Jerusalem.　When the Jews gained a new homeland in 1948, fulfilling decades of Zionist longings, Jerusalem again became the real center of Jewish geography. All the biblical overtones of the city of David lie inside the old walls. Outside the old walls is much evidence of the surrounding and hostile Arab population. Historically, Jerusalem summons images of kingship, prosperity, a golden age, a pawn of Christians and Muslims. Sociologically, Jerusalem gives the Jewish people a realized dream, a place of their own to which, next year, the Messiah just might come and all the blessed might journey.

Psychologically, contemporary Jews are apt to overflow with feelings about Jerusalem, some of them quite conflicting. On the one hand, there is a desire to support the powers in the new capital that are trying to promote Israel's survival and prosperity. On the other hand, there is the knowledge that the majority of Jews still live outside Israel, often more prosperously than if they lived inside Israel, and that not all the things done in the Knesset (parliament) merit full support. Some policies emanating from the Knesset have made barren land spring back to life. Yet on the West Bank the ecological policies have become so mixed with religious aims that they often seem to be a military weapon aimed against the troublesome Palestinians. It is hard for sensitive Jews to know where to direct their support.

Historically, Jerusalem has suffered from the conflicting aims of its leaders. The classical prophets often found themselves spiritual spokesmen, pitted against kings and opposing worldly powers. They feared that worldly reliances, above all military recourses, would keep the Jewish people from pure religion, and weaken Israel's firm faith in God. The kings often rejected the prophets' perspective, preferring to play power politics. The resulting split of the kingdom, as well as the fall of the southern portion to Babylon, stands in biblical history as a great vindication of the prophets. Through the many centuries when Jews had no power over their ancestral land, and the many more centuries when they lived mainly outside it in the Diaspora, the priests and rabbis could deal with questions of power politics rather distantly, regarding them as theoretical rather than practical issues. Today, however, conflicts between the religious and secular sides of Jewish faith have once again come to swords' point in Jerusalem, as in the 1982 Israeli slaying of hundreds of Palestinian refugees in Lebanese camps.

The Special Commission of Inquiry that reported on the Israeli slaying based their findings, in part, on a Jewish law and tradition with roots extending back to the Bible. They combined modern jurisprudence with the talmudic heritage, and the result was an arresting confluence of democratic self-criticism and religious sensitivity. While the proximate blame for the massacre fell squarely on non-Jewish shoulders (those responsible for the slayings were right-wing Christians), the Commission found leading Jewish military and political officials guilty of indifference and imprudence. Because the highly developed traditional moral code held that one who is able to avert an evil and does not do so is somewhat responsible for such evil, leading generals, the defense minister, and even the prime minister drew the Commission's blame. These findings were deeply disturbing to many Jews. But the form of the findings, their deep and honest self-criticism, was an act of healing, a step of therapy and hope. As many commentators the world over pointed out, there are only a handful of other nations in the world where such a public self-criticism would be conceivable, and few if any of them are in the Middle East.

The prophetic emphases on justice, conversion to God, and walking in the ways of truth continue to shape daily life in Jerusalem. Down the streets hurry bearded Hasidic Jews and visiting Americans, devout religionists and Jews nearly completely secularized. The land and the ethnic solidarity have become lodestones to chosen people all over the globe. The Jews of European origin (Ashkenazim) who have been the main reference point of our story increasingly find that they must accommodate the Jews of Spanish origin (Sephardim) and Oriental Jews. Within a small country, an amazing variety obtains. Fundamentalists seeking to establish new settlements believe they are fulfilling a biblical mandate. Twenty miles away in the Hebrew University, professors teach that such fundamentalism is foolish. Meanwhile, the specter of the Nazi death camps hovers outside Jerusalem at Yad Vashem, the memorial set in the nearby hills. This specter has led many to vow "Never again!"

Prophecy and the Chosen People.   Of the three key biblical figures, Moses predominated, because the Law that came through him has been the backbone of Jewish religious life. As different cultures were assimilated by Judaism, Abraham's lineage became less important than his exemplary faith. Similarly, as political sovereignty became a dim memory, David's kingship became rather metaphorical, propping future hopes more than guiding present living. Moses, however, stayed wholly relevant: He was thought to have authored the code that kept Jews united; he was the mediator of the covenant into which the community circumcised each male. When prophecy had become central to Jewish religion, Moses became the prophet par excellence.

Prophecy, which often distinguishes Western religion from Eastern wisdom religion, is not so much the predictions that appear in today's tabloids as a discernment of what the divine spirit is saying to the people of God. The great biblical prophets analyzed the contemporary state of faith and, from that analysis, shrewdly estimated political or military fortunes. A goodly portion of such recorded prophecy was, of course, written after the fact. No portion of respectable prophecy, though, pried into the divine mystery. God remained God; the prophet had only the word that God deigned to speak. The establishment of Moses as the supreme prophet testifies to the social utility that Jews have expected communication with God to bear. They expected such communication to result in communal renovation, strengthening, and redirection. Prophecy was not a display of individual virtuosity or a matter involving crystal balls.

As prophecy intimates, the ultimate bonding agent of Jewish society has been God; only the atypical, modern secular Jew would dispute this. Through history the master of the universe, the Adonai ("My

Lord," substituting for Yahweh, which was considered too holy to utter) that all prayers bless, has bound Jews together as his people. Physically and legally one is a Jew if one is born of a Jewish mother; spiritually one is a Jew if one identifies with the people fashioned at Sinai, framed by the Torah, and covenanted to God. To be sure, many problems attend election as God's people, and Jews have not been unmindful of them. Indeed, the relation between the chosen people and the gentile nations has been a constant topic for Jewish meditation. In good times, such meditation has turned over history's mysteries gratefully: Why were we chosen when we show no special merit? What are our obligations to the nations?

Indubitably, the gentile nations were under God's direction, too. It could not be that God had no fulfillment in store for them. So Jewish thinkers worked out the notion of the Noachian covenant: God made a pact with the gentile nations modeled after the promise he made to Noah, in which he stressed the need for human beings to respect life, especially by avoiding bloodshed. The Bible sees the rainbow as a symbol of God's fidelity to this pact: He will never destroy humanity, never again allow it to suffer as it did in the flood. Yet God could well have more in store for the nations than this Noachian covenant, and Israel's vocation was to be a light unto the nations—to provide them with a greater knowledge of God. In that way, being the chosen people became less a matter of honor than a matter of responsibility.

In bad times, however, reflection on being chosen by God had to probe darker mysteries. For instance, the prophets almost fixated on the horror that many Israelites refused their election. Most people wanted kings like the nations had, cults like those to Baal, fertility from the land rather than from the covenant. With some deliberateness, many Jews turned their backs on God because they could not endure living in faith; God's self-naming to Moses, "I am whatever I want to be," was too much for them. For the prophets, this flight from God was the deepest sickness of the soul, the most debilitating sin, as well as a rejection of Israel's better self. The worst of biblical times, then, occurred when people left the covenantal faith.

At such times, the prophets brought the whole question of what the Jewish people at core were into paradox. They then spoke of a remnant, of an Israel within Israel that was composed of the few who did keep faith. A major Jewish-Christian controversy has hung on this point, for Christians have claimed to succeed Israel by accepting God's later revelation (specifically, his revelation in Jesus the Christ). Within the Jewish community itself, prophetic religious leaders have always worried about the correlation between bad faith and loss of membership.

The Law.   For rabbinic Judaism, the Law helped to ease the problem of bad faith. Without abandoning their ideal of the perfect faith outlined in Maimonides' thirteen articles, the rabbis generally have focused more on performance than on motivation or thought. What one believed about God, within broad limits, has been less important than keeping the Sabbath and fulfilling one's communal obligations. This attitude encouraged considerable intellectual freedom, including lively debate, tolerance, and theological ambiguity. As well, it prevented the establishment of a clear-cut religious authority and dogma, such as that encountered by Roman Catholics in the magisterium of their councils and popes. The Law, which seemed so specific, had dozens of interpreters. On and on the Talmud grew, because most interpreters had insights worth preserving.

The result was a subtle but significant shift in the notion of the faith requisite for community membership. Faith was expressed in action, not in speculation or confession. How one used one's body, money, and time was more important than how one used one's mind or tongue. Such a practical view of faith meant that the community could bind itself through rituals, ethics, and laws without excessive concern about their meaning (although the rabbis did not ignore their meaning or the proper motivation behind ritual actions).

This emphasis on action relates to the Jewish refusal to separate mind and body and to the Jewish commitment to hallowing life. Traditionally, one obeyed the Law to express and learn that God, who is holy, wants holy people. Through the quite overt keeping of the Law, Jews reminded themselves that they were the people called to sanctify God's name. A Jew knew that his neighbor accepted this identity because he could see that his neighbor obeyed the Law. Not accidentally, withdrawal from the Law and from the traditional God whom the Law hallowed have gone hand in hand in modern times.

The Holocaust.   Last, contemporary Jewish identity has been annealed as a result of the Holocaust. While exodus and entry into the promised land characterized Jews in biblical times, suffering and persecution have characterized Jews since the expulsion from Jerusalem in 70 C.E. Jewish commentators have no consensus on what recent history and the Holocaust mean. For Richard Rubenstein, they mean the death of the traditional God.[64] For Emil Fackenheim, they mean a call to hold together both evil and divine providence.[65] For Hannah Arendt, they show that history can make evil utterly commonplace or banal.[66] Such commentators do agree that we must not ignore, deny, or explain away the evil of the Holocaust. As Elie Wiesel has said, it is better to keep silent than to depreciate the suffering of so many innocent victims with "explanations."[67] Thus, Jewish identity, the theme of so many American novels, has yet to be fully resolved.

Self

An intense community life, such as that of traditional Judaism, can heighten individualism. One can prize the individual because the richer the individual, the richer the group. Judaism appears to have appreciated this proposition.

For example, after the prophets (such as Ezekiel and Jeremiah), individual responsibility separated from collective responsibility. No longer could one hold, rather magically, that the fathers had eaten sour grapes and so set the children's teeth on edge. Furthermore, both Hellenization and internal legal development set apart individual reason. For instance, Jewish thinkers in Alexandria reflected Platonic, Aristotelian, Epicurean, and Stoic interests in mind and reason. Philo, the luminary of these thinkers, tried to correlate Mosaic teaching with a cosmic law. In the medieval period, Maimonides, Halevi, and others tried to square the Torah with rational demands for a less mythic, more analytic explanation of faith. Since the individual soul is the site of reason, such concerns inevitably clarified the personality's partial independence of group thought. That is, it underscored that any particular person might grasp or miss the divine Law.

Moreover, the Torah and the Talmud themselves inculcated something of this sensitivity. As a scriptural religion, Judaism demanded literacy and encouraged learning. But, literature and learning are obviously cultural developments deriving from a common human nature that tend to distinguish people according to their talent. Thus, the bright little boy may distinguish himself by the age of ten. Through his unique gifts he may stand out from the crowd, and even increase regard for his family. If he develops into a sage, he will join the line of masters whose commen-

taries on the Law are the classics. So, by stressing personal insight, legal study encouraged individuation.

To a lesser degree, Jewish mysticism and Jewish attitudes toward wealth also encouraged individuation. Mysticism, like study, is a personal inward phenomenon. Despite its debt to tradition and its occurrence within a community of faith, mysticism is a solitary pursuit involving an "I-Thou" relation. When mysticism flowered in Judaism, it produced revered personalities, such as the Baal Shem-Tov and the Magid of Mezritch. To their disciples, these *tzaddikim* were stunning demonstrations of the ardor that divinity could inspire. Their personalities were special, set apart, distinguished. Despite the threats that mysticism posed for the traditional rabbinic authority, the mystics were precious for strengthening the common people's faith. Thus, one could aspire to Hasidic distinction, as one could aspire to rabbinic distinction. Because mystical prowess edified the community, it was a worthy ambition.

Analogously, one could aspire to the (lesser) distinction that came with wealth. Judaism is not, comparatively speaking, an ascetic religion. As much as Hinduism, it views wealth or prosperity as a legitimate life goal. For his good fortune and financial talent, as well as for his philanthropy, a successful Jew could win recognition. True, with success he was sure to gain a host of petitioners, but their attestation to his generosity somewhat offset the burden they imposed.

This description of the self must be qualified in discussing women. Since their vocation was marriage and practicality, their distinction was basically reflected—that of being a rich man's wife or a scholar's mother. Nevertheless, women had rights to self-expression, at least regarding nonscriptural matters. The *shtetl* tradition that a woman had no soul did not mean that she had no say. In matters of the home or the shop, she probably had the dominant say. In matters of affection or emotion, she surely did. Thus, few distinguished Jews were not first signalized by women, and most *shtetl* neighborhoods recognized certain girls as being especially nubile and certain mothers as being especially benevolent.

Mind-Body Unity. Judaism has stressed the unity of mind and body, eschewing a body-soul or matter-spirit duality. Scholars usually contrast biblical Jewish notions of personhood and the then-contemporary Greek notions. This contrast can illumine the tendency of Judaism toward an existential concreteness that most of Western culture has been struggling for centuries to recapture.

For instance, Descartes, the father of modern European philosophy, worked hard to reconcile the opposition within the human being between its *res cogitans* (thinking part) and its *res extensa* (material part). In contrast, the "soul" *(nepesh)* of Hebrew biblical thought was a unity of mind and body that could not be divided into thinking and material parts. So the heart rather than the head stood for the center of thought and emotion. Out of the fullness of the heart the mouth would speak. This conviction fought against the Hellenization of Jewish theology, which would have made the mouth speak what reason dictated. It fought against the legalism possible in rabbinic theology, keeping space for aggadic tales whose appeal was more than mental. The earthiness that one finds in Hebrew literature, from biblical times to the present,[68] reflects these convictions about the heart and body.

Furthermore, through his or her body, the Jewish personality maintained contact with the natural world. In the beginning, God had formed human beings from the earth, breathing into them a living spirit. Various biblical figures, such as Job, acknowledge this connection with the earth when they humble themselves before God and say, "We are but dust and ashes." The connection with the earth is more intense in the command to be fruitful and multiply, for the command implies that living things have an inbuilt drive to survive and grow. Biblical notions of stewardship over the earth found an evolutionary aspect in the command to be fruitful and multiply. (They also subordinated nature to human need.)

The command to be fruitful and multiply also influenced Jewish attitudes toward marriage. The fulfillment of the spouses certainly was much valued, at least in talmudic times, but a strong focus also remained on procreation. As many commentators point out, the late development of the notion of personal immortality in Judaism is due not only to the lack of a clear sense of a spiritual (immaterial) soul, but also to the tendency to think that one continued to exist through one's offspring. In other words, the family line was a sort of concrete immortality. To some extent, this limited the significance of the individual.

On the other hand, marriage was a treasure of Jewish faith in part because it prevented the individual from being totally lost in the abyss of death. From this and other benefits attributed to marriage, sexual activity derived a certain dignity, even a certain obliga-

tion. It is true that in rabbinic Judaism prudery could offset the high evaluation of sexual love. For instance, rabbis counseled against raising one's eyes to a woman's face, and some desired that the sexes be segregated as much as possible. Most laid on women the same heavy burden of the temptress that one can see in other religions. Indeed, in Judaism, unchastity was not only sinful but deplorable, because it drew the mind down from the heights of the Torah and prayer.

In most traditional homes (which for the poor often had only one or two rooms), husband and wife did not sleep in the same bed. Tradition encouraged them to have relations except during the menstrual flow but to keep the sexual appetite in check. One of the customs of the Sabbath, however, was that in its leisure spouses should make love. As the cabalists stressed, the Sabbath was the bride of God. Consequently, they found in the coexistence of man and woman a supplement to the notion that human reason is an image of God. Humanity also images God through sexual love, acting in accordance with the Genesis line "male and female created he them."

The Human Spirit. In prophecy Jewish religion found understandings of God's relationship to the human spirit new to human history. That is, the ecstatic experience of the prophets, who seem to have begun as wandering bands of exultants *(nebi'im),* evolved into something other than ordinary shamanism (which we may take as the typical model of ancient ecstasy). For where shamanism usually kept the world divine and usually confused the relations between imagination and reason in the ecstatic experience (though some shamans were well aware of the divine incomprehensibility), the prophets had experiences that burned below imagination to the base of the spirit. The burning bush, for instance, occasioned the realization that we only know of God what the divine mystery shows in time. Elijah's small, still voice suggested that God comes more through spiritual recollection than through natural storms. Jeremiah, finally, went to the core of the matter: Divine creativity best expresses itself by writing its law upon the human heart.

That did not mean that the prophetic, or later the mystical, Jews did not mix myth, symbol, and imagination. The *merkabah* (chariot) imagery, as we mentioned, dominated even the philosophers' ruminations about God, while the cabalists' bliss was to imagine the divine emanations. Still, the union of the entire numinous experience (the entire experience of divinity) with ethical demands refined what it meant to be religious by stressing communion with a transcendent God. Implicit in the prophetic and talmudic program was the proposition that true religion is doing justice and worshiping purely. Implicit was the twofold commandment of loving God (who is one) and loving one's neighbor (who is another self). This outlook developed a powerful concept of individual conscience: God alone is the mystery that should dominate and constitute the human person in its being or its morality. When Jewish theologians clarified such a *monotheism,* they dealt a deathblow to all *idolatry.* History continues to unfold the implications of this ethical monotheism. From biblical times, then, Jews have cast the self, as well as the people, in partnership with a single God.

Ultimate Reality

The question of the place of ultimate reality in Judaism is difficult for Westerners, because the Jewish God is inseparable from Western culture. We can no more filter out Israelite ethical monotheism from the Western world view than we can filter out Greek reason. It requires considerable imaginative energy, therefore, to grasp the origins of Jewish divinity and trace how those beginnings developed into theological conceptualizations.

The biblical beginnings were extremely novel, constituting a "leap in being" rivaled only by the Greek clarification of reason. The biblical beginnings were deep spiritual experiences: irruptions of divinity that seized and formed the soul (more than they clarified reason). The God who was revealed was lively, personal, and free.

Perhaps because the genius of Israelite religion was not reason but spirit, the biblical Jews expressed this God's character as the world's origin and destiny in myths. That is, they expressed the truth of order, of humanity's proper place in and with nature and God, symbolically, from the "dead spot," the bottom of the soul, which revelation seizes. Moreover, having expressed its order mythologically, the Israelite religious genius hardly criticized its symbols, making little effort to interpret them in clearer, if less complete, conceptual terms. In other words, it did not attack the problems of inner coherence that today's analytic philosophy associates with meaning.[69] So the God of Moses "is" only what time shows him to be; the God of Genesis makes the world "in the beginning" from primal chaos, the status of which is quite unclear; and

the God of Isaiah is placed beyond the world by a dazzling cluster of symbols.

In the midst of a splendid reflection on the Book of Ruth, the contemporary Jewish novelist Cynthia Ozick probes the significance of the monotheism to which Ruth committed herself when, unlike her sister-in-law Orpah, she threw in her lot with their mother-in-law Naomi and committed herself to Naomi's God:

> Who will demand of Orpah—think of the hugeness of the demand!—that she admit monotheism to the concentration and trials of her mind? Offer monotheism to almost anyone—offer it as something to take seriously—and ninety-nine times out of a hundred it will be declined, even by professing "monotheists." A Lord of History whose intent is felt, whose Commandments stand with immediacy, whose Covenant summons perpetual self-scrutiny and a continual Turning toward moral renewal, and yet *cannot, may not, be physically imagined*? A Creator neither remote and abstract like the God of the philosophers, nor palpable like the "normal" divinities, both ancient and contemporary, of both East and West? Give us (cries the nature of our race) our gods and goddesses; give us the little fertility icons with their welcoming breasts and elongated beckoning laps; give us the resplendent Virgin with her suffering brow and her arms outstretched in blessing; give us the Man on the Cross through whom to learn pity and love, and sometimes brutal exclusivity! Only give us what our eyes can see and our understanding understand: who can imagine the unimaginable? That may be for the philosophers; *they* can do it; but then they lack the imagination of the Covenant. The philosophers leave the world naked and blind and deaf and mute and relentlessly indifferent, and the village folk—who refuse a lonely cosmos without consolation—fill it and fill it and fill it with stone and wood and birds and mammals and miraculous potions and holy babes and animate carcasses and magically divine women and magically divine men: images, sights, and swallowings comprehensible to the hand, to the eye, to plain experience. For the nature of our race, God is one of the visual arts.[70]

The fight of the best Jewish theologians has been to preserve the instinct, traceable to Moses and the prophets, that God is not one of the visual arts and that the nature of our race cannot be the measure of

God. God has to be beyond our measures—visual, emotional, even intellectual. God has to be allowed to be as God presents the divine nature: sovereignly free, though deeply committed to the welfare of human beings. Human beings have to suffer the fact that God is always going to be strictly mysterious: a fullness that human beings can never comprehend, let alone control. One can debate whether Torah became an infringement on this passionate Jewish instinct, a loss in the fight to preserve strict monotheism, but probably not to any good conclusion. For the weight of Jewish theological tradition has been that Torah offers guidance for how to live with the God who cannot be visualized, who must always be allowed the divine mysteriousness—guidance that divinity itself had offered as a gracious gift and kindly command. The core of some of the most significant Jewish theology lies in the intimate connection between Torah and the divine mystery—in guidance to honor above all the unimaginable Guide of Jewish existence.

Case Study: The God of Jewish Prayer.[71] Through more than 2,500 years of liturgical experience, Jews have developed the biblical notion of God. Probably the prime characteristic of the Jewish God that has emerged is his unity. As a summary of Jewish belief and prayer, the Shema has said it all: "Hear, O Israel: The Lord our God is One Lord." Thus the daily prayers of the individual Jew, as well as the communal prayers of the synagogue, have always lauded the divine unity. Nonetheless, the divine unity is not the only word in Jewish theology. The God of the Fathers has not only been One, he has also been the Creator, the revealer, and the redeemer. In his actions toward the world and his people, he has made new things, disclosed his will, again and again saved the people from dead ends.

All these motifs are manifest in the prayers that we shall describe. One should picture the community assembled in the synagogue as abuzz with these prayers, since the basic form of the Orthodox liturgy has been for each person present to say such prayers aloud. That is what the basic Jewish word for prayer *(daven)* has meant: to say the liturgy aloud yet quietly and privately.

In the Jewish Prayer Book one finds praise for the One God who is King of the Universe: "Praised are you, O Lord our God, King of the Universe." This prayer then itemizes the great things the King of the Universe does. He fixes the cycles of light and darkness. He ordains the order of all creation. He is the source of the light that shines over all the earth. His mercy radiates over all the earth's inhabitants. Because he is so good, he recreates the world day by day. His manifold works reveal his great bounty. Their beauty and order reveal his great wisdom.

And what does the devout Jew ask of the King of the Universe? That he continue to love his people. He, the only One exalted from of old, the One praised and glorified since the world began, has been all Jews' shield and protection: He has been the Lord of our strength, the rock of our defense. In his infinite mercy, may he continue to love us. His goodness is for all time, so we may hope for this mercy. Daily he renews the work of creation, so daily he may be our reliance. The Psalmist knew this and sang, "Give thanks to Him who made the great lights, for His loving-kindness is everlasting." O God, make a new light to shine on Zion. Make us worthy to behold its radiance. All praise to you, O Lord, maker of the stars.

The One God is also the revealer of the Torah. The Prayer Book expresses this conviction in connection with God's compassion: Out of tender regard for his people's needs, the Lord has taught our Fathers the laws of life. For their sakes, may he continue to teach us. May we, too, learn the divine Laws, trust more and more in the divine guidance. May we observe all the precepts of the divine Law, fulfill all its teachings. If we are to do this, God must enlighten our eyes and open our hearts. He must gather together our scattered thoughts, uniting our whole beings in reverence and love. This reverence and love will keep us from shame, and help us to feel God's aid. If we trust in God's holiness, we will come safely from the corners of the earth to the dignity of our own holy land. It is you, God, who are our deliverance, you who have chosen us from all peoples and tongues. We praise and thank you for having drawn us close to you. "We praise You and thank You in truth. With love do we thankfully proclaim Your unity, and praise You who chose Your people Israel in love."

When the Prayer Book reproduces the Shema, it includes much of the Shema's original biblical gloss. Thus after expressing the call to love God with whole mind, soul, and strength, the Prayer Book reminds the people that the words of the Shema should ever be in their hearts. They should teach these words diligently to their children. They should talk about the Shema at home and abroad, day and night. The words of the Shema ought to be a sign upon the hand, or as frontlets (browbands) between the eyes. They should be inscribed on the doorposts of the home and on every gate. If the people fulfill these injunctions, they will find God favoring. He will give them rain in the autumn and rain in the spring, that their harvests may flourish. He will provide them grain, wine, and oil. Their grass will grow thick in the field for their cattle. They will have food enough to eat in contentment.

The way away from God is the way to disaster, so the people must take care not to wander after false gods. If they forsake the true God, they will find the heavens closed, unwilling to provide them rain. They will find the earth barren, unable to provide them food. Before long, there will be no good land for the people to enjoy. The good land will disappear, and with it the once good people. So all Jews should stay mindful of God's words of the Shema, keeping them in their hearts and souls. The words should sign the hand, to guide all that the hand works. They should be stamped between the eyes, to guide all that the eye sees, all that the mind conceives.

In speaking of God as redeemer, Jewish prayer spotlights his intervention on his people's behalf. God has been the king of each generation, the people's only sovereign guide. He has been the redeemer of each generation, the One to whom all Jews must go in time of need. Creator, he has been a victorious stronghold, a fort no enemy could overrun. Through his redemptive interventions, he has shown that there is no God but he.

Though God dwells in the heights of heaven, his decrees reach all of creation. The very ends of the earth stand or fall by God's Laws. Happy is the person who takes these Laws to heart, obeying the commands of God's Torah. Such a person experiences what it really means to have a Lord, a defender and mighty king. The true God is the first and the last. The true people have no king or redeemer but him.

Addressing God directly, the weekly Prayer Book prays: "You, O Lord our God, rescued us from Egypt; You redeemed us from the house of bondage." As though retreating to a favorite haunt of memory, Jewish prayer again and again goes back to the Exodus. God slew the firstborn of the Egyptians, and saved his people's firstborn. He split the waters of the Red Sea, rescuing his faithful and drowning the wicked. When the waters engulfed the enemies of Israel, not one of the arrogant remained.

God the redeemer is therefore God the powerful, God the One not to be trifled with. In the Exodus episode, Israel received its greatest lesson in redemption. Ever since, Jews have sung great hymns of thanksgiving to God. Ever since, they have extolled God with psalms of praise. For ever since they have known that the Lord their God is a mighty king, overseeing everything from his high heaven. Great and awesome, he is the source of all blessing, the everliving divinity exalted in majesty.

As the Exodus episode revealed, the God of Israel humbles the proud and raises the lowly. He frees the captive and redeems the meek. Helping the needy and answering the people's call, he shows himself no respecter of earthly persons, a respecter only of what is right. So let all voices ring out with praise for the supreme God: Ever praised be he! As Moses and the children of Israel sang, "Who is like You, O Lord, among the mighty?" Who is like God in holiness, wonderful deeds, worthiness of praise? There is none like God, because there is only One God. The people God saved in the Exodus sensed this stunning uniqueness. They sang a chorus of praises by the sea. The Lord will reign forever. Rock of Israel, may he ever rise to his people's defense. "Our Redeemer is the Holy One of Israel." Lord of Hosts is our God's name. May the Lord be praised, the Redeemer of Israel.

Such prayer combines a remembrance of God's past deeds with a meditation on God's constant nature. Its regular accent is thankful and praising. God has made everything that exists. He has revealed his will to Israel. And he has saved Israel from its enemies. For these and all his other splendors, he deserves his people's full worship and confidence. Though king, Lord, ruler of heaven, he has deigned to concern himself with his people's needs. Though holy and righteous, he has manifested mercy and steadfast love.

When a person or a group prays in this mood, its words and images fall into an easy rhythm. One image sparks another, one memory brings another memory to mind. Phrases tend to repeat themselves, for the point is not innovation. The point is moving one's soul back to the dispositions of one's forebears in faith, who forged the canonical expressions. In their time, God was manifest in nature and was a fellow-warrior, with them against their foes. In their time, good harvests and military victories derived directly from God's hand, while bad harvests and military defeats suggested the people had faltered in their religion.

What has predominated in the Jewish liturgy, however, is the memory of God's saving deeds. In times past God has shown himself the people's redeemer. Times present and times future will reveal God to have remained faithful and true. Reviving their faith by journeying back to the biblical experiences, generations of Jews have been able to open their spirits to the God who lay ahead of them, in the mystery of the future. God has given his people a way to walk into the future with confidence. Not only has he promised he would reveal himself to Israel through time, he has given his Torah, to detail what holy living with him requires.

So Jews prayed for God's help to fulfill God's Torah. They wanted to be good, to do what was right, and they sensed that for this they needed God's help. Unless God gave them light for their minds and purity for their hearts, they would miss the path of Torah. Unless they did justice to their neighbors and worshiped God day and night, they would lose their heavenly protector. One can see how modern experiences of persecution could put this faith in God's redemptive activity to a severe test. Nonetheless, the Prayer Book has continued to promote the biblical phrases, confident that Jews of today need to worship God wholeheartedly no less than Jews of the past.

SUMMARY: THE JEWISH CENTER

The center of traditional Judaism is the Torah. That there is a law or guidance, come from God and leading to God, has been Judaism's first conviction and main treasure. With such a guidance, life is meaningful, reasonably clear. When such a guidance loses its persuasiveness, as it did for large numbers of Jews in modern times, almost all aspects of life demand rethinking. Then the zeal with which the rabbis studied Torah may shift focus to such new concerns as physical science, social justice, or simply making money. Kept under high pressure for centuries, Jewish intelligence cannot just relax and take a leisurely stroll. In old tracks or new, it has pressed forward to set things clear, gain new knowledge, redress old wrongs. So the summons to Torah has continued to echo in the modern Jewish psyche. When a Jew marshaled intellectual or moral energy, the old summons suggested that things might subserve a higher plan, society ought to succor its widows and orphans.

To summarize the biblical portions of Torah, one speaks of the Law, the Prophets, and the Writings. The Law is historical as much as juridical, a story as much as a blueprint, and its gives Jewish faith a certain

at-home-ness in the world. If God comes through time, and is the master of time's universe, then time is not samsara. True, history falls short of God's eternity, human understanding is inadequate to the divine counsels; but time itself is deeply humane. Though the sufferings that human beings inflict on one another call God's guidance of time into question, the Book of Job remains a powerful denial that human confusion or despair should be indulged. Thus Job suggests that much of the difficult trick of *feeling* time to be humane is to accept one's ignorance of time's final patterns. Then the very minutiae of the biblical and rabbinal codes can be ironic lessons in human finitude. If the greatest masters of Torah reach the grave ignorant of the total picture, the humblest lover of God may be closest to the final truth.

The prophets, biblical and later, pressed for Torah's social consequences. In their eyes, the guidance that came with the covenant asked Jews to weave bonds of justice and care. If righteousness stamped all the doings of the prophetic God, then fair measure and kind-heartedness ought to identify the devout Jewish believer. This conviction, too, was colored by traditional Jewish assumptions about time. Since the Creator's world was basically congenial, marred more by human malice than by any cracks at its core, it ought to be possible to make the human portion of creation humane and enjoyable. Were all Jews to keep the Law, remember their ancient traditions, and help their kin, things would surely go well. Did not the Sabbath give most weeks a patch of human perfection? Was not the Day of Atonement proof that new beginnings could occur? The hatred of outsiders would remain a heavy burden, but the community life itself could keep a strong halo of hope. Indeed, one righteous man might carry this hope so high that the Messiah would come to end all suffering. When the Baal Shem-Tov strode the land, the signs and portents were strong.

The Writings, both biblical and subsequent, added judicious perspectives. Turning over their wisdom literature, Jews learned that it was possible to accept the Law, admire the Prophets, and still feel weary from human vanity. Equally, it was possible to ride time like a poet, singing psalms of praise, psalms of grief, even songs of erotic love. This variety of mood, diversity of outlook, rounded out the Lord's guidance of time. What one felt for a lover, or on a day of defeat, or in vivid memory of the people's redemption from Pharaoh could take wing to the Holy One, advance yet more grounds for blessing his name. If one ascended to the highest heavens, the Holy One was a God of lights. If one fell to the lowest pit, the Holy One was an unshakable recourse. Torah therefore went beyond the borders of reason. One could believe and act far beyond what one understood.

And so the central Jewish instinct has been ethical, performative. Tongues might wag, minds work furiously, but doing has ruled the day. Words—what are they but phantoms and trial balloons? Thoughts—who can be sure they are accurate or will last? The surer coin is deeds, the more reliable religion. Do what Torah prescribes and one day you may understand your tradition. Sever yourself from the common way and surely you will find disaster. Through times of persecution without, schism within, Torah kept inviting and commanding performance. Those who went to the prayer hall, studied the texts, recited the prayers, kept the holidays, and supported the common projects were Jews in deed, members who could be relied on. The others? Well, times were hard, the flesh was weak, wisdom always was rare.

Discussion Questions

1. Why was David's kingship an ambiguous symbol?

2. What is the main theme of the history that the Hebrew Bible writes?

3. In what ways does rabbinic or talmudic religion differ from biblical religion?

4. How would you summarize the religious mentality expressed in Maimonides' thirteen articles of faith?

5. In what ways has Judaism focused more on culture than on nature?

6. Discuss the significance of celebrating a Sabbath each week.

7. Define exactly the senses in which the Jewish God is *creator* and *redeemer*.

8. Describe the faith of the prophet Jeremiah.

9. What is your impression of Jewish rituals?

10. How has the circumcision ceremony concretized Jewish faith?

11. What are the main religious questions raised by the Holocaust?

12. What has been the significance of the traditional exclusion of women from the Rabbinate and talmudic study?

13. What are the main advantages of a religion's having a clear Torah (divine guidance)?

14. What gives the story of the Baal Shem-Tov's storming heaven its charm?

15. What have been the main sources of anti-Semitism?

Glossary

aggadah: Jewish stories and teaching lore. The aggadah somewhat complements the drier, more precisely legal halakah. In the aggadah Jewish writers gave themselves imaginative license to personalize the biblical stories and draw out pious or moralistic lessons for faith in their days. Aggadah suggests the entertainment value that folk religion usually blends into its teachings, and by its vividness and storied character it made a great impact on the common people, for whom the legal treatises could seem rather abstract and remote.

Ashkenazim: Jews of German origin, who have predominated in Eastern European Jewish culture and contributed most of the founding figures of the modern state of Israel. Although many of the Ashkenazim lived in small villages and close to nature, many others entered fully into the Enlightenment streams of modern European culture as well as into commercial life. This family of Jewry suffered some cultural crisis with the rise of Nazism, because Nazism suggested that cultural sophistication was no guarantee that violent racism and anti-Semitism would not flourish.

cabala: a Jewish mystical movement that flourished during the Middle Ages. The cabalists usually considered themselves faithful followers of the Torah who were developing an esoteric wisdom to complement the esoteric wisdom of the halakic law. In their mystical writings and exercises, the cabalists emphasized the emanations of the divinity into the created world and the marriage of the divinity with the Torah, which gave religious living a nuptial or erotic aspect. Many of the rabbis worried about the gnostic possibilities latent within cabalism, but perhaps equally as many rabbis dipped into the cabalistic lore, often secretly studying such influential texts as the *Zohar*.

covenant: the semicontractual bond between Israel and YHWH, such that Israel would be his people and he would be their God. The Mosaic covenant was influenced by legal treatises of the ancient Near East by which a vassal pledged fealty to an overlord and in turn received protection. The various other biblical covenants—between God and Noah, God and David, God and Adam, and God and Christ (or the Church)— amounted to variations on this theme. Whether God was bound to the covenant regardless of human fidelity was a major question in the Hebrew Bible, while Christian faith has taken the position that the covenant, renewed and reset by the death and resurrection of Christ, is eschatological: accomplished once and for all, by God's grace.

Diaspora: a Jewish term for dispersion or exile from the homeland in Judah. Jews often lived in exile from their holy land following the Babylonian captivity or Exile of the sixth century B.C.E. After 70 C.E., however, when the Romans destroyed the Temple in Jerusalem and ousted the elite, Diaspora life became the norm. Rabbinic Judaism developed the Mishnah, the Gemara, and the Talmud in the Diaspora, the Babylonian Talmud tending to prevail over the Talmud of the land of Palestine. Zionism may be seen as the countermovement through which Judaism tried to overcome the alienations of being dispersed throughout foreign lands, and since the establishment of the modern state of Israel in 1948 the term Diaspora has had less weight, since even those Jews who lived outside Israel (in the free world) easily could visit the homeland.

exegesis: the process of elaborating the meaning of texts. Usually the term refers to biblical texts, but in principle it is applicable to the scriptures of all religions—indeed, to the elucidation of any text. As modern critical method has come to inform both historical and literary analyses of texts, exegesis has moved from rather commonsensical, mystical, and allegorical tendencies toward hermeneutics: trying to determine the meanings intended by the original authors and latent in the text as a somewhat transhistorical entity. Exegetes usually stress knowing the original language in which the text was written, informing oneself about the original historical context, and studying the symbols through which the text seems to be trying to express its assumptions, messages, hopes, and the like.

Exile: the term usually applied to the deportation of many Judeans into Babylon when Judah fell to Babylon in 586 B.C.E. This was a major divide in biblical history, everything before it qualifying as preexilic and everything after (or everything after within the pre-Common Era) qualifying as postexilic. The Exile highlighted the paradoxes of trying to give theological interpretations of history (say what were God's purposes in the Babylonian captivity, as well as the significance of autonomous rule in one's own land for the full flowering of biblical faith). Some of the most profound prophetic poetry of the Bible came from the cauldron of the Exile—parts of the present books of Isaiah, Jeremiah, and Ezekiel.

Exodus: the movement of the Hebrews out from Egypt under the leadership of Moses. This escape from the oppressive rule of the pharaoh was attributed to the intervention of YHWH and later served as the primary evidence for believing in God's will to make Israel his own special people. The Exodus so countered worldly expectations and likelihoods that it seemed a miracle. All of our accounts of it are filtered through later religious experience, so the historical core of the event is unclear, but every year Jews have celebrated the Passover as the memorial of this liberation that launched their peoplehood and the main reason they should continue to believe God would guide their lives. Christians typologized the Exodus, making it a symbol of the general liberation from sin that was accomplished through the death and resurrection of Jesus.

Gemara: comments on and discussion of the Mishnah. Gemara represents a second stage in the evolution of rabbinic Judaism, as the rabbis who gained more and more control during the Diaspora of the early centuries of the Common Era elaborated their views of the oral Law (which they thought had long accompanied the Tanak) and moved from collecting the teachings of the revered early sages (accomplished in the Mishnah) to collecting reflections, additions, and commentaries upon this first stratum of collected oral tradition.

halakah: Jewish legal tradition. The regulations, interpretations, juridical decisions, and the like that have been the backbone of rabbinic religion. Seen as continuing the priestly legislation one finds in such biblical books as Leviticus and Deuteronomy, the halakic works called for a keen memory and developed a particular sort of (religiously) legal mind. Halakah testifies to the priority that behavior or praxis has had in traditional Judaism, where people have been more interested in keeping the customary law than in developing doctrinal innovations. In modern times halakic lawyers have had to face major questions of how to adapt their tradition to a much changed culture and to face the implications of the widespread secularization of the Western cultures in which most Jews have lived.

idolatry: the worship of something less than God as ultimate reality. "Worship" implies giving one's complete loyalty and love. It implies adoration. For the monotheistic religions, the One God alone merits worship and worshiping anything other than the One God is terribly wrong. How purely monotheists in fact have lived and thought is a complicated question. In principle, however, one can see that when people have experienced God as a reality uniquely unlimited, good, and holy they are bound to feel that they can worship no other. Idolatry misleads the human spirit, and so human culture, by fixing it on things unworthy of it—money, pleasure, crude symbols of ultimacy—that are bound to distort it.

Karaism: a movement among Middle Eastern Jews of the eighth to twelfth centuries who rejected oral Torah. The movement was conservative if not puritanical, and it tried to establish the written Torah, above all the five books of Moses, as the sole authority in Jewish life. This directly attacked the power the rabbis had been accumulating, which was based on the legitimacy of claiming that an oral tradition had always accompanied the written Torah. As keepers (interpreters, developers) of this oral tradition, the rabbis claimed the power to legislate how the community ought to eat and drink, marry, and do business. The Karaites wanted greater freedom from this rabbinic authority, but mainly so as to impose their own more literalist sense that God's will was more concisely and clearly laid out in the written Torah.

kibbutz: a collective, often agricultural, settlement in Israel. The kibbutz movement usually partook of both an attachment to the land (Zionism as nostalgia for the promised land) and socialist convictions about how people would best prosper (spiritually, if not materially) by living in cooperatives, sharing child rearing and manual labor, and creating a community life that treasured learning, the arts, and other aspects of higher culture. Some of the kibbutzim were religious, but many were not. On the religious kibbutzim, orthodox or even fundamentalist views tended to prevail, one of the customary ideas being that when the Torah was fully observed in the ancestral land Jews would have the best possible chance to realize the potential of their chosenness.

kosher: fit, proper, suitable according to Jewish law. Kosher especially applied to dietary matters, but more broadly regarded actions, ideas, and moral habits that were considered consonant with the Torah. The dietary laws appear to have developed from a combination of ancient ideas about what was hygienic (apt to promote health and discourage disease) and what was fitting or normal in nature itself—for example, separating dairy and meat foods. Kosher observance became a badge of Jewishness in many periods, serving to demarcate Jews from gentiles and helping to preserve the purity of the chosen people. Probably more Jews kept the laws for this reason than out of any strong sense that certain foods were intrinsically unclean or that God from all eternity had wanted housewives to need two sets of dishes.

Messiah: the anointed king that Jews have awaited as their deliverer since the late biblical era. The present scholarly consensus is that the prophetic allusions to the Messiah had in mind an earthly leader on the model of David and did not foresee Jesus Christ, but any such judgment entails theological preconceptions about the nature of the Bible. For Christians many of the messianic passages seemed fulfilled in the life, death, and resurrection of Jesus, especially the songs of Second Isaiah about the suffering servant of YHWH. Jews probably thought of this figure as a corporate personality, standing for Israel as a whole, but Christians understandably found the passages anticipatory of what happened to Jesus. Thus, in their polemics with Jews, the early Christians argued typologically, trying to show that what had been prophesied about the Messiah had been fulfilled. The Gospels are strongly colored by this way of thinking, especially the Gospel of Matthew.

mikvah: the Jewish ritual bath. Visiting the *mikvah* became one of several Jewish rites of cleansing and purification, complementary to the kosher laws and the laws for observing the Sabbath. Women had the obligation to visit the *mikvah* at the end of their menstrual period, to help divide the times when sexual intercourse was illicit and licit. Men tended to visit the *mikvah* at times of the religious calendar when purification was encouraged. Although Judaism did not develop so strong a notion of human sinfulness as what developed in some branches of Christianity, it retained from its biblical lawyers the sense that one was to approach God with clean hands and a clean heart. The ritual bath, then, was more symbolic than physical (although in ancient and medieval times the physical washing could be culturally distinctive), the main idea being a "baptismal" renewal.

minyan: the quorum of ten needed for Jewish worship. Traditionally the ten had to be men, but recently some branches of Judaism have allowed women to be counted. The ten would be sought both for daily worship or study in the synagogue and for such memorial prayer sessions as sitting shivah for a person recently deceased. The minyan had the effect of specifying the social character of Jewish study and prayer, since official worship had a minimal number and a few scattered individuals would not suffice.

Mishnah: the collection of Jewish learning formalized by rabbis in the Diaspora around 200 C.E. The Mishnah was the first compilation of the oral tradition that had been building since the Second Temple period, and it became the core of the Talmud. The Gemara, which collected commentaries on the Mishnah, plus the Mishnah itself, yielded the Talmud. The interest of the mishnaic teachers was relatively practical, as they divided Jewish reality into different tractates and discoursed on how relationships ideally would be. For example, in the tractate on women they discussed especially the transitions that ought to occur when a woman passed from her father to her husband at marriage or when she passed from marriage to widowhood.

mitzvah: a Jewish commandment; a scriptural or rabbinic injunction. A mitzvah also could take on the connotation of a good deed—something commanded or required because it would bring good. In the Jewish community one struggled to become full of good deeds, not only by obeying the 613 commandments (for men) but also by helping the poor, feeding the hungry, teaching the ignorant, and the like.

monotheism: holding for only one God, who becomes the ultimate source, goal, and treasure of creation. Pure monotheisms are hard to find, but certain strands of biblical religion seem motivated by a genuine insight into the Oneness of a truly transcendent God, as does much of the Qur'an. The experience underlying monotheism is bound to be ineffable, and most monotheisms suffer when cast into doctrinal form, because the doctrines tend to ossify and suggest that one can map the sole deity comprehensively. Thus the mystical dimensions of the monotheisms have the constant task of calling adherents back to the wellsprings, while the metaphysical dimensions have the constant task of reminding people that the being of a truly monotheistic deity has to be of another order than anything people can grasp—indeed, that it has to be the creator of everything else from nothingness. Judaism, Christianity, and Islam all claim to be monotheistic, and in their high traditions no doubt have been. But in their little traditions, where saints and sprites have frolicked, they have been closer to the supposedly polytheistic traditions (Hinduism, Shinto) than many of their theologians have admitted.

Pharisees: Jews of the late Second Temple period who defended the oral Torah and tried to update it. The Pharisaic party triumphed after the Diaspora of the first century C.E., making them a fairly direct link to the rabbinic religion that generated the Talmud and dominated Judaism in the common era. The Pharisees usually are described as a lay group, much concerned for fidelity to the precepts of the Torah, and somewhat distant from the Temple that was the center of priestly, ritualistic Judaism. The portrait of the Pharisees in the New Testament is colored by Jewish-Christian polemics and cannot be considered objective in its charges of hypocrisy.

prophet: a spokesperson for God or a divinity. The prophet is one who delivers the divine message, sometimes quite unwillingly. For the classical biblical prophets, the divine message (Word) came as an inrush of understanding and will they could not avoid, much though they might have wished to. Prophets in other contexts deliver oracles at local shrines or speak to the people about the fate they feel is soon to arrive. Muhammad, for instance, preached a coming judgment, as had Zoroaster, John the Baptist, Isaiah, and Jesus. Popularly, prophets have been pictured as able to foretell the future, but usually the sharper import of their message has been a judgment on present times as being out of kilter with divine ethical standards.

rabbi: a Jewish title for teacher or master, most often applied to those who focused on the oral Law. The rabbinic movement shows ties to the priestly circles that were involved in the formulation of biblical law, and during the Second Temple period, after the return from Exile, the focus of much Jewish piety seems to have shifted from ritual to Law and wisdom. Torah exfoliated as the precepts whose following allowed one to keep the covenant well, and the rabbis became revered as the teachers of what would keep the chosen people worthy of their special election. They became the arbiters of how to interpret the Law, adjusting it to varying cases, and from their decisions, obiter dicta, and stories came the talmudic literature that has been the backbone of Judaism in the common era.

sabbath: a day set aside for worship; the Jewish day of worship. The origins of the tradition of making a sabbath are obscure, but biblical Judaism correlated its sabbatical traditions with the account of creation in Genesis, encoding the notion of a seventh day of rest in the foundations of the cosmos. Keeping a sabbath means maintaining a fence against this-worldly preoccupations, and so it may be seen as a line of sacrality delimiting secularity. By insisting that work is not all, and that worship, play, and recreation have their rights, traditional peoples have kept supple the imagination, feelings, and muscles necessary to fit human beings to the rhythms of nature and defend them against both overwork and a loss of wonder.

Sadducees: an ancient Jewish party of priests and upper-class members who were associated with the Jerusalem Temple and stressed the written Torah. Their main opponents for influence during the Second Temple period were the Pharisees, who were mainly laity and approved the oral Torah that explicated the scriptures. The Sadducees disappeared after the fall of the Jerusalem Temple in 70 C.E. They are presented in the New Testament as denying the notion of a resurrection and agreeing with the Roman establishment that Jesus was a threat to security in Judea.

Sephardim: Jews of Hispanic or Iberian cultural background. The Sephardim established a glorious civilization in medieval Iberia, and the expulsion of the Jews from Spain in 1492 was a trauma so great it led many cabalists to expect the coming of the Messiah. The Sephardim suffered greatly from the Inquisition, and after their expulsion from Spain many went into the Turkish Empire, which they hoped would be more benign than the Christian. Sephardim often are contrasted with Ashkenazim, who adapted Jewish culture to a Germanic and Eastern European subsoil. The two families shared most articles of faith, holidays, and law codes, but their different cultural complexes colored everything somewhat differently.

Shema: the Jewish proclamation of God's unity based on Deuteronomy 6:4–9. The Shema has served as an epitome of Jewish faith, reminding believers that they are covenanted to the unique deity responsible for the creation of the world and the guidance of history. Their relation to this God ought to be one of wholehearted love, and they have the obligation to make this God the focus of the education they give their children, the culture they develop, and all the distinctive features of their community life. The Shema could stand in contrast to the many laws of the rabbis' Torah, but usually it was considered their digest and pulse. The call to "hear" implied listening, to the divine or prophetic or rabbinic word. It also implied obedience and loyalty, as well as a regular effort to remember the great things

God had done for his chosen people, especially the victory of the Exodus and the gift of the promised land.

synagogue: a Jewish house of assembly, study, and prayer. The term, like the Christian term *church,* implies both a building and a congregation. The historical origins of the synagogue are not fully known, but it seems likely that after the destruction of the Temple of Solomon and the deportation of many Jews to Babylon in the sixth century B.C.E., the custom of gathering for common study and prayer gained momentum. The synagogue rather naturally gave rise to the rabbinic movement, in that it emphasized study of the tradition, focused in the Torah, more than ritualistic sacrifice. Following the Diaspora of 70 C.E., the synagogue became the major Jewish institution, although archaeological remains suggest that synagogues varied considerably in their architecture and their degree of involvement in the movement that led to the Mishnah, the Talmud, and the rabbinic hegemony over Judaism.

Talmud: the primary source of Jewish law and focus of rabbinic learning, composed of the Mishnah and the Gemara. The Talmud was probably virtually complete around 500 C.E. and existed in at least two important versions, that from Babylon and that from Palestine. It collected teachings, opinions, and decisions of rabbis concerned with continuing the tradition of the oral law—the ongoing interpretation of the Mosaic Torah. As talmudic scholarship grew throughout the Middle Ages, the talmudic texts became an encyclopedia of Jewish learning—science, linguistics, and theology, in addition to halakic theory. A traditional Jewish education was based on the Talmud, and it inculcated a good memory, a concern for legal precedent, a willingness to weigh authorities against one another, and a realization that interpretation was intrinsic to the Jewish experiences of both scripture and God. Modernist Jews challenged talmudic authority, but to the present day the Talmud continues to be a conduit of ongoing Jewish religious development. Partly because of the variety of opinions enfolded in the Talmud, Judaism has tended to sponsor considerable doctrinal freedom and to consider behavior a more crucial index of faith than theology.

Torah: Jewish Guidance, Revelation, or Law. The Torah came from God, most inaugurally to Moses. It was developed by successors of Moses, reaching the literary form of Tanak: Torah (Pentateuch), Prophets, and Writings. The rabbis insisted that an oral Torah had always accompanied the written Torah—tradition to interpret the scriptures. The Talmud codified many of the rabbinic opinions, and after the Talmud further rabbinic writings amplified the teachings of the Talmud. Thus Torah is a fluid concept, having stricter and broader denotations. Some rabbinic speculation thought of the Torah as eternal, having existed alongside God when he created and being something God himself loved to contemplate. Thus the study of Torah became the centerpiece of rabbinic Judaism, sometimes even more important than prayer.

Zionism: the Jewish movement to establish a homeland in Palestine. Zionism has biblical roots, from the time that Israel gained a land of its own centered on Mount Zion in Jerusalem. During the Exile Jews longed to be back in their promised land, where they alone could sing their native songs joyously. The Diaspora that occurred in the first century C.E. made nostalgia for Zion and the Western Wall that symbolized the Temple ingredient in all Jewish culture. During the nineteenth century Jews led by Theodor Herzl (1860–1904) began practical movements to resettle Palestine, which came to climax in the establishment of the modern state of Israel in 1948. The aftermath of the Second World War, and the sufferings that Jews had endured in the Holocaust (as the climax of centuries of anti-Semitism in Europe) had made conditions ripe. Recently bitter discussions have arisen about Zionist ideology, while the ties between Zionism and such doctrines as chosenness and the gift of the promised land continue to beg clarification.

Zohar: a prime text of Jewish cabalism. The *Zohar* probably was written by Moses de León in thirteenth-century Spain. Known as the "Book of Splendor," it consists of imaginative contemplations of the emanations of the divinity through the different layers of creation. The *Zohar* stimulated many mystics, Hasidim, and even orthodox rabbis to view creation as shot through with sparks of the divine seeking to return to God in redemption. It supported the notion that God is metaphysically married to the Torah and that the splendor of God *(Shekina)* is a nuptial entity that sets sexual complementarity and love at the center of the heavenly realities.

CHAPTER 5

CHRISTIANITY

Cross of Christ

If we gather all its parts, Christianity is the largest religion in the world. What began as a Jewish sect has carried its version of the Torah and prophecy around the globe.[1] We begin our study of Christianity by describing its history.

HISTORY

Jesus

Christianity developed from the life and work of Jesus of Nazareth,[2] as Buddhism developed from the life and work of Gautama. Jesus (whose historical reality is attested to by such non-Christian authors as Josephus, Tacitus, Suetonius, and Pliny the Younger) was born about 4 B.C.E. (by current calendars) in Palestine. It is likely that "Jehsus," a Greek form, derives from the Hebrew "Yeshua," which means "savior." We know little about his youth except through Gospel stories, such as those of his circumcision and his dialogues with religious teachers. (The stories of his birth are probably legendary, in the service of the various New Testament authors' theologies.[3]) One may assume that he grew up as a Jewish youth of his times. About the year 27 C.E. he started from his native Galilee on a career as an itinerant preacher. Geza Vermes has described the contemporary political and religious context, suggesting that Jesus was a preacher and healer on the model of the Jewish *hasid* (pious one) familiar to his time and locale.[4]

While Jesus' message has been interpreted in very different ways, certain essentials seem quite clear. Joachim Jeremias's careful study argues that Jesus' own voice echoes in the New Testament parables, riddles, discussions of the reign of God, the peculiar use of *amen,* and the peculiar use of *Abba* (Father) for God.[5] On etymological and historical grounds, these are the safest leads to how Jesus himself preached (with concrete, lively language) and to what he had to say (that a new time was dawning and that God is intimately parental). In their admirable digest of Christian theology, Rahner and Vorgrimler state that Jesus' main theme was an announcement that the reign of God was at hand in his (Jesus') own person.[6] That reign or kingdom was a new beginning, a time of justice and holiness.

According to the New Testament writers, this theme meant that Jesus had fulfilled Jewish religion and superseded it, making a new covenant with God. Jesus himself solicited a radical commitment to the

Christianity: Twenty-five Key Dates	
ca. 30 C.E.	*Death of Jesus of Nazareth*
ca. 65	*Death of Apostle Paul*
ca. 95	*Last of New Testament Writings*
ca. 100–165	*Justin Martyr, Leading Apologist*
ca. 185–254	*Origen, Leading Theologian*
313	*Christians Freed of Legal Persecution*
325	*First Council of Nicaea*
354–430	*Augustine, Leading Theologian*
451	*Council of Chalcedon*
ca. 480–550	*Benedict, Founder of Western Monasticism*
ca. 540–604	*Pope Gregory I, Founder of Medieval Papacy*
787	*Second Council of Nicaea (Last One That the Orthodox Church Considers Ecumenical)*
869–870	*Rome Declares Photius in Schism*
1054	*Mutual Anathemas between Rome and Constantinople*
1096–1099	*First Crusade*
1225–1274	*Thomas Aquinas, Leading Theologian*
1369–1415	*John Hus, Bohemian Reformer*
1517	*Luther's Ninety-five Theses*
1509–1564	*John Calvin, Leading Theologian*
1545–1563	*Council of Trent*
1620	*Mayflower Compact of the Pilgrims*
1703–1791	*John Wesley, Founder of Methodism*
1869–1870	*First Vatican Council*
1910	*Beginning of Protestant Ecumenical Movement*
1962–1965	*Second Vatican Council*

KEY CHRISTIAN DOCTRINES	
Trinity	God as a community of knowing and loving Father (unbegotten), Son (begotten), Spirit (breath of divine love)
Christology	Jesus one integral being, fully human and fully divine
Grace	Communication of divine life Strength to overcome sin Divine favor and forgiveness
Sin	Freely chosen evil Absence of divine life
Church	Body of Christ Community of disciples
Eschatology	Divine judgment Heaven and hell
Scripture	Word of God Norm for Church

new opportunities that God's reign offered, which included intimacy with God and friendship with other people. The morality that Jesus anticipated in the kingdom[7] is most graphic in his Sermon on the Mount. There the evangelists have him bless those who are poor, gentle, mourning, hungry, and thirsty for what is right, merciful, pure in heart, peacemaking, and suffering for the cause of justice. They are the citizens of the kingdom; dispositions or circumstances like theirs render human beings open to divine love. The gist of Jesus' own life, according to the New Testament, was just such love.

Information on Jesus' public life and ministry remains imprecise (because of the limited sources). Apparently he linked his work with that of John the Baptist, his message raised opposition from the religious establishment, he worked out only some of the particulars for living in the kingdom, and he predicted woe to those who rejected his program. Furthermore, he planted at least the seeds of the Christian Church by gathering disciples and co-workers, and he gained a reputation as a healer. His death

came by order of the Roman procurator Pontius Pilate on the dubious grounds that he threatened the peace.

Interpretations. Beyond this bare outline, historical and theological interpretations diverge. Indeed, all of the Gospels are theological interpretations of Jesus, developed in the light of at least a generation's worth of the Christian community's experience of faith, of controversies with Jews who did not accept Jesus as the Messiah, and of efforts to explain the significance of Jesus to gentiles. According to the New Testament and the orthodox faith of later centuries, the old reign of Satan and sin died with Jesus. Furthermore, after death Jesus was raised (***resurrected***) and was disclosed to be "Lord" or ruler of humanity. More tersely, Jesus was the divine Son whose dying and rising brought the world ***salvation***. The traditional interpretation thus stresses a twofold quality in Jesus: He was both human and divine. The church councils that specifically discussed and defined Jesus' being found this interpretation to be the intent of the Gospel and Epistle writers, who in turn considered themselves interpreters of the Hebrew Bible.

Another interpretation of Jesus found in the New Testament is that he was the Messiah—the anointed king of the age of grace which Judaism had long been anticipating, where *grace* came to mean not just peace and material plenty but intimacy with God and sharing in divine life. From the titles that the New Testament gives to Jesus, his own reported claims, and the miracles (healings, raisings from the dead, and so on) that the New Testament attributes to Jesus, we can conclude that the New Testament writers found him most remarkable—so remarkable that he had to be more than human. For them he was the bringer of salvation,[8] God's Word incarnate, the Christ (Messiah), and the divine Son.

In the earliest portions of the New Testament, the Pauline Epistles, Jesus is a living spiritual reality. The assumption behind Paul's directions for Church life, for instance, is that "the Lord" lives in Christians' midst. After Jesus' death, his followers apparently thought that his movement was finished, but the events of the resurrection convinced them that he had assumed a new form of existence. They stayed together in Jerusalem; at Pentecost (fifty days after Passover, when Jesus had died), they experienced what they called the Holy Spirit, whom they thought Jesus and the Father had sent. The Spirit charged them to go out and preach about Jesus. Thus, the early Christians proclaimed that Jesus' life and death were the definitive act of salvation. The disciples also preached that Jesus was the Messiah. As such he was in accordance with Jewish tradition and yet responsible for its transformation. From a historical perspective, then, the first Christians appear as sectarian Jews—Jews with a new interpretation of messianism. The early Christians thought of themselves as the new Israel because they thought that Jesus had brought, and the old Israel had rejected, the kingdom of God sought by Jewish messianic expectation.

It took some time for the first interpretations of Jesus to sift out and clarify, and a principal catalyst in that process was Paul. From the accounts in Acts and his own writings, Paul was a Pharisaic Jew whose conversion on the road to Damascus (Acts 9:3–9) was quite dramatic. After his conversion he tried to show his fellow Jews that Jesus was their Messiah, but their opposition to his preaching, plus his own further reflection on Jesus' life and death, led Paul to think that in Jesus God had opened the covenant to all people—gentiles as well as Jews.

Consequently, Paul made the *gospel* (good news) about Jesus a transformation of the Torah. Because God had fulfilled in Jesus the intent of the Law, the Law's many detailed prescriptions were passé. Adherence to an external code could not make one righteous (acceptable to God). Only by opening to God's love and healing could one stand before him acceptably. Paul called that opening "faith." For him, Jesus was the agent of a shift from the Torah to the gospel, from works to faith. The way to become right with God was to commit oneself to Jesus. Thus, for Paul, Jesus himself represented the kingdom, embodied God's grace. As Paul's vision spread, he saw Jesus' transition from death to life as the climax of salvation history. Jesus the Christ was a new Adam, a new beginning for the human race. All who clung to him, who used him to interpret their lives, became members of his "body." Christ and the Church formed a living entity.

Paul's interpretation of Jesus was the key to early Christianity's developing into a universal religion. By dropping the requirements of the Jewish Law and extending membership to all who would base their lives on Jesus, the early Church broke with Judaism irreparably. In the beginning some followers of Jesus ("Judaizers") had urged keeping the precepts of the Jewish Torah, but they lost out. The Torah had been the cornerstone of covenantal life. Most Jews, understandably, were not willing to throw the Torah over or enter a new covenant. Some who had seen Jesus heal or heard him preach joined his cause; the apostles who began the church after Jesus' death, for instance, were Jews who journeyed from the Torah to the gospel. However, most Jews had not heard or seen Jesus, and for historical, psychological, political, and religious reasons they could not accept the claims about him.

The gentiles who warmed to the gospel lived in a Hellenistic milieu that was ripe for salvation.[9] Just as Judaism was in turmoil, with Zealots, Pharisees, Sadducees, and Essenes all urging different reactions to Roman rule, so, too, were the belief systems of the gentiles. Through the mystery religions, Gnosticism, and philosophy, a large number of gentiles were pursuing salvation avidly. Jesus as a savior figure fit many of their needs. In a short while, Christianity established itself as a new wisdom, or *gnosis* (secret knowledge), too. It offered fulfillment in this life, immortality in a world to come.

A New World View. As a result of the gospel and Paul's theology, within a generation of Jesus' death Jewish and Greek thought had combined into a powerful new world view.[10] From Judaism came the concepts of prophet and messiah. From Hellenism came the notions of savior and god. In the Church's hands, they all were considerably developed. Jesus was the successor to Moses, the giver of a new Law, Daniel's Son of man come to inaugurate the messianic age, the conqueror of death and disorder, and the *Logos* (Word) of eternal divinity come into time. He was alpha and omega—the beginning and the end. All past history, from the first parent Adam, had been but a preparation for his coming. All of the future would unfold his implications, climaxing in a final judgment and a fulfillment in heaven.

At first the Christians expected the future to be short. Jesus would soon return in power and glory to consummate his work. As the years went by, the beliefs shifted. Jesus had accomplished the essentials of salvation through his death and resurrection. However long it took in God's dispensation for Jesus' salvation to work itself out, there was no doubt of the final success. The faithful would just have to endure. Living in faith and hope, they were to preach the good news to all whom they could reach.

Case Study: Jesus' Parables.   One of the main reasons Jesus has remained fresh for each generation of his followers is that the New Testament authors set down some of Jesus' lively teaching stories, his parables. Puzzling, enigmatic, and vivid, these parables have drawn the attention of preachers and audiences through all the Christian centuries. Today the parables have become a favorite topic of scholarly discussion. We can only hint at the main lines of this discussion, but studying one of Jesus' parables, that of the Great Supper (Matt. 22:1–10; Luke 14:16–24), will take us a few steps into what New Testament scholars are currently conjecturing about Jesus' own outlook.

As a background to our consideration of the parable of the Great Supper, let us first note the tendency of current New Testament scholars to emphasize the parables' underlying conviction of God's oneness. Believing in their bones that God was an absolute mystery, the sole power responsible for all of creation, the authors of the parables (Jesus and the writers who set them in their New Testament form) instinctively used a paradoxical speech, through which they might hint at God's transcendence—God's overspilling of all human conceptual containers. The parables imply that God cannot be captured in any single set of images. The best way to indicate the divine nature is to juxtapose stories that flash forth now one, now another aspect of what God seems to be like.

Moreover, some of Jesus' parables opposed the assumption of some of his contemporaries that the only way righteous people could experience the rule of God would be through a dramatic, even cosmic, overturning of the prevailing political patterns, so that the sinners presently in charge would be thrown out. Not so, Jesus' preaching suggested. God does not need earthquakes or revolutions. The reign of God is subtler, and more powerful, than any prevailing political or religious conditions. No matter how bad the times, one could always find something of God in them.

For Jesus, God was always active, always reaching out to people in need. It required no more than common human experience to find the arena of God's actions. There was no need for aggression or technical training. "Even Jesus' way of speaking is nonaggressive and avoids setting up barriers between people. But this way of speaking has a powerful edge; the forgiveness and reconciliation imaged is demanded for everyone's life. The holiness appropriate to the rule of God belongs to all."[11]

Applied to Jesus' liking for parables, this attitude meant a calm "take it or leave it." A parable was an invitation to enter the world of Jesus' Father, to open oneself to Jesus' sense of what God was doing. It was not an oppressive command. The parable of the Great Supper suggests that one could meet Jesus and not even realize that this was the most important encounter of one's life. Jesus would not beat his hearers over the head. God would not flash forth lightning or bellow thunder. The Kingdom of God was in people's midst. To find it they had only to turn around and open themselves to Jesus' good news.

The parable itself tells of a man (or a king) who once gave a great banquet. Deciding to throw this feast, he sent his servants to announce it to those he wanted to invite. The servants told the invitees, "Come, for all is now ready." But the invitees began to make excuses. Not sensing the significance of the invitation, they told the servants such lame tales as "I have bought a field and I must go take a look at it," or "I have bought five yoke of oxen, and I must go examine them," or "I have just gotten married, so I cannot come." (However, Deuteronomy 20:5–7 and 24:5 suggest that these may traditionally have been considered legitimate excuses.) In each case, they asked to be excused.

The man hosting the banquet got very angry. In Matthew's version, the invitees had treated the man's servants shamefully, even killing them, so the man (who was a king) sent his troops to destroy the murderers and burn their city. In Luke's milder account, the host simply told his servants to go out into the streets and lanes of the city and bring in the most wretched people they could find: the poor, the maimed, the blind, and the lame. When the servants came back to report that they had done this and that there still was room in the banquet hall, the host told them to go out again, this time into the highways and hedges, and make people come in, until the banquet hall was completely full. Those whom he had first invited had shown themselves unworthy of the banquet, but one way or another he would have his house filled.

For Matthew, the story is an occasion to indulge in a bit of allegory. By playing up the theme of the king's punishment of the invitees' bad treatment of the servants, he can allude to the Roman destruction of Jerusalem in 70 C.E., which perhaps he saw as a retribution for the slaying of Jesus. Luke, on the other hand, presents a simpler plot line, and he is more interested in the redoubling of the host's invitation than in any rejection and punishment. Where Matthew makes an irreparable break between the king and the original guests, Luke passes over this relation, allowing the possibility that it might mend. Accenting the good fortune of the new invitees, he stresses that they are an unlikely group, outcasts and strangers. For Luke, the drama lies in the host's seizing the occasion of the original invitees' (the Jews') refusal or inability to come and making it a chance to be generous to another class of people. Thus, when most Jews rejected Jesus' message, God offered the gospel to the gentiles. In the background of the New Testament's use of the parable is the bitterness between Jews who had accepted Jesus (become Christians) and those who had rejected him.

Although they tend to stress the literary structure of the evangelists' different accounts, today's scholars do not neglect the historical or theological dimensions of the parables. For example, they point out that Jewish lore contemporary with Jesus had a story that praised a tax collector for doing one good deed during his (otherwise hateful) life: inviting some poor people to a banquet when the original guests did not come. Similarly, research into the social customs of Jesus' day has revealed a tendency in sophisticated Jewish circles to invite people twice. Important people, at least, did not take seriously a single invitation but had to have their egos stroked a second time. One of the rabbis used a person dressed and ready to go by the time of a second invitation as an example of wisdom,

while a person not ready to go by the time of a second invitation, and so excluded from the good time, became an example of foolishness.

Moreover, by choosing the figure of a banquet, both Jesus and the gospel writers inevitably conjured up the messianic time. In the messianic time, when Israel's deliverer had come, Jewish tradition said the people would eat and drink joyously, banqueting together. It may be stretching the original intent of the parable to make it a full symbol of the messianic or heavenly time, as later Christian preachers often have, but the figure itself was bound to suggest inclusion in the occasion of celebrating God's victory or exclusion from it. If one stresses the confrontational side of the invitation and rejection, as Matthew does, one develops a rather harsh, judgmental view of Jesus' messiahship and the invitation to join the Christian community. The understated version of Luke simply hints at what a human situation—a generous host's disappointment that the people he first invited could not come—can reveal about God's ingenuity and goodness. Undaunted, the host finds new outlets for his largess.

Behind Matthew's harsher version probably lie the bitter experiences of the early Christian missionaries, who were confused and hurt that their proclamation of Jesus' good news brought them persecution rather than gratitude. However, this harsh attitude seems to contradict Jesus' own tendencies, which were to keep contact with people, avoid unnecessary ruptures, and find creative alternatives to strategies that had run into dead ends. Behind Jesus' own mission there seems to have lain a rather constant goodwill. If the members of the establishment were not interested in his message, there were always the crowds on society's margins. If the Jews proved intractable, there were always the Samaritans and the gentiles. Jesus may not have worked all this out into an explicit theology of his mission, but it seems latent in his regular style. For all that he seems to have been disappointed by the stupidity and hardness of heart he encountered, he kept speaking provocatively of the Kingdom of God, always hoping he would come upon a few people whom God's Spirit had prepared to accept his words.

In Luke's version of the parable, the social implications of the gospel also are important. It is no accident that the outcasts come into the banquet hall. Luke sees the good news of the Kingdom as especially intended for those people who have little other good news in their lives: the poor, the sick, the despised. At the least, his parable implies, those who have received much from God should share it generously with people less fortunate. The host who insists that his banquet not go to waste should be a role model for Christians.

In recent years, excavations at Nag-Hammadi in Egypt have made available to New Testament scholars gnostic versions of the gospel (see below) that they can compare with the canonical four *Gospels*. The Gospel of Thomas, for example, has a version of the parable of the Great Supper that is quite spare, more like Luke's than Matthew's account. Interestingly, however, the Gospel of Thomas makes several of the original invitees excuse themselves for monetary reasons. Thus one man has some merchants coming the evening of the banquet to pay him money they owe, while another man has bought some property and must go to collect the rent. When the host hears these excuses, he tells his servants to go into the streets and bring back whomever they find. The conclusion of the story is ominous: "The buyers and the merchants shall not come into the places of my Father." Not only does this conclusion make Jesus pass stern judgment on those who reject the invitation, it also castigates business (and by implication all this-worldly affairs) as incompatible with the Kingdom of Heaven.

Overall, the parables remain an absorbing topic for study. Because they stand so close to Jesus' own way of thinking and preaching, they offer some of the best keys to Jesus' intriguing personality. But the parables seldom admit of a clear-cut interpretation, any more than Jesus' other teachings or actions do. They contain so many different levels, possible allusions, and strata of metaphors that one is finally forced to leave off analyzing them and let them make a more synthetic, holistic impact. When one does this, it seems clear that Jesus, like many Eastern gurus, was a man filled with lively speech, because he was a man filled with God's presence, pregnant with God's love. The Word of God had burned so deeply into his soul that all his human words sizzled and warmed.

The Early Centuries

The gospel writers—Mark, Matthew, Luke, and John—all interpreted the life of Jesus.[12] Even in the most journalistic portions of the New Testament, they have cast Jesus' sayings and doings in terms of their own theologies. Matthew, for instance, works largely with Jewish notions, trying to show that Jesus is the successor to Moses, the gospel is the successor to the Torah, and so on. The other Gospels, as well as the Epistle to the Hebrews and the Book of Revelation, are similarly theological. John arranges Jesus' public life around a series of signs giving him a sacramental glow and making him a thaumaturgist (wonder worker). The second half of John's Gospel concentrates on Jesus' "glory": his intimacy with the heavenly Father and his victorious death and resurrection. Hebrews tries to show that Jesus fulfilled Jewish types of sacrifice, while Revelation is a Christian *apocalypse* (disclosure) designed to shore up faith against Roman persecution.

By the end of the first century, then, the Church had a variety of theologies. The majority were extensions of Jewish religion in the light of Jesus as the Messiah. The "apostolic age" is the period that elaborated what Jesus meant and how the Church was to organize itself. It embraces roughly the period from the death of Jesus (ca. 30 C.E.) to the last decades of the first century. A central concern in both those years and the next centuries was authority. For the early Church, an *apostolos* was a person to whom God had delegated Church authority. The term depended on the Jewish notion of *saliah*—a Hebrew legal term that meant "the authoritative representation of an individual or group in juridical or legal matters."[13]

During Jesus' ministry, his twelve intimates were the *apostles* par excellence, since they had received their commission from Jesus himself. Clearly the Twelve formed a collegial group with Peter as their head,[14] and the Church accepted their authority. However, balancing this apostolic, "official" authority was a looser, *charismatic* leadership expressed through prophecy, teaching, speaking in tongues, and so on.

The earliest Church preaching was intended to show that Jesus fulfilled the promises of Jewish scripture. In their teaching, the first apostles relied on oral tradition about Jesus' person and words. The first great problem in the apostolic age, as we saw, was the Pauline (pertaining to Paul) problem of opening the Church to the gentiles.

During the second century the leadership of the Church passed from those who had seen Jesus themselves to those who had received the gospel from eyewitnesses but had not themselves known the Lord. The "Fathers" who led the second-century Church are therefore apostolic in the sense that they had direct contact with the Twelve. One of the apostolic fathers was Clement of Rome, whom tradition calls the successor to Peter as leader of the Christian community in Rome. Clement wrote an epistle in the style of Paul that called for Church unity. Another early Father, Hermas, wrote a pastoral piece that called for tight moral discipline. Ignatius of Antioch wrote several letters about keeping faith in the face of martyrdom. These three apostolic writers and other writers from the early second century[15] reveal something of the young Church's internal and external problems. Internally, keeping discipline was obviously a major difficulty. As Christ's return was delayed, human weaknesses and individualism asserted themselves. Externally, from the time of Nero (54–68) the Church was ever liable to persecution by the Roman authorities.

A celebrated non-Christian source describing the situation early in the second century is a letter written by the Roman Pliny the Younger, governor of Bithynia south of the Black Sea, to the emperor Trajan about 112. Romans had executed some Christians (their faith seemed incompatible with the pledge of loyalty to Caesar that Rome required), and Pliny described the Christians' religious activities, to give the emperor the information necessary to ascertain what sort of a threat they really were. According to the letter, the Christians would gather before dawn one day a week, sing hymns to a certain "Chrestus" whom they treated as a god, and take an oath to abstain from crime. Then they would end their meeting with a common meal. Trajan answered that if other Christians would recant and "worship our gods," Pliny might pardon them. Clearly the Roman authorities of the time worried about secret societies that might sow seeds of revolution. Since the Romans looked on religion as the bond of their realm, they were especially sensitive to groups who did not worship the traditional Roman deities.

Christians expanded throughout the Roman Empire during the second and third centuries. By 300 they probably constituted the majority population in Asia Minor and Carthage, and they were at least a noticeable fraction of the population along the northern shore of the Mediterranean. Their major political problem, gaining sufferance from the Roman authorities, was not solved until Constantine came to power early in the fourth century.

Gnosticism.   More potentially destructive than Rome were the gnostic heresies. Their teachings varied considerably, but their common element was heterodox Judaism under the influence of Hellenistic and Iranian thought. In essence most *Gnosticism* involved a dualistic mythology. Matter, the negative principle, came from a Demiurge—a subordinate divinity whom the Father God begot as Wisdom but who fell from grace. Divinity itself was a *pleroma* (fullness) of times and

levels. Gnosticism offered a revelation to certain "elect" persons: If they would hate this lower world of material creation (which was under the fallen Demiurge) and believe in a higher spiritual and divine realm, they might return to glory with God.

To explain their revelation, the Gnostics taught that each of the elect had a hidden spark from God's eternal world. The sparks fell into matter because of a heavenly war between darkness and light (or, in other versions, because of an accident during the production of the divine emanations). The jealous, inferior god who clumsily fashioned the material realm, which is subject to time and fate, was born in the same accidental process. He was the author of carnal humanity, in which the divine spark was a prisoner. Higher beings would one day dissolve this fallen world, but in the meantime they called to people's hidden sparks by means of saviors, revelations, and rites of baptism.[16]

Gnosticism blended the Hellenistic notion of divine emanation, mystery religion notions about salvation through sacramental rites, and Jewish notions of *sin* and *redemption*. It stressed the division between this world and heaven, the evil of matter and the flesh, and the need for asceticism (celibacy and bodily discipline) to gain freedom from matter. Valentinus is the most celebrated gnostic teacher, but we know his system largely through the apostolic father Irenaeus, whose influential *Against Heresies* attacked it harshly.

Other Challenges.   Other threats to Christianity during the early period included the prophecies of Marcion, Montanus, and Mani, as well as Ebionism (an effort to restrict the understanding of Jesus to Jewish categories).[17] Marcion was a Christian excommunicate who maintained that the Christian gospel is wholly a matter of love rather than a matter of law. On that account, he completely rejected the Old Testament (Jewish scripture), finding the God of Genesis incompatible with the God of Jesus. Montanus led a heretical apocalyptic movement based on the primacy of the Holy Spirit. His followers expected the outpouring of the Holy Spirit on the Church. In its own prophets, Montanism saw the beginnings of the bestowal of the Spirit. Montanism developed an impressive asceticism, and it captured the estimable African thinker Tertullian, who found it more spiritual than Christianity under the discipline of Rome.

Mani lived from about 215 to 275 in Persia and India (to which he fled from Zoroastrian persecution).

His system supposed a primeval conflict between light and darkness, and it, too, stressed asceticism. The object of Manicheanism was to release the particles of light that Satan had stolen and placed in the human brain. Buddha, the Israelite prophets, Jesus, and Mani himself were the messengers whom God had sent to teach human beings the way to salvation. Manicheanism spread to Egypt, Africa, and even Rome. During the early years of his adult life, the great Christian thinker Augustine was a Manichean.

The first Christian centuries, then, were a time of missionary expansion, the development of Christian doctrine (largely through opposition to gnostic rivals), and persecution. The Roman emperors Decius (249–251) and Diocletian (284–305) made enough martyrs to make professing Christian faith a serious matter. Christians had to meet secretly in catacombs (caves) or private homes, and their organization had to be informal. Their leaders (bishops and elders) were indistinguishable from ordinary people, and their teaching had a *disciplina arcani*—a strict code of secrecy. Those who died giving testimony to their faith (martyrs, etymologically meaning "witnesses") were great heroes, whom heaven would greet with open arms. One of the greatest early controversies, in fact, concerned the status of those who had recanted their faith to avoid martyrdom and then, in a period of calm, asked readmission to the Christian community. Donatus led a party of rigorists who insisted that traitors had no place in the Church and that any *sacraments* (holy rites) that they administered would be invalid. Augustine successfully opposed Donatus, arguing for greater clemency and for Christ's decisive role in the inner effect of the sacraments.

Only a thin line separates the apostolic fathers from the conciliar fathers and the great theologians of the "patristic" age (age of the Fathers), for the three centuries after the deaths of the Twelve were characterized by a continuity of theological themes. First, there was the task of defending Church discipline and morality against both laxness and rigorism. Second, Church leaders had to walk a middle way between inspiration through charismata and institutional authority. Against Gnostics, the Church had to affirm the goodness of material creation. Against those who denied Jesus' humanity (the Docetists), it had to maintain that he was fully human and had really suffered and died. The Christian Church had little power in the secular world until the conversion of the emperor Constantine (312), so even when it was not suffering active persecution, it was not very influential. From the time of the Edict of Milan (313), however, Christianity was free to proselytize within the Roman Empire. Church leaders continued to reflect on the relation between Jesus and Judaism, as well as on conceptions of Jesus and God that would make most sense to educated Hellenists.

The apostolic Church developed a rule by local bishops. They became the primary teachers of doctrine, the primary defenders of *orthodox* (straight) belief. The bishops led the common worship, settled community disputes, and, to the extent that their talents allowed, fought heresies through sermons and writings. They were the main line of Fathers around whom the early Church arranged itself. The great heroes, as we mentioned, were the martyrs, and the life of the community took its liturgical pattern from the *eucharist* (weekly communal meal) and *baptism* (rite of entry into the Church). Forgiving sins raised questions of moral theology, for after baptism all were supposed to keep their faith pure, but gradually the Church allowed sinners to return to the community rituals after they had done penance. In the first three centuries, then, the Church established elements of the character that it has borne ever since.

The Conciliar Age

During the fourth and fifth centuries, a number of meetings (councils) of Church leaders were held that formally established the discipline and official doctrine (*dogma*) that any group in union with the apostolic Church had to adopt.[18] From those meetings came the name for the next period of Christian history. Above all, the meetings, many of which were called by emperors concerned about the unity of the empire, dealt with the central issues of the Christian creed, hammering out the dogmas about God, Jesus, salvation, and the like that became the backbone of Christian *theology*. Various controversies made Church leaders realize that it was imperative to determine which apostolic sources were genuine expressions of faith and which were not. That imperative resulted in the establishment of a Christian scriptural canon (list of official books).

Three main factors determined the final *canon:* whether the writing in question came from an apostle or a close associate of an apostle, whether it was accepted by the Church at large, and whether its contents were edifying for faith.[19] As early as 170, leaders in Rome had determined a canon of authoritative books in response to the canon drawn up by the heretic Marcion. Yet for many decades no list was agreed upon by the entire Church because local traditions varied.

For instance, the East long hesitated to accept Revelation, while the West was chary about Hebrews. In the early decades of the fourth century, Bishop Eusebius of Caesarea (perhaps the first significant Church historian) divided candidate books into three categories: acknowledged, disputed, and spurious. The acknowledged and the disputed books constitute the twenty-seven books of today's New Testament. In 367, Athanasius of Alexandria published a "Festal Letter" that listed these twenty-seven books and earned the approval of Fathers such as Jerome and Augustine and the endorsements of synods (councils) at Hippo (393) and Carthage (397 and 419).

The first great dogmatic (official doctrinal) council occurred at Nicaea in Bithynia (south of the Black Sea) in 325. It produced a consensus that was especially important for clarifying Jesus' divine status as Logos or Son. The Council of Nicaea was called by the emperor Constantine, and without imperial support the Nicene party would not have triumphed. Before Nicaea, most churches had been content to repeat what scripture (Jewish and Christian both) said about God and Jesus. However, Church theologians did not know how to respond to questions that scripture did not address. One such question came from Arius, a priest of Alexandria, in Egypt, who proposed that Jesus, as the Logos of God (the divine Son), was subordinate to the Father. In short, Arius' proposition was that if one drew a line between created beings and the uncreated divine substance, the Logos would fall on the side of created beings, because "there was a then when he was not." Arius' principal opponent was Athanasius.

Athanasius represented the theologians of Alexandria in Egypt, who descended from Clement of Alexandria (ca. 150–215), one of the first Christian theologians to cast faith as a philosophy that might persuade educated Hellenists, and Origen (ca. 185–254), the first great Christian speculator. (Working with Platonic philosophy, Origen had written immensely influential commentaries on scripture and expositions of Christian doctrine.)

Athanasius, drawing on this Alexandrian tradition, assaulted Arius' argument. Speaking for what he held to be orthodoxy, he said that the Logos was of the same substance as the Father, possessing the single divine nature. Nicaea agreed with Athanasius, making his position dogma. There were many political machinations, as different political factions chose different theological sides, and Arianism thrived among Germanic tribes well into the sixth century. However, the Nicene Creed, which codified the position against Arius, came into common use, with the result that the divinity of the Logos became common faith.

Trinitarian Doctrine. Athanasius also perceived that the canonical literature gave the Holy Spirit divinity equal to that of the Father and the Son. Therefore, he extended the meaning of his word *homoousios* (of one substance) to include the Holy Spirit and so set the lines of what would become, at the Council of Constantinople in 381, the doctrine of the Spirit's divinity. That completed the doctrine of the *Trinity:* one God who was three equal "persons," each of whom fully possessed the single divine nature.

Augustine, bishop of Hippo, in Africa, expressed this doctrine in terms of a psychological analogy that shaped Western Christian speculation. He proposed that as memory, understanding, and love are all mind, so (but without human imperfections) are Father, Son, and Holy Spirit all divinity. The Father is like an inexhaustible memory (from which all creation comes), the Logos is like the Father's self-awareness, and the Spirit is like their boundless love.

In the Trinitarian controversy (and perhaps even more in the subsequent Christological controversies [controversies about Jesus Christ]), the terminology that eventually became fixed was still quite fluid.[20] Bernard Lonergan has argued that the Church's decision to respond to Arius and so coin new language for new problems (problems not resolved by scripture) was a decisive advance in its self-understanding.[21] It would have been obscurantism, or anti-intellectualism, to refuse to grapple with questions as serious and legitimate as Arius'. By responding to Arius' challenge, the Church affirmed its ability to determine the meaning of scripture and to develop doctrine as new situations required.

Politics. The conciliar definitions gave Christian faith considerably more precision and at least tacitly encouraged theologians to study and speculate further on the doctrinal tracts that they had laid out. The conciliar age was also fraught with the intrusions of secular leaders into Church affairs, for after Constantine and his successors made Christianity the favored imperial religion, the emperors assumed that they had the right, even the pious duty, to intervene in Church affairs. Thus, the tension between Church and state, as we now call it, started its long and tangled history in the conciliar age. Whether this led to the Caesaropapism (domination of the Church by the emperor) that many historians think afflicted the Eastern portions of Christianity before the schism of 1054 (when East and West split) is a matter for learned specialists to decide. We need only point out here that, because of Christianity's favored status in the empire, the councils became a matter of imperial interest.

In fact, the councils were the spearhead of the advances that the Church and state made into one another's affairs.[22] No longer were Christians under the constant threat of persecution and martyrdom. They could enter worldly occupations, including government service—a situation that both weakened their faith and made it more realistic. As a result, the original feeling of urgency gave way to the realization that the Lord's return might be far down the road. Thus, Christianity decided it had to become a faith that was viable in the world.

Monasticism.   Such worldliness stimulated new religious movements within the Church that opposed the laxness or "accommodation" that worldly success easily begot. The most important reforms generated interest in monasticism and virginity (which overlapped, insofar as monks took vows of celibacy). Both males and females found a monastic life of dedication to prayer and charitable works a way of maintaining their martyrlike intensity of faith. Theirs was a "white" martyrdom, not the red one of blood, and many found that it led them to the desert for solitude and asceticism. The great hero of the day, in fact, was the desert father Antony, who made a great impression on Athanasius. Thomas Merton has gathered a good selection of the desert fathers' sayings.[23] In it one sees both a bare faith and considerable shrewdness about what happens to people when they set out to meet God.

Partly because of the dangers of desert solitude, many monks soon formed communities, and before long these communities admitted women (nuns). In the East, communal (cenobitic) monasticism took form under the guidance of Basil, bishop of Caesarea. His rule (which owed much to Pachomius, the founder of communal monasticism) became the common law. In the West the rule of Benedict predominated. So the dedication that had previously been an informal option (largely in terms of virginity or widowhood) took institutional form. Thenceforth monasteries were powerhouses of Christian faith that laity and *clerics* alike

viewed as centers of holiness. That, too, was an innovation added to New Testament religion, which had no monastic life. The Church's decision that monastic life was truly in keeping with New Testament religion was analogous to the decision to coin new doctrinal concepts. Quite consistently, the Protestant reformers of the sixteenth century opposed the development of monasticism (as being unbiblical), just as they opposed the development of the Catholic notion of authority.

Christology.   The councils not only set the pattern of Trinitarian faith that dominated the following centuries but also dealt with a host of problems that arose when people started to think about Jesus as the divine Word. Nestorius from Antioch and Cyril from Alexandria squared off in Christological controversy, and Alexandria won. Nestorius stressed the unity of the Christian God, though he affirmed Christ's two natures (human and divine). Cyril thought that Nestorius' affirmation was not strong enough to safeguard the single personhood of Jesus Christ the God-man, so he pressed for a "hypostatic" (personal) union of the two natures. The Councils of Ephesus (431) and Chalcedon (451) affirmed Cyril's doctrine of one "person" and two "natures." Later Christological development clarified that Jesus had a rational soul, two wills, and two sets of operations, human and divine. This orthodox Christology resulted from trying to systematize the scriptural teaching about God and Jesus. It stressed that only the union of the divine with the human in Jesus could save human beings from sin and give them divine life. Orthodoxy cast many groups in the shade, branding their positions as heretical, but it also developed Christ's meaning considerably.

Orthodoxy

Orthodoxy has two principal meanings. It may refer to the Eastern churches that separated from Rome in 1054 or to the "right belief" established by scripture, tradition, and the councils. In this section we address the first concept, describing the growth of Eastern Christianity after the conciliar age (most of the great councils took place in the East). The term *Orthodox* was adopted for two reasons: The Orthodox church thought of itself as keeping the traditional faith, especially regarding the episcopal (pertaining to bishops) focus of Church authority; *orthodoxy* has also meant, especially in the East, "right praise." As "right praise" the term links the Orthodox conception of faith to the glorious Orthodox liturgy (which primarily is a praise of God).

Western theologians, many of whom were monks dedicated to a rich communal worship, coined the expression *"Lex orandi, lex credendi"*—the law of prayer is the law of faith. Similarly, Eastern theologians felt that the Church expressed itself most fully in the *liturgy*. During the apostolic age this communal worship (*liturgy* means "the work of the people") had developed a sacramental system in which baptism and the Eucharist ("the Lord's Supper") were especially important. In the early medieval period, when Orthodoxy took form, the liturgy flowered. The result was a full calendar of holy days and a full ritual that involved music, art, incense, iconography, and more. Thus, communal worship became the dramatic center of Eastern church life.

As we have noted, the councils of the fourth century occasioned theological division as well as theological clarification. In the fifth century, during the Christological controversies, more deviant versions of faith arose—Nestorian, Monophysite (one nature in Christ), and others—because as the councils established accepted beliefs, they excluded other options. Often the deviant minority party continued a church life, with the result that there were large numbers of heterodox Christians in the East. As Arianism remained robust even after its rejection by the Council of Nicaea, so the Christologically heterodox groups did not simply recant or go back into the woodwork. Thus, the major split between East and West that occurred in 1054 was not without Eastern forerunners.[24]

From the ninth to the fifteenth century, a complicated, still quite obscure process of alienation between Byzantine (Eastern) Christianity and Roman Christianity resulted in their separation. Each group finally rejected the other, charging it with having broken the traditional faith. Some of the factors in the separation were the fall of the Eastern Roman Empire, the failure of the Crusades, the growing antagonism of Islam, the growth of the papacy, the stirrings of what developed into the sixteenth-century Protestant reactions against the papacy, and the rivalry between Russia and Western Europe.[25] These factors take us to the beginning of modernity in Eastern Christendom, explaining why East and West have remained divided to the present.

Religious Issues. Thus, the break between Eastern and Western Christianity owed a great deal to political and cultural conflicts. Although separating these conflicts from theological differences is virtually impossible, we can delineate some of the more clearly religious issues. For instance, the patriarch Photius, who presided at the Eastern capital of Constantinople from 858 to 886, drew up a list of what Byzantines considered to be Latin (Western) errors in faith. This list reveals how the two portions of Christendom had developed different understandings of orthodoxy. In this list Photius cited irregularities in the observance of *Lent* (the period of penance before the great feast of Easter when the resurrection of Christ was celebrated), compulsory celibacy for the clergy, denying priests the power to administer confirmation (the Christian sacrament of adulthood), and false teaching about the Holy Spirit. Clearly, the list concentrates on points of Church discipline and administration. Such points have serious theological implications (for instance, for the structure of the Church and its authority), but they do not affect the cardinal doctrines of the Christian faith: Trinity, grace (God's favor and life), and Incarnation, except for Photius' last point on false teaching about the Holy Spirit.

The most acute point of theological difference between the East and the West was this last point, which came to be known as the *filioque*. According to the Nicene Creed, within the life of the Trinity the Holy Spirit proceeds from the Father. The Western Council of Toledo (589) made an addition to the Nicene Creed: The Holy Spirit proceeds not just from the Father but also from the Son (*filioque* means "and from the Son"). East and West each became attached to its Trinitarian formula, so the filioque became a sharp bone of contention. The East claimed that it was heretical; the West claimed it merely articulated a tacit understanding of traditional faith that Nicaea had assumed. The practical significance of the difference is not clear, but it probably shows the East's tendency to appreciate the Father's primal mystery—the Father's status as a fathomless source from which *everything* issues.

In response to Photius, Western theologians composed their own list of complaints about Eastern usage. In their view the Eastern discipline that allowed clerics to marry, that baptized by immersion, that celebrated the Eucharist with leavened bread, and that had different rules for fasting deviated from tradition. The debate even descended to such details as whether bishops should wear rings, whether clergy should wear beards, and whether instrumental music was valid at the liturgy. However, the main theological issue continued to be the filioque, while the main political issue emerged as the difference in the churches' understanding of authority. The Eastern church's tradition

Figure 20 *Byzantine book cover, Syria, sixth to seventh century. Gold, rock crystal, and ruby; 8⁷/₈ × 6³/₈ in. The handsome cross suggests that the cover was meant for a Bible. The Nelson–Atkins Museum of Art, Kansas City, Missouri (Nelson Fund).*

was a loose federation of bishops, all of whom were considered successors of the apostles. The Eastern church also stressed the rights of individual churches and ethnic groups. The Western tradition was a "monarchical" leadership by the bishop of Rome. As successor to Peter, he claimed primacy over the other churches.

When the Byzantine Empire was about to fall to the Turks, the Eastern and Western factions met for the last time at the Council of Florence (1439). That was long after the mutual anathemas of 1054 (de-

scribed below), but the East hoped to secure both Church unification and Western help against Islam. On the agenda were only four points (the other disagreements having fallen away as trivial). They were the prerogatives of the bishop of Rome, the filioque clause, the doctrine of purgatory (the teaching that there is an intermediate state between heaven and hell, which the Orthodox condemned as unbiblical), and whether to use leavened or unleavened bread in the Eucharist. In retrospect, theologians have judged the last two items as relatively inconsequential. The first two were interrelated, because the Council of Florence came to focus on the question of whether the pope had the right to alter an ecumenical creed (that is, add filioque to the Nicene Creed). Because of their political problems (the menace of the Turks), the majority of the Greeks (Easterners) accepted the filioque and agreed to certain papal prerogatives. The union was confined to paper, though, because back at home Orthodox synods refused to ratify the agreements signed by their delegates.

Separation. The pivotal moment in the East-West division was the mutual excommunications of 1054, which were due more to politics (or to snappish personalities) than to theology. Pope Leo IX had sent a Western delegation to Constantinople headed by one Cardinal Humbert. The Normans were menacing Leo and also the emperor Constantine Monomachus, so a major goal was to unite the churches to oppose a common foe. Humbert seems to have been a narrow, contentious type, as was his Eastern counterpart, the patriarch Michael Cerularius. When Pope Leo died in 1054, Cerularius held that Humbert's credentials were void. Humbert responded by laying on the altar of Saint Sophia in Constantinople a letter that excommunicated the patriarch and all his associates. The patriarch then assembled his own council, which excommunicated Humbert in return. The emperor dispatched the cardinal back to Rome with presents, hoping that the next pope would appoint a new legate who could heal the breach. But the Normans prevented the popes from resuming negotiations, so the mutual excommunications stood until after the Second Vatican Council in the early 1960s.

In the opinion of many contemporary theologians and historians the division between the Eastern and Western branches of the Church was a tragic accident. (Historians now say much the same of the sixteenth-century Reformation split in Europe.) Political circumstances, differences in traditional ways of celebrating faith, and, above all, differences in temperament and cultural backgrounds were more decisive than hard theological differences. What Orthodox and Catholics (and Protestants and Catholics) held in common was far more significant than what they held apart. It took centuries for Christians to realize that millions of people (for example, Asians) knew little about their God, let alone their Christ—centuries for them to realize their own solidarity and so begin an "ecumenical (worldwide) movement" for Church unification. The sticking point through those centu-

ries was a main factor in the East-West division—papal authority. Recently some ecumenical theologians have suggested ways that Protestant and Orthodox churches might acknowledge certain papal powers, but full accord remains quite distant.

Thus, the Orthodox church represents an understanding of Christianity somewhat different than that of Western Christianity.[26] It numbers perhaps one hundred sixty million people, depending on the estimates used for the Soviet Union, and within the family of Christian churches it stresses the conciliar tradition, the federation of local churches in geographic families, and a lofty theology of the Trinity, Christology, and grace. As we noted, the liturgy is its center, and it has a rich sacramental life.[27]

At the Orthodox liturgy, one feels a Christian "pneumaticism": The Holy Spirit is dramatically present to effect the sacraments. In the invocation made over the Eucharistic gifts (the *epiclesis*), Orthodoxy stresses the Holy Spirit's role in transforming the bread and wine into Christ's substance. In its baptism and confession of sins, Orthodoxy's accent is sharing God's life—beginning divine life in baptism or repairing it in penance. Overall, Orthodoxy places the mystery of the Christian God to the fore. For the East, God is less a lawgiver or a judge than a spiritual power operating through creation. Creation ought to respond to God's power and beauty, so the Divine Liturgy becomes a song of praise, a hymn to the goodness and love that pour forth from the Father of Lights. Orthodoxy especially venerates Mary, the Mother of God, for her share in the "economy" of salvation—her share in the design of grace that raises human beings to participate in the divine immortality. Bernhard Schultze has offered a full sketch of Orthodox doctrines and a full listing of its different family members.[28] He shows that, through many political troubles, Orthodoxy has kept faith with Jesus and the Christian beginnings.

Case Study: Orthodox Spiritual Wisdom. Both major branches of Eastern Orthodoxy, the Greek and the Russian, have fostered a strong monastic life, and from this strong monastic life has come a steady stream of holy people wise in the ways of the religious spirit. For a fascinating glimpse of such holy people, one need only pick up *In Search of True Wisdom: Visits to Eastern Spiritual Fathers,*[29] a work that beautifully conveys the Eastern Orthodox sense of prayer and asceticism.

This sense of prayer is a major focus in one of the authors' visit with a Russian recluse of Usui Valamao, a monastery in Finland to which some Russian expatriates retired after the Soviet rise to power. The visit took place in 1954, and the account of it transmits the spiritual advice of one Father Michael, a noted holy man of Valamo. Sergius Bolshakoff, the interviewer, was himself an expatriate Russian, who had decided to dedicate his life to the reunion of the Eastern and Western churches, by concentrating on the common monastic life that still kept the two churches quite close in their lives of prayer.

Bolshakoff was sitting with Father Michael at the end of the day in the holy man's little cell. Twilight filled the room, and a little oil lamp flickered in the corner before the holy icons. All was quiet and peaceful. Bolshakoff asked Father Michael to tell him about the tears of grace, one of the signs of advanced prayer. Father Michael replied that the tears of grace express a perfect prayer and the forgiveness of sins, referring to the authority of St. Isaac the Syrian, who had written on this subject. Opening a tome of St. Isaac's writings, he had Bolshakoff read certain passages he had marked off. The passages tell much about the Orthodox tradition of mysticism.

St. Isaac said that when a person is starting to leave obscure prayer, in which things are still confused, the person's heart will begin to burn like fire, and this will grow stronger day by day. No longer will worldly things hold any attraction, not even food or drink. Far more delicious will be the sweet, new, fiery thoughts in the person's soul. Then suddenly tears will begin to flow. They will run like a stream while the person reads, prays, eats, drinks, or works. Such tears signal a crucial period, during which a person can make great spiritual advances. Before them, the person has not climbed the mountain of God. When they come, the person has arrived, but he or she must redouble the efforts, so as not to lose a great opportunity.

The tears mean that a person has begun to smell the perfume of a wonderful new air. They announce that the birth of a spiritual child is near. "Our common mother, Grace, wishes to produce in us in her own mysterious way the divine image so that we may see the light of the age to come." After the flow of tears, which must last two years or more, there comes perfect serenity of mind. In this peace of mind, one can begin to contemplate the divine mysteries. The Holy Spirit opens the heavens, and God comes to dwell in the person, to resurrect in him or her the fruit of the Spirit.

Father Michael admitted that he himself had wept a great deal in his life. When Bolshakoff confessed that a certain book he used to read in the British Museum always moved him deeply, because it spoke so beautifully of a boy growing up in a pious Moscow family before the Communists' seizure of power, the monk nodded in understanding. That is not surprising, he said. Our time of unbelief and carnal living has made piety a lovely nostalgia. We think that tears manifest pitiful weakness or something else to be despised. We relegate them to old women. Stony indifference, hardness of heart, and coolness of spirit have become our marks of virility. The truth is, however, that an absence of tenderheartedness is merely a sign of spiritual death. As a Byzantine mystic said long ago, those who attend the Holy Liturgy without tears and a tender heart eat and drink the body and blood of the Lord unworthily. We must cultivate tears and tenderness of heart, because only through them can we purify our thoughts.

The interview passed on to other topics, most of them connected with prayer. At one point, Bolshakoff asked Father Michael to explain to him a puzzling passage from the writings of St. Seraphim. In the passage St. Seraphim says that when the Holy Spirit overshadows us, we must cease to pray. Bolshakoff wasn't sure he understood why. Father Michael said that all mystics have taught as St. Seraphim does, understanding "prayer" to be something we do by our human efforts. In contrast, when the Holy Spirit overshadows us, our efforts cease and there is no "prayer." Rather there is only a sentiment or heartfelt impulse of love that reaches out toward God without words or images. But Father Michael bade Bolshakoff to continue reading, for St. Seraphim also makes it clear that there are different gifts from the divine grace. Some people have the gift of mystical, unceasing prayer. Others are moved to watch their thoughts and pray in the sense of making human efforts. Still other people have the gift to fast, or to gather alms, or to live a virginal life. The point is to find one's own gift, one's own congenial path to God, and use it.

The next passage they discussed was also from St. Seraphim, and it concerned the lightning that one of Seraphim's disciples saw streaming from the saint's eyes, so bright it made the disciple's eyes ache. Seraphim told the disciple that the disciple himself was equally shining, because of God's life in him. The disciple then saw Seraphim's face become like the middle of the sun at its noonday brightest, a blinding light radiating in every direction. This filled the disciple with an inexpressible peace of soul. St. Seraphim explained that this peace is what Jesus meant when he told his disciples, "Peace I leave with you; my peace I give to you; not as the world gives" (John 14:27). It proved that the disciple truly had left the world.

When Father Michael commented on this and other writings of the holy fathers about light, he interpreted them as referring to a light like that which the apostles saw emanating from Jesus when they went with him to Mount Tabor and he was transfigured before them (Matt. 17:2). Still, such light did not keep the apostles from denying and abandoning Jesus at the time of his arrest, and it did not keep the saints, such as Simeon the New Theologian, from returning to a worldly life for a time. So we should think of it as a temporary strengthening for those who need shoring up, rather than a permanent acquisition or something essential to the state of grace. One can be in the fullest grace and not perceive or externally radiate such light.

The conversation then passed from light to warmth, as though Father Michael and Bolshakoff were exploring all the spiritual dimensions of the inner senses. In this case, however, Father Michael emphasized the supernatural warmth that Seraphim had asked his disciple to describe. "What kind of warmth do you feel, lover of God?" Seraphim asked. The disciple replied that, despite the snow all around them, he felt warmth like that which arises in a Russian bath, when one pours water on the heated stones and steam rises in a column. But the smell was completely different, like no perfume one can find on earth. St. Seraphim smiled in agreement. The consolations of the Holy Spirit are like no perfume on earth. What will the consolations of heaven be like? And, contrary to the warmth of a Russian steam bath, the warmth the disciple was feeling melted none of the snow surrounding the saint's hut. That showed it was warmth of a completely spiritual order, like the warmth the liturgy asks the Holy Spirit to give. For centuries, Seraphim pointed out, hermits who trekked into the deepest Russian forests did not fear the snows and the cold, because they relied on the inner warmth of the Holy Spirit. The grace of God, God's inner life, filled their hearts and heated their bones.

Again and again Father Michael and the classical authors he was explaining to Bolshakoff returned to the theme of grace, which has always been central in Orthodox theology. As Seraphim put it: "The Lord said, 'The Kingdom of God is within you.' By this Kingdom of God the Lord means the grace of the Holy Spirit. Well, this same Kingdom of God is now within us while the grace of the Holy Spirit shines and warms us, filling the air around us with various perfumes, and sweetens our organs of sensation with heavenly pleasure and our hearts with indescribable joy."

The Orthodox mystical tradition continues, alive and well, in places like Mount Athos in Greece, where monks meditate in the old ways and read the old classics. The center of their lives is something spiritual, something the eye cannot see nor the ear hear nor can it enter the hearts of human beings to conceive. Like Hasidim lost in the world of Torah, the Orthodox holy men and women are lost in the world of the gospel. For them the gospel words are shining jewels, the gospel scenes are blazing **icons**. Contemplating those icons, the Orthodox saints have enjoyed wonderful visions of the life of God that fills the holy soul, the mercy of God that courses through the world. Their meditations have made the scriptural scenes contemporary, much the way Jewish prayer has made the Exodus contemporary.

It is shocking to enter the thought-world of the Orthodox seers, and perhaps equally shocking to realize that a similar thought-world predominated in the Christian West less than 500 years ago. Less than 500 years ago, even theologians studied the Bible more for its religious feeling than for its literary structure. Even theologians were more interested in feeling compunction than in knowing its definition. Similarly, the terms of reference in Father Michael's world are not the historical or literary aspects of the Bible, but the spiritual experiences and verities the monastic tradition tells him the Bible can promote. What the Holy Spirit did for the apostles, and for the later saints like Seraphim, the Holy Spirit is poised to do today. After all, Jesus, the eternal Son of God, came from God precisely to give us human beings God's life, which the Holy Spirit wants to nurture in us. For Father Michael, as for most of the saints, the great puzzle is why so many people seem uninterested in God's life.

God's life, the East always has emphasized, is the perfect community of the Father, Son, and Holy Spirit. It is the Trinity not as the subject of conciliar controversies, or the subject of theologians' dry reflections, but as the spiritual atmosphere in which human beings can live, move, and have their being, if they would open their souls in faith. What the Eastern liturgy has always sung, the Eastern holy people have always stressed: the substantial love of God poured out for the salvation of human beings; humanity's potential elevation to a new, heavenly mode of life.

One will not understand traditional Christianity without an imaginative effort to grasp spiritual convictions like Father Michael's. For the generations who gave their lives to praying over the gospel scenes, the Spirit offered a light, a warmth, a perfume surpassing anything the world had to offer. With the peace and joy of the Spirit, a person was infinitely blessed. Without the peace and joy of the Spirit, a person was greatly to be pitied.

The Medieval Period

In discussing the medieval period of Christianity, we shift focus from the East, where Orthodox faith took shape, to the European West, where a new historical epoch more clearly dawned. Evangelization (missionizing) of Europe progressed steadily from the time of the early councils, most of it presuming somewhat vaguely that the bishop of Rome was preeminent among the Church's episcopal leaders. During the fifth and sixth centuries, Christian missionaries made considerable inroads among the Germanic tribes. Frequently they would convert tribal leaders from paganism or Arianism, and then the entire tribe would convert. From 800 one could speak of the Holy Roman Empire—a tense mixture of political and religious drives for unity. However, Western state leaders tended to think that the Church was something for them to control. That tendency, plus problems of Church discipline, made the Western situation confusing. From the tenth century, however, there were efforts to reform the Church and increase its spiritual vitality. In the eleventh and twelfth centuries, such efforts—especially those that originated at the Abbey of Cluny in Burgundy—were fairly successful.

As well, individual Church leaders found that they could increase their freedom from local secular rulers by increasing their allegiance to the bishop of Rome. The friction between Church and state therefore shifted to the interaction between the pope and the Germanic emperor. A key issue was who should appoint local bishops. The investiture controversy, as it is called, was solved by a compromise in the Concordat of Worms (1122). Secular rulers had to recognize the independence of the local bishop by virtue of his loyalty to the pope, and the pope had to consult the emperor and appoint bishops acceptable to him.[30]

During the twelfth century the Crusades to the holy sites in Palestine riveted the Christian imagination, but they tended to increase the alienation between Eastern and Western Christendom. When the Fourth Crusade (1204) conquered Constantinople, set up a Western prince, and tried to Latinize the Eastern church, relations deteriorated to their lowest point. By 1453, after the Councils of Lyon and Florence had done little to heal the wounds of division, and after Easterners had suffered centuries of Western domination, a popular slogan circulated to the effect that Turks would be better rulers than Western Christians.

During the twelfth century, Europe developed strong cities, with a concomitant shift of economic and political power. This development slowly transformed the feudal system of which the Church had been an intimate part. As a result, considerable resistance to the established Church power and faith arose among some groups, such as the Waldenses, who urged a return to apostolic simplicity and poverty. Groups that owed a debt to the Manicheans, such as the French Albigensians, pushed dualistic views in their war on the flesh and their contempt for the material world.

To meet the challenge of such reformers, the Roman church developed new orders of priests and monks, the most important of which were the Dominicans and the Franciscans. Dominic (1170–1221) organized his group to preach against the heretics, and one of the devotions it added was the rosary—a string of beads for counting prayers to the Virgin Mary. The Franciscans stemmed from the charismatic *poverello* (pauper) Francis of Assisi (1181–1226), who dedicated himself to simple living. His angelic love of nature and of the infant Jesus made a deep impression on subsequent generations of Christians. Both Dominicans and Franciscans were innovations on the established (largely Benedictine) model of Western monasticism. Principally, they had more freedom than Benedictines to move out of the cloister and its settled, agricultural rhythms. They were mobile, and therefore quite effective in responding to different religious trouble spots.

Scholasticism. The thirteenth century was the high point of medieval intellectual life, and the movement known as *Scholasticism* reached its peak then. The Scholastics systematized the conciliar and patristic (the Fathers') theological doctrines.[31] Augustine was their great master, but where Augustine worked with neo-Platonic thought categories (worked out by thinkers such as Plotinus, who developed Plato's ideas), Thomas Aquinas (1225–1274), the greatest of the medievals, worked with Aristotelian categories. Between

Augustine and Aquinas lived Anselm (1033–1109), who developed the notion that theology is "faith seeking understanding." That is, on the basis of a firm Christian commitment (rooted in scriptural, conciliar, and patristic doctrines), the theologian ought to learn as much as the divine mysteries allowed.

Anselm's definition was a writ of intellectual emancipation. Though they accepted the disciplines of tradition and the Church's teaching office, the medieval theologians seized the right to develop reason and use it to illumine the realities of faith. Consequently, teachers such as Peter Lombard and Peter Abelard prepared lists of patristic opinions on different theological topics and started to reason them through dialectically. Franciscan theologians, such as Alexander of Hales and Bonaventure, and Dominican theologians, such as Albert the Great and Thomas Aquinas, developed the dialectics, writing voluminously on philosophical and theological topics.

After a great struggle, the position of Aquinas, who most carefully related reason and faith, gained the greatest following. Just as conciliar theology had moved beyond scriptural ideas (in order to illumine scripture), so Aquinas' scholastic theology moved beyond conciliar theology in order to illumine it through Greek philosophy. For Aquinas, philosophy was the wisdom available to reason. It was a universal basis for discussion, regardless of religious allegiance. Jews, Muslims, Christians, and pagans all had reason, and so all could philosophize. Theology, which rested on divine revelation, perfected philosophy, taking it into realms that it could not penetrate on its own (for instance, without revelation philosophy would not know of the Trinity or the Incarnation [the divine Word made flesh]). Aquinas developed a powerful system of philosophical theology, but he was by no means the only impressive medieval thinker. His school, Thomism, trusted in reason, had a hopeful view of the world, thoroughly analyzed the Trinity, Christology, and grace, made a careful analysis of human virtues and vices, and viewed the world as a hierarchy of levels of being, with matter on the bottom, humans in the middle, and God at the top.[32]

Hierarchy. Aquinas' hierarchy had counterparts in the medieval Church structure. The clergy had separated themselves from the laity, and within the clerical order there were numerous ranks: monks, priests, canons, bishops, abbots, archbishops, cardinals, and more. The papacy had a considerable bureaucracy and wielded great secular power. Because the general cul-

ture held a Christian world view, heaven and hell had a vivid reality. Thus, the papal power to bar people from Church membership and so from heaven made people fear the pope greatly. Considerable worldliness entered into the papal use of excommunication, interdict, and the like, because by medieval times the Church had largely laid aside the *parousia* (second coming of Christ) and was concentrating on shaping daily life.

The unsurpassed literary rendition of medieval Christianity is Dante's *Divine Comedy.* It shows the medievals' hierarchical thinking, their concern with heaven, hell, and purgatory, the venality of many medieval clergy, the infusion of pagan learning into medieval culture, and the sophistication of medieval moral theology, which catalogued virtues and vices quite precisely. Another wonderful source of insight into medieval Christianity is Chaucer's *Canterbury Tales,* which describes the daily habits of representative social types and the unconscious ways in which faith wove through medieval culture. From Dante and Chaucer one gathers that intellectuals of the late medieval period, especially nonclerical intellectuals, found many defects in the hierarchical Church yet basically accepted the terms of Christian faith. Their criticism focused on the discrepancy between the values that the Church professed and the all-too-human way in which many Church leaders conducted themselves.

The medieval cathedrals also exhibited hierarchy through their stretching from earth toward heaven. They instruct us about medieval faith, for towns built them to be a means of indoctrination. One can see this today in the gothic masterpieces of Notre Dame de Chartres and Notre Dame de Paris. The basic architectural thrust is toward heaven, as all commentators point out, yet within the cathedrals are windows and statues that bring God down into daily life. Most cathedrals were built over centuries, and sometimes the townspeople contributed free labor, as if they wanted the cathedral to praise God doubly. Significantly, Chartres and Notre Dame de Paris both bear Mary's name. As the Virgin Mother of God, Queen of Heaven and recourse of weak human beings, Mary was a mainstay of medieval faith.

In their battles with the Arians during the fifth and sixth centuries, Church leaders had necessarily stressed Jesus' divinity, which the Arians denied. Consequently, the Roman liturgy had come to place Christ and the action of the Mass (eucharistic celebration) apart from the people (as befit Christ-God). The size of the cathedrals, the inability of many people to see the ceremonies, the inability of many people to understand the Latin in which the ceremonies were conducted—all these factors prompted devotion to Mary and the infant Jesus, which brought God closer and made faith more human. Divinity was not fearsome if one could shelter behind a young mother's kindness, a baby's vulnerability. So such devotions balanced the rather stern official cult.

Around the cathedral walls, in wonderful stained glass, were biblical scenes, pictures of saints, and the like that told even the illiterate what faith meant. With the statues of the Virgin and Jesus, they gave comfort to the person who slipped into the cathedral's darkness to pray. In its majestic space, one gained a proper perspective on one's problems. At a time when hard work, early death, and many sufferings were the rule, the cathedrals were for many a great support.

Monastic life progressed during the Middle Ages, though new orders such as the Franciscans and Dominicans neither completely replaced the more stable Benedictines nor completely abandoned their regimes. The great work of the monastic community was to celebrate the divine "office": liturgical prayers throughout the day and a communal Mass. By the thirteenth century, the Eucharist involved a rather complex ceremony, with choral music, gorgeous vestments, and precious vessels for the bread and wine. Gregorian chants best represent the music, which was lively and alert, giving many psalms a joyous lilt. For solemn moments, such as the celebration of Christ's Passion, chant could express deep sorrow, prefiguring, for instance, the music of Johann Sebastian Bach.

As it developed, the Mass increasingly tended to represent Christ's sacrificial death. That did not deny the motif of a common meal, but it shifted emphasis to the consecration of the elements (bread and wine), because in the theologians' interpretation, the separation of the bread and wine stood for the sundering of Jesus' body on the cross. As a prayer (the "sequence") for the feast of Corpus Christi (attributed to Thomas Aquinas) shows, the consecrated host (bread transformed into Jesus' body) came to epitomize God's presence and redemptive action. The consecration was a miracle that the liturgy enacted each day. Paradoxically, the host defied the senses and nourished the soul. Because Jesus' body remained in church, the church was indeed God's house. Indeed, in the host, Jesus made himself available for reverence and prayer. Along with the cult of the Virgin (see Figure 21) and the cults of the many medieval saints, the cult of the

Eucharist gave people at the bottom of the Church pyramid another source of comfort.

Thus, the average person went through a harsh medieval life in fear and trembling but with many sources of hope that such a life would lead to heaven. The worldliness of much Church life was balanced by the sacramental ceremonies that stressed the primacy of heaven. Rather clearly, the faithful knew that they stood between heaven and earth. They were citizens of two worlds, and the best medieval theology and religious art counseled them to live their dual citizenship gracefully. For instance, the cathedral and monastic schools joined piety to learning. The mystery plays and even the *danse macabre* (dance of death) brought home to the common people that death leveled pope and pauper to strict equality. In fact, *"momento mori"* ("Remember death") was a pietistic watchword. Since death was a gateway to eternal life, *"momento mori"* had positive as well as negative overtones.

Case Study: Christian Art. As an interlude between the medieval and Reformation periods, let us consider the religious art of two great German painters of the early sixteenth century, Albrecht Dürer (1471–1528) and Matthias Grünewald (ca. 1470–1528). They show an interplay of the humanistic themes that grew out of the Renaissance (but had some forebears in medieval thought) and the emphases on human sinfulness that the Protestant Reformation spotlighted. We may note, however, that both poles of this interplay depended on faith in the Incarnation. Without a strong conviction that the Word of God had entered human history, had even assumed a body in order to suffer human sin, painters such as Dürer and Grünewald would never have seen the world as they did.

Dürer was born in Nuremberg, the son of a goldsmith. He showed great artistic ability even as a child, so his father apprenticed him to a wood engraver. In 1494–95 he visited Italy and learned about a new technique, called "linear perspective," that made all parallel lines converge at a single vanishing point. He also absorbed the growing Italian interest in human anatomy. Still, perhaps the most important aspect of Dürer's trip to Italy was his exposure to a new conception of the artist's vocation. Whereas the traditional medieval artist had thought of himself as an artisan called to reproduce God's creation, the Italian Renaissance artists were reconceiving the artist as a human genius inspired to create his own personal world.

This new conception of the artist is evident in Dürer's *Self-Portrait*, painted in 1500. The painting

Figure 21 Madonna and Child, *France, about 1475. Stone; 35¼ in. high. The Nelson–Atkins Museum of Art, Kansas City, Missouri (Nelson Fund).*

The long, flowing hair is reminiscent of traditional portraits of Jesus, while the sadness of the eyes indicates the burdens the artistic seer has to carry, his heavy vision of human suffering.

In 1498 Dürer published a famous series of woodcuts illustrating scenes from the Book of Revelation. One of them, *Saint Michael Fighting the Dragon,* shows a warfare proceeding in heaven, while earth is represented by a peaceful German plain with a small town complete with a church steeple. Michael and the other angels look quite human, having long hair like Dürer's own. The demons, however, are gruesome creatures from the swamps of the unconscious, with long snouts and scaly tails. The general impression the woodcut conveys is of a cosmic battle between good and evil, the issue of which is still in doubt. The peace seeming to prevail on the human plain is misleading, since what is going on in heaven cannot fail to affect the human order. Apparently Dürer's sense of foreboding captured the popular imagination, for the fifteen woodcuts of his *Apocalypse* series sold well. The discontents of the period, which were to erupt only twenty years later in Luther's reform, made apocalyptic visions popular.

Dürer also produced many line engravings, incising his drawings on copper plates, and in this medium he achieved amazingly rich effects. His engraving entitled *The Fall of Man,* produced in 1504, shows an idealized Adam and Eve surrounded by animals representing the sins and diseases that have resulted from the Fall. Whereas Adam and Eve retain some of the splendor of their original creation, the animals emphasize the perverse effects of human beings' having eaten the fruit of the tree of the knowledge of good and evil.

A second trip to Italy in 1505–1507 brought Dürer in contact with the Venice school, which was then producing lavishly colored paintings. Thus his *Adoration of the Trinity,* finished in 1511, shows richly robed cardinals and kings adoring the Trinity. The heavenly host of martyrs and prophets are similarly clothed, while the sublimity of the vision lifts the earthly worshipers right off their feet. In the right-hand corner Dürer himself stands in full-length portrait, as though wanting to stress that this glorious scene was his personal creation.

Colorful painting apparently could not hold Dürer's permanent interest, for he went back to engraving. His greatest engravings, produced between 1513 and 1515, included the famous *Knight, Death, and the Devil.* The knight, who may have been inspired by the

suggests "a Christlike figure rather than a prosperous German painter of the turn of the century. The effect is intentional. The lofty gaze of the eyes underlines the solemn, almost religious nature of the artist's vision, while the prominent hand draws attention to his use of the pen and brush to communicate it to us."[33]

Dutch humanist Erasmus' *Handbook of the Christian Knight*, published in 1502, represents vigilant Christian faith. He sits astride a magnificent horse, undaunted by either death, who brandishes an hourglass, or the devil, who looks like a mythical beast, complete with long snout and high horn. Beside the knight trots his faithful dog, whom some interpreters see as the tireless devotion that must accompany vigilant faith. The picture projects the great religious demands of the time, the inner warfare that Church corruption and the new humanistic ideals could provoke.

So, on the foundation of the medieval and fourteenth-century preoccupations with death, Dürer erected a new religious vision, equally serious but more appreciative of humanity's inner powers. Human beings were not sure to prevail against such powerful foes as death and sin, but Dürer's human figures said that men and women could fight great fights of faith, aided by the saints, angels, and Jesus, who were always ready to enter the picture.

Grünewald, whose given name was Matthias Gothart Neithart, worked for a while at the court of the cardinal archbishop of Mainz. In the Peasants' War of 1525 he took the side of the peasants against the ruling classes, and his enthusiasm for Luther's ideas lost him the cardinal's favor. Unlike Dürer, Grünewald's paintings show little influence from the new humanistic developments in Italy. Thus, there is little of the Italian Renaissance interest in an idealized human body and little effort to retrieve the humanistic subjects of classical Greek art. Instead, Grünewald turned to the traditional religious themes of medieval German art, suggesting the ferment of his own times through the intensity with which he painted familiar topics.

Two of Grünewald's best-known paintings are the *Crucifixion* and the *Resurrection* from the Isenheim Altarpiece, both completed in 1515. The *Crucifixion* depicts the intensity of Christ's anguish through straining hands, thorns stuck in a festering body, and a huge iron spike through the feet. The overall tortured effect is very different from the idealized humanity of Christ one finds in Italian Renaissance art. The figure of Christ so predominates over the other figures in the picture that ordinary humanity is made to seem of little account. At the foot of the cross Mary Magdalene kneels in grief, while to the left John the Apostle comforts Mary the Mother of Jesus. To the right stands a shaggy John the Baptist with an open Bible. He points to Jesus and above his hand are the

words, "He must increase, but I must decrease." At John's feet is a small lamb (a traditional symbol of Christ) with a shepherd's crook. The lamb is shedding blood into a liturgical chalice. The power of the death scene comes from the force of the huge cross and strong corpus. This is not a man who died easily. The dark background suggests the brooding melancholy of Good Friday, when the sun was blackened for three hours, and the barren plain takes the picture away from Jerusalem, or any other earthly site, as if to say that history's deepest moment was a unity unto itself.

By contrast, the *Resurrection* shows a Christ of dazzling light. As powerful as the corpus of the *Crucifixion,* the central figure of the *Resurrection* floats in midair, as though he has just burst forth from the tomb. The soldiers who were guarding the tomb lie scattered like tenpins. A circular aura of light surrounds the Resurrected One, and his wounds stand out like jewels. The absence of any natural setting and the confused perspective give the painting an unearthly quality. If the *Crucifixion* seems abstracted from history, all the more so does the *Resurrection*. Yet the soldiers and the other physical details make it plain that this unearthly moment is the climax of Jesus' life. Where the great body on the cross droops with heavy defeat, the resurrected body is too light to be kept on earth.

When one realizes that the Isenheim Altarpiece was commissioned for the church of a hospital, the juxtaposition of the *Crucifixion* and the *Resurrection* gains further power. The sick people contemplating it could see that none of their sufferings would ever equal the pain of Christ crucified, but also that all their sufferings would be outweighed by Christ's resurrection, to which faith gave them access.

Thus, traditional Western Christian art took Jesus' humanity deeply to heart. By the eve of the Reformation, the scenes of the Bible had come to illumine the humanity of ordinary people. That Jesus was the Son of God did not mean that he was far from the rest of humanity. It meant that his death and resurrection held the key to all human beings' lives. Thus Albrecht Altdorfer, a contemporary of Dürer and Grünewald, was unusual in painting landscapes that held no human figures. The Dutch painter Hieronymous Bosch, another contemporary of Dürer and Grünewald, was more typical in being fascinated by human concerns, even human depravities. Bosch's *Garden of Earthly Delight,* finished around 1510, crowds into its central panel hundreds of nude human figures engaged in erotic pursuits. The left panel of the tryptich portrays the Garden of Eden (with a naked Adam suspiciously interested in a naked Eve), and the right panel portrays an almost hallucinatory vision of hell, where the excessive pursuit of pleasure has finally received its just desserts. The middle panel, which presumably represents daily human life, is largely hell in anticipation. The final frustration and futility of hell are mainly but human pathos fully revealed.

By the early sixteenth century, Western Christian culture had become so disordered that the German and Dutch artists found little to cheer. Anticipating the pessimistic theologies of the Protestant reformers, the artists stressed the madness and sordidness that the fourteenth and fifteenth centuries had bequeathed to Europe. After the Black Death and Hundred Years' War in which millions had perished, even daily peasant life seemed twisted. Whereas the Italian humanists strove to create more optimistic images, the masters in the homeland of the Reformation brooded on folly. However, a generation later the best of them, Pieter Bruegel the Elder (1525–1569), painted human scenes with great compassion. For example, his *Peasant Wedding Feast* (1566–67) takes a kindly view of a small child enjoying some tidbits and a poor, vacant-faced bagpiper waiting to perform. "Let them enjoy a brief time of happiness," the artist seems to say. "Their daily lives are hard enough."

The Period of Reform

In the piety that dominated the period between the high Middle Ages and the sixteenth-century Protestant Reformation, the most influential work was the *Imitation of Christ* by Thomas à Kempis (1380–1471).[34] The book evidences a sober awareness of death and a general view that life is a vale of tears. Both reflect a medieval heritage. Some church historians have called the *Imitation* the second most influential book in Christian history, second only to the New Testament. It breathes a certain air of discontent—the mood of the Netherlands, where it arose. It also breathes a desire to experience religious consolation—the same desire that figured prominently in Martin Luther's spiritual biography.[35] However, the *Imitation* represents only one aspect of the period before the Reformation. Political factors certainly were a dominant influence, as was the fourteenth-century plague, which killed perhaps three-fourths of the population of Europe and Asia,[36] excited a great fear of devils and

witches,[37] and made clear humanity's impotence and mortality.

During the late fourteenth and the fifteenth centuries, the papacy was in great disarray. At one point there were two claimants to the chair of Peter, one in Rome and one in Avignon. In the East the Muslims held Asia Minor and Greece, their most dramatic victory being at Constantinople in 1453. Well into the fifteenth century, southern Spain was under Muslim control, while in Italy the spirit of the Renaissance seemed stronger than conciliar attempts to reform the papacy. In addition, there were frictions among local rulers within the Italian, French, and German realms; the middle classes emerged as a result of city life and economic changes; and the pre-Lutheran attacks on Church corruption by the Lollards (followers of John Wycliffe in England) and the Hussites (followers of John Hus in Bohemia) took place.

The spark that set the Reformation blazing was Martin Luther (1483–1546), an Augustinian monk whose study and spiritual searches had convinced him that the heart of the gospel was the Pauline justification by faith (the belief that only faith makes one right with God). Only by reviving this Pauline theme could Christianity regain its pure beginnings. As John Kent has shown, there is a link between this central Lutheran idea and the themes of religious freedom and religious certainty that preoccupied later Protestants.[38] Justification by faith meant the fall of a whole system of "works" that the Catholic church had developed by late medieval times—the Mass, the sacraments, the rosary, and so forth.

Luther was precipitated into action by the prevailing practice of **indulgences** (papal remissions of purgatorial punishment due for sins), which one could obtain for various good deeds, including almsgiving. Behind this practice lay some simple economics. The popes had spent lavishly in their Renaissance enthusiasm for art and culture. Leo X, for instance, was perhaps 125,000 ducats in debt at the time that he endorsed the preaching mission of Johann Tetzel, Luther's first adversary,[39] which mission included granting an indulgence for a contribution to the building of St. Peter's in Rome. To Luther the whole system—the pope's extravagance, his pretension to control a treasury of merits generated by the saints, out of which he might draw "credits" to cover sinners' debts, and his focusing his economics on the Mass—was blasphemous. On October 31, 1517, tradition says, Luther nailed his Ninety-five Theses to the door of the castle church at Wittenberg, which amounted to a formal challenge to the system.

Many Germans who for political or religious reasons had grievances against Rome supported Luther. As his thought expanded, he made scripture the sole arbiter of Christian faith, declared the primacy of individual conscience, upgraded the status of the layperson, and urged the use of the vernacular rather than Latin. Luther also stressed the uniqueness of Christ's death on the cross and so taught that the Eucharist principally commemorates the Last Supper, rather than representing Christ's sacrificial death. On the basis of scripture, he judged the doctrine of purgatory unfounded and the practice of monastic life an aberration. Because Luther was a fine preacher, he made these ideas matters for discussion in the marketplace. By translating the Bible into marvelous German, he put the central basis for his reform within reach of all literate people (and just about standardized High German in the process). Finally, Luther's departure from monastic life and subsequent marriage led thousands more to leave their monasteries and convents.

The Spread of Reformation.   Luther's reform in Germany quickly generated uprisings elsewhere. Not only were many people eager for religious reform, separating themselves from Rome furthered their nationalistic sentiments. In Switzerland, Ulrich Zwingli (among the German speaking) and John Calvin (among the French speaking) led movements with similar themes. In England, Henry VIII and Thomas Cranmer separated their church from Rome. Generally, these reformers' writings show the influence of humanistic movements, from the Renaissance on, that had undermined the scholastic framework.[40] As well, they show a link to the spiritualist movements that were in search of a more emotionally satisfying faith. As the Reformation worked out, Lutheranism took root in countries with a primarily agrarian economy, such as Germany and Scandinavia, while Calvinism took root in countries with a commercial economy, such as French Switzerland, France, Flanders, and the Netherlands.[41]

Calvin had the greatest influence, however, on America, since France and Flanders largely returned to Catholicism, while Dutch Calvinism mixed with both the older piety espoused by the *Imitation of Christ* and the humanism of Desiderius Erasmus. In America, the Puritans from England were inspired by Calvin's desire to honor God by consecrating all of life

to his kingship. Consequently, they tried to develop a theocratic state. Calvin's notions of God's sovereignty guided Jonathan Edwards, the first major American theologian,[42] and through Edwards much of the "Great Awakening" (the revivalist movement that Edwards sparked in New England from 1740 to 1743) and subsequent American religious life bore a Calvinist imprint. Through the preaching of John Knox, Scotland also became a home to Calvinism, and when they came to America Scottish immigrants brought their Calvinist tradition (Presbyterianism) to bear on business as well as Church life. Calvin's main work, *Institutes of the Christian Religion*, became the leading text of Reformed faith, while his efforts to establish a Reformed commonwealth in Geneva provided a model for other communities seeking to live by the gospel.

From the middle of the sixteenth to the middle of the seventeenth century, religious wars ravaged much of Europe. In France they subserved civil frictions. The Edict of Nantes (1598) preserved the status quo: Protestant areas would remain Protestant, Catholic areas (the majority) would remain Catholic. In the Netherlands the wars had the character of a rebellion against Spain. The northern Netherlands became largely Protestant, while the southern Netherlands remained under Spanish power and so Catholic. Germany was the most furious battlefield. Until the Peace of Münster (1648) there was constant carnage. The upshot in Germany was the famous dictum *"Cujus regio, ejus religio"*: Each area would follow the religion of its prince.

In England, Henry VIII found the Reformation currents useful in his struggle with the papacy to have his marriage to Catherine of Aragon annulled. Henry declared the king supreme in all matters that touched the Church in England, and he eagerly took monastic lands and income to finance his war against France. From 1553 to 1558 Mary Tudor made England papist again, but in 1571, under Henry's daughter Elizabeth I, the English bishops published their Thirty-nine Articles of Faith, which formalized their special blend of Protestantism and Catholicism.

Catholic Reform.   The Catholic response to the Protestant Reformation took place at the Council of Trent (1545–1563). Trent affirmed the reliance of the Church on both scripture and tradition, the effective power of the sacraments, the need for human beings to cooperate in the work of justification (that is, no justification by faith alone), and the possibility of sin after justification (denied by some reformers). It also provided for reforms in clerical education and a general housecleaning to remove the laxness and venality that had made the reformers' charges more than credible. Probably the most powerful single agent of the Catholic Reformation was the Society of Jesus (the Jesuits), which Pope Paul III approved in 1540. Its founder was Ignatius of Loyola, a Basque.

Ignatius' companions quickly proved themselves the best combination of learning and zealous faith around. Therefore, they were assigned many of the tasks of teaching and missionizing that were central to Catholic renewal. Peter Canisius in Germany, Robert Bellarmine in Italy, and Francisco Suárez in Spain were intellectuals and educators (the first two also became prelates) who had a great deal to do with revitalizing Catholicism in their countries. Jesuit missionaries to Asia such as Francis Xavier, Matteo Ricci, and Roberto di Nobili, also had great success. Xavier was a charismatic figure of the first order, able to stir crowds without even knowing their language. Ricci and di Nobili took on the customs of the people with whom they worked (Chinese and Indians) and confronted the vast task of forming native versions of Christianity. Jesuits also ministered underground to Catholics in England (several lost their lives in the effort), and they went to the New World to missionize Canada, the American Southwest, and Latin America.[43]

Further Developments. A century after Luther's Ninety-five Theses, Europe washed in waves of Reformation and Counter Reformation (the Catholic Reformation). In Britain, the alternation of Catholic and Protestant monarchs led to a series of repressive measures, while the Calvinism first of the Scot John Knox and then of the rigorists called Puritans made great gains. The Spanish and Portuguese were exporting Catholicism through their great trading ventures, while the Dutch and English were exporting Protestantism. Consequently, Christian division became a worldwide affair.

Seventeenth-century America became a refuge for Protestants who opposed what they considered oppressive practices in their native lands and who stressed individual rights of conscience. The Church of England was strong in Virginia, Georgia, and the Carolinas. The Dutch Reformed Church dominated New York and New Jersey. Germans and Dutch flocked to Pennsylvania, while Congregationalists dominated New England. Catholics were an important group in Maryland. As the Reformation principle of individual conscience worked its influence, more and more

groups splintered off to search out places where they could live their convictions in peace. According to Sidney Mead, the unique character of American religion has been that it formed a national culture and law on the basis of its pluralism.[44]

In its Reformation, Catholicism set new standards for its popes and clergy. It also obtained a new spirituality (largely Jesuit) that tried to adapt traditional piety to the new age of individual conscience. Commentators have nominated Loyola's *Spiritual Exercises* as the third most influential Christian book. If we substitute "Catholic" for "Christian," they are likely correct. The work is in the form of meditations on different gospel scenes, but Ignatius designed them to bring about a "discernment of spirits" and a choice of a way of life. Some commentators point out that the mysticism of the *Exercises* is a shift to the interior in keeping with the shift of the great contemporary Spanish mystics Teresa of Avila and John of the Cross, and that the *Exercises* bring the medieval mystical tradition up to date by tailoring it to a more active life. Other commentators have shown Ignatius' anticipation of a modern "mystagogy" (exercise in the experience of God) and mystical dialectics.[45] From the *Spiritual Exercises* and other works of the Catholic Reformation, the Roman church learned how people might work in the world with the hope of finding God in all things. That made it easier for Rome to bless new active orders of priests, brothers, and nuns.

As Robert McAfee Brown has shown,[46] the spirit of Protestantism that has come down from the sixteenth century stresses, first, the notion of reform itself—of always having to renew one's faith because of one's distance from God's holy will. Second, it stresses God's sovereignty, the authority of scripture, the priesthood of all believers, and the vocation of the laity to exercise their faith in the midst of the secular world. Ever since Luther and Calvin, the Bible has been the great text for both Protestant worship and Protestant theology, while, as historical sociologists such as Max Weber have suggested,[47] Protestant discipline has been a main ingredient in the rise of capitalistic culture. As capitalistic economies developed in Europe and the United States, efficiency and wealth often became considered religious virtues—even signs of salvation.

The Reformation left Protestants and Catholics at odds, and the conflict has abated only in recent years. Today most seem to agree (despite such throwbacks as Northern Ireland) that the reformers had legitimate grievances and that the reformers' return to scripture renewed faith. On the other hand, Protestant and

Catholic scholars also agree that many of the defects in modern Christianity result from its lacking the sense of a catholic tradition and common authority. The ecumenical task for the future, they would say, is for Christians to put their humpty-dumpty together again.

Modernity

In this section we concentrate on the eighteenth and nineteenth centuries, though aspects of modernity clearly are found in the seventeenth century and still persist today. From the myriad events and thinkers who shaped the eighteenth and nineteenth centuries we must select the most crucial. Clearly, the Enlightenment was crucial, as were the political revolutions in France and America, which were related to it. As well, the Industrial Revolution and the European colonization of large parts of Africa and Asia play in the background. Of the thinkers, the line from Descartes to Marx that passes through Hume, Kant, and Hegel is perhaps the most significant.

The religious life of the West changed dramatically in the modern period. It had to contend with new political, philosophical, and scientific thought. More profoundly, for the first time it met a passionate counterfaith, for as a movement or cause modernity opposed to reliance on God a deep commitment to humanity's own powers. (This was not true of Islam until the twentieth century.)

Heribert Raab has written, "The Enlightenment denotes the most revolutionary of all movements which the Occident has undergone in the course of history,"[48] making reference to Protestant historian Ernst Troeltsch's view that the Enlightenment marks the beginning of the modern period of European culture, ending the previous theological or ecclesiastical culture.

The Enlightenment began in the Netherlands and England in the mid-seventeenth century, but its most outstanding expressions arose in France and Germany. French rationalistic and materialistic philosophy (such as that of Voltaire, Helvétius, and Comte) and French revolutionary political action both derived from the Enlightenment. In Germany, Leibniz, Lessing, and Kant were its first philosophical offspring, while the "enlightened despotism" of Frederick the Great and Joseph II was a political result.

The Enlightenment thinkers saw themselves as part of a movement for progress, the watchword of which was criticism. They took as their enemy igno-

rance, intolerance, and repression, vowing to attack all such manifestations in national culture. To power this critical warfare they drew on the model of the new physical science (especially that of Newton). That meant setting goals of clarity, precision, and rational order. Thus, the Enlightenment was a tremendous affirmation of humanity's rational capacities. Furthermore, it assumed that both creation and human nature were essentially good, thus producing an expectation of great progress. Things would improve and freedom would increase as trustworthy critical reason expressed trustworthy human nature situated in a quite trustworthy natural order.

Quite obviously, the Enlightenment view of human nature clashed with that of traditional Christianity. Although reason held an important place in the medieval scholastic synthesis, the medieval mind never doubted that human nature is only perfectible through divine grace. In Reformation thought, Protestant and Catholic alike, both human reason and human love suffer the grievous effects of sin, with the result that only God can give the fulfillment they seek. The Enlightenment contested the beliefs of both periods.

In fact, Alexander Pope (1688–1744) epitomized his era when he said that the proper concern of man is man. Drawing on Renaissance humanism as well as on Reformation individualism, the Enlightenment thinkers concluded that things outside the province of human experience are of marginal concern. How we define human experience, of course, is a capital question. Enlightenment leaders tended to distrust both mystical experience and systematic reason (Hegel was an exception), preferring empiricism instead. Thus, Hume made a deep impression by limiting valid human thought to what sensation can verify. In the political sphere, the new thinkers sought to establish empirical laws of human nature that might help provide liberty, fraternity, and equality. Even when such philosophy or political science grew quite abstract (as in the case of the French revolutionary philosophies), there was agreement that theology and revelation were irrelevant.

For Kant and Hegel, the great innovators in the modern philosophy of consciousness, the reason that was to secure "the system" would not be subordinate to traditional faith. Thus, biblical, conciliar, and even Reformation notions of how things are in the world were rejected during the Enlightenment. By a turn to the thinking subject, reality became the domain that we now call the secular world. The transcendent domain, the holy world that past ages had called the most objective, had no place in the new world view. Only as a manifestation of human self-expression, individual or social, did religion merit attention.

A great many factors were at work in this subjective turn, of course, and not all of them sprang from human pride. A general disgust with religion—well deserved after a century of religious wars—certainly made a new humanistic beginning attractive. The overbearing weight of ecclesiastical institutions, which regularly stomped on individual rights and opposed free scientific inquiry, make anticlericalism rather healthy. (The Spanish Inquisition and Oliver Cromwell's massacre of the Irish are heinous instances of religion used to desecrate human beings.)

In the sciences, the excitement of empirical discoveries and the slow differentiation of canons of critical judgment were forces that seemed to oppose faith. Under the banner of religion huddled so much superstition and anti-intellectualism that simple integrity drove many educated people away from the Church. The best and the brightest frequently found themselves forced to choose between their love of human culture (the intelligence, sober judgment, and compassionate love that represent humanity at its best) and religion, Christianity, or even God.

However, applying Enlightenment beliefs to philosophy and politics did not prove to be an unqualified boon. Unfettered reason and humanism produced horrors that quite challenged those of the religious witch hunts and inquisitions. For instance, the bloodbaths of the French Revolution differed little from those of the religious wars, showing that not all fanaticism trumpeted about God. The American Constitution, despite its debt to Enlightenment humanism and its expression of democratic freedoms, was the framework of a culture that often treated nonwhites and women as less than human.[49] The Marxist-Leninist-Maoist brand of political religion, which is largely indebted to Hegel, produced inhuman totalitarian regimes. Small wonder, then, that Eric Voegelin found the path from Enlightenment to revolution a way of self-deification—a vicious way of placing selected human beings on the throne of divine mystery that they might crush all opposition.[50]

Those who defended the pre-Enlightenment order argued that the fallacies in the new order were both subtle and patent. On the subtle side, a thoroughly critical analysis of experience showed that there is more to reality than what Enlightenment philosophy acknowledged. For instance, mystical, mythical, poetic, romantic, and even creatively scientific thought all are poorly accounted for by Enlightenment epistemology (theory of knowledge). On the patent side, observation of human behavior showed that reason seldom guides public affairs. Putting these objections to the Enlightenment together, Christian apologists argued that an experience of God can take one beyond empirical reason and that an irrationality exists that is well labeled "sin." A major legacy of modernity is the continuing Western debate over the assets and liabilities of critical reason.

In our sketch of the historical development of Christianity, we have stressed the internal dynamics: how the original commitment to Jesus Christ as both the fulfillment of Jewish prophecy and the definitive Word of God offering human beings eschatological salvation developed into the great cultural force of the Western world. We have stressed this aspect because our main interest is Christian *religion*. For those more interested in Christian culture, or the interaction between ideas ultimately owed to Christian faith and such significant political developments as the rise of the Holy Roman Empire in medieval times or the rise of nation-states in modern times, greater stress on the struggles between kings and nobles, or between the upper and lower classes, or between capitalists and workers would be in order. We completely accept the principle that Christianity did not develop in a vacuum but was involved in a dialectical relationship with other cultural forces—political, economic, artistic, military. On Christianity's own terms, which lay rooted in the incarnation of divinity in space and time, everything human was relevant to religious faith, and religious faith was relevant to everything human. Thus one should picture the unfolding of religious ideas, theology, church life, and all the Christian rest as the result of an intense, ongoing, never-failing interaction between faith and worldly culture. Just as one cannot understand the significance of Jesus or the New Testament without appreciating how they were a response to the Jewish and Hellenistic cultures of their times, so one cannot understand later periods without realizing that Christianity was constantly molding and being molded by external forces. Religious ideas and practices never develop in a vacuum. Always the sociological pressures of a given time help to shape how people think about God, themselves, sin and grace, the sacraments of the Church, and so forth. If we have emphasized religious ideas more than secular currents, that is because religion is our main focus and obligation in this book. But students should never forget that throughout most of its history Christianity has been a highly complex phenomenon evolving in the cauldron of whatever was shaping its people.

The Contemporary Situation

The principles of Reformation and modernity have worked for more than four and a half centuries since Martin Luther. The reforming spirit continued both within and without Lutheranism and Calvinism, often simplifying Christianity to yield a stark biblical faith and worship. Thus, Puritanism, parts of Methodism, and Baptist religion moved Protestantism farther from Catholic dogmatic and sacramental theology. In reacting to this trend, Anglo-Catholicism tried to mediate between the ancient Catholic tradition and the Protestant instinct about the new religious needs of post-Renaissance society. However, the tide of the Protestant sectarians brought waves of individual, enthusiastic experience, which in turn promoted emotional preaching, revivalism, and biblical literalism. Meanwhile, traditional Catholic authority fought modernity tooth and nail, only accepting modern scholarship and modern conceptions of human rights in the twentieth century.

During the nineteenth century, the Enlightenment meant liberalism in religious matters. Christianity was adapted to the needs of the day, which liberals thought were primarily humanistic in character. Adolf Harnack's slogan that the Christian essence is "the fatherhood of God and the brotherhood of man" encapsules much of the liberal spirit.

On occasion, both liberals and *evangelicals* (people rooted in the gospel) pressed for social change. The Industrial Revolution produced some abysmal working conditions, and Christian exponents of the "social gospel" agreed with Karl Marx that such conditions destroyed human dignity. In the "liberation theology" of recent years, this kinship with aspects of Marxism has become explicit, for many liberation theologians are combining Marxist economic analyses with Christian beliefs. The most eloquent are Latin Americans,[51] but thought like theirs has penetrated the counsels of both Protestant Geneva and Catholic Rome. Recently Latinos, blacks, Asians, and feminists in North America who want to promote social change through radical Christian faith have all rallied around liberation theology.[52]

In American religious history, a central theme has been what Martin Marty calls "righteous empire."[53] With this phrase Marty tries to summarize the Prot-

estant experience in the New World. It entailed divine errands in the wilderness, the sacred tasks of making God's new Israel, and a manifest destiny to show the world a truly Christian society. There was some breakup of the empire due to the divisions among the many American Christian churches, and so there was a rather reluctant settling for a civic code that granted *all* citizens religious liberty, freedom of conscience, and separation of church and state.

The effort of Enlightenment figures such as Jefferson and Franklin to make a state that was both humanistic and hospitable to the Christian majority has been a striking experiment. However, American civil religion has been neither fully Christian nor fully human if measured by either Christian dogma or post-Enlightenment criticism.[54]

Puritanism, liberalism, and Marxism may all be analyzed as forms of Gnosticism. Although these three viewpoints relate to the Enlightenment (and contribute to U.S. history) in quite different ways, they all depart from the classical political theory that developed from Greek reason and Jewish-Christian revelation. In other words, the majority movements in modern politics have not been concerned with maintaining a balance between divinity and humanity, faith and reason, transcendent reality and the world at hand. For the most part, they have concentrated on the second terms in these pairings or even tried to convert the first terms into the second.

The result has been an apotheosis (divinization) of humanity, a hearty optimism and faith in human reason, and a nearly mystical commitment to political action—with little feel for the irony involved. In the domain of scholarship, the historian has wielded more power than the theologian. In the domain of popular Christian religion, there has been considerable defense of the secular. Only after Vietnam, Watergate, and a proliferation of crises (ecological, nuclear, and economic), whose interrelationships challenge our cultural values, did Americans begin to suspect that modern Gnosticism had led them far astray. Within Christianity, these crises have become a common challenge. Only people who ignore reality do not feel their impact. They require a thorough rethinking of the faith handed down as well as a thorough critique of the gospel as lived by Wall Street.

Furthermore, Christians have had to rethink their assumptions about revelation, salvation, the centrality of Christ, and the position of "pagans" as they have learned about other religions. Because of both secular and religious developments, then, the current Christian situation is complex and demanding. Science, technology, politics, and history (in other cultures as well as those that derive from Christianity) all demand reconciliation with traditional faith.

Those concerns of current Western theologians press in upon even an introductory text in world religions. First, we cannot separate them from the assumptions with which scholarship approaches any religious tradition today. That is, we cannot cite religious phenomena, separate central ones from peripheral ones, and compose historical or comparative analyses without understanding just what religious phenomena are and why some are central. Even a student or scholar with no express theory about such things has a tacit theory about them.

For instance, some people think of religion in terms of social ceremonies. For them a person who does not attend church or synagogue regularly is not religious. Other people define religion as the urge to know and love that opens onto mystery. For them the irreligious person blocks off contemplative love. We favor the second interpretation.

Second, the concerns that modernity generated often spark a quarrel between scholarship and faith. Persons committed to religious traditions may feel that detached, critical, scientific treatment of their beliefs and worship distorts them. American Indians, for instance, have said that anthropologists' comments on their sacred dances are usually trivial. Without the experience of being lost in communion with the Great Spirit, the anthropologist can only ruminate about group contagion or the therapies of rhythm. There are analogies in every religion. At the heart of the effort to describe the reality of religious experience lie the unavoidable issues of critical reason and experiential faith.

As a result of the Enlightenment, contemporary scholars test every observation, every statement, every memory—they accept nothing uncritically. From traditional faith comes the axiom that one must believe in order to understand, love in order to see. That axiom finally implies that faith is an act greater and more comprehensive than reason.

Third, these interpretational issues are especially acute in contemporary Western culture because they arose due to the effects of Christianity. Indeed, the Christian blend of Israelite revelation and Greek reason may have carried their seeds from the beginning. By the happenstance (or providence) that Christianity became the dominant European world view, and the happenstance that European culture developed sci-

ence, history, and philosophy into the massive critical apparatus that we possess today, these issues are fundamental to both contemporary Western culture and contemporary Christian faith. The result is a constant, if frequently subtle, interplay.

For instance, religion does not go away just because critical reason argues it off the property. Usually, it simply takes another form—the scientist or historian whose life turns on research becomes "religious" about his or her work. Indeed, the more creative such a historian or scientist is, the more passionate, even lyric and reverent, he or she will be about the commitment to truth and objectivity that the work demands. Similarly, the devoted social activist, whether Marxist or not, tends to survive through a largely unprovable faith that history has a meaningful direction or that giving one's life to improve other people's lot makes sense. Even the typical citizen who goes along without much reflection or passion hears a few whispers of God.

Case Study: Conversion.   Against this background, Emilie Griffin's book *Turning: The Experience of Conversion*[55] sharpens many of the themes of recent Christian religious experience. Seeking the meaning of her own life, Griffin came to the critical point of personal choice: conversion from the secular values of the prevailing culture to an ardent Christian faith. In describing the motives and processes of her conversion, Griffin suggests that the Christian gospel still has the power to connect some lives to a deep, mysterious source of satisfaction. As we consider her case study of Christian faith, we can note where it challenges the mores of current Western culture and also where the modern critiques of Christian consciousness show faith vulnerable to self-deception.

For Griffin, the conversion process began with a great longing, an ache in her heart for something she had never experienced and could not even describe. This is reminiscent of the paradoxical remark of Blaise Pascal (1623–1662) that we would not seek God had we not already found God. Be it world weariness, or the passing of childhood satisfactions, or the strange inability of even great success to satisfy them for long, a disenchantment prompts many converts to consider a new way of life.

When she began to study the lives of converts, Griffin found that many reported having had intense experiences of nature in their youth, times when the universe stood as a fresh and dazzling immensity. A hunger for such experiences surfaced later in their lives, when they found a horizon of "everydayness" cramped and unsatisfying. For example, Thomas Merton, the Roman Catholic convert who became a famous Trappist monk, remembered being five years old and hearing all the birds in the trees start singing when some church bells began to chime. He asked his father why the two of them were not also in church, but his father only said that they would go to church some other Sunday. Similarly, C. S. Lewis, the well-known British convert, reported harkening back to an experience he had when he was six. He could see the Castlereagh Hills from his window, and they filled him with a great longing to touch their beauty.

In Griffin's early life both literature and nature had furnished her great joy. When she left her adolescent world of books and trees, however, and went to New York in search of a career, the joy seemed to drain away from her spirit. This made her brief trips to places like Central Park, or her times free for poetry reading, all the more precious, yet also all the more unable to satisfy her growing hunger. Almost accidentally she bought a leather-bound volume of the Anglican Book of Common Prayer, which surprised her by the force its words carried, as though something that had informed her distant ancestors was now speaking directly to her own soul.

Before long she became a frequenter of churches. Even when their bad art repelled her, Christian churches hinted at a wisdom about life and death, suffering and joy—the great human experiences she was trying to fathom. While the Christian teaching about immortality seemed to her illogical, she admired the concise statements of faith that rang forth in such venerable Christian formulas as the Apostles' Creed. Her upbringing in Christian Science made the question of the relation between flesh and spirit especially engrossing. Slowly she came to suspect that the attraction of Christian churches lay in their materialization of spiritual truths. In their glass and stone, they made faith, hope, and love visible, tangible.

From this suspicion it was but a short step to considering the center of Christian faith, the *Incarnation*. That Jesus had healed the man born blind (John 9:1–40) by spitting on the ground, mixing the spittle with dirt, and applying it to the blind man's eyes seemed utterly human—so human that it must have been orchestrated by God. Similarly, Jesus had turned water into wine, multiplied loaves and fishes, eaten broiled fish and honeycomb after his resurrection. Again and again, Griffin ran into this fusion of matter and spirit, this axis of incarnationalism or sacramentality. The Christian way, she came increasingly to see, was to place divinity in the world, to enflesh the Word of God in human form.

These discoveries only sharpened Griffin's longing to find a spiritual home. When she began to study traditional Christianity more deeply, her study did not spring from an academic interest in Christian religion. It was deeply personal and passionate. Perhaps this life-way held the truth of happiness, the sources of deep satisfaction. Perhaps it could slake the burning thirst of her soul. Reason and dispassion had their place, since she wanted a life-way that was realistic, not a bundle of convenient illusions. But her reasoning now was in the service of a heartfelt need for a whole, very human truth. In fact, the closer she came to seeing that she really hungered for God, for reality of a more-than-worldly order, the more she feared that affirming God would be an irrational leap spurred by her own needs. Perhaps "God" was only a projection of her great longings.

Yet this familiar argument against God seemed to have an obverse side. Would people long so for God if "God" had no reality? Could nature have made us so vainly, so certain to be frustrated? Back and forth the argument waged within her. Was her desire an unusual neurosis, or an unusual call to health? Before long, though, she decided that her desire for faith was too important to ignore. Better to risk disillusionment than never to test faith's truth. Better to pursue the desire for God to a frustrating conclusion than to hang back and remain divided. So Griffin determined to see the issue through, both intellectually and emotionally.

If we now generalize from Griffin's biography to the question of contemporary Christian faith at large, we find that the intellectual portion of the project of Christian conversion includes accepting the great propositions of the Christian tradition about sin, grace, the Incarnation, and the Trinity. Even if one gets through the door marked "God" and becomes able to affirm the existence of a Creator, Christian faith demands that one accept these further specifications of the Creator's nature and the Creator's actions on human beings' behalf. Finally, on the other side of the room to which the door marked "God" gives access, there are the Christian doctrines about the Church, the scriptures, and the sacraments. If one buys the Christian claims about God and Jesus, these other articles of faith also line up for adoption. Only if they form a coherent system can a responsible person like Griffin judge them an attractive, acceptable package.

Curiously, though, the more Griffin pursued the question of God, the more the entire package became plausible. Having once seriously entertained the possibility that God exists, Griffin found the biblical descriptions of God rather credible. Once again the Incarnation was to be crucial. That God should appear in human form, suffering and rising "for us human beings and our salvation," as the traditional creed put it, was certainly strange, but somehow in keeping with a God as good as the Bible proclaimed God to be.

It was not so strange that the world should have an intelligible source. It was more strange that this source should be as good as the father of the prodigal son described in Luke 15, as willing to sacrifice his eternal Son as Paul insisted in Romans 8. None of this was necessary, automatically entailed in the concept of "God." But all of it somehow was fitting. If God were to choose to make creatures with the spiritual capacities of reason and love, he might well choose to express himself in a human form and solicit their free love by a life of exceptional goodness. At least, this is the way that many converts like Griffin have found themselves starting to reason.

Moreover, this response to the intellectual challenges of accepting Christian faith tends to supply answers to most of the emotional challenges. Once the option of joining the Christian Church became intellectually respectable, Griffin found the emotional obstacles greatly diminished. The possible ridicule from supposedly sophisticated secular friends paled in comparison to the new meaning that conversion seemed to hold out. And her great longing for coherence, beauty, and a cause worth dedicating herself to seemed on the verge of finding fulfillment. So a certain at-homeness began to overtake Griffin's emotions. More and more the instruction classes she attended, the Church services she took part in, and the circle of new friends she met rang true, outlined a life-style that seemed to fit.

She realized quite well that the Church had many foibles, that her new friends were quite imperfect, and that much of the attractiveness of Christianity depended on her making a prior commitment of faith. The sacraments were pregnant with lovely meaning only if she believed them to be life-giving actions of God's Spirit. Also, Griffin never forgot that her coming to the threshold of Christian faith and then stepping across into the Christian Church had been powered by her inner needs. She was like a sick person who had come in search of a cure, a puzzled person who had come in search of clarifications. Still, once she decided that this motivation need not discredit the help that Christian faith seemed to provide her, she could convert to Christianity in good conscience.

Griffin's sketch of the conversion process challenges the secular assumption that faith is unreasonable, in the very process of challenging the secular assumption that God is impossible. For Emilie Griffin, both Christian faith and the Christian God became more reasonable than the secular life of many of her friends. Indeed, increasingly she found secular living cramped and unsatisfying. If there was no more to life than good food, interesting work, and clever conversation, life was a cruel hoax. The issue boiled down to whether Christian faith or secularism laid out the richer world view, and for Griffin it finally was no contest. Jesus had words of eternal life and the world mainly spun its wheels.

It does not impugn this honest report on the dynamics of Christian conversion to point out that Christian faith ought to be judged more by its fruits than by its self-justification. That was Jesus' own criterion (Matt. 7:16), and it validates a certain healthy pragmatism. If Griffin's or any other convert's assumption of a religious world view produces a greater ability to love and to work (Freud's standard for psychic health), an honest observer will account that conversion a good thing. If, on the other hand, a religious world view injures or frustrates love and work, an honest observer will account that world view (or at least the particular convert's version of it) suspect.

What do these standards of "love" and "work" entail? No doubt some subjectivity enters in, but we would have "love" entail an increasing appreciation of the mystery of life, of our fellow human beings, and of ourselves. We would have "work" entail the ability to create, serve, and so make one's time advance the beautification, clarification, and betterment of one's time and space.

Admittedly, these are not precise criteria, but the ground-level question of human or religious authenticity can never be precise. Modern studies of human consciousness show that we are all very complex creatures, with many different motivations and needs. If, overall, we become creatures who are honest and loving, productive and helpful, the world view that forms us to such health deserves high praise. As well, it deserves thoughtful consideration by others, for it might just be the better way that they, too, have been seeking.

STRUCTURAL ANALYSIS

Nature

Theologians who treat the meaning of nature in Christianity often show that nature has usually signified the human essence.[56] That does not mean that Christianity has denied the reality of the physical world. On the contrary, its Greek and Israelite sources both gave Christianity a realistic orientation toward the world. Moreover, the body of Jesus, insofar as Christian faith made him the Logos incarnate, was an anchor to realism. Against the Gnostics, who were their foremost adversaries, the early Christian writers insisted on the reality and goodness of matter. If God himself had made the world, and God's own Son had assumed flesh, both the world and human flesh had to be good.

Nonetheless, because of the early controversies about the being of God and Christ, the word *physis* (nature) connoted divine and human "whatness" more than it connoted external reality. During the early controversies about free will and sin, Christian speculation finally concluded that the redemption and salvation that Christ had worked were beyond that to which human beings had any right. Thus, they were supernatural gifts that came only by grace. Grace, it followed, was a generosity that God does not owe us. Furthermore, redemption and salvation so transformed human nature that it could share in God's own divine nature (2 Pet. 1:4). By itself, apart from grace, nature was unredeemed, unsaved, something far from the glory of divinity. These beliefs dominated classical Christian theology (Catholic, Orthodox, and Protestant alike).

In discussing creation we find more extensive Christian considerations of the physical world.[57] God stands to the world as its independent, uncaused source, who made it from nothing by his simple free choice. The first mark of the natural world for the traditional Christian, then, has been its subordination to divine creativity. Considerable time passed before the full conceptualization of creation as a Divine mak-

ing of the world from nothingness developed (from a combination of biblical and philosophical sources), but from the beginning the God of the burning bush was sovereignly free.

In most periods of Christian history, nature was considered mysterious and overpowering, but the Genesis story that God gave human beings dominion over nature shaped a belief that the physical world existed for humanity's sake. Thus Christianity has taught its faithful to husband the physical world and use it. Little in the Christian message proposed that human beings should ravage the world, but equally little proposed integrating human life with nature's ecology or preserving nature's gifts through frugality and reverence. In most periods Christians found nature abundant and generous, so conservation was not a major concern.

Furthermore, the biblical fear of nature gods contributed to a semiconscious Christian effort to make nature undivine. In rural places (among European peasants, for instance), this effort succeeded only partially. Overall, though, it was quite central to the Christian theology of creation. Coming from God, the world was good. But since it came from God by his free choice, springing from nothingness, the world was definitely not divine. Thus, the Christian interest in transforming human nature combined with a continuance of the biblical prophets' objection to the nature gods; thus, the physical world was made a subordinate, even a somewhat ambivalent, concept. Inasmuch as nature and the human body could seem antagonistic to the spiritual destiny of human beings, nature could seem something that human beings had to restrain and control.

Science. The relative profanity (nonsacredness) that Christians attributed to nature played a rather complex role in the rise of Western science. When the Greek protoscientists, or early natural philosophers, developed a rude demythologizing of nature, they established the principle that the physical world is open to rational investigation. Thus, it was not blasphemous to pry into nature's secrets, and it could be profitable: Nature yields valuable information to those who pry well.

In Christian hands this demythologizing went several steps further. Pre-Renaissance scholars (many of them monks) worked at what we would call physics or biology, although such work was subordinated to theology. In other words, the basically religious culture preceding the Renaissance determined that theology would be the queen of the sciences. Thus, before the Renaissance, the Catholic church kept physical science on a rather short leash. The controversy that the new theories of Galileo Galilei (1564–1642) raised shows the Church attitude that still prevailed in the seventeenth century: Faith had to predominate over the evidence of the senses. Shoring up theological notions (that the earth was the center of the universe was a theological axiom) was more important than allowing intelligence the freedom to investigate nature as it would.

Enlightenment thinkers were reacting to that sort of dogmatism and theological control when they attacked Christian faith as irrational or anti-intellectual. Almost in the name of a higher religion (fidelity to conscience), they attacked theology as dishonest. Since the scientific method, as we now call it, that was disengaging itself from theology (despite the Church's protests) brought tangibly positive results, it drove the ecclesiastical authorities deeper and deeper into their indefensible corner. Still, the passion of their faith made the authorities fly their flag decades after it had turned to tatters. Long after the Galileo disgrace, when even the Roman Holy Office allowed the sun to be the center of the universe, the Church opposed new scientific theories on theological grounds. Thus, many Christian leaders denounced Darwin and Freud, because evolution and psychoanalysis seemed to refute the image of human nature that religious tradition had developed. The creature who was little less than an angel, the creature for whom Christ had shed his blood, the creature who was the very image of God could not have descended from an ape or have unconscious lust for its parents.

Regarding the investigation of nature, therefore, the Christian legacy has been mixed. At first Christianity supported reason, the reality and goodness of the world, and the value of scientific contemplation. However, when investigation seemed to threaten faith, Christian orthodoxy tried to check the scientific mind. In elite circles today things are much better, for theologians now analyze the implications of scientific findings for ethics and faith. For instance, they discuss genetic engineering, nuclear research, the medical definition of death, and the like from a belief in the Christian concept of human dignity. Some confusion still remains about the line between religion and science, but history has chastened theologians considerably, and they are now slow to condemn scientific research.

On the other side, a significant number of scientists doubt that the scientific method alone is a com-

prehensive way of life. Not only does scientific research tend to ignore ethical questions about the social applications of its findings (for example, its findings about nuclear energy), it also finds itself more and more appreciative of nature's complexity—indeed, of nature's mystery. Every scientific discovery raises many more questions, whether in the realm of atomic particles, the realm of life, or the realm of the stars. Nature itself, we are finding, is a collection of mysteries.[58] Thus, nature commands a respect, even awe, that is quite different from the arrogance with which earlier, mechanistic scientists attacked it. In fact, for some philosophers of science, such as Alfred North Whitehead,[59] nature is the concrete form of divinity.

Sacramentalism and Mysticism. Christian sacramentalism has somewhat closed the gap (between the place of nature in Christian religion in contrast to pagan religion) that was opened by the Western separation of reason from myth. As well, Christian mystics such as St. Francis who have sensed a divine presence in woods and birds have been rather naturalist in their style. In its worship and sacramental theology, Christian religion often has pressed the belief that God called creation good. Often, it has applied a mythic and poetic intelligence that made the world mysterious, awesome, and alive. Baptismal water, eucharistic bread and wine, wax, incense, flowers, salt, oil—they have all enriched the liturgy. On the most solemn feast of Easter, the liturgy spoke as though all of creation got into the act, joining in the *Exultet*—the song of great rejoicing. In the liturgy of Good Friday, which commemorates Christ's death, the tree of the cross (the holy rood) became a new *axis mundi*—a new cosmic pillar linking heaven and earth. Taking over Psalm 150, Christians praised God in his firmament. Taking over other psalms, they made the mountains and the beasts co-conspirators to God's praise. All creation, then, was to resound to the music of the spheres. All creation ought to sing as it labored for redemption. Nature was part of a divine drama, part of a cosmic play of sin and grace.

Partly from such liturgical encouragement, Christian mystics have often shown a delight in nature like that of their East Asian counterparts. The accents have been different, since the Christian God is not the impersonal Buddha-nature, but they have not been contradictory. For instance, Francis of Assisi felt free to praise God as manifested in nature, and he composed famous canticles to brother sun and sister moon. Indeed the legends about his intimacy with animals are a sort of Christian prefiguring of the messianic age of fulfillment, recalling Isaiah's figures of the child playing at the asp's hole and the lion lying down with the lamb. In the messianic age men and women would once more be intimate with nature, as they were when God made them "in the beginning."

For the early desert fathers, the wilderness was a place to become sanctified. For many Puritans and early Americans, the wilderness brought to mind Israel's wanderings in the desert—the place where its religion was pure. Thus, a romantic strain of Christian thought has kept nature close to God. Sometimes it has made the city less desirable for religious life than the country. Often it has made solitude close to the elements a privileged place for prayer. As a result, the Christian God has been strong as the seas, everlasting as the hills, lovely as the lilies of the field.

Society

Central to the Christian notion of how people ought to join together has been the Church. It could oppose the state, standing as the religious collectivity against the secular. It has also been the place where Christian life was supposed to show itself as something mysteriously organic—as the "body" of Christ. In the earliest periods of Church history, before Theodosius established Christianity as the official Roman faith, Church leaders led quite unpretentious lives. Meetings of the community tended to be small gatherings in members' homes, and the bishop who led the liturgy might earn his bread as a cobbler or a craftsman. New Testament models suggested that carpentry (the occupation of Jesus) and tentmaking (the occupation of Paul) were more than honorable occupations. To those who waited idly for the *parousia,* the Church said, "Work—or no community support." In fact, most Christians in the beginning were nondescript working people. Thus, the *Epistle to Diognetius,* [60] an early Christian work, portrays a Christian existence in the world whereby faith would make one a solid citizen.

Nonetheless, from early times Christians also felt that preaching the gospel was an especially honorable work and that some community leaders ought to be free to labor at it full time. The decision to have deacons care for temporal affairs (Acts 6:1–6) suggests that Christians quickly established a hierarchy of tasks parallel to the hierarchy of Christian authorities. The work that preoccupied Church leaders and that later theology regarded as the Church's basic duty was a ministry or service in terms of "Word and Sacra-

ment."[61] "Word" was, in the first instance, the scriptures. From the outset, they guided worship, theology, and private reflection. Ministry of the Word included commenting on scripture to edify the assembly and preaching to the outside world (missionizing).

The Word itself was the gospel, but also the divine Logos. Thus, it implied reciting the dramatic story of what God, out of his love, had chosen to do for humanity. The decisive episode in that story was Jesus' death and resurrection. And Jesus—the Christ, the Logos— became present in a special way through the preaching of the Gospel. Faith in Jesus was the "entry" to the gospel view or "economy" of salvation, and faith demanded "hearing."

Developing biblical categories, recent theologians have shown that Jesus himself has been the Church's primal sacrament;[62] his flesh has been the greatest sign of God's nature and God's love. The Johannine writings contain the richest New Testament sacramental theology, but all the early literature makes clear that sacramental life has been a life of union with Jesus. Sacramental life continued the incarnation of divinity; through its cyclical recall of the mysteries of Jesus' life, it purported to lead Church members ever deeper into God's love.

Polity. Christian society has centered on worship through Word and Sacrament. Still, its structural organization was rather fluid at first and varied from place to place. In those early arrangements we can discern elements of all three of the later Church polities: the episcopal, presbyterial (of the elders), and congregational forms of Church government. With time, though, came the monarchical structure of Roman Catholicism, the collegial model of Orthodoxy, and the government by elders that has characterized much of Protestantism.

In the West before the Reformation, the structure of the Catholic church was pyramidal. At the top was the pope, along the bottom were the laity. In between, in descending order, were cardinals, bishops, and priests. The "religious" (those who had taken vows of poverty, chastity, and obedience, usually in the context of a communal life) were in the middle, though technically most religious groups had both clerical and lay members. Status, naturally and unbiblically enough, was accorded those at the top. Thus, the Council of Trent, reacting against Reformation notions that all Christians are "saints," denounced any diminution of virginity in favor of marriage. As a result, for many Roman Catholics the Church long meant the clergy.

That was less true for Protestants and Orthodox, because their theologies stressed, respectively, the priesthood of all believers, and the mystical union of all believers with Christ their head. As well, the Protestant churches tended to have a strong theory, if not always a strong practice, that ministry was honorable in the measure it was a service.

Women's Status. In principle, the Christian Church was democratic in that all people, regardless of sex, race, or background, were welcome. Each Church member had her or his own gift from God, and each was a unique reflection of God. Thus, there was the Pauline dictum (Gal. 3:28) that in Christ there is neither Jew nor Greek, male nor female, slave nor free. In practice, however, women have been second-rate citizens in all branches of Christianity. Neither the Catholic nor the Orthodox churches would ordain women (that remains true today), nor would many Protestant churches. By associating women with Eve, the cause of Adam's fall (1 Tim. 2:14), the Church often suggested that they were responsible for human misery and sin. Thus, the fulminations of ascetics (usually celibate males) against women's wiles were a staple of the literature on how to avoid sin.

From the New Testament, men could buttress their supremacy by citing Pauline texts (Eph. 5:22–23; 1 Tim. 2:11–12) stating that wives were subordinate to their husbands and ought to keep silent in church. From the patristic age they could draw on what we can only call the misogyny of Jerome, Chrysostom, Tertullian, and others who portrayed woman as the gateway to hell. Augustine, perhaps from his personal experience of concubinage, made sexual congress the channel of original sin. Medieval theologians, such as the Dominican authors of the *Malleus Maleficarum (Hammer of Witches)* cited witches as being the cause of much psychological imbalance. In the name of preserving true faith, Church authorities tortured and killed thousands of witches.[63] Moreover, the Reformation did not relieve women's plight. Luther thought that woman's vocation was to "bear herself out" with children, while John Knox trumpeted against "petticoat" power in the Church. Reformation biblicism, then, meant merely a return to the patriarchy of the scriptures.

With a patriarchal God and an ambivalent role model in Mary the Virgin Mother, Christian women for the most part heard and obeyed, keeping any dissent to themselves. They had some measure of religious self-expression in their convents, and some of

them gained leadership roles in the Protestant sects, but from the standpoint of today's egalitarian sentiments, their fate through most periods of Christian history was quite dismal.[64]

Church and State. The Christian view of society outside the Church varied over time. According to the New Testament Book of Revelation, Roman society was a beast that the coming Messiah had to slay if the earth were to become worthy of God. During the Roman persecutions, which some recent scholarship has downplayed, this view was influential. As a result, earthly life was held cheap compared to heavenly life. When the Church gained security with Constantine, it changed its tune. Eusebius, for instance, practically ranked Constantine with the twelve apostles. In reaction against this secularization, as we noted, the monastic movement restored the tension between time and eternity. The Western father Tertullian, for instance, cast doubt on the worth of secular culture, asking what Athens had to do with Jerusalem. However, other patristic figures, such as Clement of Alexandria and Augustine, recognized that Christianity needed an intellectual respectability if it were to prosper, so they started to give their theology an infrastructure of Greek philosophy.

By the medieval period, a certain harmony was achieved, as most of the culture was formed in accordance with Christian ideals (if not practice). There was a balance between reason and revelation, between emperor and pope. In practice, however, the competition between the emperor and the pope was fierce, for each tended to claim ascendancy over the other. Consequently, Church leaders such as Ambrose and Hildebrand, who stood up to kings or even brought them to heel, were accounted great heroes. In the Christian East, however, the emperor had more clearly God-given rights.

The Reformation depended in good measure on the political power plays of its day. Through application of the principle that a region would follow the religion of its ruler, a great deal of religious power returned to the local prince. Theologically, Luther tended toward a dualism of powers, religious and secular, while Calvin promoted a theocratic state in which citizens would live under Christian law. Thus, the Reformation did not initially encourage the modern pluralistic state. In America the religious communities of the colonial period had to legalize pluralism if the colonies were to be united. With great reluctance on the part of many, the united colonies disestablished religion, and their act had enormous implications.

Since about the time of Voltaire (1694–1778), American pluralism has become something of a model for world government. Other nations have not formalized that model, with the slight exception of the United Nations, but its spirit has been at least a small counterweight to their nationalism. The model says that to live together well, human beings must find nondogmatic principles that can be common to all and that will generate the basic cooperation necessary for peace.

Through most of Christian history, though, the ideal society has been one that at worst allowed Christians freedom to exercise their religious convictions and at best institutionalized a Christian regimen. For instance, only recently has Roman Catholicism backed away from its teaching that it ought to be the established religion in any country with a Catholic majority. By its decree on religious liberty, the Second Vatican Council made an unprecedented acknowledgment of the rights of other religious communities. Orthodoxy has had difficulty with secular rulers through most of its history,[65] in part because of its organization as a cluster of national churches. To this day Russian Orthodoxy, the largest group, is shackled by its country's secular rulers. Protestantism has been more lay-oriented than Catholicism or Orthodoxy, so its ideas on the relations between church and state usually have been the most advanced.

What the Church ought to do for secular society, in contrast to what is has asked of secular society, has also varied historically. Generally, the Church has thought it should be a city on the hilltop—a witness to the commonweal that comes from mutual support and love. In other words the Church has thought it ought to be the place where society could see human community in action—could see love, cooperation, and mutual support. All human groups seek such community, and they have greater difficulty when they are large or their members have different values. The Church has thought it ought to manifest this community. In what Roman Catholic theologian Karl Rahner has called today's diaspora situation,[66] in which Western churches are losing members, it becomes crucial that this concept of witness replace the ambition to rule over secular society that dominated most periods of the Christian past. Many contemporary theologians therefore want the Church to be with the poor, the oppressed, the people whom Jesus named in the beatitudes, for that would be where its witness would be most vivid.

Self

The conceptions of nature and society that we have sketched above suggest the Christian view of the self. The biblical teaching that God placed human beings over nature has meant to Christians that the human person is of much greater value than the plants and animals.

Furthermore, as Christian social theory interacted with the secular elaboration of human nature through Western history, the individual acquired greater stature than in Asia. In Asia, as in ancient societies generally, the group predominated over the individual. One was most importantly a member of a tribe and only secondarily a unique person. As an image of God, the individual was more significant under Christianity. Of course, at times both secular and religious authorities crushed individuals ruthlessly. Nonetheless, because they bore the life of Christ, individuals commanded respect. In matters of ethics, for instance, the notion of individual conscience counterbalanced the finespun codes of the canon lawyers and the moral theologians. The sacrament of penance epitomized this, for penance was essentially a self-accusation in which the individual, helped by the Church's representative, passed judgment on his or her standing before God.

By standing out from nature and having personal rights, the Christian individual was conscious of being a unique self. Historically, the Church did not lay great emphasis on fulfilling one's unique self by communing with nature, but it did lay great emphasis on fitting into the social body of Christ. In fact, the charity of the community united was to be the primary sign of God's presence. Beyond social fulfillment, however, Christian theology encouraged the self to commune with divinity itself—with the Father, Son, and Holy Spirit. During the biblical period that meant putting on the "mind of Christ." During the patristic age it meant that grace was considered a share in divine nature and that religion was a process of divinization. Since the Hellenistic divinity was above all immortal, religion was also a process of immortalization.

In medieval speculation, the self's fulfillment was the "beatific vision." By directly perceiving God's essence, our human drives to know and love (Augustine's famous "restless heart") would find a restful bliss. For the Thomists, participation in the divine nature through grace meant sharing in the "missions" of the Son and Holy Spirit. Thus, one's contemplation, knowing, and loving flowed into and out from the dynamic relations that characterized God's own inner life. The Reformation returned to biblical emphases, sending people to study the Word and to work in the world. For Orthodoxy the Divine Liturgy, with special accents on the Holy Spirit and the Mother of God, nourished one throughout life.[67]

In many periods, Christians never quite found the balance between life in the world and life that looked to heaven as its true home. Before the Reformation, Christians probably gave greater emphasis to the latter. Since the Reformation and the Enlightenment, they have emphasized social and political commitments in the world.

Religious Development.   Stressing communion with God, traditional Christian spiritual masters developed certain models of what happens in the life of the serious religious person. One of the most influential traditions involved the "three ways" that the self would travel. First, one had to walk the "purgative" way, which meant purging oneself of sin and developing virtuous habits. Then one would enter the long way of "illumination," by which the Christian truths of Word and Sacrament would slowly become one's own. No longer would they be external concepts—in time they would become inner principles of judgment and action. Finally, consummating the spiritual life was the "unitive" way, by which the self would unite with God as in a deep friendship or even a marriage. Occasionally such union would produce experiences of rapture, and then one could speak of mysticism strictly so called ("infused contemplation"). Clearly, then, the paradigm of the three ways depended on the notion that final fulfillment was communion with God.

The saints who modeled Christian selfhood tended to be wholeheartedly given to communion with God. They also had to manifest charity for their fellows, but the spotlight was on their love of God. Because solitude or monastic withdrawal seemed to foster love of God, by allowing the freedom of deep, leisurely prayer, most saints went outside of family or civic life to lose themselves in devotion. That was the pattern up to the Reformation, and it took Christian selfhood some distance from the New Testament's view that prayer is important but not dominant.[68] Still, as

the world became more important, the concept of saintliness expanded to include the service of other human beings. The Church had always honored certain holy married people, certain holy civic leaders, but by late medieval times it had to contend with a more dynamic society.

Consequently, the Protestant emphasis on holy worldliness found a ready audience among many post-medievals. This emphasis did not remove the notion that one was a pilgrim trying to make progress through time toward a more lasting city. However, it did upgrade the status of family life, business, and government. Indeed, by the nineteenth century, tracts appeared with the theme that Jesus was the greatest salesman of all time. As well, one could hear Andrew Carnegie defend capitalistic wealth as God's way of keeping the poor from squandering his gifts.

Sin.   Related to the capital question of what the self should most value is the complicated Christian teaching about *original sin* (most developed in Western Christianity—Eastern Christianity has not stressed original sin to the same degree). At its crudest, the teaching said that all people not baptized were in thrall to Satan and on the road to hell. Hell was essentially the deprivation of God (the loss of the beatific vision), but because of a gruesome imagery of fire and brimstone, it was popularly conceived of as a place of physical suffering. The ceremony for infant baptism, then, contained an exorcism of Satan—to save the little one from evil and make it pure for God. (Unbaptized babies who died before reaching the age of responsibility, and so before the possibility of personal sin, went to "Limbo," a state of "natural" happiness without beatific vision. Although Limbo was never a matter of fully official Church teaching, it exerted considerable influence.)

A key moment in the development of the doctrine of original sin was Augustine's reading of the Fall as a social act. Adam's sin had alienated all human beings from God, for Adam was the head of the entire race. Augustine took the seeds of this view from Paul (for instance, Rom 5:12–14). It suggested that Christ is the head of a new holy race, but that those not baptized into Christ belong to an old human nature destined for punishment.

The classical Protestant thinkers owed a great deal to Augustine; thus, their reform of theology emphasized original sin. Like Augustine, they interpreted Genesis and Paul rather literally, thinking in terms of corporate sinners and saints. The famous double *pre-destination* of Calvinism was an attempt to explain human beings' different fates (going to hell or heaven), as members of Adam or members of Christ, without removing the mystery of God's creative vision and providence. Whom God has destined for heaven will surely end up there. Likewise, whom God has set for hell will fall into the flame.

In a fateful development of Calvinistic predestination, the signs of election to heaven became outward decorum and even material prosperity. That meant the double burden of being both poor and damned and the double blessing of being both rich and saved. Eventually more careful Bible readers recognized that this correspondence contradicted the Sermon on the Mount, but a lot of Calvinists thoroughly enjoyed storing up plenty in their barns and letting their souls wax fat.

How inherently wicked or good the self is was an important question in the Reformation debates between Protestants and Catholics. Protestants, following Luther's stress on justification by faith and Calvin's stress on God's sovereignty, tended to emphasize the corruption of human nature through sin. Catholics, partly in reaction to that Protestant position and partly from their own emphasis on the sacraments and the Incarnation, saw an essential goodness in human nature (though they spoke of sin as darkening the mind and weakening the will). Clearly, though, Christianity made the West suspicious of human instincts. Many Christians were indoctrinated with the belief that they were virtually bound to be wicked sinners. Often that led them to oscillate between self-punishment and, in compensation, self-indulgence. However, most were taught that through penance one could experience God's mercy—the almost delicious sense of being loved gratuitously. Then the Johannine promise (1 John 3:20) that even when our hearts condemn us God is greater than our hearts could break out into joyous effect.

The Pauline discussion of sin and grace in terms of "flesh" and "spirit" focused Christian understanding of the self as embodied. That Paul's original language did not intend a matter-spirit dualism was almost forgotten after Christianity took up Greek thought. As a result, extremists tended to deprecate the body, marriage, and the world of human affairs as fleshly pursuits. In response to the Manichean and Albigensian heresies, the Church affirmed the goodness of the body, but the Church's general orientation toward heaven, its introduction of celibacy for holders of high Church offices, and its preference for ascetic saints tended to make the average person regret his or her flesh. For women this caused considerable suffering, because the male Church teachers often projected their sexual problems onto women. In that case, women became by nature wanton, seductive, and dangerous.

On the other hand, a certain realism about worldly life, in which imperfection if not sin was inevitable, tended to soften this rigorism. Christian moral theologians have usually taught that sins of the flesh are less grievous than sins of the spirit (such as pride, anger, or hatred). And, although at one point Roman Catholic moralists classified all sexual offenses as serious ("mortal" as opposed to "venial" sins), there were usually effective if unauthorized counterforces in the bawdiness of Chaucer and Boccaccio and the frequent concubinage of members of the clergy.

Case Study: Christian Rituals. By means of its sacramental system, the Christian Church has ritualized its members' passage through the life cycle. The system has begun with baptism, the sacrament designed to celebrate a person's birth into divine life and Church membership. If the person was an adult, it was usual to require a profession of faith. The questions in the traditional inquiry into the candidate's faith show the transition that the sacrament of baptism was ritualizing.

First, the minister of the sacrament asked candidates whether they renounced Satan and the spiritual forces of evil that rebel against God. Assuming the answer was yes, the interrogation continued, soliciting affirmative answers to such questions as whether the candidates renounced the evil powers of this world that corrupt and destroy the creatures of God; whether they renounced all sinful desires that drew them away from God's love; whether they turned to Jesus Christ and accepted him as their savior; whether they put their whole trust in Christ's grace and love; and whether they promised to follow and obey Christ as their Lord. Along with a profession of the traditional creed, this profession of faith set the main lines of what the sacrament of baptism was enacting: a passover from a life of bondage to Satan and the world to a life of freedom in the grace of Jesus Christ.

The celebrant would then pray over the baptismal water, consecrate the oil with which the candidate was to be anointed, and finally baptize (pour water on the forehead of) the candidate in the name of the Father, and of the Son, and of the Holy Spirit. The concluding prayer summarized the effects the action was believed to have: "Heavenly Father, we thank you that by water and the Holy Spirit you have bestowed upon these your servants the forgiveness of sin, and have raised them to the new life of grace. Sustain them, O Lord, in your Holy Spirit. Give them an inquiring and discerning heart, the courage to will and to persevere, a spirit to know and to love you, and the gift of joy and wonder in all your works. Amen."[69]

The second sacramental rite in the normal Western life cycle was confirmation, the Christian celebration of coming-of-age. (The Eastern Christians celebrated along with baptism a rite called "chrismation" that bestowed the gift of the Holy Spirit.) The main motif in this celebration was asking God to give the candidates further strength from the Holy Spirit, in view of the services that adult life would require them to perform.

The Holy Eucharist has been the principal sacrament in the majority of the Christian traditions, and the ritual for the Eucharist has begun with a Liturgy of the Divine Word. After opening prayers, members of the congregation read several "lessons" from scripture, usually from both the Old and the New Testaments. There followed a sermon, to explain the scripture readings and apply them to daily life, and then a recitation of the Nicene Creed. Next came prayers for various needs, and then the eucharistic liturgy proper began.

This first offered thanks to God and praise of God's holiness. Then came the main action, a remembrance of the Last Supper that Jesus celebrated with his apostles before his death. The key words of this remembrance have been, "For in the night in which he was betrayed, he took bread; and when he had given thanks, he brake it, and gave it to his disciples, saying, 'Take, eat, this is my Body, which is given for you. Do this in remembrance of me.' Likewise, after supper, he took the cup; and when he had given thanks, he gave it to them, saying 'Drink ye all of this; for this is my Blood of the New Testament, which is shed for you, and for many, for the remission of sins. Do this, as oft as you shall drink it, in remembrance of me.' "

After these prayers of consecration, there was a recitation of the Lord's Prayer ("Our Father"), more short prayers, and a Communion service, in which worshipers received the consecrated bread and wine.

The prayers said when administering the bread and wine summarized the participants' sense of what they were receiving: "The Body of Our Lord Jesus Christ, which was given for thee, preserve thy body and soul unto everlasting life. Take and eat this in remembrance that Christ died for thee, and feed on him in thy heart by faith, with thanksgiving. The Blood of our Lord Jesus Christ, which was shed for thee, preserve thy body and soul unto everlasting life. Drink this in remembrance that Christ's Blood was shed for thee, and be thankful."

Overall, the Church celebrated the Eucharist as both a memorial of Jesus' death and a memorial of his last meal, when he gave himself to his friends under the signs of bread and wine. Since Jesus' death and resurrection were the central events in the Christian reading of history, each eucharistic memorial laid before the Christian faithful an epitome of their sense of reality. In Jesus' death and resurrection stood revealed the meaning and destiny of each human life.

Moreover, by receiving Jesus' body and blood, the believer was believed to be nourished in the divine life that Jesus' death and resurrection had made available. The Eucharist therefore was like the messianic banquet that Jews of Jesus' time had believed would accompany God's definitive victory. Celebrating the good news of Jesus' victory together, Christians renewed their spiritual strength by feeding on Jesus' substance. There was nothing cannibalistic in this. The eating and drinking were simply ways of expressing and strengthening the deep intimacy between Christ and Christians, who, according to Saint Paul (1 Cor. 12:12), were members of one body, or, according to Saint John (John 15:5), were united like a vine and its branches.

The people who found baptism, confirmation, and the Holy Eucharist insufficient to keep them from sin could have recourse to sacramental rites of penance, which were designed to reconcile sinners with God and the rest of the community. Normally the minister of this sacrament offered a prayer over the penitent, and then the penitent confessed his sins: "I confess to Almighty God, to his Church, and to you, that I have sinned by my own fault in thought, word, and deed, in things done and left undone, especially by [here the penitent would mention the specific sins most troubling him]. For these and all other sins which I cannot now remember, I am truly sorry. I pray God to have mercy on me. I firmly intend amendment of life, and I humbly beg forgiveness of God and his Church, and ask you for counsel, direction, and absolution." After whatever counsel and direction he thought appropriate, the minister would absolve the sinner of his or her sins, in the name of the Father, and of the Son, and of the Holy Spirit.

When the time came to marry, Christians have been expected to celebrate their union through a marriage ritual. The Christian theology of marriage has likened the conjunction of man and woman in matrimony to the union between Christ and the Church, and it has found in the Genesis creation account, in which God gave Eve to Adam, a prototype of the nuptial union. A Christian marriage was meant for both the mutual comfort of the spouses and the procreation of children. It had to be entered into freely by both parties, and usually the minister called upon the assembled community not only to witness the parties' vows but also to support them in their marital venture. The actual marriage took place when the betrothed said to one another, "I take you to be my wife [husband] to have and to hold, from this day forward, for better or worse, for richer or poorer, in sickness and in health, to love and to cherish, until we are parted by death." Then the couple would give one another wedding rings, as a sign of their union.

A sixth sacramental ritual deals with the ordination of the Church's ministers. In churches with several ranks of ministers, the bishop has usually presided at the ordination. After satisfying himself that the candidates were qualified, he solicited the approval and support of the community, prayed over the ordinand and then laid hands on the ordinand's head and prayed, "Therefore, Father, through Jesus Christ your Son, give your Holy Spirit to_____; fill him [or her, in churches that ordained women] with grace and power, and make him [or her] a priest in your Church."

Many churches also celebrated sacramental rituals for the healing and consolation of the sick and the dying. After prayers and scriptural readings, the sick person usually went through the penance ritual, and then the minister would lay hands upon the sick person and anoint her or him with holy oil. The prayers accompanying this anointing asked God for an inward anointing of the Holy Spirit, to forgive the sick person's sins, release the person from suffering, and restore wholeness and strength. Often the person then would receive Holy Communion.

The last stage on the Christian's way was the burial rite, which usually focused on the Holy Eucharist for the occasion of death and burial. The Liturgy of the Word featured psalms and scriptural passages concerned with death and the Christian hopes for resurrection, and the person would be buried in consecrated ground with prayers for forgiveness and the life of the blessed in heaven.

The Christian sacramental system is the basic framework of the traditional Christian's church life. While many churches of the Protestant Reformed tradition came to downplay the sacraments that Catholics and Eastern Orthodox celebrated, Protestants still assembled for baptism, a liturgy of the scriptural Word, and to solemnize such occasions as marriage, ordination, and Christian burial. Whatever reservations they had about the Catholic and Eastern Orthodox development of almost sumptuous rituals, Protestants retained the Christian conviction that God uses material things (if only words and music) to draw human beings in spirit and truth. The churches of the Catholic and Orthodox traditions extended this principle to bread and wine, oil and wax, and various "sacramentals" (signs, such as holy water and ashes, meant to solemnize smaller occasions). The result was a counterbalance to any Christian overemphasis on sin or unbridled condemnation of the world. If God's own Word had taken flesh, the body and the world had to be basically good. All of life, therefore, had "sacramental" possibilities. As the Holy Eucharist showed the deepest potentialities of an ordinary meal, so the union of Christ with the Church showed the deepest potentialities of ordinary sexual intercourse. Not every generation of Christians has preached this sacramentalism boldly, but it always has lain ready to hand in the mainstream tradition.

The sacramental system epitomizes the Christian sense of God's ways with human beings. Where God could have stood apart, in splendid isolation, God freely chose to make covenants, strike bonds, call his people not servants but friends. By enfleshing the eternal Word of his heart, God placed divinity in the very midst of human history. The death and resurrection of Jesus, which was celebrated each Sunday, said that God goes down with human beings in their deepest grief and raises human beings up beyond their wildest hopes. At its most gracious, Christian faith has become a dance that partnered time to eternity. God and humanity are joined sacramentally; through the things of matter, space, and time, the timeless Spirit of God has touched human beings and quickened them.

Ultimate Reality

The first Christian conception of God was Jewish. Jesus himself accepted the God of the Fathers—Abraham, Isaac, and Jacob. This God, as we have seen, interacted with human beings and was personal. His guidance of humanity peaked in his liberation of Israel from Egypt and his covenanting with Israel on Mount Sinai. As numerous theologians have pointed out, it was difficult for Jesus to designate himself as divine, because to do so would have confused his identity with that of his "Father." In other words, the God of Jewish faith was Jesus' Father, his source.

In dealing with the revealed God's inner nature, the concept of the Trinity became paramount. Orthodox catholic (universal) faith held that Father–Son–Holy Spirit was attested by the scriptures and defined by the councils. As we indicated, the psychological analogy that Augustine and Aquinas developed gained great respect, the West considering it the "purest" (the least material) analogy. Thus, the God of Christian speculation was a fullness of intelligence and love. He was perfection, in need of nothing outside himself. He was the Creator and Redeemer, moved only by his own goodness. The Incarnation was the main instance of his outpouring, but glimpses of God abounded everywhere. Subhuman creatures were his "vestiges" (footprints); human beings were his images. Christians were images of his great Image, for they reflected the eternal icon, the Logos-Son.

Regarding the Trinity, Christians stood in the Son's position, receiving their likeness to God from the Father and expressing it through Spirit-carried love. The similitude broke down, however, because the divine persons were only relationally distinct (that is, Son and Father differed only as begotten and begetter), while humans remained creatures distinct from God. Still, the consummation of faith, whether occurring in worldly mystical experience or in the beatific vision,[70] meant knowing with something of divinity's own knowledge, loving with something of divinity's own love.

Biblical Renewal. When Reformation thought returned to biblical conceptions, because it found the medieval synthesis too abstract and unhistorical, it revived the notion that faith is a living interpersonal relation to God. This contrasted somewhat with the position of most Scholasticism, which stressed the propositional knowledge (the information) that faith provides. As well, the reformers revived the twin notions of God's judgment and his merciful love. By faith, God became one's "rock and salvation"—the one on whom to rely. Between the time of Luther and the nineteenth-century Danish theologian Søren Kierke-

gaard, such faith became paradoxical—a leap. In the face of the "impossibility" of the Incarnation, Kierkegaard jumped into the intellectual abyss, proposing that what reason could not fathom divinity could yet do, because it moved by reasons the mind knew not, by reasons of the heart.

The Hebrew notion of *hesed* (steadfast, merciful love), which kept God to his freely chosen covenant, encouraged believers to trust that no situation in their lives was hopeless. If Ezekiel's God could raise dry bones back to fleshly life, Jesus' God could use even suffering and evil to his own inscrutable ends. Was not God's chosen way of salvation, the death of his only begotten Son, the surest sign that no one had ever understood him? As the heavens are above the earth, so were God's ways above the ways of human beings. For that reason, the Reformers wanted only a Pauline faith: God's power and wisdom are Christ crucified.

Did this finally mean a justification of God by surrender? For the deeper theologians, who had frequently wrestled with unbelief personally, the answer was yes. With Job and Paul, they said that the pot cannot tell the potter how to fashion. For the sake of their sanity, they had to affirm that God is wise and just (and even loving) in all his doings. How this worked out, however, they often could not say. Surrender was finally a matter of trust, a matter of unexpectedly feeling God's love. As the mistranslation of Job put it, "Though he slay me, yet will I trust him." The farthest reach of the Christian conception of God was an intimate marriage of lives and fortunes. What the prophet Hosea had written of God's constancy, even God's vulnerability, the new biblical theologians found in New Testament *agape* (love).

The Johannine epistles say God is this *agape*. The Pauline epistles say *agape* is the greatest of God's gifts. The biblical theologians translated *agape* as self-sacrificing love. Beyond *eros* (self-fulfilling love) or *philia* (the love of friendship), it worked through God's use of the cross. Thus, it was an attack on evil, on lovelessness. Thus, it broke the circle of tit for tat, of sin and retribution. God the judge finally yielded to God the lover. In Jesus he suffered evil to undo evil, thereby making a new creation. The lamb who was slain for this new creation was worthy of all glory and honor, because his sacrifice showed a divinity greater than one could ever imagine. Only the nursing mother who could never abandon her child, the father of the prodigal son (Luke 15:11–32), or the lover to whom the beloved is more than another self could glimpse

Figure 22 Dead Christ with Angels, *by Edouard Manet (1832–1883). Etching and aquatint; 13 × 11⅛ in. The Nelson–Atkins Museum of Art, Kansas City, Missouri (Gift of Mr. and Mrs. Milton McGreevy through the Westport Fund).*

this *mysterion*—this plan of God's love, hidden from all ages.

In contrast to other religions' versions of divinity, Christian theology has stressed the personal, loving character of God that Jesus' flesh disclosed. Jesus was God in human terms. (He was also humanity fulfilled by union with divinity.) As a result, Christianity did not appreciate the impersonal divinity of nature so dear to East Asian and Indian thought. This divinity was implicit in Christian theology, but the personalistic emphasis placed it in the shade.

At its better moments, Christianity was grateful to Judaism, since it had adopted most of Judaism's doctrine of God. As well, it was mindful of the continuing election of Israel that Paul had proclaimed (Romans 9–11). At its worst, Christianity condemned Jews as Christ killers and spoke of their responsibility for Christ's blood. Islam confronted Christianity with claims of a later, perfected revelation and prophecy, and with an adamant insistence on God's unity. For Islam, and for Judaism, the Christian doctrine of the

Trinity violated monotheism. Christian claims that God is both one and three seemed to Muslims and Jews incoherent, while Christian allegiance to Jesus clashed with Muslim allegiance to the Qur'an and Jewish allegiance to the Torah. Those clashes remain with us yet.

As the center of the Christian world view, God in Christ dominated Christian conceptions of nature, society, and self. Nature was but God's cloak. It was a lovely gift, but it sprang from nothingness and was wholly under God's control. With each extension of space and time by science, the awe of sophisticated believers increased: A more complex nature only magnified their God all the more.

Similarly, God was the norm and goal of Christian society, because his law was the source of all natural law and because eternal life with God in heaven was the goal of all people. God wanted human beings to form a community. Christ showed them the love that could bring that about. Thus, the vocation of the self was to obey the great twofold command: to love God with whole mind, heart, soul, and strength and to love neighbor as itself.

SUMMARY: THE CHRISTIAN CENTER

The Christian center is Jesus, for the God worshiped in the Christian liturgy, served in the Christian ministries, and crucial for the Christian Church is the Father known through the revelations of Jesus. In the New Testament (John 14:6) Jesus is the way, the truth, and the life. For the Christian monk, martyr, or layperson, Jesus has been the strong soldier in combat with Satan, the sacrificial victim dying for human beings' sins, or the good shepherd ever seeking his lost sheep. In the East, Jesus has been the *pantokrator,* the Lord of the World shining with heavenly glory. In the West, Jesus has been the great moral teacher, the supreme exemplar of selfless love. So it goes, in all times and places. At the center of the religion that bears his titular name, Jesus the Christ holds all things together, as Colossians (1:17) put it long ago: "He is before all things, and in him all things hold together."

The centrality of Jesus the Christ has meant that Christianity is supremely incarnational. Its theology, if not always its Church practice, has pivoted around the enfleshment of divinity. Orthodox and Roman Catholic Christians have developed this theology into rich sacramental rites. Protestant Christians have developed it into a profound reverence for holy scripture. With interesting but ultimately secondary differences, the main Christian families have agreed that God made Jesus the Christ his prime self-manifestation. Bluntly put, Jesus has been God in human terms—as much of ultimate reality as a single human being could convey. Often the startling result of this conviction has been that humanity itself has become profoundly sacramental or iconic. Not only has no one ever seen God; no one has ever seen the depth, or the height, or the breadth of the human potential to image forth God.

Thus one finds each Christian generation tending to picture Jesus, the central icon of God, according to its own interests and tastes. To a peasant age, Jesus could be a simple tradesman or a king in beggar's garb. When court ceremonial deeply impressed itself, Jesus could be clothed in elegant vestments: silk, fur, brocade. A Renaissance soldier might picture Jesus as the commander of his regiment, evoking the utmost loyalty and bravery. A passionate contemplative might picture Jesus as her spiritual spouse, the lover burning her deepest soul. Thus did the Incarnation vary, age upon age, temperament upon temperament. Jesus' preaching, healing, teaching, friendship, communing with the Father, battling with Satan, and other facets have offered artists and common folk limitless food for imagination. The New Testament portrait has been full enough to show that Jesus was completely human, an incarnation that took divinity into all of humanity's basic concerns. Yet the New Testament also has been empty enough, laconic enough, to allow readers to develop a Jesus after their own hearts.

Still, life and death have centered Christianity, as they have centered all religion, so the nub of the Christian center has been Jesus' death and resurrection.[71] That the Son of God died for human beings showed the lavishness of the Father's love. As well, it convinced millions that Jesus was indeed like them in all things save sin, did indeed know their utmost dreads. To outsiders the crucifix might be a stumbling block, or a sign of foolishness, but to believing Christians it has been a sign of God's peculiar power and wisdom. Because he completely embraced their death, Jesus made God burningly relevant to all people, a deity of blood and bone. As the Christian liturgy put it, "Dying he destroyed our death."

Rising, Jesus is believed by Christians to have restored the life for which human beings ever have longed. To be immortal, at one with the holy ultimate reality, filled with the creative love that moves the stars, has always been the human dream, the hope too good to be realistic. If Christmas has been the most popular Christian feast, because it celebrates God's nearness and humility, officially Easter has been the most profound Christian feast, because it celebrates a God so lavish he takes one's breath away.

Without Jesus' resurrection, Christian faith would only be a profound probing of life's tragic nobilities. To live for love, and so suffer injustice and misunderstanding, perhaps even cruel death, would be a very noble human way, but it would leave both God and human nature shrouded in uncertainty. If all things end in the grave, then the agony of the cross, the nobility of living for love, is pure but almost unbearably ambiguous. On the other hand, if all things end in the mystery of Jesus' resurrection, certainty beckons round the corner.

Very peculiar, this central Christian symbol of why life is worth living. The resurrection of Jesus, taken as a pledge of one's own resurrection, escapes the laws of ordinary human calculus, stands to the side in a clearing all its own. Its witnesses tell a very puzzling story. Its many abusers make the prudent very skeptical. Yet the mysterious thing itself keeps haunting the back alleys of one's soul, like a pencil of light one can neither escape nor trace down.

Discussion Questions

1. Why might Jesus have said that it is easier for a camel to pass through the eye of a needle than for a rich person to enter the Kingdom of God?

2. What is the significance of Jesus' parable of the Great Supper?

3. Elaborate on the following extract: "From Judaism came the concepts of prophet and messiah. From Hellenism came the notions of saviour and god."

4. Why were the Councils of Nicaea and Chalcedon important?

5. How did the Mass summarize medieval Christian symbolism?

6. Describe the main tenets of sixteenth-century Protestantism.

7. How does the eighteenth-century Enlightenment contrast with faith, mysticism, and symbolism?

8. How has Christianity both spawned physical science and frustrated it?

9. Compose a brief rite for Christian baptism, stressing the Orthodox reliance on the Holy Spirit.

10. Indicate the main issues a contemporary person should consider in converting to Christianity.

11. Why would you like, or not like, to have an interview with the Russian holy man Father Michael?

12. Give a brief digest of the overall Christian gospel.

13. Why has the understanding of Jesus changed from age to age?

14. What have been the main influences of the Christian doctrine of original sin?

15. What do the three ways of the Christian spiritual life—purgative, illuminative, unitive—suggest about religious maturation?

16. What has the Virgin Mary offered Christian women for a role model?

17. What have been the distinguishing features of Protestant, Orthodox, and Roman Catholic Christianity?

Glossary

apocalypse: biblical or extrabiblical literature that claims to be a revelation from God about the events that are soon to occur as the consummation of history. In the Bible the Books of Daniel and Revelation illustrate the literary genre of apocalyptic. Present-day scholars tend to emphasize the tradition—store of symbols, chain of historical influences—that one can discover the apocalyptic writers using, as well as the psychosocial roots of apocalyptic literature in anxieties or resentments about worldly times, which might be bringing either persecution or marginalization from the centers of cultural influence.

apostle: one sent forth to proclaim an authoritative message. The early Christian leaders considered themselves authoritative emissaries of Jesus Christ, the most authoritative among them being the Twelve who had been the eyewitness companions and confidants of Jesus during his ministry. New Testament literature

was associated with various leading apostles—Peter, John, Paul—and drew much of its authority from the such supposed sources. Apostolicity later became one of the four marks of the genuine Church, which was supposed to be one, holy, catholic, and apostolic.

baptism: the Christian sacrament of initiation, which proceeds by lustration—washing with water. The basic symbolism is of a cleansing from sin, but in baptism by full immersion in water the early Christians also developed the (Pauline) motif of going down into death with Christ and rising to new, divine life. Baptism has served as the rite of entrance into the Christian community, as well as the passover from sin to grace. Different churches have held different positions about the advisability of baptizing infants, which often was not done in the early centuries (yet can claim a fair antiquity). Insofar as parents and the community, as well as Christ and the Holy Spirit, have been granted primary places in the ritual action, defenders of infant baptism have claimed that such baptism is both moral and fitting.

canon: a list or body of writings considered scriptural, authoritative, or officially approved. The establishment of a canon of scriptural writings is always a momentous step in the development of a religious tradition, but usually it is not a neat, once-and-for-all process. Thus the canonization processes of both the Tanak (Hebrew Bible) and the New Testament remain somewhat obscure. Canonization implies an authority powerful enough to declare what writings authentically represent faith, and it has the effect of both narrowing the range of data that the orthodox will subsequently consider and widening the scope for creative interpretation of the group's religious traditions.

charism: a gift or talent thought to have been bestowed by God. Many religions have been reinvigorated by charismatic reformers, prophets, and mystics, whose gifts drew followers and seemed to reclarify the religious pathway. Charismatic authority usually stands somewhat in tension with official, institutional authority, and even so sophisticated a religious tradition as the Christian has never fully resolved the relation between the two types of authority. One can say that office and institutional leadership (or service) themselves are charismata, but on the whole the groups that have given special weight to charismata (eloquence, speaking in tongues, healings) have had weak institutional structures and easily splintered into smaller groups.

cleric: an official religious functionary. The word has ties to the ability of people destined for religious service to read and write, and usually it designates the group within a church or non-Christian religious body that constitutes its professional class—its full-time religious functionaries. The typical cleric is a priest, minister, or prayer-leader, and while much of the stability of religious organizations clearly has come from their clerical classes, the clergy have also been the usual target for charges of conservatism, stultification, legalism, and even corruption. So on the whole "cleric" usually stands somewhat in tension with "charismatic," and "clericalism" is not a term of praise.

dogma: official doctrine, set forth by a religious group's duly constituted authorities, that is considered binding on all who are members in good standing and so constitutes orthodoxy. In itself, dogma is a morally neutral term, having the advantage of clearly specifying what the given group believes and requires. As an adjective, however, "dogmatic" also connotes an authoritarian mind-set that is too quick to equate its own decrees with the (relatively few) truths the deity has revealed as necessary for salvation.

eucharist: a Christian term essentially meaning "thanksgiving" but regularly applied to the sacramental sacrifice and meal Christians have celebrated in memory of the Last Supper, death, and resurrection of Jesus. This meal owes debts to Jewish notions about the messianic banquet to be celebrated when God's anointed would bring deliverance and the consummation of history, as well as to the Jewish celebration of the Sabbath and Passover. It has ties with Christian views about the Incarnation of God's Word, the sacramental structure of faith, and the sense that grace has abounded over sin, making good news and thanksgiving Christian watchwords.

evangelical: referring to Christians who take an especially strong stand on the Christian scriptures, as the outward form of the "good news" (*euangellion*) of Christ. Evangelicals draw upon several principles of the Protestant Reformation, including the primacy of scripture over Church authority and the rights of the individual to interpret scripture as the Spirit inspires. Evangelicals run a considerable gamut in their degree of literalness about scripture, submission to Christian tradition and Church authority, and the like. In broadest connotation, any Christian who greatly prized the scriptures could claim to be an evangelical, while in narrow connotation neither Roman Catholics, nor

Eastern Orthodox, nor (for many evangelicals) fundamentalists would qualify, because none would nourish the proper mystique about the presence of the divine power in the scriptural Word.

filioque: the Western Christian teaching that, within the Trinity, the Holy Spirit proceeds not just from the Father but also from the Son. Historically, this represented an addition to the explicit formulas of the earliest ecumenical councils. It became a bone of contention when Eastern and Western Christianity felt themselves estranged. How significant it is in itself depends on one's theology of the Trinity. Some Western Christian theologians think that giving the Son a role in the procession (the "active spiration") of the Spirit helps to prepare an understanding of the Spirit's actions in the order of salvation and this-worldly influence, while some Eastern Christian theologians insist that the filioque represents a move away from a previously more profound appreciation of the "Father," the originating source of the Godhead, as awesomely full and prior in everything relating to the Godhead.

Gnosticism: in general, the tendency to claim a privileged, secret, esoteric teaching about the true state of the world and the true path to salvation; in particular, the movement that challenged Christianity in the early centuries of the Common Era by proposing secret interpretations of either the teachings of Jesus or the divine plan for salvation. These interpretations stressed the fall of human beings from a previous intimacy with God, the need to purify oneself of material desires and let the continuing presence of sparks of one's old divine grandeur assert themselves, and joining with other Gnostics in rites and studies that would lead one back through the heavens to restoration with God.

gospel: the Christian term for the glad tidings announced by Jesus, and then by the Church, and then in the written form of the four evangelical writings that gained canonical status. In the ministry of Jesus the gospel centered on the announcement of the reign of God—the time and state when God would directly reorder all things so that justice and love would prevail. In the ministry of the Church, the gospel became the main content of preaching and liturgical celebration, often focusing on the victory of Christ and the new life brought by Christ's Spirit. In the New Testament the Gospels are seen as so many variants (there were many other "Gospels" that did not gain official approval) of the single proclamation about the time of grace that came with Jesus and continued in Jesus' community.

Gospels: the early Christian accounts of the life, death, and resurrection of Jesus that preserved originally oral memories of what Jesus did and taught. All four of the canonical Gospels are more than mere collections of different local churches' memories, however, because each offers a distinctive interpretation of who and what Jesus was (a distinctive Christology). The Gospels are our best indications of both the historical Jesus and the Christ believed in by the early Church, but on both counts none of them offers simply historical data because each of them is a construct by believers and for believers that begins by assuming the unique holiness of Jesus and his Lordship over the Church.

grace: divine favor, help, or life. Grace can refer to the special help believers believe God gives them to deal with ordinary life and also crises. It can also refer to the gratuity of God's having offered human beings salvation, through the whole mechanism of the salvation history laid out in the Bible and, for Christians, consummated in Christ. Third, it can denote the divine life poured forth in believers' hearts by the Spirit of Christ, a life of knowing and loving that stretches forward toward an eternal consummation ("heaven"). Last, grace can also indicate the presence of God to all people, everywhere, through acts of love and support that draw people toward integrity of conscience, courage in the face of death, and faith that honesty and love are more important than any temporary gains one may make by violating them.

Incarnation: the Christian doctrine that the divine Word (Logos) was made flesh in Jesus of Nazareth. This doctrine specifies the essential mystery of Jesus. For orthodox Christian faith, he is both fully human and fully divine: one "person" possessed of two different "natures." Christian incarnationalism flows from this doctrine, viewing matter as good because worthy of being taken into union with divinity. Christian sacramentalism and iconography look to the Incarnation for their ultimate theological sanction: If God could use matter to make a primary sacrament (the flesh of Christ), then symbolizing the workings of grace and reverencing pictures of Jesus, Mary, and the saints must be legitimate, even required.

indulgence: the (largely Roman Catholic) notion of a pledge that some of the punishment due to one's sins will be remitted because of good deeds. The theology of indulgences depends on an organic notion of the

Church (as the "communion of saints") in which the merits of one may be shared with others. Thinking itself the custodian of these merits, the Catholic hierarchy felt justified in dispensing the merits. At the time of the Protestant Reformation such dispensation had become rather commercial, appearing to Luther and others as a good symbol of the corruption that had degraded biblical faith. To restore the gratuity of salvation and the primacy of the merits of Jesus, they attacked the system of indulgences as unbiblical and scandalous.

Lent: the Christian penitential period (forty days) before Easter. The forty days no doubt derived from the biblical imagery of Jesus' time in the desert (which, in turn, reflected the forty years Israel wandered in the desert before entering upon the Promised Land). When the Christian liturgical cycle centered on the celebration of Easter (the Christian Passover, when Jesus moved from death to resurrection), it no doubt seemed fitting to prepare for this holiest season by doing penance. The regular discipline focused on food, all the faithful who were in good health being supposed to fast between meals and cut down on their overall intake of food. In some periods alcohol was frowned upon, as were sexual relations. Sundays were exempt from Lent, so many Christians relaxed or even partied on Sundays. Prior to Ash Wednesday, the beginning of Lent (when Catholics would receive ashes on their foreheads as a reminder of "ashes to ashes and dust to dust"), Mardi Gras ("Fat Tuesday") often was celebrated as a last, even bacchanalian fling.

liturgy: public, official, ritualized worship. The word comes from the Greek terms for "people" and "work." Thus, the work of the Christian people (and then, by scholarly extension, the worship of other peoples such as Jews and Muslims) was in the first place to praise God. The eucharist was the center of the traditional Christian liturgy, for there people most clearly remembered the grace to which they had been called, the love that had saved them from their sins. When monasticism arose in the Church, the monastic office— singing psalms and praying prayers throughout the day—came to partake of liturgical dignity. The sacraments, as official acts of the Church, also had strictly liturgical status. But in practice even so-called paraliturgical forms of prayer, such as rosaries and novenas (nine-day sessions of prayer and renewal), carried a liturgical patina. As common prayer, done with ecclesial faith—a desire to benefit the entire community—all public worship more or less conformed itself to the pattern most clearly laid out in the eucharistic liturgy.

Logos: the divine Word that Christians identified with Jesus. The Christian doctrine of the Logos had predecessors in both Jewish and Hellenistic thought. The Word that came to the Hebrew prophets at times seemed an entity existing somewhat independently or alongside of God, much like the Wisdom celebrated in the Book of Proverbs. The Logos that interested pre-Socratic philosophers and by the end of the classical period had become part and parcel of the confluence of being and intelligibility served the Hellenistic philosophers (for example, the Stoics) in their speculations about the build of the physical and moral worlds (natural law). In Christianity, the Gospel of John was especially significant, identifying as it did the Word that was with God before the foundations of the world with the divinity that became incarnate in Jesus Christ. The overtones to the Logos included the idea of its being the Wisdom of God (a quality also associated with the Holy Spirit), its being that in which creation hung together (Col. 1:15–20), and its being the revelatory self-expression of the Godhead.

original sin: the Christian notion that the fall of Adam and Eve caused or represents a basic condition afflicting all human beings—a tilt that makes all human actions and thoughts somewhat unjust or impure. This notion owes much to Paul's Epistle to the Romans, especially chapter 5, and gained greater impact through the speculations of Augustine. It has a mirror image in Christian notions about the solidarity of believers in Christ, who like a new Adam gives the whole human race a fresh start. Paul and Augustine both taught that where sin abounded grace had abounded the more, but Western Christianity sometimes forgot this positive tilt. Eastern Christianity did better, stressing the divinization God offered and the pneumatic character of a creation filled by the Spirit of the resurrected Christ.

orthodox: straight, correct, or approved in belief or worship. Doxa can refer to either opinion or praise. Thus, orthodoxy can refer to straightness, correctness, in either doctrine or liturgy. Eastern Christianity has sensed the correlation of the two, insisting on a worship that is primarily praise of the deity and that can only be shared by those who agree in creedal faith. Western Christianity has somewhat agreed, insofar as it has accepted the notion that worship expresses faith—gives the tipoff about what believers actually confess before God. In the context of other religious traditions, the word tends to be used by accommodation to this Greco-Christian etymology, signifying what has come to be accounted acceptable, nondeviant or nonheterodox, in a given area (doctrine, ethics, political policy).

predestination: the notion that God has determined one's fate (especially one's place in heaven or hell) as part of an eternal divine plan. All religions that speak of a deity omnipotent and omniscient have to contend with the problem of predestination, which in turn implies the problem of human freedom. Christian scripture is typical in asserting both that God guides all events and that human beings have a say in their own salvation or damnation. No speculative schema has definitively resolved the relationship between God's action and that of human beings, if only because human beings can never understand God's action (or any of the other infinite divine characteristics). However, some schemata have mitigated problems by underscoring that the divine knowledge and action do not occur in time and consequently do not occur "before" or "after" human choices. For God to know something (for example, the existence of a specific person in heaven or in hell) as existing coincides with the actual existence of that something. It does not precede it and so need not cause it (although it might have to concur in the existential operations that bring that something about).

redemption: retrieval ("buying back"); deliverance from sin. Part of the imagery is that of ransoming a slave from captivity. By paying the debt the slave had incurred, the redeemer satisfies the slaveholder and sets the indentured person free. The analogy to people's religious situations is simple enough. Insofar as sin or ignorance is viewed as bondage, who or what delivers people from sin or ignorance is a redeemer. One need not develop the analogy legalistically, as such theories of redemption as that of the medieval Christian theologian Anselm of Bec threatened to do, to make "payment" a significant image. However, the people redeemed ought to appreciate that effort, even cost, was expended on their behalf. Thereby, they will not think their redemption a cheap grace but rather will appreciate it as a great mercy of their liberator.

resurrection: the Christian notion of being raised from death and transported into the divine presence. Resurrection was a notion current at the time of Jesus, so it made cultural sense to depict his passover from death to Lordship at the "right hand" of the Father as an action of the Father raising him definitively into the heavenly sphere. Theologians sometimes contrast resurrection with immortality of the soul, describing the former as not positing a dualism of matter and spirit. Resurrection bears similarities to notions of rebirth found in many ancient peoples' rites of initiation, but in the Christian understanding it seems to carry a literal core that entails thinking of the risen Jesus as possessing a physical body and being in a "place" where the raised (and transformed) physical bodies of those he saves can join him.

sacrament: a sacred, empowering action, such as the Christian baptism and Eucharist or the Hindu investiture with the sacred thread. The term has flourished in Christian circles, but clearly it may be applied to many religious rituals. Sacraments typically employ symbolic materials—water, oil, bread, wine—that are believed to be filled with a pneumatic power that impresses a spiritual meaning on the person's soul. The sacramental mentality moves by analogy, seeing many correspondences between the literal import of the material used and deeper or higher religious possibilities. Thus, the physical bread and wine of the Christian Eucharist symbolize the spiritual nurture faith requires, and the two lines of thought join in the Christian conviction that in the Eucharist the bread and wine are transformed into the body and blood of Christ.

salvation: saving from sin; making whole and healthy. Insofar as religious cultures generally depict human existence as flawed, they present a situation in which people need salvation. The imagery may be of sickness or ignorance, but regularly it implies that the ordinary human condition requires healing, enlightenment, perhaps even transformation, if it is to measure up to the best aspirations people have. Salvation may focus upon the human personality, or human society, or people's relations with God. Occasionally it even extends to dealings with nature. The saved person claims to have become a unified personality. The saved community speaks of peace and brotherly/sisterly love. Those saved by divine grace speak of being restored to friendship and good relations with the deity. Those for whom healing or enlightenment extends to people's dealings with nature speak of hurting the earth no more and experiencing both flora and fauna as friends. Salvation takes aim at the problem of evil and so is always a central religious concern. If one knows what

a given tradition finds to be saving, one knows much of its potential appeal.

Scholasticism: the medieval Christian movement to develop a rational elaboration of faith. Scholasticism had its roots in Greek philosophy, which had disciplined reason and made it systematically analytical. During the patristic era, Christian theologians began the process of elaborating a Christian world view, trying to coordinate the various insights of the scriptures. Augustine combined a powerful speculative mind with great rhetorical skill, but the Scholastics sought something more detached and scientific. Peter Lombard (ca. 1100–1160) collected the opinions of authoritative Church thinkers on key points of faith, arranging them under the four headings of the Trinity, Creation and Sin, the Incarnation and the Virtues, and the Sacraments and the Last Things. Peter Abelard (1079–1142) introduced sharp dialectical skills, reasoning carefully about the reasons for and against many propositions about faith. Thomas Aquinas (ca. 1225–1274) brought the scholastic movement to a climax, producing the most esteemed of the *summas* that attempted to survey and coordinate all the major topics of faith. Overall, the Scholastics were responsible for placing much greater rigor into Christian theology, though sometimes at the expense of losing its symbolic and mystagogic character.

sin: an offense against God or the sacred moral order. Sin is moral evil—what should not be in the realm of free choice. Though some traditions use the word sin for indeliberate offenses or transgressions of tribal laws, the word has fuller resonance when it names the mysterious twistedness of the human mind and heart. Most theistic traditions are willing to say that all human beings are sinners, but what this means differs from group to group. Christians have emphasized sin more than Jews and Muslims, while Buddhists and Hindus have spoken more of ignorance. From Christian usage, as a secular aftermath, has come the modern Western inclination to speak of all human nature as dangerously pivoted on self-interest. Thus much modern political theory has tried to contrive checks and balances meant to keep a self-serving human nature at bay. This largely translates convictions of the classical Protestant reformers about the corruption of human nature and the necessity for divine grace. But it tends to leave out the possibility of divine grace and so to shift the focus from sin, strictly so called, which is an abuse of freedom that the love of God can overcome, to a humanity so flawed by evolutionary development (laws of the jungle) that nothing can heal it or make peace and justice more attractive to it than power and profit.

theology: study or teaching about God or the gods. In traditional cultures theology tended to be inseparable from general culture, since the basic traditional myths, rituals, and mores all bore on the people's sense of divinity and supposedly expressed the divine will. As knowledge differentiated into separate, specialized areas, theology became associated with ultimate questions, or with the corpus of tradition (scripture, liturgy, speculation about the divine) considered established by revelation. One traditional Western view is that theology is "faith seeking understanding," which puts well the priority belief often has had over vision or argumentative conclusions. Insofar as it purports to bear on the genuine God who exists transcendent to human ways, theology is intrinsically shaped by mystery—the inexhaustible nature of the divinity. What therefore sometimes is called mystical or negative theology is close to the essence, although equally necessary is an affirmative theology that does its best to find language in which to say the few essentials about divinity that human beings can and must say.

Trinity: the Christian God as Father–Son–Spirit. Christians have found the Trinity implied, though not clearly articulated, in the New Testament writings and recorded speeches of Jesus, who prayed to God as to his Father and spoke of the Spirit he would send. In orthodox Christian theology, the three "persons" do not make three gods. Each possesses divinity in its entirety. Each is equally and fully divine, though their relations indicate that the divine life is a system of knowing and loving with a certain structure. The Father is the unbegotten fullness, that beyond which one cannot go in primodiality. The Son is the expression of the Father's self-knowledge, while the Spirit is the result of the love that this self-knowledge issues. Creation is conceived as a work of all three persons, as are other works (salvation, divinization) "outside" the Godhead. Yet the missions of the Son and Spirit make it fitting to associate the divine contributions to the historical processes of creation and divinization (respectively) with them. Jews and Muslims generally have not accepted Christian arguments and have felt that the doctrine of the Trinity compromised strict monotheism. Christians have agreed that none of their arguments or symbols is adequate to explain the Trinity, which they have considered a strictly supernatural mystery, but they have felt the Trinity to be an essential part of biblical revelation.

CHAPTER 6

ISLAM

Crescent and Star: Ancient Byzantine symbols taken over by victorious Islam

The prophetic religion that began with Israel and took a new turn in Christianity gained a further career in Islam. Islam, which is the world's fastest-growing religion today, arose from the visions of the prophet Muhammad. At its height, Islam stretched from India to western Spain.[1] Today it is a great force in Africa, a middling presence in China, a strong presence in the Soviet Union, a shareholder in the petropolitics of the Middle East, a huge presence in Indonesia, and the religion of more than six million North Americans. To study the religion behind the crescent flag, we begin by describing its history.

HISTORY

Muhammad

Islam stems directly from the two precepts contained in the profession of faith: "There is no God but God, and Muhammad is his Prophet." *Allah* (the Arabic term for God) is the ultimate agent of Islamic revelation and religion, but he chose to work through Muhammad. Thus, Muhammad was the spokesman,

Islam: Twenty-five Key Dates	
570 C.E.	*Birth of Muhammad*
609–610	*First Qur'anic Revelations*
622	*Hejira (Flight to Medina)*
630	*Conquest of Mecca*
632	*Death of Muhammad*
636–640	*Conquest of Damascus, Jerusalem, Egypt, Persia*
ca. 650	*Establishment of the Canon of the Qur'an*
661–750	*Umayyad Caliphate*
680	*Murder of Husain, Shiite Saint*
711	*Muslim Entry into Spain*
713	*Muslim Entry into Indus Valley*
750–1258	*Abbasid Caliphate*
762	*Foundation of Baghdad*
909	*Rise of Fatimids in North Africa*
956	*Conversion of Seljuk Turks*
966	*Foundation of Cairo*
1099	*Christian Crusaders Capture Jerusalem*
1111	*Death of al-Ghazali, Leading Thinker*
1258	*Sack of Baghdad by Mongols*
1453	*Ottoman Turks Capture Constantinople*
1492	*End of Muslim Spain*
1707	*Decline of Mogul India*
1803–1804	*Wahabism Victorious in Mecca and Medina*
1924	*Secularization of Turkey*
1947–1948	*Creation of Pakistan and Israel*

the medium, of a definitive message and book (the Qur'an). Through it Allah expressed once and for all the divine mercy and judgment.

Muhammad was born in 570 C.E., in Mecca, which is in present-day Saudi Arabia. Around 610, he began to receive revelations. At that time, the religious milieu of the Arabian Peninsula was "a rather primitive *polydemonism* and worship of stones, stars, caves and trees."[2] Most of the people identified with one of the nomadic tribes that lived in the area. Mecca was a religious and commercial center, where people came to venerate the Black Stone, set in the shrine known as the Kaaba. Today scholars surmise that the stone was a meteorite. Whatever its origin, it served as a rallying point for local soothsayers and poets, who dominated the Arab religion that Muhammad witnessed as a youth. The likeliest forerunners of Muhammad's strict monotheism were the *hanifs,* a group who took offense at the polytheism and sought a purer faith, although to what extent they inspired Muhammad is not known.

W. Montgomery Watt has stressed the commercial strife that divided the people of Mecca during Muhammad's early years.[3] The conflict of the Byzantine and Persian empires affected Mecca, because traders from those realms passed through it. Among the Arabs in the Meccan area, a difficult social transition was under

MAJOR MUSLIM BELIEFS	
Oneness of Allah	Opposition to idolatry
Prophecy of Muhammad	Consummation of revelation
	Muhammad the model Muslim
Divinity of the Qur'an	Qur'an the "incarnation" of Allah's mind and will
Judgment Day	Separation of believers and unbelievers
	Consignment to Garden or Fire
Creation	Allah the Lord of all Worlds
	Humanity the vicegerent of Allah
Ummah	All believers form a brotherhood
	Pilgrimages to Mecca an experience of unity

way from a nomadic society, in which loyalty was to one's clan, to a mercantile society, in which loyalty was to one's business partners (or simply to profit). The result was considerable upheaval. Before that time people such as orphans and widows, who fell outside of nuclear families and trading groups, could find support in their larger clans, but the social change destroyed this support. Muhammad grew up as an orphan, so he must have felt some of the suffering experienced by children not raised by their own parents. Indeed, much of the social reform in his early message was to provide a religious basis for a unity extending beyond the clan and prompting concern for all orphans, widows, and the poor. At issue also were the tribal ethics that included the notions of honor and vendetta: feeling obliged to kill any outsider who had sullied the reputation of one's tribe, especially by bloodshed.

Muhammad grew up in a branch of the ruling Kuraish family under the care of his uncle, and he probably entered his family's caravan trade as a youth. In adulthood he married a wealthy widow, Khadija, who was some years older than he and who had been his employer. They had six children, of whom four daughters survived. Whether from personal troubles, challenges in the social situation, or a positive desire to understand the world more deeply, Muhammad de-

veloped the habit of going off to the hills near Mecca. There, in a cave, he enjoyed meditative solitude and began to have visions. His first visions, according to the Qur'an (53:1–18, 81:15–25) were of someone "terrible in power, very strong."[4] That person hovered near him on the horizon and imparted a revelation. It and subsequent revelations finally convinced Muhammad that God was choosing him to be a messenger.

At first, however, he wondered if he were going crazy. Nonetheless, Khadija encouraged him to believe in the revelations, and as his thought clarified, he attributed them to the angel Gabriel. Muhammad continued to receive revelations for the rest of his life (over twenty years), and those messages, which either he or early disciples wrote down on "pieces of paper, stones, palm-leaves, shoulder blades, ribs and bits of leather,"[5] formed the basis of the Qur'an.

From what scholars conjecture to be the early revelations, given to Muhammad before he moved to Medina, five major themes emerge: Allah's goodness and power, the need to return to Allah for judgment, gratitude and worship in response to Allah's goodness and pending judgment, generosity toward one's fellow human beings, and Muhammad's own vocation to proclaim the message of goodness and judgment.

At first, Muhammad's proclamation met with considerable resistance, principally because it threatened some powerful vested interests. For example, the absoluteness of Allah threatened the traditional polytheism. However, his message was much more than just a challenge to custom and traditional religion—it was a mortal challenge to the commerce that had grown up around the Kaaba. The livelihoods of the merchants who sold amulets, the soothsayers who sold fortunes, and the semiecstatic poets who lyricized the old gods were all imperiled.[6] Second, Muhammad's call for social justice implied a revolution—if not in contemporary financial arrangements, at least in contemporary attitudes. Third, the message of Allah's pending judgment was hardly welcome, for no age likes to find itself set before divine justice, hell fire, or the sword of retribution. Last, many Meccans ridiculed Muhammad's notion of the resurrection of the body.

Rise to Power.   Initially rejected, Muhammad drew consolation from the fate of prophets who had preceded him. Increasingly, it appears, he learned about Judaism and Christianity from believers of those traditions who either lived in the area or traveled it for trade. The first converts to Muhammad's revelations came from within his own family. When he started to preach publicly, around 613, the leaders of the most powerful clans opposed him vigorously. He thus tended to be most successful among the low-ranking clans and those with young leaders ripe for a new order. Also, those who were considered "weak" (without strong clan protection) found the new prophecy attractive. Muhammad was proposing a religious association based on faith in Allah that transcended clan allegiances and so might make the weak stronger.

In 619 Muhammad suffered a personal crisis. His wife and uncle, who had been his foremost supporters, both died. *Muslims* ("submitters" to his God) were slowly increasing in number, but the future was very uncertain. In 622 he left Mecca and went to Yathrib, to the north, to arbitrate a long-standing dispute between two leading tribes. He settled there, and the town became Medina, the town of the Prophet. Muslims call Muhammad's departure or flight from Mecca the *Hejira,* and they view it as the turning point in the history of early Islam. Annemarie Schimmel interprets the Hejira as the complete breakup of Muhammad's relations with his own tribe—a definitive split from the old order,[7] which was a virtually unheard-of act in the clan-based society of the time.

Isma'il al Faruqi emphasizes the positive work that went on in Medina: the "promulgation of a constitution and the launching of the Islamic policy on its universal mission."[8] Muhammad proved to be a good politician, able to organize the immigrants who followed him from Mecca and the Medina clans into a single group.

One problem for Muhammad in Medina was the local Jewish community, which refused to accept him as a genuine prophet and ridiculed his interpretation of Jewish scripture. Apparently Muhammad either drove such Jews out of Medina or had them killed or sold into slavery.[9] After consolidating his power base and building support among the neighboring Bedouin tribes, Muhammad started to challenge his old foes at Mecca. He disrupted their trade in an effort to overturn the city's commercial base, and in 624 his vastly outnumbered troops won a surprising victory at Badr. Finally, after several further skirmishes, Muhammad won a decisive victory at the Battle of the Ditch.

Muhammad's greatest triumphs came through diplomacy among the tribes, however. Mecca finally fell in 630 without the stroke of a single sword. In control, Muhammad cleansed the Kaaba of pagan idols. He then consolidated his victory by a final military triumph over resistant Meccans at Hunayn. This settled the matter for most onlookers, and thenceforth the surrounding tribes were in Muhammad's hands.

In the two remaining years of his life, Muhammad further developed the educational program that he had set up in Medina. "The centre of all his preoccupations was the training, educating, and disciplining of his community. They were to be the leaven to leaven the whole lump—for he had no illusions about the Arab character and realized that any genuine conversion of the majority could only be the end of a long process extending far beyond his own lifetime."[10] Muhammad soon became the focus of Arab solidarity, and just before his death, he apparently contemplated action against the Byzantine powers in the north, perhaps because Muslim nationalism meant a growing hostility toward the Greeks and their Christian Arab allies. The quick military victories of his successors make most sense on the assumption that they simply executed plans that Muhammad himself had formulated.

Personality and Religious Impact.   Although critics have decried Muhammad's violence toward his enemies, he certainly demonstrated an abundant humanity. In addition to his religious sensitivity and his political and military skills, the Prophet apparently manifested a notable sympathy for the weak, a gentleness, a slowness to anger, some shyness in social relations, and a sense of humor.[11] According to the *hadith* (traditions about Muhammad), for instance, one day the Prophet's second in command, Abu Bakr, started to beat a pilgrim for letting a camel stray. Muhammad began to smile and then indicated to Abu Bakr the irony that a pilgrim like Abu Bakr (a pilgrim through life) should beat a pilgrim to Mecca.

In glimpses obtained from the Qur'an and the earliest levels of the tradition, Muhammad seems to have been an ordinary man whom Allah singled out to receive revelations. Muhammad's virtue was to accept his commission and keep faith with it until death. The emphasis in the Prophet's own preaching on the sovereignty of Allah and the divine authority for the Qur'anic message led him to stress his own ordinariness, his liability to error, and the like. For example, at one point he thought that Muslims could compromise with Satan (the "Satanic Verses"), but then he realized that only Allah could receive Muslim devotion. He made no claim to miraculous power. The central miracle was the Qur'an itself—a message of such sublimity and eloquence that it testified beyond doubt to a divine source. In keeping with Muhammad's own humility, orthodox Islam has condemned any move to exalt Muhammad above ordinary humanity or to worship him as divine.

Nonetheless, popular Muslim religion sometimes seized on hints in the Qur'an and made Muhammad superhuman. The most famous of its images is Muhammad's "night journey" (miraculous flight) to Jerusalem, after which he ascended to Paradise, talked with the prophets who had preceded him, and experienced an ineffable vision of Allah. This story became so popular that it finally entered orthodox faith. Later religious faith also elaborated on Muhammad's preaching of the coming Last Judgment and tended to think of the Prophet as its shield and intercessor on the Last Day.

Sufis (mystical Muslims) later elaborated a view of Muhammad as the supreme saint and mystic, while some Muslims given to cosmological speculation gave Muhammad an eternal existence prior to creation, which related to the eternal preexistence of the Qur'an as Allah's own Word. This belief gave Muhammad a role in creation as the intermediary between Allah and humanity. The mystic al-Hallaj, whom Islamic authorities killed because he claimed oneness with the deity, saw Muhammad as the first of the prophets—as the Light that was the source of all their lights: "He was before all, his name the first in the Book of Fate; he was known before all things and all being, and will endure after the end of all."[12] In such understandings, the Prophet became the supreme exemplar, the mediator, something close to the Word of creation.

Qur'anic Religion

After Muhammad's death, his followers collected the texts of his revelations and established the orthodox version of the Qur'an during the rule of Othman (644–656). "To this day this version remains as the authoritative word of God. But, owing to the fact that the kufic script in which the Koran was originally written contained no indication of vowels or diacritical points, variant readings are recognized by Muslims as of equal authority."[13]

The present version of the collection of revelations follows the editorial principle that the chapters (suras) should be ordered in decreasing length. The result is that the present text tells the reader nothing about the chronology of the revelations. While scholars have attempted to distinguish the Meccan utterances from the ones given at Medina, their work is often so refined (distinguishing separate verses within a sura) that no one theory of the chronology of the revelations has won universal acceptance. Therefore, it is more expeditious simply to accept the fact that Muhammad's revelations were written down and collected unsystematically and that he used them as the basis of the program that he urged on his listeners. Among the earliest themes of his preaching, as noted, were the sovereignty of Allah, the imminence of judgment, and the need for fraternal charity.

Kenneth Cragg and other commentators insist on the importance of the Arabic used in the Qur'an.[14] Muslims consider the Qur'an to be written in the purest Arabic. The style of the Qur'an, as well as its message, proves to them that it must have come directly from Allah. Scholars such as Jeffrey and al Faruqi have both given thematic presentations of the Qur'an's religious materials.[15] They organize the Qur'an's seemingly repetitious or circular presentations, and by following their analyses we may get a sense of how Islamic revelation developed.

An early Meccan passage (96:1–5) emphasizes that Muhammad experienced his call as a command to *recite,* although what he was to recite only became clear as time passed. Sura 53, lines 1–18, richly symbolizes how Muhammad experienced his call. Because of Muhammad's vision of the angel Gabriel, the Muslim theology of revelation granted Gabriel an important role as the mediator in transmitting the Qur'an. In Sura 81, lines 15–29, are suggestions that Muhammad's early preaching met with disbelief and even contempt. Indeed, the Prophet seems to have had to defend himself against the charge of *jinn* (demon) possession.

Suras 73 and 74 buttress the tradition that Muhammad regularly used to go off to a cave to pray. Wrapped in a mantle against the night cold, he would seek Allah's comfort. This image has been a model for countless Sufis and ascetics as they have sought an experiential knowledge of Allah. Other Qur'anic passages that are considered reflections of Muhammad's early experiences boom forth a praise of Allah, a sense of Allah's overwhelming majesty, that suggests Rudolf Otto's classic definition of the holy: the mystery that is both alluring and threatening.

The later passages of the Qur'an, those that likely were written in Medina, concern more practical matters. As the head of an established political and religious community, Muhammad had to deal with questions of law and order. Thus, we can find the seeds of later Islamic law on inheritance, women, divorce, warfare, and the like. These seeds, plus the *hadith,* which contain what oral tradition said the Prophet himself taught and judged,[16] are the primary sources of Islamic law. Generally, Muhammad's law and social teaching were advances on the mores of his day. They improved the lot of the downtrodden and humanized both business and war. For instance, Muhammad made widows and orphans the prime beneficiaries of the *zakat* (almsgiving) required of all the faithful. Two points on which outsiders frequently have faulted Muhammad and the Qur'an are the doctrines of holy war *(jihad)* and polygamy. Nevertheless, in both cases Muhammad's views were improvements on the pre-Muslim practices and benefited both women and prisoners of war.

The Five Pillars. On the basis of the Qur'an's prescriptions for a true Islam, a true religion of submission to the will of Allah, Muslims have elaborated five cardinal duties known as the "pillars" of true faith. They are witnessing to faith (proclaiming the creed), ritual prayer, fasting during the lunar month of Ramadan, almsgiving, and pilgrimage to Mecca. The witness to faith epitomizes the Muslim's orientation in the universe. There is no God but God, and Muhammad is his Prophet. Allah is the only fit object of worship, and Muhammad is the last of the prophets—the "seal."

What a comparativist might call the rigorous monotheism of Islam has both negative and positive aspects. Negatively, in what amounts to an attack on false religion, Islam makes idolatry (associating anything with Allah) the capital sin. At the onset, then, Muhammad's revelation implied an attack on the prevailing Arab religion. Later it led to a polemic against Christian Trinitarianism and a check on any worldly pride or mammon that might diminish God's sovereignty. Positively, Islamic monotheism generated great praise for the "Lord of the Worlds"[17]—the Creator who guided all things, who was the beauty and power by which the world moved. For the Muslim mystics, the words of the creed swelled with hidden meaning. Like the Jewish cabalists, some Muslim mystics assigned each letter a numerical value and then composed numerological accounts of how the world hung together. Some Muslim mystics pushed the concept of divine sovereignty so far that they denied the existence of anything apart from Allah. Not only was there no God beside him, there was no being apart from his Being. While the orthodox Muslims found such pantheism blasphemous, the mystics tended to stress the oneness of the Lord's domain.[18] Last, rigorous monotheism implied that Muhammad himself was not divine. His high status was to be the *rasul*—the prophetic mouthpiece. (In later devotion, as we have seen, there was a tendency to exalt Muhammad, while later theology often viewed the Qur'an as coeternal with God, much as rabbinic theology saw the Torah as coeternal with God.)

The second pillar of faith is prayer, which has worked out as an obligation to pray five times daily. Authoritative authors such as al-Ghazali went to great lengths to specify the postures, words, number of bows, and proper places and times for prayer,[19] but the primary effect of the second pillar on the common people was to pace them through the day in the great Muslim practice of remembrance *(dhikr).* At each call from the minaret (prayer tower), they were to remember the one God whom they served—remember his compassion, his mercy, and his justice. Ideally, by praying fervently at the appointed hours, one might forge a chain that linked together more and more moments of remembrance, so that God progressively came to dominate all one's thought, action, and emotion. And, in fact, witnessing Muslim prayer is a moving experience. The slow chant of the Qur'anic words becomes haunting, stirring even the non-Arabist. The voice (usually recorded today) is passionate—a lover's near sob, a tremulous witness to God's grandeur.

Third, what the prayer times are to the day, the holy month of Ramadan is to the year. *Ramadan* is the month of fasting and (interestingly enough) of celebration that helps give the year its rhythmic turning around Allah. Through all the daylight hours of Ramadan (from the time that one can distinguish a black thread from a white), no food or drink is to pass the lips. Thereby, the Muslim learns discipline, sacrifice, and the price that divine treasures cost.[20] In contrast to a secular succession of months, in which no time is finally more significant than any other, the religionist erects special times like Ramadan. These times oppose the flux, fencing off a portion of time as sacred.

Fourth, Islam has developed a similar paradigm for space by praying toward Mecca and by the obligation to make a pilgrimage to Mecca at least once in one's lifetime. For Muslims, Mecca is the center, the *omphalos* (navel) where the world was born. It is the holy city where Qur'anic revelation was disclosed to the world. Thus, the psychodynamics of the pilgrimage run deep. Without doubt, devout pilgrims feel that they are going to the holiest spot in creation.

On pilgrimage, Muslims dress alike, go through the same traditional actions tying their religion to the faith of Abraham, their spiritual father, and often experience an exhilarating sense of community.

The fifth pillar, almsgiving, focuses this sense of community in a practical, economic way. By insisting that all contribute to the support of the poor (often one-fortieth of one's wealth annually), Qur'anic religion gives its community *(Ummah)*[21] food and clothing. The Muslim alms, then, is more than a tiny dole or act of charity—it is an act of social, corporate responsibility. Furthermore, it reminds the advantaged that they are one family with the disadvantaged and that the stern Judge will demand a strict account of what they have done with his gifts.

Case Study: Mary.   Sura 19, entitled "Mary," shows some of the connections between the Qur'an and both Judaism and Christianity. The sura begins with an interpretation of the story of the birth of John the Baptist (Luke 1:5–80). Zacharias, the father of John the Baptist, approached God and prayed for an heir. He received the answer that he would have a son, to be called John, despite the fact that he and his wife were advanced in years. "It shall be no difficult task for Me, for I brought you into being when you were nothing

before."[22] Allah instructed John to observe the scriptures with a firm resolve, bestowing on him wisdom, grace, and purity. John grew up to be a righteous man who honored his father and mother and was neither arrogant nor rebellious. So the Qur'an blesses the day John was born, and blesses the day of his death: "May peace be on him when he is raised to life."

Then Muhammad receives a command to recount the story of Mary, who left her people and betook herself to a solitary place to the east. Allah tells Muhammad that he sent to Mary the divine spirit in the semblance of a grown man. Mary saw the spirit and was seized with fear. But the spirit explained that he was a messenger of Mary's Lord, come to give her a holy son. When she asked how this could be, since she was a virgin, the spirit said that nothing was difficult to God and that this miracle was God's will. The son "shall be a sign to mankind," says the Lord, "and a blessing from Ourself. That is Our decree." Thereupon Mary conceived. When her time of delivery came, she lay down by a palm tree, wishing that she had died and passed into oblivion. But a voice from below her cried out that she should not despair. God had provided her a brook to run at her feet, and if she would shake the trunk of the palm tree it would drop ripe dates in her lap.

Mary took her child to her people, who abused her as a harlot. So she pointed to the baby in the cradle, who spoke up and said: "I am the servant of Allah. He has given me the gospel and ordained me a prophet." The child explained that Allah had commanded him to be steadfast in prayer, to give alms to the poor, to honor his mother, and to be free of vanity and wickedness. Allah had blessed the day of his birth and would bless the day of his death.

The sura then makes a polemical point: This is the whole truth about Jesus, the son of Mary, which "they" (probably the Christians) are unwilling to accept. "God forbid that He himself should beget a son!" In other words, though Jesus had a marvelous birth, he was in no way the divine Son of God. Only Allah is Muhammad's Lord, and the Lord of Muslims. Therefore only Allah is to be served. That is the right path. Any other path is erroneous. The unbelievers who cling to a different view of Jesus will experience woe on the day they appear before Allah, since they are in the grossest error (idolatry).

Next the sura takes up the story of Abraham. Abraham was a prophet and a saintly man. He asked his father, "How can you serve a worthless idol, a thing that can neither see nor hear?" Furthermore, he told his father that the truth had been revealed to him (Abraham), so that if the father followed Abraham he would follow the even path, away from the worship of Satan, who had rebelled against the Lord of Mercy. But Abraham's father only became angry, banishing him from the house and threatening him with stoning. Abraham prayed that the true Lord would forgive his father, but he departed, since he could not worship idols. God rewarded Abraham with sons called Isaac and Jacob, prophets of high renown.

The next story in the sura on Mary concerns Moses, who was a prophet, an apostle, and a chosen man. Allah called out to Moses from the right side of a mountain. When Moses came, Allah communed with him in secret and gave him his brother Aaron, also a prophet. Then there was Ishmael, also an apostle, a seer, and a man of his word. Ishmael enjoined prayer and almsgiving on his people, and thereby he pleased the Lord. Last there was Idris (Enoch), another saint and prophet, whom the Lord honored and exalted.

To all these men, Allah has been gracious. They are the line of prophets, from the descendants of Adam and the people God carried in the ark with Noah. They include Abraham and Israel (Jacob), and they stand out as the line God has guided and chosen. When they received divine revelations, these prophets humbled themselves, falling down on their knees in tears and adoration. In contrast, the generations that succeeded the prophets neglected prayer and succumbed to temptation. Assuredly they shall be lost.

However, those that repent, embrace the faith that Muhammad is preaching, and do what is right will be admitted to Paradise. They shall not be wronged, but shall enter the Garden of Eden, which the Merciful has promised to his servants as their reward for faith. What God has promised, God shall fulfill. In Paradise the just will hear no idle talk, only the voice of peace. Morning and evening they shall receive their sustenance. That is the bliss which the righteous shall inherit.

The sura then interposes a strange transition: "We do not descend from Heaven save at the bidding of your Lord." Muslim commentators tend to interpret this as the voice of the angel Gabriel, answering Muhammad's complaint that the revelations he was receiving sometimes stopped, making for long intervals of silence. Gabriel reminds Muhammad that revelation like this is solely God's affair. To Allah alone belongs what is before us and what is behind us, and all that lies between.

Gabriel goes on to comfort Muhammad. His Lord does not forget his servants. Allah is the ruler of the heavens and the earth and all that is between them. Muhammad's task is simple: Worship him and be loyal in his service. After all, what god compares with Allah? To whom else can a sane or devout person go?

But all human flesh is weak, so it finds faith hard to sustain. Thus human beings regularly ask, "When I am once dead, shall I be raised to life again?" Allah's answer is a call to remembrance. Why do human beings forget that Allah once had to create them from the void? Unless they put their lives in order, Allah will call them to account, placing them in the company of the devils, setting them on their knees around the fire of hell. Each sect of dissidents will have its stoutest rebels cast down into hellfire. Allah alone knows who most deserves to burn.

Sternly, the Lord issues a dire warning: Not one of the unbelievers shall not pass through the confines of hell. This is his absolute decree. Allah will deliver those who fear him, but wrongdoers will go to their knees to endure the torments of the fire. For the conduct of the unbelievers is wanton. When Allah's clear revelations are laid out before them, they say to Allah's faithful, "Will that way add to your glory or place you in better company than ours?" Such questioning and haggling will bring them speedy destruction. Allah has destroyed many generations of unbelievers before this present one. Faithless people far richer and more splendid than they have been sent on their way to destruction.

Yet Muhammad is to tell the unbelievers that Allah is merciful. He will bear with the unbelievers until they witness the fulfillment of his threats, be that a worldly scourge or the hour of doom, when all are called to judgment. At such times of reckoning, the unbelievers will realize the comparative worth of their way and the true way of God. Their worse plight and smaller following will make it clear they have chosen unto their woe.

On the other hand, Allah will more and more guide those who have chosen the right path. Their deeds will bring them lasting merit, a rich reward in Allah's sight, and an auspicious end. The unbeliever, in contrast, has only empty boasts. He expects wealth and children, as though he had had the future disclosed to him, or the merciful Lord, who alone knows what lies ahead, had made him a solemn promise. The truth is far different. Allah will record every word of such vain boasts and determine punishments long and terrible. When the unbeliever is brought to judgment,

Figure 23   *Dome of the Rock, Jerusalem, one of Islam's most splendid shrines, built in the seventh century. Photo by J. T. Carmody.*

he shall come alone, his expected wealth and children having proven only vain imaginings. The unbelievers have chosen other gods to help them. In the end, these useless gods will reject the unbelivers' worship and turn against them. So the unbelievers will be sent down to the devils that incite their irreligion. True believers like Muhammad should be patient. The days of the unbelievers are numbered.

On the day of reckoning, Allah will gather the righteous and bring them before him. But the sinful he will drive in great hordes into the fire of hell. Then no one will be able to intercede for the wicked, save the one (Muhammad?) who has received the sanction of the Merciful.

Again the sura lashes out at those who teach that Allah has begotten a son. That is such a monstrous falsehood that the heavens should crack, the earth should break asunder, the mountains should crumble to dust. Those who ascribe to Allah a son know nothing of the nature of the Merciful. It does not become

him to beget a son. His sovereignty is beyond any such thing. For there is none in the heavens or the earth who shall not return to the Lord in utter submission. Allah keeps strict count of all his creatures. One by one, they shall all approach him on the Resurrection Day. Those he shall cherish are they who have accepted the true faith Muhammad is preaching and shown charity to their fellows.

Concluding, the sura has Allah remind Muhammad that he has revealed the Qur'an in Muhammad's own tongue so that Muhammad can proclaim good tidings to the upright and warnings to a contentious nation. How many generations has the Lord not destroyed before this one? Is one of those past generations still alive? Does any still speak so much as a whisper?

From reading this remarkable bit of the Qur'an, one senses the overwhelming sovereignty of Muhammad's God. Not to believe him, not to accept the way he lays out, is tantamount to blindness or utter corruption of heart. Muhammad finds this way prefigured in the prior prophets of Judaism and Christianity, who deserve high esteem. Jesus, the miraculous child of Mary, the great heroine of faith, was a worthy precursor.[23] But the Christian notion that Jesus was God's son is sheer blasphemy, an effort to diminish the absolute uniqueness and sovereignty of Allah. The Creator is solely responsible for all that happens in the world. Those who confess this will merit good things in the Garden of Eden. Those who reject it will go to hell, the place of punishing fire and devils. So the choice is very simple: Believe and prosper, or reject belief and perish. The Lord is merciful, so belief is offered to all. The Lord is also just, so unbelief cannot evade due punishment. Those with any wit will open their hearts to God's last Prophet and believe.

The Age of Conquest

At Muhammad's death in 632 most of Arabia had accepted Islam, though often the allegiance was superficial. Some tribes took the occasion of the Prophet's death to attempt a revolt. General Khalid al-Walid, who served the first caliph (leader), Abu Bakr, crushed them within a year. Thus, when Abu Bakr died in 634, Arabia was united and poised for adventure. The obvious foes were Byzantium and Persia, which threatened Arabian prosperity and were ripe for religious and military conquest. The Muslim armies were amazingly effective. By the end of 636 they controlled both Damascus and Jerusalem. As important in this lightning conquest as their military skill, though, was the unrest of the peoples they conquered. Those peoples "welcomed the Muslims as kin-liberators from Byzantine politics, economic exploitation, Church persecution, and social tyranny."[24] On the eastern frontier, Muslim armies spread into Persian territory, and by 649 all of Persia was in Arab hands.

The quick conquest of Syria released men for further expeditions in the west; by 640 there were conquests in Egypt. Alexandria soon fell, and despite resistance from the Roman emperor Constans, the Arabs established themselves as a marine power operating from the southeastern Mediterranean. By 648 they had conquered Cyprus; by 655 they were in charge of the waters around Greece and Sicily. On land in North Africa, the Muslims conquered the Berber region of Tripoli in 643 and then proceeded to Carthage and to the Nubian regions along the Nile, conquering the Nubian capital city of Dongola. When the Umayyad caliphate established itself in 661, the ventures became even more far-reaching. Soon Muslims were as far away as China, India, and western Europe. By 699 Islam occupied Afghanistan, while various campaigns south of the Caspian and Aral Seas brought Armenia, Iraq, Iran, and eastern India into the Muslim fold by 800.

At the beginning of the ninth century, Arab rule along the southern Mediterranean stretched from Palestine to the Atlantic. Muslims controlled three-quarters of the Iberian Peninsula, and most Mediterranean traffic had to reckon with Muslim sallies. European campaigns had brought Arab soldiers as far north as Orleans, and they strongly influenced the southern portions of the Frankish kingdom. In 732 Muslims had taken Toulouse and then the whole of Aquitaine, moving into Bordeaux and Tours. Charles Martel stopped them at Poitiers, but in 734 they crossed the Rhone and captured Arles, Saint-Remy, and Avignon. Then they fortified Languedoc and recaptured Lyons and Burgundy. In the ninth century, from their positions in southeastern France, they pushed northeast as far as Switzerland. By daring naval raids, they harassed such ports as Marseilles and even Oye on the coast of Brittany.

Toward the end of the ninth century, Islam controlled most of western Switzerland and ruled many of the Alpine passes. In the mid-tenth century Muslims were at Lake Geneva, taking Neuchâtel and Saint Gall. Only the attacks of the Huns and the Hungarians from the north and northeast and the deterioration of the Spain-based Umayyad caliphate kept them from ruling all of southern Europe. However, Muslim expansion ended after 1050, for the Normans pushed Islam out of southern France, southern Italy, Corsica, Sardinia, and Sicily.

By 1250, Islam's European presence had weakened considerably. Only southernmost Spain and eastern Anatolia (Turkey) held secure. However, Islam had spread through all of Persia, crossed northern India, and reached the western Chinese border. In East Asia, it had a discernible presence in Sumatra, Borneo, and Java. All of North Africa was securely Muslim, while down the East African coast as far as Madagascar it exerted a strong influence. In many of these regions, of course, substantial portions of the populations remained non-Muslim. For instance, in Egypt many Monophysite and Coptic Christians remained loyal to their own traditions, as did many Christians in Anatolia and Syria. Nestorian Christians in Iraq north of Baghdad held out, while portions of southern Persia remained Zoroastrian strongholds. In India the majority remained Hindu, especially in the central and southern regions.

Motivations. Through this age of conquest and expansion, the basic Muslim strategy revolved around the use of the desert.[25] Just as modern empires, such as the British, made great use of naval power, so the Arabs exploited their experience with the desert, using it for communication, transferring supplies, and retreating safely in time of emergency. In their spread through North Africa, they established main towns at the edge of the desert. In Syria they employed such conquered cities as Damascus to the extent that they lay close to the desert. Through the Umayyad period (to 750), these garrison towns at the edge of the desert were the centers of Arab government. By dominating them and by introducing Arabic as the language of government, the conquerors exerted a disproportionate influence (they usually remained a minority of the total population). The towns served as the chief markets for the agricultural produce of the neighboring areas, and around their markets clusters of artisan quarters developed. By imposing discriminatory taxes on the outlying populations, the Arabs encouraged the citizenry to congregate in the cities, making their control easier.

Historians debate the motivation for all this expansion, and we can safely say that it was complex. The Arabs were likely suffering from population pressures on the Arabian Peninsula, which incited many of them to search for more land. Precedents for such an outflow occurred in the fifth and sixth centuries, before Islam, and apparently from even earlier times the land to the northeast, especially the Fertile Crescent, served as a safety valve for overpopulation. Bernard Lewis has suggested that older historians overestimated the role of religion in the Islamic conquests and that more recent historians have underestimated it. In his own view, "its [religion's] importance lies in the temporary psychological change which it wrought in a people who were naturally excitable and temperamental, unaccustomed to any sort of discipline, willing to be persuaded, but never to be commanded. It made them for a time more self-confident and more amenable to control."[26]

Symbolically, religion served as a rallying point for the Arab cause. It stressed common bondage to a single Lord, and it dignified the Arab movement with a sort of manifest destiny. Certainly the generals who dominated the era of conquest were as accomplished in worldly affairs as they were in religion. For Khalid and Amr, two of the most outstanding, the utilitarian values of religion seem to have been clear.

The Islamic administration of the conquered territories was also quite pragmatic. Rather understandably, the interests served were not those of the conquered subjects but those of the aristocracy that conquest created—the interests of the Arab rulers. Thus, the temper of the Arab military commanders and then of the quasi-military Arab governors most determined how Islam treated its new peoples. At the beginning of the conquest in Byzantium and Persia, Muslims kept the old administrative structures. In the 640s, though, they shifted to a new format, through which the caliphs could impress their will more directly.

However, at first there was no unified imperial law. The conquerors struck different bargains with different peoples, and some stipulated that local customs or laws remain in force. The Arabs tended to take only the property of the state (and that of the new regime's enemies); other landowners who were willing to recognize the new regime could keep their holdings provided they paid a sizable tax. Nevertheless, there were opportunities for Muslim "speculators," as we might call them, to gain lands outside the garrison center on which they would have to pay only light levies.

At first, the conquered peoples were allowed to retain most of their traditional civil and religious rights. The Muslims grouped most of the conquered non-Muslims together as *Dhimmis*—members of religions that Arab law tolerated. As "peoples of the book," Jews and Christians were *Dhimmis,* with title to special respect. There were nevertheless frictions, especially if Jews or Christians were blatantly derogatory of the Prophet and his Book, but usually people were not compelled to convert to Islam. Because Arab rule regularly promised to be more just than Byzantine rule, many Jews and Christians are on record as having welcomed the change. For example, in Palestine the Samaritans actively assisted the invaders. The Arabs were not always sure how to handle such complicity, especially when it developed into a desire to convert to Islam. Islam and Arabism were so synonymous that the first converts had to become *Mawali*—clients of one of the Arab tribes. In fact, converts seldom gained status equal to born Muslims, especially regarding such material benefits as the booty that warriors received after a conquest.

Internal Strife. Despite its enormous outward success in the age of conquest, the Islamic community suffered notable internal divisions. With the exception of Abu Bakr, the first caliphs, known as the *Rashidun* (rightly guided), all left office by murder. (Despite that fact, modern Islam has considered their time the golden age.[27]) Ali, the fourth caliph, was the center of a fierce struggle for control. His main opponent was Muawiya, the head of a unified stronghold in Syria. Muawiya maneuvered to have the legitimacy of Ali's caliphate called into question. As a result, Ali lost support in his own group, and dissidents called Kharijites appeared who had a hand in many later conflicts. A Kharijite killed Ali in 661, and the caliphate passed to the Umayyad dynasty—the followers of Muawiya.

However, Ali's influence did not end with his assassination. In fact, his assassination became part of Islam's deepest division, the one between the *Shia* (party), who were loyal to Ali, and the *Sunni* (traditionalists). The "party" supporting Ali believed that the successors to Muhammad ought to come from Muhammad's family—in other words, that Islamic leadership should be hereditary. (As the cousin and son-in-law of Muhammad, Ali was his closest male relative and so his heir.) This conviction was supported by certain verses of the Qur'an, in which the Prophet supposedly indicated that Ali would be his successor. The Shia therefore consider the first three caliphs, who preceded Ali, as having been usurpers. After Ali's death, they took up the cause of his sons, Hasan and Husain.

The word that the Shia gave to the power that descended through Muhammad's family line was *imamah* (leadership). Through its history, the Shia has made it a cardinal doctrine that Muhammad's bloodline has an exclusive right to *imamah*. The slaughter of Husain in Iraq in 680 was an especially tragic event, and the Shiites (who have been strongest in Iran) have come to commemorate it as the greatest of their annual festivals. It gives their Islam a strong emphasis on sorrow, suffering, and emotion that quite distinguish it from Sunni piety.[28]

Of course, our brief summary has presented only a slice of the dense military, political, and religious history that shaped the first unfolding of Qur'anic faith. Externally, Islam's quick successes testified as much to the political vacuum within which the conquered peoples lived and to their oppression as it did to Arab military genius. Internally, Islam's great energy made for considerable strife. However, during the following centuries, religion and culture caught up with the military wildfire of the initial expansion, consolidating the empire and making it much more than just a far-flung string of garrisons.

The Golden Civilization

In his history of science, Stephen Mason states that Muslim scientific culture began in the era of the Umayyads.[29] The Umayyads had been auxiliaries of the Romans in Syria, so when they established the caliphate in Damascus in 661, they brought an enthusiasm for Hellenistic culture. In particular, they became patrons of the sciences. For example, in 700 they founded an astronomical observatory at Damascus. However, the Umayyads fell to the Abbasids in 749, Umayyid rule continuing only in Spain. The Abbasids set their caliphate in Baghdad and turned to Persian rather than Hellenistic culture, supporting the Persian specialties of medicine and astronomy. Al-Mansur, the second Abbasid caliph, was also devoted to learning, bringing Indian astronomers and doctors to Baghdad and having many Indian scientific treatises translated. Under his successors, translation continued to be a major project, any nation's heritage being fair game. As a result, many Greek treatises (for example, those of Galen and Ptolemy) became available to Muslims. Partly because of Babylonian and Zoroastrian influences, the Baghdad caliphs deemed astronomy especially important. They imported Indian mathematicians to help in astronomical calculations and made Baghdad a center of astronomical learning.

Al-Razi (865–925) collected voluminous lore on medicine from Greek, Indian, and Middle Eastern sources. Indeed, he may even have drawn on Chinese sources, for there is a story that he entertained a Chinese scholar who learned to speak Arabic, and his successors' works include what seems to be the Chinese doctrine of what one could learn from the body's pulses. A Muslim alchemy arose in the ninth century with Jabir ibn-Hayyan, but in Islam alchemy remained somewhat suspect because the authorities linked it with mystical religion. Some radical Sufis became deeply involved in alchemy, but orthodox Sunni had the works of at least one such group, the "Brethren of Purity," declared heretical and burned. Principally, the orthodox favored the rational geometry and deductive science of the Greeks.

From 970, the Spanish branch of the Muslim Empire had a distinguished scientific center in Cordoba.

Similarly, the religious authorities patronized science, especially medicine and astronomy, at Toledo from the early eleventh century. The Spanish Muslims tended to be critical of Ptolemy and to favor Aristotelian doctrines. Averroës (1126–1198) was a great Aristotelian synthesizer who composed a full philosophical corpus.

By conquering the territory between the Muslim East and the kingdom of Sung China, the Mongols expedited trade and the flow of learned information between East and West. Marco Polo (1254–1324) was able to travel to the East because of Mongol rule, which also enabled the Chinese Mar Jaballaha (1244–1317) to come West and become the Nestorian Christian patriarch. When the Mongols conquered China they left its bureaucratic structure intact. They set up an observatory in Peking and staffed it with Muslims. In the West they conquered the Abbasid capital of Baghdad in 1258, where they continued to support astronomical studies.

Albert Moore has shown the effects of Islam's monotheism in the field of art, arguing that it led to a classical concentration on the architecture and ornamentation of the mosque.[30] This art reached its peak in the sixteenth and seventeenth centuries, leaving impressive monuments in Ottoman Turkey, Safavid Persia, and Mughal India. Schuyler Cammann[31] has shown exceptions to the generally nonrepresentational character of Islamic art in Persian works, and Moore indicates that paintings of hunting and of love scenes were permitted in private Muslim homes. Nonetheless, the preponderance of Muslim art during the golden age was nonpictorial, including rugs, vases, lamps, and mosques.

A distinctively Islamic calligraphy developed from the trend to decorate pages from the Qur'an. The Qur'an itself praises the art of writing (96:4), and speaks of being written on a heavenly tablet (84:21–22). The favorite script was Kufic, which originated in the new Islamic town of Kufa near Babylon, and it was the standard scriptural model from about the seventh to eleventh centuries. It is vertical, massive, and angular, while its prime alternate, the Naskhi script, is horizontal, flowing, and rounded. A favorite subject of embellishment has been the *Bismallah,* the prefix to the Qur'anic suras ("In the name of God"). Through an extension of calligraphic swirls and loops, Muslims developed an ingenious ability to suggest flowers, birds, lions, and so on. The Sufi interest in numerology also encouraged artistic work.

Case Study: Architecture and Poetry. As we suggested, Islam also influenced architecture. The mosque was a sort of theology in the concrete. Muslim architects tried to embody the faith and conviction that all of life stands subject to Allah and so that no great distinction should be made between sacred dwellings and profane. The guiding idea in the construction of a mosque was simply to house a space for prayer and prostration. The *hadith* reported that the Prophet led his first companions outside the city, so that they could pray together in an open space. At Medina, the usual place for prayer was the open courtyard of Muhammad's own house. For convenience, the architects tried to construct a churchlike building that had the character of an open space where many faithful might go through the same rhythmic motions of bowing, kneeling, prostrating, and praying together.

Mosque architecture tended not to differ radically from that of Muslim palaces. Most of the renowned Muslim palaces have crumbled, but the Alhambra, in Granada, Spain, still stands, a glorious tribute to the Muslim golden age. The Alhambra was built between 1230 and 1354 and served as a great citadel for the Moorish kings. It was mutilated after the expulsion of the Muslims in 1492, but extensively restored from 1828 on. Its beauty suggests the Muslim notion of how religion and secular life ought to interpenetrate.

Physically, the Alhambra is located on a hill overlooking the city of Granada. Although it is surrounded by walls and has the look of a fort, only the lowest parts of the enclosure were actually used for military purposes. According to early Islamic tradition, palaces were supposed to be placed as the Alhambra is: close to the city, yet a little bit apart. Thus the Alhambra strikes us as a country villa, yet also like an urban citadel. One gets the same impression from similar palaces in Aleppo (northwest Syria) and Cairo. There, too, the effort was to retain the amenities of a royal palace while fortifying the ruler's residence against possible incursions. Such military considerations led to architectural innovations in the vaulting, gateways, and towers of the *qal'a* or urban citadel.

The Alhambra goes beyond a simple fusion of the villa and citadel traditions, however, by breaking its sizable area into a series of separate units. Some of these units are lovely gardens, in the Muslim paradisic tradition. For example, both Iranian and Indian Muslim palaces frequently sought to prefigure Paradise by developing lovely royal gardens. Of the other units of the Alhambra, the most celebrated is the Court of the Lions. The Court of the Lions has an impressive portico running along several sides, with slim, delicate pillars supporting strong arches. The open space in the center is handsomely tiled, and a small fountain with flowers at the base adds splashes of color. Off the court run complexes of square and rectangular rooms, as though the architect wanted to suggest sumptuousness. This is what one commentator calls the "additive" principle: adding room after room, to imply that the royal resources were limitless. The delicate, filigreed work on some of the wall panelings gives an impression of exquisite lace.

"The most important point is that very few of the halls and courts of the Alhambra had an architecturally definable purpose. A curious dissociation seems to have occurred between building and function, as though individual forms which are definable in architectural terms as courts, porticoes, square or oblong halls, and so forth, were merely generalized forms in which a variety of purposes, from traditional audiences to various pastimes, could be performed."[32] This dissociation, or apparent lack of precise function, was a feature of many other Muslim buildings. The masses of kiosks or pavilions in the palaces of Cairo or Istanbul, for example, were similarly "formal" constructions and did not suggest precisely what activities would take place in them. One could relate this Muslim style to recent Western tendencies toward "multipurpose rooms," which are capable of being turned into lecture halls, dining areas, or gymnasiums with little effort.

A third feature of the Alhambra, beyond its fortified and multipurpose aspects, is its extraordinary attention to decoration. When one is inside the Alhambra, the most gripping feature is the careful ornamentation of the pillars, walls, ceilings, and floors. Once again, commentators generalize from the Alhambra to Muslim buildings of Iran, Central Asia, or Turkey. In all these places, the themes and techniques of internal palace decoration were spectacular.

If one asks why Muslims lavished such care on the internal aesthetics of their palaces, the Alhambra provides an important clue to the answer. The impressive stalactite domes, and the thin pillars of the Fountain of the Lions, apparently derived from the medieval Muslim understanding of Solomon, the famed biblical king. In the medieval mythology surrounding Solo-

mon, the jinns made wonderful scenes of beauty for him and his queens. Thus medieval Muslim rulers had a certain stimulus to create scenes of an otherworldly, separate Paradise. Wanting to produce by natural means beauty such as that which Solomon achieved by supernatural power, they came to stress gardens, delicate decorations, and almost tours de force of engineering (thin pillars holding stupendous domes, for instance).

Less spectacularly, the motivations behind architecture like that of the Alhambra led to the "monumentalization" of many ordinary Muslim buildings. Thus in many urban areas, schools, shops, hostels, hospitals, baths, and even warehouses were built with great facades and intricate decorations. The caravanserais (motels, we might say) of thirteenth-century Anatolia, for example, employed the latest and most sophisticated techniques of construction. A religion that had a large place for "works"—business, pragmatic affairs, military matters—placed great stress on housing its social activities and secular affairs well. Also, in the medieval period Muslims tended to invest in land or buildings rather than trade or industry. The result was an architecture that little distinguished between the mosque and the secular building. Facades, for instance, seldom gave external viewers a basis for determining what sort of building they were entering. It was the internal decorations of the buildings, or the activity that occurred within them, that gave them their distinction.

In the history of architecture, the Muslim achievements stand out as the most significant development in the period from Roman times to the Middle Ages. Indeed, the Muslim development of monumental buildings for secular purposes was rivaled only by Roman lavishness. For the most part, this sort of construction seems to have gone forward haphazardly, out of an instinct that daily life ought to be housed well. Exceptions to this general rule stand out: for instance, the organized city planning of Samarkand, Isfahan, and Istanbul.

Curiously, even the specifically religious architecture of Islam was influenced by Islamic secular monumentalism. From the tenth century on, the growth of domes, minarets, and mausoleums was mainly due to a desire to honor and publicize the people who were building the religious constructions, rather than to a desire better to serve the religious activities the constructions would house. Thus Islamic architecture differs from European medieval architecture as consciously more secular.

From the time of the building of the famous Jerusalem Dome of the Rock (Figure 23) in 691, the decoration we stressed in the case of the Alhambra preoccupied Muslim builders. Indeed, increasing the decorative beauty of their buildings seems to have been a prime motivation in the Muslims' development of stucco, in their laying bricks to make bold designs, and in their creation of colored tiles. This concern with ornamentation leads to the question of how Muslim construction and decoration relate, a question historians of Islamic architecture debate with some vigor.

A good case to study is the mosque of Cordoba. In the *mihrab* (niche to designate the direction of Mecca) of the Cordoba mosque the domes contain such unusual features as ribs that appear to support the cupola yet form a static mass with the cupola. The squinches (a characteristic support of domes) that accompany the ribs do not really support anything. In other words, the ribs and squinches are present for decorative, rather than constructive, reasons. The north dome of the great mosque in Isfahan, Persia, built a century after the *mihrab* of the mosque in Cordoba, has an unusual articulation of supports that also seem more decorative than constructive. The supports correspond to every part of the superstructure and give the impression of being a grid or net filled with decorative masonry. Third, the Muslim use of *muqarnas,* three-dimensional shapes used in many different combinations, seems clearly intended for decorative, rather than constructive, purposes. The *muqarnas* draw attention to some principal parts of a building, but they usually have little significance in terms of engineering.

The debate among scholars of Muslim architecture seems to turn on what value one ought to give these decorative features. Perhaps the best resolution of the debate, for our lay purposes, is the one that stresses that Muslim architects apparently strove, through their engineering and ornamentation alike, to produce a distinctive overall effect. In their great masterpieces, the whole is greater than the sum of its parts. Engineering and ornamentation have so blended that one gets an effect that is more than either brilliant constructive design or artful decoration. The *muqarnas* domes, for example, often give the effect of the revolving heavens. As the source of external light moves around the base of the dome, the complex surface that the *muqarnas* produce on the cupola gives

an illumination that is always changing. Like the heavens, the top of the mosque never looks the same yet seems quite motionless.

Due to the secular impact of Muslim faith, then, Islamic architecture developed such characteristic features as a preponderance of activity (use) over form, a tendency to monumentalize buildings that served quite ordinary functions, and a tendency to fuse construction and decoration into one harmonious entity. However, Islam seldom created its architectural forms entirely from Muslim inspiration. Ordinarily it adapted non-Muslim forms influential in an area it had conquered. Thus in Iran Islamic architects made use of the pre-Islamic *aywan,* a large vaulted hall opening directly onto an open space. This became an axial feature of Iranian mosques, and of Iranian Muslim secular buildings as well. Similarly, in Ottoman Turkey the superb mosques of Istanbul adapted features of the famous Christian cathedral of Hagia Sophia (Holy Wisdom).

Since it conquered so many different areas, Islam had the opportunity, and the need, to graft Muslim ideas onto a variety of different architectural traditions. In India, for example, it tended to experiment with several different Near Eastern Muslim models, trying to adapt them to the local Indian traditions and materials. The result often was a fairly hybrid style, brilliant in such well-planned constructions as the Taj Mahal (Figure 27 on page 257), but often undistinguished in more commonplace undertakings.

Summarily, then, Muslim architecture suggests that (1) Islam tended to prize buildings as much for their versatility in being able to serve several functions as for their formal beauty, and (2) it tended to show more originality and brilliance in secular than in strictly religious constructions. Both these characteristics expressed the Muslim conviction that religion ought to breathe through all dimensions and activities of life. If one Lord ruled all of creation, overseeing each and every human activity, the distinction between sacred functions and profane was quite small.

The basic ornamental motif in much other Islamic art is repetition, seemingly endless patterns, whether representational (roses and leaves), semiabstract (vine tendrils and rosettes), or completely abstract (geometric patterns). This motif is known as the infinite pattern, and some suggest that it has theological significance. It does not want to rival God by creating anything fixed or permanent. Popular art often

Figure 24 *Courtyard of Cairo Mosque, with purification fountain. Photo by J. T. Carmody.*

violated this pattern, suggesting that it most applied to mosques and official constructions. For instance, a Persian manuscript painting of the sixteenth century portrays Muhammad's ascent to Paradise, complete with winged angels, dishes of fruit, showers of pearls, and rubies.

Poetry. A. J. Arberry has translated a representative collection of Islamic writings,[33] and it suggests a great breadth and lyricism. Poetry had always held a place of honor among Arabs, for eloquence had always been considered a trait of a great man, even before the advent of Islam. Much as the Greeks valued military prowess and the ability to persuade others, so the Arabs honored both warfare and eloquence.

The ancient poetry was born in the desert, so it was replete with desert images and themes. With expansion and conquest, however, Islam became largely an urban culture,[34] so there was need to reshape its poetry. Meter, rhyme, and new imagery became the chief tools. The result was a very complex style: "We have called this poetry arabesque, and indeed it is fully as exquisitely and delicately ornamented as the finest Saracenic architecture."[35] The thirteenth-century poet Ibn al-Khabbaza fashioned an elegy that epitomized Arab eloquence: "Your life was of the order true of Arab eloquence; the tale was brief, the words were few, the meaning was immense."[36]

The themes that dominate Arberry's poetic selections are not especially religious: the beauty of a beloved, trees, battle, and, for humor, the flanks and shanks of an ant. Still, some of the religious mystics, such as Junaid, Rumi, and the woman Rabia, gained fame for their poetic skills. Most were Sufis—devotees of religious emotion and feeling. Among the religious poets of Islam, the Persians were most eminent. Their themes and images centered on the Sufi goal of self-effacement in the divine immensity. For instance, Rumi often portrayed the soul's sense of abandonment in moments of trial when it could not feel the divine embrace: "Hearken to this Reed forlorn, Breathing ever since 'twas torn from its rushy bed, a strain of impassioned love and pain."[37] In this way, the talented Sufi writers won considerable respect from cultured people. To be able to express their religious vision with eloquence made them seem less eccentric, more representative of traditional Arab cultural ideals.

Law and Theology.   Within the inner precincts of Islam, neither science nor art constituted the main cultural development. Rather, the most important flowering of Qur'anic faith was the law (*Sharia*).[38] As the opening verses of the Qur'an suggest, a fundamental concern in Islam is guidance, and Islam went to lawyers, not to scientists, poets, or even mystics, for its most trustworthy guidance. In fact, Islam obtained little guidance from philosophical theology, which began a most promising career but foundered on the shoals of sectarian controversy and debates about the relation of reason to faith. Although numerous schools of law developed, the differences among them were relatively slight, and they usually subordinated speculative reason to faith and tradition. Thus, the authorities accounted them more trustworthy than philosophical theology—better cement for Muslim society.

Traditional Islamic law has thought of itself as derived from Allah's plan for the proper ordering of human life. Its province has extended to whatever impinged on human beings' passage to Paradise. A term equivalent to *Sharia, figh* ("understanding" or "knowledge"), implied that the laws developed by the lawyers expressed what was understood to be behavior that would keep believers on the straight path.

The classical *figh* treatises follow a similar format. First, they usually discuss people's obligations to God. For example, there are detailed rules for how to carry out daily prayers, the pilgrimage to Mecca, fasting during the month of Ramadan, and almsgiving. As well, one's obligations to God have included identifying sources of ritual pollution, carrying out ablutions to achieve ritual purity, the proper preparation of a corpse for burial, and the selection of a prayer leader for the community.

A second interest of the *figh* rules usually bears on what we might call horizontal relationships (in contrast to the vertical relationship between the be-liever and God): marriage, divorce, freeing slaves, oaths, criminal penalties, relations with nonbelievers, partnerships, contracts, the slaughter of animals, use of the land, fines, wills, sports, prohibited drinks, and much more. Some of these topics traditionally got more attention and development than others, in part because the religious courts were more able to detail and enforce laws concerning them: inheritance law, family law, and law concerning pious endowments for good works (schools, hospitals, etc.), for example.

On the whole, Islamic law has most concentrated on what sometimes is called "personal law": marriage, divorce, and inheritance. These areas continued to receive great attention and stay under the influence of religious lawyers even in the twentieth century, somewhat in contrast to the secularization of such other areas as taxation, criminal law, and constitutional law. Interestingly, however, with the rise of fundamentalist influences in many Muslim countries during the 1970s and 1980s has come a trend to rethink even these latter, secularized legal areas in terms of older traditions that assumed there was no unreligious, secular dimension in a good Muslim's life.

The early theological discussions dealt with the nature of faith. Idolatry and unbelief were the major evils for the Qur'an, so it was important to understand them well. The types of sins were also an important early theological focus. Later debates focused on the unity of God (in the context of discussing the divine attributes) and on the relation of the divine sovereignty to human freedom. While there was a full spectrum of opinions, in Sunni quarters the more moderate positions tended to win favor. Before long, however, Islam effectively curtailed speculation, favoring instead careful efforts to ascertain what legal precedents any *practical* problem had in the Qur'an, the *Hadith* of the Prophet, community consensus, or analogous situations. (These were the four main sources of religious authority).

To be sure, Muslims did not view religious law or theology as a human creation. Rather, it was divine guidance, the expression of God's own will. The goal of the teachers was to offer comprehensive guidance for all of life—much as the rabbis' goal was to apply the Torah to all of life. The lawyers classified theology among the obligations one owed to God, for theology was the science of right belief, and right belief was primary among the things that human beings owed to God. As they refined their science, the teachers also distinguished all human actions according to five headings: obligatory, recommended, permitted, disapproved, and forbidden. Thus, one had to confess the unity of God and the Prophethood of Muhammad, one was counseled to avoid divorce, and one was forbidden to eat pork. Since Muslim society was a theocracy, *Sharia* was the code of the land. While that made for a certain unity and order, it also prepared the way for the Sufi emphasis on personal devotion as a counterweight to legalism.

The Period of Division

A minor source of division within the Muslim community was the differences in law developed by the various schools. The Hanafite school came to dominate Muslim countries north and east of the Arabian Peninsula. Within Arabia itself the dominant school was founded by ibn-Hanbal. Northeast Africa was under Shafite and Hanafite lawyers, while Malikite opinions were the most prestigious in northwestern Africa. In Persia the Shia sect had its own law. On the whole, that distribution still holds today.

Given the four recognized legal codes of Sunni, the large Shia minority, and the division of the Islamic Empire into eastern and western parts centered at Baghdad and Cordoba, respectively, one can see that religious and political unity was less than perfect. Still, Muslims holding to the Five Pillars and the Qur'an had much more in common with one another than they had with any non-Muslim peoples. Thus, legal or creedal differences did not divide Muslim religion severely. In contrast, different devotional styles, such as *Sufism,* caused considerable hubbub.

Sufism. Opinions about the merits of Sufism differ. Fazlur Rahman, commenting especially on the work of al-Ghazali (1058–1111), speaks of the "fresh vitality" that al-Ghazali's devotionalism infused into the Muslim community.[39] Isma'il al Faruqi, on the contrary, cites Sufism as the first step in Islam's decline from its golden civilization.[40] It is true that al-Ghazali was not a typical Sufi (he had great learning as well as great piety), and that al Faruqi's sympathies lie with the reforming Wahabis (see below), for whom Sufism was an abomination. Still, a survey of studies shows quite mixed reactions to Sufism. Most commentators agree that its initial centuries (the ninth through thirteenth) were more creative and positive than its later ones.

At the outset, Sufism (the name likely comes from the Arabic word for wool, which Sufis wore as a gesture of simplicity)[41] stood for reform and personal piety. In a time when political and military success tempted Islam to worldliness, and the rise of the law brought the dangers of legalism, the Sufis looked to the model of Muhammad at prayer, communing with God. For them the heart of Islam was personal submission to Allah, personal guidance along the straight path. In later centuries, through its brotherhoods and saints, Sufism set a great deal of the emotional, antiintellectual, and antiprogressive tone of an Islam that had lost its status as a world power.

Several cultural streams ran together to form the Sufi movement. First was the ascetic current from traditional desert life, which was basic and simple—a daily call for endurance. Out of a keen sense of the religious values in such a harsh life, Abu Dharr al-Ghifari, a companion of the Prophet, chastised the early leaders who wanted to lead a sumptuous court life after their conquests. Second, many of the Sufi ecstatics, as we mentioned, drew on the Arab love of poetry. Their lyric depictions of the love of God, coupled with the Qur'an's eloquence, drew sensitive people to the side of a living, personal faith that might realize the beauties of Islam.

Third, the more speculative Sufis drew on gnostic ideas that floated in from Egypt and the Fertile Crescent. By the ninth century, Sufi contemplatives (especially the Persian Illuminationists) were utilizing those ideas to analyze the relations between divinity and the world. (The Sufis seem to have found most attractive the emanational ideas—the theories of how the world flowed out of the divine essence—rather than the dualistic theories of good and evil.) This kind of understanding, along with the alchemical interests noted previously, was the beginning of the esoteric and sometimes magical lore for which the orthodox theologians and lawyers held the Sufis suspect. Last, Indian (especially Buddhist) thought apparently influenced the eastern portions of the Muslim realm, and it perhaps was a source of the tendencies toward self-annihilation (loss of personal identity in God) that became important in Sufi mystical doctrine.

Taken at their own word, the Sufis desired to be faithful followers of Muhammad and the Qur'an. The more honored among them never intended any schismatic or heretical movements. Rather, they resembled spiritual writers of other traditions, such as the Christian Thomas à Kempis, in that they wanted to "feel compunction rather than know its definition." The most famous statement of this desire occurs in al-Ghazali's description of his withdrawal from his prestigious teaching post in Baghdad to settle the conflicts in his soul: "I was continuously tossed about between the attractions of worldly desire and the impulses towards eternal life."[42] Upon retiring into solitude to purify his soul, he found the peace he had sought. From being a learned philosopher, theologian, and lawyer, he became a follower of the mystical way, which the Sufis represented: "I learnt with certainty that it is above all the mystics who walk on the road of God; their life is the best life, their method the soundest method, their character the purest character; indeed, were the intellect of the intellectuals and the learning of the learned and the scholarship of the scholars, who are versed in the profundities of revealed truth, brought together in the attempt to improve the life and character of the mystics, they would find no way of doing so."[43]

In Idries Shah's collection of Sufi sayings,[44] one catches overtones of the pedagogical genius that the spiritual masters developed. Much like the Jewish Hasidim, they fashioned stories to carry their messages about the paradoxes of the spiritual life, the need for being focused and wholehearted, the way that God comes in the midst of everyday life. In these stories, the poor man turns out to be rich; the fool turns out to be truly wise. Like their counterparts in other traditions, the Sufis left no doubt that riches and prestige tend to be obstacles to spirituality. As well, they questioned the rational, "right-handed" portions of the personality, arguing that the more intuitive, "left-handed" portions must have their due if one is to achieve balance and fullness.

Predictably, this challenge to the expectations of society, of the religious authorities, and of the literally minded won the Sufis no love. Perhaps to intensify their opposition, some Sufis became even more provocative, challenging the establishment and suggesting that its religion was little more than dead convention. For instance, when Hasan of Basra was asked what Islam was and who were Muslims, he replied, "Islam is in the books and Muslims are in the tomb."[45] This oracular reply could mean that the Qur'an holds the secrets to true submission and that the earth holds the bodies of the great exemplars of the past. However, it could also mean that what people take to be Islam (the official version) is actually a dead letter, something buried and forgotten, because no one lives it anymore. Along similar lines is a story of a dervish who meets the devil. The devil is just sitting patiently, so the dervish asks him why he is not out making mischief. The devil replies, "Since the theoreticians and would-be teachers of the Path have appeared in such numbers, there is nothing left for me to do."[46]

Decline.   By the beginning of the fourteenth century, the age of some of the greatest Sufi figures was over; Sufism started to decline, and with it much of Islam's religious vitality. The orders continued to multiply, and many princes and sultans continued to patronize them, but abuse, scandal, and superstition became more and more common. In Arberry's view, "It was inevitable, as soon as legends of miracles became attached to the names of the great mystics, that the credulous masses should applaud imposture more than true devotion; the cult of the saints, against which orthodox Islam ineffectually protested, promoted ignorance and superstition, and confounded charlatanry with lofty speculation. To live scandalously, to act impudently, to speak unintelligibly—this was the easy high road to fame, wealth, and power."[47]

Still, the Sufis played a considerable role in the expansion of Islam, largely by serving as models of piety for the common people and giving them hopes of wonder working. For instance, Sufi folk literature played an important role in the expansion of Indian Islam during the fifteenth through seventeenth centuries,[48] while genuine Sufi spirituality aroused strong devotion in North Africa well into the twentieth century.[49] The organizations carrying Sufi influence were the Sufi orders, or brotherhoods. The first seems to have dated from the twelfth century. Abd al-Qadir, who began his religious career in Baghdad as a student of Hanbalite law, converted to Sufism and became a preacher of the holy life. The many converts and followers that he gathered came to call themselves Qadiris, and historians often regard their association as the first brotherhood. It has been especially influential in India, where it has a presence even today. Al-Qadir was a traditionalist who called for strict adherence to the Qur'an and condemned any antinomian (lawless) tendencies. No doubt this helped his group become acceptable.

A second great order, also influential in India, derived from al-Suhrawardi (1144–1234), a moderate. Other orders of significant number and influence were the Shadhiliya, who were especially successful in

Egypt, North Africa, Arabia, and Syria, and the Turkish order of the Mevleviya, which derived from the renowned Persian poet Rumi.

Typically, at the order's local lodge, a small number of professionals resided to teach and lead worship. Most members have been lay adherents who came for instruction when they could and who supported the lodge by contributing money, manual labor, and so on. Each order tended to have its own distinctive ritual, whose purpose was usually to attain ecstatic experience. The ritual was the group's interpretation of the general virtue of *dhikr* (remembrance) that all Muslims seek. For instance, whirling dances characterized many of the Mevlevi dervish meetings, while Saadeeyeh Sufis developed a ceremony in which the head of the order rode on horseback over prone devotees.

The writings of the contemporary theosophist Gurdjieff have introduced a number of Sufi ideas into recent American consciousness. Overall, however, Islam has been making its greatest strides among Africans who have found that it suits their traditional tribal structure and their nationalistic mood better than Christianity.[50] The divisions and declines that sundered Islam before this modern resurgence were largely due to a combination of Sufi piety and orthodox rigidity, which undermined the fusion of piety and order that any vital religion has to have.

Islam also suffered from a counterattack by the countries that it had conquered. For instance, the European countries who supported the Crusades sharply contracted the empire that Islam had forged in its golden age. Historians date the point of decline differently. Bernard Lewis, however, holds that by the eleventh century Islam was in "manifest decay."[51] In addition to what they suffered at the hands of the Crusaders in the Holy Land and from the Europeans' counterattack in southern Europe, the Arabs found themselves superseded in the East by the Turks, who became Muslims, and by the Mongols, who at first showed no interest in Islam. The latter conquered both Persia and Iraq, causing a breakdown of Muslim power.

The Turkish Mamluks established themselves in Cairo by the mid-thirteenth century, ruling Egypt and Syria until 1517. When Vasco da Gama circumnavigated Africa in 1498, much of the Muslim economic and political power, which derived from Muslim control of the trade with India, quickly faded. The Ottoman Turks replaced the Mamluks in the early sixteenth century and ruled Middle Eastern Islam for almost 400 years.[52] Only in southern Arabia (Yemen) did speakers of Arabic remain largely free of foreign domination.

Late Empire and Modernity

During the period of empire (the Mamluks of Turkey and the Middle East, Persia,[53] and the Mogul dynasty in India[54]), at least three general changes occurred in Arabic-speaking society. The first was the transformation of the Islamic Near East from a commercial economy based on money to a feudal economy based on subsistence farming. The second was the replacement in positions of authority of Arabic-speaking peoples by Turks. The Arab tribes retained their independence in the desert regions, where they held out quite well against Turkish rule. In the cities and cultivated valleys (the plains of Iraq, Syria, and Egypt), however, the Arabs became completely subjected, and the glorious language that had been the pride of Islam became the argot of an enslaved population. Psychologically, the Turks grew accustomed to taking the initiative and commanding, and the Arabs grew accustomed to passivity and subjection. The third change was the transfer of the seat of Islam from Iraq to Egypt. Iraq was too remote from Turkey and the Mediterranean to be the base for the eastern wing of Islam, so Egypt—which was on the other principal trade route and which was the most unified area geographically—became the new center.[55]

As a result of this shift, Turkish and to a lesser degree Persian became the leading languages of Islam. At first many of the subject peoples welcomed the Ottoman takeover from the Mamluks as a return to political order. By the eighteenth century, however, the Ottoman Empire was in decay—corrupt, anarchic, and stagnant. The principal religious form of revolt during this period was Sufism. At first Sufism was mainly an escape for oppressed individuals, but with the organization of more brotherhoods, it became a social movement that was especially powerful among the artisan class. The long centuries of stagnation finally ended, however, with increased contact with the West. From the beginning of the sixteenth century, European expansion brought some of the new learning of the Renaissance and the Reformation. The French in particular had considerable influence in the Middle East, and Napoleon's easy conquest of the Ottoman Turks at the end of the eighteenth century was the final blow to Islamic military glory.

The Wahabis. Also during the time of Napoleon arose an Islamic reform that was designed to check the infection of Sufism.[56] One of the first leaders in this reform was a stern traditionalist named Muhammad ibn Abd al-Wahab, whose followers came to be known as Wahabis. They called for a return to the doctrines and practices of the early generations, of the ancestors whom they venerated.

In law, the Wahabis favored the rigorous interpretations of the Hanbalite school, and they abhorred the veneration of saints, which they considered superstitious. Thus, they inveighed against supposed holy personages, living or dead, and went out of their way to destroy the shrines that had become places of popular piety or pilgrimage. They further objected that the worship of saints presumed that they were "partners" of God and so was idolatrous. The punishment due such idolatry was death. Some of the more rabid Wahabis went so far as to classify the more lenient lawyers and schools as being guilty of idolatry (and so punishable by death). The Wahabis were based in Arabia, whence they waged war on their dissenting neighbors. They went down to military defeat in their 1818 Turco-Egyptian campaign, but their puritanical reform had much ideological success and spread to other parts of the Islamic world.

An immediate effect of the Wahabi movement was great hostility toward the Sufi brotherhoods. In fact, Muslims interested in renovating orthodoxy singled out the Sufis as their great enemies, although they also attacked the Scholasticism of such theological centers as al-Azhar in Cairo. One of the leaders of the nineteenth-century reform was the apostle of Pan-Islam, Jamal al-Din al-Afghani, who proposed the political unification of all Muslim countries under the caliphate of the Ottoman sultans. While Pan-Islam has never been realized, it stimulated the widespread search for an effective Muslim response to modernity. In India and Egypt, conservative groups arose that gravitated toward the Wahabi position. Many of the Sufi organizations lost their strength, and those that survived tended to back away from gnosis and return to a more traditional theology.

Even before this conservative threat, however, the Sufis had reformed on their own, sponsoring a number of missions in Africa, India, and Indonesia. For the most part these were peaceful, but occasionally they involved military ventures. In fact, some groups quite consciously took up the Qur'anic tradition of holy war, including the "Indian Wahabis" and the Mahdists in the Sudan. However, even in decline the Sufi brotherhoods kept dear to Islam the notion of bonding together for mutual support in faith.

The organizations that have grown up in recent times, such as the Association for Muslim Youth and the Muslim Brotherhood, seem in good measure an effort to fill the void created by the demise of the Sufi brotherhoods. The new groups differ by operating primarily in pluralistic cultures, where Muslims live in the midst of non-Muslims, while the Sufi orders drew on the ardor of a homogeneous culture that was secure in its unchallenged faith.

Western Influence. A characteristic of Islamic modernity was the invasion of Western secular ideas. These ideas came on the heels of modern Western takeovers in the Middle East, at first through the administrations of the Europeans who governed the newly acquired territories and then through the educational systems, which were Westernized. The new classes of native professionals—doctors, lawyers, and journalists—frequently trained abroad or in native schools run by Westerners. One political effect of such training was to raise Muslim feelings of nationalism and to provoke cries for Westernized systems of government. The new ideas challenged the *madrasas,* or religious schools, too, for it was not immediately apparent that these new ideas could be taught along with traditional theories of revelation and Qur'anic inspiration.

From the nineteenth century on, the economics, politics, education, social habits, and even religion of Muslims were increasingly affected by the upheaval that resulted from the European Renaissance and Enlightenment. Some countries remained largely insulated from Western notions, but they tended to be backward portions of the old empire with little political impact. As we might expect, the cities bore the brunt of the challenge. In theology the outward Muslim reaction was to close ranks. Still, even in the most fiercely traditionalist schools, modern notions—such as the freedom of human beings to shape their own destinies—softened the old propositions about providence and predestination.

Indeed, when it was convenient, theologians incorporated modern science into their argumentation. For instance, some Muslim theologians justified the doctrine that God creates the world continuously by citing atomic theory. The less theologically inclined among the modern educated classes contented themselves by asserting that Islam, as submission to the Master of Truth, in principle cannot conflict with modern science or with any empirically verified truths.

Controversy over societal matters has been more heated than that over theology because the guidance provided by the traditional legal schools diverged more sharply from Western mores than Muslim theology diverged from Western theology. Slowly Islamic countries have developed civil codes and separated civil courts from religious courts. In the mid-nineteenth century, the Turkish Republic breached the wall of tradition when it abolished the authority of the *Sharia* in civil matters. In other countries the *Sharia* has remained the outer form, but new legislative codes direct the interpretations. The tactic has been to invoke the Qur'an, the *hadith,* and the traditions of the schools but to leave the legislators and judges free to choose the authority that is most appropriate. Specifically, the legal reforms have applied primarily to marriage contracts (protecting girls against child marriage), divorce proceedings, and polygamy—central factors in the traditional family structure.

What new theology will emerge from the dynamics of these changes remains to be seen. H. A. R. Gibb has pointed out that by granting jurists freedom to interpret the traditional opinions and by departing from the old norm that there had to be a uniformity of interpretation throughout the Islamic community, the reformers have introduced a "Protestant principle" into the previously "Catholic" social consciousness.[57] Indeed, through its fairly rigid law, Islam had reified (made objective) its community more thoroughly than most other religions had.[58] Whether the demise of the former practice will result in a Protestant splintering of Islam is difficult to predict. On the one hand, it is hard to recall the critical or independent spirit once it has broken loose. On the other hand, there has arisen a growing Islamic fundamentalism similar to the fundamentalism by which some Protestant Christians are battling the spirit of Enlightenment criticism.

Relatedly, even some liberal Muslim reformers attracted to Marxist thought seem to bypass the Marxist call for a new order and to desire, rather nostalgically, the old social solidarity. On the other hand, traditionalists such as the Saudis find Marxism completely repulsive because of its atheism. Whether Saudi Arabia can progress satisfactorily by means of a capitalistic economy and technology, though, is far from certain. Critical-mindedness in the laboratory and simple faith in religion are not impossible, but few people in any faith manage them without a kind of schizophrenia.

Publications of the American Academic Association for Peace in the Middle East suggest that the history of such countries ("confrontation states") as Syria and Jordan explains much of the turmoil in the Middle East.[59] These countries have been trying to adapt their economics, their politics, and their religion to the modern world. On the one hand, their models for this transition have been the Western nations, who produced modernity. On the other hand, Western nationalism has taught them to insist on their right to a nationalistic expression of their ethnicity, their history, and their religious cohesiveness. The catalysts for this process have included the creation of contemporary Israel and Muslim oil resources.

In considering recent Muslim fundamentalism, one must realize that Islamic secularism never got so advanced as Western secularism. True, fundamentalism attracts a noteworthy number of Christians and Jews, but Christianity and Judaism more clearly differentiate the civic realm, the realm shared with citizens of other religious convictions (or of none), than Islamic culture has done. Conversely, Islam has kept the sacred and the secular more tightly conjoined than Christianity or Judaism has, professing that there is no secular realm—that everything lives by the will and touch of Allah, who is as near as the pulse at one's throat.

Case Study: Lessons from Recent Iran.   The rest of the Islamic world followed the Iranian upheavals of 1979 with great interest, to say the least, and many interesting commentaries on the meaning of Islam for the late twentieth century arose because of the Iranian events. One such commentary appeared in Cairo, at the instigation of the Islamic Student Association of Cairo University. Studying the reflections of this commentary may open a window on the likely future of Islam's blend of religion and politics.

The commentary begins with a quotation from the Qur'an (3:26) to the effect that God, the possessor of all sovereignty, gives earthly sovereignty to whomever he wishes. Just as freely, God takes earthly sovereignty away. Only God is powerful over all things. If God wishes to raise someone up, he does. If God wishes to debase someone, he does.

From this theological foundation the commentary moves to the Khomeini revolution in Iran, which was then riveting the whole world. This revolution, says the article, the violence and restraint of which surpassed the calculations and wildest imaginings of most observers, deserves deep study. Muslims must ponder such marvelous happenings, if they are ever to fulfill their Qur'anic destiny (see 3:110) and "assume the reins of world leadership of mankind once again and place the world under the protection of the esteemed Islamic civilization."[60]

Beginning such study, the first lesson the commentary would underscore is the influence of the creed on the Islamic people. The Iranian people, who had appeared completely submissive to death and tyranny, exploded like a volcano, tossing their fears aside. Their spiritual conquest of the steely forces that opposed them recalls the heroes of earliest Muslim times, and it should remind everyone that faith might muster similar power in many situations. Islam is the religion with the power to redress the injustices of all peoples everywhere.

Second, the Iranian revolution reminds us that Islam is a comprehensive religion, legislating for both this world and the next. It provides alike for religion and state affairs, education and morals, worship and holy war. In fact, the Iranian revolution clarifies the errors in modern secularism, which would separate religion from state affairs. Clearly, it shows that secularism is the recourse of idolaters, who want to keep religion out of politics, so that they can plunder the wealth of the common people. The only adequate laws and constitutions are those that derive from the *Sharia* of Islam. When laws and constitutions are man-made, their status is no greater than the idols of the pre-Muslim Arabs. If the pre-Muslim Arabs got hungry, they would eat the Goddess of Pastry. In contrast, the *Sharia* of Islam, which comes from God, is permanent, just, wise, and perfect.

Third, Iranian affairs show that the true leaders of the Muslim people are the sincere, learned men of religion. These men (the *ulama*) have been the guiding lights of all the best modern Muslim liberation movements. The touchstone is justice. For forty years the tyrant shah betrayed his community and brought down on it the most repulsive forms of injustice. God takes his time with the wrongdoer, but when he takes him there is no escaping.

Fourth, shrewd observers will note how the false Iranian leaders had the courage of lions when dealing with their own people but were puppets in the hands of the rulers of the East and the West. Yet the West quickly disowned the shah, abandoning him like a worn-out shoe. To the lesson implied in this one should add the patent effort of Islam's enemies to exploit the sectarian differences between Shiites and Sunnis and tear the Muslim community apart. As well, the enemies of Islam tried to use the Iranian revolution to instigate local governments to strike out at Islamic movements.

Therefore, rulers in other Islamic locales must realize that their true strength lies in the strength of their people, and that the true strength of their people lies in Islam. Wise leaders are those that place their allegiance in God, his apostle Muhammad, and Muslim believers. As the Qur'an (5:49) teaches, only those who rule by what God has revealed can expect to be strengthened. Thus, to those who would instigate strife against Islamic movements, one should reply: God suffices for us. The Qur'an has said the last word in these matters: "God promised those of you who believe and perform good works that he would make you viceroys on earth as he did with those before and will make it possible for you to follow the religion which pleases you and will change your fear into safety. You will worship me, associating nothing else with me" (24:55).

Several concerns of the Cairo Students' Association merit special comment, because they have been present in the recent resurgence of a passionate Islam in other countries, such as Iran itself and Pakistan. First, some students obviously long for a return to traditional Muslim law. Chafing under what they think is their recent rulers' secularism, the students believe that returning to the principles of the Qur'an and traditional Muslim law will speedily redress all current wrongs. In its early stages, the revolution in Iran seemed a great vindication of this viewpoint. Even fervent Muslims were amazed that faith was able to bring down so powerful an enemy as the shah. Today, at a greater distance from the events of 1979, and with more experience of what the Ayatollah Khomeini understood the revolution to imply, even zealous students might take pause. The bloody chaos that afflicted the Muslim ranks in Iran after the revolution argues that the *Sharia* is open to markedly diverse and violent interpretations. The war between Iran and Iraq was a festering sore in the Muslim community.

Second, the chauvinism latent in the Islamic students' position paper is not likely to prove the most effective translation of the *Sharia* for the decades ahead. A great deal of the world does not want to be placed under the protection of Islamic civilization, even when one grants Islamic civilization its great due. Pluralism is a more powerful force than the students seem to realize, and any peaceful assumption of the reins of world leadership will have to handle pluralism quite sympathetically. Any forceful assumption of the reins of world leadership is almost unthinkable, both because Islam is hardly in the position to challenge the West or the East militarily and because military means to power inevitably raise the specter of nuclear war. No nations would profit from a contemporary translation of Islamic "holy war" that led to nuclear confrontations.

Third, students of religion might most profitably focus on the somewhat tacit pleas that run through the Egyptian students' commentary. For example, there is the tacit plea that the rest of the world take seriously and duly honor a proud religious tradition. Islam came on hard times when the West took charge of modernity. Its pride was wounded, and one can trace much of its strong rhetoric, even its hyperbole, to this wounded pride. Now that Islam is on the march again, more than competitive with the Western religions in Africa and other parts of the Third World, it is trying to recoup some of its emotional losses.

Another tacit plea is for an integral culture, in which religion and daily affairs might fit like hand and glove. Not only is this integration a part of Islam's traditional ideal, as we have seen, it is also a common human desire. Indeed, even the Western cultures play strains of this song. Christian and Jewish fundamentalists, for example, express a passionate desire to bring all of life under the domain of their God. Despite the cultural or religious imperialism to which this desire can lead, it is worth studying sympathetically. The rise of secular cultures in many nations of the world *has* made it more difficult to find transcendent meaning. There *are* many contemporary citizens, East and West, who feel fragmented or schizophrenic.

Probably the most viable solution to this problem is a synthesis at a higher level that avoids a fundamentalist reduction to blind faith, but such a synthesis is very demanding. One of the unfortunate features of our late twentieth-century times is the speed that evolution has reached. Whereas in the past people facing demands analogous to today's demand for a resolution of the conflict between a pluralistic secularism and a unified religious faith might have had thousands of years at their disposal, today we cannot be sure we have more than a generation. This should incline us to get on with the task, but also to comfort ourselves with a proper estimate of the task's magnitude. Nothing less than a truly ecumenic, universal humanity will solve our worldwide religiopolitical problems, and achieving a truly ecumenic, universal humanity is almost more than we can imagine.

Still another plea running through the students' manifesto is for simple justice. This plea is not at all tacit; it is quite express and eloquent. Iranians had been suffering injustice. Enough of them had been tortured and abused by the shah to make his regime hated. The popular support for the Khomeini revolution was only explainable on the basis of this hatred. Had the shah's innovations, his programs for modernization and economic development, not been perceived as brutally unjust, as well as destructive of the people's cherished religious heritage, the shah probably would not have become the Iranian Satan. Even when one allows for a considerable emotional excess in the rhetoric of the shah's opponents, and their considerable manipulation by religious leaders quite ambitious for power, the political facts seem clear. The clarion call of the religious revolutionaries was for a restoration of justice. A major attraction in the prospect of restoring a Qur'anic government was the possibility of achieving a much greater justice.

As statements by the Ayatollah Khomeini himself have suggested, the revolutionaries' ideal was a religious government free of the human caprice that so easily leads to injustice: "The venerable prophet, may God's peace and prayers be upon him, was appointed ruler on earth by God so that he may rule justly and not follow whims." However, things become ominous when Khomeini goes on to say, "The *Shari'a* and reason require us not to let governments have a free hand. The proof of this is evident. The persistence of these governments in their transgressions means obstructing the system and laws of Islam whereas there are numerous provisions that describe every non-Islamic system as a form of idolatry or a ruler or an authority in such a system as a false god."[61] For many Western observers, Khomeini's authoritarianism soon became precisely a demand for idolatrous obedience, precisely the arbitrary rule of a false god.

STRUCTURAL ANALYSIS

Nature

The key to the Muslim notion of nature is Islam's concept of creation. As much as the biblical religion on which it built, Islam sees Allah as the maker of all that is. Several Qur'anic passages establish this doctrine. For instance, Sura 10 describes the Lord as "God, who created the heavens and the earth in six days, then sat Himself upon the Throne directing the affair." This is the biblical imagery of creation: Genesis spreading God's work over six days. Moreover, the Qur'an finds significance in this creation in that through creation Allah has given God-fearing people signs of his dominion. By making the sun a radiance and the moon a light, by giving them "stations" so that astronomers can calculate time, and by alternating night and day, Allah has set over humankind a heaven full of signs. Just as the modern German philosopher Immanuel Kant spoke of the starry heavens above as a wonder that can incite a true grasp of the human condition, so Muhammad unself-consciously expressed the sovereignty of his God by referring to the divine guidance of the stars, the heavenly circuits by which the Creator periodizes our time.

Sura 13 repeats this theme, adding earthly phenomena: It is he who stretched out the earth, set firm mountains and rivers, and placed two kinds of every fruit. The abundance of nature testifies to the abundance of nature's source and ought to remind human beings of Allah's power and provision. Thus, the Creator is not only strong but also admirable in his design of the world and praiseworthy in his concern for human welfare as evidenced by his bounty. In this way the best features of nature become analogies for Allah in the Qur'an. The "Light-Verse" of Sura 24 gives one of the most famous of these analogies: God is the light of the heavens and the earth. His light is as a niche where there is a lamp. The lamp is in a glass, the glass is like a glittering star. The lamp is kindled from a Blessed Tree, an olive neither of the East nor of the West, whose oil would shine even if no fire touched it. Light upon light, God guides to the light whom he will.

Religiously, then, nature is replete with signs in which wise people discern Allah's creative presence. However, nature is not itself a divinity or a form of Allah's presence. Unlike East Asian thought, Islamic thought does not mix divinity with the cosmos. Islam separated from the ancient cosmological myth, in that Allah transcends the world. One may say that the biblical prophets' critique of nature gods combined with Muhammad's negative reaction to the polytheism of his times to correlate transcendence and anti-idolatry. So the signs that nature gives to the God-fearing are not themselves sacraments. They point beyond themselves; the divinity does not come in them. Water, oil, bread, wine—they are not miniature incarnations of

divinity. The God of Islam has no incarnation, no personal or material forms by which he becomes present.

Isma'il al Faruqi tries to establish that Islam is rationalistic, meaning that Islam's highest religious certainty *(iman)* is not merely an act of believing, an "act of faith," but "a state in which religious knowledge produces an intuition of its certainty as a result of the consideration and weighing of all possible alternatives."[62] Then, in treating what he considers Islam's second essential quality (that it is "transcendentalist"), al Faruqi argues that Islam rejects all forms of immanentism for the divine. In other words, Creator is Creator, creature is creature, and never the twain shall meet. This transcendentalism provides the context for al Faruqi's discussion of the Muslim view of nature, the lead sentence of which is "Nature is not transcendent and constitutes an autonomous realm."[63] From this it follows that nature contains no divinity in its materials or its forces. It is totally real, wholly created. It is actual and objective, and "it contains no mystery."[64]

Thus, for al Faruqi, Islamic nature is utterly profane, in no way sacred (since nothing is sacred without mystery). That interpretation seems considerably more rationalistic than what most Muslims themselves have thought, for, as we suggested above, most Muslims have not followed Western Enlightenment by separating the sacred from the secular. When al Faruqi says that nature must be unmysterious to be autonomous, regular, and knowable, we are tempted to say that he protests overmuch. The mechanistic scientist of the nineteenth century could write such a description of nature, but few contemporary scientists and few traditional Muslims would do so.

Some Muslim thinkers might have lost contact with nature's mystery, but they were not in the majority, for that would have made Islam a comparative anomaly. For example, Jews and Christians, despite sharing with Islam the notion of a transcendent Creator, used psalms that glorified God's provision of food in due season. With Job, they found that the world and its train of strange animals were marvelous indeed. The Hasidim looked to the world for divine sparks, and the Christian poets drew on the sacraments and on the model of saints such as Francis of Assisi to consider the world pregnant with God's power. Both of Islam's sister faiths did develop veneration of nature less than the Eastern religions did, and both did fear the forces of fertility, the polytheism, that afflicted the lands of their origin. But in the actual exercise of their faiths, nature was alive with the mystery of God and was neither profane nor autonomous.

Still, al Faruqi is right in implying that nature never dominated Islam or Arab culture. For instance, the earliest poetry deals more with war and nomadic life than with father sky and mother earth. Pre-Muslim Arabia worshiped natural and agricultural forces, but Qur'anic monotheism attacked them harshly. In religious art, as we have seen, the prohibition on images was not absolute, although religious art tended to avoid representations of natural scenes, let alone representations of Allah.

Still, the prime material for worship, the Qur'an itself, contained natural figures and not merely in the context of creation. Thus, it embellished its theme of judgment and recompense with naturalistic imagery. For instance, if one denied God's bounties—did not live the truth that Allah ever labors creatively for human benefit—then "against you shall be loosed a flame of fire, and molten brass" (55:35). Judgment is a day when "heaven is split asunder and turns crimson like red leather" (55:37), when sinners will go to Gehenna and hot boiling water. However, those who fear Allah will enter Paradise. The main image for Paradise is the Garden. There the virtuous will find two fountains running with water, fruits of all kinds, virgin maidens lovely as rubies and coral. Paradise has green pastures, gushing water, fruits, palm trees, pomegranates, and cool pavilions (55:50–70).

Thus, the Qur'an considered nature a factor in the mysteries of judgment, punishment, and reward as the images of Fire and Garden clearly show. Moreover, mythological elaboration of these themes in popular religion was quite unrestrained. "Hell, sometimes imagined as a terrible monster, is described as filled with fire and stinking water, and awful trees with poisonous fruits grow there."[65] In the popular conception, angels presided over hell, meting out punishments, while heaven became a place for enjoying fruit, wine, and the charming black-eyed virgins.

Like other religions, Islam maintained that justice would be served in the afterlife through reward for the pious faithful and punishment for the unbelievers. Sex was high on the list of pleasures, so Paradise was rich with sex. Islam depicted sex from the male point of view, with details of "maidens restraining their glances, untouched before them by any man or jinn" (55:55). As we shall see below, Islam did not declare the goodness of sex so loudly and clearly for women. In fact, there has often been ambiguity, puritanism,

and a double standard concerning sex in Muslim society. Still, the basic fact that Islam does not paint heaven as an ethereal, wholly spiritual realm shows that it blesses human nature.

In summary, nature for Islam is one locus of Allah's signs to humanity. Nature is less prominent than in East Asian or ancient religion. Rather, Islam configures itself socially and theologically, focusing on the community and the sovereign Lord.

Muslim spirituality manifests something of this emphasis, in that one of its interests is to keep nature under control. By fasting, a Muslim tames the nature closest to the self. By confessing that there is no God but God, a Muslim clears the world of competitors to the Creator and Judge. That means that many devout Muslims' ideal is a bare vista. The Sufis manifested this ideal most fully, for many of them saw life as a pilgrimage to union with an Allah much more valuable than anything worldly. In less deliberate but still consoling ways, the poor merchant or soldier learned from misfortune how precarious a worldly vista was. Although the physical world was definitely real and on occasion quite good, the human being's role was to observe it closely enough so that it served as a guidepost to heaven. A Muslim can be comfortable in the natural world, then, but only as a visitor. Life in the natural world soon passes, and Judgment depends on higher things, such as one's faith, one's prayer, and one's generosity in giving alms. The tradition does not teach people that the Judge will ask them how they treated the environment or whether they tore the bosom of mother earth. Those issues are far less important than whether they remembered Allah and his Prophet.

Society

The Muslim social ideal has never distinguished between secular and sacred aspects of community life. Thus Islamic countries have been ambivalent about modernity, which usually sought to develop secular (nonreligious) codes of law and other cultural entities. Estimates of the social innovations that Islam introduced into prior Arab society and the degree of social perfection that it achieved vary considerably.

The proponent of Islam, Isma'il al Faruqi, begins with the thesis that Muslim society existed so that human beings might realize that "divine pattern." Elemental in that pattern was the family. Marriage was a civil contract, not a sacrament, and a man could marry more than one wife so long as he provided justice, equity, and loving care. Private property and the pursuit of wealth were inviolate rights, but wealth brought the obligation to care for the deprived. Concerning the right to life: "The life of one's fellowman is inviolate, except by due process of law. Nothing may henceforth be decided by force or violence. Such recourse is legitimate only in self-defense and in the safe-guarding of the security of missionaries. For the Muslim is duty-bound to bring his faith to the knowledge of mankind with sound preaching and wise counsel, to convey with warning and command of his Lord."[66]

The Muslim political unit has been the *Ummah,* which is as comprehensive a notion as the broadest notions of church or synagogue. Tradition says that the Qur'an teaches that the Prophet and his successors bore a theocratic power. That is, they had authority in both the religious and the secular spheres, because Islam does not much distinguish the two. Due to the concept of the *Ummah,* Muslims had to fight for brethren in other places who suffered tyranny (Qur'an 4:75). For Muslim leaders, the consensus of the community was an important goal, for they wanted a single divine rope to bind the *Ummah* together. Strong faith was to create an equality among all believers, and Allah would reward every man and woman who was faithful through difficulties and trials. Muslims were to bring their disputes to the Prophet or his successors, and they all had a common duty to worship Allah, to obey Allah's commands, and to do good and avoid evil.

Members were to be to one another as brothers and mutual guardians (9:71), respecting life and enjoying its good things. Woman came from the soul of man (4:1). Both men and women had the right to what they had earned, and both could enter Paradise, although "men have priority over women, by virtue of what God has endowed to them and by what they spend on women of their wealth" (4:34). Men were to provide their women tenderness and affluence if they could. Marriage was the usual state, and Islam did not support celibacy. Almsgiving was a primary obligation, and one was to go beyond justice to charity and forgiveness. From the call that Allah gave the Prophet, ideally all human beings would come to reason and felicity. Since Allah clearly did not compel non-Muslims to believe, Muslims themselves had no right to force others to believe (10:99, 108). However, the Qur'an regards balefully non-Muslims who contract with Islam and renege: "Lesser than the beasts in the eye of God are the unbelievers for they have covenanted with you and violated their covenant shamelessly in every case. If you lay hold of them in war, make of them a lesson to the others" (8:55).

The covenant of Medina that Muhammad composed gave Jews explicit rights: "To the Jews who follow us belong assistance and equal treatment from us without either injustice or discrimination."[67] The basic status of non-Muslims within the state that Muhammad envisioned was what might be called "colleagueship"—peaceful cooperation. The democratic principles applying to Muslim citizenship were individual responsibility, equality, the leaders' responsibility to run the government, and the mutual security of all citizens. In its law the state was to regard itself as a replica of the cosmic state that Allah runs by strict and unalterable laws. In effect, this meant buttressing Islamic convictions with a sure faith in divine justice on Judgment Day. The imam, or leader, led the community in upholding the law. This was the basis for his quasi-contractual relationship with the *Ummah.*

The Islamic state made a threefold division of humanity: Muslims, covenanters, and enemies. The Muslim peoples who constituted the *Dar al-Islam* (House of Islam) could not legitimately resort to war against one another. Covenanters were non-Muslims who had made compacts of peace, and their rights and duties were the same as those of Muslims. Al Faruqi does not specify the fate of enemies, although he notes the Qur'anic teaching that Muslims are to preach to them but not force them to convert. Presumably, holy war only resulted when enemies rejected both conversion and covenant. If an enemy responded with hostility, Muslim security necessitated war. What happened when the enemy simply wanted to be left alone or considered a Muslim takeover of its area unacceptable is not clear. However, clearly it was not blameworthy for Islam "to combat with the sword the sword which stands between it and man, preventing Islam from conveying its call and man from listening to or receiving it."[68]

Ethics. Annemarie Schimmel has sketched Muslim ethics, which presumably directed Muslim actions.[69] The guiding principle was to serve Allah as though you saw him in front of you. In other words, belief in Allah, Judgment, and the necessity of right deeds were the bases of Islamic ethics. Religious bonds rather than blood bonds, pure faith rather than idolatry, and sexual restraint rather than indecency—these were notable advances made by the Qur'an over Arab paganism. In addition to the exhortations to justice and charity found in the Meccan suras and the detailed legislation of the Medinan suras, those who survived Muhammad looked back on the Prophet's own life as the key to how a Muslim ought to live.

The early disputes about the fate of a sinner and the place of good works, which divided the theological and legal schools, suggest that human beings were considered free and responsible. As we noted, the law distinguishes five kinds of action, from the commanded to the forbidden. The Qur'an deals with adultery, murder, and theft, prescribing stern punishments for them. Women had the right to refuse a proposed marriage, but men had greater rights than women in divorce. The wife had to obey her husband, who could punish her, and she always had to be at his disposal. "If a husband kills his wife and her lover *in flagrante delicto* [in the act of adultery itself] he is not punishable. Sodomy is likewise forbidden (though often practiced in a society that excluded women largely from daily life. The object of Persian and Turkish love poetry is generally masculine)."[70]

The Qur'an takes slavery for granted, but it commends humane treatment and commends freeing slaves. Only non-Muslim prisoners of war could legally become slaves. Discrimination because of color and race was unlawful, though some racial prejudice mars Islamic history. When the law reached its final stage of development around 1000, its detailed specifications tended to become mechanical. The mystics therefore tried to make ethics spring from a deeper relationship with God. The first virtue they taught was *wara*—abstention from everything unlawful or dubious. In other words, one was not to nitpick but to act from the heart and turn away from anything that might displease God. Masters such as al-Ghazali developed a shrewd psychology of virtue and vice, which they deployed to bring about the highest perfection. That perfection was living every moment in the presence of Allah. Finally, the general effect of Muslim ethics was to heighten awareness of one's distance from the divine purity and so lead one to beg Allah's mercy and forgiveness.

Women's Status. The status of women in Islam says a great deal about Muslim society.[71] In the Qur'an there is some basis for sexual equality: Reward and punishment in the afterlife depend on deeds, not gender; marriage and conjugal life are precious; women have dowry rights in some divorces, inheritance rights, rights to remarry, and rights to protection in

time of pregnancy and nursing. However, women's rights are not equal to those that the Qur'an gives males in either divorce or inheritance. Moreover, the Qur'an does not even consider the possibility that women might assume leadership roles in the community, receive an education equal to that of males, teach law or theology, or engage in polygamy (as males could).

Furthermore, the misogyny latent in most patriarchal religions had dark effects in Muslim society. As late as 1970, an Arab sheik offered the opinion that "educated or not a woman is a woman and the Prophet—God's prayers and peace on him—had said that women are lacking in mind and religion."[72] The tradition placed more women in the Fire than in the Garden, and the prime determinant of their destiny was their treatment of their husbands. In legend Muhammad virtually despised female nature as stupid and irreligious. Its specific defects were menstruation, which interfered with prayer and fasting, and unreliability, which made a woman's witness worth only half a man's in court. Obedience to her husband was the woman's first duty; failure to obey can still get her killed today.[73]

The Muslim woman regularly was considered erotic and empty-headed. Thus she was subject to purdah (seclusion and veiling), polygyny, concubinage, and the harem. Women were not to be taught to read and write ("a great calamity"), and they were morally "bent" because they came from Adam's bent rib. Thus, in many men's eyes, they had a dismal existence: "It were best for a girl not to come into existence, but being born she had better be married or buried."[74] Recent Muslims, especially Africans, have defended clitoridectomy and kindred operations, frequently with the following sort of rationale: "Circumcision of women releases them from their bondage to sex, and enables them to fulfill their real destiny as mother."[75] As she has done in the cases of Indian suttee, Chinese foot binding, and Christian witch burning, Mary Daly has vividly described African genital mutilation, writing more vividly than most scholars find comfortable.[76]

Another revealing view of women in Islamic society comes from the imagery of the Garden.[77] For many men, the best part of the heavenly Garden was the *hur*: dark-eyed, buxom virgins. In addition to his earthly wife, each male in heaven could expect to have seventy *hur*. They would never be sick, menstruating, pregnant (unless he wished), bad-tempered, or jealous. He would be able to deflower a thousand each month and find them all intact when he returned to them. In descriptions of the Judgment scene, one sees the reverse of this fantasy: Women are in charge of men, which is a sure sign of disorder.

In fairness, Islam improved the lot of Arab women considerably, and certain parts of the community allowed women a function in the *Hadith*,[78] in scholarship, and in saintliness.[79] Some Muslim cultural areas had traditions more benign toward women than Arab culture was, and many modern Muslims deplore the injustices that women have suffered in the past. As well, they interpret Qur'anic religion in a way that gives women great dignity, and they bitterly oppose the drive of fundamentalists to return to such traditions as marrying girls off when they reach thirteen.

The recent resurgence of Muslim traditionalism in both Sunni and Shiite centers of learning (Cairo, Tehran) has brought more restrictions into many women's lives.

Variety.   The different Islamic cultures have all been bonded by the Qur'an despite their geographic, linguistic, ethnic, and even theological differences. The principal theological division, as we noted, has been between the Shiites and the Sunnis. However, as W. Montgomery Watt has shown, the formative period of Islamic thought saw a variety of controversies and then "heterodoxies."[80]

In India, as noted, Islamic elements fused with Hindu elements to create Sikhism, and Islam was also the inspiration behind Baha'i. Baha'i is a universalist religion that stresses the unity of all traditions and the basic oneness of the human race. It arose in nineteenth-century Persia when a Shiite Muslim, Sayyid Ali Muhammad, declared that he was the twelfth imam—the last, messianic leader whom the Shia awaits. Sayyid took the designation *Bab* ("gate"), and his follower Baha Ullah produced writings that became classic works of Baha'i faith. Today Baha'i has about five million adherents. Its world center is on Mount Carmel in Haifa, Israel, where there is a lovely garden and shrine to the Bab (Figure 25).[81]

Case Study: Islamic Rituals.[82]   Yoruba Muslims of West Africa have ritualized their religion for the life cycle, the religious year, and the ordinary week. By studying these rituals, we may glimpse not only how Muslims have expressed their faith over the centuries, but also how Islam has adapted itself to such new geographic areas as West Africa.

The life cycle of Yoruba Muslims begins on the day they become members of the worshiping community. This may be the day when, as adults, they formally convert to Islam, or the eighth day after their birth, when they receive their name. The major action in the adult conversion ceremony is an ablution, to symbolize the pure life the convert is entering upon. The candidates take off their clothes and don loin cloths. The presiding cleric washes each one's right hand three times, the left hand three times, the right leg three times, and the left leg three times. Then three times he washes the elbows, blows each one's nose, and washes the ears. Concluding, he pours water on the head and chest of each candidate, who, having been washed and become clean, is a true Muslim.

For the naming ceremony of a newborn child, the presiding cleric receives money in a covered dish. The cleric prays for the child, preaches a solemn sermon (often in Arabic), and then gives the child its name. Some West African Muslims also sacrifice a sheep or cut the infant's hair. (The Yoruba practice circumcision, as well as the drawing of tribal marks on the face or body. Apparently Islam did not introduce these customs but rather gave them a new interpretation.)

The second major stage on the Yoruba Muslim's way is marriage. The presiding cleric must divine that the proposed match is a good one and pray for the marital partners. Before the wedding, the groom has to pay the bride's family several monies and gifts. In modernized West African Muslim rituals, the presiding cleric asks the groom: "Do you take Miss _____ as your wedded wife? Will you love her, honor her, feed her, clothe her, and lodge her in proper lodging?" Then he quotes the Qur'an (4:34), to the effect that one of the signs God has given human beings is creating mates for them, that they may find quiet of mind. Putting love and compassion between these mates, God gives reflective people a sign of his goodness and care. The presiding cleric also asks the bride similar questions, including whether she will love, honor, and obey her husband. He repeats most of the quotation from the Qur'an, and reminds the bride that "the good women are therefore obedient, guarding the unseen as Allah has guarded." The ceremony concludes with prayers to Allah that he bless this wedding. (Most of the West African Muslim community supports the traditional polygyny.)

Funeral rites complete Islam's ritual impact on the Yoruba life cycle. When a person has died the neighbors come together and dig a grave. They then

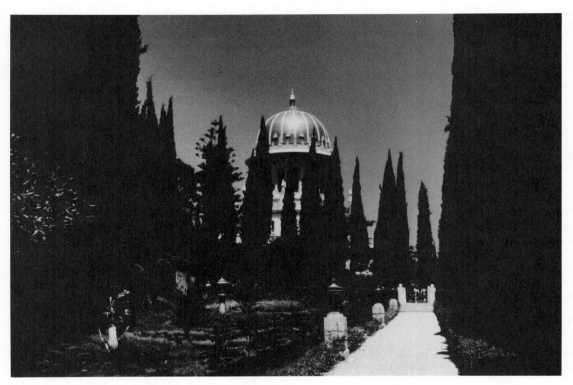

Figure 25 *Shrine to the Bab, Haifa. Photo by J. T. Carmody.*

wash the corpse, repeating the ablutions of the conversion ceremony. They dress the corpse in a white cap, loin cloth, and sewn sheet, and then put it into the grave and cover it with earth. The presiding cleric prays for the deceased person, that God may forgive its sins. The dead person's family is expected to pay the cleric handsomely, with food as well as money. Some modernized sects hold a second ceremony, on the eighth day after the burial, with readings from the Qur'an, a sermon, and a eulogy of the deceased.

In addition to these three major ceremonies for the life cycle, Yoruba Islam has an annual cycle of feasting and fasting. The cycle begins with the Muslim New Year, which is a day for hearty eating in most sects and for orgiastic nude bathing and mock battles in a few. The New Year festival recalls Noah, who disembarked from the ark very hungry.

The next festivals in the annual cycle are two celebrations of Muhammad, his birthday and the night of his heavenly journey to Jerusalem and Paradise. The more conservative Yoruba Muslims have made much of the Prophet's birthday, using it as an occasion to display their learning. In their circles children act out scenes from the Prophet's life, and those who teach the Qur'an receive special stipends. The Yoruba do not understand the Prophet's heavenly journey well, so they tend to make little of it.

The month of Ramadan is the great time of fasting, but many of the Yoruba elderly fast during the month of Rajab as well. The last Friday of Ramadan is especially important, because then one may ask forgiveness for one's laxities in worship during the past year. Among the modernizing Yoruba Muslims the Ramadan ceremonies include the prayer, "O Allah! whom our obedience does not benefit and our disobedience does not harm, please accept from us what does not benefit you, and forgive us what does not harm you."

The two greatest feasts in the Yoruba Muslim calendar are the Feast of the Breaking of the Fast and the Feast of the Immolation. Each entails two days of public holidays in Nigeria. For the Feast of the Breaking of the Fast, worshipers dress elaborately and bring expensive prayer rugs. The ceremony includes an almsgiving, to solemnize gratitude for a successful conclusion to Ramadan, a visit to the ruler of the Yoruba, and a visit to the graves of the first two imams (religious leaders) of the community. The Feast of the Immolation reminds the Yoruba that their fellow Muslims in Arabia are performing this sacrifice in Mecca, as part of their pilgrimage. The immolation itself usually is the sacrifice of a small goat. After the communal ceremony many individuals also sacrifice goats or rams at the entrances to their own houses.

The last feast of the annual cycle is the *hajj*, the pilgrimage to Mecca. Since Nigerian independence, the government has supported the pilgrimage, making the *hajj* available to the prosperous farmer, shopkeeper, or local leader. If the individual can make an initial outlay of money, he or she usually will receive supplementary gifts from friends. Once the pilgrims return to their local communities, they enjoy great status, since they have been to the center of the Muslim world. Usually the experience of Islam as a worldwide fellowship greatly broadens the Yoruba pilgrim's horizons. Not all Yoruba Muslims have the opportunity to travel to Mecca, but each year at the time of the *hajj* all turn their imaginations to the holy city and picture what is taking place there.

In the weekly religious cycle of Yoruba Muslims, Friday is the crowning day, but Wednesday and Thursday also have special significance. The last Wednesday of each lunar month is esteemed as a day of special blessings. All are encouraged to increase their prayers, that they may protect themselves from the evil every month contains. The darkness of the moon at the end of the month is probably the spark for this attitude. A prayer of Muslim reformers expresses the last Wednesday mood: "In the name of God, the Merciful, the Compassionate: O God, O Terrible in power, O Terrible in cunning, O Strong One, O Thou Who guidest by Thy might everything in Thy Creation, shield me from the evil of everything Thou has created."

In folk Islam, Wednesday is considered replete with blessings, as is Thursday. Most Yoruba groups have adopted this folk attitude. Thus, most marriages, celebrations of a student's completion of the Qur'an, and groundbreakings occur on Wednesdays or Thursdays. One of the many functions of the Yoruba *alfa* (presiding cleric) is to divine an auspicious date for these celebrations. Conservative Muslims, who tend to

be better educated, downplay such divinations, and do not attribute any special significance to particular days of the week.

However, Thursday evening has a special significance, because it is the threshold to Friday, the Muslim Sabbath. Indeed, most Yoruba Muslims offer prayers for the dead on Thursday night. A popular tradition says that on Thursday evening God allows the dead to come back to the world and see what is going on. This ties into a Yoruba tradition of leaving gifts for the deceased. If a dead person does not have gifts left for him, he loses prestige among his peers.

A certain conflict between traditional, pre-Muslim notions about the dead and Muslim ideas confuses many Yoruba Muslims. The traditional pictures show the dead existing in a shadowy heaven *(orun),* where they need the care of those they have left behind. The Muslim beliefs in judgment and resurrection do not square with these pictures, so the status of the dead is rather murky. Some Yoruba Muslims translate resurrection so that it becomes a state much like *orun,* but others accept the more orthodox Muslim notion that resurrection is a wondrous event that will occur in the future.

Friday is the center of the weekly cycle, when all good Muslims are supposed to gather at noon in the main mosque for communal worship. In the large towns the mosques are crowded with male worshipers. (A smaller number of women is allowed to worship, segregated from the males, at the back of the mosque.) The service begins with the call to prayer and then has a sermon in the vernacular. Often this "sermon" turns out to be more like a group session of petitionary prayer. People come up to the prayer leaders and whisper their intentions, which "megaphonists" then repeat in a loud voice, so that God and the community at large can hear them. The sermon sometimes amounts to no more than a few moral exhortations tossed in as editorial comments on the prayers people have offered. The people also contribute money.

After the sermon comes the heart of the Friday service, the communal *salat* or ritual prayer. Together the group go through the actions of the fivefold daily prayer—bowing, kneeling, and touching their foreheads to the ground. Muslim prayer is essentially this doing, this performative act. So "a mosque in the last resort is not a building: It is a place of prostration and any patch of ground in ritual purity suffices where a human frame may stretch itself—a fact about Islam which accounts in large measure for the naturalness of its occasions and the contagion in its expansion. A faith that does not need to house its worshipers has no walls to hide its creed."[83]

Through the life cycle, the annual cycle, and the weekly cycle, the great lesson the Yoruba or any other Muslims are learning is the lesson of prostration. Bowing before God, the Almighty, the Muslim deepens her or his sense that only one power is in charge of the world. To be at peace with God is life's greatest accomplishment; to be at war with God is life's greatest tragedy.

Self

The strong control of the Muslim community by religious law has had two primary effects on the individual or self. First, the common code that governed external behavior shaped and constrained the majority. In other words, most Muslims accepted the ethics sketched above. Second, the Sufis and mystics drew a substantial minority to a more internal doctrine of the self shaped by personal devotion. Such devotion sought to unite the individual with God experientially. Thus, the first lesson that it taught was that the human person has a spiritual substance or capacity that can unite with God.

These two effects on selfhood produced a balance in Muslim religion: The self learned that membership in the House of Islam depended on observing the common law, which led to merit and the Garden, and that it could anticipate the Garden and taste God's joy in the present life.

The orthodox conception of the self began with the notion of creation. In Sura 96 the self is described essentially as a small thing that God made from a blood clot or a drop of sperm. The essence of Islam and of being a Muslim was to recognize the creator-creature relation: a sovereign God who is completely the Lord of a very insignificant vassal. The basic scriptural message of Islamic anthropology is submission, even a certain holy slavery.

This attitude was no false humility. Rather, it was the bare truth of the human condition. Human beings came from God, and their destiny depended on living out the pattern that God had in making them. Thus, they had no basis for self-glorification. Thus, the exclamations of an al-Hallaj, who claimed identification with God (through mystical union), could only sound blasphemous to the majority, who were immersed in the literal text. Between the divine Lord and the human vassal stretched an impassable gulf. However much genuine love might have drawn the spirit up to God, however much God's intimate mercy might have descended toward human flesh, the essential difference in their states remained.

From other Qur'anic accounts of creation one can gather the impression that, despite their lowliness, human beings have a special status among all creatures. Al Faruqi calls this status being God's "vicegerent" on earth.[84] The word *lakum* ("for you") appears in the stories of how God made the earth to produce herbs, crops, and animals and of how God made the sea to carry ships and the camels and sheep to bring forth their offspring.[85] In the stories of Adam's creation (for instance, 2:28, 15:29, 32:8), the angels object to God's making human beings, but God forms this first man from clay and water, gives him a most beautiful form, and breathes his spirit into him. Then he makes the angels bow before Adam, for Adam is to be the *khalifa* (vicegerent) on earth, having in this capacity the right and duty to carry out God's orders. Echoing Genesis, Sura 2:31 speaks of God's teaching Adam the names of all things, which means giving him power over all things, since to control a being's name was to have power over it. The end God had in mind for such a creature, the recompense that He expected, was adoration: "We have created men and jinn only for adoration" (51:51).

We can see, therefore, the basis for the Islamic view that God made the earth subject to human control. Along with the doctrine of God's transcendence, this anthropocentricity in creation helped to deemphasize nature. As we argued above, naming and ruling the world did not remove nature's mystery. Even with nature's mystery, however, the Muslim felt that the earth had been given into his (and to a lesser extent her) control. Nonetheless, Muslim teachings about human nature honored its ties with the earth, its creation from clay and water.

Anthropology. In traditional Muslim anthropology (view of human nature) the spiritual faculties had several names. The *nafs* was essentially the animal soul, the source of concupiscence (desire). It had the connotation of belonging to the lower part of the personality—to the flesh that incites evil. (Sometimes, though, it just means "self.") The *ruh* was the spirit, come from Allah, that animates the human body. Muslims often pictured it as a subtle matter that permeates the human body. Reason *(aql)* was the spiritual faculty

Figure 26 *The Meeting of the Theologians, by 'Abd Allah Musawwir, Persia, mid-sixteenth century. Colors on paper; 11³/₈ × 7¹/₂ in. The Nelson–Atkins Museum of Art, Kansas City, Missouri (Nelson Fund).*

by which human beings discern right and wrong. Finally, the mystics spoke of the *qalb*—the heart that is the faculty by which one obtains direct knowledge of God.

For some of the Sufis, the doctrine of creation in God's image was crucial. On occasion, neo-Platonic or gnostic notions colored this doctrine to mean that the soul wanders in exile. It can return to its home, though, if it appropriates secret teaching or learns certain meditative techniques. From the notion of creation in God's image, the Sufis also developed their concept of the *insan kamil,* the perfect man. Usually they applied it to Muhammad, who contained all the divine attributes and served as a microcosm of divinity.

The destiny of the human being, as we have seen, was either the Fire or the Garden. Islam did not con-

sider man and woman to be laboring under a "fallen" human nature, for Muslims did not regard the sin of Adam and Eve as being contagious or passed on to their offspring. Thus, Islam did not speak of redemption. The prophet was a revealer or a medium of revelation; he was not a ransom, a victim, or a suffering servant. Instead of sin (in the deep sense of alienation from God by irrational actions), Islam tended to stress human forgetfulness (of God's goodness). Human nature was weak—prone to a kind of religious amnesia. In the Prophet's own conception of human destiny, men and women have a common responsibility to remember God's goodness and to respond by fulfilling his will. Originally, both men and women were to offer prayer and alms; however, in later times women's status deteriorated, and they did not have this obligation.

The self that was faithful to the identity set by the community could expect to gain Paradise. God would forgive sins (violations of religious law), so they did not mean a loss of community membership. (However, the dissident Kharijites said that every Muslim who committed a grave sin was an unbeliever.) What separated one from the *Ummah* in the orthodox view was to deny that the injunctions of the Qur'an came from God and thus were eternally binding. Among the Shia, who have predominated in Iran, faith also has included acknowledging the mystical imam of the time—the hidden successor to Ali whom the Shiites expect to come as the Messiah. By uniting with this hidden imam, one partook of salvation.

Historically, the major theoretical question concerning the self was the relation of human freedom to divine will. At least in the Meccan sections, the Qur'an takes human freedom for granted. Muhammad's call and his preaching make no sense without a capacity to respond. Similarly, the scenes of Judgment Day assume that human beings have been responsible for their actions—that they could have done otherwise than they did. However, later Qur'anic passages emphasize God's omnipotence. As a result, the question arises: Does God lead some people astray—or at least leave them in error?

In the Umayyad period a group of strict predestinarians (the Jabriya) stressed God's complete control. Opposing them were the Qasriya, who defended human responsibility. A third group, the Mutazilites, defended both human freedom and God's perfect justice.

Still another position, that of al-Ashari, satisfied many people with the following formula: "God creates in man the will to act and the act, and man acquires the act by performing it." To say the least, the issue vexed Islam. In later times the common people frequently felt that life was fated—that it was out of their hands. Among the few monistic mystics, human freedom was lost in the divine nature.

In summary, Islam has given the self rather complex directives. The core message is that membership in the Prophet's community and submission to Allah fulfill the human duties. The way to realize oneself is to follow the community law. In the present, such self-realization means spiritual security; in the future, it will mean Paradise. While waiting for Paradise, one can work the earth, trade, fight, or enjoy the pleasures of the senses, so long as the chosen activity does not divert one from the ultimate reality of Allah. If one is submissive to God, most things are licit. More things are licit for men than for women, as we have seen, but many commentators think the Qur'an did improve the Arab woman's lot considerably.

Still, the popular image of Muhammad as a man who could satisfy nine wives and still receive revelations greater than those of Jesus inculcated a certain bravado in all but the most ascetic males. Since Islamic education deals primarily with religious lore, it does not necessarily demythologize Muhammad's popular image. As well, historically most Muslim women have been denied education. Therefore, tradition has tended to describe sexuality mainly from a male point of view. That point of view, in turn, has tended to meld with the patterns set forth in the eternal Qur'an. Following these patterns, one would let God more and more dominate the entire self.

Case Study: Muslim Saints.[86] When we considered the life cycle rituals, the annual rituals, and the weekly rituals of Yoruba Muslims, we glimpsed Islam's accommodation to the West African religious traditions that predated it. We get another glimpse of such cross-cultural accommodation by studying the different ways the different Muslim ethnic groups have conceived sainthood, the peak achievement of Muslim selfhood. For example, the Indonesian Muslims, who have been greatly influenced by Indian culture, have focused their religious imagination on saints whose style is markedly quieter than the style of the saints Moroccan Muslims have venerated. Since "Islam"

starts to come into focus only when one begins to find the unity underlying such differences, let us attempt a comparative study of the Indonesian and Moroccan Muslim saints.

In Indonesian Muslim lore, Sunan Kalidjaga is the most important of the group of nine "apostles" considered to be the founders of Indonesian Islam. Legend has it that he was born the son of a high royal official of Madjapahit, one of the greatest and last of the Indonesian Hindu-Buddhist kingdoms, which dominated most of Eastern Java during the fourteenth and fifteenth centuries. In the sixteenth century Madjapahit declined, caught between the old Hindu-Buddhist order and the new Muslim order that was emerging. Pressured by this change, Kalidjaga moved to the new harbor state of Djapara, where he met another of the early apostles, Sunan Bonang, and was converted to Islam. Later Kalidjaga so greatly influenced Javanese politics that he is credited with Java's having become solidly Muslim. Symbolically, therefore, Kalidjaga serves as a bridge between the old Indic world of god-kings, ritual priests, and Indian shrines and the new Islamic world of pious sultans, Qur'anic scholars, and austere mosques. Indonesians love to contemplate the story of his conversion, for it recapitulates their good fortune in having gained access to the world of Allah, and it drives home the conviction that Islam is the best flower of the new phase of their history.

When Kalidjaga arrived in Djapara, he was a ne'er-do-well, accomplished in stealing, drinking, whoring, and gambling. So deep were his vices, he stole all his own mother's money, and when he had dissipated this he set out to steal from the public at large. Eventually he became a highwayman of such renown that people were afraid to go to the Djapara market lest they encounter him and lose all their goods.

Into this scene strolled Sunan Bonang, a Muslim (probably an Arab) dressed in gorgeous clothes and expensive jewels, and carrying a cane of solid gold. Naturally he attracted the attention of Kalidjaga, who put a knife to his throat and demanded all his finery. But, to Kalidjaga's amazement, Bonang laughed in his face. Calling Kalidjaga by his name (though he had never met Kalidjaga before), Bonang chided him as though he were a little boy: "Don't always be wanting this thing and that thing. Such material desires are pointless. We live but a moment. It is foolish to be attached to worldly goods. Look: there is a whole tree full of money."

Kalidjaga turned and saw a banyan tree transformed to gold and hung with jewels. At a stroke, he realized that material things were nothing compared with Bonang's power. What sort of a man must Bonang be, to be able to turn trees into gold and jewels and yet not care about gold and jewels at all? With this thought, Kalidjaga's life of vice repulsed him, and he begged Bonang to teach him spiritual power. Bonang agreed, but he warned Kalidjaga that such teaching was very difficult. Kalidjaga vowed he would persist until death, but Bonang merely told him, "Wait here, by the side of the river, until I return." Then he took his leave.

Kalidjaga waited by the side of the river for forty years, lost in thought. Great trees grew up around him, floods arose and receded, crowds jostled him back and forth, buildings went up and were torn down. Still he waited, lost in thought. Finally Bonang returned, and he saw that Kalidjaga had indeed been steadfast. So instead of teaching Kalidjaga the doctrines of Islam, Bonang simply told him that he had been a good pupil—indeed, that he had come to surpass Bonang himself. To prove this, Bonang asked Kalidjaga difficult questions about religious matters, and Kalidjaga answered them all correctly. Then Bonang told him to go forth and spread the truths of Islam, which Kalidjaga did with unsurpassed effectiveness.

What a remarkable story! The master apostle of Javanese Islam becomes a great saint without ever having seen the Qur'an, entered a mosque, or prayed a Muslim prayer. His conversion comes directly from a change of heart deepened by yoga-like meditation. It is not so much a change in belief (taking that word to refer mainly to matters of thought) as a change in will.

Because he had reformed his life, and penetrated the implications of his reform, Kalidjaga had become a Muslim. When he walked the meditative way that Indian culture had been impressing on Indonesia for centuries, he came out a Muslim—the new holy man forged in the fires of Indonesia's cultural transformation. So the message that was trumpeted whenever the legend of Java's greatest saint was told was that Islam is the obvious expression of the reformed, converted, highly developed religious personality. If one finds the depths of human authenticity, one eventually realizes that the Qur'an, the mosques, and the Muslim scholars are human authenticity's best expressions.

The Moroccan saint Sidi Lahsen Lyusi is quite a contrast to Kalidjaga. Lyusi was born into an obscure tribe of shepherds in the Middle Atlas Mountains of Morocco in 1631. Although he probably was of Berber descent, he claimed to be a *sherif* or direct descendant of Muhammad. Lyusi died in 1691, so the sixty years of his life coincided with the rise of the Alawite dynasty (which still rules today in Rabat, the capital of Morocco) from the chaos of a preceding sectarian strife. Like Kalidjaga's, therefore, Lyusi's sainthood was intimately tied to a difficult time of transition, when people were looking for models of a new social order. However, where Kalidjaga functioned as a miniature of the new harmony that Indonesia sought, Lyusi directly opposed the power he saw rising in his times. Thus Clifford Geertz, whose description of these two saints we are following, characterizes Lyusi's approach as moralistic, in contrast to the aesthetic approach of Kalidjaga.

The chaos of Lyusi's lifetime is sometimes called the Maraboutic Crisis, and it arose after the collapse of the last of the Berber dynasties, the Merinid. A *marabout* is a holy man, and during the Maraboutic Crisis Morocco splintered into different political groups clustered around different holy men. Lyusi wandered from political group to political group, always restless and on the move. When he arrived in Tamgrut, a desert oasis, he encountered the famous Muslim saint Ahmed ben Nasir. Ben Nasir was sick with smallpox, and so he asked his disciples, one by one, to wash out his loathsome nightshirt. Each disciple refused, repelled by the disgusting garment and afraid for his health. Lyusi, who had just arrived and was not known to ben Nasir, approached the saint and volunteered for the job. He took the shirt to a spring, rinsed it, wrung it out, and then drank the foul water it produced. When he returned to the master his eyes were aflame, not with sickness but with what Moroccans call *baraka:* the supernatural power that makes a marabout.

The story summarizes the Moroccan notion of sainthood. The main forces at work in Lyusi's transformation into a man of *baraka* were his extraordinary physical courage, his absolute personal loyalty to his "teacher," his moral intensity, and an almost physical passage of sainthood from teacher to disciple. Thus the Moroccan notion of Muslim sainthood seems more energetic than the Indonesian. Whereas Kalidjaga was transformed by forty years of meditation near a river, Lyusi was transformed by a single act of heroic courage.

Thirty years after this event, Lyusi had a momentous confrontation with Sultan Mulay Ismail, the great consolidator of the Alawite dynasty. In 1668 the Alawites had put an end to the Maraboutic Crisis and gained power in Morocco. The confrontation took place in the Sultan's new capital of Meknes, and it reveals the delicate relation between strongman politics and Maraboutism that has dominated Moroccan history. The warrior and the saint have been the two basic forms of heroism in Morocco, and this epic confrontation pitted a great warrior against a greater saint.

When Lyusi arrived in Meknes, Mulay Ismail received him as an honored guest. Indeed, he brought Lyusi to the court and made him his spiritual adviser. The sultan was building a large wall around the city and treating the men working on the wall cruelly. When one of the workmen fell from exhaustion and was sealed into the wall, some of the other workers came to Lyusi secretly to complain. Lyusi said nothing, but that night, when his supper was brought to his chamber, he broke all the dishes. He continued to do this, night after night, until all the dishes in the palace were broken.

Eventually the sultan learned what was happening and ordered Lyusi brought to him. When he asked the saint why he was acting so outrageously, the saint asked in return whether it was better to break pottery of clay or the pottery of Allah (human beings). Then he proceeded to upbraid the sultan for his cruelty to the workers. The sultan was not moved. Lyusi had abused his hospitality (a high crime in Moroccan culture), so he ordered Lyusi out of the city.

Lyusi left the palace and pitched his tent near the wall that was being built. When the sultan asked why the saint had not obeyed the royal order, Lyusi said that he had left the sultan's city and taken up residence in God's city. At this answer the sultan was so enraged that he charged out on horseback. Interrupting the saint's prayers (another high crime), he again asked why the royal order had been disobeyed. Again he received the answer that Lyusi was now in the city of God. Wild with fury, the sultan advanced to kill the saint. But the saint drew a line on the ground and when the sultan's horse crossed the line the horse's legs began to sink into the earth. Terrified, the sultan begged mercy and promised that he would reform. Lyusi said he only wanted a decree acknowledging that he was a *sherif,* entitled to the honors of a direct descendant of the Prophet. The sultan gave him this

decree and Lyusi left Meknes (fearing for his life) to preach to the Berbers in the Middle Atlas forests. After his death a great cult developed at his tomb, and he has since been revered as a most powerful marabout. In Lyusi, Moroccan Islam has found an ideal embodiment of its moral passion, just as in Kalidjaga Indonesian Islam has found an ideal embodiment of its meditative passion.

Ultimate Reality

Islam is perhaps the most theocentric of the major religions.[87] In Muhammad's revelation, Allah emerged to become the sovereign Lord. Before Muhammad, some Arabs had spoken of a high god "Allah" who was above the numerous idols. The divine name itself seems to fuse two words: al-Ilah ("the God"). It was an attempt to designate an ultimate divinity, a God who was beyond all demigods. From his visionary experience, Muhammad recognized that Allah is the only divinity, and that his primary designations are "Creator" and "Judge." As such, Allah leaves no place for other deities to function in either the world's creation or in the destiny of humankind.

Islam polished its theocentricity through controversy with polytheistic Arabs and then with Christians committed to the Incarnation and the Trinity. Sura 112, which Schimmel calls the logical end of the Qur'an,[88] puts the matter succinctly: "Say: He is Allah, One; Allah, the Eternal; He brought not forth nor hath He been brought forth; Coequal with Him there hath never been anyone."

The Creator made the world in six days (or in a single moment, according to Sura 54:50). Muslims trust that he guides the world wisely and unfailingly. Allah's knowledge of all creatures is total, and his mercy extends to all who acknowledge him. It is Allah in whose name every work is being begun and upon whose will every future action depends. Thus, one has to add "insha Allah" ("if God wills") to every sentence that refers to a future act or a new direction of thought. To try to indicate Allah's fullness, the Qur'an encircles him with "most beautiful names." He is the First and the Last, the Inward and the Outward. Above all, he is Merciful and Compassionate. He is the All-Holy, the Peace, the Light of Heaven and Earth. Transcendent though he be, he is also as near as the jugular pulse. Wherever one turns, there is his Face (the Qur'anic expression for Allah's essence).

Many scholars find the negative portion of the creed ("no God but Allah") very important, since it unequivocally rejects other peoples' gods. As well, it determined that the greatest sin in the Muslim code would be *shirk*—idolatry or "association" (of other objects of worship with Allah). The mystics sometimes took this to mean that nothing but Allah exists—that God alone is real. Among modern Muslims, anti-idolatry on occasion has worked against ideologies such as Marxism, capitalism, and nationalism, which some orthodox Muslims find incompatible with pure monotheism. Insofar as such ideologies gain the ultimate concern of many human beings, they amount to new kinds of paganism.

However, the theology of the Qur'an itself is not without ambiguity. After Muhammad's death, debates arose about Allah's nature. At the beginning, the orthodox clung to the letter and imagery of the received text. That meant accepting descriptions of Allah that gave him a face, hands, and the like. The Mutazilites, who had contact with Hellenistic rationalism, pointed out the dangers latent in such anthropomorphism: When we think of Allah in human terms, we think of him as finite.[89] Thus, the Mutazilites clung to the absolute unity of Allah, accepting as a consequence that Allah cannot be imagined. In other words, they prized Allah's difference—the gulf that lies between the Creator and everything created. In Western terms, that made them "negative" theologians. Indeed, to safeguard Allah's unity, the Mutazilites even questioned the doctrine of the divine attributes (that Allah has speech, sight, and so on). For that reason, the orthodox described the Mutazilites as "those who deny the attributes," a charge of heresy.

In these debates, Muslims shared with Jews and Christians the consequences of an exposure to Greek reason. They had to ask whether their descriptions of Allah could be reconciled with what they could infer from the divine transcendence. For instance, they could infer that a Creator would be independent of the world, unlimited, unimaginable in created terms. From that it followed that any picture of Allah would be at best a happy convenience—a more or less useful fiction that might help some people's faith. As a further extension of such rationalism, the Mutazilites denied that the Qur'an is Allah's uncreated word. To them that would have made it a coeternal attribute, something ever existent with Allah. However, calling the Qur'an "created" deeply offended the orthodox, for whom the Arabic text expressed a heavenly prototype. The human Qur'an was unalterable (which led the orthodox to resist all attempts to translate it from Arabic), because it derived from eternity. Thus, the Mutazilites and the orthodox clashed in their theologies of revelation.

Furthermore, the Mutazilites insisted that Allah has to be just and true. For the divine will to be arbitrary would violate Allah's own inner consistency. Consequently, Allah has to reward the just with heaven and punish the evil with hell. As well, Allah cannot be the author of sin, so human beings must have free will. To the less intellectual Muslim majority, this logic seemed rarefied, and they could not follow its deductive chain. "Limiting" Allah's freedom jarred with their sense of the divine sovereignty. Indeed, popular orthodoxy never fully accepted either human freedom or the notion that Allah had to obey rules for creation, even if they were his own. Popular orthodoxy preferred to leave all things in Allah's hands and saw little reason to puzzle over human freedom, Allah's noncontradiction, or the other problems that vexed the Mutazilites.

Al-Ashari, who had mediated the debate on the question of divine providence and human freedom, also mediated the question of the divine attributes. To the Mutazilites, he insisted that Allah has attributes (thereby saving the picture in the Qur'an). To the traditionalists, he insisted that we cannot say precisely how Allah has his attributes. In al-Ashari's eyes, both anthropomorphism and the denial of attributes were grave sins.

Among the Arab philosophers,[90] such as Avicenna, Greek doctrines stimulated the conception of Allah as a first cause whose being is pure existence. In contrast, the Sufis tended to forego philosophical speculation, favoring instead a personal experience of the divine. For them the profitable way was not reasoning but intuition. Furthermore, the Sufis opposed Qur'anic fundamentalists by proposing that we should obey Allah out of love. To the fundamentalists, such a personal relationship seemed novel, for they admitted only a relationship of obedience: The Creator commanded and the creature obeyed. Because the Sufis were more ecstatic than either the fundamentalists or the philosophers, they are a richer source for ascertaining the beauty of the Islamic God—the allure of Allah's mystery and its fearsomeness. The Shiites also have been quite ecstatic, praying in remembrance of their martyred saints and for the coming of the seventh Imam, their Messiah.

The basic Islamic program for worshiping God has always been the Five Pillars. In the daily prayer *(salat),* one expressed one's submission to God and so one's faith in God's Lordship. Historically, men attended the Friday common worship in the mosque, while women prayed at home. Sufi circles developed unstructured prayer, which frequently involved a repetition of Allah's holy names. On the folk level, magical practices mixed with worship. The Qur'an gave such practices some foundation by saying that the (bad) angels Harut and Marut taught the Babylonians magic (2:96). Ordinarily, the magician knew formulas that could conjure up the jinns or the angels. This has led to an expansion of the ways in which one can imagine the spirits and call them to one's aid. Amulets, reproductions of verses from the Qur'an, reproductions of God's names, and so on, are popular expressions of Muslim interest in attaining good luck. Similarly, Muslims continue to dread the "evil eye." To ward off its malignant influence, people constantly intersperse their conversation with "as Allah wills." As well, they wear amulets or give their children ugly names to keep the evil ones away.

Popular religion also retains a considerable interest in astrology, prophecy, and fortune-telling. A favorite technique for divining the future is to open the Qur'an at random and take the first verse that one's eye falls on as a cipher for what is to come. Other popular methods are reading palms or coffee grounds.

Sacrifice also has a place in Muslim worship of Allah. Those who can afford it immolate a sheep on the Day of Slaughtering during the annual pilgrimage to Mecca. This sacrifice is in memory of Abraham, who was willing to sacrifice his son Ishmael. People also make votive offerings—cocks, sheep, and so on—at holy places such as the tombs of saints. The animal should be slaughtered ritually, by cutting its jugular vein and its trachea in one stroke; tradition recommends giving it to the poor. Finally, sacrifice is appropriate on almost any important occasion, such as starting construction of a house, celebrating a child's birthday, or expiating an offense.

Although Islam places no mediators between Allah and human beings, it has made both Muhammad and many saints quite important objects of devotion. The members of Muhammad's family have enjoyed special privileges, and Ali, his cousin and son-in-law, became a cult figure to those who considered him to be Muhammad's legitimate heir. The Shia expanded the creed to include the words "Ali is the Friend of God." The Shia also venerated the line of imams, with special emphasis upon the currently hidden imam. He is the ruler of the age, and he will return at the end of the world to fill the world with justice. In Iran this imam's name accompanies the promulgation of laws, and he is for pious Shiites an object of intense personal devotion.[91] Ali's son Husain also plays an important role, for the celebration of his assassination is a day of deep mourning.[92] Among the Sufis, the leaders of the orders were venerated, as were holy people who gained a reputation for miracles. The latter often received special tombs to which the faithful would go for cures and favors.[93]

Angels are also essential objects of Muslim faith. According to tradition, Allah created them from light. The Qur'an stresses that they are neither children of Allah nor female beings. They are intelligent and can become visible. From the Qur'an, Muslims know Gabriel as the angel of revelation. Israfil will blow the trumpet at Doomsday, and Azrael is the angel of death. Iblis is the fallen angel. Like Harut and Marut, he is a source of evil. Harut and Marut taught humankind witchcraft, but a beautiful woman seduced them and then imprisoned them in a well in Babylonia.[94] Thus, the sacred space between the creature and the Creator has been abuzz with personages of interest.

The Islamic divinity is similar to that of the other theistic religions. Though official Islamic doctrine insists on Allah's uniqueness, the comparativist finds that its popular practice also greatly honors Muhammad, angels, and saints. Muslims perhaps have read the Qur'an more literally than other religionists have read their respective scriptures, since Islamic orthodoxy reified it into Allah's eternal Word, but there are analogies in Judaism, Christianity, and Hinduism. Clearly, though, Muslim faith regularly has aspired to make things simple; a black-and-white doctrine of God, Muhammad, and Judgment; a program of genius (the Five Pillars) for reducing this faith to practice; a single community of believers dedicated to filling the earth with true religion—with submission to the Grand Lord of the Worlds.

SUMMARY: THE MUSLIM CENTER

Allah is certainly the Muslim center, and because the Qur'an is the definite expression of Allah, the Qur'an is the central place where the invisible Muslim God has become visible. How, then, does the Qur'an portray the Lord of the Worlds, the most ultimate and holy Muslim reality? It portrays him majestically, as a sovereign beyond compare, a power nothing earthly can approach. When Allah commands, the heavens thunder and the earth quakes. When Allah consoles, the winds quiet and the soul feels bliss. Were Allah not compassionate, merciful, life would be utterly terrifying. He is a severe judge, and none can abide the day of his coming. Yet he has sent prophets to warn humanity of his coming, has reset the strict boundaries of his laws. Muhammad is the seal of these prophets, in whom their work has come to complete fulfillment. As there is no God but God, so there is no final prophet but Muhammad. The eternal Qur'an that has been at Allah's side from the foundations of the world has taken definitive voice in Muhammad's recitals. All the *hadith*, ponderings of the lawyers, visions of the saints, and virtuous living of the pious depend on this one ever-flowing font. Apart from the Qur'an, there would be no house of Islam.

For Qur'anic religion, the world is bare of idols. If we rightly perceive the Lord of the Worlds, nothing stands between divinity and creation. Whatever exists in space and time depends utterly on Allah. To Allah belongs all praise and worship; any worship of creatures is a wicked blasphemy. This does not mean that one should be an ascetic. The austerities of some of the Sufis are understandable, but they have never been the Muslim mainstream. The Muslim mainstream has rather been a sober, almost fated acceptance of whatever life brings. Thus wealth, power, or even plunder need not take a Muslim from healthy religion. Similarly, poverty and illness need not interfere with a solid holiness, since they too can be accepted "as Allah wills." The will of Allah dominates the Muslim psyche. What so splendid a Lord chooses to dispense obviously is one's true fate.

The best dispensation of Allah, his sovereign Word, has been the pious Muslim's fated solace. Thus small children memorizing the Qur'an, often without knowing its language, have slowly been formed to a passionate love of Islam's Arabic cadences. The rhythms of the Qur'an have become the rhythms of their souls. Muslim piety is poetic, rhapsodic, both burning and disciplined. When one bows and lets the verses sing through one's whole being, becoming like the Reed of whom the Sufis wrote, one's piety is almost instrumental. The poetry of God uses devout submission as its musical instruments—strings and drums of flesh and blood.

As a result, the Muslim mystics seem almost intoxicated with the Qur'anic God. His poetic voice fills their spirits like heady wine. In the stark clearing of Islam's powerful monotheism, the Muslim soul can see and feel divinity everywhere. The mystics who claimed strict union with Allah, utter identification, went beyond what orthodoxy would allow, but they built on an experience that mainstream Muslim piety fostered. An Allah as near as the pulse at one's throat, utterly in control of one's world, easily could invade one's spirit, break down the barriers between mine and thine. That usually he did not is a strong tribute to the effectiveness of the Qur'anic stress on his sovereign transcendence. Though he controlled all events, none captured more than a fraction of his power or being.

As a result, no event or creature could stand for Allah sacramentally, as the rites or icons of other theisms could stand for their people's God. Muhammad could not be an incarnate divinity, as Jesus could be for Christians. (This is most true of Sunnis. Sufis have a more charismatic Muhammad, and Shiites make the seventh Imam close to divine.) No baptism or Eucharist could mediate the divine life, just as no meditation could actuate the divine enlightenment. The light of Allah was indeed a shining lamp. The path of Allah was indeed the Way that was straight. But the life of Allah, the being of Allah, dwelt beyond all this-worldly metaphors, ceremonies, or other means of conveyance. They even dwelt beyond all this-worldly experiences: The most intense mystical raptures did not allow one to claim possession of the divine nature. There is no God but God. There is no connection to God, no understanding of God, no commission from God that clouds the clear Muslim heaven. Allah is like the sun at its apex, blazing down on a beautiful desert stripped of all competitors to him.

Psychologically, then, the Muslim center is the submission in which one expresses one's creaturehood. God is great and the submitter is small. In the world of fellow human beings the submitter may be weak or strong, wealthy or poor, a simple soul or a complex tyrant. Under the aspect of Allah's eternity, the submitter remains but a creature of a day, a grain of sand along an endless shore. The best fruits of this psychology are the freedom and objective humility it has fostered. If one really lives under the aspect of eternity, few earthly tyrannies are impressive. The worst fruits of this psychology, showing its negative potential, have been its stuntings of human growth.

Discussion Questions

1. Contrast Muhammad with Jesus.

2. In what sense is Islam the preeminent religion of the Book?

3. Why do the Five Pillars make a comprehensive, fully adequate religious program?

4. Explain briefly how Qur'anic religion could inspire the golden age of Arabic civilization.

5. What does Sufism contribute to the family of Islam?

6. Compare the position of women in Islam, Judaism, and Christianity.

7. How well does submission describe the relation between the Muslim and Allah?

8. Contrast the sainthood of Lyusi and Kalidjaga.

9. Why is Islam so fervently opposed to God's having a son?

10. What are the assets and liabilities in the Muslim idea of a theocracy with no separation between religion and politics?

11. What are the main implications of believing Allah to be as near as the pulse at one's throat?

12. What are the main implications of believing that Judgment Day is soon to arrive?

13. What are the main psychodynamics you would expect to see at work during the pilgrimage to Mecca?

14. Why has Islam had no official sacraments?

15. How can God be all-powerful and human beings have free will?

16. How does Islam deal with the problem of evil?

17. What model of sanctity has Muhammad encouraged?

Glossary

Allah: the Muslim deity, singular for the degree to which Muhammad and Muslims have insisted he is the sole possessor of divinity, the Lord of the Worlds beside whom everything else pales into insignificance.

dhikr ("zicker"): a Muslim term for remembrance or recollection. This virtue became all-important when one linked it with the Muslim conviction that forgetfulness (rather than sin) was the main reason people disregarded Allah, fell into idolatry, violated the *Sharia,* and so forth. Thus the Qur'an called for constantly remembering the goodness of Allah, the promises and favors Allah had vouchsafed, the teachings of the Prophet, and the like. The call to pray five times a day externalized the importance of *dhikr,* and in general much Islamic spirituality sought to keep the disciple in the presence of the Qur'anic word or attentive to the presence of Allah to both human beings and the signs of physical nature.

hadith: Muslim traditions about Muhammad. The *hadith* function in Islam as one of the principal sources of authoritative teaching, standing with the Qur'an, community consensus, and analogical reasoning. They imply the paradigmatic faith of the Prophet, whose life believers have taken as the model or template for Muslim existence. Complicated rules govern how sayings became authenticated and entered the collections of *hadith.* Muslims tend to be confident that what is housed in the several authoritative collections accurately reports what the Prophet said and did, but scholars using the detached techniques of textual criticism find much that seems folkloric and mythic.

hajj: the Muslim pilgrimage to Mecca. One of the Five Pillars that summarize the practice of Islamic faith, the *hajj* has the special objective of binding believers to the birthplace of Islam and convincing them that all believers form a universal brother- and sisterhood. Pilgrims repeat ritual gestures more than a thousand years old, wear common, nondistinctive garb that levels their wealth and signs of worldly station, and regularly experience what the anthropologist Victor Turner has called "communitas": the sense of being a unified people that only can flourish in special circumstances, when one feels called out of the workaday world and has one's human relationships reset by direct experience of the divine holiness.

Hejira: Muhammad's flight or departure from Mecca to Medina in 622. The Hejira may be considered Muhammad's definitive realization that he would never get through to his fellow Meccans and so his striking out on a new chapter in his mission to spread Qur'anic revelation. In Medina he was given control of a community and so could develop a blueprint for a Muslim state. Having consolidated both his own thought and considerably more power, Muhammad then returned to Mecca and conquered his prior enemies, making the Hejira the prelude to the wholesale victory that established Islam as what would become a great religious empire and culture.

imam: a spiritual guide in Shiite Islam. Imams may be human teachers, offering the faithful instruction in Qur'anic religion. Or they may be mystical teachers ruling over given ages. The last of these mystical imams, ruling the final age in secret, is an object of great yearning in Shiite Islam. When he comes, Shiites will be justified in having followed Muhammad's bloodline for their successors and they will be recompensed for the sufferings of their great saints.

Islam: the faith, obedience, and practice of Muslims. The word has overtones of "submission," implying that the Muslim is in the first instance the one who submits to Allah. In practice this means submitting to the revelation of Allah (the Qur'an), to the Prophet of Allah (Muhammad), and to the community Allah had Muhammad form through the Qur'an (the *Ummah*). Islamic piety carries through this notion of submission by having worshipers bow low at daily prayer and think of their relation to Allah as compassionate and merciful. Allah may be loved and may be experienced as love. But probably the stronger overtones in Islam are that Allah is the Lord and human beings are the servants, those who should hear and obey.

jihad: a Muslim term meaning holy struggle, warfare in defense, or pursuit, of a good cause. Muslims frequently make the point that jihad is broader than simply "holy war." It can connote the whole range of effort necessary to promote the faith in both personal and social life. Moreover, even when it refers to military matters, it need not primarily be offensive. The more ordinary reason for going to war, in the Muslim view of past history, was opposition that would have denied Muslims the chance to practice or spread their faith. Seeing such a denial as opposition to God, the Qur'an, and the Prophet, Muslims have felt obliged to fight, as they could feel obliged to fight on behalf of brother and sister Muslims who came under attack. The unity of the Muslim community justified such a sense of social solidarity, believers having ties among themselves that relegated their relations with unbelievers or outsiders to a lower level.

jinn: an Arabic term for a demon or spirit. Arab religion before Muhammad's time generally was polytheistic and animistic, believing in many spirits, both good and evil. The evil spirits or demons had to be warded off with prayers, sacrifices, amulets, and spells. Muhammad tried to cleanse the Arab psyche of its polytheistic impulses but he himself accepted the existence of angelic spirits and jinn. The jinn and angels certainly were not on the same level as Allah, but they had influence in human life and had to be dealt with. Popular Islamic religion frequently remained quite involved with fighting the jinn, retaining long-standing beliefs in the influence of the evil eye and the need to protect oneself against bad spirits by prayers and regular submission of one's fate to the will of Allah.

Muslim: a submitter to Allah; a follower of Islam and the Prophet Muhammad. Muslims accept the prophecies of Abraham and Jesus, but the Qur'an is their great charter. They think of Muhammad as the seal of prophecy—the definitive revealer. Islam correlates the submission of the believer bowing low in prayer with submission of the nonidolatrous mind. Just as the body bends and prostrates itself, so the mind should accept the sole Lordship of Allah and submit to the divine will manifested in the Qur'an.

polydemonism: the reverence or fear of many demons, spirits, or jinn. Polydemonism is simply a further specification of the animistic tendency to populate the world with frightful spirits. Witchcraft and black magic tend to abound in a polydemonistic world view, and usually the psychology of the people in question is troubled, even paranoid. In such cases, missionaries of either a single transcendent God or of a simplifying message such as the Buddhist call to enlightenment can seem liberators, offering people a way to escape thrall to irrational principalities and powers.

Ramadan: the Muslim lunar month during which the faithful are expected to fast from sunup to sundown. Keeping the fast of Ramadan is one of the Five Pillars basic to the superstructure of Islamic faith. Yet the fast is as much joyous as penitential, for in many Muslim countries those fasting celebrate each evening. Because lunar months move through the solar year, Ramadan may occur when the days are either short and cold or when they are long and hot, which means the severity of the exercise can vary considerably. The fast is supposed to discipline both body and mind, reminding all Muslims that their first obligation is to the will of Allah, and that to fulfill the will of Allah they need to be masters of their own personal beings.

rasul: Muhammad as the prophet or messenger par excellence. Islam admits that other prophets—Abraham, Jesus—preceded Muhammad, and it sees Muhammad as completing the prophecy of such predecessors. But with Muhammad has come the Qur'an, the Recital that "seals" prophecy. In other words, Qur'anic revelation is definitive. It completes what was begun but remained imperfect prior to Muhammad, and it itself will never be superseded. As the *rasul,* Muhammad is also the great exemplar of what God wants human beings to become. He is the compleat Muslim, modeling both proper piety and human maturation. Although Islam insists Muhammad was not divine, it has accorded him great honor and taken much offense whenever outsiders denigrated him.

Sharia: the path, teaching, canon law, and guidance of Islam. *Sharia* is analogous to Jewish Torah, Buddhist dharma, and Christian doctrine. Historically it rose from reflections on the Qur'an and the *hadith* that passed on the example and teachings of the Prophet. Generally it tends to connote the orthodox law codes Islam developed, which codified the consensus of the community and the conclusions the Muslim teachers had reached by reasoning from precedents. Traditional Muslims have looked to *Sharia* for guidance on the path to salvation, although they have admitted notable debate among their teachers over fine points of interpretation. *Sharia* has been the backbone of traditional Muslim culture, developing the revelations of the Qur'an and the example of the Prophet so that they could inspire a full body of architectural, scientific, political, and ritualistic expressions.

Shia: sectarian Islam that has opposed Sunni orthodoxy. The Shia arose from early disputes about succession to Muhammad in leadership of the Muslim community. It was the group championing Ali and the rights of blood relatives of the Prophet. It has usually been the Islamic minority and from its minority status, as well as specific historic sufferings such as the murder of the sons of Ali, has developed a religious consciousness dominated by suffering, persecution, and martyrdom. The Shia has predominated in Iran, which in some historical periods has been the cultural luminary of the Muslim world. Recently its relations with Sunni Islam have been tense, even combative. Shiites and Sunnis share more doctrines and practices than they hold separately, although the Shiites do have certain distinctive doctrines, such as the expectation of the return of the hidden imam to consummate history, and certain distinctive festivals, such as the commemoration of the martrydom of the sons of Ali.

Sufism: devotional, ascetic, or mystical Muslim traditions whose adherents often are members of a lodge or brotherhood. Sufism appears to have arisen shortly after the Muslim military expansions and political successes, in good part as a protest movement. Fearing that worldly success would taint adherence to Allah, the Qur'an, and the Prophet, the Sufis turned their backs on worldly concerns to devote themselves to prayer and spiritual purification. Yet they did not advocate celibacy, and they usually did profess to be keeping faith with *Sharia.* Their critics have considered their support of saints and their sometimes eccentric, even credulous, religious practices a source of Muslim decline, comparing them disadvantageously with the sober demands of *Sharia.* The Sufis somewhat parallel the Jewish Hasidim, both groups seeking religious fervor and rejecting official legalism. Sufi mysticism added to the staple Muslim submission to Allah new notes of love, most notably in such writers as Rabia and Rumi. Sufi teachers, like Zen roshis, sometimes have spoken paradoxically, used pointed or parabolic stories, and employed theatrical gestures to prod their students.

Sunni: the majority denomination in Islam. The Sunnis have considered themselves both more traditional and more moderate than either the Shia or the Sufis. They have tended to think the *Sharia* the backbone of Muslim culture and to favor religious life that balanced between profession of the uniqueness of Allah and conviction that Allah had made the material world good for human beings to develop. Sunnis have predominated in most cultural areas other than Iran. Historically, they supported the view that the successors to Muhammad in leadership of the Muslim community need not be members of the Prophet's bloodline—a position with some foundations in pre-Islamic Arab political custom. Sunnis certainly are not monolithic, but the similarity of the several official Sunni law codes and the common rejection of doctrines peculiar to the Shia tend to harmonize them.

Ummah: the Muslim community. Islam thinks of all believers as comprising a brother- and sisterhood. The Prophet was the head of the entire community in his day, but after his death the question of headship of the community became entangled in political and cultural battles. Historically, the community has been led by different dynasties and has been divided geographically. In addition, the differences between Shiites and Sunnis have complicated estimates of how the *Ummah* actually subsists in time. But such occasions as the annual pilgrimage to Mecca have allowed Muslims to affirm their solidarity, while the common hold that the Prophet, the Qur'an, the *Sharia,* the Five Pillars, and other Muslim staples have kept on all the faithful has meant the community has been a solid reality, not just an unrealized ideal.

zakat: the Muslim alms. The *zakat* is one of the Five Pillars of Islam, not a charitable gift but a matter of obligation. How much it should be has varied with local custom, but everywhere it has symbolized the community all Muslims share and the obligations they carry to care for one another. In Muhammad's day clan society had broken down, with considerable suffering for widows, orphans, and others who had no immediate family. The alms in the first place was aimed at helping such unfortunates, but it can also take the form of endowing hospitals, schools, and mosques.

CHAPTER 7

ALTERNATIVES TO RELIGION—SECULARISM AND HUMANISM

A modern symbol suggesting human control

HISTORY

Traditional Sources of Secularization

In this chapter we look directly at the challenge the world religions have received—largely, but not exclusively, in modern times—from thinkers and social trends that have deprecated the significance of divine mystery and cut back the influence of religious professionals, institutions, doctrines, and behavioral patterns.[1]

Perhaps the first thing we should note is that the religious traditions themselves have always housed forces with a potential to decrease their hold on the common people and lessen the public perception that religion was the most important factor in anyone's life. For example, when Akhenaton promoted a "monotheistic" reform of Egyptian religion, he ran into opposition from the Egyptian priesthoods, because he threatened the existence (and so influence) of their particular gods. Somewhat similarly, when the Buddha preached the Four Noble Truths, he implied that the Indian gods were much less significant than popular Indian religion then held. People of the ancient Near East who heard about the Israelite God YHWH sensed that that God threatened their many naturalistic deities. Eurowhen it focuses on experiences, ideas, or spiritual powers that suggest ways of finding life to be beautiful, meaningful, something one can preserve from death and tragedy. So nowadays mythology usually commands considerable respect.[2]

Several generations ago, mythology commanded less respect because observers tended to focus on its irrational, unscientific, magical aspects. Often mythology seemed the enemy of an intellectual understanding of nature, rational attempts to improve health care and economics, and emancipation from taboos, superstitions, and crippling fears. We have mentioned the negative estimates of Sufism that many Muslim modernizers held—how they considered Sufism a bastion of backwardness. Much the same has applied to modernizers of other traditions: reforming Jews or rationalistic rabbis confronting the mythology indulged by Hasidim, Christian progressives confronting fundamentalist snake-handlers or pilgrims flocking to shrines in hopes of cures, Communist Chinese trying to rid rural villagers of their faith in demons, river sprites, and folk medicine.

Again and again, such attitudes, whether promoted by religious or antireligious people, have combined demythologizing with rationalization. Demythologizing is the effort to replace a storied, rather imaginative or magical view of reality with something more critical, more insistent on hard facts and rigorous logic. Rationalization, as social scientists such as Max Weber have used the term, is the effort to organize social institutions and culture generally in more reasoned—detached, disciplined, objective—ways. For example, when groups move from somewhat hit-or-miss family (clan) sources of help for the poor to government agencies operating according to clear laws or public policies, one can speak of welfare efforts being rationalized. Insofar as such rationalization can mean that the welfare efforts become more efficient, that they reach more people and distribute a group's resources more fairly, one can praise rationalization. Insofar as aid becomes depersonalized, cold, hampered by bureaucratic details, one can long for the less rationalistic, more spontaneous old days.

Relatedly, increasing the quotient of reason in a people's world view and religious existence can bring both benefits and losses. Reason can clear up a lot of untidiness that irritated the thoughtful in the group. It can bring the focus back on important things—love of God, love of neighbor—and away from devotion to the saints or concern with cures that had taken center stage. Moreover, it can aid the reform of religious in-

pean tribes who received Christian missionaries learned that if they embraced Christ their fields and streams would have less powerful natural spirits.

In none of these cases did popular religion change so radically that the world lost its mysteriousness and divine power ceased to be significant. Also, each of these reforms or innovations proposed a new object of worship or intense concentration that the innovators hoped would intensify people's efforts to find wholeness by communing with the most significant, sacred powers. Yet, in the maturation of every religious tradition, one can find seeds that only needed certain technological and social developments to manifest their potential for challenging the mythological outlook of the culture at large.

Nowadays scholars tend to be more appreciative of myth than they were a few generations ago, realizing that the stories people have told themselves about their origin, destiny, and identity have been mainstays of their cultures and sanity. By their very concreteness and holism, their very power to grip the imagination and fire the emotions, stories, dances, rites of passage, and the like have made ultimate questions things people could feel very deeply. Deep, intense feeling helps people enjoy being alive. Certainly it can be terrifying, when it focuses on all that is unknown, destructive, or threatening. On the other hand, it can be exhilarating,

INGREDIENTS OF MODERN ALTERNATIVES TO TRADITIONAL RELIGION	
Natural science and technology	New power over nature Need for independence from Church authority
Political liberalism	Focus on individual rights Sense that modern people had come of age Rejection of Church authority
Historical criticism	Realization that all texts and institutions are historically conditioned
Global exploration	Sense that European theism is only one of many different cultural options
Evolutionary theory	Human beings merely a part of nature Modernity far advanced over ages of faith
Humanism	Primary concern for human affairs
Secularism	Primary interest in "this world" Evil seen as proof there is no God
Marxism	Religion a source of alienation and oppression Concentration on economics and politics

stitutions and the lives of religious professionals, lessening the impact of unthinking custom, longtime systems of patronage, longtime assumptions of autocratic powers. Once again, however, people subjected to too sweeping or sudden a demythologizing or reform can feel that they have lost precious old friends. If they were used to praying to the saints or reverencing the clergy as presences of supernatural power, they may find the reformed religion thin beer.

To be sure, it is a far distance from religious reforms to secularism. Most of those who seek to make religious traditions more rational, less mythological in the pejorative sense, have no desire to oust divinity and make the world *(saeculum)* seem the be-all and end-all. But whenever one focuses the powers of reason, starts to ask the old myths to make logical sense, wonders whether new ways being tried outside the tribe wouldn't be worth testing, one begins to tinker with the machinery that up to that point had kept the

people relatively content and secure. Certainly that should not make people refuse to initiate any innovations, but it suggests why older people tend to become conservative. With experience, they have realized that change often is more radical in its implications than those proposing it realize.

Nonetheless, change is inevitable, as the historical record everywhere shows. Certainly change is not inevitably a move from mythology to rationalization, from a religious immersion in nature's mysteries to a secularist rejection of such mysteries. The lines can go forward or back, up or down, and applying values ("better," "worse") to "forward" and "back" is a perilous venture indeed. So we are not proposing that secularization is necessarily progress (or regress). But we are proposing that lines of change there will be, and as we see in the next sections, the changes associated with the modern period of Western history generally brought demythologizing, rationalization, and a lessening of the influence of traditional religious authority. More and more, this-worldly matters attracted people's energies, while otherworldly matters receded from center stage. More and more countries secularized their law codes and considered public affairs—business, entertainment, even education—something better kept out of the hands of religious professionals. If not considered dead, then, God seemed to be taking more vacations.

Modern Science

One can document the introduction of disciplined, critical, "scientific" reason in the history of several religions. For example, the Buddhist *Abhidhamma* literature, which pored over the experiences of meditation, shows that early Buddhists soon developed a scholastic mind—one passionate about precise definitions, catalogues, and close reasoning. By the time of the fourth-century Christian councils, technical terms had entered the discussion of Christ's nature, and Greek philosophy had become the infrastructure of Christian theological speculation. The rabbis who developed the Mishnah, Gemara, and Talmud show the final results of Second Temple Jewish efforts to establish the religious law as the center of Jewish life.[3] The Neo-Confucians who attempted a philosophy of nature to make their tradition competitive with Buddhist philosophy brought a rationalizing, demythologizing mind to their task. So did the Muslim lawyers and philosophers who tried to make *Sharia* something precise and tried to give Islam a world view clarified by Greek reasoning.

Nonetheless, the only place where what we mean by modern science developed was in the Christian West. Historians of science debate the whys and wherefores of this phenomenon, but it seems clear that neither Greece, India, nor China was fully hospitable to the blend of *empirical* observation and rigorous analysis that developed in the medieval West and flowered with such early moderns as Francis Bacon and Isaac Newton. Greece and India seem to have been inhibited by their sense that the cosmos went through endless cycles, repeating over and over again the same constant trends. True enough, the investigations of nature one finds in the pre-Socratics and the naturalistic works of Aristotle display many of the intellectual characteristics one associates with modern science. But in fact Greece apparently did not generate sufficient faith in the intelligibility of empirical nature to launch the audacious enterprise begun in the later

medieval to early modern West. Similarly, while India and Islam came to house considerable mathematical talent, as well as interesting technologies, their science never became the systematic investigation of nature intrinsic to the institutions of modern science. China certainly developed great technological ingenuity, but again one finds that the world view apparently could not undergird the modern patterns of detailed observation, bold hypotheses, and rigorous verifications.[4] Modern science may in fact have come in recent years into a postmodern phase, in which it requires a more nuanced and less mechanistic philosophy of nature than that which empowered it in the seventeenth, eighteenth, nineteenth, and early twentieth centuries. But it gained its present shape in significant part because its cultural underpinnings included a belief that nature was the creative work of an omniscient deity and human beings were images of that deity through their powerful faculties of reason and will.

The above is certainly a simple-minded sketch of the origins of modern science, and no doubt historians could dispute it at many points. But the exposition of this view that one finds in such distinguished works as Stanley Jaki's Gifford Lectures makes it a reputable hypothesis.[5] What is less questionable and more germane for our purposes is the character and the effects of modern science. Whereas originally the investigation of nature had been a branch of religious philosophy or theology, by the time modernity had become well launched in the *Enlightenment,* science was well on its way to becoming an independent, autonomous enterprise. To be sure, various other branches of knowledge gradually differentiated themselves from the compact medieval world view in which theology was the queen of the sciences and philosophy (which comprised much of what we would now distinguish as physical science, social science, logic, ethics, and political science) was the handmaid. Still, the most dramatic differentiation came through the emancipation of first the philosophy and then the empirical science that studied physical nature.

The dynamics of this differentiation of physical science reveal many of the roots of modern Western secularization. If at first late medieval scientists (some of them monks and clerics) went to nature thinking it a warehouse of of God's works (St. Augustine had said that nature everywhere showed the vestiges of God), gradually the divine origin of nature or the presence of divine power in nature receded into the background. In the foreground, commanding more and more of the interest, were the data and patterns of the natural phenomena themselves. As telescopes and microscopes improved, the range of the data broadened. As speculative naturalists saw the need for more powerful theoretical tools for handling the data and explicating the patterns, mathematics made leaps into such areas as calculus. True, the early modern scientific giants—Newton, Pascal, Leibniz—were philosophers as much as what we would call natural scientists. But large portions of their work and thought treated nature as a somewhat autonomous realm possessing laws that human reason (relatively or completely unaided by special divine graces) could master.

Such mastery had a twofold significance. On the one hand, there was the pure desire to know how nature was constituted—to understand how the planets moved, how peas changed genetically, how the blood circulated through the human body. On the other hand, there was the desire to bring nature more fully under human control. Francis Bacon, especially, proposed the thesis that scientific knowledge amounted to power. Modern technology owes much of its origin to this thesis, since everything from modern medicine to modern engineering could be promoted as research and application geared to increasing humanity's power to bend nature to its service.

In the controversy between the astronomer Galileo and the authorities of the Catholic church early in the seventeenth century, the old theological ways clashed with the new scientific ways quite dramatically. Galileo has been vindicated and made a champion by later modernity, but it is important to realize that in his own day his proposals were bound to seem impious. God then was thought much more immediately involved in the running of the natural world, and the priority of divine revelation (necessary for salvation from sin) was considered much more important than any understanding or practical benefits the investigation of nature might bring. Certainly most present-day theologians would say the Catholic authorities were unwise to connect a geocentric view of the solar system with Christian orthodoxy, but historians of ideas know that everywhere traditional peoples have tied their sense of how the cosmos came into being and was structured with their doctrinal and ethical systems.[6] Certainly the vindication of Galileo was a victory for intellectual honesty, and certainly intellectual honesty should be high among the virtues religion defends. But in historical perspective it is not surprising that redefining faith so that it proved compatible with an intellectual honesty on the model of the autonomous investigations and speculations of modern science turned out to be a painful, traumatic business.

At any rate, their immersion in the data of physical nature, their sometimes intoxicating experience of the speculative powers of the human mind, and their witness of the practical changes to which scientific discoveries could lead when transmuted into modern technology all increased the scientists' conviction that they were the wave of the future. So science steadily developed its own canons of procedure, indeed its own orthodoxies.[7] The success of this development, combined with the greater wealth and health people came to enjoy from the labors of scientists and engineers, made the reservations of religious professionals seem either sour grapes or sheer timidity. Not until recent decades, when nuclear power burst on the scene with terrifying prospects of annihilation, chemistry and biology revealed horrible possibilities for polluting the earth, and military weaponry became unimaginably lethal, did confidence in modern science and technology take a significant body blow. Even now, huge portions of Western culture continue to cope with these and vast other problems (hunger, homelessness, drugs, economic dysfunctions, widespread criminality) as though physical science, technology, and behavioral science were the best sources for remedies. Religious believers, many of them fundamentalists, certainly oppose such an assumption, but it remains to be seen whether antiscientific religion proves any more effective than antireligous scientism and secularity. Religion that affirms the independence and value of science, and science that honors the mystery at the core of religion, could be good neighbors.

Liberalism

If modern science was the great arena in which independence of traditional religious authorities seemed to prove fruitful, modern political thought was the great arena in which the rights of human beings began to be defined apart from humanity's debts to the grace of God. There are many words and movements one could use to describe this political turn away from traditional, supposedly divine norms to rights defined by human beings themselves, but "liberalism" can stand duty for a goodly number of them. Probably the most influential liberal thinker was the Englishman John Locke (1632–1704), but other thinkers in England, France, Germany, and the United States both drew upon his thought and advanced it in new directions.

Locke studied the classics, lectured on moral philosophy, and then took training as a physician. He became a political confidant of Lord Ashley, Earl of Shaftesbury, who led the parliamentary opposition to the Stuart kings. In 1675 Locke made a prolonged visit to France, where he deepened his understanding of the ideas of the French philosopher René Descartes, and in 1683 he was forced to follow Shaftesbury into political exile in Holland.

Locke's political philosophy ran to a constitutional monarchy, a parliamentary government, and an enumeration of human rights. Life, liberty, and property summarized much of his platform, which had great influence in the eighteenth-century revolutions in both the United States and France. While Locke wrote treatises in defense of the reasonableness of Christianity, his understanding of human nature in fact was considerably more empiricist (considerably less mythological) than that of traditional Christianity. Although raised as a Puritan, he tended to treat of theological themes (the existence of God, revelation) in a rather restrained way, separating faith from what one can determine by empirical reason. This helped him undergird an instinct that true religion is tolerant of others' religious opinions. Relatedly, Locke was skeptical of the claims of any one church or religious group to know with certainty the way to salvation. In the trade-off between institutional authority and the rights of individual conscience, he came down for individual conscience.[8]

One can see, then, that while Locke kept ties to prior views of religion and the priority of the divine, he paved the way for the later liberal stress on humanism. As science seemed to place more and more of the natural world under the influence of human beings, and as religious institutions showed themselves conservatively opposed to progress in either physical science or political efforts to emancipate people from the destructive control of kings or aristocratic classes, Lockean principles justified emphasizing the truth human beings could discover on their own and the political freedoms that ought to flow from considering the individual conscience something precious, indeed, something sacred. Many liberals in fact assumed that social morality would continue to follow patterns indebted to Christian culture, but liberalism itself tended to erode the doctrinal bases of that morality.

Two centuries after Locke, John Stuart Mill advanced the liberal outlook, writing persuasively about individual liberties (which included the emancipation of women). In France, Jean Jacques Rousseau had brought forward romantic notions of the benefits that would accrue were human beings left free to have their unspoiled (relatively unsocialized) natures develop. In the economic sphere, Adam Smith, the Scottish economist (or moral philosopher), had advocated laissez-faire policies that would give maximum play to individual initiative, trusting that a free market would somehow manage the best possible development and distribution of wealth.

What these various "liberal" thinkers held in common was a stress (now more, now less, exclusive) on the freedom of individual human beings to run their own lives. Often they assumed social agreements and controls that their later successors did not assume, but in general they wanted to move away from strict controls by either Church or state that would inhibit people from choosing to become what they thought best. Theological traditionalists tended to criticize such liberalism by arguing that sin made human beings much less trustworthy than the liberals assumed, while political conservatives argued that power was well handled by only a few and liberalism opened the door to anarchy. On the whole, the religious and political establishments supported one another in offering cautions against liberal views.

Whether or not they explicitly cast aside traditional religious guidance and traditional religious views of God and human nature, liberals tended to put divinity in the shade. They were more interested in such this-worldly questions as political freedoms, educational reforms, and license to develop entrepreneurial projects. The Industrial Revolution was an ambiguous phenomenon, for on the one hand it brought this-worldly expertise and drive to bear on creating previously unknown disbursements of wealth, while on the other hand it severely limited the actual liberty of thousands of workers. Behind the liberal stress on individual conscience lay the stress of the Protestant reformers on the rights of individual conscience in religious matters, but the reformers and their heirs certainly had assumed the priority of divine revelation.

Insofar as liberalism meant being free of oppressive authorities, it ran in tandem with many themes of the eighteenth-century Enlightenment. Both movements were excited at the prospect of human beings coming of age sufficiently to think for themselves, depend on their own resources, and solve their main political, economic, and technological tasks with energy and confidence. For both, traditional religion often seemed a source of ignorance and repression, so both contrasted human autonomy with an older, religiously based heteronomy, arguing that it was more honest, profitable, and fitting that human beings look to themselves.

As one can easily imagine, such a call to self-reliance tended to produce both fits of enthusiasm and fits of depression. While people who had chafed under what they took to be repressive theological or political regimes found the humanistic message emancipating, people who found human ingenuity or human goodness unequal to the tasks of producing wealth in which all might share and developing a fully inclusive political system could despair of life apart from divine assurances and controls. The freedom to which the liberal thinkers called their fellow human beings held both terrors and joys. To those who felt strong enough to depend on themselves, it was good news, pressed down and overflowing. To those who longed for a tidy sense of reality, a map through time that would lay things out quite neatly, the liberal call could seem a siren song portending disaster.

Nonetheless, liberal thought gained sufficient influence in modern Europe and modern America to become a dominant political outlook. For example, the instinctive belief of the typical citizen of the United States that one has the right to run one's own life with little outside interference owes much to the liberal tradition. Through history, of course, many notions originally associated with the liberal thinkers have been transferred to latter-day "conservatives," this instinct for individual autonomy primary among them. Under whatever label, however, originally liberal ideas have challenged the traditional religious systems that made God's laws the major determinant of everyday behavior and gave religious institutions the main say in determining what was real or how people ought to live.

Marxism

In the nineteenth century, Karl Marx (1818–1883) was the main influence in shifting liberal ideas into the sphere of economics. For Marx, *atheism* was a necessary postulate of human freedom, while the principal subjugation human beings suffered came from the exploitation of the working classes by their capitalist bosses. Marx saw history as a dialectical interplay of such forces as evolutionary matter and class conflicts. Although he borrowed considerably from the German idealistic philosopher G. W. F. Hegel (1770–1831), Marx had little patience with Hegel's interests in the operations of the divine Spirit. To his mind, the worlds of politics and economics, which mutually determined one another, were the things upon which to concentrate.

All this might have been peaceful enough had Marx not added the further notion that philosophy itself ought to be changed. Whereas in the past philosophers had thought of their task as being to understand or interpret the world, in modern times it had become clear that the great task was to change the world. In other words, Marx gave a certain priority to action or praxis over thought. But where other thinkers of such a practical bent, including the American pragmatists (Dewey, Peirce, James), refrained from advocating violent or revolutionary programs, Marx, his associate Engels, and his most influential interpreters Lenin and Mao all wanted to embody Marxist principles in strikes, uprisings, and revolutions that would take power from the oppressive ruling classes and place it in the working classes (whom they themselves would direct).

Scholars debate the extent to which Marx would have opposed a religion that made justice toward the poor a primary goal, but there is little debating about the general impact of Marxist thought upon the religious attitudes of those who espoused it. Marxist groups became the leading representatives of a wider socialist movement that regularly targeted religious bodies as props of an oppressive status quo. In the name of human progress toward justice and prosperity, they regularly denounced old religious beliefs and practices. For some, God and Jesus were not great problems, because they could be interpreted as champions of the poor. But for others, anything religious, otherworldly, dealing with spirituality and the sacred was atavistic—a throwback to the days of superstition and degenerate myth. Now that human beings had come of age, as modern science and technology surely showed they had, such backwardness was immoral. Those who indulged in it were either hopeless fools or knowing manipulators of forces designed to keep the common people in thrall to the owners—factory workers, upper-class nabobs—who were so handsomely profiting from their sweat.

Although Marxist groups often have been better at rhetoric than hard analysis, and although often their own accession to power has brought worse repressions than those they had promised to end, much of the Marxist vision has entered into the liberal humanistic tradition, as a sort of further transfusion of energy and idealism. Whereas the original liberals were rather individualistic and did not criticize the socioeconomic construction of reality with great penetration, Marx and his followers studied labor and capitalism with considerable acumen. In line with many of the ideas of the biblical prophets, they denounced piety that did not pay off in justice, indeed did not produce mercy and helpfulness toward society's least well-off. In their critiques of religion, they tended to demonstrate how religion could be an ideology: a scaffolding of ideas that supported current economic and political arrangements and so went hand in glove with the interests of the wealthy classes.

This sense of "ideology," according to which every group puts forward ideas, even a systematic world view, that works to its own advantage, of course could be turned back on the Marxists themselves, but usually they exempted their own positions, calling them expositions of such supposedly unassailable truths as the laws of class conflict, the determinism of economic factors, and the necessity of atheism. Of course this made the Marxists as dogmatic as any religious or politically conservative group they were attacking, but somehow they regularly managed to keep themselves from confronting such countercharges. Where they might have availed themselves of the insights of Friedrich Nietzsche (1844–1900) that all philosophers tend to build thought-systems that defend themselves, and that European culture by the mid-nineteenth century in effect had killed the living God (the God who called for creativity and spiritual life) by its hypocrisy and mediocrity, the Marxists preferred to style themselves "scientific" and so shied away from such poetry.

Marxism of course has changed shape considerably in the twentieth century, but what has remained constant in its many incarnations as the inspiration of political revolutions has been its assurances that history is on the side of the lower, working classes, who have only to rise up and fight their oppressors to advance the day when there will be a classless, egalitarian society. The Soviet and Chinese Communist regimes have been the two outstanding examples of wholesale efforts to remake states by Marxist principles, and the successes and failures of both have proved highly illuminating. For on the one hand both have certainly improved the material lot of their common people, while on the other hand neither has scrupled to shed rivers of blood in putting down any individuals or groups they felt threatened their dogmatic programs.

In these two Marxist regimes, the twentieth century has had object lessons in the assets and liabilities of a humanism defined as a break with traditional recourse to divine laws about human behavior. The third great object lesson, the Nazi regime of the 1930s and 1940s, certainly stemmed from different philosophical (or mythical) foundations, but it furnished an equally powerful lesson. The wrath of the movement was particularly directed against the Jews, whom the Nazis blamed for all modern evils, but Christians soon realized that Nazism was equally antithetical to their own views, requiring them to choose between Christ and the Führer.

Marxism, Nazism, and other forms of this-worldly, secularistic thought (scientific humanism, for example) certainly require careful study as individual developments, but for our purposes in this chapter they mainly are significant as examples of the rapidity with which modernity raced away from traditional religion. By the middle of the twentieth century, only four hundred years or so from the beginnings of the modern scientific, political, and philosophical stirrings, the mainstreams of Western art, science, and general culture serenely ignored God and traditional religious doctrines. Darwinian biology, modern geology, Einsteinian physics, Freudian psychology, and the sociology indebted to Comte, Weber, and Durkheim all inclined moderns to think that nature, society, and the self were all there was. "God" was at best a projection of human ideals, while religious tradition was at best a hodgepodge of commonsensical observations about humanity's place in a mysterious world. The experience of war and political unrest in the first half of the twentieth century had been enough to convince many moderns that meaning was nowhere to be found. History, whether recent or ancient, showed mainly a record of barbarities, while the new powers that science and technology were unveiling gave more reason for fear than hope. The result was the great wasteland dramatized somewhat self-indulgently by the existentialist literature that flourished after World War II. Human beings, in the phrase of Jean-Paul Sartre, were nothing but useless passions. They had no definite essence, nothing by way of a nature fashioned by God (which might have given them guidance). Their burden was to be completely free, and so completely responsible for what they made of themselves.

In contrast, much psychology and sociology was deterministic, teaching that early family life or social conditioning left people little if any freedom. Religion therefore found itself disregarded on two sides. Existentialists said that human freedom was incompatible with the existence of God, while much social science said that freedom, and so choice about ultimate destiny, were largely illusory.

Industrialization, urbanization, and the increasing complexity of business and national life all served to reinforce the secularist tendency not to accept the stimulus from physical nature to contemplate the turning of the seasons. Relatedly, the rush and relative superficiality of urban and suburban life tended to deflect people from pondering the mysteries of human community and selfhood, perhaps for fear they would glimpse the void or feel human life to be like vapor over a volcano.

Paradoxically enough, therefore, by the end of the third quarter of the twentieth century humanistic, this-worldly intellectual currents themselves were inclining many people to take up religious questions again. Although often they did not realize it, when such people tried to find ways to assure human existence some ultimate meaning they rejoined the great stream of what some have called the perennial philosophy—the sense of the whole that had made wonder at the mystery of existence the primary foundation of culture.[9]

STRUCTURAL ANALYSIS

Nature and Divinity in Humanistic Perspective

Humanism is a term we have left undefined to this point, because we wanted to set it alongside secularism and let them both pick up rough and ready connotations from history. However, at this point it would be well to focus more clearly on both terms. Since the Italian Renaissance, *humanism* has connoted a turn to the human figure in art, a return to the classical literature of Greece and Rome that celebrated human pathos, and an assertion that human experience is worthy of interest and concern (in contrast to theological tendencies to deprecate human experience as disfigured by sin and overshadowed by the death and judgment soon to terminate one's passage through this vale of tears). One can connect humanism with religious views, as Christian humanists especially

have done, in which case it tends to mean celebrating the grandeur of what God has done in making men and women of flesh and spirit. So, for example, the Christian father Irenaeus sang that God's glory was human beings fully alive. In recent years, humanism has become the bugbear of religious fundamentalists, who have contrasted it with a faith-filled acceptance of the primacy of God. Where religion has said life ought to be God-centered, arrogant humanists have said that human beings ought to be the measure and interest of all our doings. Thus humanism (or "secular humanism") has been taken to be atheistic, in fact if not in outright profession.

Secularization is the process by which this-worldly things have become more important and heavenly things have faded into the background. Industrialization, urbanization, and the demythologizing effects of scientific and critical thinking usually are nominated as major reasons why secularization has occurred in the modern West (and, through the cultural exports of the modern West, in other parts of the globe). Secularization is ethically neutral—whether it has been good or bad depends on further premises and judgments. *Secularism* is the viewpoint, the philosophical position, that secularization has been good because otherworldliness was a distraction or a vitiation of human development. In other words, secularism assumes or argues that God, grace, salvation, sin, and the other staples of the religious world views that have urged people to look beyond the here and now for their ultimate meaning have all been misguided notions.

Once again, one can make some distinctions and point out that many religious traditions have sponsored a sort of this-worldliness and so a sort of secularism. Christians claiming that the incarnation of Christ and the sacramental system made space and time God's chosen theater of salvation have been religiously this-worldly. Buddhists urging people to concentrate on the here and now, to find nirvana in the midst of samsara, to realize there is no self or Brahman behind or beyond the network of dharmas, have also been religiously this-worldly. But both usually have denied that human beings are the ultimate norm and measure. Rather, both usually have argued that human beings only find their full, proper measure when they realize they are situated in something greater than themselves: the mystery of God or the grandeur of the cosmic buddha-nature.

Through these semantic forays, we have suggested much of what secular humanists tend to think about nature and divinity. For those who do make human beings and/or this world of space and time the be-all and end-all, physical nature tends to be given rather than created. It did not arise from the creative fiat of a supreme power transcending the world. It is a fascinating system of material forces, but where it is going or what brought it into being is beyond our reckoning. It has no moral implications, and how human beings interact with it should be determined by such factors as the value one places on its beauty, its being the matrix of all life and thought, its having preexisted human beings, and its potential services to human beings, both present and future. Some secular humanists do find nature dwarfing human concerns and restoring perspective. Others find contemplating nature ultimately depressing, because the icy wastes of space and the infinities of both subatomic and cellular beings reveal nothing that cares about humankind. Insofar as all of nature heads toward destruction (entropy) and death, the matrix of humanity can seem casual—without either purpose or care. On the other hand, the grandeur of sunrise and sunset, the immensities of space and time, the variety and staggering beauty of the myriad species, and even the wonders of the human body and mind can all cause secular humanists to break out in praise. How far such praise is from what religious people do in acclaiming the Lord of the Worlds is a nice question.

The divinity of secular humanism either is completely missing—nonexistent—or lodges in the implications of behavior (such as acclamation of physical nature) that in fact seems to hunger for a purpose for human existence. When God is missing from people's world views, emotions, and practical calculations, the other three basic dimensions of reality tend to collapse together. Either nature, society, or the self may predominate, pulling the others more fully into its orbit by an intellectual gravity, but all three have only implicit grounding. For "God" and its equivalents function in human mentality as the ground and context for all other thought. They indicate, however vaguely, the horizon, the backdrop, the whence and whither that neither nature, nor society, nor the self provides. One may say that concern about such a whence and whither is illusory or profitless. One may readily confess that questions about them move one to a transempirical realm where the mind may well be making up its data. But the fact remains that limiting one's constructions of reality to what sense and reason can produce by focusing on the phenomenal aspects of nature, society, and the self doesn't match what past cultures have dealt with nor what any healthy mind can be shown to vector toward.

Hindu, Buddhist, Taoist, Jewish, Christian, and Muslim cultures (to cite only the most obvious) all have concerned themselves with questions, experiences, perhaps realities that transcended "nature," "society," and "self" understood in empirical (sense-experienced) terms. Any healthy mind can be brought to a quiet and wonder that realize they are on the frontier of what may be a different sort of reality by placing it before a dead person and asking what the person's life has meant, or where the spirit of the person has gone, or why someone who enjoyed life should have to die, or what the outreach of the human mind and heart toward an understanding and love greater than mortality signifies. One doesn't have to answer these questions to sense the realm of *transcendence* that has meant so much to traditional religious cultures. One has only to raise them—only experience one's spirit move out toward them or be enveloped by their mystery. To be sure, many nominal atheists, humanists, and secularists have felt their spirits move into such mysterious matters. The question, then, is whether in fact they have lived apart from divinity and whether in consequence their world views have adequately accounted for their own spiritual experiences.

Society and Self in Humanistic Perspective

Areligious humanism may exalt society as the proper focus of human interest and endeavor, or it may view society as the source of most human corruption. By and large, the modern totalitarianisms have taken the first option, making "the people" the justification for their policies, whether benign or murderous. What has tended to suffer in modern humanistic social thought is the notion that "community" itself is a mysterious creation, a whole much greater than the sum of its parts and so a wonder suggesting divine aid.[10] To be sure, people who share military, political, or cultural ventures usually experience bonding. The question remains, however, what makes such bonding sacred—valuable enough to warrant reverence and sacrifice. Much the same question attends human love, as we shall see when we come to humanistic perspectives on the self.

On their own terms, most humanists do not raise such further questions. A few reflective humanists do not raise them as a matter of principle, having judged or postulated that such questions bring no profit or deal with a transcendent realm about which we can at best be agnostic. The majority of secular humanists, however, simply don't have the spiritual interest, need, or drive to press their first views of community toward something foundational. In this they are like the majority of believers, whose faith is equally uncritical. Nonetheless, secular humanism certainly can be developed into an impressive view of human community, if only by a logic such as the following.

Assume that there is no God demanding to be set at the center of one's system. Then survey what remains of human experience for what seems most valuable. You may decide that nature is the most valuable portion of reality, and so dedicate yourself to understanding, conserving, or developing nature. You may decide that personal freedom, individual autonomy, is the most precious thing you know, and so hymn the life of the artist, or the entrepreneur, or any other species of self that relies mainly on its own resources and tries to create meaning through its work or its love. If you choose either of these two courses, you certainly will not be alone. But probably you will find yourself with more company if you decide that helping suffering fellow human beings, or trying to create peaceful and beautiful human communities, best expresses your sense of where a godless world seems most worth inhabiting.

So one finds dedicated but humanistic doctors, lawyers, teachers, social workers, politicians, and the like who give their lives to helping other people or trying to bring peace and justice to a given portion of global society. One finds internationalists, even diplomats and soldiers, who have made their own the cause of trying to stay the forces of evil that ruin life for so many. Certainly it is rare to find someone both completely dedicated and fully convinced that all such social effort in no way reaches beyond the grave, but it is not unknown, perhaps not even extraordinary.

In a brave sort of *agnosticism,* many good people place brackets around ultimate questions and content themselves with doing here and now something they can be sure will make a positive difference. So they set broken bones, try to repair broken marriages, arbitrate grievances between owners and workers, try to smooth relations between alienated or warring nations. Realizing that most societies are much less just and enjoyable than they might be, such humanists decide they will spend themselves playing midwife to the birth of a somewhat better world. However slight

their success, it will justify their time spent as police, firefighters, nurses, ministers of a gospel they believe centers on brother- and sisterhood.

The self emerges in humanistic perspective no less mysteriously than it does in religious perspective, because any probing of the self—psychological, artistic, medical—runs into reams of unknown factors. We have learned a great deal about the physical and psychological mechanisms that go into a human identity, yet we are so far from understanding the whole that what we have learned clearly is but a fraction of all there is to know. How our brains work, how our hormones interact with our brains, whether we have souls, how our nerves quicken our bodies, what causes some people to have brilliant memories, or imaginations, or computational skills, what causes other people to suffer severe depression, or schizophrenia, or to be idiot savants—these and hundreds of other aspects of selfhood await full understanding. We don't know why some people are shy and other people extroverted. We don't understand how children acquire language so easily, so naturally. Biological clocks, bodily intelligence, intuition, orgasm, mystical experience, loss of confidence, the acquisition of a social persona, the processes of aging—these research topics only skim the surface.

But perhaps the greatest of the self's mysteries continues to be the encounters with other selves that bring the healing and fulfillment associated with "love." Love is so common a phenomenon, and yet so precious a flower, that we understandably find it bruited about everywhere, advertised in the cheapest of bookstores, collapsed into sex to sell automobiles. Romantic love, the love of friendship, parental love, love of nature, love of God, love of creative work, the love that arises when two or three gather in the name of a common cause, suffering love, self-love—on and on the varieties go. Love is the foremost energy of the self, not to be divorced from the self's eros for knowledge but more central and profound. Children who are not loved do not thrive. Adults who are not loved and do not love in return do not thrive. Love naturally overflows into teaching, guiding, caring for, trying to heal, trying to help make amends. It takes form as forgiveness, reconciliation, peacemaking. And all of these forms of love, all of these facets of the self's adventure in search of love, of course intrigue humanists as much as religious people—sometimes more.

The humanistic self may be in special danger of turning narcissistic, but the religious self is in special danger of alienation—prematurely surrendering the self to "God" and so never maturing, becoming responsible, developing a healthy self-esteem. The humanistic self may be in special danger of despairing, since its philosophy offers it no ultimate reason for its brief time in the sun. On the other hand, the religious self can be repulsively full of answers, a know-it-all confusing the mystery of God with the doctrines of its little church, synagogue, mosque, or sect. On its own terms, the humanistic self has to consider the religious self liable to the same anxieties it is and so a fit object for compassion. On its own terms, the religious self has to say that the divine mystery plays in all people's lives, wooing them at the center where they occasionally go still and wonder about the whole. Neither humanistic wholeness nor religious grace can rightly be considered the exclusive preserve of a favored few.

Everywhere, people who enter into themselves, center down, and face both their terrors and their joys find an ambiguous darkness. Is it the blank nothingness of nature's muteness, the near side of a cosmic and personal meaninglessness? Or is it the cloud of unknowing about which the mystics speak, the presence of a God who can never be understood and always must be accepted in trust? Positioned this way, the two selves, humanistic and religious, seem more alike than different. The honest humanist who does not know about ultimacy and fears that professing faith would be hypocritical seems little different from the honest believer who confesses that God or the buddha-nature can never be mastered, will always force human hearts to abide in mute hope.

SUMMARY: THE HUMANISTIC CENTER

Although there are many varieties of humanists (people who do not configure reality in terms of God or a transcendent ultimate reality), they all qualify as humanists because they make humankind the main treasure or focus of their lives. A few think that the natural world onto which human intelligence opens is the most important consequence of there being a species that can understand and reflect, but more are preoc-

cupied with social and personal questions. Indeed, probably the most typical center in a humanistic world view is the border between society and the self, where the group and the individual interact to construct "reality." Let us muse about this interaction.

Among the unreflective, who one is and for what one should strive tend to come from informal public opinion. "Image" is a great interest and influence, shaping young women to aspire toward beauty and power on the model of what they see in glamour magazines, studies of women's impact in the business world, or more traditional projections of what it might mean to be a wife and mother. Young men are manipulated by images of success in the work world, on the athletic field, with foxy ladies who admire their looks, muscles, brains, or tenderness. These many variations on the theme of the images laid out by one's society determine much of what plays in people's heads as they work at the main task of late adolescence and early adulthood: fashioning a self, a personal identity and sense of the world.

In traditional, premodern societies, most people gained their personal identity and sense of the world through dramatic rites of passage. At puberty and marriage they appropriated their people's sense of how reality was configured, of what the ultimate powers expected of a man or a woman. With the demise of the great, guiding myths typical of premodern societies, the social shaping of personal identities has become more diffuse and confused. Indeed, at times it seems that young people are the main targets in a war for influence over the future generation. Certainly parents, teachers, coaches, and friends continue to exert major influences, but the lack of heroic role models means that many young people will have only middling confidence that they know what they would like to become.

What is it that the typical secular humanist wants to become? Our estimate is someone self-reliant, realistic, and free. There being no privileged revelation in the humanistic world view, one has to make do with the best wisdom one can glean from either past humanistic traditions or personal experience. The best educated of humanists working with these tools soon find that little has changed in their project since the time that Plato or the Buddha ventured forth. Drop the few trappings of myth and divinity one finds in the Platonic dialogues or the sutras of the Buddha and you have two interesting models of the effort to find meaning without recourse to religious institutions. In fact, both Plato and the Buddha ended with visions of transcendent reality, but their methods seem quite amenable to adaptation by modern humanists.

In creating the literary identity of Socrates, Plato described a man bent on wringing wisdom from his experience, deflating the pompous fools who trumpeted unthinkingly about tradition, and listening to the inner voice of conscience, which he called his *daimon*. Socrates became the wisest man in Athens because he learned how much he didn't know—most of his wisdom was negative. For Plato the death of Socrates was a telling judgment on Athenian society. If the polis could not see the worth of the one man who might have saved its culture, it was blind unto spiritual death. The Platonic notion that one would only have a decent polis if one gained a philosopher-king extrapolated from the death of Socrates: the chance that a truly wise person would come to secular power was slim indeed.

The Buddha was humanistic in not relying on past Indian tradition but basing his teaching on his personal experience. Certainly he was formed by Indian meditation techniques and philosophical assumptions, but the crucial aspects of his medicinal program drew their authority from his own enlightenment experience. Above all, the proposition that the way to escape suffering is to eliminate desire went to the heart of every person's existence, presenting itself as something anyone might test at home.

In latter days, humanists have been most true to their own principles when they have followed Socrates and the Buddha in focusing on personal experience. In arguing that religious tradition was folly, they were most persuasive when they challenged religious institutions to show how religious doctrines formed people who were happy, productive, and left the world better for their having passed through it. In the light of such a challenge, the religions that had been responsible for slaughter in warfare, repression in sexual life, poverty in subjugation to wealthy upper classes, and crippling fear of divine wrath stood revealed as inhumane, perhaps even antihuman. On the other hand, the religions that could point to mystics rapt in love of a good God, to men and women spending themselves in caring for the poor, the sick, and the uneducated, and to thinkers who took away some of the sting of death and injustice, stood up to the humanists' challenge. Usually they had already accepted a pragmatism such as that of Jesus and agreed that one could know any group or intellectual position by the fruits it grew.

The perennial value of humanistic approaches to life resides in such pragmatism. By focusing intensely on what happens to human beings, how they are hurt or helped by the thought-systems they indwell, humanists have reminded all with ears to hear that what people promise is less significant than what people do. For a philosophical theologian, the implication of this reminder is that positions, theories about nature, society, self, and divinity, are best developed from what people who operate successfully in those areas must assume.

For example, no less a master in the realm of nature than Albert Einstein advised that one pay more attention to what successful scientists do than to what they say (about either the nature of science or the construction of nature). Applied in the political realm, this advice would imply that one should construct theories of human community from the instances of success—the times and places when people in fact have lived together peacefully, justly, making a profound culture in which buying and selling were in the service of art, science, and social service. Applied to the realm of the self, it would imply that one pay more attention to the dynamics at work in creative artists, creative scientists, signally successful parents, and people signally whole than to psychoanalytic, behavioristic, or other theories about human selfhood. Last, one would best explore the significance of divinity by examining the lives of the saints, the mystics who have communed with God, and the reformers who have spent themselves redeeming people from sin.

In all such experientially focused studies, one of course would run smack into evil, destruction, the dark side of human existence. The pessimistic humanisms pay such heed to this admittedly gigantic side that they come away with little hope that peace or justice will ever prevail. Perhaps the best question then becomes why light has continued to shine in the midst of such darkness, why the darkness has failed to snuff it out. For the metaphysician, the thrust of this question is toward the roots of existence, where one must wonder why there is something rather than nothing. For the anthropologist, the question becomes why creativity, goodness, and even holiness continue to emerge, generation after generation.

Are the light we have, the being that keeps nothingness at bay, the positive aspects of human nature sufficient to make life worth living? Humanists, no less than religious believers, all have to answer that question for themselves. No doctrinaire answer, humanistic or religious, cuts the mustard. At the heart of the human being, in the inalienable voice of conscience, all of us find our lives spelling out and boiling down to a radical choice. Will we say—are we saying—yes or no to the hands we have been dealt, the world in which we have been placed, the self we have received and made, the mystery into which all intimations of ultimacy usher us? Because this is the question we authors find at the center of the humanistic perspective, we think (with some amusement) that the center of the humanistic perspective is another window onto transcendence and ultimate mystery.

Discussion Questions

1. How has the tendency toward rationalization within the world religions contributed to demythologizing and secularization?

2. What are the advantages and disadvantages in bringing reason to bear on divine mystery?

3. Why did the empirical turn of modern science tend to dilute the premodern awe about nature?

4. How might empiricism coexist with a myth-making mind?

5. From what have most of the modern political liberals wanted to be free?

6. For what have most of the modern political liberals wanted to be free?

7. Why was classical Marxism dogmatically atheistic?

8. How has Marxism joined its analyses of work, ideology, and class conflict?

9. What are the main characteristics of a scientific humanism that makes nature and scientific method the kingpins of its world view?

10. What do the humanistic philosophies tend to put in the place of divinity when they try to configure the major dimensions of reality?

11. What should be the consequences of a humanistic philosophy that is pessimistic about the effects of socialization (formation by the common mores of one's group)?

12. Is there a core to the self that ties it to something or someone transcending its biology and culture formation? Why?

13. What should one conclude from the capacity and inclination of the human being to keep raising further questions?

14. How different would a balanced religious humanism be from a balanced secular humanism, and what would "balanced" mean in each case?

Glossary

agnosticism: the position that one does not know the ultimate structure of things. While there have always been some agnostics, Western modernity was the first historical period to associate agnosticism with a mainstream secularistic humanism. Within religions, agnosticism can suggest a mature theological or philosophical appreciation of the mysteriousness bound to attend God or ultimate reality.

atheism: the position that there is no God (or that none of the theologies or religions renders what would be worthy of a true God). While atheism has always had a small presence in developed religious cultures, because skeptics have always had intellectual or social reasons for thinking that no worthy deity could have sponsored the popular religion of the time, only in modern Western culture did a significant portion of the intelligentsia make atheism the prevailing assumption. Modern science and technology seemed to remove the need for a transcendent divinity, while the ambiguity of modern religious groups (their warfare, opposition to progress, and occasional venality or philistinism) made it easy to mock religion's claims to be representing the Creator or Savior of the world.

empiricism: the philosophical outlook that stresses sense experience and limits speculation. While one may point to instances in which empiricism has been religiously motivated, for instance, as an effort to live out a Christian incarnationalist view of reality, or a Hindu sacramental view, or a Buddhist conviction that nirvana is best found in the midst of the particulars of samsara, generally empiricism is a foe of religion, insofar as it finds little basis for the transcendental speculations that probe the nature of ultimate reality or God and finds equally little basis for the contemplative activities that try to deal with a formless, nonparticular, or specific whole.

Enlightenment: the eighteenth-century European movement that stressed the untrammeled use of human reason. Spurred by discoveries in natural science, many Enlightenment philosophers (Voltaire, Kant) urged human beings to take charge of their own lives, throwing off the constraints of Church authorities and traditional dogmas and becoming more autonomous. Through this Enlightenment modern critical history, social science, and other humanistic disciplines came to assume that their independent researches could produce valuable, perhaps definitive insights into the human condition and the build of reality itself.

humanism: an appreciation of human virtues and needs that leads on to focus on human concerns, sometimes to the neglect of divinity or ultimate reality. Humanism may go hand in hand with religion, or it may appear to be religion's enemy. The social programs of the religions, and their appreciation for the wonders of human nature, tend to make them humanistic. However, when humanism becomes delimiting—a way of saying that human beings are the measure or the limit—religion usually must protest. Religion lives from transcendence: going beyond any present attainment, reaching out to the infinite. Humanism can define itself so as to be compatible with such transcendence, but frequently it does not. Secular humanism expressly does not, taking its name from the this-worldly horizon that at best brackets divine transcendence.

Marxism: the politicoreligious system of philosophical thought and socioeconomic practice that has devolved from the work of Karl Marx. What Marx himself set out in germ regarding labor, capital, ideology, religion, class conflict, and the like has served as the basis for Marxist developments, but present-day Marxists often use terms and work with theories unknown in Marx's day. V. I. Lenin and Mao Zedong have probably been the most influential Marxist thinkers, each taking the thought of Marx (and Engels) in new directions. "Marxism" is now a quite protean notion, almost as much in need of further specification as "Christianity." It always denotes some debt to the thought of Karl Marx, and usually it connotes a dialectical materialism and commitment to achieving a classless society. Beyond that, convictions sometimes seem as numerous as there are Marxist writers.

secularism: the worldly view of existence that tends to deprecate transcendence and so be at odds with tradi-

tional religion. Secularism can have a healthy connotation, in which it is close to sacramentality in insisting on the worth and significance of this-worldliness: the human body, social justice, the production of culture. So doing, it rightly combats an otherworldliness that would deprecate the body, sexuality, social justice, beauty, and the other entailments of an incarnational religion. However, secularism regularly runs aground on the questions of death and evil, for which its this-worldliness provides no explanation or healing. The religious response that does claim to provide an explanation of sorts and healing would insert divine, more than worldly powers into space and time. Calling such an insertion grace or enlightenment, it would argue that the human being, human culture, and even the whole physical world cannot be themselves—realize their potential—on their own. What they postulate for fulfillment and beg for healing must come to them from an otherness, outside or within, that is free of the limits (physical, intellectual, moral) one finds in all creation.

transcendence: going beyond the usual limits, often out to the divine. One source of the human tendency to associate transcendence with divinity is the drive of the human spirit to know more and love more. A certain limitlessness in the human makeup suggests that the goal of human intentionality has to be a limitless intelligibility and love. Relatedly, human images of growth and maturation suggest that people ought always to be making progress, spiritually if not physically. The barriers human beings run into—death, ignorance, moral weakness—raise the question whether there is anything on the other side. Thus Buddhists have longed for the wisdom that has gone beyond the stream of human suffering. Other traditions, such as Judaism, Christianity, and Islam, have made divinity transcendent of the world and have spoken of a Judgment that would mediate human beings' way to living with the divinity definitively. Transcendence would seem to be polar to immanence (the inward presence of divinity), but most theologians find no contradiction in predicating both of God. God could go beyond even the barriers raised by human identity, being, as Augustine said, more intimate to us than we are to ourselves.

CONCLUSION: SUMMARY REFLECTIONS

A contemporary sign for friendship between man and woman

At the outset, we postulated that the religious life of humanity is a vast and diversified spectacle. Perhaps you now find that postulate only too well verified. The ancient religious mind, the wisdom religions of the East, and the prophetic religions of the West all combine to make a tapestry of unmanageable proportions. We have tried to discern some of this tapestry's principal patterns. We have tried to present the information and the themes that might make such terms as Judaism or Islam intelligible. Our final task is to review the whole and suggest its implications.

UNITY AND DIVERSITY

The unity of the phenomena we have studied is religion—the common quest for a way to the center. The diversity of the phenomena makes the religions—the distinctive traditional ways in which sizable numbers of people have worked at this quest together.

The quests are all deeply humanistic, in that they all focus intensely on human welfare. For instance, according to C. G. Jung,[1] the American Indian or African who greets the sun as a daily miracle performs

Year	Event
1492	About 10 Million American Indians Living North of Rio Grande
1565	Roman Catholic Colony in New World
1619	Beginning of Black Slavery
1620	Mayflower Compact
1654	First Jewish Settlement in New Amsterdam
1683	William Penn Founds Philadelphia
1734	Great Awakening in New England
1776	Declaration of Independence Expresses Nonconformist, Enlightenment-Influenced Religious Outlook
1784	Death of Shaker Leader Ann Lee
1799	Creation of Russian Orthodox Diocese in Alaska
1801	Beginnings of Western Revivalism
1836	Founding of Transcendentalist Club in Concord, Massachusetts
1847	Bushnell's Christian Nurture
1848	Mormons Found Salt Lake City
1850	Oberlin College Grants First Theological Degree to a Woman
1863	Emancipation Proclamation
1866	Second Roman Catholic Plenary Council in Baltimore
1876	Mary Baker Eddy Founds Christian Science Association
1885	Pittsburgh Platform of Reformed Rabbis
1890	Massacre at Wounded Knee
1901–1902	William James's Gifford Lectures, The Varieties of Religious Experience
1917	Rauschenbush's A Theology for the Social Gospel
1920–1933	Prohibition
1945	Peak of Protestant Neo-Orthodoxy
1964	Civil Rights Act; Martin Luther King, Jr., Receives Nobel Peace Prize

deep psychic work. The Hindu who makes *puja* (worship) or whom *bhakti* (devotionalism) carries to Krishna constructs a world that makes sense and provides emotional comfort. The same is true of Buddhists who ponder koans, Taoists who try to confect the elixir of immortality, and Hasidic Jews who learn diamond cutting to preserve what they can of the old *shtetl* life. In most times and places, the religions have supported or developed meaning unpretentiously, unobtrusively. For most people the traditions have worked subtly as sets of largely unquestioned assumptions.

Still, the traditions have varied in their subtleness. People who ate bean curd sensed the world differently from people who ate roasted lamb. The Prophet who recited, "There is no God but God," oriented Arabs away from the world that the Greek philosopher Thales saw when he exclaimed, "The world is full of gods." The recent introduction of social scientific and critical historical methods has made religious studies more empirically minded and so more sensitive to such variety. Thus, the differences among the religions have been in the spotlight.

Quite properly, we have seen that Judaism and Islam are vast concepts. Indeed, they are quite abstract, for Jews and Muslims have lived out their Torah and Qur'an very differently depending on time, place, and station. Therefore, to talk about Judaism or Islam requires finding common qualities among great diversity, such as a regard for the Torah or the Prophet, for mitzvoth or the Garden. Increasingly scholars debate whether there is a common quality among all the traditions, a common religion at the traditions' cores.[2]

If one can see the sacred, it breaks through the iron, bamboo, and other curtains that have divided our modern world. Perhaps the only traces of the sacred we can see are the anxieties on which the tranquilizer industry trades. Or perhaps we are able to appreciate it in the Nobel Prize–winning efforts of outstanding scientists and writers. Either way, with or without overt theology, ultimacy is always at hand. We may choose not to embrace it, not to call mystery our inmost vocation. However, as surely as we suffer and die, it will embrace us. All people by nature desire to know, Aristotle declared. Our mortal condition makes Aristotle's dogma existential: All people by nature desire to know the mystery from which they come and to which they go. All people are by nature set for religion.

Religion

The word *religion* refers to the inmost human vocation. By empirical fact as well as theoretical interpretation, *religion* pertains to all life that is reflective, that heads into mystery. Largely for that reason, the word *religion* was seldom uttered by the great teachers.[3] They rather spoke of meaning, the way to "walk," the traditional wisdom, the balance called justice, and the fire called love. Because they were embodied spirits speaking to other embodied spirits, they used familiar figures: mountains, rivers, widows giving alms. Furthermore, their speech led to common action: rhythmic prostrations, gutsy resistance to the emperor, dancing with the Torah, helping a friend. All these actions, though, were religious.

People organized communities around the great teachers' speech and actions. The communities expressed their religion (their venture after meaning into mystery) in ways that Joachim Wach has labeled theoretical, social, and active.[4] That is, they made theologies, brotherhoods and sisterhoods, and liturgies and laws. Regularly, the communities lost the spirit of their founders, as succeeding generations repeatedly prized order more than charisma, control more than inspiration, and orthodoxy more than creativity. Just as regularly, reformers tried to find their way back to the original vision. In China it was "Back

to the ancients." In the Christian West it was "Back to the Word."

The various traditions have shaped their peoples in endless ways. Some have spoken rather simply—Judaism and Islam, for instance. Others have made strange bedfellows and cultures more complex, such as the religions of China and Japan. Still, all traditions have used the past to decipher the present and to prepare for the future. All have received and handed on.

That handing on is what we mean by *tradition*.[5] None of us fashions meaning free of external influences. All of us receive a cultural inheritance, meager or rich, to which we add. We do this willy-nilly—by having children, teaching students, working with colleagues, supporting friends. Original sin is the dark side of such a sense of tradition. According to this concept, we all take our first breath in air that is polluted, in a game that is tilted against us. How polluted or tilted the world is has been a matter of vigorous debate. The only consensus seems to be that evil is a sad fact and that there is sufficient good to justify hope. The handing on therefore leads all the religions to revile evil and buttress hope—a process that can be called a concern for salvation.

For instance, ancient peoples banded together for evolutionary salvation—against the evil of extinction and in hope that the race would go on. Close to the earth, they thought in concrete terms, undifferentiatedly, telling stories of life and death. Life came from the fatherly sky and the motherly earth. Life was as possible, as renewable, as heavenly water and productive dirt. Death was breathtakingly near, but perhaps the dead were as seed falling in the ground. Perhaps they were but a link in the chain of generations. Or maybe they passed to a new form of life. As smoke passes from burning wood, so perhaps the subtle part of a person, the part that thinks and travels in dreams, could pass to a new state. In those ways, perhaps, ancient peoples fought for hope, tried to block out absurdity.

To suffer, lose, rejoice, or trust—such acts know no religious, ethnic, or national bounds. We all walk a way (if only a way to death) that we cannot name. We all seek (if only covertly) a path that is straight, a path that mystery blesses. If some of our predecessors have been Nordic berserks, who heated up to feel mystery boil, others have been Eastern yogis, who so slowed themselves that they could be buried alive. If some of our predecessors have been erotics, convinced that the force of the way is sexual *shakti,* others have been lonely ascetics, convinced that meat clouds the spirit.

Figure 27   Taj Mahal: Islam on Hindu soil. Photo by J. T. Carmody.

There are few roads that no one has taken, few options that no one has tried. Though the options make all the difference for the individual, we can see from others where we might have gone. Indeed, that is a major reason why we study the humanities. There would be no basis for studying the humanities were there no unity called human nature. Likewise, there would be no religious studies were there no unity called religion.

Contending with nature, society, the self, and whatever ultimacy they have known, all human beings have mused about their sunrise and sunset. For all of them, the cosmos and the group have had effects, the self and ultimacy have beguiled. Without and within each person, the world has taken shape, changed, occasionally threatened to slip away. Since we are "synthetic" beings, whose incarnate spirits include the lowest matter and the heights of thought, we cannot escape religion's full span. Madness comes when the span tilts and the synthesis comes unglued. Boredom comes when we lose the span's tension, when imagi-

nation goes stale. In health, we find nature, society, and the self fascinating. In health, science, politics, and art are all essential, all deeply humanistic. If they become so specialized, so arcane, that their essential humanity is not apparent, we must speak of disease—of dysfunction, pathology, alienation.

Though disease has terrible power in our time, as nuclear arms and the prison systems show, it has always written arguments for despair. Parents who wept over dead children heard despair at Stonehenge, Gettysburg, and My Lai. Every woman raped, every man tortured, has heard voices within counseling her or him to abandon hope. Amazingly, though, human beings will not live by despair alone. Their very sense that the times are out of joint is a cry that there ought to be health.

Until we give up completely, we label health as normal. Disease, we say, is the lack of health. Evil, we say, is the lack of good—of proper order, right being, justice, and love. Indeed, so deep is our drive toward health that we cannot think of nonbeing and evil directly. They are irrational, absurd, and void. In their hope, then, the religions uncover more religion. In their hope, Marxists and religious believers can dialogue.

Meaning and Idiosyncrasy

The themes above are some of the constants that all the traditions carry. If they are general, it is because they pertain to all of humanity. In religious perspective, our human characteristics comprise a common condemnation (or consecration) to meaning. Thus, the differences among traditions are simply *how* their peoples have sought, conceived, and enacted meaning. That affirms, of course, that differences do differentiate.[6] It affirms that a Buddhist is not a Hindu and a Christian is not a Jew.

Because he or she is always dealing both with religion as a whole and with the individual religions, the student of religion must develop a peculiar balance. If she or he is blind to the unity behind all religions, the student will miss the deep humanity that the traditions can offer us. On the other hand, if the student sweeps all the information together, making all Buddhists anonymous Christians or all Christians renegade Jews, he or she will miss the grainy texture that religion always has in people's lives. As is often the case, the ideal involves a duality: *both* cutting to the heart of the matter, where all human beings are siblings, *and* respecting the idiosyncrasies that differentiate people as nations, tribes, sexes, individuals, and traditional religionists.

The idiosyncrasies are mysterious. Why should the Buddha have proposed no-self? A first answer might be because no-self answered the question of suffering that the Buddha's personal life and the life of his Indian culture posed. Fine, but this is hardly an end to the matter. Why should death, disease, and putrefaction have troubled this particular prince so deeply? Presumably many other princes saw corpses without deciding to leave their palaces, wives, and children to adopt a life of asceticism; similarly, many other cultures experienced suffering. Why, then, did the Indians penetrate the psychology of suffering so profoundly? Why not the Babylonians, Chinese, Aztecs, or Mayans?

As those questions show, there is a limit to historical analysis. It can explain some of the differences among individuals or cultures, but their real origin lies beyond it. For the real origin of differences is the incomprehensible world order[7]—St. Paul's *mysterion*. We did not set the cosmic dust spinning. We don't know why it wove the combinations it did. Therefore, when we respect differences, we respect the totality of history and its mystery. We respect the ultimacy behind the facts, the often very brutal facts, that just this universal drama has played and no other.

Let us again try to be concrete. The Australian dream world, as scholars imperfectly reconstruct it from artifacts and interviews, reflects the peculiar landscape of the Australian continent. The aboriginal myths are similar to those of other areas that explain how the ancestors or demiurges fashioned the world, yet the aboriginal world is unique. The Australian use of the *tjurunga,* the sacred wooden boards, for instance, is distinctive. Other ancient peoples painted and carved, but none (that we know) with just the Australian concern for totemic ancestors. Or consider African peoples' use of masks. That, too, has analogies—with the American Indian use of *kachinas* and even the Greek use of theater masks. Yet in Africa masks relate to thought, such as Ogotemmeli's Dogon thought,[8] that speaks of man and woman, fox and ant hill, smithy and granary as the people of no other continent do. Again, the Chinese divination practice of *feng-shui* (geomancy) is like the complex basket divination of the Africans, yet they differ greatly. The two types of divination have the same purpose (to determine what will happen in nature and time), but they express it differently. *Feng-shui* would not seem appropriate in the Congo.

Differences also appear among religions about which we have more historical information. For instance, Judaism memorialized the Exodus (flight from Egypt) in a Passover ritual. Something happened to get the people out of Egypt, and Jewish religious memory attributed it to God and Moses. In time the happening became a paradigm for interpreting Jewish history. Because of what had happened in the past, faithful Jews endured their trials with hope. God would deliver them again somehow. That sort of historical memory, that "anamnesis," gave Jews an identity different from that of the Canaanites, Egyptians, Romans, or Germans. Indeed, without their religious memory, Jews today would have little identity crisis. It is the Exodus that makes the Holocaust so shattering. It is the Exodus and the Holocaust together that make the current state of Israel so taut.

For Christians, the Exodus was a prefigurement of the liberation that Jesus' death and resurrection worked. In their eyes, Jesus' "passover" made a new creation, Jesus' Spirit formed a new Israel, Jesus' teaching established a new covenant. The lamb of the old Passover was a figure of Jesus the victim and conqueror. In the heavenly Jerusalem, Jesus the lamb received all power, glory, and honor. In fact, the lamb had married the heavenly Jerusalem. Moreover, the heavenly Jerusalem had no temple, because "the Lord God Almighty and the Lamb were themselves the temple, and the city did not need the sun or the moon for light, since it was lit by the radiant glory of God and the Lamb was a lighted torch for it" (Rev. 21:22–23). This imagery—this radical reinterpretation of Exodus and Passover—developed within a century of Jesus' death. By then Christians and Jews had irrevocably separated. For nineteen centuries, they have thought of themselves as mutually opposed.

For Muslims, Muhammad makes a reality different from the reality that Moses makes for Jews or Jesus makes for Christians. The difference is rooted in pre-Islamic Arab culture and took form in Muhammad's own psyche, where he received visions not of a burning bush or a dove descending from heaven but of the angel Gabriel. This difference flowered in Islamic conquest, which made the Prophet's people imperial in ways that Jews and Christians never were. Muslims swept across the Mediterranean world as Jews never thought to do, and they rejected priests, monks, and sacraments. Even their version of the religions' general abuse of women was distinctive: a peculiar blend of polygyny, purdah, the harem, clitoridectomy, and the *hur.*

A mosque, a synagogue, and a church all show likenesses to a Hindu or a Buddhist temple. All five enclose sacred space. But the first three have a family likeness that separates them from the latter two. Principally, their space reverberates with the Word of a Creator God. Still, one is not likely to confuse a mosque with a church or a synagogue. The Word takes different forms in St. Peter's, Rome, a synagogue in Skokie, Illinois, and a mosque in Cairo, Egypt.

Differences, then, are real. We could develop that theme for Hinduism contrasted with Jainism or Buddhism, for Catholics contrasted with Orthodox or Protestants. How great differences are, how divergent they make their adherents' realities, is difficult to determine. Often it seems as much a matter of the analyst's temperament as of the adherents' realities. In the terms of a recent debate,[9] the analyst who has an "esoteric" (inner-directed) personality tends to stress the unity in the traditions, while the "exoteric" (outer-directed) personality tends to stress the diversity.

Esoteric types respond to innermost notions and innermost realities. For them, a common mystery is as real as distinctive facts, even more real. Therefore, esoteric types tend to the negative way—the Hindu *"neti, neti"* ("not this, not that"). They may downplay or even disparage the diverse ways that people have chosen to pursue the supreme value. In contrast, exoteric types respond to outer phenomena—to the actual births, hungers, murders, orgasms, and deaths that make people's lives colorful, intense, palpably real. They fear that moving away from such realities ignores the way things are.

Besides exoteric blood, sweat, and tears, God does seem esoteric, pale and abstract. Looking closely, though, we find that esoterica have given religions most of their life. For instance, what would American Indian ceremonies—the Sun Dance, the vision quest, the potlatch (gift-giving feast)—have been without Wakan Tanka, the Great Spirit? What would the Egyptian pyramids have been without Osiris and Re? Those pale gods gave the ceremonies and massive stones their meaning. Apart from such meaning, exoterica are mute. The same applies in other traditions. Hindu popular festivals make no sense without a Krishna to play the flute, a Kali to wield the sword. In the West, circumcision, the Eucharist, and the Muslim *hajj* (pilgrimage to Mecca) depend on the covenant, redemption, and the eternal Word. In the lives of religious people, the exoteric is a body for the esoteric. We think it should be the same in the writings of religion scholars.

COMPARING THE WESTERN TRADITIONS

Listening for meaning offers a first handle for comparing the Western traditions. American Indians, Egyptians, Iranians, Greeks, Jews, Christians, and Muslims have all had priests, shamans, or sages who have listened for the meaning of their peoples' lives.

For the nonliterate traditions of the West, the main meaning of the peoples' lives was to live harmoniously with nature. Nature was virtually coextensive with reality, and what was sacred, worthy of supreme veneration, was more nature's depth than something standing apart from the cosmos, from the world of space and time. To be sure, the Great Spirit was something that fleshly thoughts could never fathom. But the tribal peoples' many efforts to reach the Great Spirit almost always came to fruition as a vision or sense of communion that brought harmony with the natural world.

The Egyptian concern with life and death somewhat extended this tribal sense of reality. Although the Egyptians enjoyed the pleasures of their life in the sun and their good fortune to live by the Nile, they pondered the afterlife so intensely that they left the pyramids as massive memos. As the pyramid texts suggest, the Egyptians sensed that the afterlife would be fortunate only if one could pass the test of a strict judgment on one's days of earthly life. Unless the soul were light and clean, it would gain no good immortality. The brief Egyptian flirtation with "monotheism" proved less powerful than an instinct that all the forces of nature, all the vectors of life and death, had to be represented, written large as divinities, if the people were to understand the tensions of earthly life and reach the depth their spirits sought.

Iranians who flocked to Zoroaster heard a different message about the spirit's wishes. To their great seer, the primal forces were Truth and the Lie—the human spirit as open to the light or the human spirit as closed. Thus Zoroaster seems to have meditated with his "topmost" mind, while his naturalistic predecessors in Egypt and among the Western tribes burrowed down toward the roots of the unconscious. Zoroaster's concerns with light, ideas, and images of heavenly forces all suggest a person aware of the human spirit's "transcendent" inclinations, its drive to rise higher and higher, go farther and farther beyond what it had conceived in the past.

The Greeks are remarkable for the fullness of their religious life, which spanned from the deepest roots of the unconscious to the most transcendent inclinations of the topmost mind. The riches of Greek mythology are a remarkable treasury, full of experiences of nature, family relations, and the struggles of the unconscious mind. The great Greek tragedians used this treasury most artfully, leaving the West unsurpassed renditions of humanity's most basic conflicts. The Greek philosophers seem to have taken the dazzling physical light of the Greek islands as a challenge to find dazzling mental counterparts. Building on the work of the early philosophers of nature, Socrates, Plato, and Aristotle finally accomplished the monumental feat of differentiating human reason. Following the light of the mind, the logos that made human beings a unique species, they saw that this light is the inreach of divinity, whose Light is coincident with any creature's reason-to-be. Although Hellenistic religion largely lost the classical philosopher's great achievement, enough of their differentiation remained to turn Western culture in a distinctively rational direction.

Along with Greek reason, biblical revelation also pushed Western culture to find its reason-to-be in God. However, where the Greek accent was the Divine Light, the biblical accent was the Divine Love. Thus Judaism formed a people around the free overtures of a God who wanted to make a people uniquely covenanted to himself. As biblical Jews understood this relationship, it was not the product of any special merit on their part. It was completely the product of God's own love. From his own goodness God decided to reveal himself over time, walking with the Jews as a fellow traveler. The Exodus was the warrant for Jewish faith that God could make the walk a liberation, while the covenant was the codification of the traveling relationship. Through the permutations of biblical history, biblical prophecy, biblical wisdom literature, rabbinic reflection, cabalistic lore, and Hasidic piety, Judaism retained this sense of being bonded to a loving God. The Master of the Universe had shown the people a personal face. He had pledged them his mercy and steadfast love. This revelation and pledge held the deepest mystery of time.

Christianity accepted Judaism's stress on God's love, but by the fourth century it had added more of Greece's stress on God's Light. Jesus himself had preached and taught as a Jew, quite aware of the biblical traditions. For him the deepest mystery of time was on the verge of a definitive self-expression. The Kingdom of God, in which God's love and mercy would become dominant in many people's hearts, was as near as his intimate heavenly Father. When Christians reflected on Jesus' life and death, they moved the Kingdom into his person. This singular man, they said, himself embodied what God's love and mercy could do. Indeed, his resurrection was the pledge and first fruits of the Kingdom's cosmic import. Whoever clung to Jesus as Jesus had clung to the Father could hope to rise with Jesus to the Father's right hand. There Father, Son, and Spirit, the fullness of the Christian

God, would give one a full understanding of time's mysteries, a full experience of love's beatitude.

The Jewish and Christian experiences of God's revelation somewhat shaped Islam, but the visions of Muhammad really determined the Muslims' world view. For Muhammad, Allah was Light and Love, but more powerfully Allah was the sole Creator, the omnipotent Lord of the Worlds. Thus Islam has accented human beings' need to submit completely to Allah. When Allah speaks, every creature ought to bow low, as in the daily prayer. When any creature considers the world, she or he ought to revere the many signs the world gives of Allah's great wisdom and power. Allah is a stern judge, demanding a full recognition of these truths. People who will not listen to Muhammad's recital are surely marked for the Fire. So for Islam the great disaster is unbelief. Sin and error play their woeful parts, but the core ruin to which human beings are prey is unbelief, which usually shows itself as idolatry. In all aspects of life, from Friday worship in the mosque to daily business in the street, the One God has set the standards. The devout Muslim prays each day to stay on the sole path that is straight, the path of Allah's guidance.

There are other strands in the history of Western religion, of course, but these traditions certainly account for most of the Western configurations. In modernity they ran up against a powerful atheistic revolt, so we "postmodern" Westerners tend to experience these religious traditions as somewhat strange. For example, the changes in Western consciousness that the Enlightenment and Marxist philosophies have worked suggest to many of our contemporaries that traditional religion is at best a curio, at worse an impediment to human growth. For the Enlightenment philosophers, the crux was our human capacity to make "reality." They saw that much that we think is "out there" comes from "in here," our own minds. For the Marxist philosophers, such speculative matters have been less important than the practical business of overthrowing current injustices. Understanding an imperfect reality, they have said, is only half the job. The full job includes building a new, better reality.

The traditional Western religions could agree with one part of the Enlightenment/Marxist program, but they would have to disagree with another part. Accepting the Greek understanding of humanity's vocation to follow the light of reason, the Western religious traditions could listen to the modern antireligionists quite sympathetically, marveling at how the moderns'

rejection of traditional faith has helped them to make many splendid discoveries in physical science, epistemology, psychology, biological science, and sociology. These are all further disclosures of the inreaching Divine Light, so what is true and noble in them deserves religious veneration.

Accepting the biblical understanding of humanity's vocation to follow the love of covenantal sharing, the Western traditions could also listen quite sympathetically to the modern pragmatists. There is a biblical imperative to do justice and make a world fit for human beings to live in. There is a Qur'anic call to fellowship that transcends all boundaries of nations and races. Therefore, much in the modern Enlightenment/Marxist program preaches in terms almost identical with the Western religious traditions' own sacred scriptures.

On the other hand, the Western religious traditions could not agree with the modern antireligionists' hatred of God, nor with their murky view of human nature. For the religious traditions, only God gives human beings prosperity. Islam has driven this home like a stake into the heart: Idolatry is utter ruin. Unless the Creative Love and Power that makes the world afresh every day dominates human consciousness, human consciousness errs grievously and strews cruel wreckage left and right. Thus a clear view of human nature balances on a thin edge. It is neither optimistic nor pessimistic. It is hopeful, because open to God. Human beings have a limited capacity to follow the Light and understand. They have a limited capacity to give and receive love and so build peaceful communities. When they open themselves to God's help, human beings can do justice, make beauty, prosper in truth. When they close themselves to God, they truncate and warp their limited powers, and so produce trash, injustice, and great suffering. As the religious forms of arrogant closure to God have given the West many dreadful "holy" wars, so the irreligious forms of arrogant closure to God have given the West Gulag Archipelagos, Nazi concentration camps, Latin American butchery, and North American greed. To be human, our species needs the Light that Plato saw, the Love that Jeremiah hoped would make a new covenant. Without these, we treat one another worse than wolves. Without these, it does not matter whether we call ourselves religious or irreligious, for our true names are simply "Ruined."

When confronted by godless modernity, the Western traditions tend to pull together. For Judaism,

Christianity, and Islam, the Creator is the creature's inmost definer. For the other Western traditions we have studied, the case is a little more complicated, but the upshot is much the same: Human beings are not the measure of reality.

In the eighteenth and nineteenth centuries, the Western religious traditions were thrown on the defensive, forced to grow beyond their insular, and in many ways self-serving, understandings of revelation. In the second half of the twentieth century, the irreligious humanisms have been thrown on the defensive, shown by their totalitarian tyrannies and nuclear horrors to be precipitous paths to hell. The question for the twenty-first century will be whether these two strains of current Western humanity can grow or purify themselves enough to cooperate and make the full circle of checks and balances that survival surely will demand.

The Prophet as Western Archetype

For the Asian traditions, it is relatively clear that the dominant personality, the religious ideal, has been the sage. Buddha, Confucius, Lao-tzu, and the various Hindu holy men have all been philosophic contemplatives, concerned with ordering or saving human life by penetrating the structures of the cosmos. For the Western religious traditions, the case is not so clear. The prophet seems to be the strongest personality, but often the sage and the mystic run a close second and third.

Among the nonliterate Western tribes, the dominant personality has been the shaman. Specializing in ecstatic techniques, the shaman has gone out of himself (less frequently, herself), to make contact with the sacred forces running the world. Thus the Eskimo shaman might go into trance to travel to Sedna, the goddess of the undersea who had fenced in the seals.

For Egypt, the priest, officiating at religious ceremonies, and the king, mediating divine order (*maat*), were highly visible personalities. Egypt also produced an interesting wisdom literature, most of it rather stoical. The message of Egyptian wisdom usually was that human experience teaches the value of prudence. The person who wants to prosper should keep the mouth shut and the eyes open.

For Iran, the Zoroastrian prophecies placed a high premium on the inner spirit of light. As the fire burned in the Zoroastrian rituals, so the truth should blaze in the human heart. The magi who later spoke for Zoroastrian wisdom earned a handsome reputation in the Middle East, much of it for their astrological learning. True to the continued immersion of their tradition in the cosmological myth, they set human affairs under the influence of the stars.

In Greece the philosopher, the lover of wisdom, ruled the psychological stage. Shamanist types and priests played strong roles in the days of Olympian religion, but after historians, natural scientists, political thinkers, and dramatists had come to the fore, the philosophers' search for the unseen measure prepared to take the place of honor. When Socrates, Plato, and Aristotle assumed this place, philosophy became a way of life, not an academic discipline. Speaking of their illuminations in religious terms, they would have dismissed any strong distinction between philosophy and revelation. In their experience, when the soul took wing and rose toward the idea of the good, God was the prime mover and drawer.

In both Judaism and Islam, prophets dominated the first stages of the tradition. Moses struck the covenant because he had received the Word of the Lord, while Muhammad was simply the *rasul,* the messenger commanded to recite God's Qur'an. In later periods both religions developed a less prophetic, more jurisprudential understanding of God's guiding Word (Torah or *Sharia*). Then the rabbis and lawyers dealt with an ethics both more complex and less explosive than the original prophetic Word. As well, both the Jewish rabbis and the Muslim lawyers assumed something of the philosopher's mantle, and both their cultures opened to Greek rationalism, though seldom to the point where prophetic revelation was endangered. For when rabbinical theology or Muslim law seemed in danger of running dry, the Hasidim, cabalists, and Sufis rose up to water it with devotion. Thus Sufi teaching lore enlivened the Muslim lawyers' codes, while aggadah enlivened the Talmudists' halakah.

Overall, the biblical prophets and Muhammad *the* Prophet kept the notion of the Divine Word central. If both Judaism and Islam strike the comparativist as more ethical than metaphysical, it is because both thought of the Divine Word as more an imperative than an indicative. Revelation of God commanded that the people be holy, since they were to consort with the Holy One. In both traditions' understanding of this holiness, what one thought was less important than what one did. Such "doing" included worship as well as morality, but it had a distinct priority over speculative or purely contemplative theology. Speculation and contemplative theology had their places, but their potential for division was large. For the community to hold together, the people had first to keep the same Sabbath and kosher laws, to depend on the same Five Pillars.

In the case of Christianity, Jesus, also, seems more a prophet than a sage, despite the fact that the New Testament significantly casts Jesus in the lines of Old Testament wisdom. Jesus teaches the crowds, but what he teaches is mainly a view of God leading to a new mode of living. The centrality of love in Jesus' preaching somewhat distinguishes his prophecy from that of the Hebrew prophets, and even more from that of Muhammad, but we should not exaggerate this distinction. The love of God and love of neighbor that epitomize Jesus' program have strong analogues in both Judaism and Islam.

Where Christianity departs from the prophetic typology of Judaism and Islam is in divinizing its main prophet. Neither Moses nor Muhammad became Sons of God, sharers in the divine creative nature. Moreover, an infusion of Greek philosophy made Christianity quite ontological about Jesus and the Trinity. True, the conciliar controversies of the fourth and fifth centuries were passionate, rather than detached, bouts of speculation, but they determined that the Logos related intimately with the world's reason-to-be. The Christian God expressed his being in both an ongoing act of creation and the Incarnation of the Logos. Picking up hints from Pauline and Johannine literature (Col. 1:15–20, John 1:1–14), the Christian theologians came to think that creation occurred in the Divine Word, whom God had planned to incarnate from eternity.

The Incarnation made Christianity a prophetic religion instinctively sacramental. Where Judaism and Islam prohibited the representation of God, Christianity was fundamentally iconographic. Since God had made an icon of himself, uttering his Word into human flesh, all material things were open to the inspiration of God's Spirit. When the Spirit moved over the waters, the waters became baptismal. When the Spirit moved over the bread and wine, the bread and wine became the body and blood of the Lord. Above all, human affairs became the primary arena of God's action. Accepting the Jewish notion of covenant, Christianity said that Jesus and his people were bonded like a groom and bride. The story of the Church therefore was like the saga of an extended family, relating the increases and diminishments the original marriage had produced. To be sure, the marital compact would come to full fruition only in heaven, where the glory of the lamb (Rev. 5:12) would blaze forth, but even the days of earthly time could bring touches of conjugal union.

Although they rejected Christian incarnationalism and sacramentality, Judaism and Islam developed their own equivalents. Both became this-worldly religions, Judaism in large part by adding marriage and good deeds to Torah to make a trinity of holy blessings. As a result, Jews have influenced Western culture, literary and scientific alike, out of proportion to their small numbers. Since the Lord had made history his chosen field of interest, temporal things ranked high on the Jewish agenda. Islam largely agreed, sponsoring a splendid, full-bodied culture during its golden age. The Islamic stress on Judgment and afterlife probably made it more eschatological than Judaism, more preoccupied with heaven and hell, but the Muslim theocratic ideal assured that politics, business, and war would all seem inseparable from religious practice.

Furthermore, neither Judaism nor Islam approved of celibacy, so neither had a corps of monks testifying to the rights of eternity. While the rabbis and Sufis hardly were robust in their encouragement of sexuality, they felt that God's command to increase and multiply, as well as ordinary human psychology, made marriage the healthiest estate. So, unlike their counterparts in much of Christianity, the prophetic and legal masters of Judaism and Islam felt a constant pressure to provide for wives and children. While this did not promote women to equal status with men, it did assure that family life received a thorough consideration. Thus the rabbis saw that the Genesis account of creation made humanity male-female, and that it suggested the Fall was in part a sexual awakening. Thus the cabalists spoke of redemption in sexual terms, hoping that one day the fragmented world would return to God's full embrace.

In hindsight, neither Judaism, Christianity, nor Islam gave physical nature the appreciation it deserved. Although the trail from the beginnings of these religions to today's ecological crises is tangled, there is little doubt that the biblical and Qur'anic subordination of nature to human beings helped the prophetic religious cultures to ravish the earth. Neither the Bible nor the Qur'an said to ravish the earth, but both so feared fertility religion and idolatry that they downplayed nature's sacredness. They knew the Creator had to be present to rocks and trees, if rocks and trees were to exist at all, but the prophetic religions shied away from the implications of creation, not wanting to say that whatever exists is inviolable.

Figure 28 Three Apostles, *Spanish (1140–1170). Limestone; 31 in. high. The apostles are Paul, Andrew, and John, part of a group of twelve. The Nelson–Atkins Museum of Art, Kansas City, Missouri (Nelson Fund).*

Today the most important legacy of the prophetic religions probably is their cry for justice. The Word of God the West has trumpeted is a shout for honesty and love. Through the Israelite prophets, Jesus, and Muhammad, God demanded that human beings treat one another well. Even though Judaism, Christianity, and Islam often have narrowed this demand, becoming ethnocentric and insular like other tribes, the demand itself is virtually their constitution. "If you would worship the true God," they all have heard, "you must do justice to your neighbors." So all the prophetic religions stand against the exploitation or oppression—capitalist, Marxist, or other—that denies the sanctity of human beings. So the racism, sexism, and religious bigotry that have spawned in the prophetic religions denounce them before their God. In evolutionary terms, this may be the prophetic religions' great significance. Imperfect though all their peoples have been, the prophetic religions have still nursed an ideal of just, genuine living.

ON BEING AN AMERICAN CITIZEN OF THE RELIGIOUS WORLD

We have not paid special attention to America in this book, because in the history of religion, America has occupied only a small fraction. In general handbooks such as *The Historical Atlas of the Religions of the World, Historia Religionum, The Concise Encyclopedia of Living Faiths,* and *The Encyclopedia of Religion,* American religion does not receive 2 percent of the space. The first lesson that the world religions offer Americans, then, is that America is not as important as Americans tend to think. Our 400 years of religious experience are not much beside India's 5,000. If our 5 percent of the world's population and almost 33 percent of the consumption of the world's raw materials are disproportionate, we need all the help we can get to become less important.

We are not advocating the suppressing of patriotism. Few existing cultures are very old. Europeans or Asians who sniff because their cultures go back more centuries than ours are hardly less ridiculous than we. All nations need a perspective on world history. All

So only at their most confident times did the prophetic religions make sacraments and humanisms that welcomed nature kindly. No doubt rural peoples of these traditions always sensed God's coming through the seasons, but the main word of the prophets stressed God's transcendence of the world, implying that God cared little for the seasons. (Therefore, high on the agenda of East-West religious dialogue should be discussing the East's greater appreciation of nature, and its greater appreciation of the impersonal side of God with which nature is allied.) The Western prophetic religions all experienced God as fiercely personal, a Word and Will impressing themselves mightily. Although the mystics in these traditions (especially the Christian mystics who were influenced by Greek spirituality) went beyond words and feelings to the naked divine immensity, the mainstreams in these traditions (especially the Christian mainstream) pictured God as a human person.

nations need to see things "under the aspect of eternity."

For most Americans, religion has been Christianity, and Christianity has often pivoted on Jesus and the founder of their own church. In some cases the dark ages between those two personages stretch 1,800 years. For such people, Catholics are not considered Christians, and Orthodox are beyond the pale. True, Americans have modified this intolerance by coexisting with their neighbors. Many Americans, though, could profit from a breath of cosmopolitan air.

The root of provincialism is what Erik Erikson calls *"pseudospeciation"*—pretending that we are the only true human beings. In the past, that "we" has been Chinese, Japanese, and Eskimos. It has been Boston Brahmins and Oklahoma dirt farmers. It has been Catholics who would never darken a Protestant church door, Orthodox who would never visit a synagogue. Fortunately, we now know enough about the psychodynamics of pseudospeciation, largely through analyses of prejudice, to show that it has little to do with genuine religion. In fact, we now know that genuine religion directly opposes pseudospeciation.

In most cases, pseudospeciation stems from a combination of fear and self-interest. We fear the universal humanity, the radical equality, that a pluralistic world implies. It would force us to shed our shells; it would snatch away our platform for boasting. Similarly, we fail to grasp notions such as the Christian Church because it is to our advantage that "in Christ" there be male and female (Gal. 3:28). We fail to enact the notion of a union of all nations, because it is to our advantage to dictate prices to the world. Few of us are magnanimous willingly, textbook writers included.

If we Americans are to gain stature in religion's golden eye, we will have to become more realistic about time and space than we have tended to be. Throughout all time, most people have not been Americans, Christians, or whites, and any true God has blessed more lands than just ours. By today's standards, the colonial Puritans' "errand in the wilderness" was terribly naive. Those who launched it simply did not have our facts about human prehistory and human diversity. It was largely ignorance, then, that led them to locate salvation in New England. The same is true of those who proposed that America be God's new Israel. Sober students of American history wonder to what extent such notions were used to justify ravaging the Indians. Historians of religion stumble over

Approximate Membership Data on Major American Religious Groups (1986)*

Adventists, Seventh-Day	640,000
Baptists	27,000,000
Buddhists	100,000
Christian Church (Disciples of Christ)	1,132,000
Christian Churches and Churches of Christ	1,050,000
Church of Christ, Scientist[†]	250,000
Church of the Nazarene	516,000
Churches of Christ	1,600,000
Eastern Churches (Orthodox)	3,500,000
Episcopal Church	2,775,000
Friends United Meeting (Quakers)	100,000
Jehovah's Witnesses	700,000
Jewish congregations	5,000,000
Latter Day Saints (Mormons)	3,600,000
Lutherans	8,500,000
Mennonites	185,000
Methodists	13,500,000
Muslims	about 3,000,000
Pentecostals	3,500,000
Presbyterians	3,300,000
Roman Catholics	52,250,000
Salvation Army	420,000
Unitarian Universalist Association	170,000
United Churches of Christ	1,700,000
Total: ca. 60% of population	142,000,000

*Source: *The World Almanac and Book of Facts 1987.*
[†]1936 data. Since 1936, American membership data have not been made public.

the obvious fact that God's old Israel was perfectly well.[10]

If we deflate our egos, we may see things in better perspective. From the vantage point of an astronaut or the sun god Re, Americans have never been *the* holy people. Long before the whites, reds revered every striking American locale. Shortly after the whites, blacks became America's suffering servants. Unbeknownst to our pioneers, peoples in Asia were living lives of grace under pressure.

The only holy people, in religious perspective, are of the single race, the single species. All divisions make but partial stories. There is a dictum in religious studies that he or she who knows just one religion knows no religion. By that dictum Americans urgently need to study world religions; if only to determine our own identity, we need to know what others have been, what alternatives there were.

In addition, the world religions can suggest what in American religious experience has been distinctive. This topic is immense, so we can only offer a few leads. First, the Reformation and Enlightenment had a marked effect on American religion. Together, they led to a peculiar blend of pietism and rationalism. Of course, pietism and rationalism have been present in other cultures. For instance, India embraced both bhakti and Vedanta; Islam embraced both Sufism and Law. In America, the mixture tended to set the Bible against the brain. Evolution and the Scopes trial of 1925 dramatized this tension. In colonial times, Calvinists made syntheses of biblical faith and intellectualism that pleased at least themselves. During the drafting of the Constitution, it appears that reason ousted piety—unless we should call the founding fathers pietistic.

One way of looking at American pietism and rationalism is aesthetic. William Clebsch has recently elaborated that point of view.[11] In his opinion, such representatively American thinkers as Jonathan Edwards, Ralph Waldo Emerson, and William James were most moved by the world's beauty. Another way of approaching American religion is to emphasize religious liberty. Sidney Mead has argued that the American experiment in religious pluralism proved as momentous as the establishment of Christianity in imperial Rome.[12]

Both these views owe much to the Enlightenment's advances on the Reformation. The Reformation established the principles of individual conscience and individual interpretation of scripture. The Enlightenment proposed that reason—nondogmatic thought common to all—should be the judge when individual interpretations shattered civic peace. In this new land, where individual opportunity was rich, reason sat in the official driver's seat.

In the matter of religious liberty through law, Americans made quantum leaps over their European forebears. There was much less than full political equality, as generations of blacks and women have underscored, but something novel was present that we have come to call pluralism. In religious terms, it was an attempt to live together as equals despite differences in creed. In secular terms, it was a search for a common sense to ensure economic and political cooperation. In theological terms, it conjured up natural theology—speculation about God apart from scripture or dogma. For Roman Catholics, the implications of American pluralism hit Europe only in the "Decree on Religious Liberty" of the Second Vatican Council, where the American model was accepted for the whole Church.

Despite its faults, America has done much that is commendable. In a world where the majority still seek basic human rights, including the right to religious liberty, America looks quite good. Even in the perspective of the world religions, our civic tolerance is remarkable.[13]

Has our agreement to disagree about fundamentals relegated them to the private sphere? If religion is absent from the public places where we forge our national culture, our center may not hold. On the other hand, if religion is pursued only by the pious, genuine traditionalists will not want it to hold. Eric Voegelin has said that a crucial test of a culture is whether it enlists the best of its youth or alienates them. For both United States government and United States religion, that can be a hard saying.

We have become used to speeches telling us that our government has only to be as good as its citizens for America to prosper. In too many political assemblies, churches, and synagogues, that is a palliative, a placebo. It brings no health or distinction to the speaker or the audience. To a religious guru, it shows that the speaker ignores the human condition—the beginner's mind, the nature of enlightenment. Unreflective, unmeditative, the speaker cannot be terse, poetic, evocative; he or she can only pour forth the old, stale, placating language. Ignorant of ignorance and sin, the speaker sees no tragedy. Lacking rigor, stupid in the reasons of the heart, the speaker thinks hope is the same as good cheer.

Much the same is true of the audience, of ourselves. Not having gone down in spiritual death, we do not fly to the gods. Not set for spiritual combat, we do not resent that the seats are plush, the rhetoric easy. In part, that is because our culture tells us that only eggheads knit their brows and ponder. In part, it is because we are too lazy to live. In many cases it is a major accomplishment for us to endure ten minutes of silence.

Figure 29 **The Sleep of Reason Produces Monsters,**
*by Francisco Goya, Spanish (1746–1828). Etching
and aquatint; 7³/₁₆ × 4³/₄ in. The Nelson–Atkins Museum of Art, Kansas City, Missouri (Nelson Fund).*

People who say things that others do not want to
hear, no matter how true such things may be, will
suffer for their indiscretion. Socrates stands as the
paradigm of their fate, and Socrates shows that in the
political realm, prophets and sages are one. He also
shows that prophets and sages cannot live for audience
applause. They must do what they have to do, say what
they have to say, because it is their truth, their good,
their charge. Shamans, for further instance, must
sing—because it relieves their sadness, because it
makes them whole. Plato's "Seventh Letter" says that
the philosophical soul must live by a love of the Good,
that it can deny the Good only by denying its self.
Religious people, creative people, humanity's benefac-

tors have all found something more precious than human praise. Better, they have all been found by
something more precious.

That something is the sacred, the numinous, the
holy, the really real. It is Wakan Tanka, the Tao, Buddha-nature, God. Commonly, it is the essence of any
conviction significant in the ultimate order, in the
world as it finally is. The world as it finally is is the
one place where you get what you are. It is where someone may finally tell you, "If you do not believe in mystery, God, or the *Tao*, be honest about it." By being
honest you will reap two benefits. First, you will not
bring ultimate realities into further disrepute. Second,
you will take the first step in the pilgrimage toward
wisdom, which is acknowledging the truth.

A second step is no less simple or heroic. It is to
love the truth that you acknowledge. That may be the
truth that mystery is beautiful or the truth that the
religions often cant. It may move you to sound the
ram's horn or to void at the flag. The point is not so
much the content as the act. The dynamic of human
consciousness, on which any genuine wisdom takes its
stand, is a movement from one's present light to wherever that light leads. "Lead kindly light," Cardinal
Newman and others have prayed. Go to your light's
source, Augustine and others have counseled. Your
light shines in the darkness, and the darkness cannot
overcome it—as long as you want to be human, as
long as samsara is not your all.

Whatever is noble, whatever is good, whatever is
honest—think on it, St. Paul said. Whatever is your
current belief about American religion, face it and
start to love it. If it is a solid truth, your personality
will ripen, your social circle will take fire. If it is
a rotten pseudo-truth, you will hear a call to turn
and change your heart. In the spiritual life, the
only disaster is avoidance. Because they will not
face their own beliefs, whether solid or rotten, many
stay half-asleep.

Awakened, human consciousness reveals its intrinsic religiousness by pursuing the light to where it
is love. Worthy religious traditions and patriotism
have nothing to fear from this pursuit. The pursuer
does have some things to fear, but they pale in comparison with what there is to gain. In Eastern terms,
the pursuer learns about ignorance: how much is sam-
saric in his or her starting "truth." In Western terms,
the pursuer learns about sin: how difficult it is to follow only the light. Why we do not know the good we
should know, why we do not do the good we should

do—they are among our deepest mysteries. Only when you ponder them can you call yourself mature, let alone wise. Still, understanding these mysteries is the major therapy that any self needs. Understanding them is the heart of traditional political science.

However, the religions' dharma and prophecy illumine much more than ignorance and sin. Ultimately they lead to enlightenment and grace. Enlightenment happens: It is an empirical fact. Light floods some people, bringing them inexpressible joy. Similarly, grace happens: There are marvelous saints. They love God with whole mind, heart, soul, and strength. They serve sisters and brothers more than themselves.

In a dark and troubled time (that is, in any historical time), saints and enlightened people save our beleaguered hope. Just one of them is stronger than all the rubbish, all the valid ground for cynicism. For a single really holy, really religious, really humane person says that what we want and need is possible. We want and need light and love. Light and love are possible. By definition, light and love are buddha-nature and God. By saintly testimony, they are our center.

Discussion Questions

1. To what extent do the religions share a common attraction toward mystery?

2. Explain the following: "The final utility of religion is that it can teach us how to die and how to live."

3. What have been the principal strengths and weaknesses of American religion?

4. Write a brief definition of *religion* that takes into account the traditions' unity and the traditions' diversity.

5. What is the permanent lesson in the Western traditions' elevation of the prophet?

6. On what grounds might one defend "profit"?

7. How have the religions fostered or defended pseudospeciation?

8. Why does the experience of enlightenment or grace tend to lessen greed?

9. How valid is it to study a religion without personally confronting its call for conversion?

10. What have been the benefits of civil religions?

11. What is the mystical dimension in every human life?

Glossary

pseudospeciation: a term employed by the psychologist Erik Erikson to denote the tendency of people to deny the humanity of groups outside their own cultural circle. Erikson's point was the gap between psychology and biology at this point, as people who manifestly belong to the same biological species (who could, for instance, mate and reproduce) contrive to deny that the "others"—foreigners, aliens—are as human as their own kind. The extreme form of pseudospeciation is xenophobia—fear of foreigners to the point of hatred. Pseudospeciation thrived when peoples were isolated and so somewhat plausibly could keep their myths to the effect that creation had occurred in their neighborhood and they were the center of the earth. With the development of a planetary culture in recent decades, pseudospeciation stands revealed as more pathological than was first appreciated, and the religious contributions to pseudospeciation (bigotry, crusades, holy wars) stand revealed as dubious expressions of an estimable divinity.

NOTES

Introduction

1. This story is adapted from the Dutch Catholic bishops' work, *A New Catechism* (New York: Herder and Herder, 1967), p. 3.

2. See Michael Polanyi, *Personal Knowledge* (New York: Harper Torchbooks, 1964); Stephen Toulmin, *Human Understanding* (Princeton, N.J.: Princeton University Press, 1977). For a discussion of Western religion and the distinctive rise of Western science, see Stanley L. Jaki, *The Road of Science and the Ways to God* (Chicago: University of Chicago Press, 1978).

3. Philip Kapleau, *The Three Pillars of Zen* (Boston: Beacon Press, 1967), pp. 189–291.

4. For example, Heinz Robert Schlette, *Toward a Theology of Religions* (New York: Herder and Herder, 1966).

5. Another view of theology, geared to its easier practice in the university, is Shubert Ogden's "Theology and Religious Studies: Their Difference and the Difference It Makes," *Journal of the American Academy of Religion,* 1978, *46*(1):3–17.

6. John Carmody, "Faith in Religious Studies," *Communio,* 1976, *3*(1):39–49.

7. W. Richard Comstock, *The Study of Religion and Primitive Religions* (New York: Harper & Row, 1971), pp. 13–17.

8. See Erik Erikson's *Gandhi's Truth* (New York: Norton, 1969).

9. See Clifford Geertz, *The Interpretation of Cultures* (New York: Basic Books, 1973), pp. 412–453.

10. For a several-methoded approach to Judaism, see *Take Judaism, for Example: Studies toward the Comparison of Religions,* ed. Jacob Neusner (Chicago: University of Chicago Press, 1983). The methods are not precisely the five we have sketched, but the book's four stages (Analysis, Description, Interpretation, and Comparison) cover much the same ground. For a good introduction to the several different extensions of Torah, see *Back to the Sources,* ed. Barry W. Holtz (New York: Summit Books, 1984). As a way into the methodology most influential in recent studies of world religions, see Ugo Bianchi, "History of Religions," *The Encyclopedia of Religion,* vol. 6, ed. Mircea Eliade (New York: Macmillan, 1987), 399–408. (Hereafter cited as *ER.*) Other stimulating sources include *The World's Religious Traditions,* ed. Frank Whaling (New York: Crossroad, 1986); and Jonathan Z. Smith, *Imagining Religion* (Chicago: University of Chicago Press, 1982). What these methodological studies most suggest is the crying need for a theory of consciousness that could map their different questions and coordinate

them. We favor the views of Bernard Lonergan and Eric Voegelin. See Lonergan's *Insight* (New York: Philosophical Library, 1958) and *Method in Theology* (New York: Herder and Herder, 1972). See Voegelin's *Anamnesis* (Notre Dame, Ind.: University of Notre Dame Press, 1978) and *In Search of Order: Order and History,* vol. 5 (Baton Rouge: Louisiana State University Press, 1987).

11. See 1989 *Britannica Book of the Year* (Chicago: Encyclopaedia Britannica, 1989), p. 289.

12. Florinda Donner, *Shabono* (New York: Delacorte, 1982), pp. 163–164.

Chapter 1

1. Shunryu Suzuki, *Zen Mind, Beginner's Mind* (New York: John Weatherhill, 1970), p. xxx.

2. See John Bowker, *The Sense of God* (Oxford: Clarendon Press, 1973), pp. 57–58, 228. On prehistoric religion generally, see Mary Edwardsen, James Waller, et al., "Prehistoric Religions," *ER,* 1987, *11,* 505–522.

3. Sherwood Washburn, "The Evolution of Man," *Scientific American,* 1978, *239*(3):196–197.

4. E. O. James, "Prehistoric Religion," in *Historia Religionum, I,* ed. C. J. Bleeker and G. Widengren (Leiden: E. J. Brill, 1969), p. 23.

5. Mircea Eliade, "On Prehistoric Religions," *History of Religions,* 1974, *14*(2):141. (Hereafter cited as *HR.*)

6. Eric Neumann, *The Origins and History of Consciousness* (Princeton, N.J.: Princeton University Press, 1971), pp. 5–101.

7. Jacques Waardenburg, ed., *Classical Approaches to the Study of Religion* (The Hague: Mouton, 1973), pp. 3–78.

8. Barre Toelken, "Seeing with a Native Eye: How Many Sheep Will It Hold?" in *Seeing with a Native Eye,* ed. Walter H. Capps (New York: Harper & Row, 1976), p. 9.

9. E. G. Parrinder, "Religions of Illiterate Peoples," in *Historia Religionum, II,* ed. C. J. Bleeker and G. Widengren (Leiden: E. J. Brill, 1971), p. 550.

10. James, "Prehistoric Religion," p. 23.

11. Bowker, *Sense of God,* pp. 44–65.

12. Merlin Stone, *When God Was a Woman* (New York: Dial Press, 1976), pp. 1–18. Behind this conception may well lie a more central role for women in biological evolution than they have hitherto been accorded. Recent studies suggest that women were the primary socializers of developing humanity, as well as the source of from 50 to 90

percent of its food. See Nancy Tanner and Adrienne Zihlman, "Women in Evolution, Part I: Innovation and Selection in Human Origins," *Signs,* 1976, *1*(3):585–608; Adrienne I. Zihlman, "Women and Evolution, Part II: Subsistence and Social Organization among Early Hominids," *Signs,* 1978, *4*(1):4–20. On the rise of feminine deities, see James J. Preston et al., "Goddess Worship," *ER,* 1987 *6,* 35–59. For perspectives on why goddess worship did not necessarily improve the social lot of women, see Gerda Lerner, *The Creation of Patriarchy* (New York: Oxford University Press, 1986).

13.   Adolf E. Jensen, *Myth and Cult among Primitive Peoples* (Chicago: University of Chicago Press, 1963), pp. 135–146.

14.   Mircea Eliade, *A History of Religious Ideas,* vol. 1, *From the Stone Age to the Eleusinian Mysteries* (Chicago: University of Chicago Press, 1978).

15.   Ibid., p. 4.

16.   See Joseph Campbell, *The Masks of God: Primitive Mythology* (New York: Viking, 1970), pp. 173–176; Jensen, *Myth and Cult,* pp. 107–112.

17.   Eliade, *History of Religious Ideas,* vol. 1, pp. 38–39.

18.   Ibid., p. 115. For megalithic religion in general, see Marija Gimbutas and J. Stephen Lansing, "Megalithic Religion," *ER,* 1987, *9,* 336–346. On Stonehenge in particular, see Benjamin C. Ray, "Stonehenge: A New Theory," *HR,* February 1974, *26*(3):225–278.

19.   Björn Kurtén, *Dance of the Tiger* (New York: Berkeley Books, 1981), pp. 198–199.

Chapter 2

1.   Mircea Eliade, *Cosmos and History* (New York: Harper & Row, 1959), pp. 8–16.

2.   Rudolf Otto, *The Idea of the Holy* (New York: Oxford University Press, 1958), pp. 12–40; see also Carsten Colpe, "Sacred and Profane, The," *ER, 12,* 511–526; Joel L. Brereton, "Sacred Space," ibid., 526–535; Barbara C. Sproul, "Sacred Time," ibid., 535–544.

3.   G. Van der Leeuw, *Religion in Essence and Manifestation, I* (New York: Harper & Row, 1963), p. 23.

4.   Bruce Lincoln, "Treatment of Hair and Fingernails among the Indo-Europeans," *HR,* 1977, *16*(4):351–362.

5.   Manabu Waida, "Symbolisms of the Moon and the Waters of Immortality," *HR,* 1977, *16*(4):407–423.

6.   Theodore M. Ludwig, "Gods and Goddesses," *ER, 6,* 59–66.

7.   Mircea Eliade, *From Primitives to Zen* (New York: Harper & Row, 1967).

8.   Hartley Burr Alexander, *The World's Rim* (Lincoln: University of Nebraska Press, 1953), pp. 63–99.

9.   Joseph Campbell, *The Masks of God, I: Primitive Mythology* (New York: Viking, 1970), p. 151.

10.   Durango Mendoza, "Summer Water and Shirley," in *American Indian Authors,* ed. Natachee Scott Momaday (Boston: Houghton Mifflin, 1972), pp. 96–105.

11.   Clyde Kluckhohn, *Navaho Witchcraft* (Boston: Beacon Press, 1967), pp. 13–61.

12.   Ruth M. Underhill, *Red Man's Religion* (Chicago: University of Chicago Press, 1965), p. 51.

13.   Carlos Castaneda, *Tales of Power* (New York: Simon & Schuster, 1974), pp. 118–162.

14.   Annie Dillard, *Pilgrim at Tinker Creek* (New York: Harper's Magazine Press, 1974), pp. 163–164.

15.   Adolph E. Jensen, *Myth and Cult among Primitive Peoples* (Chicago: University of Chicago Press, 1963), pp. 1–79. W. Richard Comstock, *The Study of Religion and Primitive Religions* (New York: Harper & Row, 1971), pp. 28–72; John J. Collins, *Primitive Religion* (Totowa, N.J.: Littlefield, Adams, 1978), pp. 55–158; Kees W. Bolle et al., "Myth," *ER, 10,* 261–285; Evan M. Zuesse, "Ritual," *ER, 12,* 405–422.

16.   Marcel Griaule, *Conversations with Ogotemmeli* (London: Oxford University Press, 1965), pp. xi–3.

17.   Joseph Epes Brown, ed., *The Sacred Pipe* (Baltimore: Penguin, 1971), pp. 116–126. Black Elk's exposure to Christianity makes it difficult to consider him a pure representative.

18.   Colin Turnbull, *The Forest People* (New York: Simon & Schuster, 1962), pp. 184–200.

19.   Mircea Eliade, *Myths, Dreams, and Mysteries* (New York: Harper & Row, 1960), pp. 174–175.

20.   Mircea Eliade, *Shamanism* (Princeton, N.J.: Princeton University Press, 1964), pp. 3–13.

21.   Odd Nordland, "Shamanism as an Experiencing of the 'Unreal,' " in *Studies in Shamanism,* ed. Carl-Martin Edmans (Stockholm: Almquist and Wiksell, 1967), pp. 166–185.

22.   Arthur Waley, *The Nine Songs* (London: Allen & Unwin, 1955).

23.   Ichiro Hori, *Folk Religion in Japan* (Chicago: University of Chicago Press, 1968), p. 181.

24.   I. M. Lewis, *Ecstatic Religion* (Middlesex, England: Penguin, 1971).

25.   John Neihardt, *Black Elk Speaks* (Lincoln: University of Nebraska Press, 1961), p. 20.

26.   Napoleon Chagnon, *Yanomamo: The Fierce People* (New York: Holt, Rinehart and Winston, 1968), p. 52.

27.   Carl-Martin Edmans, ed., *Studies in Shamanism* (Stockholm: Almquist and Wiksell, 1967; see also Mircea Eliade et al., "Shamanism," *ER, 13,* 201–222.

28.   Robert Coles, *Children of Crisis,* vol. 4, *Eskimos, Chicanos, Indians* (Boston: Little, Brown, 1977).

29.   Ibid., p. 522; see also Werner Müller, "North American Indians," *ER, 10,* 469–525; Catherine L. Albanese, "Exploring Regional Religion: A Case Study of the Eastern Cherokee," *HR,* May 1984, *23*(4):344–371.

30.   See C. G. Jung, *Memories, Dreams, Reflections* (New York: Vintage, 1963), pp. 246–253.

31. Weston La Barre, "Amerindian Religions," in *Historical Atlas of the Religions of the World,* ed. I. al Faruqi and D. Sopher (New York: Macmillan, 1974), pp. 51–57.

32. J. R. Fox, "Religions of Illiterate People: North America," in *Historia Religionum, II,* ed. C. J. Bleeker and G. Widengren (Leiden: E. J. Brill, 1971), pp. 593–608.

33. A. Clos, "Religions of Illiterate People: Asia," in *Historia Religionum, II,* ed. C. J. Bleeker and G. Widengren (Leiden: E. J. Brill, 1971), pp. 573–592.

34. Eliade, *From Primitives to Zen,* p. 88.

35. Paul Radin, *The Trickster: A Study in American Indian Mythology* (New York: Philosophical Library, 1956); see also Klaus-Peter Koepping, "Absurdity and Hidden Truth: Cunning Intelligence and Grotesque Body Images as Manifestations of the Trickster," *HR,* February 1985, *24*(3):191–214.

36. Underhill, *Red Man's Religion,* p. 104.

37. Charles A. Eastman, *The Soul of the Indian* (Boston: Houghton Mifflin, 1911), pp. 6–8.

38. See La Barre, "Amerindian Religions," p. 52.

39. Emory Sekaquaptewa, "Hopi Indian Ceremonies," in *Seeing with a Native Eye,* ed. Walter H. Capps (New York: Harper & Row, 1976), p. 39.

40. La Barre, "Amerindian Religions," p. 53.

41. Dee Brown, *Bury My Heart at Wounded Knee* (New York: Holt, Rinehart and Winston, 1971).

42. Carl F. Starkloff, *The People of the Center: American Indian Religion and Christianity* (New York: Seabury, 1974).

43. Ake Hultzkrantz, "The Contribution of the Study of North American Indian Religions to the History of Religions," in *Seeing with a Native Eye,* ed. Walter H. Capps (New York: Harper & Row, 1976), pp. 86–106.

44. Sam D. Gill, "Native American Religions," *Council on the Study of Religion Bulletin,* 1978, *9*(5):125–128.

45. Ake Hultzkrantz, "North American Indian Religion in the History of Research: A General Survey," *HR,* 1966, *6*(2):91–107; 1967, *6*(3):183–207; 1967, *7*(1):13–34; 1967, *7*(2):112–148.

46. Margaret Atwood, *Surfacing* (New York: Popular Library, 1976).

47. N. Scott Momaday, "Native American Attitudes to the Environment," in *Seeing with a Native Eye,* ed. Walter H. Capps (New York: Harper & Row, 1976), pp. 79–85.

48. See Coles, *Children of Crisis,* vol. 4, pp. 216–217; see also Inge Kleivan, "Inuit Religion," *ER, 7,* 270–273; and Daniel Merkur, "Eagle, the Hunter's Helper: The Cultural Significance of Inuit Mythological Tales," *HR,* November 1987, *27*(2):171–188.

49. Kaj Birket-Smith, *The Eskimos* (London: Methuen, 1959), p. 161.

50. Franz Boas, *The Central Eskimo* (Lincoln: University of Nebraska Press, 1964), p. 175.

51. Ibid., pp. 178–179.

52. Birket-Smith, *The Eskimos.*

53. Knud Rasmussen, *Across Arctic America* (New York: Putnam's, 1927), p. 385.

54. Ibid., p. 386.

55. Ibid., p. 81.

56. Ibid., p. 86.

57. Eliade, *Shamanism,* p. 58.

58. Barry Lopez, *Arctic Dreams* (New York: Charles Scribner's Sons, 1986), brings the reader into this traditional Eskimo sensitivity to the environment.

59. Clos, "Religions of Illiterate People: Asia," p. 576.

60. Birket-Smith, *Eskimos,* p. 166.

61. Collins, *Primitive Religion,* pp. 65–66.

62. Peter Freuchen, *Book of the Eskimos* (Cleveland: World, 1961).

63. Boas, *Central Eskimo,* p. 201.

64. Rasmussen, *Across Arctic America,* p. 261.

65. See Turnbull, *The Forest People,* p. 252.

66. John Mbiti, "Traditional Religions in Africa," in *Historical Atlas of the Religions of the World,* ed. I. al Faruqi and D. Sopher (New York: Macmillan, 1974), pp. 61–68; see also Benjamin C. Ray et al., "African Religions," *ER, 1,* 60–96.

67. See 1990 *Britannica Book of the Year* (Chicago: Encyclopedia Britannica, 1990), p. 316.

68. For moving literary presentations, see Hamidou Kane, *Ambiguous Adventure* (New York: Collier Books, 1969), on Islam; and Chinua Achebe, *No Longer at Ease* (New York: Fawcett, 1969), on Christianity.

69. Evan Zuesse, "Divination and Deity in African Religions," *HR,* 1975, *15*(2):167, note 15.

70. Henri Frankfort, *Kingship and the Gods* (Chicago: University of Chicago Press, 1978), pp. 33–34. (Originally published 1948.)

71. Geoffrey Parrinder, *African Traditional Religion,* 3rd ed. (New York: Harper & Row, 1976), p. 17.

72. Geoffrey Parrinder, "Religions of Illiterate People: Africa," in *Historia Religionum, II,* ed. C. J. Bleeker and G. Widengren (Leiden: E. J. Brill, 1971), p. 556.

73. John Mbiti, *African Religions and Philosophy* (Garden City, N.Y.: Doubleday, 1969), p. 67.

74. Parrinder, "Religions of Illiterate People: Africa," p. 561.

75. W. Richard Comstock, *The Study of Religion and Primitive Religions,* p. 80; see also Luc de Heusch, *Sacrifice in Africa* (Bloomington: Indiana University Press, 1985).

76. This paragraph is adapted from Denise Lardner Carmody, *Women and World Religions* (Nashville: Abingdon, 1979), p. 34. See Carol P. MacCormack, "Biological Events and Cultural Control," *Signs,* 1971, *3*(1):93–100; also Mbiti, *African Religions and Philosophy,* pp. 165–171.

77. Turnbull, *The Forest People,* p. 217.

78. See Ian Barbour, ed., *Finite Resources and the Human Future* (Minneapolis: Augsburg, 1976), especially pp. 55–114.

79. Parrinder, "Religions of Illiterate People: Africa," p. 564.

80. Eliade, *From Primitives to Zen,* p. 269.

81. Ibid., p. 268.

82. Parrinder, "Religions of Illiterate People: Africa," p. 567.

83. Zuesse, "Divination and Deity," pp. 158–182.

84. Ibid., p. 167, note 15.

85. See Parrinder, *African Traditional Religion,* p. 124.

86. This is dramatically portrayed in the anthropological novel by Elenore Smith Bowen, *Return to Laughter* (Garden City, N.Y.: Doubleday, 1964).

87. Geoffrey Barraclough, ed., *The Times Atlas of World History* (Maplewood, N.J.: Hammond, 1979), p. 236.

88. See Patrick White, *A Fringe of Leaves* (New York: Viking, 1977). Also, see White's earlier novel *Voss* (New York: Viking, 1957), especially pp. 237 ff; see also Ronald M. Berndt et al., "Australian Religions," *ER, 1,* 529–570.

89. See Mircea Eliade, *Australian Religions* (Ithaca, N.Y.: Cornell University Press, 1973), p. 194.

90. T. G. H. Strehlow, "Religions of Illiterate People: Australia," in *Historia Religionum, II,* ed. C. J. Bleeker and G. Widengren (Leiden: E. J. Brill, 1971), pp. 609–628.

91. Emile Durkheim, *The Elementary Forms of the Religious Life* (New York: Free Press, 1965).

92. Eliade, *Australian Religions,* p. 68.

93. Eliade, *From Primitives to Zen,* pp. 140–141.

94. Ibid., p. 162.

95. Rita M. Gross, "Menstruation and Childbirth as Ritual and Religious Experience in the Religion of the Australian Aborigines," *JAAR,* 1977, *45*(4):1147–1181.

96. Eliade, *Australian Religions,* p. 88.

97. Ibid., p. 92.

98. Ibid., p. 122.

99. Eliade, *From Primitives to Zen,* p. 424.

100. See William Richardson, *Heidegger: Through Phenomenology to Thought* (The Hague: Martinus Nijhoff, 1967).

101. Walker Percy, *The Thanatos Syndrome* (New York: Farrar, Straus & Giroux, 1987).

102. Bernard Lonergan, *Method in Theology* (New York: Herder and Herder, 1972), pp. 101–103.

103. Erik Erikson, *Toys and Reasons* (New York: Norton, 1977), pp. 67–118.

104. Carol P. Christ, "Why Women Need the Goddess: Phenomenological, Psychological, and Political Reflections," in *Woman-spirit Rising,* ed. Carol P. Christ and Judith Plaskow (New York: Harper & Row, 1979), pp. 273–287.

105. E. F. Schumacher, *Small Is Beautiful* (New York: Harper Torchbooks, 1973).

106. Sam Gill, *Beyond the Primitive: The Religions of Non-literate Peoples* (Englewood Cliffs, N.J.: Prentice-Hall, 1982), p. 111.

107. See Michael Harner, *The Way of the Shaman: A Guide to Power and Healing* (New York: Harper & Row, 1980).

Chapter 3

1. See James B. Pritchard, ed., *Ancient Near Eastern Texts,* 3rd ed. (Princeton, N.J.: Princeton University Press, 1969), pp. 37–41; Thorkild Jacobsen, "Mesopotamian Religions: An Overview," *ER, 9,* 447–466.

2. Ibid., pp. 60–61; Tikva Frymer-Kensky, "Enuma Elish," *ER, 5,* 124–126.

3. Jacobsen, ibid., pp. 72–100.

4. See William L. Moran, "Gilgamesh," *ER, 5,* 557–560; Tzvi Abusch, "Ishtar's Proposal and Gilgamesh's Refusal," *HR,* November 1986, *26*(2):143–187.

5. Henri Frankfort, *Kingship and the Gods* (Chicago: University of Chicago Press, 1978), pp. 15–214.

6. See Eric Voegelin, *Order and History, I, Israel and Revelation* (Baton Rouge: Louisiana State University Press, 1956), pp. 88–95; John A. Wilson, *The Culture of Ancient Egypt* (Chicago: University of Chicago Press, 1956), pp. 58–60; Leonard H. Lesko, "Egyptian Religion: An Overview," *ER, 5,* 37–54.

7. Voegelin, *Order and History, I,* p. 99.

8. C. J. Bleeker, "The Religion of Ancient Egypt," in *Historia Religionum, I,* ed. C. J. Bleeker and G. Widengren (Leiden: E. J. Brill, 1969), pp. 47–49.

9. Voegelin, *Order and History, I,* p. 108; for an overview of opinions about Akhenaton, see Virginia Lee Davis, "Akhenaton," *ER, 1,* 169–170.

10. James B. Pritchard, ed., *Ancient Near Eastern Texts,* 3rd ed. (Princeton, N.J.: Princeton University Press, 1969), p. 370.

11. Voegelin, *Order and History, I,* p. 86.

12. Hans J. Klimkeit, "Spatial Orientation in Mythical Thinking as Exemplified in Ancient Egypt: Considerations toward a Geography of Religions," *HR,* 1975, *14*(4):266–281.

13. Frankfort, *Kingship and the Gods,* pp. 148–212.

14. C. J. Bleeker, *Egyptian Festivals* (Leiden: E. J. Brill, 1967), pp. 91–123.

15. C. J. Bleeker, *The Rainbow: A Collection of Studies in the Science of Religion* (Leiden: E. J. Brill, 1975), pp. 167–173.

16. Pierre Montet, *Everyday Life in Egypt* (Westport, Conn.: Greenwood Press, 1974), p. 51.

17. Vern L. Bullough, *The Subordinate Sex* (Baltimore: Penguin, 1974), pp. 32–33; for an overview of women's lot in Egypt and other ancient Near Eastern cultures, see Gerda Lerner, *The Creation of Patriarchy* (New York: Oxford University Press, 1986).

18. Bullough, ibid., p. 39.

19. John A. Wilson, *The Culture of Ancient Egypt* (Chicago: University of Chicago Press, 1956), p. 78.

20. James B. Pritchard, ed., *Ancient Near Eastern Texts* (Princeton, N.J.: Princeton University Press, 1969), p. 34.

21. Ibid., p. 35.

22. Jacques Duchesne-Gullemin, *The Hymns of Zarathustra,* trans. M. Henning (Boston: Beacon Press, 1963), p. 1.

23. R. Ghirshman, *Iran* (Baltimore: Penguin, 1954), p. 27; Bruce Lincoln, "Indo-European Religions: An Overview," *ER, 7,* 198–204; Gherardo Gnoli, "Iranian Religions," ibid., 277–280.

24. Arnold Toynbee, *Mankind and Mother Earth* (New York: Oxford University Press, 1976), pp. 91–116.

25. See Richard Frye, *The Heritage of Persia* (New York: World, 1963), pp. 19–20; Jarich G. Oosten, *The Way of the Gods: The Social Code in Indo-European Mythology* (London: Routledge and Kegan Paul, 1985).

26. R. C. Zaehner, *The Dawn and Twilight of Zoroastrianism* (New York: Putnam's, 1961), pp. 60–61.

27. Duchesne-Gullemin, *The Hymns of Zarathustra,* p. 135.

28. Ibid., p. 137.

29. Isma'il R. al Faruqi, "Zoroastrianism," in *Historical Atlas of the Religions of the World,* ed. I. al Faruqi and D. Sopher (New York: Macmillan, 1974), pp. 133–134.

30. Zaehner, *Dawn and Twilight,* p. 99.

31. Frye, *Heritage of Persia,* p. 190; William R. Darrow, "Zoroaster Amalgamated," *HR,* November 1987, *27*(2):109–132.

32. Ghirshman, *Iran,* p. 269.

33. On Manicheanism, see J. P. Asmussen, "Manicheanism," in *Historia Religionum, I,* ed. C. J. Bleeker and G. Widengren (Leiden: E. J. Brill, 1969), pp. 580–610.

34. See Gherardo Gnoli, "Zorastrianism," *ER, 15,* 589–590.

35. Jacques Duchesne-Gullemin, "The Religion of Ancient Iran," in *Historia Religionum, I,* ed. C. J. Bleeker and G. Widengren (Leiden: E. J. Brill, 1969), pp. 366–367.

36. Emily E. Culpepper, "Zoroastrian Menstruation Taboos," in *Women and Religion,* rev. ed., ed. J. Plaskow and J. A. Romero (Missoula, Mont.: Scholars Press, 1974), pp. 199–210.

37. Mary Boyce, "Zoroastrianism," in *Historia Religionum, II,* ed. C. J. Bleeker and G. Widengren (Leiden: E. J. Brill, 1971), pp. 228–229.

38. Eric Voegelin, *Anamnesis* (Notre Dame, Ind.: University of Notre Dame Press, 1978), p. 92.

39. Arnold Toynbee, *Mankind and Mother Earth,* (New York: Oxford University Press, 1976), pp. 77–78.

40. Phillipe Borgeaud, "The Open Entrance to the Closed Palace of the King: The Greek Labyrinth in Context," *HR,* 1974, *14*(1):1–27; Raymond Christinger, "The Hidden Significance of the 'Cretan' Labyrinth," *HR,* 1975, *15*(2):183–191.

41. Mircea Eliade, *A History of Religious Ideas,* vol. 1, *From the Stone Age to the Eleusinian Mysteries* (Chicago: University of Chicago Press, 1978), p. 136; K. Kerenyi, "Voraussentzungen in der Einweihung in Eleusis," in *Initiation,* ed. C. J. Bleeker (Leiden: E. J. Brill, 1965), pp. 59–64; M. Mehauden, "Le secret central de l'initiation aux mystères

d'Eléusis," ibid., pp. 65–70; Olivier Pelon, "Aegean Religions," *ER, 1,* 32–39.

42. B. C. Dietrich, *The Origins of Greek Religion* (New York: de Gruyter, 1974), pp. 191–289; see also Louis Gernet, *The Anthropology of Ancient Greece* (Baltimore: Johns Hopkins University Press, 1981); and Jean-Pierre Vernant, *The Origins of Greek Thought* (Ithaca, N.Y.: Cornell University Press, 1982).

43. Eliade, *History of Religious Ideas,* vol. 1, pp. 247–250.

44. W. K. C. Guthrie, *The Greeks and Their Gods* (Boston: Beacon Press, 1955), pp. 73–87; Claude Calame, "Facing Otherness: The Tragic Mask in Ancient Greece," *HR,* November 1986, *26*(2):125–142; Jean-Pierre Vernant, "Greek Religion," *ER, 6,* 99–118.

45. E. R. Dodds, *The Greeks and the Irrational* (Berkeley: University of California Press, 1966), pp. 76–82.

46. Ibid., pp. 270–282.

47. Eliade, *History of Religious Ideas,* vol. 1, p. 360.

48. H. J. Rose, *A Handbook of Greek Mythology* (New York: Dutton, 1959), pp. 91–94.

49. Edith Hamilton, *Mythology* (New York: New American Library, 1942), pp. 103–105.

50. Guthrie, *Greeks and Their Gods,* p. 318.

51. Ibid., pp. 217–253.

52. See Eric Voegelin, *Order and History, II: The World of the Polis* (Baton Rouge: Louisiana State University Press, 1957), pp. 203–331.

53. Ibid., pp. 332–373; Eric Voegelin, *Order and History, IV: The Ecumenic Age* (Baton Rouge: Louisiana State University Press, 1974), pp. 178–183.

54. John Carmody, "Plato's Religious Horizon," *Philosophy Today,* 1971, *15*(1):52–68.

55. Voegelin, *Order and History, IV,* pp. 187–192; Werner Jaeger, *Aristotle* (New York: Oxford University Press, 1962), pp. 366–406.

56. Bernard Lonergan, *Verbum* (Notre Dame, Ind.: University of Notre Dame Press, 1967).

57. Murray, *Greek Religion,* pp. 119–165; Dodds, *Greeks and the Irrational,* pp. 236–269; Walter Burkert, *Ancient Mystery Cults* (Cambridge, Mass.: Harvard University Press, 1987).

58. M. J. Vermaseren, "Hellenistic Religions," in *Historia Religionum, I,* ed. C. J. Bleeker and G. Widengren (Leiden: E. J. Brill, 1969), p. 495; J. Gwyn Griffiths, "Hellenistic Religions," *ER, 6,* 252–266.

59. Sharon Kelly Heyob, *The Cult of Isis among Women in the Graeco-Roman World* (Leiden: E. J. Brill, 1975), pp. 111–127.

60. See Vermaseren, "Hellenistic Religions," pp. 522–533.

61. Ibid., pp. 523–528.

62. See Mircea Eliade, *From Primitives to Zen* (New York: Harper & Row, 1967), p. 55.

63. See Eliade, *History of Religious Ideas,* vol. 1, p. 256.

64. See Bullough, *Subordinate Sex,* p. 59.

65. Eliade, *From Primitives to Zen,* p. 540.

Chapter 4

1. R. J. Zwi Werblowsky, "Judaism," in *Historia Religionum, II,* ed. C. J. Bleeker and G. Widengren (Leiden: E. J. Brill, 1971), p. 1; Eugene B. Borowitz, "Judaism: An Overview," *ER, 8,* 127–148.

2. Herbert May, ed., *Oxford Bible Atlas,* 2nd ed. (New York: Oxford University Press, 1974), p. 57; G. Widengren, "Israelite-Jewish Religion," in *Historia Religionum, I,* ed. C. J. Bleeker and G. Widengren (Leiden: E. J. Brill, 1969), p. 226.

3. Isadore Epstein, *Judaism* (London: Penguin, 1959), pp. 12–14; Eric Voegelin, *Order and History, I: Israel and Revelation* (Baton Rouge: Louisiana State University Press, 1956), pp. 188–195.

4. I. al Faruqi and D. Sopher, eds., *Historical Atlas of the Religions of the World* (New York: Macmillan, 1974), p. 286.

5. See E. E. Urbach, "Torah," *ER, 14,* 556–565; "Torah," *Encyclopedia Judaica (EJ),* vol. 15 (Jerusalem: Keter, 1972), pp. 1235–1246; Barry W. Holtz, ed., *Back to the Sources* (New York: Summit, 1984); Jonathan Rosenbaum, "Judaism: Torah and Tradition," in *The Holy Book in Comparative Perspective,* ed. Frederick M. Denny and Rodney L. Taylor (Columbia: University of South Carolina Press, 1985), pp. 10–35; Richard Elliott Friedman, *Who Wrote the Bible?* (Englewood Cliffs, N.J.: Prentice-Hall, 1987).

6. William Foxwell Albright, "The Biblical Period," in *The Jews: Their History,* ed. Louis Finkelstein (New York: Schocken, 1970), pp. 15–19.

7. See Samuel Sandmel, *The Enjoyment of Scripture* (New York: Oxford University Press, 1972), pp. 164–175.

8. For example, Roland Murphy, "Introduction to Wisdom Literature," *The Jerome Biblical Commentary,* vol. 1, ed. R. Brown, J. Fitzmyer, and R. Murphy (Englewood Cliffs, N.J.: Prentice-Hall, 1968), p. 487.

9. John J. Collins, "The Jewish Apocalypse," in *Apocalypse: The Morphology of a Genre,* ed. John J. Collins (Missoula, Mont.: Scholars Press, 1979), pp. 21–59.

10. Eric Voegelin, *Order and History, IV: The Ecumenic Age* (Baton Rouge: Louisiana State University Press, 1974), pp. 117–133, 153–165.

11. Victor Tcherikover, *Hellenistic Civilization and the Jews* (New York: Atheneum, 1974), pp. 152–234.

12. Joseph Fitzmyer, "A History of Israel," in *The Jerome Biblical Commentary,* vol. 2, ed. R. Brown, J. Fitzmyer, and R. Murphy (Englewood Cliffs, N.J.: Prentice-Hall, 1968), p. 692; Judah Goldin, "The Period of the Talmud," in *The Jews: Their History,* ed. Louis Finkelstein (New York: Schocken, 1970), pp. 121–129.

13. *Encyclopedia Judaica,* s.v. "Talmud, Babylonia."

14. See Jacob Neusner, "Form and Meaning in the Mishnah," *JAAR,* 1977, *45*(1):27–54; "History and Structure: The Case of the Mishnah," *JAAR,* 1977, *45*(2):161–192; "Stable Symbols in a Shifting Society," *HR,* November 1985, *25*(2):163–175.

15. R. Travers Herford, *Pirke Aboth: The Ethics of the Talmud* (New York: Schocken, 1962).

16. Renée Bloch, "Midrash," in *Approaches to Ancient Judaism,* ed. William Scott Green (Missoula, Mont.: Scholars Press, 1978), pp. 19–50; Nahum N. Glatzer, ed., *Hammer on the Rock* (New York: Schocken, 1962).

17. Epstein, *Judaism,* pp. 121–194. On the Talmud's view of prophecy (which its law was somewhat trying to replace), see Nahum G. Glatzer, "A Study of the Talmudic-Midrashic Interpretation of Prophecy," in his *Essays in Jewish Thought* (University: University of Alabama Press, 1978), pp. 16–35.

18. See Jacob Neusner, ed., *The Life of Torah: Readings in the Jewish Religious Experience* (Encino, Calif.: Dickenson, 1974), pp. 17–24.

19. Epstein, *Judaism,* p. 140.

20. See Robert Goldenberg, *The Sabbath Law of Rabbi Meir* (Missoula, Mont.: Scholars Press, 1978), pp. 159–264.

21. For a contemporary view of the Sabbath, see Richard Siegel et al., *The Jewish Catalogue* (Philadelphia: Jewish Publication Society of America, n.d.), pp. 103–116.

22. For an overview of the medieval period, see Jacob B. Agus, *The Meaning of Jewish History,* vol. 2 (New York: Abelard-Schuman, 1963), pp. 232–297; Martin A. Cohen, "Judaism: Judaism in Southern Europe," *ER, 8,* 172–180; Ivan G. Marcur, "Judaism: Judaism in Northern and Eastern Europe to 1500," ibid., 180–186.

23. Epstein, *Judaism,* p. 180.

24. On this whole question, see S. D. Goitein, *Jews and Arabs* (New York: Schocken, 1955).

25. Epstein, *Judaism,* p. 191.

26. See Julius Gutmann, *Philosophies of Judaism* (New York: Holt, Rinehart and Winston, 1964).

27. Moses Maimonides, *The Guide for the Perplexed,* 2nd ed., trans. M. Friedlander (New York: Dover, 1956), p. 11; see also Ralph Lerner, "Maimonides' *Treatise on Resurrection,*" *HR,* November 1983, *23*(2):140–155.

28. R. J. Zwi Werblowsky, "Judaism, or the Religion of Israel," in *The Concise Encyclopedia of Living Faiths,* ed. R. C. Zaehner (Boston: Beacon Press, 1967), pp. 45–48; Arthur Green, "Religion and Mysticism: The Case of Judaism," in *Take Judaism, for Example,* ed. Jacob Neusner (Chicago: University of Chicago Press, 1983), pp. 67–91.

29. Gershom G. Scholem, *Major Trends in Jewish Mysticism* (New York: Schocken, 1961).

30. See J. Doresse, "Gnosticism," in *Historia Religionum, I,* ed. C. J. Bleeker and G. Widengren (Leiden: E. J. Brill, 1969), pp. 536–537.

31. Werblowsky, "Judaism," p. 24.

32. See Gershom G. Scholem, ed., *Zohar: The Book of Splendor* (New York: Schocken, 1963), pp. 12–21.

33. Agus, *Jewish History,* pp. 300–485; Cecil Roth, *A History of the Jews* (New York: Schocken, 1961), pp. 235–424.

34. Roth, *History of the Jews,* pp. 180–294.

35. Leon Poliakov, *The History of Anti-Semitism* (New York: Schocken, 1974).

36. See Elie Wiesel, *Souls on Fire* (New York: Vintage, 1973).

37. Mark Zborowski and Elizabeth Herzog, *Life Is with People* (New York: Schocken, 1962); Steven J. Zipperstein, "Judaism: Judaism in Northern and Eastern Europe since 1500," *ER, 8,* 186–195.

38. Meyer Levin, *Classic Hasidic Tales* (New York: Penguin Books, 1975), p. 125. We have adapted Levin's version of the story, found on pp. 125–131.

39. Martin Buber, *Hasidism and Modern Man* (New York: Harper Torchbooks, 1966).

40. Abraham J. Heschel, *Man's Quest for God* (New York: Scribner's, 1954), *God in Search of Man* (New York: Farrar, Straus & Giroux, 1955).

41. Agus, *The Meaning of Jewish History,* p. 152.

42. Jacob Neusner, *The Way of Torah,* 2nd ed. (Encino, Calif.: Dickenson, 1974), pp. 68–71.

43. Arthur Green, "The *Zaddiq* as Axis Mundi in Later Judaism," *JAAR,* 1977, *45*(3):327–347.

44. Martin Buber, *Tales of the Hasidim,* 2 vols. (New York: Schocken, 1947–48).

45. Elie Wiesel, *The Gates of the Forest* (New York: Avon, 1966), pp. 6–10.

46. On this conflict in the United States, see Sydney Ahlstrom, *A Religious History of the American People* (New Haven, Conn.: Yale University Press, 1972), pp. 969–984; also Neusner, *Life of Torah,* pp. 156–203.

47. Agus, *The Meaning of Jewish History,* p. 154.

48. Eva Fleischner, "A Select Annotated Bibliography on the Holocaust," *Horizons,* 1977, *4*(1):61–83; *Encyclopedia Judaica,* vol. 8 (Jerusalem: Keter, 1972), pp. 828–918.

49. See, for example, Rosemary Ruether, *Faith and Fratricide* (New York: Seabury, 1974).

50. See, for example, John L. McKenzie, *Dictionary of the Bible* (Milwaukee: Bruce, 1965); Paul J. Achtemeier, ed. *Harper's Bible Dictionary* (San Francisco: Harper & Row, 1985). *The Encyclopedia Judaica,* vol. 12 (Jerusalem: Keter, 1972), does have a three and one-half column article, but only twelve lines deal with the biblical period.

51. Werblowsky, "Judaism, or the Religion of Israel."

52. Geoffrey Wigoder et al., *Jewish Values* (Jerusalem: Keter, 1974).

53. Voegelin, *Order and History: IV,* chaps. 1, 3, 7.

54. Salo Wittmayer Baron, *A Social and Religious History of the Jews,* vol. 1, *Ancient Times,* 2nd ed. (New York: Columbia University Press, 1952), pp. 4–16.

55. Sherry B. Ortner, "Is Female to Male as Nature Is to Culture?" in *Woman, Culture and Society,* ed. M. Z. Rosaldo and L. Lamphere (Stanford, Calif.: Stanford University Press, 1974), pp. 67–88.

56. Phyllis Bird, "Images of Women in the Old Testament," in *Religion and Sexism,* ed. Rosemary Radford Ruether (New York: Simon & Schuster, 1974), pp. 41–88.

57. Judith Hauptmann, "Images of Women in the Talmud," in *Religion and Sexism,* ed. Rosemary Radford Ruether (New York: Simon & Schuster, 1974), pp. 184–212. On Mishnaic menstrual taboos, see Jacob Neusner, *A History of the Mishnaic Law of Purities* (Leiden: E. J. Brill, 1977), p. 22.

58. I. Epstein, "The Jewish Woman in the Responsa: 900 C.E.–1500 C.E.," *Response,* Summer 1973, no. 16, pp. 23–31.

59. For an overview of women in Judaism, see Denise Lardner Carmody, *Women and World Religions* (Nashville: Abingdon, 1979), pp. 92–112. For current issues, see Carol P. Christ and Judith Plaskow, eds., *Woman-spirit Rising* (New York: Harper & Row, 1979); Elizabeth Koltun, ed., *The Jewish Woman: New Perspectives* (New York: Schocken, 1976).

60. See his contributions to *The Life of Torah: Readings in the Jewish Religious Experiences,* ed. Jacob Neusner (Encino, Calif.: Dickenson, 1974), p. 104; see also Elliot R. Wolfson, "Circumcision, Vision of God, and Textual Interpretation," *HR,* November 1987, *27*(2):189–215.

61. Judith Plaskow, "Bringing a Daughter into the Covenant," in *Woman-spirit Rising,* ed. Carol P. Christ and Judith Plaskow (San Francisco: Harper & Row, 1980), p. 181.

62. See *The Jewish Catalogue,* ed. Richard Siegel et al. (Philadelphia: Jewish Publication Society of America, 1973), p. 158.

63. On this point, Robert L. Cohn reminded us of Hillel's saying, "Sever not thyself from the congregation" (*Pirke Avot,* 2:5). (Private communication.)

64. Richard L. Rubenstein, *After Auschwitz* (Indianapolis, Ind.: Bobbs-Merrill, 1966).

65. Emil Fackenheim, *God's Presence in History* (New York: New York University Press, 1970).

66. Hannah Arendt, *Eichmann in Jerusalem* (New York: Viking, 1965).

67. See Elie Wiesel, *The Oath* (New York: Random House, 1973).

68. See, for example, Joel Blocker, ed., *Israeli Stories* (New York: Schocken, 1965).

69. Michael Polanyi and Harry Prosch, *Meaning* (Chicago: University of Chicago Press, 1975). That does not mean, however, that the Talmud did not meditate deeply on Jewish divinity. See A. Cohen, *Everyman's Talmud* (New York: Schocken, 1975), pp. 1–26. For a contemporary view, see Leo Baeck, *The Essence of Judaism* (New York: Schocken, 1961), pp. 83–150.

70. Cynthia Ozick, "Ruth," in *Congregation,* ed. David Rosenberg (New York: Harcourt Brace Jovanovich, 1987), p. 373.

71. See Neusner, ed., *Life of Torah,* pp. 17–24.

Chapter 5

1. For a brief study of Christianity that includes fine maps of its spread, see Gerald Sloyan, "Christianity," in *Historical Atlas of the Religions of the World*, ed. I. al Faruqi and D. Sopher (New York: Macmillan, 1974), pp. 201–236; see also Jaroslov Pelikan, "Christianity: An Overview," *ER*, *3*, 348–362; and Williston Walker et al., *A History of the Christian Church*, 4th ed. (New York: Charles Scribner's Sons, 1985).

2. One of the most thorough recent treatments of the critical and theological issues concerning Jesus is Edward Schillebeeckx, *Jesus* (New York: Seabury, 1979).

3. See Raymond E. Brown, *The Birth of the Messiah* (New York: Doubleday, 1977).

4. Geza Vermes, *Jesus the Jew* (London: Fontana, 1976), pp. 18–82.

5. Joachim Jeremias, *New Testament Theology: The Proclamation of Jesus* (New York: Charles Scribner's Sons, 1971), pp. 29–36.

6. Karl Rahner and Herbert Vorgrimler, *Theological Dictionary* (New York: Herder and Herder, 1965), pp. 236–241.

7. A succinct discussion of New Testament ethics is J. L. Houden, *Ethics and the New Testament* (New York: Oxford University Press, 1977); see also Wayne A. Meeks, *The Moral World of the First Christians* (Philadelphia: Westminster, 1986).

8. Jeremias, *New Testament Theology*, pp. 250–257.

9. See Eric Voegelin, "The Gospel and Culture," in *Jesus and Man's Hope*, vol. 2, ed. D. Miller and D. Hadidian (Pittsburgh: Pittsburgh Theological Seminary, 1971), pp. 59–101.

10. Joseph A. Fitzmyer, "Pauline Theology," in *The Jerome Biblical Commentary*, vol. 2, ed. R. Brown, J. Fitzmyer, and R. Murphy (Englewood Cliffs, N.J.: Prentice-Hall, 1968), pp. 810–827.

11. Pheme Perkins, *Hearing the Parables of Jesus* (Ramsey, N.J.: Paulist Press, 1981), p. 94. Our treatment adapts pp. 94–98.

12. Recent and readable is Stephen Neill, *Jesus through Many Eyes* (Philadelphia: Fortress, 1976). For a literary stress, see Leonard L. Thompson, *Introducing Biblical Literature* (Englewood Cliffs, N.J.: Prentice-Hall 1978), pp. 213–307. For an overview of Jesus that includes a comparison with other great world religious figures, see Denise Lardner Carmody and John Tully Carmody, *Jesus: An Introduction* (Belmont, Calif.: Wadsworth, 1987); see also Jaroslav Pelikan, *Jesus through the Centuries* (New Haven, Conn.: Yale University Press, 1985).

13. Antonio Javierre, "Apostle," in *Sacramentum Mundi*, vol. 1, ed. Karl Rahner et al. (New York: Herder and Herder, 1968), p. 77.

14. Raymond E. Brown et al., eds. *Peter in the New Testament* (Minneapolis, Minn.: Augsburg, 1973).

15. See Maxwell Staniforth, trans., *Early Christian Writings* (Baltimore: Penguin, 1968).

16. J. Doresse, "Gnosticism," in *Historia Religionum, I*, ed. C. J. Bleeker and G. Widengren (Leiden: E. J. Brill, 1969), pp. 536–537.

17. Succinct information on personages such as these is available in F. L. Cross, ed., *The Oxford Dictionary of the Christian Church* (New York: Oxford University Press, 1966).

18. See Jaroslav Pelikan, *The Christian Tradition, 1: The Emergence of the Catholic Tradition* (Chicago: University of Chicago Press, 1971).

19. J. G. Davies, "Christianity: The Early Church," in *The Concise Encyclopedia of Living Faiths*, ed. R. C. Zaehner (Boston: Beacon Press, 1967), pp. 60–69; W. H. C. Frend, *The Rise of Christianity* (Philadelphia: Fortress, 1984).

20. On patristic terminology, see G. L. Prestige, *God in Patristic Thought* (London: Society for the Promotion of Christian Knowledge, 1959).

21. Bernard Lonergan, *The Way to Nicaea* (Philadelphia: Westminster, 1976); Charles Kannengiesser, S.J., "The Athanasian Decade 1974–1984: A Bibliographical Report," *Theological Studies*, September 1985, *46*(3):524–541; Francis M. Young, *From Nicaea to Chalcedon* (Philadelphia: Fortress, 1983); Robert C. Gregg and Dennis E. Groh, *Early Arianism: A View of Salvation* (Philadelphia: Fortress, 1983).

22. William A. Clebsch, *Christianity in European History* (New York: Oxford University Press, 1979), pp. 29–84; Stephen Reynolds, *The Christian Religious Tradition* (Encino, Calif.: Dickenson, 1977), pp. 35–77.

23. Thomas Merton, *The Wisdom of the Desert* (New York: New Directions, 1960).

24. Nicholas Zernov, "Christianity: The Eastern Schism and the Eastern Orthodox Church," in *The Concise Encyclopedia of Living Faiths*, ed. R. C. Zaehner (Boston: Beacon Press, 1967), p. 86; Stanley Samuel Harakac, "Christianity: Christianity in Eastern Europe," *ER*, *3*, 372–378.

25. Donald W. Treadgold, *The West in Russia and China*, vol. 1 (Cambridge: Cambridge University Press, 1973), pp. 1–23.

26. On classical Eastern theology, see Jaroslav Pelikan, *The Christian Tradition, 2: The Spirit of Eastern Christendom* (Chicago: University of Chicago Press, 1974); see also G. P. Fedotov, *The Russian Religious Mind* (Cambridge, Mass.: Harvard University Press, 1966).

27. See Timothy Ware, *The Orthodox Church* (Baltimore: Penguin, 1964).

28. Bernhard Schultze, "Eastern Churches," in *Sacramentum Mundi*, vol. 2, ed. Karl Rahner et al. (New York: Herder and Herder, 1968), pp. 120–130.

29. Sergius Bolshakoff and M. Basil Pennington, *In Search of True Wisdom: Visits to Eastern Spiritual Fathers* (Garden City, N.Y.: Doubleday, 1979).

30. C. W. Monnich, "Christianity," in *Historia Religionum, II,* ed. C. J. Bleeker and G. Widengren (Leiden: E. J. Brill, 1971), p. 65.

31. Jaroslav Pelikan, *The Christian Tradition, 3: The Growth of Medieval Theology* (Chicago: University of Chicago Press, 1978), pp. 268–307.

32. Anthony Kenney, ed., *Aquinas* (New York: Doubleday, 1969); see also H. Francis Davis, "St. Thomas and Medieval Theology," in *The Concise Encyclopedia of Living Faiths,* ed. R. C. Zaehner (Boston: Beacon Press, 1967), pp. 108–112.

33. Lawrence Cunningham and John Reich, *Culture and Values: A Survey of the Western Humanities,* vol. 2 (New York: Holt, Rinehart and Winston, 1982), p. 99. Our treatment adapts pp. 99–103.

34. On the history of the notion of reform, see Gerhart B. Ladner, *The Idea of Reform* (Cambridge, Mass.: Harvard University Press, 1959).

35. Erik H. Erikson, *Young Man Luther* (New York: Norton, 1962).

36. *The New Columbia Encyclopedia,* s.v. "plague."

37. See Pennethorne Hughes, *Witchcraft* (Baltimore: Penguin, 1965).

38. John Kent, "Christianity: Protestantism," in *The Concise Encyclopedia of Living Faiths,* ed. R. C. Zaehner (Boston: Beacon Press, 1967), pp. 117–149; Martin E. Marty, "Protestantism," *ER, 12,* 23–38.

39. Owen Chadwick, *The Reformation* (Baltimore: Penguin, 1964), p. 41.

40. See Lewis Spitz, ed., *The Protestant Reformation* (Englewood Cliffs, N.J.: Prentice-Hall, 1966).

41. C. W. Monnich, "Christianity," p. 72.

42. See William A. Clebsch, *American Religious Thought* (Chicago: University of Chicago Press, 1973), pp. 11–56; Edward S. Gaustad, ed., *A Documentary History of Religion in America,* vol. 1 (Grand Rapids, Mich.: Erdmans, 1982).

43. James Brodrick, *The Origin of the Jesuits* (London: Longmans, 1940); *The Progress of the Jesuits* (London: Longmans, 1946).

44. Sidney E. Mead, *The Lively Experiment* (New York: Harper & Row, 1976); *The Nation with the Soul of a Church* (New York: Harper & Row, 1975); see also Sydney E. Ahlstrom, *A Religious History of the American People* (New Haven, Conn.: Yale University Press, 1972), pp. 121–229.

45. Harvey D. Egan, *The Spiritual Exercises and the Ignatian Mystical Horizon* (St. Louis: Institute of Jesuit Sources, 1976); Gaston Fessard, *La dialectique des exercices spirituels de Saint Ignace de Loyola* (Paris: Aubier, 1956); Antonio T. De Nicolas, *Powers of Imagining: Ignatius de Loyola* (Albany: State University of New York Press, 1986).

46. Robert McAfee Brown, *The Spirit of Protestantism* (New York: Oxford University Press, 1965); Jaroslav Pelikan, *The Christian Tradition,* vol. 4 (Chicago: University of Chicago Press, 1984).

47. Max Weber, *The Protestant Ethic and the Spirit of Capitalism* (New York: Charles Scribner's Sons, 1958).

48. Heribert Raab, "Enlightenment," in *Sacramentum Mundi,* vol. 2, ed. Karl Rahner et al. (New York: Herder and Herder, 1968), p. 230; see also Crane Brinton, "Enlightenment," in *The Encyclopedia of Philosophy,* vol. 2, ed. Paul Edwards (New York: Macmillan, 1967), pp. 519–525; Allen W. Wood, "Enlightenment, The," *ER, 5,* 109–113; George Alfred James, "Atheism," *ER, 1,* 479–490.

49. See the articles by Sidney E. Mead, Sydney E. Ahlstrom, Vincent Harding, and Robert Bellah in *Soundings,* 1978, *61*(3):303–371.

50. Eric Voegelin, *From Enlightenment to Revolution* (Durham, N.C.: Duke University Press, 1975).

51. The breakthrough work was Gustavo Gutierrez, *A Theology of Liberation* (Maryknoll, N.Y.: Orbis, 1973). Especially provocative is Jose Miranda, *Marx and the Bible* (Maryknoll, N.Y.: Orbis, 1974). A fine survey that brings liberation thought to the United States is Robert McAfee Brown, *Theology in a New Key* (Philadelphia: Westminster, 1978).

52. See Sergio Torres and John Eagleson, eds., *Theology in the Americas* (Maryknoll, N.Y.: Orbis, 1976).

53. Martin E. Marty, *Righteous Empire* (New York: Dial Press, 1970).

54. Robert Bellah, *The Broken Covenant* (New York: Seabury, 1975).

55. Emilie Griffin, *Turning: The Experience of Conversion* (Garden City, N.Y.: Doubleday, 1980). We especially draw on pp. 31–49; see also Walter E. Conn, *Christian Conversion* (New York: Paulist Press, 1986).

56. Jorg Splett et al., "Nature," in *Sacramentum Mundi,* vol. 4, ed. Karl Rahner et al. (New York: Herder and Herder, 1969), pp. 171–181.

57. Pieter Smulders et al., "Creation," in *Sacramentum Mundi,* vol. 2, ed. Karl Rahner et al. (New York: Herder and Herder, 1968), pp. 23–37; Conrad Hyers, *The Meaning of Creation* (Atlanta: John Knox, 1984).

58. See Harold K. Schilling, *The New Consciousness in Science and Religion* (Philadelphia: United Church Press, 1973).

59. Alfred North Whitehead, *Process and Reality* (New York: Harper Torchbooks, 1960).

60. See Staniforth, *Early Christian Writings,* pp. 171–185.

61. See Bernard Cooke, *Ministry to Word and Sacrament* (Philadelphia: Fortress, 1976); Monika K. Hellwig, "Christian Sacraments," *ER, 12,* 504–511.

62. Edward Schillebeeckx, *Christ: The Sacrament of Encounter with God* (New York: Sheed & Ward, 1963).

63. Mary Daly, *Gyn/Ecology* (Boston: Beacon Press, 1979), chap. 6.

64. Denise Lardner Carmody, *Women and World Religions* (Nashville: Abingdon, 1979), pp. 113–136; Carol P. Christ and Judith Plaskow, eds., *Woman-spirit Rising* (New York: Harper & Row, 1979); Elizabeth Clark and Herbert

Richardon, eds., *Women and Religion* (New York: Harper & Row, 1977); Rosemary Radford Ruether, ed., *Religion and Sexism* (New York: Simon & Schuster, 1974); Mary Daly, *The Church and the Second Sex* (New York: Harper Colophon, 1975); Elisabeth Schüssler Fiorenza, *In Memory of Her* (New York: Crossroad, 1983); George H. Tavard, *Women in Christian Tradition* (Notre Dame, Ind.: University of Notre Dame Press, 1973); Rosemary Radford Ruether and Rosemary Skinner Keller, eds. *Women & Religion in America,* 3 vols. (San Francisco: Harper & Row, 1983).

65. Steven Runciman, *The Orthodox Churches and the Secular State* (Auckland: Auckland University Press, 1971).

66. Karl Rahner, *The Shape of the Church to Come* (New York: Seabury, 1974).

67. See Vladimir Lossky, *The Mystical Theology of the Eastern Church* (Crestwood, N.Y.: St. Vladimir's Seminary Press, 1976); Alexander Schmemann, ed., *Ultimate Questions* (Crestwood, N.Y.: St. Vladimir's Seminary Press, 1977); Marina Warner, *Alone of All Her Sex* (New York: Alfred A. Knopf, 1976).

68. John L. McKenzie, S. J., *The Power and the Wisdom* (Milwaukee, Wis.: Bruce, 1965), pp. 252–255.

69. *The Book of Common Prayer* (New York: Seabury, 1977), p. 308. Our description of the sacramental rituals depends on the *Book of Common Prayer;* see also Charles L. Rice, "Preaching," *ER, 11,* 494–501.

70. A profound interpretation is Karl Rahner's "Thomas Aquinas on the Incomprehensibility of God," *Journal of Religion,* 1978, *58,* supp., 107–125; see also Paul Ricoeur, " 'Response' to Karl Rahner's Lecture on the Incomprehensibility of God," ibid., 126–131; for early Christian background, see Robert M. Grant, *Gods and the One God* (Philadelphia: Westminster, 1986).

71. On the Christian life as a reflection of Jesus' death and resurrection, see Alan Paton, *Ah, But Your Land Is Beautiful* (New York: Charles Scribner's Sons, 1982).

Chapter 6

1. There are good maps on the spread of Islam in Geoffrey Barraclough, ed., *The Times Atlas of World History* (Maplewood, N.J.: Hammond, 1979), pp. 104–105, 134–135, 138–139; see also I. al Faruqi and D. Sopher, eds., *Historical Atlas of the Religions of the World* (New York: Macmillan, 1974), pp. 237–281.

2. Annemarie Schimmel, "Islam," in *Historia Religionum, II,* ed. C. J. Bleeker and G. Widengren (Leiden: E. J. Brill, 1971), p. 127; Fazlur Rahman, "Islam: An Overview," *ER, 7,* 303–322; Isma'il R. al Faruqi and Lois Lamya' al Faruqi, *The Cultural Atlas of Islam* (New York: Macmillan, 1986).

3. W. Montgomery Watt, *Muhammad: Prophet and Statesman* (New York: Oxford University Galaxy Books, 1974), pp. 45–55; W. Montgomery Watt, "Muhammad," *ER 10,* 137–146.

4. We have used the translation by A. J. Arberry, *The Koran Interpreted* (New York: Macmillan, 1973).

5. Watt, *Muhammad,* p. 7.

6. On the pre-Islamic background, see Ignaz Goldziher, *Muslim Studies,* vol. 1 (Chicago: Aldine, 1967), pp. 11–44; Marshall G. S. Hodgson, *The Venture of Islam,* vol. 1 (Chicago: University of Chicago Press, 1974), pp. 103–145; M. M. Bravmann, *The Spiritual Background of Early Islam* (Leiden: E. J. Brill, 1972).

7. Schimmel, "Islam," p. 129.

8. Isma'il al Faruqi, "Islam," in *Historical Atlas of the Religions of the World,* ed. I. al Faruqi and D. Sopher (New York: Macmillan, 1974), p. 241.

9. Charles J. Adams, "The Islamic Religious Tradition," in *Judaism, Christianity and Islam,* ed. J. O'Dea, T. O'Dea, and C. Adams (New York: Harper & Row, 1972), p. 166.

10. H. A. R. Gibb, *Mohammedanism,* 2nd ed. (New York: Oxford University Press, 1962), p. 30.

11. See Watt, *Muhammad,* pp. 229–231.

12. H. A. R. Gibb, "Islam," in *The Concise Encyclopedia of Living Faiths,* ed. R. C. Zaehner (Boston: Beacon Press, 1967), p. 179.

13. N. J. Dawood, trans., *The Koran* (Baltimore: Penguin, 1968), p. 10.

14. Kenneth Cragg, *The House of Islam,* 2nd ed. (Encino, Calif.: Dickenson, 1975), pp. 30–34; Arberry, *Koran Interpreted,* p. 28; Charles J. Adams, "Qur'an: The Text and Its History," *ER, 12,* 156–176; Mahmoud M. Ayoub, "Qur'an: Its Role in Muslim Piety," ibid., 176–179.

15. Arthur Jeffrey, ed., *Islam: Muhammad and His Religion* (New York: Bobbs-Merrill, 1975); Isma'il al Faruqi, "Islam," in *The Great Asian Religions,* ed. W. T. Chan et al. (New York: Macmillan, 1969), pp. 307–395.

16. On the development of the *Hadith,* see Ignaz Goldziher, *Muslim Studies,* vol. 2 (Chicago: Aldine, 1975), pp. 17–251; L. T. Librande, "Hadith," *ER, 6,* 143–151.

17. Cragg, *House of Islam,* pp. 5–18.

18. See Martin Lings, *A Sufi Saint of the Twentieth Century,* 2nd ed. (Berkeley: University of California Press, 1973), pp. 121–130; R. C. Zaehner, *Hindu and Muslim Mysticism* (New York: Schocken, 1969), pp. 86–109; Annemarie Schimmel, *The Mystical Dimension of Islam* (Chapel Hill: University of North Carolina Press, 1978); Seyyed Hossein Nasr, ed., *Islamic Spirituality: Foundations* (New York: Crossroad, 1987).

19. W. Montgomery Watt, *The Faith and Practice of al-Ghazali* (London: Allen & Unwin, 1953), pp. 90–130.

20. See Cheikh Hamidou Kane, *Ambiguous Adventure* (New York: Collier, 1969).

21. Cragg, *House of Islam,* pp. 73–108; Frederick Mathewson Denny, "The Meaning of *Ummah* in the Qur'an," *HR,* 1975, *15:*34–70.

22. Dawood, trans., *The Koran,* p. 32. Our treatment of this sura draws on pp. 32–37.

23. See Geoffrey Parrinder, *Jesus in the Qur'an* (New York: Oxford University Press, 1977).

24. al Faruqi, "Islam," in *Historical Atlas*, p. 248.

25. Bernard Lewis, *The Arabs in History*, rev. ed. (New York: Harper Torchbooks, 1966), p. 55; see also Edmund Bosworth, "Armies of the Prophet," in *Islam and the Arab World*, ed. Bernard Lewis (New York: Knopf, 1976), pp. 201–224; V. J. Parry, "Warfare," in *The Cambridge History of Islam*, vol. 2, ed. P. M. Holt et al. (Cambridge: University Press, 1970), pp. 824–850.

26. Lewis, *Arabs in History*, p. 56.

27. See Hodgson, *The Venture of Islam*, pp. 187–217.

28. See W. Montgomery Watt, *The Formative Period of Islamic Thought* (Edinburgh: University Press, 1973), pp. 253–278.

29. Stephen F. Mason, *A History of the Sciences*, rev. ed. (New York: Collier, 1962), p. 95; see also A. I. Sabra, "The Scientific Enterprise," in *Islam and the Arab World*, ed. Bernard Lewis (New York: Alfred A. Knopf, 1976), pp. 181–200; G. Anawati, "Science, in *The Cambridge History of Islam*, vol. 2, ed. P. M. Holt et al. (Cambridge: University Press, 1970), pp. 741–779.

30. Albert C. Moore, *Iconography of the Religions: An Introduction* (Philadelphia: Fortress, 1977), pp. 213–226; see also Richard Ettinghausen, "The Man-Made Setting," in *Islam and the Arab World*, ed. Bernard Lewis (New York: Alfred A. Knopf, 1976), pp. 57–88; G. Fehervari, "Art and Architecture," in *The Cambridge History of Islam*, vol. 2, ed. P. M. Holt et al. (Cambridge: University Press, 1970), pp. 702–740; al Faruqi, *The Cultural Atlas of Islam*, pp. 336–440.

31. Schuyler V. R. Cammann, "Religious Symbolism in Persian Art," *HR*, 1976, *15:*193–205.

32. Oleg Grabar, "Architecture," in *The Legacy of Islam*, 2nd ed., ed. Joseph Schacht and C. E. Bosworth (New York: Oxford University Press, 1979), p. 263.

33. A. J. Arberry, *Aspects of Islamic Civilization* (Ann Arbor: University of Michigan Press, 1967); see also Charles Pellah, "Jewellers with Words," in *Islam and the Arab World*, ed. Bernard Lewis (New York: Alfred A. Knopf, 1976), pp. 141–160; Irfan Shahid et al., "Literature," in *The Cambridge History of Islam*, vol. 2, ed. P. M. Holt et al. (Cambridge: University Press, 1970), pp. 657–701.

34. Oleg Grabar, "Cities and Citizens," in *Islam and the Arab World*, ed. Bernard Lewis (New York: Alfred A. Knopf, 1976), pp. 89–116.

35. Arberry, *Aspects of Islamic Civilization*, p. 257.

36. Ibid.

37. Ibid., p. 111.

38. See J. Schacht, "Laws and Justice," in *The Cambridge History of Islam*, vol. 2, ed. P. M. Holt et al. (Cambridge: University Press, 1970), pp. 539–568; Ann Elizabeth Mayer, "Islamic Law: Shari'ah," *ER, 7*, 431–446; M. Hashim Kamali, "Islamic Law: Personal Law," ibid., pp. 446–453.

39. Fazlur Rahman, *Islam* (Garden City, N.Y.: Doubleday, 1968), p. xxii.

40. al Faruqi, "Islam," in *Historical Atlas*, p. 267.

41. Martin Lings, *What Is Sufism?* (Berkeley: University of California Press, 1977), pp. 45–46; A. J. Arberry, *Sufism* (New York: Harper Torchbooks, 1970), p. 35; Peter J. Awn, "Sufism," *ER, 14*, 104–122.

42. Watt, *Al-Ghazali*, p. 57.

43. Ibid., p. 60.

44. Idries Shah, *The Way of the Sufi* (New York: Dutton, 1970).

45. Ibid., p. 162.

46. Ibid., p. 169.

47. Arberry, *Sufism*, p. 119.

48. Richard M. Eaton, "Sufi Folk Literature and the Expansion of Indian Islam," *HR*, 1974, *14:*117–127.

49. Lings, *Sufi Saint;* see also Clifford Geertz, *Islam Observed* (Chicago: University of Chicago Press, 1971).

50. See Roger Le Tourneau et al., "Africa and the Muslim West," in *The Cambridge History of Islam*, vol. 2, ed. P. M. Holt et al. (Cambridge: University Press, 1970), pp. 209–405; Benjamin Ray, *African Religions* (Englewood Cliffs, N.J.: Prentice-Hall, 1976), pp. 174–191; Nehemiah Levtzion, "Islam: Islam in Sub-Sahara Africa," *ER, 7*, 344–357.

51. Lewis, *Arabs in History*, p. 144.

52. See Norman Itzkowitz, "The Ottoman Empire," in *Islam and the Arab World*, ed. Bernard Lewis (New York: Alfred A. Knopf, 1976), pp. 273–300.

53. Roger M. Savory, "Land of the Lion and the Sun," in *Islam and the Arab World*, ed. Bernard Lewis (New York: Alfred A. Knopf, 1976), pp. 245–272.

54. S. A. A. Rizi, "Muslim India," in *Islam and the Arab World*, ed. Bernard Lewis (New York: Alfred A. Knopf, 1976), pp. 301–320; see also I. H. Qureshi et al., "The Indian Sub-Continent," in *The Cambridge History of Islam*, vol. 2, ed. P. M. Holt et al. (Cambridge: University Press, 1970), pp. 1–120; Peter Hardy, "Islam: Islam in South Asia," *ER, 7*, 390–404.

55. Lewis, *Arabs in History*, pp. 158–159.

56. See Rahman, *Islam*, pp. 237–260.

57. Gibb, "Islam," p. 207.

58. See Wilfred Cantwell Smith, *The Meaning and End of Religion* (New York: Mentor, 1964), p. 79.

59. Anne Sinai and Allen Pollack, *The Syrian Arab Republic* (New York: American Academic Association for Peace in the Middle East, 1976); *The Hashemite Kingdom of Jordan and the West Bank* (New York: American Academic Association for Peace in the Middle East, 1977).

60. Islamic (Student) Association of Cairo University, "Lessons from Iran," in *Islam in Transition*, ed. John J. Donohue and John L. Esposito (New York: Oxford University Press, 1982), p. 246.

61. Ayatullah Ruhullah Khumayni (*sic*), "Islamic Government," *Islam in Transition*, ed. John J. Donohue and John L. Esposito (New York: Oxford University Press, 1982), p. 318 (both quotations).

62. al Faruqi, "Islam," in *Great Asian Religions*, p. 308.

63. Ibid., p. 310.

64. Ibid.

65. Schimmel, "Islam," p. 186.

66. al Faruqi, "Islam," in *Great Asian Religions*, p. 359.

67. Ibid., p. 366.

68. Ibid., p. 374.

69. See Schimmel, "Islam," pp. 160–166.

70. Ibid., p. 163.

71. For an overview, see Denise Lardner Carmody, *Women and World Religions* (Nashville: Abingdon, 1979), pp. 137–155; Jane I. Smith, "Islam," in *Women in World Religions*, ed. Arvind Sharma (Albany: State University of New York Press, 1987), pp. 235–250. On recent attitudes, see Elizabeth Warnock Fernea and Basima Qattan Bezirgan, *Middle Eastern Muslim Woman Speak* (Austin: University of Texas Press, 1977).

72. Joseph Graziani, "The Status of Women in The Contemporary Muslim Arab Family," *Middle East Review*, 1976–77, *9*:48.

73. *Ms.*, March 1977, p. 112.

74. Kari Ka'us Iskander, *A Mirror for Princes* (London: Cresset, 1951), p. 125.

75. George Allgrove, *Love in the East* (London: Gibbs and Phillips, 1962), p. 128.

76. Mary Daly, *Gyn/Ecology* (Boston: Beacon Press, 1979), chap. 5.

77. Jane I. Smith and Yvonne Haddad, "Women in the Afterlife: The Islamic View as Seen from the Qur'an and Tradition," *JAAR*, 1975, *43*:39–50.

78. See Goldziher, *Muslim Studies*, vol. 2, pp. 366–368.

79. On scholarship and saintliness, the Sufis somewhat sponsored women, though their overall view of women was ambivalent; see Schimmel, *Mystical Dimensions of Islam*, pp. 426–435.

80. Watt, *Formative Period of Islamic Thought*.

81. See J. E. Esslemont, *Bahaa'u'llah and the New Era: An Introduction to the Baha'i Faith* (Wilmette, Ill.: Baha'i Books, 1970); Alessandro Bausani, "Baha'is," *ER, 2*, 40–42.

82. This section adapts Patrick J. Ryan's *Imale: Yoruba Participation in the Muslim Tradition* (Missoula, Mont.: Scholars Press, 1978), pp. 249–270; see also John Pemberton III, "Yoruba Religion," *ER, 15*, pp. 535–538.

83. Cragg, *House of Islam*, p. 60.

84. al Faruqi, "Islam," in *Great Asian Religions*, p. 347.

85. Schimmel, "Islam," p. 179.

86. This section draws on Clifford Geertz, *Islam Observed* (Chicago: University of Chicago Press, 1971), pp. 25–35; see also James L. Peacock, "The Creativity of Tradition in Indonesian Religion," *HR*, May 1986, *25*(4):341–351.

87. For a sensitive study of the meaning of *Islam*, more suitable for the end of our survey than the beginning, see Jane I. Smith, *An Historical and Semantic Study of the Term Islam as Seen in a Sequence of Quran Commentaries* (Missoula, Mont.: Scholars Press, 1975).

88. Schimmel, "Islam," p. 142.

89. On the Mutazila, see Watt, *Formative Period of Islamic Thought*, pp. 209–250.

90. See S. Pines, "Philosophy," in *The Cambridge History of Islam*, vol. 2, ed. P. M. Holt et al. (Cambridge: University Press, 1970), pp. 780–823.

91. Earle Waugh, "En Islam Iranien," *HR*, 1975, *14*:322–323.

92. See Gustave Thaiss, "Religious Symbolism and Social Change: The Drama of Husain," in *Scholars, Saints, and Sufis*, ed. Nikki R. Kiddie (Berkeley: University of California Press, 1972), pp. 349–366.

93. Fatima Mernissi, "Women, Saints, and Sanctuaries," *Signs*, 1977, *3*(1):101–112.

94. Schimmel, "Islam," p. 168.

Chapter 7

1. See Bryan Wilson, "Secularization," *ER, 13*, 159–165; Phillip Hammond, ed., *The Sacred in a Secular Age* (Berkeley: University of California Press, 1985); Mary Douglas and Steven Tipton, eds., *Religion and America; Spirituality in a Secular Age* (Boston: Beacon Press, 1983).

2. See Kees Bolle, "Myth: An Overview," and Paul Ricoeur, "Myth and History," *ER, 10*, 261–273, 273–282.

3. See Shaye J. D. Cohen, *From the Maccabees to the Mishnah* (Philadelphia: Westminster, 1987).

4. See Joseph Needham, *Science and Civilization in China* (Cambridge: University Press, 1969).

5. See Stanley Jaki, *The Road of Science and the Ways to God* (Chicago: University of Chicago Press, 1978).

6. See Robin W. Lovin and Frank E. Reynolds, ed., *Cosmogony and Ethical Order* (Chicago: University of Chicago Press, 1985).

7. See Stephen Toulmin, *Human Understanding* (Princeton, N.J.: Princeton University Press, 1972), and Thomas S. Kuhn, *The Structure of Scientific Revolutions*, 2nd ed. (Chicago: University of Chicago Press, 1970).

8. See James Gordon Clapp, "Locke, John," *The Encyclopedia of Philosophy*, vol. 4, ed. Paul Edwards (New York: Macmillan, 1967), pp. 487–503.

9. See Robert Heilbroner, *Marxism: For and Against* (New York: Norton, 1980); Eric Voegelin, *Science, Politics and Gnosticism* (Chicago: Henry Regnery, 1968), and *From Enlightenment to Revolution* (Durham, N.C.: Duke University Press, 1975); Karl Löwith, *From Hegel to Nietzsche* (Garden City, N.Y.: Doubleday Anchor, 1967); Charles C. West, "Marxism," *ER, 9*, 240–249.

10. See Rosemary Haughton, *The Transformation of Man* (Springfield, Ill.: Templegate, 1967), pp. 153–280.

Conclusion

1. C. G. Jung, *Memories, Dreams, Reflections* (New York: Vintage, 1963), p. 235.

2. In our view, Mircea Eliade shows that persuasively; see his *Shamanism* (Princeton, N.J.: Princeton University Press/Bollingen, 1972); *Yoga* (Princeton, N.J.: Princeton University Press/Bollingen, 1970).

3. See Wilfred Cantwell Smith, *The Meaning and End of Religion* (New York: Mentor, 1964); on the rise of the term *religio* with Cicero, see Eric Voegelin, *Order and History,* vol. 4 (Baton Rouge: Louisiana State University Press, 1974), pp. 43–48; Winston L. King, "Religion," *ER, 12,* 282–293.

4. See Joachim Wach, *The Comparative Study of Religions* (New York: Columbia University Press, 1961).

5. Three recent works that illumine religious traditioning are Huston Smith, *Forgotten Truth: The Primordial Tradition* (New York: Harper & Row, 1976); E. F. Schumacher, *A Guide for the Perplexed* (New York: Harper & Row, 1977); Peter Slater, *The Dynamics of Religion* (New York: Harper & Row, 1978).

6. This is a theme in John Bowker, *The Sense of God* (Oxford: Clarendon Press, 1973).

7. See Voegelin, *Order and History,* vol. 4, pp. 330–335.

8. See Marcel Griaule, *Conversations with Ogotemmeli* (New York: Oxford University Press, 1965).

9. Huston Smith, "Frithjof Schuon's *The Transcendent Unity of Religion:* Pro," and Richard C. Bush, "Frithjof Schuon's *The Transcendent Unity of Religion:* Con," *JAAR,* 1976, *44:*715–719, 721–724.

10. On religious interpretations of American destiny, see Conrad Cherry, ed., *God's New Israel* (Englewood Cliffs, N.J.: Prentice-Hall, 1971).

11. William A. Clebsch, *American Religious Thought* (Chicago: University of Chicago Press, 1973).

12. Sidney Mead, *The Lively Experiment* (New York: Harper & Row, 1976); R. Laurence Moore, *Religious Outsiders and the Making of Americans* (New York: Oxford University Press, 1986); *The Bible in America,* ed. Nathan O. Hatch and Mark A. Noll (New York: Oxford University Press, 1982).

13. On American pluralism, see *Soundings,* 1978, *61*(3), entire issue.

ANNOTATED BIBLIOGRAPHY

Introduction:
On the Study of World Religions

Carmody, Denise Lardner. *Women and World Religions,* 2nd ed. Englewood Cliffs, N.J.: Prentice-Hall, 1988. A survey of female images and roles in the major religious traditions that describes what being religious as a female has meant in the past and means today.

Carmody, Denise Lardner, and Carmody, John Tully. *Religion: The Great Questions.* San Francisco: Harper & Row, 1983. A comparative study of the major traditions in terms of their positions on the central existential questions of evil, the good life, and so on.

Eliade, Mircea. *The Sacred and the Profane.* New York: Harcourt, Brace & World, 1959. A concise statement of Eliade's view that human beings try to find meaning by making sacred the primary realities of their lives.

Hall, T. William, general editor. *Introduction to the Study of Religion.* San Francisco: Harper & Row, 1978. A team of scholars from Syracuse University tackles the major conceptual topics.

Hick, John H. *Philosophy of Religion,* 3rd ed. Englewood Cliffs, N.J.: Prentice-Hall, 1983. A good survey of the main problems and concepts involved in the study of religion.

Lovin, Robin W., and Reynolds, Frank E., ed. *Cosmogony and Ethical Order.* Chicago: University of Chicago Press, 1985. Studies dealing with how numerous religious traditions have tried to root their ethical systems in the order given at the birth of the physical world.

Smart, Ninian, and Hecht, Richard D., eds. *Sacred Texts of the World: A Universal Anthology.* New York: Crossroad, 1982. A good collection of primary sources on all the traditions that we treat.

Stewart, David, ed. *Exploring the Philosophy of Religion.* Englewood Cliffs, N.J.: Prentice-Hall, 1988. A reader of selections from primary sources in the history of Western thought about religious experience, God, faith, religious language, evil, and death.

Whaling, Frank, ed. *The World's Religious Traditions.* New York: Crossroad, 1986. Essays in honor of Winfred Cantwell Smith, a pioneer in elucidating the function of religious traditions, which examine both what "tradition" has tended to mean in the major world religions and how scholars now tend to approach the study of religious traditions.

Wilson, John F. *Religion: A Preface.* Englewood Cliffs, N.J.: Prentice-Hall, 1982. A short overview of the problems and traditions that one must consider in studying world religion—weak on the East but good on modernity.

Chapter 1:
The Ancient Religious Mind

Auel, Jean M. *The Clan of the Cave Bear.* New York: Bantam, 1981. A persuasive novel about Neanderthal life that focuses on women's roles.

Campbell, Joseph. *The Masks of God: Primitive Mythology.* New York: Viking, 1970. A readable interpretation of prehistoric culture from a Jungian point of view.

Carmody, Denise Lardner. *The Oldest God: Archaic Religion Yesterday and Today.* Nashville: Abingdon, 1981. A study of the ancient religious mentality from prehistoric times to the present.

Gimbutas, Marija. *The Goddesses and Gods of Old Europe: 6500–3500 B.C.* Berkeley: University of California Press, 1982. Reports and guarded speculation about the findings of archeological excavations of prehistoric sites in Eastern Europe. Primary focus is on the varieties of goddesses and fertility figures found.

Jensen, Adolf E. *Myth and Cult among Primitive Peoples.* Chicago: University of Chicago Press, 1963. A rather speculative account of the interaction of stories and ritual actions in terms of the primary mysteries of the lives of hunter-gatherers.

Kurtén, Björn. *Dance of the Tiger.* New York: Berkeley Books, 1981. A good novel focused on the interaction of Neanderthals and Sapientes, by a leading European paleontologist.

Maringer, Johannes. *The Gods of Prehistoric Man.* New York: Knopf, 1960. A dated but lucid reconstruction of religion from early Paleolithic to late prehistoric times.

Marshack, Alexander. *The Roots of Civilization.* New York: McGraw-Hill, 1972. Studies in the cultural significance of archeological remains suggesting early human beings' efforts to calculate the seasons of nature and correlate them with the habits of the game they hunted.

Roe, Derek. *Prehistory.* Berkeley: University of California Press, 1972. A basic survey of the period from the Old Stone Age to the Iron Age.

Tanner, Nancy Makepeace. *On Becoming Human*. New York: Cambridge University Press, 1981. An anthropological study of the evolution from apes to human beings.

Chapter 2:
Religions of Recent Nonliterate Peoples

Coles, Robert. *Children of Crisis*. Vol. 4: *Eskimos, Chicanos, Indians*. Boston: Little, Brown, 1977. Case studies of Eskimo, Chicano, and American Indian children that beautifully describe their current share of their rich traditions.

Eliade, Mircea. *Australian Religions*. Ithaca, N.Y.: Cornell University Press, 1973. A somewhat demanding application of Eliade's theories to the data available on Australian aborigines.

Gill, Sam D. *Beyond the Primitive: The Religions of Nonliterate Peoples*. Englewood Cliffs, N.J.: Prentice-Hall, 1982. A good theoretical orientation to the study of nonliterate peoples, informed by recent cultural anthropology and laced with many examples.

Harner, Michael. *The Way of the Shaman*. San Francisco: Harper & Row, 1980. A clear presentation of the nonordinary reality used by shamans, with many tips on how to adapt shamanic techniques to current Western life.

Hultkrantz, Ake. *The Religions of the American Indians*. Berkeley: University of California Press, 1979. A topical study of the main ideas, institutions, and ritual concerns of both the tribes of North and South America and the high cultures of the Incas, Mayas, and Aztecs.

Rasmussen, Knud. *Across Arctic America*. New York: Putnam's, 1927. A firsthand account of Eskimo customs by an explorer sensitive to the richness of Eskimo religion.

Turnbull, Colin M. *The Forest People*. New York: Simon & Schuster, 1962. A study of the pygmies of the Congo by an anthropologist who came to know and love them well enough to be adopted into their tribe.

Turnbull, Colin M. *The Human Cycle*. New York: Simon & Schuster, 1983. Studies illuminating the key moments of the human life cycle from the author's anthropological experience among several African tribes.

Underhill, Ruth M. *Red Man's Religion*. Chicago: University of Chicago Press, 1965. A readable introduction, rich in details, to the principal beliefs and practices of American Indians north of Mexico.

Zahan, Dominique. *The Religion, Spirituality and Thought of Traditional Africa*. Chicago: University of Chicago Press, 1979. An interesting attempt to sketch the general belief system and ritualistic world views of Africans not greatly influenced by Islam or Christianity.

Chapter 3:
Religions of Ancient Near Eastern Civilizations

Burkert, Walter. *Structure and History in Greek Mythology and Ritual*. Berkeley: University of California Press, 1979. An historical investigation that finds a continuous tradition evolving from Paleolithic to Hellenistic times.

Eliade, Mircea. *A History of Religious Ideas*, I–III. Chicago: University of Chicago Press, 1978, 1982, 1985. These volumes have chapters on Greece, Iran, and Egypt that place these countries in the overall history of religious ideas.

Foy, Whittfield, ed. *Man's Religious Quest: A Reader*. New York: St. Martin's, 1977. This volume includes interesting texts from Greece and Iran.

Frankfort, Henri, et al. *Before Philosophy*. Baltimore: Penguin, 1949. A classic popular presentation of the mythical thought of Egypt and Mesopotamia.

Frye, Richard. *The Heritage of Persia*. New York: World, 1963. An informative if rather fact-laden history of ancient Iran.

Guthrie, W.K.C. *The Greeks and Their Gods*. Boston: Beacon Press, 1955. A thorough commentary on the religion of classical Greece.

Jacobsen, Thorkild. *The Treasures of Darkness: A History of Mesopotamian Religion*. New Haven, Conn.: Yale University Press, 1976. A solid overview by one of the leading scholars and interpreters of Mesopotamian mythology.

Pritchard, James B., ed. *Ancient Near Eastern Texts Relating to the Old Testament*, 3rd ed. Princeton, N.J.: Princeton University Press, 1969. The standard source for key Mesopotamian and Egyptian texts, arranged according to genres for easy comparison.

Renault, Mary. *The Last of the Wine*. New York: Pocket Books, 1964. One of her several historical novels that absorbingly reconstruct the classical Greek world—in this case, that of Socrates and Plato.

Ringgren, Helmer. *Religions of the Ancient Near East*. Philadelphia: Westminster, 1973. A good introduction to Mesopotamian religions.

Wilson, John A. *The Culture of Ancient Egypt*. Chicago: University of Chicago Press, 1956. A general history, not too difficult and good on the principal ideas.

Chapter 4:
Judaism

Carmody, John, Carmody, Denise Lardner, and Cohn, Robert L. *Exploring the Hebrew Bible* (Englewood Cliffs, N.J.: Prentice Hall, 1988). A basic text that analyzes all the books and suggests their lasting significance.

Cohen, A. *Everyman's Talmud*. New York: Schocken, 1975. A topical presentation of rabbinic Judaism's main teachings, rich in quotations and details.

Cohen, Arthur A. *The Tremendum*. New York: Crossroad, 1981. A theological reflection on the significance of the Holocaust.

Encyclopedia Judaica. 16 vols. Jerusalem: Keter, 1971. The standard comprehensive reference work, with articles on all aspects of Jewish history, faith, and practice.

Heilman, Samuel C. *Synagogue Life*. Chicago: University of Chicago Press, 1976. A sociological study of the interactions among Jews at synagogue gatherings.

Neusner, Jacob. *The Life of Torah*. Encino, Calif.: Dickenson, 1974. A selection of readings that illustrate basic aspects of Jewish faith, both traditional and modern.

Neusner, Jacob. *The Way of Torah*, 2nd ed. Encino, Calif.: Dickenson, 1974. A readable introduction to Judaism that delineates its classical structure, the Torah, and the modern situation.

Roth, Cecil. *History of the Jews*. New York: Schocken, 1961. A lucid presentation of Jewish experience from biblical times to World War II.

Rubenstein, Richard L. *After Auschwitz*. Indianapolis: Bobbs-Merrill, 1966. One of the first and most radical interpretations of the implications of the Nazi Holocaust of six million Jews for Jewish faith.

Scholem, Gershom. *Major Trends in Jewish Mysticism*. New York: Schocken, 1961. A classical brief treatment of the evolution of Jewish mysticism stressing Cabalistic and Hasidic developments.

Zborowski, Mark, and Herzog, Elizabeth. *Life Is with People*. New York: Schocken, 1962. An absorbing portrait of *shtetl* life before World War II, based on interviews and personal reminiscences.

Carmody, John, Carmody, Denise Lardner, and Robbins, Gregory A. *Exploring the New Testament*. Englewood Cliffs, N.J.: Prentice-Hall, 1986. A comprehensive introduction to the New Testament stressing the ideas on which later Christian faith built.

Clebsch, William A. *Christianity in European History*. New York: Oxford University Press, 1979. A somewhat demanding but stimulating view, set in terms of religious studies rather than Church history.

Farmer, David Hugh. *The Oxford Dictionary of Saints*, 2nd ed. New York: Oxford University Press, 1987. A handy reference to many of the great personalities who shaped Christian faith and piety.

Frend, W. H. C. *The Rise of Christianity*. Philadelphia: Fortress, 1984. A massive but readable narrative of the first six hundred years of Christian history when most of the formative ideas and institutions took shape.

Jones, Cheslyn, Wainwright, Geoffrey, and Yarnold, Edward, eds. *The Study of Spirituality*. New York: Oxford University Press, 1986. An excellent handbook guiding readers through the historical development of the major Christian schools of devotion.

Pelikan, Jaroslav. *Jesus through the Centuries*. New Haven, Conn.: Yale University Press, 1985. A good survey of how Christian views of Jesus developed through interaction with succeeding historical cultures.

Schmemann, Alexander. *The Historical Road of Eastern Orthodoxy*. Crestwood, N.Y.: St. Vladimir's Seminary Press, 1977. A view of the development of Orthodoxy from New Testament times, originally written for Russian Christians.

Walker, Williston, et al. *A History of the Christian Church*, 4th ed. New York: Charles Scribner's Sons, 1985. A standard text that has the advantage of offering all the major chronological periods roughly equal space.

Chapter 5:
Christianity

Brown, Robert McAfee. *The Spirit of Protestantism*. New York: Oxford University Press, 1965. A lucid analysis of the major emphases in Protestant theology and faith.

Carmody, Denise Lardner, and Carmody, John Tully. *Christianity: An Introduction*, 2nd ed. Belmont, Calif.: Wadsworth, 1988. A basic text that offers an analysis of the Christian world view, a succinct history, and sketches of current schools of Christian religious thought.

Carmody, Denise Lardner, and Carmody, John Tully, *Jesus: An Introduction*. Belmont, Calif.: Wadsworth, 1987. New Testament, historical, recent theological, and comparative studies of Jesus that situate him in both Church history and the full spectrum of the founders of the world religions.

Chapter 6:
Islam

Al Faruqi, Isma'il. *Islam*. Niles, Ill.: Argus, 1979. A simple introduction that offers an overview of Islamic thought and practice. Well illustrated.

Al Faruqi, Isma'il R., and Al Faruqi, Lois L. *The Cultural Atlas of Islam*. New York: Macmillan, 1986. A large, comprehensive work stressing institutional and cultural themes more than history or theology.

Arberry, A. J. *Aspects of Islamic Civilization*. Ann Arbor: University of Michigan Press, 1971. Selections that illumine major themes of Muslim culture, including science, law, poetry, and mysticism.

Bosworth, C. E., and Schacht, Joseph, eds. *The Legacy of Islam*, 2nd ed. New York: Oxford University Press, 1974. Studies of such major cultural areas as Islamic art and architecture by leading scholars of the previous generation.

Cragg, Kenneth. *The House of Islam,* 2nd ed. Encino, Calif.: Dickenson, 1975. An analysis of major topics in Islam, such as its view of God, the role of Muhammad, liturgy, and Sufism.

Donohue, John J., and Esposito, John L., eds. *Islam in Transition.* New York: Oxford University Press, 1982. Texts from Islamic commentators on recent social changes.

Geertz, Clifford. *Islam Observed.* Chicago: University of Chicago Press, 1968. A brief, somewhat difficult, but rewarding analysis of religious development in Morocco and Indonesia by a leading cultural anthropologist.

Lings, Martin. *A Sufi Saint of the Twentieth Century,* 2nd ed. Berkeley: University of California Press, 1973. A somewhat cumbersome analysis of the impact and teaching of a leading North African sheik.

Rahman, Fazlur. *Islam,* 2nd ed. Chicago: University of Chicago Press, 1979. A solid, fact-filled history of Islam from Muhammad to the present.

Rahman, Fazlur. *Major Themes of the Qur'an.* Chicago: University of Chicago Press, 1980. Systematic presentations of the view of the Qur'an on such themes as God, human nature, and revelation.

Chapter 7:
Alternatives to Religion—
Secularism and Humanism

Buckley, Michael J. *At the Origins of Modern Atheism.* New Haven, Conn.: Yale University Press, 1987. A demanding study of the origins of modern atheism in the shift of Christian apologetics from general appeals to what the life of faith generated to philosophical inferences from the orderliness of nature to the existence of an omniscient God.

Douglas, Mary, and Tipton, Steven, eds. *Religion and America: Spirituality in a Secular Age.* Boston: Beacon Press, 1983. Essays by social scientists and humanists focusing on the resurgence of conservative religious feeling that astounded secularistic observers of American culture during the early 1980s.

Hammond, Phillip, ed. *The Sacred in a Secular Age.* Berkeley: University of California Press, 1985. Studies covering some of the same ground as the book edited by Douglas and Tipton but with more interest in civil religion as the background for the recent contest between secularity and sacrality.

Heilbroner, Robert. *Marxism: For and Against.* New York: Norton, 1980. Analyses by a liberal economist impressed by Marxist insights into the relations between labor and product value but unimpressed by what Marxist economic systems to date have produced.

Jaki, Stanley. *The Road of Science and the Ways to God.* Chicago: University of Chicago Press, 1978. Jaki's Gifford Lectures on the origins of modern science from Christian foundations and the implicitly theistic postulates of even recent scientific geniuses.

Kuhn, Thomas S. *The Structure of Scientific Revolutions,* 2nd ed. Chicago: University of Chicago Press, 1970. Kuhn's thesis that science proceeds by observing normative paradigms until something revolutionary creates a new paradigm (which then becomes normative) aroused great controversy among historians and philosophers of science. As well, historians of other disciplines, theology among them, soon adapted the notion of paradigms and normal science to study the evolution of their own fields.

Löwith, Karl. *From Hegel to Nietzsche.* Garden City, N.Y.: Doubleday Anchor, 1967. A well-regarded, staple study of the evolution of European philosophy in the nineteenth century, when many of the postulates of secularist humanists became fixed.

Toulmin, Stephen. *Human Understanding.* Princeton, N.J.: Princeton University Press, 1972. A study of human cognition greatly indebted to the philosophy of science and ordinary language analysis that deals sufficiently with the historical rise of the institutions that guide formal thought to illustrate the secularization of the modern West.

Voegelin, Eric. *From Enlightenment to Revolution.* Durham, N.C.: Duke University Press, 1975. A portion of Voegelin's discarded history of political ideas that focuses on Marx and other modern political thinkers who were revolting against intellectual and social constraints associated with Christian theism.

Voegelin, Eric. *Science, Politics and Gnosticism.* Chicago: Henry Regnery, 1968. A readable version of Voegelin's thesis that much modern political philosophy amounts to a gnostic effort to direct human development by privileged but nontranscendent revelations about human nature and the laws of history.

Conclusion:
Summary Reflections

Ahlstrom, Sydney. *A Religious History of the American People.* New Haven, Conn.: Yale University Press, 1972. A massive, authoritative treatment of American religion from precolonial times to the end of the 1960s.

Daedalus, Volume 111, Number 1 (Winter 1982). A collection of essays by leading scholars who try to interpret the current significance of religion, both in the United States and on the world scene.

Daedalus, Volume 117, Number 2 (Spring 1988). A discussion among educators about the current function of religion and religious studies in American higher education.

Johnston, William. *The Inner Eye of Love.* New York: Harper & Row, 1978. Shows the contemplative foundations of religion, with special reference to Christianity and Buddhism.

Moore, R. Lawrence. *Religious Outsiders and the Making of Americans.* New York: Oxford University Press, 1986. Chapters on the history of the process by which many groups, either sectarian or marginal to the cultural mainstream, were Americanized.

Neville, Robert C. *Soldier, Sage, Saint.* New York: Fordham University Press, 1978. Typological studies of some of the dominant religious personalities.

Voegelin, Eric. *Order and History,* Vol. 5, *In Search of Order.* Baton Rouge: Louisiana State University Press, 1987. A brief, demanding, but brilliant conclusion to Voegelin's epic study of how human beings have pursued the structures of history and consciousness.

APPENDIX A

ONE HUNDRED KEY DATES IN WORLD RELIGIOUS HISTORY

4.6 billion years ago	Formation of the earth
500,000 years ago	Homo erectus using fire
100,000 years ago	Homo sapiens: ritual burial
50,000 years ago	Homo sapiens in Australia
30,000 years ago	Prehistoric painting and sculpture; Mongoloid peoples cross Bering Strait
8,000–6,000 B.C.E	Agriculture, domestication of animals, rise of towns
4500	Early Jomon period of hunting and gathering in Japan
4000	Casting of bronze
3500	Invention of wheel; Megalith cultures in Britain and Iberia
3100	Unification of Egypt; Invention of writing in Sumer
3000	Farming in central Africa
2750	Growth of civilization in Indus Valley
1600	Shang Bronze Culture in China
1570–1165	New Kingdom in Egypt
1500	Vedas, Rise of Iranian-speaking peoples
1200	Exodus of Hebrews from Egypt
1000	Colonization of Arctic
900	Nubian kingdom of Kush
800–400	Upanishads
750	Homer and Hesiod written down
750–550	Hebrew Prophets
ca. 628–551	Zoroaster
599–527	Mahavira, founder of Jainism
586	Fall of southern kingdom (Judah)
551–479	Confucius
536–476	Buddha
525	Persian conquest of Egypt
525–406	Aeschylus, Sophocles, Euripides
500–200	*Mahabhrata, Ramayana, Bhagavad Gita*
427–347	Plato
350	*Tao Te Ching*
331	Alexander conquers Palestine
273–236	Asoka
200	Rise of religious Taoism
80	Buddhist decline in India
50	Formation of Buddhist canon
5 C.E.	Building of Japanese National Shrine at Ise
30	Death of Jesus of Nazareth
50–95	New Testament writings
70	Romans destroy Jerusalem
80–110	Canonization of Hebrew Bible
220–552	Buddhist missions to China and Japan
304–589	Huns fragment China
325	First Ecumenical Council at Nicaea
400	Fall of Indian Gupta dynasty
451	Council of Chalcedon
500	Compilation of Babylonian Talmud
570–632	Muhammad
637	Islamic invasion of Persia
645	Taika reform—Japan takes Chinese model
650	Canonization of Qur'an
700	Golden Age of Chinese poetry
712–720	Shinto Chronicles
749	First Buddhist monastery in Tibet
750–1258	Abbasid caliphate
762	Foundation of Baghdad
787	Second Council of Nicaea
788–820	Shankara
800–900	Rise of Hindu orthodoxy
845	Persecution of Chinese Buddhists
966	Foundation of Cairo

1054	Mutual anathemas of Rome and Constantinople
1058–1111	Al-Ghazali
1130–1200	Chu Hsi, leading Neo-Confucian
ca. 1135	Maimonides
1175	First Muslim empire in India
1175–1253	Introduction of Pure Land, Zen, and Nichiren schools in Japan
1225–1274	Thomas Aquinas
1453	Ottoman Turks capture Constantinople
1469–1539	Nanak, founder of Sikhism
1473–1543	Nicolaus Copernicus
1492	Expulsion of Jews from Spain
1517	Luther's ninety-five theses
1526–1707	Islamic Mogul Dynasty in India
1549	Francis Xavier in Japan
1565	Roman Catholic colony at St. Augustine
1585	Matteo Ricci in China
1619	Beginning of black slavery in colonial America
1620	Mayflower Compact
1654	Jewish settlement at New Amsterdam
1734	First Great Awakening in New England
1801	Beginnings of revivalism in western United States
1809–1882	Charles Darwin
1818–1883	Karl Marx
1856–1939	Sigmund Freud
1868–1871	Meiji persecution of Buddhism
1869–1948	Mahatma Gandhi
1879–1955	Albert Einstein
1880–1913	Partition of Africa by Western powers
1893	World Parliament of Religions in Chicago
1893–1977	Mao Tse-tung
1894–1905	Japanese victorious in wars with China and Russia
1910	Beginning of Protestant ecumenical movement
1933–1945	Nazi persecution of Jews
1945	Japanese surrender; Disestablishment of Shinto
1947	Partition of Pakistan from India
1948	Creation of state of Israel
1954–1956	Sixth Buddhist Council, Rangoon
1962–1965	Second Vatican Council
1964	Civil Rights Act in United States

APPENDIX B

APPROXIMATE MEMBERSHIP DATA ON MAJOR AMERICAN RELIGIOUS GROUPS (1985)

Adventists, Seventh-Day	623,000
Baptists	30,000,000
Buddhists	250,000
Christian Church (Disciples of Christ)	1,157,000
Christian Churches and Churches of Christ	1,041,000
Church of the Nazarene	500,000
Churches of Christ	1,250,000
Eastern Orthodox Churches	4,000,000
Episcopalians	2,768,000
Friends United Meeting (Quakers)	57,500
Jehovah's Witnesses	697,660
Jewish Congregations	5,817,000
Latter-Day Saints (Mormons)	3,602,000
Lutherans	8,500,000
Mennonites	90,000
Methodists	13,000,000
Pentecostals	3,300,000
Presbyterians	3,300,000
Roman Catholics	52,000,000
Salvation Army	420,000
United Universalist Association	175,000
United Churches of Christ	1,700,000

Sources: Constance H. Jacquet, Jr., ed., *Yearbook of American and Canadian Churches 1986* (Nashville: Abingdon, 1986), and Frank S. Mead and Samuel S. Hill, *Handbook of Denominations in the United States* new 8th ed. (Nashville: Abingdon, 1985).

INDEX OF
NAMES AND PLACES*

Boldface numbers indicate pages on which glossary definitions appear.

INDEX OF SUBJECTS*

Boldface numbers indicate pages on which glossary definitions appear.